M000313608

Government and the Economy

Government and the Economy

AN ENCYCLOPEDIA

David A. Dieterle and Kathleen C. Simmons, Editors

AN IMPRINT OF ABC-CLIO, LLC
Santa Barbara, California • Denver, Colorado • Oxford, England

Copyright © 2014 by ABC-CLIO, LLC

All rights reserved. No part of this publication may be reproduced, stored in a retrieval system, or transmitted, in any form or by any means, electronic, mechanical, photocopying, recording, or otherwise, except for the inclusion of brief quotations in a review, without prior permission in writing from the publisher.

Library of Congress Cataloging-in-Publication Data

Government and the economy : an encyclopedia / David A. Dieterle and Kathleen C. Simmons, editors.

pages cm

ISBN 978-1-4408-2903-1 (hardback) — ISBN 978-1-4408-2904-8 (ebook) 1. United States—Economic policy—Encyclopedias. 2. Economic policy—Political aspects. I. Dieterle, David Anthony. II. Simmons, Kathleen C.

HC102.G59 2014

330.973—dc23 2014010822

ISBN: 978-1-4408-2903-1

EISBN: 978-1-4408-2904-8

18 17 16 15 14 1 2 3 4 5

This book is also available on the World Wide Web as an eBook.
Visit www.abc-clio.com for details.

Greenwood
An Imprint of ABC-CLIO, LLC

ABC-CLIO, LLC
130 Cremona Drive, P.O. Box 1911
Santa Barbara, California 93116-1911

This book is printed on acid-free paper ∞

Manufactured in the United States of America

Contents

Alphabetical List of Entries

Entries in Alignment with National Content Standards in Economics

Council for Economic Education, "Voluntary National Content Standards in Economics, 2nd Edition," http://www.councilforeconed.org/wp/wp-content/uploads/2012/03/voluntary-national-content-standards-2010.pdf.

Standard 1: Scarcity

Productive resources are limited. Therefore, people cannot have all the goods and services they want; when they choose some things they must give up others.

Arrow, Kenneth

Buchanan, James

Democratic Socialism

Economic Rent

Federal Home Loan Mortgage (Freddie Mac)

Immigration Reform and Control Act of 1986

Interstate Commerce Act of 1887

Kelo v. City of New London, Connecticut, 545 U.S. 469 (2005)

Lochner v. New York, 198 U.S. 45 (1905)

Mankiw, Gregory

Market Capitalism

Market Failure

Mercantilism

National Deficit vs. Debt

Okun, Arthur

Private Property

Protectionism

Public Goods

Samuelson, Paul

Smith, Adam

Sowell, Thomas

Taxes

Theory of Public Choice

Trade-Offs

Tullock, Gordon

Youngstown Sheet & Tube Co. v. Sawyer, 343 U.S. 579 (1952)

Standard 2: Decision Making

Effective decision making requires comparing the additional costs of alternatives with the additional benefits. Many choices involve doing a little more or a little less of something; few choices are "all or nothing" decisions.

Arrow, Kenneth

Buchanan, James

Coase, Ronald

Command Economy

Contracts

Crony Capitalism

Deflation

Demand-Pull Inflation

Democratic Socialism

Economic Rent

Expansionary Fiscal Policy

Expansionary Monetary Policy

Externalities

Fascism

Federal Home Loan Mortgage (Freddie Mac)

Inflation

Kelo v. City of New London, Connecticut, 545 U.S. 469 (2005)

Keynesian Economics

Majority Rule

Mankiw, Gregory

Market Capitalism

Menominee Tribe v. United States, 391 U.S. 404 (1968)

National Deficit vs. Debt

Okun, Arthur

Olson, Mancur

Private Property

Protectionism

Samuelson, Paul

Smith, Adam

Sowell, Thomas

Taxes

Theory of Public Choice

Trade-Offs

Tullock, Gordon

Voluntary Exchange

Williams, Walter

Standard 3: Allocation

Different methods can be used to allocate goods and services. People acting individually or collectively must choose which methods to use to allocate different kinds of goods and services.

Affordable Health Care Act Cases, 567 U.S. ___ (2012)

Arrow, Kenneth

Buchanan, James

Coase, Ronald

Command Economy

Contracts

Crony Capitalism

Democratic Socialism

Economic Rent

Externalities

Fascism

Federal Home Loan Mortgage (Freddie Mac)

Federal National Mortgage Association (Fannie Mae)

Federal Trade Commission

Financial Reform Act of 2010 (Dodd-Frank Act)

Fiscal Policy

Great Society

Helvering v. Davis, 301 U.S. 619 (1937)

International Monetary Fund (IMF)

Interstate Commerce Act of 1887

Kellogg Co. v. National Biscuit Co., 305 U.S. 111 (1938)

Kelo v. City of New London, Connecticut, 545 *U.S. 469 (2005)*

Keynesian Economics

Laffer Curve

Lochner v. New York, 198 U.S. 45 (1905)

Mankiw, Gregory

Market Capitalism

MCI Telecommunications Corp. v. American Telephone and Telegraph Co., 512 U.S. 218 (1994)

Menominee Tribe v. United States, 391 U.S. 404 (1968)

Olson, Mancur

Ostrom, Elinor

Pollock v. Farmers' Loan & Trust Company, 157 U.S. 429 (1895)

Protectionism

Public Goods

Simons, Henry

Smith, Adam

Standard Oil Co. of New Jersey v. United States, 305 U.S. 111 (1911)

Supply-Side Economics

Taxes

Theory of Public Choice

Trade-Offs

Tullock, Gordon

Voluntary Exchange

Youngstown Sheet & Tube Co. v. Sawyer, 343 U.S. 579 (1952)

Standard 4: Incentives
People usually respond predictably to positive and negative incentives.

America Invents Act of 2011 (Leahy-Smith Act)

Coase, Ronald

Command Economy

Crony Capitalism

Deflation

Demand-Pull Inflation

Democratic Socialism

Economic Rent

Expansionary Monetary Policy

Externalities

Fascism

Federal Home Loan Mortgage (Freddie Mac)

Federal National Mortgage Association (Fannie Mae)

Federal Reserve Act of 1913

Financial Reform Act of 2010 (Dodd-Frank Act)

Fiscal Policy

Friedman, Milton

Great Society

Inflation

Inflation, Measures of

International Monetary Fund (IMF)

Kellogg Co. v. National Biscuit Co., 305 U.S. 111 (1938)

Kelo v. City of New London, Connecticut, 545 U.S. 469 (2005)

Laffer Curve

Market Capitalism

Market Failure

Ostrom, Elinor

Private Property

Protectionism

Servicemen's Readjustment Act of 1944 (GI Bill)

Smith, Adam

Sowell, Thomas

Taxes

Trade-Offs

Transaction Costs

Voluntary Exchange

Williams, Walter

Youngstown Sheet & Tube Co. v. Sawyer, 343 U.S. 579 (1952)

Standard 5: Trade

Voluntary exchange occurs only when all participating parties expect to gain. This is true for trade among individuals or organizations within a nation, and among individuals or organizations in different nations.

Contracts

Crony Capitalism

European (Economic) Community

Federal Trade Commission

Federal Trade Commission Act of 1914

Financial Reform Act of 2010 (Dodd-Frank Act)

George, Henry

Group of Eight (G8)

International Monetary Fund (IMF)

Interstate Commerce Act of 1887

Lochner v. New York, 198 U.S. 45 (1905)

Mercantilism

North American Free Trade Agreement (NAFTA)

Protectionism

Smith, Adam

Tariff Act of 1930 (Smoot-Hawley Tariff Act)

Voluntary Exchange

World Bank

World Trade Organization (WTO)

Standard 6: Specialization

When individuals, regions, and nations specialize in what they can produce at the lowest cost and then trade with others, both production and consumption increase.

Cyclical Unemployment

Democratic Socialism

Immigration Reform and Control Act of 1986

Indian Gaming Regulatory Act of 1988

International Monetary Fund (IMF)

Labor Force

Lechmere, Inc. v. National Labor Relations Board, 502 U.S. 527 (1992)

Lochner v. New York, 198 U.S. 45 (1905)

Market Capitalism

Private Property

Smith, Adam

Trade-Offs

Voluntary Exchange

World Bank

Youngstown Sheet & Tube Co. v. Sawyer, 343 U.S. 579 (1952)

Standard 7: Markets and Prices

A market exists when buyers and sellers interact. This interaction determines market prices and thereby allocates scarce goods and services.

Affordable Health Care Act Cases, 567 U.S.___ (2012)

Command Economy

Crony Capitalism

Deflation

Demand-Pull Inflation

Democratic Socialism

Expansionary Monetary Policy

Externalities

Fascism

Federal Trade Commission

Federal Trade Commission Act of 1914

Friedman, Milton

Great Depression (1929–1939)

Immigration Reform and Control Act of 1986

Inflation

Inflation, Measures of

Interstate Commerce Act of 1887

Kelo v. City of New London, Connecticut, 545 U.S. 469 (2005)

Lechmere, Inc. v. National Labor Relations Board, 502 U.S. 527 (1992)

Lochner v. New York, 198 U.S. 45 (1905)

Market Capitalism

Market Failure

MCI Telecommunications Corp. v. American Telephone and Telegraph Co., 512 U.S. 218 (1994)

Money

National Labor Relations Board (NLRB)

North American Free Trade Agreement (NAFTA)

Olson, Mancur

Private Property

Prohibition

Protectionism

Public Goods

Smith, Adam

Standard Oil Co. of New Jersey v. United States, 305 U.S. 111 (1911)

Steelworkers Strike of 1919

Tariff Act of 1930 (Smoot-Hawley Tariff Act)

Taxes

Telecommunications Reform Act of 1996

United States v. South-Eastern Underwriters Association, 322 U.S. 533 (1944)

Standard 8: Role of Prices

Prices send signals and provide incentives to buyers and sellers. When supply or demand changes, market prices adjust, affecting incentives.

Crony Capitalism

Deflation

Demand-Pull Inflation

Democratic Socialism

Externalities

Federal Reserve System

Federal Trade Commission

Galbraith, John Kenneth

Inflation

Inflation, Measures of

Interstate Commerce Act of 1887

Market Capitalism

Mises, Ludwig von

Money

Olson, Mancur

Protectionism

Tariff Act of 1930 (Smoot-Hawley Tariff Act)

Standard 9: Competition and Market Structure
Competition among sellers usually lowers costs and prices, and encourages producers to produce what consumers are willing and able to buy. Competition among buyers increases prices and allocates goods and services to those people who are willing and able to pay the most for them.

Affordable Health Care Act Cases, 567 U.S. ___ (2012)

Citizens United v. Federal Election Commission, 558 U.S. ___ (2010)

Clayton Antitrust Act of 1914

Coase, Ronald

Command Economy

Crony Capitalism

Democratic Socialism

De Soto, Hernando

Economic Systems

Externalities

Fascism

Federal Home Loan Mortgage (Freddie Mac)

Federal National Mortgage Association (Fannie Mae)

Federal Trade Commission

Federal Trade Commission Act of 1914

Friedman, Milton

Galbraith, John Kenneth

Government Failure

Immigration Reform and Control Act of 1986

Indian Gaming Regulatory Act of 1988

International Monetary Fund (IMF)

Interstate Commerce Act of 1887

Kellogg Co. v. National Biscuit Co., 305 U.S. 111 (1938)

Labor Force

Laffer Curve

Lechmere, Inc. v. National Labor Relations Board, 502 U.S. 527 (1992)

Market Capitalism

Market Failure

Marx, Karl

Marxism

McCulloch v. Maryland, 17 U.S. 316 (1819)

MCI Telecommunications Corp. v. American Telephone and Telegraph Co., 512 U.S. 218 (1994)

Menominee Tribe v. United States, 391 U.S. 404 (1968)

Mercantilism

National Labor Relations Act of 1935 (Wagner Act)

New Deal

Private Property

Prohibition

Protectionism

Regulated Monopolies

Samuelson, Paul

Seminole Tribe of Florida v. Florida, 517 U.S. 44 (1996)

Sherman Antitrust Act of 1890

Smith, Adam

Sowell, Thomas

Stalin, Joseph

Standard Oil Co. of New Jersey v. United States, 305 U.S. 111 (1911)

Steelworkers Strike of 1919

Tariff Act of 1930 (Smoot-Hawley Tariff Act)

Taxes

Telecommunications Reform Act of 1996

Thatcher, Margaret

Theory of Public Choice

United States v. South-Eastern Underwriters Association, 322 U.S. 533 (1944)

Voluntary Exchange

Welfare State

Williams, Walter

Standard 10: Institutions

Institutions evolve and are created to help individuals and groups accomplish their goals. Banks, labor unions, markets, corporations, legal systems, and nonprofit

organizations are examples of important institutions. A different kind of institution, clearly defined and enforced property rights, is essential to a market economy.

Bureau of Economic Analysis
Bureau of Engraving and Printing
Bureau of Labor Statistics
Congressional Budget Office
Department of Commerce
Department of Labor
Environmental Protection Agency (EPA)
Federal Deposit Insurance Corporation (FDIC)
Federal Home Loan Mortgage (Freddie Mac)
Federal National Mortgage Association (Fannie Mae)
Federal Reserve System
Federal Trade Commission
Group of Eight (G8)
Internal Revenue Service (IRS)
International Monetary Fund (IMF)
Juilliard v. Greenman, 110 U.S. 421 (1884)
Kahn, Alfred
National Bureau of Economic Research (NBER)
Okun, Arthur
Reich, Robert
Rivlin, Alice
Romer, Christina
Schwartz, Anna
Securities and Exchange Commission (SEC)
Shultz, George
Summers, Lawrence
Supreme Court
Tennessee Valley Authority (TVA)
Tyson, Laura
United States Census Bureau
United States Mint
United States Treasury

World Bank
World Trade Organization (WTO)

Standard 11: Money and Inflation

Money makes it easier to trade, borrow, save, invest, and compare the value of goods and services. The amount of money in the economy affects the overall price level. Inflation is an increase in the overall price level that reduces the value of money.

Banking Act of 1933 (Glass-Steagall Act)
Central Banking
Contractionary Fiscal Policy
Deflation
Demand-Pull Inflation
Expansionary Fiscal Policy
Expansionary Monetary Policy
Federal Reserve Act of 1913
Federal Reserve System
Financial Reform Act of 2010 (Dodd-Frank Act)
Fiscal Policy
Friedman, Milton
Inflation
Inflation, Measures of
Juilliard v. Greenman, 110 U.S. 421 (1884)
Keynesian Economics
Monetary Policy
Money
Schwartz, Anna
Taxes
United States Mint
U.S. Treasury Bills, Notes, and Bonds

Standard 12: Interest Rates

Interest rates, adjusted for inflation, rise and fall to balance the amount saved with the amount borrowed, which affects the allocation of scarce resources between present and future uses.

Central Banking
Deflation

Demand-Pull Inflation

Expansionary Monetary Policy

Federal Home Loan Mortgage (Freddie Mac)

Federal National Mortgage Association (Fannie Mae)

Federal Reserve Act of 1913

Federal Reserve System

Friedman, Milton

Inflation

Inflation, Measures of

Keynesian Economics

Monetary Policy

U.S. Treasury Bills, Notes, and Bonds

Standard 13: Income

Income for most people is determined by the market value of the productive resources they sell. What workers earn primarily depends on the market value of what they produce.

Crony Capitalism

Cyclical Unemployment

Deflation

Immigration Reform and Control Act of 1986

Inflation

Internal Revenue Service (IRS)

Interstate Commerce Act of 1887

Keynesian Economics

Labor Force

Lechmere, Inc. v. National Labor Relations Board, 502 U.S. 527 (1992)

Lochner v. New York, 198 U.S. 45 (1905)

Market Capitalism

Pollock v. Farmers' Loan & Trust Company, 157 U.S. 429 (1895)

Seminole Tribe of Florida v. Florida, 517 U.S. 44 (1996)

Social Security Act of 1935

Steelworkers Strike of 1919

Taxes

U.S. Treasury Bills, Notes, and Bonds

Welfare State

West Coast Hotel Co. v. Parrish, 300 U.S. 379 (1937)

Williams, Walter

Standard 14: Entrepreneurship

Entrepreneurs take on the calculated risk of starting new businesses, either by embarking on new ventures similar to existing ones or by introducing new innovations. Entrepreneurial innovation is an important source of economic growth.

America Invents Act of 2011 (Leahy-Smith Act)

Financial Reform Act of 2010 (Dodd-Frank Act)

Kellogg Co. v. National Biscuit Co., 305 U.S. 111 (1938)

Labor Force

MCI Telecommunications Corp. v. American Telephone and Telegraph Co., 512 U.S. 218 (1994)

Private Property

Protectionism

Seminole Tribe of Florida v. Florida, 517 U.S. 44 (1996)

Smith, Adam

Youngstown Sheet & Tube Co. v. Sawyer, 343 U.S. 579 (1952)

Standard 15: Economic Growth

Investment in factories, machinery, new technology, and in the health, education, and training of people stimulates economic growth and can raise future standards of living.

Command Economy

Crony Capitalism

Cyclical Unemployment

Democratic Socialism

Economic Growth, Measures of

Economic Systems

Expansionary Fiscal Policy

Expansionary Monetary Policy

Federal Reserve System

Financial Reform Act of 2010 (Dodd-Frank Act)

Fiscal Policy

Friedman, Milton

Government Failure

Gross Domestic Product (GDP)

International Monetary Fund (IMF)

Kellogg Co. v. National Biscuit Co., 305 U.S. 111 (1938)

Keynesian Economics

Kuznets, Simon

Laffer, Arthur

Laffer Curve

Market Capitalism

Mises, Ludwig von

Monetary Policy

Okun, Arthur

Phillips, A. W. H.

Protectionism

Romer, Christina

Servicemen's Readjustment Act of 1944 (GI Bill)

Smith, Adam

Supply-Side Economics

Taxes

Thatcher, Margaret

Transaction Costs

Unemployment

Welfare State

World Bank

Standard 16: Role of Government and Market Failure

There is an economic role for government in a market economy whenever the benefits of a government policy outweigh its costs. Governments often provide for national defense, address environmental concerns, define and protect property rights, and attempt to make markets more competitive. Most government policies also have direct or indirect effects on peoples' incomes.

America Invents Act of 2011 (Leahy-Smith Act)

Banking Act of 1933 (Glass-Steagall Act)

Central Banking

Ostrom, Elinor

Protectionism

Public Goods

Regulated Monopolies

Sherman Antitrust Act of 1890

Smith, Adam

Social Security Act of 1935

Supreme Court

Taxes

Tennessee Valley Authority (TVA)

Theory of Public Choice

Tobin, James

Unemployment

United States Census Bureau

United States v. South-Eastern Underwriters Association, 322 U.S. 533 (1944)

Vickrey, William

Welfare State

West Coast Hotel Co. v. Parrish, 300 U.S. 379 (1937)

Standard 17: Government Failure

Costs of government policies sometimes exceed benefits. This may occur because of incentives facing voters, government officials, and government employees; because of actions by special interest groups that can impose costs on the general public; or because social goals other than economic efficiency are being pursued.

Command Economy

Crony Capitalism

Entitlements

Externalities

Fascism

Federal Home Loan Mortgage (Freddie Mac)

Federal National Mortgage Association (Fannie Mae)

Free Rider

Friedman, Milton

Government Failure

Laffer, Arthur

Laffer Curve

Pollock v. Farmers' Loan & Trust Company, 157 U.S. 429 (1895)

Prohibition

Protectionism

Sowell, Thomas

Supply-Side Economics

Williams, Walter

Standard 18: Economic Fluctuations

Fluctuations in a nation's overall levels of income, employment, and prices are determined by the interaction of spending and production decisions made by all households, firms, government agencies, and others in the economy. Recessions occur when overall levels of income and employment decline.

Contractionary Fiscal Policy

Contractionary Monetary Policy

Cyclical Unemployment

Deflation

Demand-Pull Inflation

Expansionary Fiscal Policy

Expansionary Monetary Policy

Fascism

Federal Reserve Act of 1913

Federal Reserve System

Fiscal Policy

Friedman, Milton

Gross Domestic Product (GDP)

Inflation

Inflation, Measures of

Keynes, John Maynard

Keynesian Economics

Klein, Lawrence

Laffer, Arthur

Laffer Curve

Mises, Ludwig von

Monetary Policy

National Deficit vs. Debt

New Deal

Phillips, A. W. H.

Protectionism

Romer, Christina

Smith, Adam

Supply-Side Economics

Unemployment

Standard 19: Unemployment and Inflation

Unemployment imposes costs on individuals and the overall economy. Inflation, both expected and unexpected, also imposes costs on individuals and the overall economy. Unemployment increases during recessions and decreases during recoveries.

Bernanke, Ben

Burns, Arthur

Central Banking

Contractionary Fiscal Policy

Contractionary Monetary Policy

Cyclical Unemployment

Deflation

Demand-Pull Inflation

Department of Labor

Discouraged Workers

Entitlements

Expansionary Fiscal Policy

Expansionary Monetary Policy

Federal Reserve System

Fiscal Policy

Friedman, Milton

Government Failure

Greenspan, Alan

Heller, Walter

Inflation

Inflation, Measures of

Keynes, John Maynard

Keynesian Economics

Labor Force

Lechmere, Inc. v. National Labor Relations Board, 502 U.S. 527 (1992)

Lochner v. New York, 198 U.S. 45 (1905)

Monetary Policy

Phillips, A. W. H.

Protectionism

Unemployment

United States Census Bureau

Welfare State

West Coast Hotel Co. v. Parrish, 300 U.S. 379 (1937)

Yellen, Janet

Standard 20: Fiscal and Monetary Policy

Federal government budgetary policy and the Federal Reserve System's monetary policy influence the overall levels of employment, output, and prices.

Banking Act of 1933 (Glass-Steagall Act)

Bernanke, Ben

Burns, Arthur

Central Banking

Command Economy

Contractionary Fiscal Policy

Contractionary Monetary Policy

Deflation

Demand-Pull Inflation

Expansionary Fiscal Policy

Expansionary Monetary Policy

Federal Reserve Act of 1913

Federal Reserve System

Fiscal Policy

Friedman, Milton

Greenspan, Alan

Heller, Walter

Inflation

Inflation, Measures of

International Monetary Fund (IMF)

Keynes, John Maynard

Keynesian Economics

Klein, Lawrence

Laffer, Arthur

Laffer Curve

Meltzer, Allan

Monetary Policy

Money

National Deficit vs. Debt

Simons, Henry

Supply-Side Economics

Taxes

Unemployment

Volcker, Paul

Yellen, Janet

Entries in Alignment with United States History Content Standards

National Center for History in the Schools, UCLA, "United States History Content Standards for Grades 5–12; Overview of U.S. Standards, by Eras," http://www.nchs.ucla.edu/Standards/us-history-content-standards.

Era 1: Three Worlds Meet (Beginnings to 1620)

Standard 1

Comparative characteristics of societies in the Americas, Western Europe, and Western Africa that increasingly interacted after 1450

Standard 2

How early European exploration and colonization resulted in cultural and ecological interactions among previously unconnected peoples

Mercantilism

Era 2: Colonization and Settlement (1585–1763)

Standard 1

Why the Americas attracted Europeans, why they brought enslaved Africans to their colonies, and how Europeans struggled for control of North America and the Caribbean

Standard 2

How political, religious, and social institutions emerged in the English colonies

Standard 3

How the values and institutions of European economic life took root in the colonies, and how slavery reshaped European and African life in the Americas

Classical Economics

Era 3: Revolution and the New Nation (1754–1820s)

Standard 1
The causes of the American Revolution, the ideas and interests involved in forging the revolutionary movement, and the reasons for the American victory

Standard 2
The impact of the American Revolution on politics, economy, and society

Standard 3
The institutions and practices of government created during the American Revolution and how they were revised between 1787 and 1815 to create the foundation of the American political system based on the U.S. Constitution and the Bill of Rights

Classical Economics

Smith, Adam

Supreme Court

United States Census Bureau

United States Mint

Era 4: Expansion and Reform (1801–1861)

Standard 1
United States territorial expansion between 1801 and 1861, and how it affected relations with external powers and Native Americans

Standard 2
How the Industrial Revolution, increasing immigration, the rapid expansion of slavery, and the westward movement changed the lives of Americans and led toward regional tensions

Standard 3
The extension, restriction, and reorganization of political democracy after 1800

Standard 4
The sources and character of cultural, religious, and social reform movements in the antebellum period

Gibbons v. Ogden, 22 U.S. 1 (1824)

Marx, Karl

Marxism

McCulloch v. Maryland, 17 U.S. 316 (1819)

Era 5: Civil War and Reconstruction (1850–1877)

Standard 1
The causes of the Civil War

Standard 2
The course and character of the Civil War and its effects on the American people

Standard 3
How various reconstruction plans succeeded or failed

Internal Revenue Service (IRS)

National Bank Act of 1863

Era 6: The Development of the Industrial United States (1870–1900)

Standard 1
How the rise of corporations, heavy industry, and mechanized farming transformed the American people

Standard 2
Massive immigration after 1870 and how new social patterns, conflicts, and ideas of national unity developed amid growing cultural diversity

Standard 3
The rise of the American labor movement and how political issues reflected social and economic changes

Standard 4
Federal Indian policy and United States foreign policy after the Civil War

Bureau of Engraving and Printing

Bureau of Labor Statistics

George, Henry

Interstate Commerce Act of 1887

Era 7: The Emergence of Modern America (1890–1930)

Standard 1
How Progressives and others addressed problems of industrial capitalism, urbanization, and political corruption

Standard 2

The changing role of the United States in world affairs through World War I

Standard 3

How the United States changed from the end of World War I to the eve of the Great Depression

Clayton Antitrust Act of 1914

Command Economy

Congressional Budget Office

Department of Commerce

Department of Labor

Fascism

Federal Reserve Act of 1913

Federal Reserve System

Federal Trade Commission

Federal Trade Commission Act of 1914

Internal Revenue Service (IRS)

Lochner v. New York, 198 U.S. 45 (1905)

National Bureau of Economic Research (NBER)

Pollock v. Farmers' Loan & Trust Company, 157 U.S. 429 (1895)

Prohibition

Sherman Antitrust Act of 1890

Stalin, Joseph

Standard Oil Co. of New Jersey v. United States, 305 U.S. 111 (1911)

Steelworkers Strike of 1919

Tariff Act of 1930 (Smoot-Hawley Tariff Act)

Era 8: The Great Depression and World War II (1929–1945)

Standard 1

The causes of the Great Depression and how it affected American society

Standard 2

How the New Deal addressed the Great Depression, transformed American federalism, and initiated the welfare state

Standard 3

The causes and course of World War II, the character of the war at home and abroad, and its reshaping of the U.S. role in world affairs

Banking Act of 1933 (Glass-Steagall Act)

Bretton Woods Agreement

Coase, Ronald

Federal Deposit Insurance Corporation (FDIC)

Federal National Mortgage Association (Fannie Mae)

Great Depression (1929–1939)

International Monetary Fund (IMF)

Kellogg Co. v. National Biscuit Co., 305 U.S. 111 (1938)

Keynes, John Maynard

Keynesian Economics

National Labor Relations Act of 1935 (Wagner Act)

New Deal

Roosevelt, Franklin Delano

Servicemen's Readjustment Act of 1944 (GI Bill)

Simons, Henry

Social Security Act of 1935

Tennessee Valley Authority (TVA)

United States v. South-Eastern Underwriters Association, 322 U.S. 533 (1944)

West Coast Hotel Co. v. Parrish, 300 U.S. 379 (1937)

World Bank

Era 9: Postwar United States (1945 to early 1970s)

Standard 1

The economic boom and social transformation of postwar United States

Standard 2

How the Cold War and conflicts in Korea and Vietnam influenced domestic and international politics

Standard 3

Domestic policies after World War II

Standard 4

The struggle for racial and gender equality and the extension of civil liberties

Arrow, Kenneth

Bureau of Economic Analysis

Burns, Arthur

European (Economic) Community

Friedman, Milton

Galbraith, John Kenneth

Great Society

Heller, Walter

Klein, Lawrence

Kuznets, Simon

Menominee Tribe v. United States, 391 U.S. 404 (1968)

Mises, Ludwig von

Phillips, A. W. H.

Samuelson, Paul

Schwartz, Anna

Tobin, James

Vickrey, William

Youngstown Sheet & Tube Co. v. Sawyer, 343 U.S. 579 (1952)

Era 10: Contemporary United States (1968 to the present)

Standard 1

Recent developments in foreign and domestic politics

Standard 2

Economic, social, and cultural developments in contemporary United States

Affordable Health Care Act Cases, 567 U.S. ___ (2012)

Bernanke, Ben

Buchanan, James

Command Economy

De Soto, Hernando

Environmental Protection Agency (EPA)

Federal Home Loan Mortgage (Freddie Mac)

Financial Reform Act of 2010 (Dodd-Frank Act)

Greenspan, Alan

Immigration Reform and Control Act of 1986

Indian Gaming Regulatory Act of 1988

Kahn, Alfred

Kelo v. City of New London, Connecticut, 545 U.S. 469 (2005)

Laffer, Arthur

Laffer Curve

Lechmere, Inc. v. National Labor Relations Board, 502 U.S. 527 (1992)

Mankiw, Gregory

MCI Telecommunications Corp. v. American Telephone and Telegraph Co., 512 U.S. 218 (1994)

Meltzer, Allan

Mirrlees, James

North American Free Trade Agreement (NAFTA)

Ostrom, Elinor

Reagan, Ronald

Reich, Robert

Rivlin, Alice

Romer, Christina

Seminole Tribe of Florida v. Florida, 517 U.S. 44 (1996)

Shultz, George

Sowell, Thomas

Summers, Lawrence

Supply-Side Economics

Telecommunications Reform Act of 1996

Thatcher, Margaret

Tyson, Laura

Volcker, Paul

World Trade Organization (WTO)

Yellen, Janet

Preface

Today's economic environment is in constant change, as is the role of the governments that oversee it. Governmental agencies, whether local, state, national, or global, have taken on new roles—sometimes larger, sometimes smaller—with both positive and negative economic consequences. It is more important than ever to have a sound understanding and appreciation of a government's various roles at all levels of economic activity.

A central component of any developed economy is a government that actively protects the interests of consumers, businesses, and financial institutions, setting "the rules of the game" and serving as referee to ensure that everyone plays by the rules in a competitive marketplace. What the rules should be, how involved government should be in an economy, and who sets the rules or who plays by the rules have been issues and challenges for every government. The limits of and answers to these issues have been discussed, debated, and argued for centuries, and will continue to be. *Government and the Economy: An Encyclopedia* is not about solving those age-old questions.

It is, however, meant to serve as a "travel guide" into the role of government in an economy. *Government and the Economy: An Encyclopedia* is a comprehensive collection of over 160 entries on the concepts, issues, ideas, writings, people, lessons, and resources on the influence of government's role on the economy for students, researchers, teachers, and writers.

The encyclopedia's purpose is to present and broaden our understanding of government's role from economic, historical, and foundational perspectives. The encyclopedia is a readable, easy-to-understand, general one-stop reference on the world of a government's role in the economy. The encyclopedia appeals to the general readers, students, scholars, and any person interested in the field of economics and government.

Much like the evolution of technology in manufacturing, the role of government in an economy has evolved into economic subdisciplines complete with economists and political leaders who have created a foundation, the principles, and a heritage of government's role in an economy. We believe that we have created the most comprehensive encyclopedia on the market with a focus specifically on the role of government in the economy. More important, we believe that we have written this encyclopedia with the general reader foremost in mind. Yet it is comprehensive enough for the student, teacher, and researcher.

Whether the economy is a developed economy, one that is developing to join the global economy, or one that is making inroads as a transitional economy, in *Government and the*

Economy: An Encyclopedia we have created several ways for exploring the role of governments in all economic systems. The introductory essay, "Government and the Economy: The Ultimate Macroeconomic Pair," outlines the various roles of government in any economy and the philosophies on which the role of government in an economy is based. Many of today's economic decisions are policy decisions at the local, state, and national government levels. *Government and the Economy: An Encyclopedia* provides you a ready reference road map with the A–Z list of entries, the glossary, and special appendices.

The 160-plus A–Z entries introduce you to the many events, people, documents, and concepts that help you gain a better understanding of government's economic role. The entries are written by over 20 contributors who are leading scholars, practitioners, and practicing teachers and academics. The entries are written with a broad-based, politically neutral approach so that the reader does not have to be concerned about any hidden political or economic agenda on the part of the editors or contributors.

Each entry includes cross-references to other entries in the encyclopedia, further related readings, and topic finders to broaden the reader's knowledge. The A–Z entries include economic events, Supreme Court cases, critical legislation by Congress, ideas, concepts, economists, movements, organizations, and documents on the role of government in the economy. As you read the entries, you will notice we have tried to include important maps, photos, tables, and graphs. Additional sources have been provided for ready-reference content for readers with little to no prior knowledge of government's role in the economy.

We have included a comprehensive collection of appendices applicable for the general reader and educator. They are led by a comprehensive glossary to familiarize you with key economics terms that might be unknown to a nonspecialist. A special appendix of Supreme Court cases categorized by their economic impact will give you an "at a glance" look at how some of the most important Supreme Court cases have impacted the U.S. economy. Another appendix highlights the legislation passed by Congress and signed by the president that has altered and changed our economic way of life. A government is responsible for collecting and analyzing a significant amount of economic data. One appendix identifies some of the different data sets and measures of the economy, and looks at who does the measuring and how, as well as the pros and cons and nuances of these measurements, which makes a handy reference on measuring an economy.

For teachers and professors, we have developed two special appendices. The first is the timeline for the encyclopedia's entries. What is so special about this appendix is that we used the "Eras" timeline from the *United States History Content Standards for Grades 5–12 Overview of U.S. Standards, by Eras*. The second special appendix for educators is the classroom materials and sources for the educator, which we have aligned with the high school National Content Standards for Civics and Government, adapted from the Center for Civic Education, and the National Content Standards in Economics from the Council for Economic Education.

One source always welcome among educators is a central location for sources of lessons and ideas for lessons to implement in their classrooms. Our "Resources for Educators and Researchers" appendix is a listing of Web sites and sources providing classroom lessons, materials, and sources on the government's role in the economy.

Finally, to broaden the reader's understanding of government's role, we have created a selected bibliography. This bibliography provides you with references on many of the peripheral topics, issues, and people relevant to government's role in the economy.

We have brought together a diverse group of over 20 scholars and economic educators to create a contributor team with the breadth of experience, expertise, and skills to make such a commanding project possible. Of course, any project of this importance and magnitude would not have been possible without their diligence and dedication. We owe all of them a very heartfelt thank you. As always, we could not have devoted the time and attention as coeditors without a great deal of patience and understanding from our families and friends. To them we owe the most special thank you.

Kathleen C. Simmons
David A. Dieterle

Introduction

Government and the Economy: The Ultimate Macroeconomic Pair

Life is full of pairs. There are the obvious pairs such as a pair of socks, a pair of shoes, or a pair of pants, each part of which must have the other to be functional. There are many things in life that have their "pair." When they reach for the salt, most people also reach for the pepper. If one grew up with peanut butter, most assuredly jelly was also there. In the world of a single person, there are many pairs. In the world of many, many people there are also a few pairs, some more important than others. In the new macroeconomic world of a global economy the most important role for a nation or society is the relationship between its government and its economy.

While one can discuss the government of a nation without discussing the economy, one cannot discuss the nation's economy without discussing its government. The late Nobel laureate Milton Friedman made this point on many occasions. He often spoke of the link between the type of economic system of a nation and the form of government running the nation at the time. Michael Novak, the Catholic theologian turned political commentator, wrote the classic *The Spirit of Democratic Capitalism* (1982) making the same connection between government and economy with the addition of societal norms.

Economic populism has shown conclusively that it is successful only in the short run. In both instances, Friedman and Novak submitted that economic systems and styles of government are paired. If society wants capitalism, it must be willing to have a government functioning as a democracy. On the other side of the spectrum, a dictator with absolute singular political power will not risk that power by conceding the economic power of market freedoms to the people. Capitalism and dictatorship do not mix, like democracy and a centrally planned economy do not make a good pair in the long run.

Experiments to cross-breed the two have been tried throughout history and still are being tried today. Some would contend that China is an experiment in cross-breeding a market economy with a one-voice (single political party) government rule. Many feel that Europe has pushed the rules with its highly socialized yet mostly democratic governments. While functioning success may seem apparent now in the short run, what about in the long run? Therein lies a second important question: How does one distinguish between short run and long run? For the United States, that distinction was settled by one man, John Maynard Keynes—a British economist, no less.

In 1936, in the midst of the Great Depression, John Maynard Keynes published a text that was to change the relationship between government and the economy in the United States forever. When Keynes's *General Theory on Employment, Interest, and Money* (1936) was published, he became the instant expert on the role of government in an economy. He also settled, or appeared to settle, the timing issue with his now-famous response to an interview question on whether his theories would pass the long-run test. To this, Keynes famously replied, "In the long run we are all dead." Question answered, at least for many.

Those who believe Keynes was the beginning of government's role in an economy have been misinformed. While governments throughout history dating back to biblical times and beyond have been the impetus for a functioning economy, even the United States government's role did not begin with Keynes. Alexander Hamilton pressed for government to establish a national bank. Tariffs were instrumental in the early eras of the U.S. economy. There is a commerce clause in the Constitution of the United States. Keynes may have broadened the role of government in an economy, but certainly did not initiate it.

Move the calendar forward to the beginning of the twenty-first century. As the twenty-first century begins government's role in the economy has broadened to include being the consumer police, provider of public goods and services, and distributor and redistributor of the nation's wealth to provide for the less fortunate. While a few of the roles are the exclusive responsibility of the federal government, many of these roles are conducted at the state and local levels as well.

How the Pair Align: The Role of Government in the Economy

Define and Enforce the "Rules of the Game"

Government defines property rights and establishes the law upholding contracts. It also defines the terms of voluntary exchange defining competitive behavior versus noncompetitive behavior and recourse for consumers.

Correct for "Market Failures"

Government alters or produces the quantity of a good or service the public deems appropriate by political consensus if the private market will not provide it in appropriate quantity. The kinds of goods involved in these decisions include collective or public goods such as national defense, a lighthouse, goods with extremely high costs such as highways, or extremely risky ventures like space travel.

A second role for government is to "referee" goods that have a "neighborhood" effect, or externalities. In these instances the market prevents the costs and benefits of a transaction from being totally internalized. The costs or benefits of their production are not borne exclusively by the parties to the exchange (internalized). If such goods emit external or neighborhood costs, they will be produced beyond the socially optimal amount. If the goods emit external or neighborhood benefits, they will not be produced in sufficient quantity to satisfy society. Externalities result from the inadequate assignment of property rights in resources used in the production of final goods. Externalities can have spillover costs or benefits. It is government's role to provide avenues to internalize costs or expand benefits.

Provide Goods with Extremely High Transaction Costs

Government has a role in providing economic goods whose sale involves very high transaction costs. Government may either provide the good directly or provide a subsidy. City parks or general access highways are examples for which a private producer would find it prohibitively expensive to charge individual users, even though a charge for these services could be handled by a private firm. Often these goods, such as utilities, are provided by government giving a regulated monopoly to one firm and avoiding overdistribution and misallocation of resources to one industry.

Provide Goods with Extraordinary Risks

Some goods have such high risks in their provision that no private firm would take on such a venture. One such venture is space exploration. The movie *The Right Stuff* (1983) exhibited very clearly the extremely high risk of space flight when it was in its infancy. No private firm would commit the high costs to such a high-risk venture. Government filled the void.

Allocate "Merit" Goods: Social Goods

Government often provides workplace safety, equal opportunity of employment, and nondiscrimination in the workplace or in employment practices. These are often referred to as "merit" goods and require government intervention on the grounds that the public does not know its own best interests or cannot determine the benefits of these goods efficiently. Often the argument for these "merit" goods is that businesses are not responsive to consumers' or workers' wishes, or exert an influence on consumers or workers that is counter to their interests.

Examples of "merit" goods provided by government include setting work standards through the Occupational Safety and Health Administration (OSHA), or the standards government has set to make us safer in our automobiles. The Federal Drug Administration (FDA) provides a comfort of safety and effectiveness with our drugs or nutritional content in food. Governments provide a standard of performance in certain occupations with licensing requirements.

There are times when a good is offered by the private sector, but government interferes with consumer sovereignty and attempts to alter consumer behavior. Government may use its taxing to levy a "sin tax" on goods such as tobacco and alcohol in an attempt to reduce consumption of these private goods. Gasoline has also been taxed at times to alter behavior by changing driving habits to reduce driving.

Regulate Natural Monopolies

Firms whose costs decline over a relevant range of production need what is called economies of scale to be viable to the consumer. If two or more firms were to compete in these industries, they would divide the total output so their individual output levels would not be sufficient and the costs of supplying the good much higher. This scenario calls for government to designate one company as the provider of the good. This, of course, equates to giving the designated company a monopoly. For this solution to be palatable to the consumer, government then regulates the monopoly and monitors the output of the firm and controls the price the firm can charge.

Stabilize Aggregate Economic Activity

John Maynard Keynes argued that government needs to be an active participant in an economy during times of recession, and less active during times of growth. Government can use fiscal and monetary policy tools to stabilize an economy, accelerating the economy during times of recession or slowing it down during times of rapid expansion. Since no one individual has the adequate resources to do this, or even the inclination to do so, government needs to intercede during such economic times. Government has the power to tax, to spend, and to supply currency to move the economy in a desired economic direction.

Redistribute Income to Provide a Social Safety Net

Government can use its power to tax and its tax structure to redistribute income, thus providing a social safety net for those less fortunate or in temporary need. As a society, we do not like to see people go hungry, not have a place to sleep, or be denied access to education. Government takes on a more pragmatic role in an economy by providing basic services.

Engage in Public Enterprise

Somewhat similar to several roles above, government's role in public enterprise differs in that government does not need to be the deliverer of the good itself. The only enterprise listed above that government can do exclusively is supply currency. For all the others, the private sector can be delegated to in order to carry out the various tasks. Or the government and society may find it is more expedient for government to provide the merit good. These goods include education, public health, and the postal service for first-class mail.

This involvement by government results in its influencing the quantity of goods produced involving externalities, high transaction costs, or extremely high risks. Government unilaterally decides the private market does not produce a sufficient supply for total public consumption, determining which goods the private market does not value sufficiently. Government engages in the economy to oversee natural monopolies, stabilize the economy, supply the currency, redistribute income, stabilize the aggregate economy, or produce certain products. While government produces very little for the economy, it funds a great deal of private-sector activity to produce public goods; for example, a private construction company might build a public school and be paid using public funds generated through taxes or public municipal bonds.

"Regulate" Private Industry: Enforce Property Rights

Government regulates the economy by policing the activity of private firms. Government enforces property rights by enforcing antitrust and collusion activities. It attempts to internalize costs (minimize the effects of externalities) by either regulating a firm or providing subsidies and incentives to correct the externality. As mentioned before, government influences the regulation and provision of "merit" goods, controls regulated monopolies, and redistributes income to provide a social safety net for the less fortunate.

From Alexander Hamilton's federalism to President Franklin Roosevelt's New Deal to President Lyndon Johnson's Great Society, the role of government has broadened and deepened with regard to the economy. Many discussions, debates, and arguments have taken place from family kitchen tables to local pubs to the halls of Congress about the limits of government's role in an economy and the successes and failures of such involvements. What is certain is that government does have a role to play. Government sets private property laws in Congress, the rule of law is upheld in the Supreme Court, and the executive branch executes and upholds private property and rule-of-law statutes. Without government serving as referee and provider of certain services, our lives would be very different. For example, without national defense, we would not feel as safe. We could not travel without access to highways. We would not feel comfortable as consumers without government regulations. And we would not have the world role we have without total access to education. The pairing of government and the economy is integral to the fabric of our life.

to internalize costs (to minimize the effects of externalities) by either regulating a firm or providing subsidies and incentives to correct the externality. As mentioned before, government influences the regulation and provision [illegible] regulated [illegible] policies and redistributes income to [illegible] social safety net [illegible] less fortunate.

[illegible]

Affordable Health Care Act Cases, 567 U.S. ___ (2012)

Economic Concepts

Opportunity costs; taxes; fiscal policy; markets; role of government; income redistribution

Economic Impact

The Supreme Court upheld the power of Congress to change the market of an economic good; in this instance, the health care market by requiring most Americans to purchase health insurance.

Economic Summary

It is rational to assume that virtually all Americans at some time in their lives will enter the health care market. In addition, it is safe to infer that without health insurance (the financial means to pay for products and services in the health care market) many Americans will experience economic hardship during this exchange. Some will not be able to pay at all. For them, the products or services are provided without cost. The cost is shifted to those with the means to pay. Thus, the consequences of this market on the nation are to economically burden the individuals who have the ability to pay and redistribute income to pay the cost of health care for those who cannot. As in the case of Social Security, the authority of the federal government to attempt to remedy the financial shortcomings and aid the general welfare comes into question with *Health and Human Services v. Florida et al.* This case was a combination of two other cases, all three of which posed fundamental constitutional questions. The Court viewed this case not in terms of whether it was good or poor public policy, but rather from the perspective of whether Congress had adhered to constitutional principles.

Case Summary

There is an adage that history tends to repeat itself; however, people learn little from history, and in the future repeat the arguments of the past. This was a case where the United States headed straight back to the future. In both *Pollock v. Farmers' Loan and Trust Company* (1895, income tax) and *Helvering v. Davis* (1937, Social Security tax), when government exercised its taxing power, the debate began anew. In 2010, Congress passed the Patient Protection and Affordable Care Act (ACA). Congress crafted this piece of legislation and the accompanying taxes to deal with negative externalities and social issues related to the health care market. This sparked a national debate on the appropriate role of government within the market system, as well as a lively discourse on what constitutes taxes, commerce, and states' rights.

Historically, the roots of health care in the United States were in private enterprise, subject to the rules of the marketplace. The majority of the nation's health care infrastructure was owned by private companies, either for profit or nonprofit. Health care was delivered through practitioners in medical fields that, over the years, have increased and specialized. These providers functioned within a market system and were vital in promoting the general health and well-being of citizens. Any intervention deemed appropriate for the government was restricted to state legislatures. Two centuries later, this structure has evolved into a joint effort, both public and private. The facilities and practitioners have remained mostly private. The unique factor that differentiates this market is the means by which payment is made. Today, this is known as health insurance. The time when a physician could be paid with a chicken and Aunt Sophie's apple pie has mostly disappeared.

The health care market and the health insurance industry are inextricably entwined. Private and public health care facilities and insurance companies exist together. Currently, government programs provide the majority of health insurance. These include Medicaid (government health insurance for the indigent); Medicare (government health insurance for the elderly); Children's Health Insurance (government health insurance for indigent children); TRICARE (civilian health benefits for military personnel, retirees, and their dependants); and the Veterans Health Administration (government health care for disabled veterans). Most Americans not covered by these programs purchase health insurance through their employers or other private companies. In all cases, whether private or public sources, the choice to purchase insurance had always been up to the consumer. This free entry into the market changed with the passage of the ACA.

The cost impact of the existing mixed public-private system is controversial, but what remains constant is that health care as a percentage of the U.S. GDP (Gross Domestic Product) is substantial. From a market perspective, this system of third-party payment removes the consumer from the role of main determinant affecting the cost of products and services. Instead, government health insurance providers reimburse at rates that may not reflect the natural equilibrium of the market. Add to this other medical factors, such as higher-priced technologies, more extensive diagnostic testing, new treatments with various nonmedical practices, and the result is cost shifting from government rates to higher rates for the same services from private payers. As a consequence, the overall cost of health care in the United States has increased.

In March 2010, the ACA became law, creating considerable changes in health insurance. The goals of the act included making affordable health insurance available for all Americans and reducing the costs of health care for individuals and the government. It proposed mandates, subsidies, and insurance exchanges as mechanisms to reach these goals. The main tools for increasing insurance coverage were creating state-based insurance exchanges and expanding Medicaid eligibility. A central component of this legislation was the health insurance mandate, requiring all Americans to buy health insurance or pay a fine for not participating.

Soon after the ink dried on President Obama's signature, Florida and 25 other states, two individuals, and the National Federation of Independent Business (NFIB), among others, filed lawsuits against the federal government challenging the constitutionality of the individual mandate. They claimed that the expansion of Medicaid, wherein the states either followed federal directive or lost their original money from Washington to provide health care for the indigent, was unconstitutional. Judge Roger Vinson of the U.S. Federal Court for the Northern District of Florida agreed with the plaintiffs that the commerce clause of the Constitution limits Congress's authority and declared the entire law unconstitutional. This case, along with others, was appealed to the Eleventh Circuit Court of Appeals, where a three-judge panel affirmed Judge Vinson's decision regarding Medicaid and the individual mandate, claiming that it exceeded Congress's authority as enumerated in the Constitution. This set the stage for a showdown in the U.S. Supreme Court.

The Supreme Court took the appeal and combined three cases, *Florida et al. v. Department of Health and Human Services et al.*; *National Federation of Independent Business et al. v. Kathleen Sebelius, Secretary of Health and Human Services, et al.*; and *Department of Health and Human Services et al. v. Florida et al.* The responsibility of the Roberts Court in this case was to determine whether or not Congress had exceeded its constitutional powers by requiring the individual mandate, and whether the requirement to the states to expand Medicaid or lose funding was coercion. In addition, there was a discussion of whether or not the right to sue the government over a tax before the tax had been paid was even admissible under the Anti-Injunction Act of 1867.

The Court scheduled an unprecedented six hours of oral argument (a normal case would take only one hour) in an effort to anticipate the complexity and significance of this case. The justices listened to and questioned seven different attorneys. At the end of the day, the Court ruled that the Anti-Injunction Act did not bar the Court from hearing this petition. It also found that Congress does have the authority under the commerce clause and the taxing and spending clause of the Constitution to require that most Americans purchase health insurance. Finally, the Court ruled that Congress did exceed its powers of federalism when it pressured states into the conditions imposed on states if they did not expand Medicaid, as proposed by the guidelines of the ACA.

Chief Justice Roberts wrote the majority opinion. He stated clearly that the Court did not impose an opinion as to the law itself, but rather determined if the law was constitutional. With regard to the mandate, the Court held that the goal of affordable health coverage would not be obtainable without nationwide participation. This was how insurance companies functioned, having enough healthy participants to cover those in need. This provided for the general welfare and was within the realm of Congress's power. However, the idea that states could be coerced into compliance with federal mandates by withholding funds to crucial services was indeed a violation of states' rights.

In politics, a national crisis is often seen as an opportunity to pursue an agenda. This was not an easy agenda. Health care never has been. But neither was the Sixteenth Amendment or Social Security, and some would argue that the crisis for that legislation was even more acute. In his dissent, Justice Kennedy, along with Justices Scalia, Thomas, and Alito, stated that the commerce clause of the Constitution did not permit Congress to create commerce where it did not already exist, but rather to regulate it where it was already happening. They thought that the Framers would not condone this type of intrusion upon the market. Scalia argued that mandating that all Americans purchase funeral insurance because eventually we would all die was absurd. The Constitution protected the right of consumers to decide what products or services they would purchase and Congress did not have the police power to preempt this right.

There has been much political discourse regarding health care. There will be much more. What is clear is that this case established as constitutional the most significant health care reform in a generation.

Kathleen C. Simmons

See Also Constitution of the United States (see Appendix); Entitlements; Gross Domestic Product (GDP); Public Goods; Social Security Act of 1935; Supreme Court; Taxes

Related Cases

Pollock v. Farmers' Loan and Trust Co., 157 U.S. 429 (1895) (Upheld the Sixteenth Amendment)

Helvering v. Davis, 301 U.S. 619 (1935) (Upheld Social Security)

National Federation of Independent Business v. Sebelius, 567 U.S. (2012) (Included in this decision)

Florida v. Department of Health and Human Services, 567 U.S. (2012) (Included in this decision)

Further Readings

"#11-398, In the Supreme Court of the United States." http://now.iscotus.org/healthcare/11-398_brief-in-opposition_1.pdf. (Petition of certiorari from Florida to the Supreme Court)

"#11-398, In the Supreme Court of the United States." http://now.iscotus.org/healthcare/11-398_brief-in-opposition_1.pdf. (Brief in response for private respondents)

"#11-398, In the Supreme Court of the United States." http://now.iscotus.org/healthcare/11-398_brief-in-opposition_2.pdf. (Brief for state respondents)

"#11-398, In the Supreme Court of the United States." http://now.iscotus.org/healthcare/11-398_reply.pdf. (Reply brief for petitioners)

"#11-398, In the Supreme Court of the United States." http://now.iscotus.org/healthcare/States%20brief%20as%20petitioner%20(Medicaid).pdf. (Brief of state petitioners on Medicaid)

"#11-398, In the Supreme Court of the United States." http://now.iscotus.org/healthcare/U.S.%20brief%20(11-400%20Medicaid).pdf. (Brief for respondents on Medicaid)

"#11-398, In the Supreme Court of the United States." http://now.iscotus.org/healthcare/11-398_petition_appendix.pdf. (Appendix A, B, C, D, E for a writ of certiorari [court of appeals decision; order granting summary judgment; district court order; order on motion to dismiss; constitutional and statutory provisions])

"In the Supreme Court of the United States." http://www.justice.gov/healthcare/docs/hhs-v-florida-petition-certiorari.pdf. (Copy of the petition for a writ of certiorari)

Resources for Teachers

OYEZ, ITT Chicago, Kent College of Law. N.d. "The Affordable Care Act Cases." http://www.oyez.org/cases/2010-2019/2011/2011_11_400. (Summary of the Affordable Care Act cases)

Scotusblog. N.d. "*National Federation of Independent Business v. Sebelius.*" http://www.scotusblog.com/case-files/cases/national-federation-of-independent-business-v-sebelius/. (The Supreme Court blog Web site on health care)

The Court and Healthcare Reform. N.d. "The Cases." http://now.iscotus.org/healthcare/.

Alaska Dept. of Environmental Conservation v. EPA, 540 U.S. 461 (2004)

A Supreme Court Case on the Environment, Economic Growth, and Federalism

Economic Concepts

Economic growth; federalism

Economic Impact

Balancing economic growth with the economic and social costs involved in protecting the environment is a challenge for industries as well as state and national governments.

Economic Summary

Standards for safeguarding the environment are set at both the state and national levels. Most of the economic burden associated with protecting the environment and economic growth is incurred by local industry. Meeting clean air standards includes expenses that increase the cost of doing business. In a competitive market, these added expenditures to clean up existing factories and build new ones have long-term effects on a state's economic development. In addition, there is a political relationship between economic growth and protecting the environment. In the case of *Alaska Dept. of Environmental Conservation v. EPA*, the relationship between the state of Alaska and a federal bureaucratic agency snowballed into a classic battle between states' rights and federal power.

Case Summary

Red Dog Mine is one of the largest zinc mines in the world. It is located in the Northwest Arctic borough of Alaska, almost 50 miles from the Chukchi Sea. Red Dog is operated by Teck Cominco Alaska Incorporated and owned by NANA, a regional Alaska native corporation formed in 1971 under the Alaska Native Land Claims Settlement Act (ANCSA). NANA (not an acronym) is a for-profit corporation owned by thousands of Inupiat (indigenous people who inhabit northwest Alaska) and is one of Alaska's largest employers. The partnership between Teck and NANA over the last three decades has been a serious contributor to Alaska's economy. Mine operations provide hundreds of jobs for the local and regional economy as well as key economic benefits to Alaska's Native population through shareholder dividends and community support.

The method Red Dog Mining uses to extract zinc and lead is an open pit process where there is drilling, blasting, and separating. To secure future productivity, a plan for expansion of the mining industry included the completion of a new diesel-fired power generator to fuel operations. Mining can have negative impacts on the surrounding environment, including air, soil, and water. However, this case was concerned with air pollution from the stacks connected with the power generator.

During President Lyndon Johnson's administration, the Clean Air Act of 1963 was signed into law. This Act authorized the U.S. Public Health Department to research techniques that would monitor and control air quality. The Clean Air Act of 1970 (CAA) changed the focus from research and monitoring to setting standards and enforcement. At the same time, the 90th Congress passed the National Environmental Policy Act (NEPA), which took effect in January 1970. This landmark piece of legislation was passed unanimously in the Senate and almost as favorably in the House, reflecting an increased national appreciation for the environment and attention to its safekeeping. Following this stream of legislation, in December 1970, President Nixon signed an executive order (presidential power that enables the operation and management of the federal government) consolidating the administration and enforcement of environmental law to the Environmental Protection Agency (EPA).

At the onset of this case, Alaska had not seen 30 legislative sessions. In terms of developing bureaucratic agencies, statutory history, and political encounters, Alaska is a youngster. The fledgling Alaska Department of Environmental Conservation (ADEC) has a division of Air Quality that manages stationary out-of-stack discharges of air pollution through a permit and compliance program. In addition, it monitors, measures, and alerts the public to any health concerns. These standards were developed with the federal EPA guidelines in mind but reflect the unique idiosyncrasies of Alaska, i.e., an occasional volcanic eruption or glacial ice dust storm. As well as the federal and state duty to the environment, industries such as Teck and Red Dog Mining assert that they also take seriously their responsibility to care for the land and to ensure the future of these natural resource benefits.

Red Dog Mining applied for a permit through ADEC to comply with local and federal air quality standards at its construction site. The Clean Air Act states that new facilities must use the "best available control technology" (BACT) to limit pollution, especially in areas still relatively free of contamination. Alaska had a legal obligation to meet this standard, but on final review, the state decided that the BACT was too costly and gave a permit for a less expensive alternative. The EPA disagreed, and after much-documented memo tag, ordered a halt to construction of the Red Dog generator in February 2000. Alaska challenged the EPA in the Ninth Circuit Court of Appeals in San Francisco. The appellate court upheld the EPA's authority to require a stricter interpretation of the standards and frowned upon the pressure put on states by industries feeling the economic weight of added costs. Alaska appealed to the Supreme Court.

In October 2003, the Supreme Court heard arguments in the case of *Alaska Dept. of Environmental Conservation v. EPA*. The plaintiff argued that the EPA did not have the authority to override a discretionary determination by the state of Alaska. Moreover, it was never Congress's intention to allow such encroachment of the federal government into what should be decided by local priorities and local control. Furthermore, if the EPA did not agree with Alaska's interpretation of the law, the correct procedure was a review by courts. The EPA disregarded states' rights and overstepped its congressional authority when it barred the construction of the facility.

The EPA responded by stating that nothing in the CAA allowed states a shield from arbitrary and unreasonable decision making. In the EPA's view, Alaska was arguing the letter of the law—procedure—and ignoring the spirit of the law—clean air. As for the former, the EPA had a due process drill that Alaska chose not to follow. In the EPA's opinion, air quality suffered and procedural due process was not a valid excuse. The EPA recognized that state agencies had the power to make discretionary decisions as to what constituted the BACT based on what the costs would mean to the mine in terms of profitability, employment, or global competitiveness. The problem was that Alaska admitted that the Red Dog Mining Company had failed to bring this evidence to trial. Alaska thereby conceded that it had made the discretionary decision without substantive facts. The EPA claimed the authority to stop such random acts of disregard for air quality, as Congress gave it a mandate to carry out the intent of the law.

The responsibility of the Supreme Court in this case was to determine if under the CAA, the EPA had the authority to overrule a state agency's discretionary decision in determining the BACT. The Court questioned the EPA's implication that in this case Alaska was not the depository of best judgment as to what would work in local communities and federal law requirements. On the other hand, the Court examined the extent of Congress's intention to give the EPA the enforcement authority to prevent significant deterioration of ambient air, especially in areas where early prevention would be key to maintaining air quality.

In January 2004, in a 5–4 vote, the Court decided to uphold the findings of the Ninth Circuit Court. Justice Ginsburg wrote in the opinion of the court that ADEC should have stayed with its original permit suggestion to Red Dog Mining, whereby emissions would be reduced by 90 percent, as opposed to its final decision, allowing only a 30 percent reduction. The Court conceded that states have the discretionary power to make these decisions, though not untethered to the federal requirements of BACT as stated in the CAA. In this case, the justification of this choice lacked evidentiary support and was therefore unreasonable. In addition, it assumed hypothetical usage of various smoke stacks to justify the lower standards, again not providing enough substantive evidence. In the opinion of the Court, the EPA properly exercised its authority when it stopped construction at the Red Dog Mine.

James Madison cautioned in the Federalist Papers #46 that intrusion of the federal government on the power of state governments would be cause for serious alarm. Justice Kennedy echoes Madison's forewarning in his dissent. He states that the majority opinion rests its findings on principles that do not preserve the integrity of the states in our federalist system. Furthermore, Kennedy continues, the EPA exceeded its power by executing administrative fiat and not allowing a review by the courts to take place. By definition, BACT presumes that the states will take into consideration all criteria and apply a more comprehensive lens to the decision-making process.

However, preceding the federal intervention in Alaska was a chain of events from Love Canal to the publication of Rachel Carson's *Silent Spring*. The balance of environment and economic growth involves an evolution of circumstances. Indeed, James Madison continues his analysis in the Federalist Papers #10, stating that the Constitution is a "happy combination" in which the national government takes the aggregate interest and the states care for the local and particular concerns. Whether or not the Clean Air Act anticipated the local and particular concerns to be accommodated by the agents of the state legislatures remains part of this precarious balancing act. The outcome in this case suggests that the federal government must be vigilant in safeguarding standards that Congress established to protect the environment.

Kathleen C. Simmons

See Also Environmental Protection Agency (EPA); Supreme Court

Related Cases

Vermont Yankee Nuclear Power Corp. v. Natural Resources Defense Council, Inc., 435 U.S. 519 (1978) (State agencies have authority to fashion their own rules of procedure even when a statute does not specify what process to use)

Barnhart v. Walton, 535 U.S. 212 (2002) (Court supports procedural due process as deferred to administrative agencies)

Further Readings

Legal Information Institute. Cornell University Law School. N.d. "*Alaska Dept. of Environmental Conservation v. EPA* (02-658) 540 U.S. 461 (2004) 298 F.3d 814, affirmed. Opinion of the Court Delivered by Justice Ginsburg." http://www.law.cornell.edu/supct/html/02-658.ZO.html.

Legal Information Institute. Cornell University Law School. N.d. "*Alaska Dept. of Environmental Conservation v. EPA* (02-658) 540 U.S. 461 (2004) 298 F.3d 814, affirmed—Transcript Kennedy, J. Dissenting." http://www.law.cornell.edu/supct/html/02-658.ZD.html.

OYEZ, ITT Chicago, Kent College of Law. N.d. "*Alaska Dept. of Environmental Conserv. v. EPA*: Facts of the Case." www.oyez.org/cases/2000-2009/2003/2003_02_658.

OYEZ, ITT Chicago, Kent College of Law. N.d. "*Alaska Dept. of Environmental Conserv. v. EPA*: Full Transcript Text of Oral Argument and Opinion Announced." http://www.oyez.org/cases/2000-2009/2003/2003_02_658.

Resources for Teachers

Constitution USA with Peter Sagal. N.d. "Federalism." http://www.pbs.org/tpt/constitution-usa-peter-sagal/federalism/#.U3uFYfldWSo.

Legal Information Institute. Cornell University Law School. N.d. "Federalism." http://www.law.cornell.edu/wex/federalism.

The Library of Congress. N.d. "The Federalist Papers." http://thomas.loc.gov/home/histdox/fedpapers.html.

America Invents Act of 2011 (Leahy-Smith Act)

The America Invents Act of 2011 updates the patent system to encourage innovation, job creation, and economic growth. The last major patent reform took place with the Patent

Act of 1952. The America Invents Act of 2011 was sponsored by House Judiciary Committee chairman Lamar Smith (a Republican representative from Texas) and Senator Patrick Leahy, Democrat from Vermont. On September 16, President Obama signed the America Invents Act of 2011 into law.

Patents encourage innovation and business growth, providing inventors and innovators protection from duplication and copycat theft. The act helps the nation's innovators and job creators, who rely on the patent system to make new products. The act implements a first-inventor-to-file (FITF) standard for patent approval and creates a post-grant review system to filter out bad patents.

The America Invents Act affects three main parts of the economy: job creation, patent office reforms, and legal reform. For job creation, the act protects the rights of inventors for their original inventions and encourages business growth by speeding up the patent process so that entrepreneurs and innovators can quickly turn their inventions into businesses. The adoption of the FITF system ends the need for expensive discovery and litigation to establish priority dates, while also ensuring priority dates through simple and inexpensive provisional applications. The act also builds on the Bayh-Dole Act, which permits universities and small businesses to keep title to their inventions in exchange for fulfilling a series of obligations: disclosing the invention to the federal agency funding the research, electing to retain title, and filing patent applications. The 2011 America Invents Act adds extra patent protections to the previously mentioned Bayh-Dole Act while also changing various timing requirements, such as the contractor having to file a patent application before the expiration of a one-year period. The America Invents Act also assists the Patent and Trademark Office (PTO) in addressing the backlog of patent applications. Its 15 percent surcharge (which became effective September 26, 2011) aided the PTO's hiring of new examiners and other personnel. The act also provides some relief to patent owners to practice their inventions. Before this act, failure to mark the product as patented meant the patent-marking statute operated as a forfeiture of damage. Since the act was implemented, however, patent owners no longer have to include the patent number on the product. Instead, they can merely put "patent," along with an address of a Web site that posts the patented article with the patent number, saving the cost of new manufacturing equipment every time the patent changes. Finally, the America Invents Act of 2011 influences legal reform. The act not only creates an administrative program for review of business method patents, but it also provides additional options to challenge the validity of an issued patent. It adds a new procedure called the post-grant review (PGR). A petition for PGR can be based on lack of enablement, lack of utility, and/or failure to comply with written description requirements. If the petition is granted, the proceedings may allow for oral proceedings and a chance for the patent owner to amend.

Lastly, the America Invents Act affects patent office reform. It creates an anti-fee diversion (before this act, the patent application fees were diverted by congressional appropriators to other government programs), and ends the practice of fee diversion at the PTO. This effectively lowers taxes on innovators and innovation. It also ensures continued congressional oversight by both the Judiciary and the Appropriations Committee in the House and Senate. The act allows the PTO director to adjust fees to better accommodate market conditions and help reduce the time it takes to review and issue a patent to get the product into the market quickly and efficiently. To summarize, the America Invents Act creates cost-effective alternative legal forums that will provide a simpler way to review questions of patentability, reducing the costs of frivolous litigation against job creators.

Shima Sadaghiyani

See Also Protectionism

Further Reading

Bryant, Tracie L. 2012. "The America Invents Act: Slaying Trolls, Limiting Joinder." *Harvard Journal of Law & Technology* 25: 687–711.

Jeruss, Sara, et al. 2012. "The America Invents Act 500: Effects of Patent Monetization Entities on U.S. Litigation." *Duke Law & Technology Review* 11: 357–89.

Rantanen, Jason, and Lee Petherbridge. 2011. "Toward a System of Invention Registration: The Leahy-Smith America Invents Act." *Michigan Law Review First Impressions* 110: 24–62.

Resources for Teachers

America Invents Act. N.d. "Leahy-Smith America Invents Act." http://www.aiarulemaking.com/about.php.

Stanford University Office of Technology Licensing. N.d. "The America Invents Act (AIA)." http://otl.stanford.edu/inventors/resources/inventors_aia.html.

The United States Patent and Trademark Office. N.d. "Leahy-Smith America Invents Act Implementation." http://www.uspto.gov/aia_implementation/.

Arrow, Kenneth

Born: August 23, 1921, in New York City; general equilibrium theory, welfare theory, economic growth, Nobel Prize (1972); Major work: *Social Choice and Individual Values* (1951).

Kenneth J. Arrow is an American economist. In 1972, he, along with Sir John Hicks, won the Nobel Prize in Economics for work on general equilibrium and welfare economics. Arrow is also known for his work in the area of public choice, for he introduced and defended the impossibility theorem in his dissertation.

Kenneth Joseph Arrow was born on August 23, 1921, in New York City. He did his undergraduate work at the City College of New York, where he received a bachelor of science in social science with a major in mathematics in 1940. He received an MA in mathematics from Columbia University in 1941. At that point, he switched to the Economics Department at Columbia for further graduate work, having completed his PhD course work in 1942, although he was still in search of a dissertation topic. His dissertation research was interrupted by military service during World War II in the U.S. Army Air Corps, where he served as weather officer, rising to the rank of captain. It was here that he had his first published paper, "On the Optimal Use of Winds for Flight Planning."

Upon his return from the military, Arrow was at Columbia for a brief period before joining the Cowles Commission at the University of Chicago in 1947. Time spent with other young econometricians and mathematically oriented economists proved to be a significant influence.

Arrow became affiliated with the RAND Corporation in 1948 and continued that relationship into the 1970s. It was early in his time at RAND that he arrived at an idea for his dissertation. He sought to apply the newly emerging field of game theory to large groups, such as countries. His research was published in 1951 under the title *Social Choice and Individual Values*. The work introduced the "impossibility theorem," which stated that, given certain assumptions, it was impossible to find a voting construct that would provide an outcome that most voters preferred. This provided and continues to provide great insights into social welfare theory, as well as voter behavior in the public arena.

In 1949, Arrow joined the Economics Department at Stanford University, where he would stay until leaving to join the faculty at Harvard in 1968. While at Stanford, some of his most significant early works were published: the aforementioned *Social Choice and Individual Values*, several articles on competitive equilibrium with Leonid Hurwicz from 1958 to 1960, and his contribution to "Toward a Theory of Price Adjustment" in *Allocation of Economic Resources*, edited by Moses Abramovitz, in 1959. Also while at Stanford, Arrow won the John Bates Clark Medal in 1957. It was while at Stanford that he also began his research into economic growth. His article "The Economic Implications of Learning by Doing" is a precursor to modern growth theory and the role of human capital.

In 1968, Arrow accepted a position at Harvard University. He would remain on the faculty at Harvard until returning to Stanford in 1979. While at Harvard, Arrow continued his work in the areas of information, market efficiency, and public choice, producing several articles and books of note. These include *Public Investment, the Rate of Return, and Optimal Fiscal Policy* (with Mordecai Kurz) in 1970; *Essays on the Theory of Risk-Bearing* in 1970; *General Competitive Analysis* (with Frank Hahn) in 1971; and *The Limits of Organization* in 1974. Each of these provided insights into the role of information in markets or decision making. Arrow also produced significant research on the economics of discrimination and of health care.

Upon his return to Stanford in 1979, he became the Joan Kenney Professor of Economics and professor of economic research. During this second period at Stanford, Arrow continued his work on the impact of information in the market and in decision making, as well as providing important insights into topics as widely divergent as income distribution and globalization.

Arrow retired in 1991, but remains professor emeritus at Stanford. He continues his research into areas of information economics, growth, and the environment.

Timothy P. Schilling

See Also Fiscal Policy; Welfare State

Selected Works by Kenneth Arrow

Arrow, Kenneth J. 1983. *Behavior under Uncertainty and Its Implications for Policy*. No. TR-399. Stanford, CA: Center for Research on Organizational Efficiency, Stanford University.

Arrow, Kenneth J. 1971. *Essays on the Theory of Risk-Bearing*. Chicago: Markham.

Arrow, Kenneth J., and Frank H. Hahn. 1971. *General Competitive Analysis*. Amsterdam, NL: North Holland.

Arrow, Kenneth J. 1974. *The Limits of Organization*. New York: Norton.

Arrow, Kenneth J. 1987. *Handbook of Mathematical Economics*. Vol. 1. Handbooks in Economics. Amsterdam, NL: North Holland.

Arrow, Kenneth, and Mordecai Kurz. 1970. *Public Investment, the Rate of Return, and Optimal Fiscal Policy*. Washington, DC: RFF Press.

Arrow, Kenneth J. 1973. *Theoretical Issues in Health Insurance*. Essex, UK: University of Essex.

Arrow, Kenneth J. 1959. "Toward a Theory of Price Adjustment." In *Studies in Resource Allocation Processes*, edited by Kenneth Joseph Arrow and Leonid Hurwicz, 380–90. Cambridge: Cambridge University Press.

Arrow, Kenneth J. 1951. *Social Choice and Individual Values*. Hoboken, NJ: Wiley.

Selected Works about Kenneth Arrow

Arrow, Kenneth J. 1972. "Autobiography." Nobelprize.org. http://www.nobelprize.org/nobel_prizes/economics/laureates/1972/arrow-autobio.html.

Chichilnisky, Graciela, ed. 1999. *Markets, Information and Uncertainty: Essays in Economic Theory in Honor of Kenneth J. Arrow*. Cambridge: Cambridge University.

Hammer, Peter J., Deborah Haas-Wilson, Mark A. Peterson, and William M. Sage., eds. 2003. *Uncertain Times: Kenneth Arrow and the Changing Economics of Health Care*. Durham, NC: Duke University Press.

"Kenneth Arrow." In *The Concise Encyclopedia of Economics*, ed. David R. Henderson. The Library of Economics and Liberty. http://www.econlib.org/library/Enc/bios/Arrow.html.

"Kenneth Arrow." The RAND Corporation. Accessed February 2011. http://www.rand.org/pubs/authors/a/arrow_kenneth.html.

"Kenneth Arrow." Stanford University. Accessed March 2011. http://economics.stanford.edu/faculty/arrow.

Scheib, Ariel. N.d. "Kenneth Arrow." Jewish Virtual Library. http://www.jewishvirtuallibrary.org/jsource/biography/arrow.html.

B

Banking Act of 1933 (Glass-Steagall Act)

The Banking Act of 1933, also known as the Glass-Steagall Act, was introduced as a response to the stock market crash of 1929. It established the Federal Deposit Insurance Corporation (FDIC) and enforced many other banking reforms. The congressional sponsors of this act were Senator Carter Glass, a Democrat from Virginia, and Representative Henry Steagall, a Democrat from Alabama. The Banking Act of 1933 combined two congressional projects: 1) the creation of a federal system of bank deposit insurance, and 2) the regulation of commercial and investment banking. Although at the time, the Roosevelt administration and many in Congress resisted and criticized the act for introducing inefficiency and limiting competition, today many of its supporters consider the act to be the possible explanation for a long period of financial stability in U.S. banking history.

Contrary to the commercial banking theory prevalent during the 1920s, many economists and politicians argue that the stock market crash of 1929 happened mainly because banks were loosely regulated and were actively involved in security market speculation. Following its inception in 1913, the Federal Reserve System had minimal control over the activities of U.S. commercial banks. Senator Glass was one of the proponents of the commercial banking theory, which suggests that commercial banks should limit their lending to short-term loans to finance only the production and sale of goods (versus securities such as stocks or bonds) in commercial transactions. Glass believed that if this theory had been followed and enforced, the crash of 1929 could have been avoided. Senator Glass introduced his first bill on June 17, 1930, to investigate the operations of the National and Federal Reserve banking systems.

Furthermore, Glass and his long-term adviser Henry Willis opposed the engagement of commercial banks in real estate lending, a practice that decades later crippled the U.S. economy during the recession of 2007–2009. Glass criticized banks for lending to stock market speculators and for engaging in risky security transactions, and criticized the Federal Reserve for not applying better regulatory policy.

In 1933, Senator Carter Glass and Representative Henry Steagall introduced the Banking or Glass-Steagall Act. The main purpose of this historic legislation was to limit conflicts of interest between the banks and individual investors caused by the involvement of commercial banks in underwriting activities related to the security exchange. The new law prohibited commercial banks from underwriting securities. In addition, the banks had to choose between being a commercial or an investment bank. The Glass-Steagall Act also introduced the Federal Deposit Insurance Corporation (FDIC) to insure deposits of all commercial banks and to increase the control of the Federal Reserve over them. The deposit insurance and most provisions of the act were severely attacked during congressional debate, mainly for limiting competition and introducing inefficiency into the U.S. banking industry. Despite all opposition, the Banking Act of 1933 was signed into law by President Roosevelt on June 16, 1933.

The law imposed numerous banking reforms and established the FDIC in the U.S. banking system. The Banking Act of 1933 had a significant number of provisions, many of which were changed or repealed over time. The provision that required all FDIC-insured banks to be members of the Federal Reserve System was repealed in 1939. In 1956, the Bank Holding Company Act extended banking regulations by restricting banks that owned other banks from engaging in nonbanking activities or acquiring banks in other states. During the 1960s and 1970s, bank lobbyists persuaded Congress to allow commercial banks to enter the securities market. By the 1970s, a number of investment firms started introducing some of the traditional commercial banking services, offering services such as money market accounts with interest, allowing check writing, and offering credit or debit cards.

In 1986, the Federal Reserve Board bent the law by allowing commercial banks to earn up to 5 percent of their gross revenue from investment banking. Later, the Federal Reserve Board allowed the Banker Trust, a commercial bank, to actively participate in short-term credit transactions and underwriting activities. Finally, in 1987, after more than five decades of strong lobbying of big commercial and investment firms against the Banking Act of 1933, the Federal Reserve Board voted three to two in favor of easing the restrictions imposed by the act. In March 1987, despite strong opposition from Paul Volcker, the Federal Reserve Board chair at the time, the Fed approved an application by Chase Manhattan to participate in underwriting securities. In addition, the Fed increased the limit for participation of commercial banks in securities investment from 5 percent to 10 percent of their gross revenue.

In August 1987, Alan Greenspan became the new chair of the Federal Reserve Board of Governors. A former director of J. P. Morgan, Greenspan firmly advocated for banking deregulation. In 1989, the Federal Board approved additional applications by J. P. Morgan, Chase Manhattan, and other national banks to allow them to expand their transactions to debt and equity securities. In 1990, J. P. Morgan became the first bank to participate in underwriting activities, with the condition that it not exceed the newly imposed 10 percent limits. After the Senate's numerous failed attempts to repeal the Glass-Steagall Act of 1933, in December 1996, supported by Chairman Alan Greenspan, the Federal Reserve Board increased the limit for engaging in securities business to 25 percent of the gross revenue of commercial banks. Finally, in 1999, Congress passed the Financial Services Modernization Act, repealing the Banking Act of 1933.

Elham Mahmoudi

See Also Federal Deposit Insurance Corporation (FDIC); Federal Reserve System; Great Depression (1929–1939); Greenspan, Alan; Roosevelt, Franklin Delano; Volcker, Paul

Further Reading

Landis, James M. 1959. "Legislative History of the Securities Act of 1933." *George Washington Law Review* 28: 29.

Preston, Howard H. 1933. "The Banking Act of 1933." *The American Economic Review* 23, no. 4 (December): 585–607.

Westerfield, Ray B. 1933. "The Banking Act of 1933." *The Journal of Political Economy* 41, no. 6: 721–49.

Resources for Teachers

Federal Reserve Bank of Philadelphia. N.d. "A Day in the Life of the FOMC." http://www.philadelphiafed.org/education/teachers/resources/day-in-life-of-fomc/.

federalreserveeducation.org. N.d. "History of the Federal Reserve." http://www.federalreserveeducation.org/about-the-fed/history/.

National Archives-DOCS Teach. N.d. "Act of June 16, 1933 (Banking Act of 1933), Public Law 73-66, 48 STAT 162." http://docsteach.org/documents/299834/detail.

Bernanke, Ben

Born: December 13, 1953, in Augusta, Georgia; American; monetary policy, chairman of the Federal Reserve System 2006–2014; Major Works: "Nonmonetary Effects of the Financial Crisis in the Propagation of the Great Depression" (1983), *Essays on the Great Depression* (2004).

Ben Bernanke is an American economist who served as chairman of the Federal Reserve System Board of Governors from 2006 to 2014. Bernanke directed the Federal Reserve's response to the financial crisis of 2007–2009. He served on the Federal Reserve Board of Governors from 2002 to 2005. He was first appointed chairman by President George W. Bush, and was reappointed by President Obama in 2010. Prior to being named chairman of the Federal Reserve Board of Governors, he had been a board governor since 2002. Prior to joining the Board of Governors, Bernanke was a tenured professor and chair of the Princeton University Department of Economics. Bernanke also served President George W. Bush as chairman of the Council of Economic Advisers.

Benjamin Shalom Bernanke was born on December 13, 1953, in Augusta, Georgia. Growing up in Dillon, South Carolina, as the grandson of Jewish immigrants, he graduated as high school class valedictorian. Bernanke earned his BA in economics from Harvard University with honors in 1975. He received his PhD in economics from Massachusetts Institute of Technology (MIT) in 1979. His dissertation adviser was future Bank of Israel central bank counterpart, Stanley Fischer.

Bernanke's dissertation, "Long-Term Commitments, Dynamic Optimization, and the Business Cycle," launched his career as a Depression-era economic historian. Upon graduation from MIT, Bernanke began his academic career in the Stanford University Graduate School of Business. Bernanke joined the faculty at Princeton University in 1985, becoming department chair in 1992—a position he would hold till 2002.

Bernanke's expertise and research on the economic causes and consequences of the Great Depression elevated his reputation as an equal to Milton Friedman and Anna Schwartz. In 1983, Bernanke published "Nonmonetary Effects of the Financial Crisis in the Propagation of the Great Depression." Bernanke made the case that the key causes and eventual collapse of the economy in 1929 and subsequent depression of the 1930s was a failure of the banking system to provide sufficient credit. This view goes beyond Friedman's response, which laid blame directly on the Federal Reserve and the government. Later, in 2004, he would provide a summation of his views in *Essays on the Great Depression.*

Beyond his work on the Great Depression, he is the coauthor of two successful economics textbooks, both in their multiple editions. Bernanke has delivered lectures at the London School of Economics on monetary policy and theory. He directed the Monetary Economics Program of the National Bureau of Economic Research and edited the *American Economic Review.*

Ben Bernanke entered public service in 2002, when he accepted an offer from President George W. Bush to join the Federal Reserve Board of Governors. He remained on the Board of Governors until 2005, when he chaired President Bush's Council of Economic Advisers until 2006. In 2006, he was a top candidate to replace the retiring Alan Greenspan as chairman of the Federal Reserve Board of Governors. On February 1, 2006, Ben Bernanke succeeded Greenspan as chair, becoming the most important monetary economist in the nation. He also chaired the Federal Open Market Committee, the committee responsible for key monetary policy decisions.

Though he soundly defended the Federal Reserve's actions, Bernanke was not without his critics. He was criticized for the Federal Reserve's role in backing J. P. Morgan Chase in order for Chase to buy Bear Stearns, the Troubled Asset Relief Program (TARP), and with the U.S. Treasury bailout of AIG.

An avowed monetarist and student of the Great Depression, Bernanke feared deflation more than inflation. As a result, he publicly advocated supplying as much money as necessary to the monetary system to avoid a deflationary spiral. Using a helicopter analogy in a speech to describe his monetary views, Bernanke was labeled (mostly by his critics) "Helicopter Ben."

Known as "quantitative easing" on three different occasions (QE I, II, III), the Fed went into the business of buying and adding depreciated assets to the Federal Reserve's balance sheet. In return, the Federal Reserve supplies sufficient quantities of dollars to the monetary system, keeping interest rates at historic lows. In responding to these crises, under Ben Bernanke, the Federal Reserve took on more direct actions than quite possibly at any time since its inception in 1913.

Bernanke's honors included being named a fellow of the American Academy of Arts and the Econometric Society, and a Guggenheim fellow. He also was a member of the National Bureau of Economic Research (NBER) and NBER's Business Cycle Dating Committee.

David A. Dieterle

See Also Friedman, Milton; Greenspan, Alan; Schwartz, Anna; Volcker, Paul; Yellen, Janet

Selected Works by Ben Bernanke

Bernanke, Ben S. 2004. *Essays on the Great Depression.* Princeton, NJ: Princeton University Press.

Bernanke, Ben S. 1983. "Nonmonetary Effects of the Financial Crisis in the Propagation of the Great Depression." *American Economic Review* 73, no. 3, June: 257–76.

Bernanke, Ben S., Andrew B. Abel, and Dean Croushore. 2007. *Macroeconomics*. 6th ed. Boston: Addison-Wesley.

Bernanke, Ben S., and Alan S. Blinder. 1992. "The Federal Funds Rate and the Channels of Monetary Transmission." *American Economic Review* 82, no. 4, September: 901–21.

Bernanke, Ben S., and Robert H. Frank. 2007. *Principles of Macroeconomics*. New York: McGraw-Hill.

Bernanke, Ben S., Mark Gertler, and Mark Watson. 1997. "Systematic Monetary Policy and the Effects of Oil Price Shocks." C. V. Starr Center for Applied Economics, New York University, May 27.

Bernanke, Ben S., Thomas Laubach, Frederic S. Mishkin, and Adam S. Posen. 2001. *Inflation Targeting: Lessons from the International Experience*. Princeton, NJ: Princeton University Press.

Selected Works about Ben Bernanke

"Ben Bernanke." N.d. *Forbes*. http://www.forbes.com/profile/ben-bernanke/.

"Ben Bernanke's Greatest Challenge." *60 Minutes*. CBS News, March 12, 2009. http://www.cbsnews.com/stories/2009/03/12/60minutes/main4862191.shtml.

"Ben S. Bernanke." Board of Governors of the Federal Reserve System. http://www.federalreserve.gov/aboutthefed/bios/board/bernanke.htm.

Harris, Ethan S. 2008. *Ben Bernanke's Fed: The Federal Reserve after Greenspan*. Cambridge, MA: Harvard Business Press.

Lowenstein, Roger. "The Education of Ben Bernanke." *New York Times*, January 20, 2008. http://www.nytimes.com/2008/01/20/magazine/20Ben-Bernanke-t.html.

Wessel, David. 2009. *In Fed We Trust: Ben Bernanke's War on the Great Panic*. New York: Crown Business.

Bretton Woods Agreement

The Bretton Woods Agreement was an international monetary contract for exchanging one currency for another. In 1944, representatives from 44 nations came together in Bretton Woods, New Hampshire, to establish an agreement to monitor exchange rates and lend funds to member nations with trade deficits. The agreement was followed by the creation of the International Monetary Fund (IMF) and the International Bank for Reconstruction and Development, now known as the World Bank. In 1971, President Richard Nixon put an end to the Bretton Woods Agreement by discontinuing the link between gold and the dollar, known as the gold standard.

In 1944, as World War II was drawing to a close and after more than two years of planning and negotiation, 44 allied nations came together in Bretton Woods, a resort village in New Hampshire, to discuss postwar monetary reconstruction. Two competing plans dominated the meeting: that of Henry Dexter White, from the United States, and that of John Maynard Keynes, from England. Except for differences on issues related to future access to international liquidity, the two plans were almost identical. The final agreement, however, was much closer to the one offered by the United States, which, considering the increasing power of the United States at that time, was not surprising.

The Bretton Woods Agreement was based on four fundamental factors. First, the negotiators agreed on a new par value exchange rate system, which allowed member countries to declare a par value for their national currencies and, if required, to limit exchange rate fluctuations within a certain set of margins. All participating nations agreed that the unrestricted floating exchange rates of the 1930s would not attract trade and investment in the post–World War II era. On the other hand, they knew that the fixed exchange rates of the nineteenth century would not be applicable either. The par value system was basically a compromise between a completely fixed and a floating exchange rate, where nation members could, based on agreed-upon procedures, change their par value for reasons such as a domestic financial crisis or reserve currency crisis.

Second, because exchange rates were not to float freely (as they had in the past), member countries needed a guarantee of enough emergency supply of monetary reserve. Negotiators did not change the international liquidity system, which was mainly based on national stocks of gold or gold exchange (currencies that could easily be converted to gold). Therefore, the Bretton Woods Agreement created a system of subscriptions and quotas, which was a fixed basket of national currencies and gold subscribed to by each member country. Accordingly, each country had to pay 25 percent in either gold or currency convertible into gold (at the time, only the dollar had this status) and 75 percent in the member country's currency. Thus, if needed, each member country was entitled to borrow foreign currency based on the size of its quota.

Third, in order to prevent the economic conflicts of the 1930s, all member countries were prohibited from getting involved in discriminatory currency or exchange regulation. The Bretton Woods Agreement removed the pre–World War II exchange control, which limited currency convertibility between the member nations. There were two exceptions to this agreement: 1) the agreement only applied to existing international transactions in goods and services, not the capital account, and 2) if the member country decided, the agreement could be put off during the post–World War II transitional period.

Fourth, all members agreed that there was a need for an institutional assembly to monitor and regulate international monetary issues. The member countries decided to set up a voting system among participant countries based on the proportion of each country's quotas. Therefore, the United States, providing 75 percent of the Institute of Monetary Fund (IMF) quotas, gained tremendous international power over all other member countries.

In summary, the Bretton Woods Agreement was an international monetary policy based on the same gold standard of the past but with a new par value exchange rate system; it created the IMF as an international institution to centralize a reserve of gold and national currencies for emergency monetary needs of the member countries. The IMF was the result of the Bretton Woods Agreement and had three important tasks: 1) administrative and regulatory responsibilities, 2) financial responsibilities, and 3) advisory responsibilities.

As it turned out, contrary to what members of the Bretton Woods Agreement expected, the transition period during the post–World War II era was long and unstable, and the IMF initial fund was not enough to cover various funding requests. Hence, for over a decade, the IMF's lending power declined to a minimal amount. Due to its financial and economic power, the United States became the only global monetary stabilizer for decades after World War II.

Despite the fact that Bretton Woods was an international agreement, in practice, its initiation, its future developments, and finally its termination were directly under the influence of the United States. The agreement offered strong evidence of the growing international power of the United States in the post–World War II arena. The U.S. dollar enjoyed a powerful position in international trade for a long period of time after the agreement. However, it was the United States that put an end to the Bretton Woods Agreement. On August 15, 1971, President Nixon ended the convertibility of the dollar into gold by setting it free to float independently in the global currency market. Eighteen months later, all industrial countries followed suit.

Elham Mahmoudi

See Also International Monetary Fund (IMF); Keynes, John Maynard; Keynesian Economics; World Bank

Further Reading

Eichengreen, Barry. 2004. "Global Imbalances and the Lessons of Bretton Woods." *Economie internationale* 4: 39–50.

Hammes, David, and Douglas Wills. 2003. "Black Gold: The End of Bretton Woods and the Oil Price Shocks of the 1970s." *Independent Review* 9, no. 4: 501–11.

Helleiner, Eric. 1996. *States and the Reemergence of Global Finance: From Bretton Woods to the 1990s*. Ithaca, NY: Cornell University Press.

Resources for Teachers

Council on Foreign Relations. 2013. "Teaching Module: The Battle of Bretton Woods." http://www.cfr.org/europe/teaching-module-battle-bretton-woods/p31080.

Shand, Robert. N.d. Understanding Fiscal Responsibility Blog: "What Really Happened at Bretton Woods." http://teachufr.org/admin/what-really-happened-at-bretton-woods/.

Teaching American History. 1944. "United Nations Monetary and Financial Conference at Bretton Woods." http://teachingamericanhistory.org/library/document/conference-at-bretton-woods/.

Buchanan, James

Born: October 2, 1919, in Murfreesboro, Tennessee; Died: January 9, 2013, in Blacksburg, Virginia; American; public choice theory, Nobel Prize (1986); Major Work: *The Calculus of Consent: Logical Foundations of Constitutional Democracy* (1962).

James Buchanan is an American economist who founded the subdiscipline of economics called public choice theory. Public choice theory analyzes the actions of individuals in a democracy, and seeks to explain what they do by examining their individual goals. By studying the incentives of politicians, voters, and other people in public functions, Buchanan believed that we could gain a more real and less ideal understanding of how our society works. Buchanan died in 2013.

James McGill Buchanan was born October 2, 1919, in Murfreesboro, Tennessee, to a family that was both important and poor. His grandfather, John P. Buchanan, had been governor of Tennessee, which brought prestige to the family but not wealth. Buchanan's family expected him to continue the proud family tradition by becoming a lawyer-politician. However, the onset of the Great Depression meant that they would be unable to send him to Vanderbilt University, which was their first choice, opting instead for Middle Tennessee State Teacher's College in Murfreesboro. Buchanan milked cows throughout all four years of college to pay for school. He graduated from Middle Tennessee State in 1940. Shortly thereafter, he was drafted into the navy with the U.S entry into World War II.

After the war, Buchanan attended graduate school at the University of Chicago. After earning a doctorate from Chicago and spending a research year in Italy, he launched into a career as a political economist that lasted his whole life, during which he has held professorships at the University of Virginia, UCLA, Florida State University, the University of Tennessee, Virginia Polytechnic Institute, and George Mason University. He was awarded the Nobel Prize for Economics in 1986.

Buchanan believed all economic analysis had to begin with the study of individual choices. He wrote that governments, nations, communities, ethnic groups, and any other type of group cannot be said to make decisions or choices; rather, all groups are made up of people who are trying to get the most benefit for the least cost. In short, he applied the economic concept of cost-benefit analysis to politics. Therefore, in Buchanan's analysis, one would consider not what the government or a policy would do in a certain situation, but what politicians seeking reelection, voters seeking public money, or bureaucrats seeking a larger budget would do.

A second piece of Buchanan's economic thought was the importance of free exchange in economics. He emphasized that the main way people get what they want is through trade. On the other hand, people can also get what they want through force. To analyze how people might choose whether to trade or whether to use force, he thought of an imaginary world that is in a state of nature in which no government exists—the same philosophical approach used by Thomas Hobbes and John Locke.

Buchanan reasoned that in a state of nature, people would divide their time between production, predation (taking things by force), and protection of their property. In such a situation, everyone could become wealthier if they did not have to worry about predation and protection and could simply focus on producing things. Therefore, people would have an incentive to create a government that could protect people and their property. A good government with a good constitution would allow for the maximum amount of trade because people would not have to worry about defending themselves. Therefore, he claimed, the creation of the "rules" of politics, or the constitution, was the most important part of the political process.

However, he also saw problems on the horizon. Buchanan noted that in a democracy, each citizen has an incentive to try to vote money out of other citizens' pockets and into his or her own. This would not be a problem if a constitution prevented it, as he believed the U.S. Constitution did in fact do. However, in *Democracy in Deficit: The Political Legacy of Lord Keynes* (1977), he wrote that the Keynesian idea that a government could use public debt to produce goods and services for the common good ignored the principle that politicians and bureaucrats act just as everyone else does—in their own self-interest. Rather, public debt was more likely to be used to make projects that would get politicians reelected and bureaucrats better funding. When the government goes beyond its role of protecting its citizens, it takes society back to the state of nature. People will cease to pursue their self-interest through production and trade. They will begin to pursue self-interest by gathering political force and take the fruits of others' work.

To limit the government, Buchanan recommended nothing less than change on the constitutional level. He suggested a balanced-budget rule, larger majority requirements for the spending of public money, and the creation of specific taxes for specific projects. He opposed the concept of broad-based taxes that are funneled into a pool of government revenue.

In Buchanan's works, the state is viewed as a combination of self-interested individuals, similar to a market, but with different incentives. Buchanan best summarized his work as the notion that people, given a set of constraints, will seek the best position for them personally regardless if they are a producer or consumer in the marketplace, a politician, or a government bureaucrat.

James Buchanan died on January 9, 2013, in Blacksburg, Virginia, at the age of 93.

Stephen H. Day

See Also Keynes, John Maynard

Selected Works by James Buchanan

Buchanan, James. 1962. *The Calculus of Consent: Logical Foundations of Constitutional Democracy*. Ann Arbor: University of Michigan Press.

Buchanan, James, and Richard E. Wagner. 1977. *Democracy in Deficit: The Political Legacy of Lord Keynes*. Indianapolis, IN: Liberty Fund.

Buchanan, James, and Gordon Tulloch. 1999. *The Logical Foundations of Constitutional Liberty*. Vol. 1. Indianapolis, IN: Liberty Fund.

Buchanan, James. 1958. *Public Principles of Public Debt: A Defense and Restatement*. Homewood, IL: Irwin.

Buchanan, James. 1979. *What Should Economists Do?* Indianapolis, IN: Liberty Fund.

Selected Works about James Buchanan

Brennan, G., H. Kliemt, and R. D. Tollison, eds. 2002. *Method and Morals in Constitutional Economics: Essays in Honor of James M. Buchanan*. Berlin: Springer.

Reisman, David. 1990. *The Political Economy of James Buchanan*. Basingstoke, UK: Macmillan.

Younkins, Edward W. 2008. *Champions of a Free Society*. Lanham, MD: Lexington Books.

Bureau of Economic Analysis

The Bureau of Economic Analysis (BEA) is an agency of the Department of Commerce. The Census Bureau and the BEA are two divisions of the department's economic and statistics administration. The BEA's main responsibility is to promote an accurate picture of the U.S. economy by providing key economic statistics including the national income and product accounts (NIPAs) and Gross Domestic Product (GDP). These estimates are then used to provide important information about essential issues such as economic growth rate, industry-specific and regional development, and, most importantly, the economic strength of the nation in the world's economy. The BEA's mission is to promote an enhanced understanding of the U.S. economy by developing and providing timely, relevant, and accurate economic accounts statistics in an objective and cost-effective manner.

In 1972, the BEA was officially established in the Social and Economic Statistics Administration (SESA) within the Department of Commerce. However, the function of developing and interpreting the economic accounts of the United States goes back to 1820, when the Division of Commerce and Navigation (1820–1866) was responsible for developing and publishing annual statistics on U.S. foreign trade. By 1844, this responsibility had expanded to include domestic trade within the United States.

During the twentieth century, the important task of deriving and analyzing national economic statistics evolved and expanded. Today, the BEA is one of the most important statistical agencies in the world and the main agency of the Federal Statistical System in the United States. The BEA collects and manages data from various segments of the U.S. economy, conducts research, develops statistical estimates, and disseminates statistics to the public. The BEA offers statistical information in five different categories: 1) national, such as GDP, personal income, consumer spending, corporate profits, and fixed assets; 2) international, such as balance of payments, trade in goods and services, international services, international investment, direct investment and multinational companies, and survey forms and related materials; 3) regional, such as GDP by state and metropolitan area, personal income by state and local area, and economic information for coastal areas; 4) industry, such as annual industry accounts, benchmark input-output accounts, research and development satellite accounts, travel and tourism satellite accounts, and supplemental statistics; and 5) Integrated Accounts, such as integrated income, product, and Federal Reserve Financial Accounts, integrated BEA GDP-BLS productivity accounts, and integrated BEA-BLS industry-level production accounts.

GDP and national accounts statistics are used by the White House and Congress to prepare budget estimates, by the Federal Reserve to define appropriate monetary policy, by Wall Street to provide accurate economic projections, and by business communities for financial strategies. The industry data are used by both industry and academia to estimate productivity, by the U.S. International Trade Commission to analyze trade policies, and by national and local leaders to evaluate the impacts of economic shocks. International trade and investment data are mainly used by trade policy officials to negotiate international agreements and by analysts and policymakers to evaluate the effects of international investment. Regional estimates are used by federal and local government agencies as well as businesses to track various economic activities and develop the best strategies for the future.

One of the most closely watched of all economic statistics that is developed by the BEA is the Gross Domestic Product (GDP). GDP is the market value of all legally recognized final goods and services produced within a country in a given period of time. GDP per capita is recognized as one of the indicators of a country's standard of living. GDP is also related to national accounts, and it is an important macroeconomic indicator. Another primary set of macroeconomic estimates that is widely used for economic and policy analysis is the integrated macroeconomic accounts (IMAs). The IMAs consist of several macroeconomic accounts that connect production and income to the change in net worth in the U.S. economy. The accounts define the sources and expenditures of the funds that are made available for capital formation or lending. Furthermore, they track assets and liabilities of the major segments of the economy. IMAs provide enough information regarding changes in the market values of assets and liabilities to be able to draw conclusions regarding changes in the net worth of each economic segment or the entire U.S. economy.

Elham Mahmoudi

See Also Bureau of Labor Statistics; Department of Commerce; Gross Domestic Product (GDP); National Bureau of Economic Research (NBER); United States Census Bureau

Further Reading

Bureau of Economic Analysis. 2012. Available from http://www.thecre.com/pdf/20021014_commerce-bea-final.pdf.

Resources for Teachers

Bureau of Economic Analysis. N.d. "Interactive Data." http://www.bea.gov/itable/index.cfm.

Haskell, Doug. 2013. "Focus on Economic Data: U.S. Real GDP Growth, Q1 2013 (First Estimate)." econedlink. http://www.econedlink.org/lessons/index.php?lid=1163&type=educator.

Wall Street Journal. N.d. "Economic Analysis." http://topics.wsj.com/subject/E/economic-analysis/2515.

Bureau of Engraving and Printing

The Bureau of Engraving and Printing (BEP) is an agency of the Department of the Treasury. The BEP's most important task is to produce paper currency. In addition, the BEP produces treasury securities, military commissions, and a variety of other security documents. The BEP has two large production facilities in Washington, D.C., and Fort Worth, Texas.

Prior to the Civil War, the production process for paper currency was completely manual. A private company produced bills in sheets of four. Then, the sheets were transferred to the Treasury Department, where clerks signed the bills and other workers cut them by hand. In 1861, in order to help fund the Civil War, Congress empowered the secretary of the Treasury to produce paper currency instead of coins. The paper currency served as government IOUs and was redeemable in coins at specific treasury locations. In 1863, Congress created the Office of Comptroller of the Currency, which was responsible for the production of currency. In 1874, the Bureau of Engraving and Printing was officially established.

The Bureau of Engraving and Printing has produced a variety of different documents, such as passports, money orders, bonds, refunding certificates, and treasury notes. In

1894, the BEP officially started producing postage stamps for the U.S. government. During the first year, the BEP produced more than two billion stamps. For the next 111 years, the BEP was the sole producer of stamps in the United States. Because it became more cost effective, the U.S. Postal Service moved stamp production to the private sector. In 2005, the Bureau of Engraving and Printing produced its last set of postage stamps for the U.S. Post Office. After more than 100 years of monopolizing stamp production, the bureau terminated its postage stamp production entirely. The main task of the Bureau of Engraving and Printing was to print paper currency.

In 1918, following World War I, the production of paper currency increased from the initial four notes per sheet to eight. In 1929, the design of the paper currency standardized and it became much smaller than its original size. The bureau could increase the number of notes per sheet from 8 to 12. Over the years, mainly by reducing the size, the bureau was able to lower the cost of producing paper money.

Counterfeit deterrence has improved dramatically through the bureau's application of better engraving and security techniques and the general public's improved recognition of paper note features. In 1952, after new developments in the production of non-offset inks, the bureau was able to increase the number of notes per sheet even further. The use of new ink that dried faster enabled the bureau to reduce the rate of damage and distortion in its money production. Since paper notes have to be printed on both the front and the back, this faster drying ink made it possible for the sheets to be kept moist until both the back and the front were printed. By avoiding the re-wetting process and therefore decreasing the damage rate, in 1952, the bureau was able to switch from 12-note printing plates to 18-note plates.

In 1957, the bureau started using the dry intaglio method, which is a printing technique in which the image is marked into a surface. The areas created by the marked lines hold the ink. The bureau had to use special paper and non-offset inks to switch to the intaglio printing technique. This enabled the bureau to increase the number of notes from 18 to 32 per sheet and to be more efficient. Using the intaglio method made wetting the paper prior to printing an unnecessary step in the process. Since 1968, all paper monies have been printed using the intaglio method. After both faces are printed, the sheets are printed with serial numbers and U.S. Treasury seals.

The Bureau of Engraving and Printing has two production locations: Washington, D.C., and Fort Worth, Texas. The Washington, D.C., building is listed in the U.S. National Register of Historic Places. It has a neoclassical architectural style with fireproof concrete. In 1938, because of an increase in number of personnel and in size of production, the bureau added another building, opposite the main building, to its original facility. In 1987, the bureau started building a new facility in Fort Worth, Texas. The Fort Worth facility was mainly built not only because of an increase in production size, but also to be used in case of an emergency in the Washington, D.C., area. In December 1990, the Fort Worth facility officially started production.

Elham Mahmoudi

See Also Money; United States Treasury; U.S. Treasury Bills, Notes, and Bonds

Further Reading

Gelinas, Ulric J., Jr., and Janis L. Gogan. 2006. "Accountants and Emerging Technologies: A Case Study at the United States Department of the Treasury Bureau of Engraving and Printing." *Journal of Information Systems* 20, no. 2: 93–116.

Ichikawa, Ieyasu. 1976. "Special Intaglio Printing Process for Preventing Forgery of Securities." www.google.com.tr/patents/US3980018?hl=tr.

United States Bureau of Engraving and Printing. 1929. *A Brief History of the Bureau of Engraving and Printing: With a Description of Its Work*. Washington, DC: US Government Printing Office.

United States Bureau of Engraving and Printing. 1909. *Annual Report of the Director of the Bureau of Engraving and Printing*. Washington, DC: US Government Printing Office.

Resources for Teachers

Bureau of Printing and Engraving. N.d. "Home-Featured Sections." www.moneyfactory.gov/home.html.

United States Mint. N.d. "Lesson Plans for Grades K-12, Including Common Core and National Standards." www.usmint.gov/kids/teachers/lessonPlans/index.cfm.

United States Mint. N.d. "Web Site References." www.usmint.gov/kids/teachers/library/libraryWebSite.cfm.

Bureau of Labor Statistics

The Bureau of Labor Statistics (BLS) is an agency within the Department of Labor. The BLS formed in 1884, and it has been the main statistical agency responsible for collecting, managing, analyzing, and disseminating statistical data to the public, the U.S. Congress, other federal agencies, state and local governments, businesses, and labor representatives. The BLS is the main statistical source of the U.S. government.

On June 27, 1884, the Bureau of Labor Act established the Bureau of Labor within the Department of the Interior. The main purpose of this establishment was to collect information on labor and employment. In 1888, the Bureau of Labor became an independent department, but in 1913, it joined the Department of Labor and has remained there ever since. It is located in the Postal Square Building, close to the United States Capitol in Washington, D.C. A commissioner who serves a four-year term heads the BLS.

The BLS produces a wide range of surveys and statistics that can be divided into three main divisions: 1) prices, 2) employment and unemployment, and 3) compensation and working conditions. The U.S. Consumer Price Index (CPI), the Producer Price Index (PPI), the U.S. Import and Export Price Indices (IEPI), and the Consumer Expenditure Survey (CES) track statistics related to prices. For employment and unemployment, there are various surveys and statistics such as the Current Population Survey (CPS), the Current Employment Statistics (CES), the Job Openings and Labor Turnover Survey (JOLTS), the Business Employment Dynamics (BED), and the Mass Layoff Survey. For compensation and working conditions, the BLS produces the National Compensation Survey; the Injury, Illnesses, and Fatality (IIF) program; and the Productivity Report. All the reports, surveys, and statistics produced by the BLS are categorized into four geographic regions that are known as census regions: Northeast, South, Midwest, and West. Each region then is divided into many census divisions.

The reports and statistics produced by the BLS must be of the highest accuracy, relevance, and timeliness. Furthermore, impartiality in both content and presentation of the reports is of the utmost importance to the Department of Labor.

The following are the main sections within the BLS:

1. Office of Employment and Unemployment Statistics: This office analyzes and publishes data on employment, labor demand, work hours, earnings, and employment by occupation and industry. Every two years, this office publishes a career handbook covering the outlook for employment in many occupations.
2. Prices and Living Conditions: This office analyzes and publishes data on the CPI and the PPI, U.S. import and export processes, consumer spending patterns, and sources of consumer income.
3. Office of Compensation and Working Conditions: This office analyzes and publishes data on wages and benefits (such as health insurance, retirement plans, paid vacations, paid holidays), and occupational safety (such as workplace injuries or occupational hazards).
4. Productivity and Technology: This office analyzes and publishes indexes of labor productivity for each industry, as well as for large economic sectors. In addition, this office compares U.S. productivity measures, labor costs, and benefits with those of other countries.
5. Survey Methods Research: This office has two centers: 1) the Mathematical Statistics Research Center (MSRC), and 2) the Behavioral Sciences Research Center (BSRC). The MSRC is responsible for accuracy and efficiency of the BLS survey methods and its statistical analyses. The BSRC is responsible for increasing survey response rates, reducing nonsampling errors, and improving applied survey methods.
6. Publications and Special Studies: This office is mainly responsible for public relations, media contact, and dissemination of all that is produced in the BLS.
7. Field Operations: This office trains field economists who are responsible for collecting data throughout the United States. The office also conducts quality assurance and provides technical direction regarding how to collect data.
8. Administration: This office manages the administrative tasks of the BLS in areas such as financial management and human resources.
9. Office of Technology and Survey Processing: This office uses information technology to promote the mission of the BLS. Project managers and information technology specialists in this office provide a reliable and efficient system to be used for the BLS's advanced and highly technical computational tasks.

Elham Mahmoudi

See Also Bureau of Economic Analysis; National Bureau of Economic Research (NBER); United States Census Bureau

Further Reading

Cunningham, Jim. 1998. "Bureau of Labor Statistics." *Behavioral & Social Sciences Librarian* 16, no. 2: 73–75.

Goldberg, Joseph P., and William T. Moye. 1985. *The First Hundred Years of the Bureau of Labor Statistics*. Washington, DC: United States Bureau of Labor Statistics.

Resources for Teachers

Bureau of Labor Statistics. N.d. "Occupational Outlook Handbook." http://www.bls.gov/ooh/education-training-and-library/high-school-teachers.htm.

Bureau of Labor Statistics. N.d. "Resources for: Student of Teacher." http://www.bls.gov/audience/students.htm.

Bureau of Labor Statistics. N.d. "Teacher: What Is This Job Like?" http://www.bls.gov/k12/help01.htm.

Burns, Arthur

Born: April 27, 1904, in Stanisławów, Galicia (now Ivano-Frankivsk, Ukraine); Died: June 6, 1987, in Baltimore, Maryland; American; monetary policy, economic growth; Major Works: *Economic Research and the Keynesian Thinking of Our Time* (1946), *Prosperity without Inflation* (1957), *Reflections on an Economic Policy Maker* (1978).

Arthur Burns was the chairman of the Board of Governors of the Federal Reserve System from 1970 until 1978. Though his record of academic work and government service continued on far beyond his time as head of the nation's central bank, he is most commonly remembered for his work at the Federal Reserve, particularly for his part in creating the policies that led to economic stagnation and inflation during the 1970s. Burns died in 1987.

Arthur Frank Burns was born on April 27, 1904, in Stanisławów, Galicia (now Ivano-Frankivsk, Ukraine). He emigrated with his parents to New Jersey when he was a little boy. Burns earned both his bachelor's and doctoral degrees from Columbia University. After earning his PhD, he was hired at the new National Bureau of Economic Research, located at Columbia. Here, he gathered copious amounts of data on various industries, which he used to predict economic business cycles.

Burns's research during this period focused on booms and busts in the U.S. economy. He carefully measured aspects of the business cycle, looking into the behavior of many different industries to create a complex yet somewhat predictable view of the economy. Burns believed that recessions occurred not so much because of lack of aggregate demand, as the popular Keynesian theory posited, but because several industries happened to slump at the same time. Such theory promised to be valuable for macroeconomic forecasting, and it gave Burns the reputation as a respectable, impartial scientist.

Burns's nuanced and moderately conservative work got the attention of the Eisenhower administration, and he was recruited to serve on the Council of Economic Advisers in 1953, which he did until 1956. Burns is credited with convincing President Eisenhower not to attempt an aggressive fiscal policy when responding to a recession. When the economy improved in 1954 without significant fiscal stimulus, Burns's fame as an approachable, wise adviser grew. In 1968, this reputation served to elevate Burns as a counselor to the newly elected President Richard Nixon, and in 1970, Burns was appointed chairman of the Board of Governors of the Federal Reserve System.

Burns inherited an economy beset by both rising unemployment and rising inflation. He embarked upon a policy of fighting unemployment with "easy" monetary policy (i.e., keeping interest rates low in order to stimulate economic activity) while fighting inflation with a variety of schemes to discourage large companies from increasing wages and prices. He failed on both counts, as both unemployment and inflation continued to increase. Throughout his tenure as chairman of the Federal Reserve, Burns kept interest rates at a level that is now considered dangerously low. In 1978, Burns was replaced briefly by G. William Miller prior to Paul Volcker's tenure as Fed Chair, in which he fought skyrocketing inflation not with wage and price controls (as Nixon and Burns had done), but with tighter monetary policy. This policy worked, and the Burns era of the Federal Reserve became known as a lost decade.

During the time of Arthur Burns's tenure as Federal Reserve chair, it was not clear that inflation was mostly about money. Many economists believed that inflation had to do with factors such as the power of unions and the price of oil. Attributing inflation to "real" factors such as these made monetary policy of secondary importance. More interesting, however, was the influence of President Nixon and Treasury Secretary John Connally. Nixon was convinced that he had lost the 1960 presidential election because tight monetary policy had raised unemployment, and he did not intend to lose the 1972 election for the same reason. He was recorded in the White House tapes in 1971 as saying, "I've never seen anybody beaten on inflation in the United States. I've seen many people beaten on unemployment." Nixon and Connally cynically urged, threatened, and manipulated Burns to keep an expansive monetary policy. They leaked hints to the press that Burns would no longer be an adviser and that the Federal Reserve might lose its independence if interest rates were not kept low. These threats seem to have been effective in convincing Burns to agree to a looser monetary policy than he would have held without their persuasion.

Thus, throughout the 1970s, inflation surged despite wage freezes, price freezes, and federal anti-inflation councils, and without a significant drop in unemployment. Since that time, economists have refocused on the importance of controlling the money supply as a means to stop inflation. Burns was appointed ambassador to West Germany by President Ronald Reagan in 1981, a post in which he served effectively until 1985.

Arthur Burns died in Baltimore, Maryland, on June 6, 1987.

Stephen H. Day

See Also Greenspan, Alan; Volcker, Paul; Yellen, Janet

Selected Works by Arthur Burns

Burns, Arthur, and Jacob Koppel Javits. 1968. *The Defense Sector and the American Economy.* New York: New York University Press.

Burns, Arthur. 1946. *Economic Research and the Keynesian Thinking of Our Time*. Washington, DC: National Bureau of Economic Research.

Burns, Arthur. 1966. *The Management of Prosperity*. New York: Carnegie Institute.

Burns, Arthur, and W. C. Mitchell. 1946. *Measuring Business Cycles*. Washington, DC: National Bureau of Economic Research.

Burns, Arthur. 1957. *Prosperity without Inflation*. New York: Fordham University Press.

Burns, Arthur. 1978. *Reflections of an Economic Policy Maker*. Washington, DC: American Enterprise Institute for Public Policy Research.

Selected Works about Arthur Burns

"Arthur Burns." N.d. Columbia 250. Accessed April 7, 2012. http://c250.columbia.edu/c250_celebrates/remarkable_columbians/arthur_burns.html.

"Arthur Burns, 1904–1987, Economist." N.d. HistoryCentral.com. Accessed April 7, 2012. http://www.historycentral.com/Bio/people/burns.html.

Wells, Wyatt C. 1994. *Economist in an Uncertain World: Arthur F. Burns and the Federal Reserve, 1970–78*. New York: Columbia University Press.

C

Central Banking

A central bank is an independent institution granted the legal authority by a government or group of governments to manage a nation's or region's money supply and regulate its credit markets. A central bank can also be the legal authority for a group or region of nations such as the European Central Bank, for the European Union's Eurozone.

Dating back to at least 1668 with the founding of Sweden's Riksbank, central banks initially loaned governments funds for commerce and wars, or to quell recurring monetary crises. In the beginning, central banks were privately owned.

Modern central banking in the United States arguably had its genesis in 1913, when the Federal Reserve (Fed) was formally established as a private institution owned by member banks, yet authorized by Congress to create and destroy currency to maintain an appropriate money supply to facilitate daily economic transactions without significantly affecting prices. It was formally charged with regulating and safeguarding the nation's banking system and employing monetary policy with a dual mandate: price stability (maintaining the real value, or purchasing power, of the currency) and high and sustainable economic growth (noninflationary full employment). Implicitly, a central bank is thus expected to maintain financial stability by offsetting economic shocks and crises and smoothing out greater business cycles.

Learning from the Great Depression, which ensued from a financial panic generated by banks' inability to meet depositors' immediate demands for withdrawals, the Fed subsequently required member banks to hold a percentage of all deposits in reserve, unavailable for loans. This would greatly reduce the likelihood of future panics.

Within this fractional reserve banking system, a central bank employs monetary policy in three primary (and many lesser) ways. One, a central bank can manipulate the required reserve ratio. This action would legally change the amount of funds available for banks to lend. In reality, this tool is rarely used by the Federal Reserve. If the reserve ratio is lowered, banks can make more loans, which eventually become deposits in other banks. New money, or reserves, is created for further loans (and so on), thus increasing the money supply by a multiple of the original deposit. A higher reserve ratio will require greater reserves, thereby reducing funds available for loans, and thus restricting the supply of money.

The second tool of a central bank is to alter the discount rate, which is the interest rate the Fed directly charges banks for overnight loans in order to maintain legal reserve requirements. If the discount rate is increased, banks must pay more for short-term loans, thus requiring them to charge more for their own longer-term lending to customers.

Finally, a central bank can influence the key interest rate and implement policies for the interest rate to remain within a preferred target range. This can be accomplished through open-market operations of buying and selling government securities. This key interest rate is the market-based interest rate charged to banks for overnight loans by other banks with excess reserves. If the rate strays too low, the central bank will sell government securities, which requires payment, thereby reducing funds available for other interbank loans, thus pushing the rate upward. On the other hand, the central bank will purchase government securities (largely held in members' reserve accounts) and inject new money into the economy, thereby pressuring rates lower, incentivizing more borrowing.

Monetary policy intended to stimulate an economy is termed "easing," while restrictive policy (generally meant to combat inflationary forces) is referred to as "tightening." Other significant monetary tools central banks might employ include raising or lowering capital requirements for bank lending and margin requirements for investing. Additionally, money can be created by purchasing foreign currencies with new reserve dollars, or withdrawn from the economy's circular flow through sales (requiring payment in dollars). There are limitations to monetary policy. Like the metaphorical horse that can be led to water but not forced to drink, banks can be incentivized to loan (or borrow) through interest rate policies, but they cannot be forced to actually loan.

Steven J. Eschrich

See Also Federal Reserve Act of 1913; Federal Reserve System; Great Depression (1929–1939); Monetary Policy; Money

Further Reading

Blinder, Alan S. 1998. *Central Banking in Theory and Practice.* Boston: The MIT Press.

Bordo, Michael, D. 2013. "A Brief History of Central Banks." Federal Reserve Bank of Cleveland, Cleveland, Ohio, November 26. Accessed December 1, 2013. www.clevelandfed.org/research/commentary/2007/12.cfm.

"So You Want to Be in Charge of Monetary Policy." N.d. Fed Chairman Game. Accessed December 1, 2013. sffed-education.org/chairman/.

Resources for Teachers

Bivens, Josh. 2013. "The Fed Turns 100: Lessons Learned from a Century of Central Banking." Economic Policy Institute. www.epi.org/publication/fed-turns-100-lessons-learned-century-central/.

Federal Reserve Education. N.d. "Constitutionality of a Central Bank." www.federalreserveeducation.org/resources/detail.cfm?r_id=fedd7ffa-dd86-4779-ae4c-b904655071c1.

Federal Reserve Education. N.d. "History of Central Banking: From 1791 to the 21st Century." www.federalreserveeducation.org/resources/detail.cfm?r_id=99715b95-6b72-4064-888b-608366208b23.

Citizens United v. Federal Election Commission, 558 U.S. ___ (2010)

Supreme Court Case Upholding First Amendment Rights

Economic Concepts

Private property; economic rent

Economic Impact

A Supreme Court Case upholding the First Amendment rights of corporations, nonprofits, and unions to include unlimited financial contributions for the purpose of electioneering.

Economic Summary

The Bipartisan Campaign Reform Act of 2002 (BCRA) was passed by Congress in an effort to change the manner in which money is obtained and used for political campaigning in America, hopefully for the better. The focus in the *Citizens United v. Federal Elections Commission* case was on corporations, nonprofits, and labor unions and their right, without government restraint, to contribute to these political campaigns. However, when an individual votes or contributes to a politician's campaign, it is with the expectation he or she will be looked out for as a constituent.

Large corporations or unions are not like people who can cast a ballot. When they contribute to campaigns, the expectation is much different. The quid pro quo could include a corporation's receiving economic rent through special legislation that will benefit its business; less severe regulation; tax credits; or perhaps some political appointments. In an effort to adjust this imbalance and limit the contributions these organizations could make toward getting leaders elected to political office, Congress abridged their First Amendment right to free speech. The constitutional question before the Court was whether or not Congress had the authority to stifle free speech by these legal organizations whose contributions had external economic effects on the nation.

Following this decision, changes indeed did take place in the manner in which money was channeled toward and spent on political campaigns in an effort to obtain economic rents. Large firms, sensitive to government policies, are able to contribute unlimited assets to the political economy with few restrictions. The economic and political results of this case still remain to be seen. Nevertheless, it can be argued that the impact of this case has altered the finances of the political landscape more than any other in recent history.

Case Summary

The race for the White House is the most expensive political race in the world. Some have suggested that presidential candidates wear outfits like racecar drivers, where corporations advertise their support and no sponsor secrets are hidden. These garments would make more than just a fashion statement. In the case of racecar drivers, their right to wear such apparel is protected by the First Amendment to the Constitution. In the *Citizens United v. Federal Election Commission* case, the First Amendment, politics, and economics collided at the intersection of Hillary Clinton and 1600 Pennsylvania Ave., resulting in an explosion of the political economy.

In his progressive campaign during 1905, President Theodore Roosevelt called for Congress to ban corporate contributions for political purposes. The evolution of regulatory policies aimed at limiting the richest Americans from influencing the outcome of federal elections has continued. In February 1972, the Federal Election Campaign Act (FECA) was designed to focus on disclosure of contributors. In 1974, it was amended to tighten limits on these contributions. In addition, this amendment created the Federal Election Commission (FEC). The FEC is an independent regulatory agency led by six members, appointed by the president and confirmed by the Senate, who by law are half Republican and half Democrat. Their duty is to disclose, enforce, and oversee federal elections legislation passed by Congress.

During the 2004 presidential campaign, Citizens United, a wealthy nonprofit corporation that runs a political action committee (PAC), produced a 90-minute movie (*Hillary: The Movie*) about Senator Hillary Clinton. This was not a musical. On the contrary, it listed character traits and background evaluations, and scrutinized her political vita in a manner that would discourage voters from casting their ballot for her as the next president. Citizens United paid over a million dollars from funds in its general treasury to have it aired on pay-per-view cable television within 30 days prior to the primaries. However, according to the amended section of BCRA, no electioneering communication that clearly identifies a candidate could be funded by the general treasury of a corporation and broadcast 30 days prior to a primary election. The law made it a felony punishable with up to five years in jail for corporations that violate this law. The FEC banned Citizens United from airing the broadcast. The corporation then filed suit in the Federal District Court of Washington, D.C., for an injunction (legal stop to an action) to lift the ban. The District Court denied the injunction based on *McConnell v. FEC, 540 U.S. 93 (2003)*, in which the Supreme Court upheld BCRA, stating that not all political speech was protected by the First Amendment.

The plaintiff appealed the case to the Supreme Court. The Roberts Court heard the first round of arguments in March of 2009. Theodore Olson, arguing on behalf of the petitioner, claimed that political speech was a core principle guaranteed in the First Amendment. The punishment for a corporation that expressed its political opinion in film was five years in jail. Olson argued that the First Amendment is there to guarantee intense political debate and participation. That process of expression is fundamental, and therefore government limitations on corporate political speech are a violation of the Constitution.

The fact that there was an exemption for media corporations added to the unconstitutionality of the issue. If your name was Disney or National Public Radio, you did not have to follow the same rules. In addition, the 90-minute documentary speech was not only offered by the speaker but also invited by the listener, who had to choose to hear it and was thereby entitled to heightened First Amendment scrutiny.

On behalf of the defense, Malcolm Stewart countered with the legislative statutes included in BCRA. Congress did not ban political corporate speech, but rather how the speech was funded and in what time frames it was to be presented. The law was not intended to take away constitutional freedoms, but rather to level the playing field of political influence in a democracy where corporations did not get the high ground simply because they could afford it. Whether the subject is a book, newsletter, sign, or film, the ban on using corporate treasury funds is a clear violation of the law and within the constitutional powers of Congress to enact. It was also within the power of Congress, according to the *McConnell* case (which upheld BCRA and claimed that not all political speech is protected) to grant exemptions to media corporations. In fact, the media exemption for publishing corporations is an effort to safeguard First Amendment rights.

The Supreme Court heard arguments a second time on this case in September 2009. Again, Olson brought forth the argument that this fundamental right to free political speech was denied to corporations, even the vast number of small, single-shareholder-owned businesses. However, Solicitor General Elena Kagan, who a year later would be an associate justice on the Supreme Court, contributed to the government's defense, stating that there was great concern for the overall corrupting influence that campaign finance had on the political system, and that BCRA may well have been the most unselfish act of Congress in a very long time. To this she added that there had been compiled before Congress a great number of records indicating the validity of this corruption and the need to address it through legislation regulating political expenditures, particularly by corporations. Seth Waxman spoke as well on behalf of Senators John McCain et al. as amicus curiae (friends of the court) in support of the government. In his brief time, he reminded the Court of the historical dangers involved in allowing corporations to contribute to and spend within political elections without regulation.

In January 2010, the Court decided 5–4 for Citizens United. The Court overruled *Austin v. Michigan Chamber of Commerce*, which had upheld a restriction on corporate speech and portions of the *McConnell* case. The conservative justices Roberts, Scalia, Alito, Thomas, and Kennedy, who wrote the opinion, held that the First Amendment supported corporate funding of independent political broadcasts in elections and cannot be limited. The more liberal Justice Stevens dissented, and was joined by Justices Ginsburg, Breyer, and Sotomayor, all of who maintained that narrow disruption to a corporation's right to free speech was the lesser evil, considering the danger it posed to the political process.

Nevertheless, the majority also held that the BCRA's disclosure of contributors' identities was constitutional because it served a justifiable government interest in educating the people as to resources behind the spending. In addition, the Court maintained the ban on direct contributions to candidates from corporations and unions with regard to the appearance of impropriety.

Between the original oral arguments and the second round of oral arguments, the Court saw the retirement of Justice Souter and the addition of Justice Sotomayor. Since the outcome was divided on ideological lines, changing one liberal justice for another did not change the end vote. Nonetheless, anyone who listened to the oral arguments would have heard the passion with which these principles were discussed. This case revealed a true concern for the electoral process—a desire to balance rights with guidelines, and a deep respect for judicial and legislative traditions—and it had a dramatic effect on the political economy of U.S. democracy. The decision is new and more time is needed before we fully understand the impact it has had on the relationship between the political power of wealthy corporations, free and fair elections, and First Amendment free speech rights.

Kathleen C. Simmons

See Also Constitution of the United States (see Appendix); Economic Rent; Supreme Court

Related Cases

Buckley v. Valeo, 424 U.S. 1 (1976) (Upheld limits on campaign contributions; ruled that spending money on elections is a form of free speech)

Austin v. Michigan Chamber of Commerce, 494 U.S. 652 (1990) (Upheld the restriction on corporate speech: "Corporate wealth can unfairly influence elections")

McConnell v. Federal Election Commission, 540 U.S. 93 (2003) (Upheld BCRA; not all political speech is protected by the First Amendment)

Federal Election Commission v. Wisconsin Right to Life, Inc., 551 U.S. 449 (2007) (Held that issue ads may not be banned from the months preceding a primary or general election)

Further Reading

Legal Information Institute, Cornell University Law School. N.d. "*Citizens United v. Federal Election Commission* (No. 08-205)." http://www.law.cornell.edu/supct/html/08-205.ZO.html. (Transcript of Justice Kennedy's opinion of the Court)

Legal Information Institute, Cornell University Law School. N.d. "*Citizens United v. Federal Election Commission* (No. 08-205)." http://www.law.cornell.edu/supct/html/08-205.ZC.html. (Transcript of Justice Roberts's concurring opinion)

Legal Information Institute, Cornell University Law School. N.d. "*Citizens United v. Federal Election Commission* (No. 08-205)." http://www.law.cornell.edu/supct/html/08-205.ZC1.html. (Transcript of Justice Scalia's concurring opinion)

Legal Information Institute, Cornell University Law School. N.d. "*Citizens United v. Federal Election Commission* (No. 08-205)." http://www.law.cornell.edu/supct/html/08-205.ZX.html. (Transcript of the opinion of Justice Stevens)

Legal Information Institute, Cornell University Law School. N.d. "*Citizens United v. Federal Election Commission* (No. 08-205)." http://www.law.cornell.edu/supct/html/08-205.ZX1.html. (Transcript of the opinion of Justice Thomas)

Teacher Resources

Citzens United. N.d. "Home." Accessed November 24, 2013. http://www.citizensunited.org/.

Supreme Court of the United States. N.d. "Syllabus, *Citizens United v. Federal Election Commission*, Appeal from the United States District Court for the District of Columbia." http://www.supremecourt.gov/opinions/09pdf/08-205.pdf. (Supreme Court syllabus and transcripts of opinions in the case)

Vogel, Kenneth P. 2011. "Year after Ruling: Right Gloats, Left Vows Fight." *Politico*, January 21. http://www.politico.com/news/stories/0111/47955.html#ixzz2lseYsDzy.

Classical Economics

The term "classical economics" denotes a philosophical system that dominated economic thought and policy from the end of the eighteenth until the middle of the nineteenth century. This system, with many contributors and characteristics, was influenced most especially by the writings of Adam Smith (1723–1790), Thomas Robert Malthus (1766–1834), David Ricardo (1772–1823), Jean Baptiste Say (1767–1832), and John Stuart Mill (1806–1873).

Sometimes referred to as a system of natural liberty, classical economics described government as having a circumscribed role in the economy. Classical economics emphasized the importance of natural law, natural rights, and a Newtonian order of society. The essential features of classical economics include the following concepts: *laissez-faire*, economic growth and competition, value and utility theory, the population principle, and Say's Law. Economic growth and competition are additional cornerstones of the system, incorporating private property rights, arguments in favor of free trade, the encouragement of emerging markets, and an expanding division of labor and a wage-earning class. As the factory system developed and manufacturing began to exert a greater influence on the economy beginning in the eighteenth century, use and exchange value of a good or service was incorporated in the classical theory of value. This theory, which maintained a "paradox of value"—an expression that stressed the dichotomy between "use" value and "exchange" value for each good or service—would be subsequently replaced by a more complete value analysis by three important marginalist writers: William Stanley Jevons (1835–1882), Leon Walras (1834–1910), and Carl Menger (1840–1921), during the latter half of the nineteenth century. Utility, the idea that value comes from the pleasure or benefit produced by a good and not the good itself, was refined throughout the classical period. The population principle, which later led to the notion of a "Malthusian trap," provided the classical paradigm with subsistence wage rates and a stationary state, leading many later writers to label economics as the "dismal science." Finally, the general acceptance of Say's Law, or the law of markets, also pervaded classical discussions. Although controversial and somewhat limiting in its description, the law implies that in a state of equilibrium, and generally in the long run, goods and services are simply bought with other goods and services.

Adam Smith, the first major classical writer, was born in Kirkcaldy, Scotland. Smith entered the University of Glasgow at the age of 14 and also studied at Oxford. In 1751, he was appointed a professor of logic at Glasgow. He was appointed chair of moral philosophy in 1752. Smith's first publication, *Theory of Moral Sentiments* (1759), was a widespread success. In 1776, Smith's seminal work, *An Inquiry into the Nature and Causes of the Wealth of Nations*, was published. The global success of *The Wealth of Nations* was the beginning of the classical period. Smith's focus on growth and development exemplified the ideas of the Scottish Enlightenment. In *The Wealth of Nations*, Smith attacked mercantilism, the popular economic system of his day. As the originator of the classical school of economics, Smith developed the theory of value, wages, rents, and profits. Smith promoted the natural liberty of the individual and the free enterprise economic system, making him the originator of classical economics philosophy.

Smith identified three roles for government: national defense, the maintenance of law and order, and the building and maintenance of a public infrastructure and public institutions. Smith is arguably most popular for his economic concept of the invisible hand, the idea that each individual promotes the general welfare by seeking to advance their individual welfare.

Thomas Robert Malthus, born in Surrey, England, studied at Cambridge and became a clergyman in the Church of England. He later assumed the post of professor of history and political economy at the East India College. His most famous work, *Essay on the Principle of Population as It Affects the Future Improvement of Society* (1798), was initially published anonymously and created a controversy in the academic community of his day. In response to the assertion by many contemporary writers of the inexorable ascent of human happiness and prosperity, Malthus's work denied this claim, arguing that ultimately, a country's population would outstrip its food supply, thereby dampening future economic growth and development. The policy implication of this population principle, even with positive and preventive checks, was an eventual subsistence wage rate and economic stagnation.

David Ricardo, born in London, England, entered his father's brokerage firm at the age of 14 after a short business education in Holland. After leaving the firm at 21 after his marriage and subsequent conversion to Christianity from Judaism, Ricardo, with the financial support of numerous members of the exchange, eventually became extremely wealthy on his own as a trader and stockbroker on the London Exchange. In 1814, he retired from business and later became a member of Parliament. It was in this capacity that he took an active part in the public policy debates of his day, including bank reform, tax proposals, the resumption of specie payments, and the national debt. Ricardo contributed numerous articles and pamphlets pertaining to various pressing issues in monetary and fiscal policy of the early nineteenth century, especially his spirited debate with Malthus regarding the repeal of the Corn Laws. His most important work, however, was *On the Principles of Political Economy and Taxation* (1817). Improving and borrowing from classical rent theory, Malthus's population theory, and the wages-fund doctrine of Adam Smith, Ricardo forged a highly abstract analytical system that focused on the problem of income distribution. Additional insights included his recognition of an imperfect measure of value, a long-run stationary state, and an analysis of comparative advantage.

French-born Jean Baptiste Say was a businessman in England before he returned to France. Upon his return, he edited a magazine promoting ideas of the French Revolution. In 1799, he promoted his laissez-faire philosophy publicly when he was appointed to the Tribunate. He was later relieved of his duties by Napoleon, who did not agree with Say's views. His *Treatise on Political Economy* was published in 1803. It was widely read through many editions in both the United States and Europe. While the phrase "supply creates its own demand" is incorrectly attributed to Say, the book is credited with spreading the ideas of Adam Smith to the mainland European continent.

John Stuart Mill, the oldest son of James Mill, published *Principles of Political Economy with Some Application to Social Philosophy* in 1848. *Principles* was the most-used economics textbook in the English-speaking world until the late 1800s, when it was replaced by Alfred Marshall's *Principles of Economics* (1890). Mill's philosophy was a combination of the utility theory of Jeremy Bentham and the intellectual ideas of David Ricardo. Mill addressed many microeconomic topics and public policy issues of his day. He supported social change through his support of inheritance taxes, women's suffrage, and compulsory education.

Although classical economics had declined in importance as a system of thought by the end of the nineteenth century due to the rise and importance of marginalism, the emergence of socialist and historicist critics, and its inability to adequately answer some of the great policy debates of the day, it continues to be the starting point for modern micro- and macroeconomic analysis.

Joseph A. Weglarz

See Also Smith, Adam

Selected Works about Classical Economics

O'Brien, D. P. 2004. *The Classical Economists Revisited.* Princeton, NJ: Princeton University Press.

Rothbard, Murray N. 1995. *Classical Economics*. Cheltenham, UK: Edward Elgar.

Sowell, Thomas. 2006. *On Classical Economics*. New Haven, CT: Yale University Press.

Resources for Teachers and Researchers

Liberty Fund. 2005. "The Industrial Revolution." Indianapolis, IN: Liberty Fund.

Sandoz, Ellis, ed. 1998. *Political Sermons of the American Founding Era: 1730–1805*. 2 Vols. Indianapolis, IN: Liberty Fund.

Smith, Adam. 1982. *The Wealth of Nations*. R. H. Campbell and A. S. Skinner, eds. 2 vols. Indianapolis, IN: Liberty Press.

Clayton Antitrust Act of 1914

The Clayton Antitrust Act of 1914 was written to further strengthen the government's control of monopolies and monopolistic activities that weakened trade in the United States. The Clayton Act further strengthened the antitrust laws originally expressed in the Sherman Antitrust Act of 1890 by allowing a person to sue if he or she could prove damage by an illegal arrangement to restrain trade. According to the Clayton Act, a successful plaintiff in such a case would be allowed to recover three times the damages sustained. The purpose of this rule of triple damages was to encourage private lawsuits against conspiring oligopolists.

Historical Antitrust Legislation

For centuries, throughout England and the United States, judges have deemed agreements among competitors to reduce quantities and raise prices to be contrary to the public good and the free-enterprise system. They have therefore refused to enforce such agreements. The Sherman Antitrust Act of 1890 codified and reinforced this policy. The Sherman Act established a legal boundary for contract law. The act also stated that every contract or attempt to restrain trade or commerce among states or with foreign nations was illegal.

Under this original antitrust legislation, any person who monopolized or attempted to monopolize any part of the trade or commerce among states or with foreign nations would be deemed guilty of a misdemeanor with a punishment of a fine not exceeding 50,000 dollars or by imprisonment not exceeding one year, or both punishments, at the discretion of the Court.

The Clayton Antitrust Act, signed into law in 1914 by President Woodrow Wilson, supplemented the Sherman Antitrust Act. The Clayton Antitrust Act made illegal price cutting, rebates, or exclusive contracts that are specifically for the purpose of eliminating the competition. The act excluded two groups: labor unions and agricultural cooperatives.

So long as they were peaceful, the act allowed strikes, pickets, and boycotts. It also restricted the courts to issue injunctions against organized labor for the purpose of strike-breaking. This particular piece of the Clayton Act expressly defined labor as not a commodity or "article of commerce." This was seen as a win for the labor force in the United States. Workers hailed the law as labor's backing force. Businesses, however, continued to assert that labor should not be protected in this way.

The act further increased the punishment for breaking said antitrust legislation. It became more punitive with the introduction of the triple damage rule. It also strengthened the government's powers and authorized private lawsuits. The antitrust laws give the government various ways to promote competition. They allow the government to prevent mergers, and prevent companies from coordinating their activities in ways that make markets less competitive.

It has been the job of the Federal Trade Commission and the Department of Justice's Antitrust Division to watch firms closely to ensure that unfair trade practices are not taking place. Actions such as predatory pricing, the formation of cartels and/or monopolies, and the breaking up of existing monopolies are all actions that are considered illegal under the current antitrust legislation.

Even the prevention of mergers that might lead to reduced competition and higher prices is a power given to the government under the Clayton Antitrust Act. The government must act carefully to make the right decision when considering the merging of two or more companies. While some mergers hurt consumers by reducing competition, others can actually leave the consumer better off. Mergers that lower prices, provide more reliable products or services, and create a more efficient industry are allowed.

Antitrust Laws in Modern Times

Since the 1980s, government officials have had a difficult time in the courts proving monopoly power. Judges have mostly held that large companies are not bad just because they are large. If the market is promoting competition, then company size should not be an issue and the government should not interfere.

In 1997, the Justice Department and the Federal Trade Commission released new guidelines for proposed mergers. Now, companies that want to merge have the chance to prove that the merger would lower costs and consumer prices or lead to a better product.

Before the Justice Department rules on allowing a merger, they try to predict the effects of a merger on prices and service. It is a fine balance between allowing market freedom and protecting consumers. The Supreme Court has embraced many antitrust principles that began in the 1980s.

Tracy L. Ripley

See Also Sherman Antitrust Act of 1890

Further Reading

Mankiw, N. Gregory. 2011. *Principles of Microeconomics*. Cincinnati, OH: South-Western-Cengage Learning.

McNeese, Tim. 2009. *The Robber Barons and the Sherman Antitrust Act*. New York: Chelsea House.

O'Sullivan, Arthur, and Steven M. Sheffrin. 2007. *Economics Principles in Action*. Upper Saddle River, NJ: Pearson: Prentice Hall.

Resources for Teachers

eNotes-Study Smarter. N.d. "Antitrust Acts and Laws." http://www.enotes.com/antitrust-acts-laws-reference/antitrust-acts-laws.

Street Law Inc. N.d. "Lesson 1: Why Do We Have Antitrust Laws?" Accessed June 16, 2013. http://www.fairfightfilm.org/lessons/lesson1.pdf.

Coase, Ronald

Born: December 29, 1910, in Willesden, England; Died September 2, 2013, Chicago, IL; English; property rights, economics of law, Nobel Prize (1991); Major Works: "The Nature of the Firm" (1937), *British Broadcasting: A Study in Monopoly* (1950), "The Problem of Social Cost" (1960)

Ronald Coase wrote little compared to other famous economists, but what he did write made a tremendous impact on economic thought. Two of his journal articles have started new subfields of economics: the economics of property rights and the economics of law.

Ronald Harry Coase was born on December 29, 1910, in Willesden, England, just outside London. His parents were not well educated, both of them having dropped out of school by the age of 12. As a boy, his weak legs required him to wear metal braces; as a result, he was sent to a school for physically handicapped children. When he was 12 years old, he was admitted to a quality grammar school, and in 1929, he enrolled in the London School of Economics. In his last year at school, he took a study tour to the United States. During his visit he examined the structure of American industries. It was here, before he even graduated from college, that he gained his essential insight into the workings of companies for which he was to become famous, and the concept of "transaction costs."

Upon graduation, Coase taught at various British universities and, with the onset of World War II, entered government service, first for the Forestry Commission and then for the Offices of the War Cabinet. After the war, he continued to teach college classes and also worked on a doctoral dissertation. Upon earning his PhD in 1951, he emigrated to the United States, where he taught at the University of Buffalo, the University of Virginia, and finally the University of Chicago, from which he retired in 1979. After retirement, however, his work did not stop. He continued as a researcher at the University of Chicago in law and economics—a field that he himself created.

When Coase visited the United States in 1931–1932, he collected data and made observations about how firms really work. In doing so, he stumbled across a question to which no one had produced an adequate answer: "Why do firms (companies) exist?" If people can specialize in whatever job gets them the most value, how could it possibly be efficient to hold workers captive in large companies? Should it not be more efficient to make individual contracts with individual workers for each necessary task? Coase pointed out that all firms are like little socialist economies: instead of individuals deciding what kind of economic activity to pursue, they have to follow orders from their managers.

In an article entitled "The Nature of the Firm," Coase solved this problem by discussing the idea of transaction costs. Each economic exchange has certain built-in costs, like bargaining costs, the costs to gather and interpret information, and the costs to protect trade secrets. These transaction costs interfere with market activity and provide an incentive for entrepreneurs to produce goods and services in-house by hiring workers and forming a company. Creating a hierarchy inside a firm can lower transaction costs, but only to a certain degree. Coase also noted that as a company gets larger, it becomes more difficult to manage, a problem called diseconomies of scale. Because of this, there is a limit to the size to which companies can grow (contrary to what Karl Marx believed). Rather, according to Coase, firms will begin to make contracts with individuals and smaller companies to do the work that is inefficient for the firm to do itself.

Coase's second groundbreaking article, "The Problem of Social Cost," was published in 1960, 23 years after "The Nature of the Firm." In "The Problem of Social Cost," Coase attacked a generally held theory about how people interact in society, first posited by Arthur Pigou in 1920.

Externalities (spillover costs) are the costs and consequences of one decision imposed upon third parties external to the transaction. According to Pigou, the government can tax the entity creating the externality (such as pollution) to make it stop or at least reduce the behavior. The government could then use the tax money to deal with the effects of the behavior, in this case to clean up the pollution.

Coase's insight into externalities was that the situation could be resolved by simply assigning clear property rights, or if that is not possible, by making one of the parties legally liable for the spillover costs incurred. The surprising conclusion is that the final amount of spillover will be the same regardless of who is liable for it. If the two parties involved are free to negotiate and trade with one another, they will make a deal to get the end result they both desire.

For example, if a factory is made liable for polluting the nearby neighborhood, then the factory will pay the neighbors for the right to pollute. Conversely, if the neighbors are held liable, then they will pay the factory to pollute less. If there are no transaction costs (and this is a big "if"), then the same amount of pollution will be produced either way, though the wealth of the parties involved may be different. This became known as the "Coase theorem," and it has had a definite real-world impact. Because of Coase's theorem, legislators and judges are now encouraged to define ownership (property rights) before issuing taxes or injunctions.

Primarily for his work on social costs and the Coase theorem, Ronald Coase was awarded the Nobel Prize in Economics in 1991. Coase spent much of the rest of his professional career editing the University of Chicago's *Journal of Law and Economics*.

Ronald Coase died on September 2, 2013, in Chicago, Illinois.

Stephen H. Day

See Also Externalities; Public Goods

Selected Works by Ronald Coase

Coase, Ronald. 1950. *British Broadcasting: A Study in Monopoly*. London: London School of Economics and Political Science.

Coase, Ronald. 1994. *Essays on Economics and Economists*. Chicago: University of Chicago Press.

Coase, Ronald. 1988. *The Firm, the Market, and the Law*. Chicago: University of Chicago Press.

Coase, Ronald. 2011. *How China Became Capitalist*. London: Palgrave MacMillan.

Coase, Ronald. 1937. "The Nature of the Firm." *Economica* 4, no. 16: 386–405.

Coase, Ronald. 1960. "The Problem of Social Cost." *Journal of Law and Economics* 3: 1–23.

Selected Works about Ronald Coase

Coase, Ronald. 2011. "Autobiography." Nobelprize.org. http://nobelprize.org/nobel_prizes/economics/laureates/1991/coase-autobio.html.

Overtweldt, Johan van. 2007. *The Chicago School: How the University of Chicago Assembled the Thinkers Who Revolutionized Economics and Business*. Chicago: Agate B2.

Command Economy

In a command economy, also known as a centrally planned economy, the factors of production or resources are owned by a central authority, usually government. Government has the responsibility to determine how to solve the economic problem of scarcity. Government planners or central committees answer the economic questions: *What to produce? How to produce?* and *For whom to produce?*

Command economies are usually combined with a highly authoritative political system. The ideas of socialism or communism are most often used in reference to a command economy. Socialism is an economic theory where most resources are publicly owned, and general assemblies along with workers and consumers make economic decisions. Communist nations have an authoritarian government or a single political party or dictator. Communism is a centrally planned economy with the government owning all economic and political power.

Central planners try to allocate the best use of land, labor, and capital to provide a basic standard of living for all peoples within the society. Central planners create production and hiring targets to achieve economic goals such as price stability, economic growth, and full employment. To achieve these goals, they determine the levels of production for capital goods and consumer goods.

A command economy functions on short- and long-term goals devised by the central authority. Often plans are set for five-year periods with additional smaller targets to achieve objectives. In contrast to a market economy, where the interactions of consumers and producers establish prices and determine signals, planned economy prices do not signal the value or distribution of goods or services, as the central authority has already established prices and allocations within their plan.

Advantages

Due to the central decision-making process, a centrally planned economy is usually able to mobilize economic resources for large-scale projects with relative ease. Historically, this has allowed such economies to transform large societies and encourage rapid industrialization, especially in developing a military complex. A short-term advantage is their emphasis on full employment and equitable distribution of goods. This advantage is very appealing to the voters of developing nations when proposed by their populist politicians. A second advantage is the emphasis placed on economic security, with promises that all citizens will have jobs, and that basic needs like medical care, housing, and education will be met. Societies that do not normally practice command economies have also found a centrally planned economy useful and advantageous during wartime, as it allows focused production on those goods and services deemed necessary for success.

Disadvantages

Consumer sovereignty does not play a role in a planned economy. In a command economy, it is common for production targets not to be clearly communicated between the government and manufacturer, leading to a lack of coordination resulting in low product quality and inaccurate production quantities. This coordination problem highlights the emphasis of quantity over quality. Five-year plans and smaller target goals make it difficult to predict consumer wants and needs, leading to market misallocations and frequent shortages. Personal limitations and a lack of consumer goods facilitate the rise of shadow economies and/or political corruption.

In addition, a goal of full employment may force people to work in an industry or job they did not choose. There is a loss of individual innovation and incentive as all effort is focused on the production target or five-year state goal, rather than on market interactions between business and labor or producer and consumer.

History and Examples

Planned economies existed as long ago as the Incan empire of sixteenth-century Peru. The Viennese economist Otto Neurath used this method to control hyperinflation after World War I. The Mormons in nineteenth-century Utah, Maoist China, Castro's Cuba, and the

United States during World War II mobilization have all used planned economies. The former Soviet Union is considered the essential case study.

The Union of Soviet Socialist Republics

The story of the USSR begins with German economist Karl Marx and philosopher Frederick Engels. The two wrote *The Communist Manifesto* in 1848 after observing the numerous deplorable working conditions common during the Industrial Revolution. Marx and Engels wrote of an alternative system in which the proletariat or working class would rise up and overthrow the bourgeoisie or factory owners. In its place, society would form a classless society or utopia.

Vladimir Lenin led the Bolsheviks to try this great social experiment in Czarist Russia of 1917. The state claimed ownership of the means of production, and government committees began planning and performing the prior functions of the market. Lenin quickly realized that some ownership of private property (the New Economic Policy) was necessary for a smooth economy, yet the government would maintain control of what Lenin termed the commanding heights or major infrastructure industries, such as coal, steel, and transportation.

After the Bolshevik Revolution and the communist consolidation of power following the Russian Civil War, Soviet leaders decided to move away from Lenin's New Economic Policy. Stalin rose to power upon Lenin's death in 1924, and embarked on a rapid industrialization movement known as the First Five-Year Plan in 1928. A number of other five-year plans followed, with differing amounts of success. However, the Soviet Union was successful in becoming one of the major industrial and military powers in the world in the 1930s.

While the Soviet Union put an emphasis on the production of capital goods in the industrial sector, it moved toward collectivization in the agricultural sector. During 1927–1937, the state took control of the country's agricultural inputs. These collectivization efforts led to a famine in 1932–1933, resulting in millions of deaths due to starvation. The production of agricultural goods was slow to recover and the Soviet Union was forced to import large quantities of these goods for years afterward.

After World War II, the Soviet Union exerted its influence over the nations of Eastern Europe by creating Soviet-style governments throughout the region. The Soviet Union forced the economies of these nations to specialize in the creation of certain goods under the Council for Mutual Economic Assistance (Comecon). Under both Nikita Khrushchev and Leonid Brezhnev, the Soviet Union placed emphasis on creating more consumer goods than in the Stalin era.

By the 1980s, the inefficiencies of central planning were having disastrous effects on the Soviet economy. When Mikhail Gorbachev took over the reins of leadership in the Soviet Union in 1985, he embarked on a policy called "perestroika," which introduced more market principles into the Soviet economy. However, crippling shortages and massive military spending because of an arms race with the United States helped contribute to the end of the Soviet Union in 1991.

Jeremy Robinson
Kathryn Lloyd Gustafson

See Also Economic Systems; Market Capitalism; Marx, Karl; Marxism

Further Reading

Amadeo, Kimberly. 2013. "Command Economy." About.Com US Economy. Accessed November 24, 2013. http://useconomy.about.com/od/US-Economy-Theory/a/Command-Economy.htm.

Ericson, Richard E. N.d. "Command Economy." Accessed November 24, 2013. http://econ.la.psu.edu/~bickes/rickcommand.pdf.

How Stuff Works? N.d. "Union of Soviet Socialist Republics-Economic System." Accessed November 24, 2013. http://history.howstuffworks.com/asian-history/union-of-soviet-socialist-republics2.htm.

Marx, Karl, with Frederick Engels. 2008. *The Communist Manifesto*. Stillwell, KS: Digireads Publishing.

Merriman, John. 2004. *A History of Modern Europe: From the Renaissance to the Present*. 2nd ed. New York: W. W. Norton.

Resources for Teachers

Council for Economic Education. N.d. "Lesson 2: What? How? For Whom?" Accessed November 24, 2013. http://www.councilforeconed.org/lesson-resources/lessons/sample-lessons/Master_Curriculum_Guides_56_Sample_Lesson.pdf.

EcEdWeb. N.d. "Lesson on Economic Systems, Andersonville Prison: An Economic Microcosm." Accessed November 24, 2013. http://ecedweb.unomaha.edu/ecedweek/lesson2.htm.

Fraser Institute. N.d. "Pencils or Candies? Planned Economies and Market Allocation." Accessed November 24, 2013. http://www.fraserinstitute.org/uploadedFiles/fraser-ca/Content/education-programs/teachers/classroom-resources/Lesson-Plan-Economic-Systems.pdf.

Herman-Ellison, Lisa C. 2007. "Comparative Economic Systems." econedlink. Accessed November 24, 2013. http://www.econedlink.org/lessons/index.php?lid=322&type=educator.

Congressional Budget Office

The Congressional Budget Office is a nonpartisan agency within the federal government that produces analytical budgetary and economic reports. These analyses are then used to assist Congress in maintaining and balancing the federal budget.

The power to maintain the federal budget is an enumerated power in the United States Constitution and the responsibility is given to the Congress. Despite this, with the passage of the Budget and Accounting Act of 1921, the president became increasingly involved in planning the budget. The Budget and Accounting Act caused two things to occur. First, the Bureau of the Budget was created, giving the president greater authority over budget information. Second, the Budget and Accounting Act gave the president the power to plan a yearly budget that needed to be given to Congress for approval.

Conflicts between the legislative and executive branches of the government gave rise to the Congressional Budget and Impoundment Control Act of 1974, otherwise known as the Budget Act. The Budget Act returned the responsibility of maintaining the federal budget to Congress. In so doing, Congress enacted several changes.

First, new procedures were established for Congress to develop, coordinate, and enforce budgetary priorities without presidential oversight. Second, the House and Senate

Budget Committees were created to direct the budgeting process. Lastly, the Congressional Budget Office was formed to provide objective and impartial information on budgetary and economic issues for use by the House and Senate Budget Committees and the rest of Congress. The Congressional Budget Office also assists the Appropriations, Ways and Means, and Finance Committees.

The director of the Congressional Budget Office is selected jointly by the president pro tempore of the Senate and the Speaker of the House of Representatives. The rest of the approximately 235-member staff of the Congressional Budget Office is made up of non-partisan economists and policy analysts who are selected on a basis of professional competence, not political association. The Congressional Budget Office also employs lawyers, information technology specialists, and editors.

The Congressional Budget Office is organized into the Office of the Director as well as the following eight divisions:

- Budget Analysis Division
- Financial Analysis Division
- Health, Retirement, and Long-Term Analysis Division
- Macroeconomic Analysis Division
- Management, Business, and Information Services Division
- Microeconomic Studies Division
- National Security Division
- Tax Analysis Division

The Office of the Director houses several agents who are essential to running the office smoothly. The Director of the Congressional Budget Office works closely with:

- Associate Director for Economic Analysis, who contributes to all aspects of the agency's analytic work;
- Associate Director for Legislative Affairs, who serves as the Congressional Budget Office's central liaison with the Congress;
- Associate Director for Communications and the members of the Office of Communications, who are responsible for all of the public affairs activities of Congressional Budget Office, including relations with the media and with the public; and
- Office of the General Counsel, which performs the agency's legal work and acquisitions.

Each division is responsible for compiling information based upon its category. Information and data from one agency are often used by other divisions for their reports. The Budget Analysis Division is responsible for gathering both formal and informal cost estimates for every bill proposed or approved by Congress, as well as coming up with a baseline federal budget. This division also makes important contributions to the

Congressional Budget Office's reports on items such as the Analysis of the President's Budget and the Monthly Budget Review. The Financial Analysis Division's responsibility is to focus on the federal government's financial commitments and offer information on financial valuation, modeling, and accounting. The Macroeconomic Analysis Division studies changes in the economy, such as labor force participation, international trade, and the recent economic recovery, to name a few.

The Congressional Budget Office produces several reports and economic analyses for the Congress. These reports are created with the intent to assist the Congress in making the best decisions to maintain a healthy federal budget. The Congressional Budget Office selects what to research and analyze based upon what is needed by Congress. One of the most important reports created is the *Budget and Economic Outlook*, which includes projections of spending and revenues over 10-year periods and an economic forecast for those periods as well. These projections provide Congress with a measure of how changes in spending and taxes may affect the future. The Congressional Budget Office generates most of its projections from government-produced data, such as the surveys of labor market conditions and prices, the Current Population Survey, and health care surveys. The Congressional Budget Office also uses information from state and local governments, industry groups, professors, and government agencies, to name a few.

Ekaterini Chrisopoulos-Vergos

See Also Office of Management and Budget (OMB)

Further Reading

Congressional Budget Office (CBO). N.d. "Congressional Budget Office (CBO)." http://cbo.gov.

Office of Management and Budget. N.d. "The President's Budget for Fiscal Year 2014." http://www.whitehouse.gov/omb/budget.

Resources for Teachers

economics21.org, Economic Policies for the 21st Century. N.d. "Ten Things the Latest CBO Report Tells Us about Federal Finances." Accessed May 11, 2013. http://www.economics21.org/commentary/ten-things-latest-cbo-report-tells-us-about-federal-finances.

Graduate School USA. N.d. "Congressional Budget Process." Accessed May 11, 2013. http://graduateschool.edu/course_details.php?cid=budg8175D.

Contractionary Fiscal Policy

Contractionary fiscal policy is a policy enacted by the government to slow economic growth by increasing tax rates, decreasing government spending, and lowering transfer payments. This policy is only used when there is fear that very fast economic growth is causing inflation, which economists call the inflationary or expansionary gap. The goal of using contractionary fiscal policy is to close this gap.

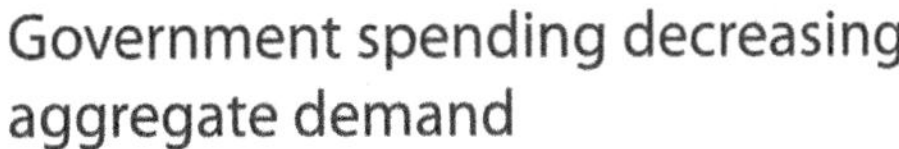

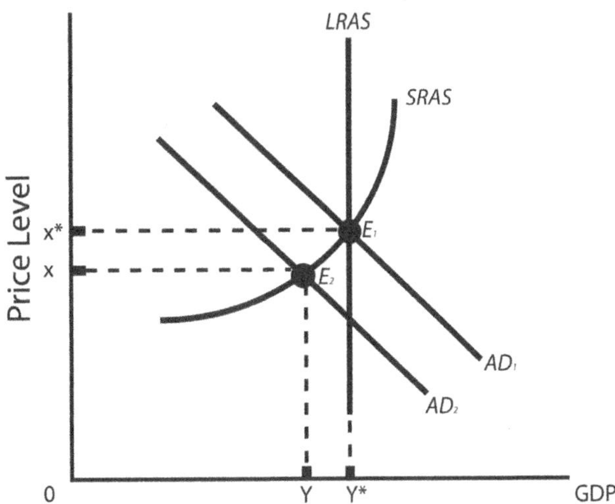

Aggregate demand decreases (AD1 to AD2) when government spending decreases (x* to x)

Fiscal policy's ultimate goal is to ensure that the economy is performing at its best. There are two conflicting viewpoints on handling the economy when inflation is high. Classical economists believe that the government should not get involved in the economy because the market will balance out naturally. Fiscal policy is based on the theories of John Maynard Keynes (1883–1946), a British economist. Keynesian economists believe that the government should step in and make policy changes when the economy is growing too quickly and causing inflation to rise. It calls for the government to employ a mix of raising taxes and decreasing government spending in order to slow the economy.

Changes in fiscal policy occur to stabilize inflation, balance employment, and uphold the value of currency. The most important element of fiscal policy is maintaining and balancing the federal budget by examining tax revenues compared to government expenditures. Contractionary fiscal policy is used when the government is looking to decrease the budget deficit or needs to increase its budget surplus.

When enacting a contractionary fiscal policy, economists illustrate this by saying it shifts the aggregate demand curve to the left, which lowers economic output along with inflation. Aggregate demand is the level of demand for goods and services by consumers, businesses, and the government. When contractionary fiscal policy goes into effect, it works to slow aggregate demand for goods and services.

There are three main tools utilized by the government to enact a contractionary fiscal policy: increasing taxes, decreasing government purchases, and reducing transfer payments.

When using increased taxation as a contractionary fiscal policy tool, the government typically only focuses on an individual's personal income taxes, though it can also include property taxes and sales taxes. An increase in taxes can either be a one-time payment to the federal government or an overall increase in income tax rates. Either way, when taxes increase, the amount of disposable income an individual has decreases. Thus, with a decrease in disposable income comes less spending power, which in turn causes decreased production of consumer goods. Overall, this slows the economy and helps to combat inflation.

Of the three contractionary fiscal policy tools that can be used, increased taxation is fairly easy to implement, though it is not favored by taxpayers or by politicians. Politicians do not like to implement tax increases because the politicians are then viewed negatively by taxpayers, who may not reelect a candidate for supporting such a fiscal policy. Another reason paying more in taxes is viewed negatively by taxpayers is due to the fact that the people with the least amount of disposable income are the hardest hit by this increase.

Reducing government spending means decreasing funds available across several different government agencies, and can include cuts in military expenditures, teacher salaries, and road construction, for example. When these government agencies have funding cuts, they are no longer able to purchase as much. When an agency has decreased income, this lowers its overall production and this assists in reducing the inflation rate.

Lowering the amount of transfer payments is also a useful tool of contractionary fiscal policy. Transfer payments are payments made by the government directly to individuals. Those who receive transfer payments fall into three categories: the elderly and disabled who are on Social Security, people who are unemployed and receive unemployment benefits, and the poor who are on welfare. Lowering transfer payments can be done either by decreasing the amount of payment one or two of the categories receive, or using a blanket percentage reduction across the three categories. Decreasing transfer payments lowers the disposable income of those who receive these benefits. Less disposable income, similar to when taxes are increased, leads to a decrease in production, when people no longer can purchase as many goods and services. This also helps to decrease inflation. Though it can be effective, lowering transfer payments is not usually used as a tool. Since the elderly, poor, and unemployed are the ones receiving these benefits, they are already at a disadvantage economically. Just as with increasing taxes, lowering payments further for those who need Social Security, welfare, or unemployment assistance could have a negative consequence for politicians who vote for these policies.

In summary, contractionary fiscal policy slows the economy to a pace that allows inflation to stabilize by lessening aggregate demand. Using policy tools such as increasing taxes, decreasing government spending, and lowering transfer payments either separately or together can work to balance the budget.

Ekaterini Chrisopoulos-Vergos

See Also Contractionary Monetary Policy; Entitlements; Expansionary Fiscal Policy; Expansionary Monetary Policy; Inflation; Social Security Act of 1935; Taxes; Unemployment

Further Reading

AmosWEB. N.d. "Contractionary Fiscal Policy." Accessed July 16, 2013. www.amosweb.com/cgi-bin/awb_nav.pl?s=wpd&c=dsp&k=contractionary+fiscal+policy.

Hall, Shane. N.d. "Contractionary Fiscal Policies by Shane Hall." *eHow Money*. Accessed July 16, 2013. www.ehow.com/info_7745738_contractionary-fiscal-policies.html.

McEachern, William A. 2010. *Macroeconomics: A Contemporary Introduction*. Mason, OH: South-Western Cengage Learning.

Resources for Teachers

Khan Academy. N.d. "Monetary and Fiscal Policy." Accessed July 16, 2013. www.khanacademy.org/economics-finance-domain/macroeconomics/aggregate-supply-demand-topic/monetary-fiscal-policy/v/monetary-and-fiscal-policy.

Nash, Jon. N.d. "Contractionary Fiscal Policy and Aggregate Demand." Education Portal. Accessed July 16, 2013. education-portal.com/academy/lesson/contractionary-fiscal-policy-and-aggregate-demand.html.

Yopp, Martha. 2012. "The Role of Government: The Federal Government and Fiscal Policy." econedlink. Accessed July 16, 2013. http://www.econedlink.org/lessons/index.php?lid=190&type=educator.

Contractionary Monetary Policy

Contractionary monetary policy is a policy in which the central bank of a country decides that it is necessary to decrease the money supply to prevent inflation or slow economic growth. Monetary policy works together with fiscal policy, which is controlled by the government, to ensure economic growth in the economy. The most frequent tool used by a central bank to implement contractionary monetary policy is the selling of government bills, notes, and bonds. The buyer of the treasuries pays the central bank with money which reduces the amount of money in the system.

In the United States, contractionary monetary policy is under the direction of the chair of the Federal Reserve. The Board of Governors of the Federal Reserve System decides when contractionary monetary policy is necessary. The Federal Reserve accomplishes contractionary monetary policy using three primary tools: raising the reserve requirement; raising the discount rate; or selling government bills, notes, and bonds. Implementation of the latter tool is done through the Federal Open Market Committee (FOMC). The FOMC implements contractionary monetary policy by raising interest rates.

In order to implement the monetary policy decisions of the Federal Reserve Board of Governors, the FOMC carries out open-market operations. To implement contractionary monetary policy, the Federal Reserve sells government bonds. The decrease in demand decreases the price and increases the interest rate. The higher interest rates create incentives for financial institutions to decrease loans, slowing economic growth, but may increase unemployment.

The Federal Reserve sells government bonds by taking cash from the purchasers of the treasuries. With less cash, commercial banks make fewer loans. If any banks are offering loans, the interest rates on these loans are higher and restrict business expansion and home purchasing. In this way, the Federal Reserve selling government bonds raises interest rates, which in turn decreases monetary supply.

When increasing the discount rate to accomplish contractionary monetary policy, the Federal Reserve is increasing the interest rate it charges banks to borrow money directly from the central bank, or more specifically one of the 12 regional banks. This discourages banks from borrowing more reserves, thus decreasing the money supply. The decreased money supply leads banks to lend less to businesses and households. In summary, increasing the discount rate decreases the money supply, which encourages higher nominal interest rates and decreases in business and household borrowing.

Increasing the reserve requirement increases the amount a bank must have in its end-of- day reserves to satisfy the Federal Reserve's reserve requirement regulations. Reserves include vault cash as well as Federal Reserve deposits. When banks have their reserve requirement increased, the supply of loanable funds is decreased, which raises nominal interest rates. The higher rates create a disincentive for banks to supply more loans to businesses and households.

A risk in utilizing a contractionary monetary policy is an economic slowdown, which leads to higher unemployment. When unemployment is higher, fewer households are participating in the purchasing of goods and services.

Utilizing open market operations to sell government bonds, increasing the discount rate, and raising the reserve requirement are actions that can be taken by the Federal Reserve to decrease the money supply and fulfill contractionary monetary policy. Each is key in contractionary monetary policy to prevent inflation.

Ekaterini Chrisopoulos-Vergos

See Also Bernanke, Ben; Contractionary Fiscal Policy; Expansionary Fiscal Policy; Expansionary Monetary Policy; Federal Reserve System; Greenspan, Alan; Monetary Policy; Volcker, Paul

Further Reading

Business Dictionary.com. N.d. "contractionary policy." http://www.businessdictionary.com/definition/contractionary-policy.html.

Hetzel, Robert L. 2008. *The Monetary Policy of the Federal Reserve (Studies in Macroeconomic History)*. Cambridge: Cambridge University Press.

Resources for Teachers

DeLong, J. Bradford. 2009. *Macroeconomics*. New York: McGraw-Hill Higher Education.

federalreserveeducation.org. N.d. "Monetary Policy Basics." http://www.federalreserveeducation.org/about-the-fed/structure-and-functions/monetary-policy/.

Haskell, Doug. 2013. "Focus on Economic Data: The Federal Reserve and Monetary Policy, May 1, 2013." econedlink. http://www.econedlink.org/lessons/index.php?lid=1144&type=educator.

Contracts

A contract is a legally binding agreement that creates an obligation. Contracts may be oral or written, and both forms are enforceable and damages may be sought if either form is breached.

For a contract to exist, one party must make a detailed offer to do something and the other party must accept the terms. A contract is formed when one party, the offeror, makes an offer, and another party, the offeree, accepts this offer. The formation of a contract generally involves two (or more) parties that agree to provide each other with some type of benefit, known as consideration. Consideration is what an offeror demands and receives as the price for the promise made by a contract. Both an offer and the acceptance of an offer must be present for a contract to exist, and both parties must intend that their agreement is binding.

Contracts can be formal or informal in nature. Formal contracts come in three types: contracts under seal, contracts of record (i.e., agreements recognized by a court), and negotiable instruments. A formal contract is enforced based on its terms that state that the involved parties seek to be bound by their terms.

A contract under seal implies that there is a seal affixed to the document, or a signature may appear followed by the word "seal." These contracts were commonly used prior to the use of consideration, and therefore required a seal to show the intention of each party and to be binding. Today, a seal is not mandatory to make a contract binding. A contract of record is an agreement that has been recorded by a court and may detail the record of someone paying a certain sum of money based on a judgment. In addition, it can also be in the form of a promise for someone to appear in court and pay a fine if he or she fails to do so. A negotiable instrument promises or orders the payment of a fixed amount of money either on demand or at a specified time. Checks, promissory notes, and certificates of deposits (CDs) are common examples.

Informal contracts can be in the form of express or implied contracts. An express contract can be either a spoken or written contract. An implied contract is defined by the actions of the parties rather than based on written or spoken words.

Though some contracts are considered valid in either a written or oral format, certain contracts must be put in writing to be considered valid. For example, land or real estate sales, marriage contracts, and contracts agreeing to pay someone else's debts must be put into writing to be valid. In some cases, even if a written contract is not created, the parties can be bound by their oral contract. For example, if two parties agree to an oral contract regarding personal property, this contract is enforceable if it is below the value identified in a statute. Contracts come in many different forms, including employment contracts, a contract to build a home, a contract for the sale of land, or a contract to perform a specific task.

A contract is discharged when the terms of the agreement have been met and the promises made by the parties have been carried out. A contract may also be discharged when the term identified in the contract has expired.

Breach of contract occurs when one party fails to uphold its part of the agreement. Depending on the breach, the party may be liable under contract law and/or criminal law. When a contract breach occurs, the wronged party seeks damages in the amount that party would have received had the terms of the contract been fulfilled. In the case of a material breach of contract, the wronged party may seek to rescind the contract. For example, a homeowner pays a contractor to install better quality copper piping, but after the piping is installed, the homeowner sees the contractor installed plastic piping, which was not agreed to in the contract. In some cases, things do not qualify for a material breach of contract—for example, if a homeowner pays a contractor to rewire a light switch and believes he or she is getting blue wiring because it is seen as the highest quality, but instead the electrician uses green wiring because he or she knows it is of the same quality.

This is a nonmaterial breach of contract because the terms of the contract were still carried out. In some instances, a party may be willing to ignore or waive the breach and the contract will continue as if the breach never occurred. Contract regulation is often done by a judge, jury, or arbitrator. Remedies for breach of contract vary and can be in the form of monetary damages or equitable damages.

Angela M. LoPiccolo

See Also Market Capitalism; Voluntary Exchange

Further Reading

Anderson, Ronald A., Ivan Fox, David P. Twomey, and Marianne M. Jennings. 1999. *Business Law and the Legal Environment*. New York: West Educational Publishing Company.

Chen-Wishart, Mindy. 2012. *Contract Law*. Oxford: Oxford University Press.

Cornell University Law School. N.d. "Contracts." Accessed July 16, 2013. http://www.law.cornell.edu/wex/contract.

Koffman, Laurence, and Elizabeth Macdonald. 2007. *The Law of Contract*. Oxford: Oxford University Press.

McKendrick, Ewan. 2012. *Contract Law: Text, Cases, and Materials*. Oxford: Oxford University Press.

Resources for Teachers

Beesley, Caron. 2013. "Contract Law—How to Create a Legally Binding Contract." SBA.gov. Accessed July 16, 2013. http://www.sba.gov/community/blogs/contract-law-%E2%80%93-how-create-legally-binding-contract.

OneCLE. N.d. "Sample Business Contracts from SEC Filings." Accessed July 16, 2013. http://contracts.onecle.com/.

Corning Glass Works v. Brennan, 417 U.S. 188 (1974)

A Supreme Court Case on Equal Pay for Women

Economic Concepts

Labor; value of labor; value of marginal product; inputs; outputs; productivity; wages

Economic Impact

This case determined that wage differences between female and male workers for the same work violated the Equal Pay Act of 1963.

Economic Summary

Traditionally, women have struggled to gain equality in the workplace with men. The wage gap has been lessening since the Fair Labor Standards Act of 1938, but despite such federal legislation, pay disparities have continued between female and male workers and in various demographic groups. *Corning Glass Works v. Brennan* was the first time the Supreme Court considered an Equal Pay Act claim based on an employer paying women less than men for the same work. While some wage discrepancies are due to differences in occupations, experience, skills, and other legitimate factors, there is still a considerable gap that exists without explanation between men and women. This case is a milestone in the long journey to remedy this market phenomenon.

Case Summary

Adam Smith expressed in *The Wealth of Nations* (1776) that the compensation of workers was the encouragement of production. Historically, women have struggled with enormous wage disparities. This unfair discrimination throughout the nineteenth century was exceptionally difficult for women. However, during the twentieth century, much has been accomplished. The Industrial Revolution ushered in manufacturing and commercial industries and moved women into the labor force in unprecedented numbers. The sweatshops and factories where women earned their wages were not always safe and secure environments. Work for women varied, but their pay remained unequal to that of men.

Corning Glass Works was a glass company started by Amory Houghton Sr., in the 1800s. Houghton helped Thomas Edison make the electric light a business success by producing the first glass light bulbs. Ever since, the company has invented and built an assortment of items, from baking dishes to missile nose cones. Corning's home office is in Corning, New York. In addition, Corning opened a plant in Wellsboro, Pennsylvania. In 1925, Corning plants operated production during the day and hired women to inspect the finished products. By 1930, Corning upgraded its manufacturing process and needed to hire night shift inspectors to keep pace with the increased productivity. This included an additional night shift. However, New York and Pennsylvania state laws did not allow women to work at night. Furthermore, inspecting finished products had been the main job held by women and labeled by male coworkers as "women's work." Men expressed the attitude that night shift inspection work was demeaning, and they did not want to take a job that earned a woman's pay. Corning signed up men to work the night shift by agreeing to pay them more than their daytime female counterparts. In 1944, unionization of Corning Glass Works brought collective bargaining agreements that took the pay disparity away from day shift workers, but did not end the higher pay for night shift inspection workers due to prohibitions still in place pertaining to women working between the hours of midnight and six in the morning.

In 1963, President John F. Kennedy signed the Federal Employees and Labor Laws Equal Pay Act of 1963 (EPA) as part of his New Frontier Program. In passing the Act, Congress added to the Fair Labor Standards Act of 1938. The act stipulated that companies were to pay men and women equally for similar work. By 1953, laws prohibiting women working at night had been rescinded in both states. After midyear of 1964, the Equal Pay Act was in effect, and the better-paying night inspection jobs opened up to women through process and replacement. In 1969, Corning agreed to pay dayshift and night shift inspectors the same wage. However, there was an exception made for workers who were hired before 1969, most of whom were men, which still allowed them to earn wages higher than the day shift inspectors. In the view of Secretary of Labor Peter Brennan, this clearly constituted a violation of the Equal Pay Act. Brennan filed two lawsuits, one in New York and one in Pennsylvania, claiming in each that Corning had violated the act. The New York plant cases were heard in the Court of Appeals for the Second Circuit, and found that Corning was in violation of the EPA for paying different wages to men and women doing the same job for no other reason except gender. However, the Court of Appeals for the Third Circuit heard the Pennsylvania plant cases and reached the opposite conclusion. There was no violation in its opinion because night work was different from day work; time of day thereby created a pay differential, not gender.

In *Corning Glass Works v. Brennan*, the Supreme Court was asked to reconcile the conflict between two federal circuit courts, both involving cases against the Corning Glass Works plants in regard to wage inequities. The Supreme Court granted certiorari (a request by the Supreme Court to the lower court for the files of the case to be sent up for review). Corning Glass Works argued that the Equal Pay Act said companies could pay employees different wages if they worked under different conditions. The company claimed working the night shift was less desirable and therefore constituted different conditions. The attorney for the labor secretary argued that "condition" referred to manufacturing facility and environment, not the time of day one worked. Furthermore, this was, in the opinion of the Department of Labor, a blatant case of gender discrimination, and short of equalizing pay, there was no other remedy.

In question was what the Equal Pay Act included as working conditions. In this case it was incumbent upon Corning Glass Works to show that the facts of the case fit within one of four exceptions that did not constitute discrimination of pay. Those included a seniority system; a merit system; a system based on the amount or quality of production; and some other factor besides gender. Corning chose to emphasize the last exemption. It claimed that working at night was a different condition than working during the day. In addition, it claimed that the men were also paid more due to seniority. The burden was too much. In a 5–3 vote, the Supreme Court ruled that different times of day did not fit the exemption status. The Court stated that the act was clear in stating that working conditions included physical surroundings and hazards. The seniority system only served to perpetuate past discrimination. Justice Thurgood Marshall delivered the majority opinion, stating that the Equal Pay Act was constructed to end the idea that men could get paid more for doing the same work as a woman because of their role in society.

However, Chief Justice Burger joined with Justice Blackmun and Justice Rehnquist to write the dissenting opinion. He argued the laws of New York and Pennsylvania had established barriers that did not allow Corning to hire women for the night shift. After these night prohibitions were lifted, there were transportation barriers that did not permit women to travel to and from evening work facilities without meeting particular guidelines. These barriers were not completely lifted until July 1965. Therefore, it was necessary to hire men for those positions due to exogenous legal circumstances. The only competitive hourly wage at which to hire a male was higher than any female wage at that time and therefore Corning was adapting to the dictates of the market. The intention was not to violate the Equal Pay Act but to adapt to state mandates and bring the factories into compliance as soon as possible. Justice Steward abstained from the case.

Women have worked alongside their male counterparts in many segments of American industry, and all too often have been the victims of serious and endemic wage discrimination. The solution—to pass a law that requires equal work to be rewarded with equal wages—is simple in principle, but has been just the opposite in practice. This landmark case lifted up the rule of law to the practices of ancient outmoded beliefs, contributing to the evolution of equality in the workplace.

Kathleen C. Simmons

See Also Department of Labor; Smith, Adam; Supreme Court

Related Cases

United States v. Universal C.I.T. Credit Corp., 344 U.S. 218 (1952) (Cited an earlier interpretation of the Fair Labor Standards Act)

Reed v. Reed, 404 U.S. 71 (1971) (Extended the Equal Protection Clause of the Fourteenth Amendment to gender-based discrimination)

Hodgson v. Miller Brewing Co., 457 F.2d 221 (CA7 1972) (An appellate court upheld women's right to equal pay for equal work and legal compensation)

Further Reading

AAUW. N.d. "Resources: Overview of Title VII of the Civil Rights Act of 1964." Accessed April 12, 2013. http://www.aauw.org/resource/title-vii-of-the-civil-rights-act-of-1964/.

Legal Information Institute, Cornell University Law School. N.d. http://www.law.cornell.edu/supremecourt/text/417/188. (Includes transcripts of majority opinion and dissenting opinions)

Smith, Adam. 1776. *An Inquiry into the Nature and Causes of the Wealth of Nations*. London: J. J. Tourneisen and J. L. Legrand.

United States Department of Justice. N.d. "Title IX of the Education Amendments of 1972." http://www.justice.gov/crt/about/cor/coord/titleix.php.

U.S. Equal Employment Opportunity Commission. N.d. "Overview." http://www.eeoc.gov/eeoc/.

Resources for Teachers

Library of Congress. N.d. "Labor Unions and Working Conditions: United We Stand." http://www.loc.gov/teachers/classroommaterials/lessons/labor/.

OYEZ, ITT Chicago, Kent College of Law. N.d. "*Corning Glass Works v. Brennan*." http://www.oyez.org/cases/1970-1979/1973/1973_73_29.

Wasnich, Wendy. 2008. "A Fair Wage." econedlink. http://www.econedlink.org/lessons/index.php?lid=203&type=educator.

Crony Capitalism

A capitalist market is when individuals choose their roles as producers and consumers in an economy. Producers succeed or fail based on their ability and skills to participate in the market and successfully conduct market transactions with buyers. In contrast, the transactions of a crony capitalist system are based on government officials selecting who will participate as producers by providing special treatment to a select group or groups, usually political allies and the friends of government officials. Crony capitalism is a form of capitalism in which government officials have chosen certain market participants for special favors such as subsidies, grants, or special payments to give the preferential business an extra advantage over its competitors.

The potential for crony capitalism behavior is higher the larger a government's budget and regulatory powers. Crony capitalism exists even in a democracy, as those with the financial means to influence the government seek to do so. The more the government becomes involved in the selection and designation of certain businesses, the more businesses depend on government favors and support to be successful. This leads to a system of bribes to government officials and increased government corruption as businesses and special interest groups vie for the government preferences. This often leads to instability in the government, sustaining a system of bribes and corruption. Since the participants—government officials and businesses receiving the special favors—have no incentive to change the system, crony capitalism reinforces the current corrupt political and economic structures and provides no incentives to change.

Crony capitalism often results in the misuse or misallocation of resources. It also emphasizes the use of economic rent (or rent-seeking behavior), which will be higher than necessary, leading to inefficiencies. Economic rent is a system in which the government grants favors to businesses while businesses must devote some resources to obtaining those favors. A business, for example, might ask the government for tariffs or quotas in an effort to protect domestic manufacturers and in exchange, the business supports the politicians providing the favors.

Crony capitalism perpetuates the influence of the political elite. The system also gives immense power to bureaucrats who make decisions on how to spend money that can benefit some people or groups over others. Even when the government seeks to provide public goods, such as roads, crony capitalism is present, as private interests seek to benefit.

Crony capitalism threatens the distribution of income, as profits remain high for the few and is at the expense of both producers and consumers. This system favors and benefits smaller groups of people and the burdens of this will be placed on the rest of society. In addition, those who are better off may be against projects that assist the poor because they would then be faced with higher taxes.

One is less likely to find a strong legal system or agencies that regulate markets when crony capitalism has a strong presence in an economy. Lenders assume more risk as they interact, and have close relationships, with their borrowers.

Corruption is much more common in economies with a strong crony capitalism component. It disrupts the efficient allocation of resources in an economy, and may affect both foreign and domestic investments.

There are also advantages to crony capitalism. One advantage is that it encourages investment in growth within an economy even when economic times are not especially strong. The presence of crony capitalism has also aided different world economies to grow in the short run, including those in Asia. There are many stakeholders, such as banks and businesses, that can remain insulated from economic problems as a result of crony capitalism.

Crony capitalism is prevalent in developing nations where populist political leaders dispense of political and economic favors to maintain control and power. Crony capitalism has been blamed in part for the economic problems of developing nations such as those in sub-Saharan Africa and South America. The Asian economic crisis that occurred in 1997 has in part been blamed on crony capitalism. A close relationship between business, the government, and banks may have actually caused the crisis that affected Thailand, Indonesia, and South Korea, as well as several other Asian countries.

In the United States, the Federal National Mortgage Association (Fannie Mae) and the Federal Home Loan Mortgage (Freddie Mac) are organizations established by government but operating in the private sector. As private businesses established by the federal government, they often take their business mission, direction, and role in the housing market from Congress. As a result of this close relationship between government and a private sector business, with the special preferential treatment they receive from government, they have often been labeled as the result of crony capitalism behavior. They benefit from their relationship with the government, which allowed them to promote and purchase below-market, substandard mortgages. Many consider this the primary cause of the housing bubble that led to the 2008 financial crisis. With the pressure of a financial collapse, the government bailed them out by purchasing some of their stock and guaranteeing loans to prevent homeowners from foreclosures where a private business without preferential government benefits would have been allowed to fail.

As mentioned, when both businesses and government officials benefit from crony capitalism, there are no incentives to change the structure. Additional government intervention and regulation often make the situation worse, which often leads to another government problem, that of moral hazard. Private businesses determine it is not a problem if they fail, for the government will bail them out as it did Fannie Mae and Freddie Mac. It is difficult to prevent or even regulate crony capitalism.

Angela M. LoPiccolo

See Also Economic Rent; Federal Home Loan Mortgage (Freddie Mac); Federal National Mortgage Association (Fannie Mae); Market Capitalism

Further Reading

Enderwick, Peter. 2005. "What's Bad about Crony Capitalism?" *Asian Business & Management* 4: 117–32.

Holcombe, Randall G. 2013. "Crony Capitalism: By-Product of Big Government." *The Independent Review* 17: 541–93.

Labaton, Stephen, and Edmund L. Andrews. 2008. "In Rescue to Stabilize Lending, U.S. Takes Over Mortgage Finance Titans." *New York Times*, September 7. http://www.nytimes.com/2008/09/08/business/08fannie.html?pagewanted=all&_r=0.

Lewis, Hunter. 2013. *Crony Capitalism in America*. Edinburg, VA: Praktikos Books.

Resources for Teachers

EDvantage. N.d. "Public Choice." http://www.theedvantage.org/economics/public-choice.

University of Puget Sound. N.d. "Corruption & Crony Capitalism." http://www.pugetsound.edu/academics/departments-and-programs/undergraduate/ipe/resources/ipe-of-the-asian-crisis/corruption-crony-capitalism/.

Wheeler, Bert. 2013. "Crony Capitalism, by Bert Wheeler." *Bereans @ The Gate*. Accessed November 24, 2013. http://bereansatthegate.com/2013/08/23/crony-capitalism-4/.

Cyclical Unemployment

Cyclical unemployment is a temporary state of unemployment that changes with the expansion and contraction of the business cycle. Cyclical unemployment is job loss that occurs when the economy enters into a period of recession and there are more people seeking work than there are jobs available. In reaction to less consumer demand for goods and services, businesses lay off workers as production need decreases. These workers are then temporarily unemployed until the business cycle reverses and employers can rehire when the economy expands and consumer demand increases.

Cyclical unemployment is one of four categories of unemployment recognized by economists. The other three are structural, frictional, and seasonal. This form of unemployment is called cyclical because it changes with a nation's business cycle. The business cycle has four segments, and has natural fluctuations in response to changes in the Gross Domestic Product (or GDP, the total final value of goods and services produced by a country). When the business cycle begins to contract and GDP drops, consumers are not spending as much and businesses find they are producing more than what is demanded. Businesses begin to lay off employees as demand decreases, causing cyclical unemployment.

The most common method used by economists to calculate the cyclical unemployment rate is to use the unemployment rate at the peak of the business cycle and then subtract the unemployment rate at the bottom of the business cycle. The difference between these two numbers is what economists call the cyclical unemployment rate.

The way to combat cyclical unemployment is to try to control the variability of the business cycle by employing both expansionary fiscal policy and expansionary monetary policy. Expansionary fiscal policy is what the government uses when it wishes to stimulate the economy during an economic downturn. The tools used by the government include decreasing tax rates, increasing government spending, and increasing transfer payments. Expansionary monetary policy is used by the central bank when it seeks to keep the economy from recession and does this by increasing the monetary supply. Increasing the monetary supply can be done by utilizing open market operations, decreasing the discount rate, and lowering the reserve fund requirement. The goal is for expansionary fiscal policy and monetary policy to work together to increase aggregate demand. When more money is available to consumers, they are able to make purchases of goods and services. When this occurs, businesses seek to increase production and seek to rehire those who they had laid off. These policies help ease cyclical unemployment.

Cyclical unemployment usually lasts for only a short time if expansionary fiscal and monetary policies are implemented properly and time lags are not a constraint. In most cases, cyclical unemployment will last approximately 18 months during a period of recession. However, it has been known to last for a number of years, as it did during the Great Depression. After the stock market crash of 1929, the economy took a turn for the worse when consumers panicked and stopped spending money. Businesses suffered as demand decreased and production came to a halt. As businesses closed their doors, thousands of Americans lost their jobs. Without jobs, aggregate demand decreased even further when consumers could no longer make purchases of goods and services.

Cyclical unemployment can be very difficult for those who have lost their jobs. It can also help former employees find new avenues for work and careers. Unskilled labor is usually the hardest hit with cyclical unemployment. On a positive note, some who have lost their jobs due to cyclical unemployment find the opportunity to pursue other interests that may lead to a new profession.

For businesses, cyclical unemployment is beneficial because those who are laid off are sometimes those who are least productive. Trimming away these positions actually helps to make the business stronger because it allows that business to save money.

Ekaterini Chrisopoulos-Vergos

See Also Expansionary Fiscal Policy; Expansionary Monetary Policy; Great Depression (1929–1939); Gross Domestic Product (GDP); Unemployment

Further Reading

Amadeo, Kimberly. N.d. "Cyclical Unemployment." Accessed April 15, 2013. http://useconomy.about.com/od/Employment/p/cyclical-unemployment.htm.

AmosWEB. N.d. "Cyclical Unemployment." Accessed April 15, 2013. http://www.amosweb.com/cgi-bin/awb_nav.pl?s=wpd&c=dsp&k=cyclical+unemployment.

Federal Reserve Bank of San Francisco. 2007. "How Is Unemployment Measured and What Are Different Types of Unemployment? Also, What Are the Economic Disadvantages Associated with High Employment?" Accessed June 2, 2014. http://www.frbsf.org/education/publications/doctor-econ/2007/may/unemployment-employment-disadvantages-types.

Johnson, Rose. N.d. "The Types of Unemployment: Cyclical, Frictional and Structural." Accessed April 15, 2013. http://www.ehow.com/info_8614302_types-unemployment-cyclical-frictional-structural.html.

Resources for Teachers

Foundation for Teaching Economics. N.d. "Inflation and Unemployment." http://www.fte.org/teacher-resources/lesson-plans/rslessons/inflation-and-unemployment/.

Herman-Ellison, Lisa C. 2010. "Unemployment in My Hometown." econedlink. www.econedlink.org/lessons/index.php?lid=351&type=educator.

Morton, John S., and Jean B. Rae Goodman. 2003. *Advanced Placement Economics: Teacher Resource Manual; Unit 2-Macroeconomics, Lesson 4, Unemployment*. New York: National Council on Economic Education.

Riley, Jeff. 2012. "Unemployment: Introduction." tutor2u. tutor2u.net/economics/revision-notes/a2-macro-unemployment.html.

D

Deflation

Deflation is a term used to describe a drop in prices across the economy as a result of long-term decrease in demand for goods and services. The opposite of deflation is inflation. An example of deflation can clearly be seen during the time of the Great Depression in the United States. Deflation can be stopped by the Federal Reserve System utilizing expansionary monetary policy tools and the federal government implementing an expansionary fiscal policy.

Deflation is a decline in price levels of goods and services across the economy due to lessened demand from the government, consumers, and businesses. There are several reasons why deflation occurs. It is mostly caused by either a decrease in the supply of money or contractionary fiscal policies that result in lower demand for goods and services.

John Maynard Keynes, a noted economist and founder of Keynesian economics, theorized that aggregate demand is the key factor in determining the health of the economy. If aggregate demand decreases, as it does during deflation, this is a sign that consumers are not purchasing goods and services, and a surplus of goods may become available. This could be a result of the government enforcing contractionary fiscal policy tools to help control growth and counter inflation, or the Federal Reserve Bank using contractionary monetary policy tools to decrease the money supply. Whenever there is low demand and high supply, price levels begin to drop as businesses try to encourage consumers to make purchases. In addition to selling products at lower prices, a business may decide to lay off workers to make up for lost revenues, decrease employee wages, or halt production of goods and services entirely. Since lost wages and high unemployment stifle the purchasing power of consumers, a deflationary cycle is created.

A good example of deflation can be found by examining the economy of the United States during the Great Depression. The economy in the late 1920s suffered from inflation, categorized by a rapidly increasing economy while currency was losing real value. To combat this, the Federal Reserve put a contractionary monetary policy into place, which helped at first. After the stock market crashed in 1929, however, the Federal Reserve continued to raise interest rates out of fear that investors would try to sell their cash for gold, creating a run on the dollar. Since the United States was still on the gold standard, a depletion of the Fort Knox reserves would send the economy into an even bigger crisis. When the Federal Reserve raised interest rates even more to preserve the value of the dollar, less money was available to businesses for loans. In addition, the Federal Reserve did not increase the amount of money in circulation creating a shortage in the money supply. According to Ben Bernanke, former chairman of the Federal Reserve System's Board of Governors, keeping a contractionary monetary policy in place during the Great Depression made the Great Depression of the 1930s longer and worse. It had created a deflationary cycle.

Deflation can be halted when expansionary monetary policy and expansionary fiscal policy are implemented by the Federal Reserve and Congress, respectively. Expansionary monetary policy is undertaken by implementing one of the Federal Reserve Bank's three main tools: decreasing the discount rate, utilizing open market transactions to lower interest rates, or lowering the reserve requirement. Using each tool separately or together, expansionary monetary policy works to increase the money supply, which helps to inflate currency during a recession.

Expansionary fiscal policy is utilized by Congress. It involves decreasing tax rates, increasing government spending, and raising transfer payments. As in expansionary monetary policy, expansionary fiscal policy tools can be used either separately or together to help stimulate the economy. Together, expansionary monetary policy and expansionary fiscal policy seek to increase demand for goods and services. When consumers have more discretionary money available, they are more likely to make more purchases. When consumers begin spending again and businesses begin to increase their production of goods and services, prices begin to stop their downward trend, thus halting deflation.

Deflation is measured through the use of the Consumer Price Index, or CPI, a report developed by the Bureau of Labor Statistics (BLS). The CPI measures the average change over time in the prices paid by consumers for a market basket of goods and services.

Ekaterini Chrisopoulos-Vergos

See Also Bureau of Labor Statistics; Contractionary Fiscal Policy; Contractionary Monetary Policy; Expansionary Fiscal Policy; Expansionary Monetary Policy; Great Depression (1929–1939); Inflation; Keynes, John Maynard; Keynesian Economics

Further Reading

Amadeo, Kimberly. 2010. "The Great Depression of 1929: Causes, Duration and How It Ended." *US Economy*. Accessed June 2, 2014. http://useconomy.about.com/od/grossdomesticproduct/p/1929_Depression.htm.

Bernanke, Ben S. 2002. "Speech, Bernanke—Deflation." Board of Governors of the Federal Reserve System, November 21. http://www.federalreserve.gov/boarddocs/speeches/2002/20021121/default.htm.

Wu, Tao. 2004."Understanding Deflation." Federal Reserve Bank of San Francisco, April 2. Accessed June 2, 2014. http://www.frbsf.org/economic-research/publications/economic-letter/2004/april/understanding-deflation/.

Resources for Teachers

Bordo, Michael D., John Landon Lane, and Angela Redish. 2004. "Good versus Bad Deflation: Lessons from Gold Standard Era." NBER Working Paper No. 10329. Cambridge, MA: National Bureau of Economic Research. http://www.nber.org/papers/w10329.

Khan Academy. N.d. "Deflation." Accessed June 2, 2014. https://www.khanacademy.org/science/macroeconomics/inflation-topic/macroecon-deflation-tutorial/v/deflation.

Demand-Pull Inflation

Inflation is the rate at which the overall price level of goods and services rises over time. First introduced by John Maynard Keynes, the concept of demand-pull inflation is present during times of economic growth when aggregate demand is higher than aggregate supply. The increase in demand for goods and services over the supply available causes the overall price level to increase. During inflationary periods, the purchasing power of currency decreases, since consumers must spend more on most goods and services across the economy.

In his 1936 book *General Theory of Employment, Interest, and Money*, John Maynard Keynes theorized that aggregate demand is the key factor in determining the health of the economy. When aggregate demand is increasing, this is a sign that consumers are making purchases of goods and services. He equated high aggregate demand to a growing economy with low unemployment, and consequently an adequate supply of goods and services being produced and available for the marketplace.

Aggregate demand may also be increasing if the government has enacted expansionary fiscal policy tools and/or the Federal Reserve Bank has initiated expansionary monetary policy tools to help stimulate the economy. In order to accommodate the increased aggregate demand for goods and services suppliers will produce more, resulting in additional purchases of raw materials and hire more employees. These are the signs of a healthy economy. Demand-pull inflation is a result of low unemployment rates, increased spending by consumers, and/or increased government purchases leading to higher demand for goods and services.

Whenever the economy is expanding, it runs the risk of developing a demand-pull inflation cycle. When aggregate demand is higher than the availability of the product or service in the economy, producers respond with their willingness and ability to produce goods and services by raising prices. This drives the price up more, causing demand-pull inflation.

If the Federal Reserve implements expansionary monetary policy, the supply of money in the economy increases. Assuming consumers spend their additional dollars on goods and services, more and more people seek to purchase a limited supply of goods and services. The increased demand pulls prices up artificially. This demand-pull inflation is generally described by economists as "too many dollars chasing too few goods."

Demand-pull inflation is no longer an encumbrance on the economy when producers increase aggregate supply to equal aggregate demand; the government reduces spending or increases taxes, or the Federal Reserve contracts the money supply to create a balance between the value of aggregate supply and the value of aggregate demand.

Ekaterini Chrisopoulos-Vergos

See Also Bureau of Labor Statistics; Contractionary Fiscal Policy; Contractionary Monetary Policy; Expansionary Fiscal Policy; Expansionary Monetary Policy; Inflation

Further Reading

Agarwal, Prateek. 2011. "Causes of Inflation: Demand-Pull Inflation." *Intelligent Economist*, October 9. Accessed May 21, 2013. http://www.intelligenteconomist.com/causes-of-inflation-demand-pull-inflation/.

Amadeo, Kimberly. 2012. "Causes of Economic Inflation." *U.S. Economy News Articles and Statistics*. Accessed June 2, 2014. http://useconomy.about.com/od/inflationfaq/f/Causes-Of-Inflation.htm.

Keynes, John Maynard. 1936. *The General Theory of Employment, Interest, and Money*. New York: Macmillan.

Kulkarni, Arjun. 2010. "Demand Pull Inflation." *Buzzle*, June 1. Accessed June 2, 2014. http://www.buzzle.com/articles/demand-pull-inflation.html.

Resources for Teachers

Florian, Tim. 2008. "What Causes Inflation?" econedlink. http://www.econedlink.org/lessons/index.php?lid=615&type=educator.

Mindbites. 2010. "Economics: Demand-Pull and Cost-Push Inflation" by Thinkwell. Accessed May 21, 2013. http://mindbites.com/lesson/7452-economics-demand-pull-and-cost-push-inflation.

Quizlet. N.d. "Economics Lesson 4(2): Aggregate Demand: Total Demand for an Economy's Goods and Services." Accessed May 21, 2013. http://quizlet.com/17131765/economics-lesson-42-flash-cards/.

Democratic Socialism

Democratic socialism is the political philosophy where a democratic government is also used to redistribute wealth to achieve social goals. Real equality, according to democratic socialists, requires that political equality and economic equality go hand in hand. Economic equality is possible only if government controls the centers of economic power collectively. As a result, a democratic socialist government uses a significant amount of central planning to achieve its goals even though it may be perceived as a democratic government.

Socialists reject the strong emphasis on individualism and competition for profit that lie at the heart of capitalism. Instead, their policies strive for collective, as opposed to individual, social and economic responsibility to achieve income equality. In nations structured under this type of system, the government often owns major industries, such as utilities, public works, and property.

Democratic socialism exists to varying degrees in different nations throughout the world. Even though some nations have more government control, the officials in all democratic socialist nations are elected by the people. Therefore, the elected government officials manage the most important factors of production in the name of the people. If the government mismanages the people's resources, the people can elect a new government. Thus, in effect, the people do control the centers of economic power.

The roots of socialism lie deep in history, evolving through the nineteenth century and the Industrial Revolution. Most early socialists foresaw a collective economy that would arise out of, and then be managed by, voluntary private action, without government intervention. This early idea of socialism is often called "private socialism."

Many observers of nineteenth-century British factories and cities were appalled by the conditions they found. Men and women often worked 14 to 16 hours a day in filthy, noisy, and unsafe conditions for low pay. Small children regularly worked alongside their parents for even less pay. Most factory workers and their families lived in dank, crowded slums. These conditions led many to seek social and economic reforms.

Leaders of Democratic Socialism

Karl Marx was the most significant critic of capitalism to emerge in the nineteenth century. Much of his work and most of his writings were done in collaboration with Friedrich Engels. In 1848, Marx and Engels wrote *The Communist Manifesto* (1848). The *Manifesto* was a political document that condemned the miseries caused by the Industrial Revolution. It called upon oppressed workers across Europe to free themselves from "capitalist enslavement." Marx believed that capitalism was fatally flawed. According to Marx, the major flaw of capitalism was the exploitations of the workers by the business owners. He predicted that these exploitations would lead to a labor uprising against the capitalists.

During the mid to late nineteenth century, Marx's prediction appeared to be coming true. European workers began to organize a significant socialist movement. While Marx's views were widely accepted, the means to accomplish the socialist agenda were divided, by revolution or through the peaceful democratic process. Today, the terms "socialism" and "socialist" are usually used to identify the latter of the two ideals.

Modern-Day Democratic Socialism

The British Labour Party and the major "social democratic" parties in Europe are leading examples of current democratic socialists. At various times in recent history, those parties have controlled their governments and have instituted many socialist programs through democratic means. Countries with a democratic socialist government typically achieve their democratic socialist goals through nationalized industries and nationalized public services such as health care. To achieve these goals, democratic socialist governments do a significant amount of central planning and need to levy high taxes to pay for the national policies.

Even though democratic socialist governments are command economies by nature and definition, their main interest is in controlling only major sectors of an economy, leaving the more minor sectors to the market. The major sectors of an economy include utilities, steel and other major industries, transportation, and communication. Small businesses such as retail and light manufacturing will be private. Yet the true democratic socialist government insures the voice of the laborer is heard in the workplace. Sweden's Social Democratic Party, for example, has a plan for gradually transferring ownership of private companies to their workers. Elected worker representatives now sit on many companies' board of directors.

One main social goal of democratic socialist governments is that everyone in society has proper housing and food. Many of their income redistribution policies are aimed to achieve modest and proper housing, sufficient food distribution for all, proper health care, and education. They also provide government payments for those who lose their jobs or who are physically unable to work. The payments these individuals receive are nearly as high as their former salaries. All people of retirement age receive government pensions. Also, workers in Europe receive paid maternity leave and at least four weeks of paid vacation each year. Of course, each nation varies in degree of benefits, but the majority of these benefits are received throughout Europe.

With all of these social services and benefits, taxation in democratic socialist nations is quite high. Taxes may take 50 to 60 percent of an individual's total income. Democratic socialists tend to place most of the burden of tax on the upper and middle classes, which is consistent with their philosophy of achieving a more equal distribution of wealth. Tax rates for some individuals may reach 90 percent.

Critics of democratic socialist nations say that they have a tendency to develop too many layers of bureaucracy. They believe that this complicates decision making and has a deadening effect on individual initiative. Critics also believe that this type of government structure deprives people of the freedom to decide for themselves how to use their income. They further state that it deprives their citizens of motivation and incentive to work harder or be more innovative, when government ownership and high taxation are a major part of this system.

In response, democratic socialists reply that it is fairer to supply everyone with basic needs. They point to the inequalities of wealth and power that exist under capitalism. Socialists believe that political democracy runs more smoothly by supplementing it with economic democracy.

Tracy L. Ripley

See Also Economic Systems; Marx, Karl; Marxism; Taxes

Further Reading

Corfe, Robert. 2000. *Reinventing Democratic Socialism: For People Prosperity*. Edmunds, UK: Arena Books.

McClenaghan, William A. 2007. *American Government*. New York: Pearson Prentice Hall.

Mehta, Asoka. 1963. *Democratic Socialism*. New Delhi, IN: Bharatiya Vidya Bhavan.

O'Sullivan, Arthur, and Steven M. Sheffrin. 2007. *Economics Principles in Action*. New York: Pearson Prentice Hall.

Resources for Teachers

Public Broadcasting Service. N.d. "Heaven on Earth: The Rise and Fall of Socialism Lesson Plans." *PBS.org*. http://www.pbs.org/heavenonearth/teachers_lesson1.html.

TeachingAmericanHistory.org. N.d. "Socialism and Democracy." Accessed June 16, 2013. http://teachingamericanhistory.org/library/document/socialism-and-democracy/.

Department of Commerce

The United States Constitution states in Article 1, Section 8, Clause 3, that Congress has the power "[t]o regulate Commerce with foreign Nations, and among the several States, and with the Indian Tribes." In the latter part of the 1800s, the United States made huge strides in business and economic development. Many businesspeople and industrialists felt they needed closer ties to and protection by the federal government. They pushed the government for a specific department to fulfill their needs and interests. Congress called for the creation of such a department.

On February 14, 1903, under the presidency of Theodore Roosevelt, the Department of Commerce and Labor was founded. The Department of Commerce and Labor had grown too large to be contained under one secretary, and on March 4, 1913, was split into two separate entities: the Department of Labor and the Department of Commerce. The Commerce Department is dedicated to promoting economic growth, job creation, and a higher standard of living for all Americans.

The Department of Commerce is a cabinet department of the federal government's executive branch. As a cabinet position, the secretary of commerce reports directly to the president of the United States. The department works with businesses, communities, universities, and workers. The Commerce Department employs over 47,000 employees worldwide and operates with an annual budget of over $7 billion (see www.commerce.gov/about-department-commerce).

Throughout its history, the Commerce Department has grown and changed to accommodate the needs of the American society and people. As a response to these needs, the Commerce Department instituted the establishment of several subagencies that are designed to, among other things, support businesses, promote economic growth, and protect the environment.

The Department of Commerce is made up of 12 bureaus:

1. Bureau of Economic Analysis (BEA)
2. Bureau of Industry and Security (BIS)
3. Economic Development Administration (EDA)
4. Economics and Statistics Administration (ESA)
5. International Trade Administration (ITA)
6. Minority Business Development Agency (MBDA)
7. National Oceanic and Atmospheric Administration (NOAA)
8. National Telecommunications and Information Administration (NTIA)
9. National Institute of Standards and Technology (NIST)
10. National Technical Information Service (NTIS)
11. United States Census Bureau
12. United States Patent and Trademark Office (USPTO)

Each of these bureaus serves a specific function within the Commerce Department. The U.S. Census Bureau shows the Commerce Department's commitment to maintaining a wide array of useful data on and about the economy, people, and population residing within the United States, and this information has a variety of functions. Some examples of how the U.S. Census Bureau data are used include how Congressional districts are created, how over $400 billion in federal funds are allocated within communities, and what community services to provide, such as the building of schools and roads, and services for the elderly.

The U.S. Patent and Trademark Office highlights the Commerce Department's promise to protect American businesses by granting patents and generating trademarks. Patent and trademark security ensures that intellectual property created by Americans nationally and internationally is not infringed upon. Patents and trademarks emphasize an economy's property rights. Protection of property rights through patents and trademarks helps to create a strong economy through job creation.

The National Oceanic and Atmospheric Administration (NOAA) reflects the Department of Commerce's commitment to maintaining economic and environmental health by monitoring weather patterns, preserving coastlines, and supporting marine commerce. NOAA's products and services affect more than one-third of the United States' Gross Domestic Product (GDP).

Ekaterini Chrisopoulos-Vergos

See Also Bureau of Economic Analysis; Department of Labor; Gross Domestic Product (GDP)

Further Reading

American Business. N.d. "U.S. Department of Commerce—History of Business in the U.S." Accessed April 12, 2013. american-business.org/2397-us-department-of-commerce.html.

Department of Commerce. N.d. "About the Department of Commerce." Commerce.gov. www.commerce.gov/about-department-commerce.

Department of Commerce. N.d. "Milestones." 20012009.commerce.gov/About_Us/Milestones/index.html.

NOAA. N.d. "About NOAA." National Oceanic and Atmospheric Association. www.noaa.gov/about-noaa.html.

United States Census Bureau. N.d. "About Us." www.census.gov/aboutus/.

United States Patent and Trademark Office. N.d. "USPTO: About Us." www.uspto.gov/about/index.jsp.

Resources for Teachers

Haskell, Doug. 2013. "Focus on Economic Data U.S. Real GDP Growth, Q1 2013." econedlink. http://www.econedlink.org/lessons/index.php?lid=1163&type=educator.

Herman-Ellison, Lisa C. 2007. "How Is Our Economy Doing?" econedlink. http://www.econedlink.org/lessons/index.php?lid=353&type=educator.

Department of Labor

In 1903, President Theodore Roosevelt had established the Department of Commerce and Labor. As a response to labor's growing lobbying efforts for a position of influence within the president's cabinet and the growth of responsibilities of the Department of Commerce and Labor, the decision was made to separate it into two cabinet posts. The Department of Labor was created by President William Howard Taft on March 4, 1913, when he signed the Organic Act. This was the same year as the signing of the Federal Reserve Act by President Woodrow Wilson.

The main charge of the new department when it was created in 1913 was to promote and advance the working conditions and opportunities of employment for the average working person. The responsibilities and scope of the department have expanded significantly since those early days.

Four bureaus became the center of activity within the Department of Labor: the Bureau of Labor Statistics, the Bureau of Immigration, the Bureau of Naturalization, and the Children's Bureau. The Bureau of Labor Statistics (BLS) is the oldest, established in 1884. The BLS produced its first report in 1886, while it was a part of the Department of the Interior. With the creation of the new Department of Labor, the BLS was moved to its new home in the Labor Department. As it is today, the primary function of the BLS is to collect, assemble, report, and analyze economic and employment data on the labor force. The Bureau of Immigration is responsible for the laws that applied to foreigners. It also serves as an employment agency helping new immigrants find employment. The Bureau of Naturalization administers the laws for foreigners who wanted to become naturalized U.S. citizens, and the Children's Bureau, as its name suggests, had oversight of the welfare of children. It was the newest of the bureaus, established in 1912, serving as a predecessor to Child and Protective Services in caring for the welfare of children.

As the department grew in those early years, it took on the footprint of its first secretary, William B. Wilson. Wilson was not related to President Wilson, who appointed him, but he was a former labor leader and one of the members of Congress responsible for the creation of the department. Secretary Wilson was always quick to point out the department was created to serve the average wage earner but it was first and foremost a federal department devoted to fairness for everyone.

With Wilson as secretary, the department conducted many mediation and labor dispute interventions early in its existence. This one function grew so much that by 1916, conciliation had become a single item budgeted for by Congress. A second major charge early on was unemployment. Using existing personnel and resources from other bureaus, Secretary Wilson built a national framework for finding jobs for the unemployed. President Wilson was so impressed he funded the effort out of the president's office, not Congress.

As U.S. participation in World War I became more and more apparent, Secretary Wilson shifted the department's resources to aid the war effort as labor became in short supply and labor disputes increased. The Department of Labor became the primary source for administering labor policies during the war. The department was charged with the bulk of the government's programs on labor, including the all-important War Labor Board. The Department of Labor was also responsible for interring German sailors from German ships in U.S. harbors.

During the presidency of Warren G. Harding, the Department of Labor took on much less of an activist role in labor disputes. New restrictive immigration policy implementation took on a more prominent role. President Harding and the new labor secretary, James

Davis, expanded the role of the Children's Bureau. The Women's Bureau, which had been created during the war and made permanent in 1920, advanced the welfare of women in the work force. In 1931, during the Depression, the department was responsible for passage of the Davis-Bacon Act. The act required federal contractors to pay the local standard rate on federal construction projects.

The first woman to serve in a president's cabinet was a secretary of labor. Appointed by President Franklin Roosevelt in 1933, Frances Perkins became the new secretary of labor and first female member of the president's cabinet. The Bureau of Immigration and Naturalization had, to some, become overzealous in its deportation strategies. Secretary Perkins took on a popular special corps devoted to deportation and disbanded the group. The Bureau of Immigration and Naturalization was eventually transferred to the Department of Justice.

As President Roosevelt's secretary of labor, Frances Perkins was instrumental in creating and implementing many of the president New Deal programs as they related to labor. She was especially involved in the development of the Civilian Conservation Corps (CCC) and Social Security. The CCC was a labor program for young men to work on federal projects in rural America. Secretary Perkins was instrumental in the promotion and eventual passage of the Social Security Act in 1935. Perkins also revitalized the United States Employment Service (USES), instituting a nationwide network of employment services. As opposed to its involvement in World War I, the department's role in World War II was minimal.

Following World War II, the department's energies were mostly devoted to leveling the workplace landscape between labor and management. New presidential administrations added their individual agendas and Congress added laws to retain collective bargaining and maintain adequate working conditions. New programs for the Department of Labor began to emerge under President Johnson and his Great Society initiatives. President Johnson created the Manpower Administration to oversee his new programs that focused directly on labor issues. The passage of the Civil Rights Act in 1964 also changed the landscape of the department. It now devoted energies to enforcing new nondiscriminatory policies in the workplace and within federal contracts.

Through the 1960s and 1970s, major restructuring occurred within the Department of Labor. President Johnson's Manpower Administration was restructured in 1969. That same year, the Job Corps, whose programs were aimed at youths, was moved to the Department of Labor. The Comprehensive Employment and Training Act (CETA) was created in 1973 as a training and revenue-sharing mechanism for local activities. In 1971, during an economic downturn, the Emergency Employment Act was created, providing jobs in the public sector. A second 1971 initiative for the Department of Labor was a new charge of job safety, with the creation of the Occupational Safety and Health Administration (OSHA) to oversee workplace safety. The Employment Retirement Income Security Act (ERISA) was created in 1974 to protect private retirement systems.

One of the main responsibilities of the Department of Labor is administering and enforcing over 180 federal laws regarding employment and wages. The Wage and Hour Division, for example, regulates the Fair Labor Standards Act, or FLSA, which requires employers to pay their employees the federal minimum wage for most public and private sector jobs. This division also administers the Family Medical Leave Act, or FMLA, guaranteeing employees up to 12 weeks of unpaid, job-protected leave for the birth, adoption, or serious illness of a loved one. The Veterans' Employment and Training Service, or VETS, protects deployed service members by administering the Uniformed Services Employment and Reemployment Rights Act. This Act ensures that military members who are deployed can return to their jobs when they return from duty.

While most of the programs have been revised or altered throughout the years and presidential administrations, the Department of Labor continues to administer many programs to protect, educate, or provide access for the U.S. labor market. The Department of Labor serves a very important role through the various programs, services, and acts it administers. At some point in every person's life, he or she is probably somehow affected by a Department of Labor–administered program. By protecting workers and workers' rights, these programs help ensure that the American public is able to maintain gainful employment in a safe, ethical environment.

Ekaterini Chrisopoulos-Vergos
David A. Dieterle

See Also Bureau of Labor Statistics; Great Depression (1929–1939); New Deal; Roosevelt, Franklin Delano

Further Reading

United States Department of Labor. N.d. "Chapter 1: Start-Up of the Department and World War I, 1913–1921." http://www.dol.gov/dol/aboutdol/history/dolchp01.htm.

United States Department of Labor. N.d. "Chapter 2: The 1920s and the Start of the Depression, 1921–1933." http://www.dol.gov/dol/aboutdol/history/dolchp02.htm.

United States Department of Labor. N.d. "Chapter 3: The Department in the New Deal and World War II, 1933–1945." http://www.dol.gov/dol/aboutdol/history/dolchp03.htm.

United States Department of Labor. N.d. "Chapter 4: Post-War Era and Korean War Mobilization, 1945–1953." http://www.dol.gov/dol/aboutdol/history/dolchp04.htm.

United States Department of Labor. N.d. "Chapter 5: Eisenhower Administration, 1953–1961." http://www.dol.gov/dol/aboutdol/history/dolchp05.htm.

United States Department of Labor. N.d. "Chapter 6: Eras of the New Frontier and the Great Society, 1961–1969." http://www.dol.gov/dol/aboutdol/history/dolchp06.htm.

United States Department of Labor. N.d. "Chapter 7: Nixon and Ford Administrations, 1969–1977." http://www.dol.gov/dol/aboutdol/history/dolchp07.htm.

United States Department of Labor. N.d. "Chapter 8: Carter Administration, 1977–1981." http://www.dol.gov/dol/aboutdol/history/dolchp08.htm.

United States Department of Labor. N.d. "Chapter 9: Reagan Administration, 1981–1988." http://www.dol.gov/dol/aboutdol/history/dolchp09.htm.

United States Department of Labor. N.d. "The Leadership Team." http://www.dol.gov/dol/contact/contact-phonekeypersonnel.htm.

United States Department of Labor. N.d. "Mission." http://www.dol.gov/opa/aboutdol/mission.htm.

United States Department of Labor. N.d. "Summary of the Major Laws of the Department of Labor." http://www.dol.gov/opa/aboutdol/lawsprog.htm.

Resources for Teachers

Bureau of Labor Statistics. N.d. "K-12." http://www.bls.gov/bls/k12_history_prototype.htm.

United States Department of Labor. N.d. "A Brief History: The U.S. Department of Labor." http://www.dol.gov/dol/aboutdol/history/dolhistoxford.htm.

U.S. Department of Labor, Bureau of Labor Statistics. N.d. "Occupational Outlook Handbook—High School Teachers." http://www.bls.gov/ooh/education-training-and-library/high-school-teachers.htm.

De Soto, Hernando

Born: 1941 in Arequipa, Peru; Peruvian; property rights; Major Works: *The Other Path* (1987), *The Mystery of Capital: Why Capitalism Triumphs in the West and Fails Everywhere Else* (2000).

Hernando de Soto is a Peruvian economist who believes that property rights are key to a working capitalist society. De Soto believes that the poor in Third World countries are unable to realize their economic potential because of their inability to obtain property rights. He founded the Institute for Liberty and Democracy in 1981 to act as a platform for research and to communicate his economic findings and beliefs. De Soto has won numerous awards for his work and has been an adviser to many world leaders.

Hernando de Soto Polar was born in Arequipa, Peru, in 1941 to a Peruvian diplomat father. His father was exiled in 1948 after a military coup, and moved the family to Europe. Raised in Europe with his younger brother, Álvaro, de Soto was educated in Switzerland, where he completed his postgraduate work at the Graduate Institute of International Studies. He became a successful economist, executive, and consultant in Europe before he earned enough money to retire at the age of 38. In 1979, de Soto returned to his native Peru to devote his life to solving the issue of global economic inequality.

De Soto had long wondered why, given intellectual and skill equality, Europe, North America, and Western nations thrived while Third World nations remained poor. When he moved back to Peru, he set out to research what made the difference. He found that in Third World countries, the legal system, in particular access to property rights, was not available to everyone. Third World citizens are subject to a legal system that will not allow them to accumulate and transfer capital. This, de Soto claims, is the key to making capitalism work as well in Third World countries as it does in other areas of the world.

In 1981, de Soto created the Institute for Liberty and Democracy (ILD) in Lima, Peru. The ILD's mission is to equip governments with knowledge, expertise, and resources to employ institutional reforms in property and business rights allowing citizens to be participants in using the market economy to elevate them out of poverty. He and his fellow ILD researchers initiated an investigation into the process of obtaining property rights in countries such as Peru, Egypt, and the Philippines. They discovered it to be extremely difficult. They found that in Lima, Peru, it would take over 200 bureaucratic steps and 21 years to obtain the title to a piece of land. In Egypt, it would take 17 years to get authorization to build on a sand dune, and in Manila, it might take 50 years to receive a land title.

In Peru in the 1980s, many of the poor were joining the murderous terrorist group the Shining Path to combat the government. De Soto published his book *The Other Path* in 1987 to reach out to potential Shining Path members and the Peruvian government. In it, he works to convince Peru's farmers that they are future entrepreneurs and should join the legal economy instead of fight it. Because they did not have access to the capitalist system, the poor would operate extralegally in black or shadow markets. De Soto argued that if the black markets were legalized and provided the same protection that was given to legal markets, the free market could thrive. His efforts were unpopular with the terrorist group, and they made several attempts against his life before finally losing most of their power in 1992.

In his book *The Mystery of Capital*, de Soto explains the political responsibility of implementing a legal process for making property systems work for all citizens. He finds that because the poor do not own their land and cannot access capital, they are unable to expand their businesses. If the poor were given the land that they occupy, they would have the collateral needed for a loan and therefore could enjoy business growth. He also points out that the system that works so well in the United States has been established for only 100 years, and contends that now that the formula is known, it can be copied expeditiously in other countries.

De Soto was chosen one of the five leading Latin American innovators of the century in 1999, and was named in the top 100 most influential people in the world in 2004 by *Time* magazine. He was named one of the 15 innovators in *Forbes*'s 85th-anniversary edition. He has won numerous prizes for his work including the Freedom Prize (Switzerland), the Fisher Prize (United Kingdom), the Goldwater Award (United States), the Adam Smith Award (United States), the CARE Canada Award for Outstanding Development Thinking (Canada), the Americas Award (United States), the Academy of Achievement's Golden Plate Award in 2005, and the Most Outstanding of 2004 by the Peruvian National Assembly of Rectors.

De Soto gained early support from Margaret Thatcher, Richard Nixon, and Dan Quayle. He has also been an adviser to governments in Mexico, Egypt, Peru, El Salvador, Ghana, Russia, Afghanistan, and the Philippines. His foundation, the Institute for Liberty and Democracy, has been responsible for more than 400 laws and regulations in Peru that have opened up their economic system to the majority of citizens. De Soto's plans are being adopted by the unrecognized Eurasian country of Pridnestrovie and are gaining the attention of leaders worldwide.

Aimee Register Gray

See Also Economic Systems; Market Capitalism; Ostrom, Elinor; Private Property; Welfare State

Selected Works by Hernando de Soto

De Soto, Hernando. 2000. *The Mystery of Capital: Why Capitalism Triumphs in the West and Fails Everywhere Else*. New York: Basic Books.

De Soto, Hernando. 1987. *The Other Path: The Economic Answer to Terrorism*. New York: Basic Books.

Selected Works about Hernando de Soto

Berlau, John. 2003. "Providing Structure to Unstable Places; Hernando de Soto Puts Destabilized Countries on the Right Path by Securing Citizens' Confidence in Property Rights and Easing Legal Hurdles to Market Entrance." *Insight on the News*, July 8: 42

Fernandez-Morera, Dario. 1994. "Outlaws and Addresses: Hernando de Soto's Path to Property Rights." *Reason Foundation* 25, no. 9, February: 28.

Wolverton, Marvin. 2003. "Review of *The Mystery Capital*." *Appraisal Journal*, July 1: 272.

Discouraged Workers

A discouraged worker is an individual of working age who is unemployed and is not pursuing a position in the current job market. Usually this person is willing and able to work but has given up finding gainful employment due to a variety of factors. Due to these real or perceived limitations in the job market, these individuals have become "discouraged." Discouraged workers are not included in the unemployment rate and they are not considered to be in the labor force.

The Bureau of Labor Statistics of the United States Department of Labor compiles information on the labor force using the monthly Current Population Survey, or CPS. The CPS assesses data including and pertaining to unemployment, employment, those not in the labor force, and labor force characteristics. Based on a recommendation by the Committee to Appraise Employment and Unemployment Statistics, the CPS began gathering information on people not in the labor force starting in January 1967. Since these individuals were considered neither employed nor unemployed, the CPS sought to gather reasons why they were not in the labor force.

To determine why individuals are not in the labor force, the CPS asks four specific questions to gauge the person's ability to work, desire to work, job search process, and reasons why he or she has not looked for work in the previous four weeks. The answers to the questions are then used to decide whether these individuals should be a part of the marginally attached labor force measure. Those who are marginally attached to the labor force are available to work, want to work, and have been looking for work within the last 12 months.

Discouraged workers are a subsection of those who are marginally attached to the labor force. The difference between those who are marginally attached to the labor force and discouraged workers is that discouraged workers state that they have not looked for unemployment in the previous four weeks despite wanting to work and being able to work. The CPS has determined four reasons discouraged workers give as to why they are not seeking employment. These reasons include:

1. They believe no job is available to them in their line of work or area.
2. They had previously been unable to find work.
3. They lack the necessary schooling, training, skills, or experience.
4. Employers think they are too young or too old, or they face some other type of discrimination.

Discouraged workers are sometimes referred to as the "hidden unemployed" because they are not counted in the total unemployment number since they are not in the labor force. During times of economic growth when businesses are doing well and are hiring workers, discouraged workers are motivated to seek employment. When this happens, the CPS reports slightly higher levels of unemployment, as discouraged workers are then stating they are looking for work. During periods of recession when employers are laying off employees, discouraged workers are even more dejected and the CPS reports even higher levels of unemployment.

Ekaterini Chrisopoulos-Vergos

See Also Bureau of Labor Statistics; Department of Labor; Labor Force; Unemployment

Further Reading

AmosWEB, Economics with a Touch of Whimsy! N.d. "Discouraged Workers." Retrieved March 15, 2013. http://www.amosweb.com/cgi bin/awb_nav.pl?s=wpd&c=dsp&k=discouraged+workers.

Castillo, Monica D. 1998. "Persons outside the Labor Force Who Want a Job." *Monthly Labor Review* 121, no. 7: 34–42.

Flaim, Paul O. 1973. "Discouraged Workers and Changes in Unemployment." *Monthly Labor Review* 107, no. 8: 95–103.

Resources for Teachers

Bureau of Labor Statistics: Discouraged Workers. N.d. "Labor Force Characteristics: Discouraged Workers." http://www.bls.gov/cps/lfcharacteristics.htm#discouraged.

Federal Reserve Bank of San Francisco-Education. 2007. "How Is Unemployment Measured and What Are Different Types of Unemployment? Also, What Are the Economic Disadvantages Associated with High Employment?" Accessed June 2, 2014. http://www.frbsf.org/education/publications/doctor-econ/2007/may/unemployment-employment-disadvantages-types.

U.S. Bureau of Labor Statistics. N.d. "How the Government Measures Unemployment." Accessed March 15, 2013. http://www.bls.gov/cps/cps_htgm.htm.

Dodd-Frank Act (See Financial Reform Act of 2010)

E

Economic Growth, Measures of

Economic growth is the measure of an economy's productivity. Economic growth is one of the three goals every economic system aims to achieve along with price stability and low unemployment. There are several methods in which economic growth is measured. Which one is the dominant method often depends on the purpose for the measure and what specific measure is important. Each economic growth measure has its own characteristic and personality. There are three major measures of economic growth: Gross Domestic Product (GDP), Gross National Product (GNP), and Personal Consumption Expenditures (PCE).

Gross Domestic Product (GDP)

Gross Domestic Product (GDP) is the leading report and considered the most important indicator on the health of an economy. It is considered the best indicator of an economy's achieving economic growth, one of the three major goals of every economy (with price stability and low unemployment). GDP measured over time (quarter to quarter, year to year) is considered the major indicator of how fast or slow an economy is growing or contracting. In the United States, virtually all participants of the economy are impacted by the GDP reports. GDP is closely related to the other major economic goal of low unemployment. A growing GDP reflects the need for labor, capital, and land resources, which reflects lower unemployment in the future.

GDP measures the final value of goods and services produced within the borders of a nation, irrespective of who produced the good or service. GDP is not a measure of what is sold, but what is produced within an economy's borders. Toyota, even though a Japanese company, assembles automobiles in the United States. Those Toyota automobiles are counted as part of the U.S. GDP data. Conversely, a Chevrolet whose final assembly is in Canada is not counted. Another example of what counts as GDP would be a tire company that has produced eight tires. Four of the tires are shipped to an automobile manufacturer and used in the assembly of an automobile. The other four tires are shipped to a tire company's retail outlet for sale. Only the four tires sold at the tire company's retail outlet are counted toward GDP. If the four used on the automobile were counted at the time they were produced they would be double counted, as their value to the economy is counted in the final value of the automobile, assuming the automobile was assembled in the United States. If the automobile was assembled outside the United States, they would not be counted.

In the United States, GDP data are collected, measured, and reported by the Bureau of Economic Analysis, a part of the Department of Commerce. It is reported quarterly (end of January, April, July, and October) with revisions each month. The monthly revisions report marginal changes with an annual revision in July, the completed report for a given year. GDP is reported in both nominal dollars (present dollars) and real terms (constant or "chained" dollars). The Bureau of Economic Analysis collects information and data from thousands of an economy's governments and private companies within its borders including home purchases, retail sales, and auto sales to report initial GDP estimates.

GDP is measured in two ways. One measure is the expenditures of an economy in four major areas of the economy's products of goods and services; the personal consumption by households (C) on durable and nondurable goods and services, the gross private investment of businesses including changes in inventory (I), government's purchases of goods and services and investment (G), and the net trade balance between exports and imports of an economy's foreign participation (X-M). This is often shown as GDP=C+I+G+(X-M). GDP measures what is produced, not what is sold. Unsold inventory is a measure of GDP at the time of its production. Government is defined as all government entities including federal, state, and all local governmental entities.

The second measure is the income earned by laborers (w), profits earned from capital (p), interest earned by savers and investors (i), and the rents earned by landowners (r). This is often shown as GDP = w+p+i+r. Economists often measure an economy's health based on an equilibrium model of GDP=C+I+G+(X-M) = w+p+r+i and the discrepancy between these two measures.

Gross National Product (GNP)

Gross National Product (GNP) is similar to GDP with one significant distinction. GNP is more concerned with "who" is producing and not the "where." GNP measures a U.S. company's production anywhere in the world the production occurs. Using the above GDP example, the Toyota produced in the United States is not counted as GNP for the United States because Toyota is a Japanese company. It would be counted for the GNP of Japan. Likewise, the Chevrolet is counted in the U.S. GNP as a product of General Motors, a U.S. company.

Personal Consumption Expenditures (PCE)

In the United States, the largest component of GDP is personal spending on goods and services. It comprises up to 70 percent of the U.S. GDP. By contrast, China's personal spending as a component of GDP is only approximately 30 percent. Consumer expenditures are the key dynamic influence of the U.S. economy. If consumers are not purchasing goods and services, businesses are not using resources (including labor) to produce goods and services, and the economy does not grow or even regresses. The stock market and other economic indices react to the reports of how much households are spending on goods and services.

As a component of GDP, the reporting of Personal Consumption Expenditures (PCE) is a function of the Bureau of Economic Analysis (BEA). Personal spending is reported monthly with several months of revisions. The monthly reports are also annualized to reflect year-long income or expenditure trends. A major revision in data may occur to reflect new reporting and/or data collecting methodologies. Personal income is measured before taxes are deducted. BEA measures income from several sources: wages and salaries, rental income, interest and dividend income, income of the self-employed (proprietor's income), transfer payments, and other income. Personal Consumption Expenditures and personal income are reported in nominal dollars (current dollars) and real dollars (adjusted for inflation).

PCE are measured in three major categories: durable goods (goods lasting three or more years), nondurable goods (goods lasting less than three years), and services. Durable goods are major items purchased by households, such as cars, refrigerators, and televisions. Because they are items households do not purchase often they only account for 12 to 14 percent of PCE. Nondurable goods such as food and clothing account for approximately 30 percent of PCE, as they are purchased more often. Services comprise the final 40 percent, accounting for the purchases of haircuts, movies, medical expenses, etc.

One either purchases goods and services (expenditures) or saves income. Personal savings is also calculated from this information. Once all spending is measured, interest on credit cards and car loans is taken into account, and taxes deducted leaving disposable income, the remainder is considered personal savings. It has been calculated that over time the average household spends 95 cents of each dollar received and saves 5 cents. This very high percentage of consumption is the key reason the PCE receives attention from the media and economists.

Collecting personal income data is one of the most complicated tasks undertaken by the BEA. The BEA collects data from many sources to calculate both personal consumption and personal savings. Wages and salaries are collected from employment reports and transfer payments are reported by the Social Security Administration along with the Departments of Treasury and Labor. Interest and dividend payments to households are estimated from reports of the Internal Revenue Service (IRS), U.S. Census Bureau, the reports of corporations who pay dividends, and the Federal Reserve.

Measuring PCE is also complicated and involves many government departments, organizations, and companies. For example, medical expenses come from the Labor Department (a government agency), but expenditures on automobiles involve the manufacturers. Many measures of consumer expenditures are estimates after many years of data collecting.

David A. Dieterle

See Also Bureau of Economic Analysis; Department of Commerce; Department of Labor; Gross Domestic Product (GDP); United States Treasury

Further Reading

Baumohl, Bernard. 2008. *The Secrets of Economic Indicators*. 2nd ed. Philadelphia: Wharton School Publishing.

Bureau of Economic Analysis. N.d. www.bea.gov.

Department of Labor. N.d. www.bls.gov.

Resources for Teachers

Economics Network. N.d. "Online Text and Notes in Economic Growth." http://www.economicsnetwork.ac.uk/teaching/Online%20Text%20and%20Notes/Economic%20Growth.

Foundation for Teaching Economics. N.d. "Lesson 1: Economic Growth and Scarcity." http://www.fte.org/teacher-resources/lesson-plans/efllessons/lesson-1-economic-growth-and-scarcity/.

Haskell, Doug. 2013. "Focus on Economic Data: U.S. Real GDP Growth, February 28, 2013." econedlink. http://www.econedlink.org/lessons/economic-lesson-search.php?type=educator&cid=32.

Riley, Jim. N.d. "Economic Environment—Economic Growth." tutor2u. http://www.tutor2u.net/business/strategy/economy-economic-growth.html.

Economic Rent

Economic rent is the price paid for the use of land and other natural resources that are completely fixed in total supply. Land exists as a free and nonreproducible gift of nature with a perfectly inelastic supply. In other words, there is only a finite amount of land. It is not necessary to ensure that land is available to the economy as a whole.

Rent is considered a surplus or excess payment made for a factor of production (land, labor, or capital) over and above the amount expected by its owner. It is a payment that is in addition to that needed to keep it in its present use—sometimes called its transfer earnings or opportunity cost. This could be due to its unique characteristics or its scarcity. Price discrepancies for labor in the real world illustrate this idea, such as exorbitant salaries for rock stars compared to those who simply sing along in their cars, or payments for workers belonging to professional guilds versus those who do not. Payments for most factors of production usually involve both transfer payments and economic rent.

Economists of the Classical school of economic thought, such as David Ricardo (1772–1823), looked specifically at the productivity of a piece of land and that of the most marginal (farthest from town center) and the most beneficial (most fertile) using the same inputs of labor and capital. The difference between the production costs and the market price for the goods the land produced is known as the economic rent. It is the surplus payment given to the factor of production over and above what it could earn in its next best use.

Factors such as the price of the product produced on the land, the productivity of the land, and the prices of the other resources that are combined with the land determine the demand curve. The supply curve for land remains inelastic. Price for the land is then determined where these two curves intersect. The Ricardo theorem implies rent to mean payment for any such "surplus" to a factor of production over and above what was necessary to maintain that factor in its present use or form of production, above its opportunity cost.

Socialists argue that land rents are unearned incomes, as land exists on its own. It is not fair that some people, through inheritance or good fortune, should profit from rising land values. They point out that there is an unequal distribution in the tax burden meaning that a significant amount of economic rent is not taxed. Economist Henry George (1839–1897) argued in his book *Progress and Poverty* (1879) that economic rent could be heavily taxed, or even taxed away, without diminishing the available supply of land or the productive potential of the economy as a whole. As the population grows, the landowners enjoy larger rents. These rents should belong to the common good and be spent for public uses. George proposed that taxes on rental income be the only tax the government levied. Shifting the tax burden away

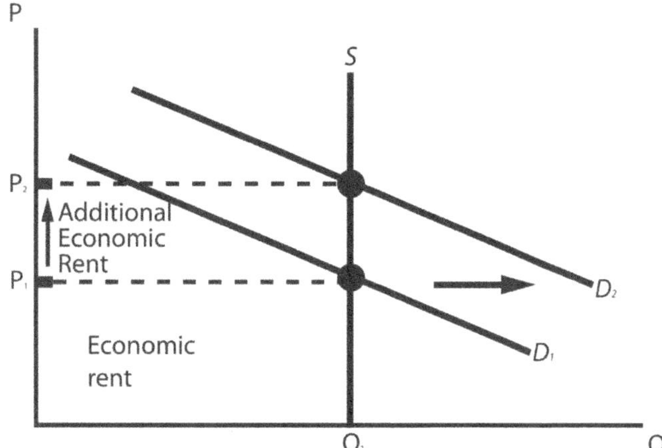

When demand increases (D_1 to D_2) and Q_s is inelastic, economic rent increases (P_1 to P_2)

from labor and capital, which is variable in supply, toward land, which is fixed in supply, can fuel a better allocation of resources and enhance economic activity. Critics argue that it would be an economically efficient tax, but would not bring in enough revenue for current government spending, and it is difficult to distinguish true rent from improvements.

Jeremy Robinson
Kathryn Lloyd Gustafson

See Also George, Henry; Market Capitalism

Further Reading

The Economist. N.d. "Economics A-Z Terms Beginning with R." www.economist.com/economics-a-to-z/r#node-21529784.

George, Henry. 1886. *Progress and Poverty*. New York: D. Appleton & Co.

Henry George Foundation. N.d. "Economic Rent." http://www.henrygeorgefoundation.org/the-science-of-economics/economic-rent.html.

McConnell, Campbell, and Stanley Brue. 2008. *Economics: Principles, Problems, and Policies*. 17th ed. New York: McGraw-Hill Irwin.

Resources for Teachers

Hawks, Douglas. N.d. "David Ricardo: Economic Theories, Lesson & Quiz." Education Portal. education-portal.com/academy/lesson/david-ricardo-economic-theories-lesson-quiz.html#lesson.

Penn State College of Mineral and Earth Sciences. N.d. "Lesson 9: Government Intervention." www.e-education.psu.edu/ebf200up/node/159.

Economic Systems

An economic system determines the way in which a country manages the production and distribution of goods and services. Every economic system functions by answering three basic questions: what to produce; how to produce; and for whom will the goods and services be distributed. The more fundamental economic question is that of who will answer these three questions. One option is the interaction of buyers and sellers in the marketplace. A second option is a central authority or government. Third is some combination of the two.

The "what to produce" question is an allocation of resources question. One decision by a society in determining the economic system is what goods and services will be produced for the marketplace. What goods and services will be produced for the marketplace, however it is defined, suggests the allocation of an economy's land, labor, and capital, i.e., the resources available for producing the goods and services. The one who answers the first question (market, government, or combination) will determine the uses of an economy's resources.

The "how to produce" question is an efficiency question. The second question defines the rate of innovation and change in the ratios of land, labor, or capital used to produce the goods and services. Will the economy use a horse and plow in the field or a tractor? Will manufactured goods be made by labor-intensive industries or capital-intensive industries? The answer lies in the decisions of the individuals, government, or some combination.

The "for whom" question is a question on the distribution of goods and services and who should receive the goods and services. Will the goods and services of an economy be distributed to those who are willing and able to pay for them, or will they be distributed to a select few, or to everyone regardless of ability to pay? Answering this third question ultimately defines the distribution of goods and services in the market as private, public, or selective. Again, the answer lies in who makes the decision; individuals, government, or some combination.

Answering the basic economic system questions has several alternatives. They can be answered because of cultural or historical tradition within a culture or society. They can be answered totally in the marketplace by the interaction of buyers and sellers. Or, at the other extreme, they can be answered by one central authority making all the economic system decisions for the entire economy. The fourth alternative is some mix between market decisions and a central authority. There are numerous combinations of a mixed economy.

Traditional Economic System

In a traditional economic system the three questions are answered by a long-standing tradition in a culture or society. This usually means one vocation or type of work is handed down from generation to generation. If one's great-grandfather was a farmer, in a traditional economic system, one's grandfather and father were also farmers. One can count on being a farmer. The tradition would continue as one's son and future generations to come will also be farmers.

Traditional economic systems are generally subsistence economies and do not experience economic growth. Since there is no mobility in labor or resources, these economies are stagnant and standards of living do not change from generation to generation. They are often very isolated and do not trade with others outside their traditional system. The lack of mobility also makes the future of a traditional economic system very predictable. The interests of the whole often supersede individual interests. As a result, property rights are often absent or lightly regarded.

Historically, traditional economic systems were a major form of economic organization. The feudal systems of early Europe, many towns and regions of early U.S. western expansion were traditional in nature. Today, traditional economic systems are confined to isolated tribes and cultures such as the aborigines in Australia.

Market Economic System

In market economies, the three economic system questions are answered by individual producers and consumers. The allocation question of what to produce is answered by the interaction of producers and consumers in the product market. Buyers (consumers) determine what they are willing and able to consume and it is up to the sellers (producers) to adequately provide those goods and services at both a price and quality the buyers desire. If buyers demand three-legged stools, it is an incentive for the producers to supply three-legged stools at a price the buyers are willing and able to pay and quality they want.

The efficiency question in a market economy is answered by the interaction of producers and consumers in the resource market. Businesses need the land, labor, and capital (resources) to produce the goods and services consumers desire. In a market economy, private property and property rights are paramount to the proper functioning of a market economic system. Individuals decide the level and participation in the economy through education, and individuals decide how to invest their resources in land and capital. All the resources are privately owned.

Privately owned resources are then sold to the businesses in the resource market so they can produce goods and services for the product market. In the resource market, the producers are private individuals and the consumers are businesses. Businesses respond to the incentives of producing goods and services using resources in the most efficiently. They also have incentives to innovate and invent new ways and methods of using resources more efficiently to be more competitive in the production of goods and services.

In a market economic system, the "for whom" question is also answered in the marketplace. In a purely market-driven economy, the question of who is going to receive the goods and services is entirely based on who are the willing and able buyers. A central authority, like government, is not involved in any economic decisions. While historically pure market economic systems existed during certain eras, such as the late nineteenth century, pure market economic systems do not exist today.

Command (Planned) Economic Systems

At the other end of the range of economic systems is the economy where the three basic economic system questions are answered by one single authority, usually the government. The government decides what will be produced, how it will be produced, and who is going to receive the economy's goods and services. In so doing, the government regulates prices, distribution, and allocation of the economy's resources. In a pure command economy, the resources are not privately owned but owned by the government. As such, the government makes all decisions regarding the allocation of resources, including designation of labor. One's job selection is determined by the government, not the individual.

Command economies have existed throughout history. Lenin introduced a command economy to Russia based on the writings of Karl Marx. A command economy in Russia eventually led to the Soviet Union and command economies of Eastern Europe. North Korea and Cuba continue to be model examples of command economies.

Mixed Economic Systems

Pure market and pure command economies are rare in today's global economy. Today, most economies answer the three basic economic system questions as some combination of market and command. These are known as mixed economies. In so doing, the questions of what, how, and for whom are answered by either individuals in the market or by government. How the questions are answered also determines whether an economy's goods and services are either private goods and services or public goods and services.

Most economies in today's global economy, including the United States, are mixed economies. The major question for most mixed economies is the degree of private influence versus the degree of public influence in answering the three economic questions. Economies such as Russia today have a high degree of command economy; they also include a degree of market economy decisions. Economies such as that of the United States have a high degree of market economy decisions with the inclusion of command economy decisions. Regardless of where each economy currently is along the economic system spectrum, all economies are in a dynamic state of change. Some economies are transitioning from a primarily command economy to a more market-oriented economy, with some transitioning from a primarily market economy to a more command economy influence.

David A. Dieterle

See Also Command Economy; Democratic Socialism; Fascism; Hayek, Friedrich von; Lenin, Vladimir; Market Capitalism; Marx, Karl; Marxism; Smith, Adam; Welfare State

Further Reading

Carson, Richard L., and Baerbel M. Traynor. 1998. *Comparative Economic Systems: Transition and Capitalist Alternatives*. Vol. 2. Armonk, NY: M. E. Sharpe.

Gardner, H. Stephen. 1998. *Comparative Economic Systems*. New York: Dryden Press.

Rosefielde, Steven. 2002. *Comparative Economic Systems: Culture, Wealth, and Power in the 21st Century*. Malden, MA: Blackwell Publishers.

Resources for Teachers

Gooru. N.d. "Economic Systems Types." Accessed November 24, 2013. http://www.goorulearning.org/#resource-play&id=2a171ea1-431b-4847-9bfe-3821f7e4730b&pn=resource.

Herman-Ellison, Lisa C. 2007. "Comparative Economic Systems." econedlink. http://www.econedlink.org/lessons/index.php?lid=322&type=educator.

Knight, Jim. N.d. "Closed or Open: That Is the Question." Teaching Channel-Great Teaching, Inspiring Classrooms. https://www.teachingchannel.org/videos/teaching-economic-systems.

Shmoop Editorial Team. 2008. *Types of Economic Systems*. Retrieved January 10, 2014. http://www.shmoop.com/economic-systems/types.html.

Entitlements

"Entitlement" is a term used to describe a group of government programs in which recipients satisfy a set of criteria to qualify to receive the benefits of the particular program. If one meets the eligibility requirements for one of these programs, one is "entitled" to receive the benefits the program provides. Examples of federal government programs that fit into this category of programs include Social Security, Medicare, Medicaid, the Supplemental Nutrition Assistance Program (SNAP), and the National School Lunch Program. State government programs would include housing assistance, the federal-state partnership for unemployment insurance, and special college tuition programs. Local governments may offer some housing assistance if one qualifies, but generally local governments do not offer programs that can be considered entitlements.

As government programs, entitlements are usually funded through tax revenues. They are considered automatic government expenditures because receiving the benefits is based on qualifications, not selection. With increases in benefits automatic, entitlements are often labeled the uncontrollable part of government budgets. Entitlements at both the federal and state levels are included in their general budgets. Especially at the federal level, entitlement programs are a larger percentage of the general budget. However, there are certain programs funded through the governments offering bonds.

The most notable entitlement programs are the federal programs Social Security, Medicare, and Medicaid. Recipients must meet the requirements for each. For Social Security and Medicare, age is the major criteria. To qualify for Social Security, one must be at least 62 years old to qualify for minimum benefits and must have paid into the Social Security System for a minimum of 40 "credits," or 10 years. Social Security benefits also extend to the family survivors from a death in a family, or if one becomes disabled and cannot work. A second Social Security eligibility requirement is that of paying into the Social Security insurance program for a minimum of eight quarters through one's employment. For Medicare, one becomes eligible on one's sixty-fifth birthday. Medicaid eligibility is based on a minimum income level. While Social Security and Medicare participation is not limited by income level, Medicaid is a medical insurance program designed to aid low-income individuals and families.

Federal spending on the entitlement programs or Social Security, Medicare, and Medicaid make up the largest components of the federal budget. They are also the fastest growing. Since the 1990s, entitlement programs have been growing between 7 and 8 percent per year, with Medicare and Medicaid growing the fastest. Projections into the future by the Congressional Budget Office project entitlement programs will continue growing as a percentage of the federal budget as more citizens qualify, especially the big three: Social Security, Medicare, and Medicaid.

Social Security

Social Security was established in 1935 when the Social Security Act was passed by Congress and signed by President Roosevelt. When passed, the intent for Social Security was to be a retirement supplement or social safety net for those whose retirement savings were not sufficient. Social Security is not just for older U.S. citizens. In 1956, the law was amended to include benefits for people with disabilities. Social Security benefits also extend to workers who become disabled and the survivors of a family in which either a spouse or parent has died. Social Security was originally established to replace approximately 40 percent of one's income at retirement. Eighty-five cents of every Social Security tax is paid to retirees or their dependents. Fifteen cents goes to those receiving disability benefits and their families.

How Social Security Works

When an employer participates in the Social Security System, an employee pays taxes into the Social Security System. The money pays the benefits to those who are entitled to receive retirement, disability, or survivor's benefits from the Social Security System. All Social Security taxes paid are held in one federal government trust fund, not in individual accounts. The taxes are used to pay those receiving benefits. Social Security taxes are paid on income up to $113,700 as of 2013.

An employee becomes eligible to receive Social Security benefits when he or she has earned a total of 40 "credits" ($1,160 per credit, maximum 4 credits per year). Forty credits equates to 10 years of employment and participation to qualify for the Social Security retirement entitlement. Fewer credits are needed to qualify for the disability and survivor benefits.

Medicare and Medicaid

The other two major entitlement programs, Medicare and Medicaid, were signed into law on July 30, 1965, by President Lyndon B. Johnson. Medicaid was originally part of the Social and Rehabilitation Services Administration. In 1977, Medicare and Medicaid were combined into one federal agency, Centers for Medicare and Medicaid Services (CMS). While there have been many changes to the original program since 1965, the most significant change occurred on December 8, 2003, with the signing of the Medicare Modernization Act (MMA) by President George W. Bush. It added several changes, the most significant being the outpatient prescription drug benefit addition.

Medicare is a federal health insurance program for individuals 65 and older. Younger individuals may qualify due to disability or End-Stage Renal Disease (ESRD). Medicare has three parts: Part A includes hospital, skilled nursing, hospice, and some home health care costs; Part B includes medical costs including doctor's services, outpatient care, medical supplies, and some preventive services; Part C includes health maintenance organizations (HMOs), preferred provider organizations (PPOs), or private fee-for-service, special needs, or Medicare medical savings accounts; and Part D includes prescription drugs. Parts C and D are offered by private companies who have contracted with federal government for Medicare services.

Individuals pay Medicare taxes on all income earned, including those self-employed. Those who work for someone else pay half (6.2%) and employers pay half (6.2%). Self-employed workers pay the entire 12.4 percent. Medicare taxes go into a trust fund to pay for hospital costs and other medical costs of Medicare recipients. Medicare and Medicaid are managed by the Centers for Medicare and Medicaid Services.

States are required by federal law to provide Medicaid health coverage to qualifying individuals with disabilities, seniors, children, pregnant women, and parents who are entitled under income requirements. The entitlement is based on the federal mandate to cover certain population groups with states having the option to include other groups. States set the eligibility requirements based on federal minimum income standards. One income eligibility standard is based on a percentage of the federal poverty level (FPL). In 2013, the FPL for a family of four was $23,550; the level is changed annually. Many state minimum eligibility levels exceed the federal minimum. Other nonfinancial criteria such as U.S. citizenship, immigration status, or residency are used to determine Medicaid eligibility.

Beginning in 2014, the Affordable Care Act of 2010 expanded Medicaid eligibility. Signed by President Barack Obama on March 23, 2010, the minimum eligibility level nationally became 133 percent of the federal poverty level. In 2011, the poverty level for a family of four was $29,700. While the new guidelines went into effect January 1, 2014, states had the option to accept the federal guidelines earlier if they chose to do so.

David A. Dieterle

See Also Affordable Health Care Act Cases, 567 in U.S. (2012); Great Society; New Deal; Roosevelt, Franklin Delano; Social Security Act of 1935

Further Reading

CMS.gov, Centers for Medicare and Medicaid Services. N.d. "History." http://www.cms.gov/About-CMS/Agency-Information/History/index.html?redirect=/history/.

Medicaid.gov: Keeping America Healthy. N.d. "Eligibility." http://www.medicaid.gov/Medicaid-CHIP-Program-Information/By-Topics/Eligibility/Eligibility.html.

Medicare.gov, the Official U.S. Government Site for Medicare. N.d. "What Is Medicare?" http://www.medicare.gov/sign-up-change-plans/decide-how-to-get-medicare/whats-medicare/what-is-medicare.html.

Social Security: Understanding the Benefits. 2013. Social Security Administration. http://www.ssa.gov/pubs/EN-05-10024.pdf.

Resources for Teachers

Just Facts, a Resource for Independent Thinkers. N.d. "Social Security." Accessed December 10, 2013. http://www.justfacts.com/socialsecurity.asp.

PBS. N.d. "NOW with Bill Moyers: Medicare Reform." Accessed December 10, 2013. http://www.pbs.org/now/classroom/medicare.html.

Practical Money Skills for Life. N.d. "Medicare and Medicaid." Accessed December 10, 2013. http://www.practicalmoneyskills.com/personalfinance/lifeevents/retirement/medicare.php.

Environmental Protection Agency (EPA)

The Environmental Protection Agency (EPA) was created on December 2, 1970, through an executive order signed by President Richard M. Nixon. The EPA reorganized the federal government's environmental programs and agencies under one entity. The EPA was created as an independent organization to supervise and control pollution, waste, air and water quality, pesticides, hazardous waste disposal, toxic substances, and wildlife in the United States. It was believed that as the country's population grew, these issues would become increasingly important and that a regulatory agency was needed to implement policies and regulations.

Prior to the creation of the EPA only sporadic attention was paid to the environment. President Theodore Roosevelt was a conservationist. During his presidency he set aside lands for national parks. Under Franklin D. Roosevelt's New Deal, soil conservation measures were put into effect with the creation of the Civilian Conservation Corps. The Tennessee Valley Authority was established in 1933 authorizing the construction of dams to generate hydroelectric power. In 1916, President Woodrow Wilson oversaw the creation of the National Park Service.

Rachel Carson's 1962 book *Silent Spring* drew widespread attention to the effects the use of pesticides was having on the environment. Carson's work helped increase public awareness of the need for environmental protection, which led Presidents John F. Kennedy and Lyndon B. Johnson to include the environment as part of their legislative agendas.

President Nixon took things further and expanded the nation's environmental policy. In 1969, Nixon established the Environmental Quality Council to oversee issues related to the environment as part of the National Environmental Policy Act (NEPA). NEPA made the government the protector of earth, land, air, and water. This act established a national environmental policy and set goals for protecting and maintaining the environment through federal agencies. In July 1970, President Nixon announced his desire to create an independent regulatory agency to oversee the implementation and enforcement of environmental policy. This agency would be called the Environmental Protection Agency, and its duties would include:

1. Recommending environmental policies to the president for implementation;
2. Enforcement of environmental standards;
3. Researching pollution and its effects and recommending policies to reduce pollution;
4. Working with state and local agencies as well as federal agencies to coordinate pollution policies;
5. Assisting other federal organizations that deal with environmental quality related issues; and
6. Developing reports for the president and Congress regarding the environment.

Furthermore, the EPA sought to identify potential pollution problems by investigating factories and manufacturing facilities. The EPA pursued an examination of agricultural pesticides and their effect on the environment. The agency also wanted to locate and address pollution in cities, rural areas, oceans, and lakes.

Countries around the world are also concerned with environmental standards. Britain's Environmental Protection Act of 1990 sought to update and refine pollution controls and standards as well as implement harsher penalties for violations. In 1998, Canada sought to strengthen its Environmental Protection Act by making it more stringent as well as providing a review of the act every five years.

Today, the Environmental Protection Agency employs over 17,000 people in fields that vary from scientists to engineers. The organization has changed with the environmental issues of the time. Most recently, the EPA has focused its attention on greenhouse gases and fuel emissions standards, as it continues to be concerned with its original charge for air and water quality.

Angela M. LoPiccolo

See Also New Deal; Roosevelt, Franklin Delano; Tennessee Valley Authority (TVA)

Further Reading

Collin, Robert W. 2006. *The Environmental Protection Agency: Cleaning Up America's Act.* Westport, CT: Greenwood Press.

Environmental Protection Agency. 1970. "Ash Council Memo." http://www2.epa.gov/aboutepa/ash-council-memo.

Environmental Protection Agency. 1970. "EPA Order 1110.2." http://www2.epa.gov/aboutepa/epa-order-11102.

Gibson, John. 1991. "The Integration of Pollution Control." *Journal of Law and Society* 18: 18–31.

Resources for Teachers

Environmental Protection Agency. N.d. "The Guardian: Origins of the EPA." http://www2.epa.gov/aboutepa/guardian-origins-epa.

Environmental Protection Agency. N.d. "Students." http://www.epa.gov/students/.

Environmental Protection Agency. N.d. "Teacher Resources and Lesson Plans." http://www.epa.gov/students/teachers.html.

European (Economic) Community

The Economic Community (EC) was established by the Treaty of Rome in 1957. There were six original member countries: Belgium, France, Italy, Luxembourg, the Netherlands, and West Germany. In 1993, the Economic Community was renamed the European Community.

The EC is a combination of three communities: the European Coal and Steel Community (ECSC, established in 1951); the European Atomic Energy Community (EURATOM, formed in 1957); and the European Economic Community (EEC, created by the Treaty of Rome in 1957).

The Economic Community (EC) was formed in the post–World War II era in an effort to unify and preserve Europe. The organization sought to provide both political and economic stability to the region rather than fostering competition among European nations. The original member countries sought to create a closer union among themselves as well as to rid Europe of the barriers that had once existed and divided them. This was necessary in order for the countries to become strong and powerful again, and it was believed that a union of several countries was the best way to accomplish this.

The member nations developed a treaty that outlined the main elements of the Economic Community. Those provisions included:

1. Economic cooperation and stability among member nations, including a common economic policy;
2. The elimination of customs duties and taxes on both imports and exports among member nations;
3. Common agricultural and transport policies;
4. The establishment of a European Investment Bank to aid developing regions;
5. The free movement of people, services, and capital among member nations;
6. Maintaining relationships with overseas territories and allowing the goods of these countries to enter free of tariffs; and
7. The creation of several institutions, including an assembly, a council, a commission, and a court of justice.

One of the most significant accomplishments of the EC was the abolition of all customs duties. By 1968, the six member nations did not impose tariffs or quotas on one another and established a common tariff on the rest of the world. In 1973, Great Britain, Ireland, and Denmark joined the EC. In 1993, the Treaty of Maastricht established the European Community, replacing the Treaty of Rome. Today, the European Community has evolved into the European Union (EU), and is composed of 28 member nations that share common political and economic features.

Angela M. LoPiccolo

See Also International Monetary Fund (IMF); Protectionism; World Trade Organization (WTO)

Further Reading

Hallstein, Walter. 1963. "The European Economic Community." *Political Science Quarterly* 78: 161–78.

"Treaty Establishing the European Economic Community. 1957. *The American Journal of International Law* 51: 865–954.

"Treaty Establishing the European Economic Community." N.d. Accessed July 16, 2013. http://www.ab.gov.tr/files/ardb/evt/1_avrupa_birligi/1_3_antlasmalar/1_3_1_kurucu_antlasmalar/1957_treaty_establishing_eec.pdf.

"The Treaty for a European Economic Community: A Critical Analysis." 1958. *The World Today* 14: 304–15.

Resources for Teachers

Eichengreen, Barry. N.d. "European Economic Community." Accessed July 16, 2013. http://www.econlib.org/library/Enc1/EuropeanEconomicCommunity.html.

"European Economic Community." N.d. Accessed July 16, 2013. http://www.princeton.edu/~achaney/tmve/wiki100k/docs/European_Economic_Community.html.

Expansionary Fiscal Policy

Expansionary fiscal policy occurs when the government attempts to stimulate the economy by decreasing taxes, increasing government spending, and increasing transfer payments. This policy is used when unemployment is high, when consumer spending is low, or when the economy is in a recession.

There are two conflicting viewpoints on handling the economy when inflation is high. Classical economists believe that the government should not get involved in the economy because the market will balance out naturally. Fiscal policy is based on a theory developed by John Maynard Keynes, a British economist. Keynesian economists believe that the government should step in and make policy changes when the economy is not growing, or worse, is in decline, and unemployment is high. It calls for the government to employ lowering taxes along with increases in government spending to "prime the pump" of the economy. Expansionary fiscal policy is aimed at stimulating the economy and increasing employment. The most important element of fiscal policy is maintaining and balancing the federal budget by examining tax revenues compared to government expenditures. Expansionary fiscal policy is used when the government seeks to increase the budget deficit or must decrease the budget surplus.

When enacting an expansionary fiscal policy, economists illustrate this by saying it shifts the aggregate demand curve to the right, which encourages economic output. Aggregate demand is the level of demand for goods and services by consumers, businesses, and the government. When this policy goes into effect, it works to increase aggregate demand for goods and services. There are three main tools utilized by the government to enact an expansionary fiscal policy: decreasing taxes, increasing government spending, and raising transfer payments.

When decreasing taxes is an expansionary fiscal policy tool, the government typically only focuses on an individual's personal income tax rates, though it can also include property tax and sales tax. A decrease in taxes can either be in the form of a one-time stimulus payment or an overall decrease in income tax rates. Either way, when taxation decreases, an individual's amount of disposable income is increased. Thus, with an increase in disposable income comes more spending power, which in turn causes increased production of consumer goods. When more production is necessary, businesses hire employees to meet the needs of growing consumer demand. Overall, this causes the economy to grow. The increase in disposable income indirectly causes an increase in aggregate demand when consumers make more purchases of goods and services.

Increasing government spending means raising funds available across several different government agencies, and can include giving more money for military expenditures, teachers' salaries, and road construction, for example. When these government agencies have increased funds available, they are able to make more purchases, which then increases an agency's income and raises its overall production. Aggregate demand is increased directly when the government spends more money because of increased output.

Raising the amount of transfer payments is also a useful tool of expansionary fiscal policy. Transfer payments are payments made by the government directly to individuals.

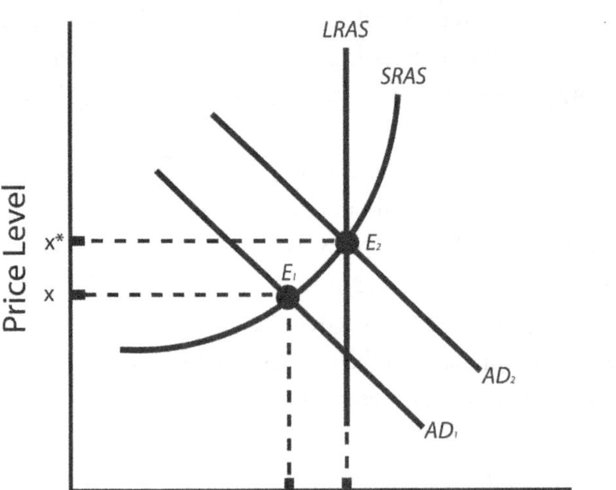

Aggregate demand increases (AD_1 to AD_2) when government spending increases (x to x*)

Those who receive transfer payments fall into three categories and include the elderly and disabled who are on Social Security, people who are unemployed and receive unemployment benefits, and the poor who are on welfare. Raising transfer payments can be done either by increasing the amount of payment one or two of the categories receive or via a blanket percentage increase across the three categories. When transfer payments are increased, this raises the disposable income of those who receive these benefits. More disposable income, like when taxes are decreased, leads to an increase in production when people are able to purchase more goods and services. Once again, an increase in production means that more people can be hired to meet increased consumer demands. This also is an increase in aggregate demand indirectly.

One issue with using expansionary fiscal policy is an occurrence known as the "crowding out effect." Whenever the government spends its own money to stimulate the economy and borrows money to pay for it, interest rates go up because of more demand in the money market. When interest rates go up, people do not invest as much, which means that economic growth slows down. While the crowding out effect is more evident when demand for money is high from the private sector, it is a risk when using expansionary fiscal policy tools.

Ekaterini Chrisopoulos-Vergos

See Also Contractionary Fiscal Policy; Entitlements; Expansionary Monetary Policy; Fiscal Policy; Keynes, John Maynard; Keynesian Economics; Taxes

Further Reading

AmosWEB: Economics with a Touch of Whimsy! N.d. "Expansionary Fiscal Policy." Accessed April 7, 2013. http://www.amosweb.com/cgi-bin/awb_nav.pl?s=wpd&c=dsp&k=expansionary+fiscal+policy.

CliffsNotes. N.d. "Fiscal Policy." Accessed April 7, 2013. http://www.cliffsnotes.com/more-subjects/economics/fiscal-and-monetary-policy/fiscal-policy.

Resources for Teachers

Liber8 Economic Information Newsletter. 2011. "Monetary and Fiscal Policy in Times of Crisis, March 2011, Classroom Edition." http://research.stlouisfed.org/pageone-economics/uploads/newsletter/2011/201103_ClassroomEdition.pdf.

Nash, Jon. 2013."Expansionary Fiscal Policy and Aggregate Demand." Education Portal. Accessed April 7, 2013. http://education-portal.com/academy/lesson/expansionary-fiscal-policy-and-aggregate-demand.html.

Practical Money Skills for Life. 2009. "Economy 101: Fiscal Policy." Accessed April 7, 2013. http://www.practicalmoneyskills.com/foreducators/econ101/20090710_fiscal_policy.php.

Yopp, Marty. 2012. "The Role of Government: The Federal Government and Fiscal Policy." econedlink. http://www.econedlink.org/lessons/index.php?lid=190&type=educator.

Expansionary Monetary Policy

Expansionary monetary policy is a policy in which the central bank of a country decides that it is necessary to increase the monetary supply to prevent recession, decrease unemployment, or increase economic growth. Monetary policy works together with fiscal policy, which is controlled by the government, to ensure economic growth in the economy. The most frequent tool used by a central bank to implement expansionary monetary policy is the buying and selling of government bills, notes, and bonds.

In the United States, expansionary monetary policy is under the direction of the chair of the Federal Reserve. The Board of Governors of the Federal Reserve System decides when expansionary monetary policy is necessary. The Federal Reserve accomplishes expansionary monetary policy using three primary tools: lowering the reserve requirement; lowering the discount rate; or buying government bills, notes, and bonds. Implementation of the latter tool is done through the Federal Open Market Committee (FOMC). The FOMC implements expansionary monetary policy by lowering interest rates.

In order to implement the monetary policy decisions of the Federal Reserve Board of Governors, the FOMC carries out open-market operations. To implement expansionary monetary policy, the Federal Reserve buys government bonds. The increase in demand increases the price and decreases the interest rate. The lower interest rate creates incentives for financial institutions to increase loans, promoting economic growth and reducing unemployment.

The Federal Reserve pays for government bonds by giving a credit to the purchasers in the form of deposits at regional Federal Reserve banks. Commercial banks then use the deposits to make more loans and accept more deposits. If many banks are offering loans, the interest rates on these loans are lowered in order to maintain competition between banks. In this way, the Federal Reserve purchasing government bonds lowers interest rates, which in turn increases monetary supply.

When decreasing the discount rate to accomplish expansionary monetary policy, the Federal Reserve is decreasing the interest rate it charges banks to borrow money directly from the central bank, or more specifically one of the 12 regional district banks. This encourages banks to borrow more reserves, increasing the money supply. The increased money supply allows banks to lend more to businesses and households. In summary, decreasing the discount rate increases the money supply, which encourages lower nominal interest rates and increases in business and household borrowing.

Reducing the reserve requirement decreases the amount a bank must have in its end-of-day reserves to satisfy the Federal Reserve's reserve requirement regulations. Reserves include vault cash as well as Federal Reserve deposits. When banks have their reserve requirement decreased, the supply of loanable funds is increased, which lowers nominal interest rate. The lower rate creates an incentive for banks to supply more loans to businesses and households.

A risk in utilizing an expansionary monetary policy is overstimulation of the economy, which leads to inflation. When inflation is high, the purchasing power of money is decreased.

Utilizing open market operations to buy government bonds, decreasing the discount rate, and lowering the reserve requirement are actions that can be taken by the Federal Reserve to increase the money supply and fulfill expansionary monetary policy. Each is key in expansionary monetary policy to prevent a recession and increase economic growth.

Ekaterini Chrisopoulos-Vergos

See Also Bernanke, Ben; Federal Reserve System; Greenspan, Alan; Monetary Policy; Volcker, Paul

Further Reading

Business Dictionary.com. N.d. "Expansionary Monetary Policy." Accessed May 12, 2013. http://www.businessdictionary.com/definition/expansionary-monetary-policy.html.

Hetzel, Robert L. 2008. *The Monetary Policy of the Federal Reserve.* Studies in Macroeconomic History Cambridge: Cambridge University Press.

Horobin, William. 2013. "OECD Calls on Europe to Loosen Monetary Policy." *Wall Street Journal*, March 28. http://online.wsj.com/article/SB10001424127887324685104578388000735651838.html.

Moffet, Mike. N.d. "Expansionary Monetary Policy vs. Contractionary Monetary Policy: What Effects Does Monetary Policy Have?" About.com Economics. Accessed May 12, 2013. http://economics.about.com/cs/money/a/policy.htm.

Resources for Teachers

DeLong, J. Bradford. 2009. *Macroeconomics*. New York: McGraw-Hill Higher Education.

Economics Center for Research and Education. N.d. "Why Money Matters: Understanding Monetary Policy and Interest Rates." Accessed May 12, 2013. http://www.whymoneymatters.org/educators/resources/lessons/understanding-monetary-policy-and-interest-rates.

Haskell, Doug. 2013. "Focus on Economic Data: The Federal Reserve and Monetary Policy, May 1, 2013." econedlink. http://www.econedlink.org/lessons/index.php?lid=1144&type=educator.

Externalities

Externalities are unexpected consequences of an activity that affect people external to an economic activity. Externalities can be positive or negative, but both forms are considered to be market failures, meaning that a market has not allocated its resources efficiently to achieve optimum satisfaction to either the producer or the consumer of a good or service.

Economists recognize two different costs: private costs and social costs. These costs can also be seen as internal costs and external costs. Ideally, economists would like all the costs of an economic transaction to be borne internally by the parties involved in the transaction. However, this is not always possible. With some economic transactions, some of the costs are external to the transaction and borne by a third party. These costs are external to the transaction; thus they are referred to as an externality. Being a cost external to the transaction denotes a negative externality. While there are costs to every economic transaction, there are also benefits. Applying the similar correlation to benefits, when the benefits of a transaction are received by a third party external to the transaction, there is a positive externality from the transaction.

Private costs can be seen as the cost the producers expected when creating and using their product, whereas social cost is the total cost of the product, including the private cost and any externalities. Social costs include all the costs that are part of the production process of the product, including possible externalities such as pollution. Private costs are also known as the internal costs of a company on which profits are derived. When producers fail to account for the true social costs, this is a market failure. Likewise, if producers do not account for all the benefits, this too is a market failure.

Negative externalities are a cost external to the original economic transaction. The costs are borne by someone other than the producer or consumer. Costs may include simply undesired effects or can also be monetary in nature. An example of a negative externality is pollution. In the process of conducting an economic transaction, a factory may be producing a good for a customer (the consumer), yet some of the transaction costs cause harm to a neighboring waterway and negatively impact citizens outside the original transaction. Some of the costs of the transaction are external to the production process. The pollution may cause harm to the waterway and keep residents from enjoying the downstream park and beach.

Another example of a negative externality is a neighbor near your home playing music at very loud volume. The fact that you can hear the music is an externality, as you were not the intended beneficiary of the music. If the music keeps you up at night and you are unable to sleep, this makes it a negative externality. This example becomes a positive externality, however, when the music being played is music you enjoy. The fact that you can hear the music is an externality, as you were probably not the intended beneficiary of the music. However, in this scenario, if you enjoy the music you are listening to and the music stops at a respectable hour for you to also enjoy your sleep, this is a positive externality.

Positive externalities can be seen as a benefit that someone other than the producer or consumer may enjoy. Another example of a positive externality would be when a homeowner decides to have the lawn in front of his or her home professionally landscaped. The homeowner may have spruced up the yard for his or her own personal enjoyment, but also unintentionally increased the value of the neighborhood.

Ekaterini Chrisopoulos-Vergos

See Also Market Capitalism; Market Failure; Public Goods

Further Reading

Caplan, Brian. N.d. "Market Failures, Public Goods, and Externalities." Library of Economics and Liberty. http://www.econlib.org/library/Topics/College/marketfailures.html.

Cornes, Richard, and Todd Sandler. 1999. *Externalities, Public Goods, and Club Goods.* Cambridge: Cambridge University Press.

The Environmental Literacy Council. N.d. "Externalities by Dawn Anderson." Accessed June 12, 2013. http://www.enviroliteracy.org/article.php/1289.html.

Resources for Teachers

tutor2u. N.d. "What Are Externalities?" Accessed June 12, 2013. http://www.tutor2u.net/economics/content/topics/externalities/what_are_externalities.htm.

Yetter, Erin. 2012. "Green Eggs and . . . Economics." econedlink. http://www.econedlink.org/lessons/index.php?lid=966&type=educator.

F

Fascism

"Fascism" was a term coined by Benito Mussolini from the Latin word *fasces*, which the Romans used as a term to symbolize unity and authority. In 1919 he formed the Fascist Party with discontented Italians and other veterans. In the 1920s and 1930s fascism meant different things in different countries. Today, it usually describes an authoritarian national government with a command economy. A fascist government elevates the priorities of the government over the individual and fundamental human rights.

There are several basic characteristics of fascism. First and foremost is extreme nationalism. The individual in a fascist nation is meant to devote blind loyalty to the country and its leaders. Fascist leaders will use violence, aggression, and strict discipline without reservations to demand this loyalty to the state. They see war and foreign expansion as necessary and preferable as a means to promote nationalism.

Such a strong national government fervor at all costs is definitely against individualism and democracy. Fascists indiscriminately reject individual liberty and freedom. The fascist views democracy, individual freedom, and liberty as weak and corrupt. For the fascist, the only goals worth striving for are the goals, power, and authority of the national government.

A second characteristic of fascism is the national rule by a one-party dictator. The dictator controls all aspects of the state including the economy. The economy was centrally planned and controlled by the dictator to the point of using spies and violence to be sure the people adhered to their decisions. As with the economy, the dictator had full control of the media for the express purpose of indoctrination and proselytizing the national viewpoint. A popular form of indoctrination for the fascist was the use of youth groups and schools. Finally, total control of the nation's way of life by the dictator did not forget the artists, books, and teaching in the schools. All were severely censored so that the fascist view of nationalism was always before the people. Fascism differed from communism in that a fascist society was very class focused, as opposed to the Marxist view of total equality.

Upon the creation of the Fascist Party in 1919, Benito Mussolini rose to power and was asked to form a government as prime minister in 1922. He thus obtained a nominally legal constitutional appointment from King Victor Emmanuel III to lead Italy. In 1925, Mussolini took the title Il Duce. As "the Leader," he immediately quashed opposition political parties through terror, silenced the media and the press, corrupted elections to serve his purposes, and brought fellow Fascist Party members to power, all while Italy was still officially a parliamentary monarchy. He imprisoned, killed, or exiled all detractors and members of the opposition. In Italy, the era of the dictator—in the person of Benito Mussolini—was coming quickly.

As a dictator, Mussolini centralized the economy under the state. Fascist Party members were put in leadership roles of businesses, labor, agriculture, and industry. The economy was class driven, favoring the upper class and leaders of Italy's industrial complex, all at the expense of the workers. Strikes were made illegal and all wages were kept low by the state.

Under the fascist philosophy, the power of the state was the only important view, at the expense of the individual. All citizens of the state were constantly fed propaganda and ideas that uplifted the importance of the state and downplayed individualism. To achieve an all-powerful state, men were told that fighting for the success of the state was an ultimate calling. Women were to be full-time mothers for the state. Mussolini strongly believed in increasing the population. He personally presented a medal to mothers who gave birth to 14 or more children.

Mussolini devoted major energy to influencing and changing the youth of Italy to the fascist philosophy and way of life. His youth groups were conducted as military training and military discipline for youths. The youth marched in parades in military formations and sang patriotic songs; they would chant, "Mussolini is always right." As the Great Depression continued to spread throughout Europe in the 1930s, Mussolini had created a military generation to spread fascism.

In the wake of World War I in Europe and the Great Depression, fascism promoted a solid, stable government, and Benito Mussolini rekindled national pride. Besides Mussolini in Italy, fascism spread throughout Europe in the 1920s and 1930s. Even though the type of fascism may have varied, the fundamental characteristics remained in places such as Germany under Adolf Hitler (1933–1945) and Spain under Francisco Franco (1939–1975). From 1936 to 1945, even Japan fostered fascist beliefs in the uniqueness of the Japanese spirit and taught subordination to the state and personal sacrifice.

Fascism in Spain under the dictatorship of Francisco Franco is a unique example of how fascism can fluctuate. One of Franco's first actions as leader was to kill or imprison thousands of former Loyalists, which was the political party in Spain that wished to preserve the republican government. Spain, much like Italy, was ruled as a strict fascist state until after World War II. After World War II, Spain became anticommunist and aligned with the United States. Even though independent political parties and trade unions remained banned, by the late 1950s, pressure for economic stabilization forced Spain to open its doors for massive foreign investments, thus loosening some government control. With foreign influences pouring in, social and ideological influences from the West soon followed. This gradual change of beliefs and economic windfall led to extraordinarily rapid economic growth and a less rigid form of fascism.

Much like Mussolini, Adolf Hitler relied on the economic crisis in Germany following World War I, and his powerful speaking ability, to influence the German population to believe in fascist ideology. As unemployment rose throughout Germany and a financial crisis spread due to Germany's massive World War I debt, Hitler promised to end reparations, create jobs, and defy the Treaty of Versailles. His primary focus was on creating a great united nation that must expand for its people. He appealed to nationalism by recalling past glories and boasted of a master race that would dominate Europe for a thousand years.

Whether in Spain, Germany, or France, the nationalism and patriotism of fascism partnered with a strong, driven, influential leader who promised to make his nation the greatest in the world, made the ideology of fascism very appealing to those in need and hopeful for change.

Tracy L. Ripley

See Also Democratic Socialism; Marx, Karl; Marxism

Further Reading

Downing, David. 2008. *Political and Economic Systems*. Chicago: Heinemann Library.

Ellis, Elisabeth Gaynor, and Anthony Esler. 2007. *World History*. New York: Pearson-Prentice Hall.

Griffiths, Richard. 2000. *Fascism*. New York: Continuum.

Resources for Teachers

Libertas Film Magazine. 2011. "Experiment in Fascism at an American High School: The Lesson Plan @ The Newport Beach Film Festival." May 10. http://www.libertasfilmmagazine.com/experiment-in-fascism-at-an-american-high-school-the-lesson-plan-the-newport-beach-film-festival/.

Mr. Donn's Social Studies Site: Free Lesson Plans, Games, Activities, Powerpoints."Fascism." Accessed August 15, 2013. http://government.mrdonn.org/fascism.html.

Federal Deposit Insurance Corporation (FDIC)

The Federal Deposit Insurance Corporation (FDIC) is a federal agency created in 1933 under the direction of President Franklin D. Roosevelt. The FDIC was created to insure customer deposits in the event of a bank failure. At first, FDIC insurance covered losses up to $2,500. The amount has grown over time and is currently at $250,000 per depositor, per insured bank.

During the 1920s, U.S. banks loaned large sums of money to many high-risk businesses. Many of these businesses proved unable to pay back their loans. The October 1929 stock market crash caused many panicked investors to sell their stocks, resulting in the collapse of the stock market. Banks had invested heavily in the stock market and lost huge sums. Farmers were also unable to pay back loans due to crop failures and hard times on the nation's farms. Fearful that banks would run out of cash, people rushed to their banks demanding their money. To pay back these deposits, banks had to recall loans from borrowers, but they could not do so fast enough to pay all the depositors.

The combination of the stock market crash, unpaid loans, and bank runs resulted in the failure of thousands of banks across the country. By the early 1930s, the Great Depression had hit the United States. Many people lost their life savings due to bank failures and closings. The American people had lost faith in the banking industry.

When Franklin D. Roosevelt took office in 1933, he needed to encourage citizens to deposit their money in banks once again and restore confidence in the nation's banking system. On March 5, 1933, Roosevelt declared a national "bank holiday" and closed the nation's banks. The "bank holiday" was not a time of festivities or celebration, but a desperate last resort move to restore trust in the nation's financial system. The "holiday" was a time for the banks to replenish their reserves and reestablish a healthy money system. Within a matter of days, sound banks began to reopen. As a result of the many bank failures of the Great Depression, banks were closely regulated from 1933 through the 1960s.

Later in 1933, Congress passed the Banking Act that established the Federal Deposit Insurance Corporation. Roosevelt was hopeful that with this act citizens would trust in the banking industry again and be willing to deposit their money in the nation's banks. The act guaranteed that even if a bank failed, deposits would be guaranteed by the federal government.

Meanwhile, banks became extremely cautious. They made fewer loans and kept enough cash on hand in case depositors all came at once to withdraw their funds. Banks began to hold substantial reserves, far in excess of those required by the Federal Reserve.

The FDIC is an independent agency of the federal government. It employs more than 7,000 people. It is headquartered in Washington, D.C., but conducts most of its business in six regional offices and field offices throughout the nation. The FDIC is managed by a five-person board of directors, all of whom are appointed by the president and confirmed by the Senate. No more than three can be from the same political party as the president.

In addition to insuring deposits, the agency also identifies, monitors, and addresses risks with deposits in participating banks. It directly examines and supervises more than 4,500 banks and savings banks for operational safety and soundness. It also monitors banks for compliance with consumer protection laws that have been created by the federal government.

To protect insured depositors, the FDIC responds immediately when a bank fails. Failed institutions are generally closed and the FDIC helps to resolve the failure, usually through the sale of deposits and loans to other thriving banking institutions. Customers of the failed institution automatically become customers of the bank that acquired the deposits and/or loans. Most of these transitions are seamless from the customer's point of view. Since the start of the FDIC insurance on January 1, 1934, no depositor has lost a single cent of insured funds as a result of a bank failure.

Tracy L. Ripley

See Also Banking Act of 1933 (Glass-Steagall Act); Federal Reserve System; Roosevelt, Franklin Delano

Further Reading

Bair, Sheila. 2012. *Bull by the Horns: Fighting to Save Main Street from Wall Street and Wall Street from Itself.* New York: Free Press.

Konstas, Panos. 2005. *Reforming FDIC Insurance with FDIC-Sponsored Deposit Self-Insurance.* Darby, PA: Diane Publishing Co.

O'Sullivan, Arthur, and Steven M. Sheffrin. 2007. *Economics Principles in Action.* New York: Pearson-Prentice Hall.

Resources for Teachers

Banking. N.d. "Lesson Plans, Games, Activities, Presentations." Accessed August 20, 2013. http://economics.mrdonn.org/banking.html.

Federal Deposit Insurance Corporation (FDIC). 2004. "Learning Bank." http://www.fdic.gov/about/learn/learning/lpindex.html.

Federal Home Loan Mortgage (Freddie Mac)

The Federal Home Loan Mortgage Corporation (FHLMC), also known as Freddie Mac, has a public mission to stabilize the nation's residential mortgage markets and expand opportunities for home ownership and affordable rental housing. Congress chartered Freddie Mac, located in Tysons Corner, Virginia, as a stockholder-owned, government-sponsored enterprise (GSE) through the Emergency Home Finance Act of 1970. Freddie Mac purchases loans from lenders to allow them to make more mortgage loans to other borrowers. They then guarantee and securitize these mortgages to form mortgage-backed securities. These securities are very liquid and carry a credit rating close to that of U.S. Treasury notes, bills, and bonds. Freddie Mac does not make loans directly to homebuyers, nor does it pay state and local income tax. The FHLMC also works to educate homebuyers and home owners through financial education programs like their "Considering a Home" and "CreditSmart" curricula.

In 1989, the Financial Institutions Reform, Recovery and Enforcement Act revised and standardized the regulation of Freddie Mac and the Federal National Mortgage Association, known as Fannie Mae. The U.S. Department of Housing and Urban Development (HUD) then oversaw Freddie Mac and created an 18-member board of directors.

In the early 1990s, Congress encouraged Freddie Mac and Fannie Mae to increase their purchases of mortgages for low- and moderate-income borrowers. These factors, along with Freddie Mac's implicit guarantee of government support, left it attractive to investors and vulnerable to the impending housing bubble.

During the financial crisis of 2008, Treasury Department officials and leading industry experts concluded that neither Freddie Mac nor Fannie Mae had enough money to sustain the crisis. Then Treasury Secretary Henry M. Paulson Jr. created a plan of "conservatorship" under the Federal Housing Finance Agency (FHFA). Boards and chief executives were fired and new chief executives were appointed. As both agencies had funded about 70 percent of home loans at the time, many saw this as a crucial step necessary for the recovery of the housing market. The government changed them from commercial entities with a goal of making money for stockholders into quasi-public service companies intended to help the housing mortgage market function.

Criticism of Freddie Mac stems from the fact that the U.S. government allows it to borrow money at interest rates lower than those available to other financial institutions. It can issue a large amount of debt, purchase and hold a large portfolio of mortgages known as its retained portfolio. Due to the size of the retained portfolio relative to the size of the total housing market, many believe it poses a systemic risk to the U.S. economy.

Freddie Mac has strengthened its credit and eligibility standards to produce better quality loans that foster sustainable home ownership.

Kathryn Lloyd Gustafson

See Also Federal Home Loan Mortgage (Freddie Mac); Federal National Mortgage Association (Fannie Mae); United States Treasury

Further Reading

Davidoff, Steven M. 2013. "Dealbook: In the Markets, at Least, Fannie and Freddie Still Astound." *New York Times*, April 10. query.nytimes.com/gst/fullpage.html?res=9F0DE3D8153FF933A25757C0A9659D8B63&ref=freddiemac.

Federal Home Loan Mortgage Corporation. N.d. www.fhfa.gov/GetFile.aspx?FileID=30.

Min, David. 2011. "For the Last Time, Fannie and Freddie Didn't Cause the Housing Crisis." *The Atlantic*, December 16. www.theatlantic.com/business/archive/2011/12/for-the-last-time-fannie-and-freddie-didnt-cause-the-housing-crisis/250121/.

Nocera, Joe. 2011. "The Big Lie." *New York Times*, December 23. www.nytimes.com/2011/12/24/opinion/nocera-the-big-lie.html?_r=0.

Roberts, Russell. 2008. "How Government Stoked the Mania." *Wall Street Journal*, October 3. http://online.wsj.com/news/articles/SB122298982558700341.

Resources for Teachers

Federal Housing Finance Authority. N.d. "History of the Government Sponsored Enterprises." fhfaoig.gov/LearnMore/History.

MoneyInstructor.org. N.d. "Mortgage Lender Types." Accessed December 15, 2013. www.moneyinstructor.com/doc/lendertype.asp.

Practical Money Skills for Life. N.d. "Understanding Mortgages." Accessed December 15, 2013. http://www.practicalmoneyskills.com/personalfinance/lifeevents/home/mortgage.php.

Federal National Mortgage Association (Fannie Mae)

President Franklin D. Roosevelt and Congress chartered the Federal National Mortgage Association, also known as Fannie Mae, in 1938 as part of the New Deal. Prior to this time, the private sector issued home loans with large down payments (about half the home's purchase price) and short time frames for payment, thus limiting home ownership. These lending institutions—banks, thrifts, credit unions, and savings and loans—held the mortgage themselves. After the Great Depression, private lenders did not want to invest in risky home loans. The National Housing Act of 1934 offered federally backed insurance for home mortgages from Federal Housing Administration–approved lenders. The Federal National Mortgage Association was established as an amendment to the National Housing Act.

Fannie Mae's purpose is to buy mortgages from banks so that they may then loan capital to other borrowers. This works to keep the mortgage market liquid and keep lenders providing mortgages. This strategy has allowed many lower- and middle-class Americans to borrow money from banks and improve the level of home ownership and the availability of affordable housing. Fannie Mae saw much growth with the advent of the Serviceman's Readjustment Act (GI Bill), and specifically the Veterans Administration mortgage insurance program, in 1944.

In 1954, the Federal National Mortgage Association and Charter Act of 1954 moved Fannie Mae from a government agency into a public-private corporation. Facing the financial pressures of Vietnam, Lyndon B. Johnson also reorganized Fannie Mae to eliminate its debt portfolio from the balance sheet through the Housing and Urban Development (HUD) Act of 1968. Congress split Fannie Mae into two companies. One was Fannie Mae. The second, and new, company was named the Government National Mortgage Association, or Ginnie Mae. Ginnie Mae continued to buy government-issued loans and remained a government entity.

The new Fannie Mae was converted into a publicly traded investor-owned company with federal government support, or a government-sponsored enterprise (GSE). This designation directed Fannie Mae to maximize shareholder profits for its private owners and support home ownership via its congressional or public mandate. Fannie Mae was now allowed to buy conventional mortgages in addition to those issued by the government from the Veterans Administration and the Federal Housing Administration. Fannie Mae also still had access to a line of credit from the U.S. Treasury, and was exempt from state and local income taxes and SEC oversight. The president was authorized to appoint 5 out of 18 members of Fannie Mae's board of directors. HUD also had the authority to require Fannie Mae to direct a larger portion of its business to low- and moderate-income housing. In 1970, Congress correspondingly created the Federal Home Loan Mortgage Corporation, Freddie Mac, to compete with Fannie Mae.

The unique identity of Fannie Mae between a private corporation and a government entity created an implicit belief that the U.S. government guarantees loans backed by Fannie Mae and Freddie Mac. Fannie Mae has been criticized for its close government ties that might lead to an unfair advantage within the industry. It has been able to borrow money from foreign investors at low interest rates because of this U.S. government support. This then allows Fannie Mae a funding advantage and an ability to earn large profits. Congress passed the Federal Housing Enterprises Financial Safety and Soundness Act in 1992 to conduct routine examinations of Fannie Mae and Freddie Mac.

In 1995, the Department of Housing and Urban Development began to specify mortgage purchase goals for both Fannie Mae and Freddie Mac in response to an inclusion of affordable housing as part of its mission. Both Fannie Mae and Freddie Mac turned to subprime securities with lax underwriting standards to meet these goals. This also helped to maximize their profits for shareholders.

Fannie Mae weathered several accounting scandals in 2003 and 2004, ultimately paying a $400 million civil penalty of $10.6 billion for overstating reported income and capital. The Securities and Exchange Commission directed Fannie Mae to restate its financial results for 2002 through 2004 and replace both its chief executive officer and chief financial officer.

In addition, the ultimate default and collapse of the subprime mortgage market forced Fannie Mae and Freddie Mac toward a government bailout. The Federal Housing Financing Agency placed Fannie Mae and Freddie Mac into conservatorships in July

2008, dismissing their chief executive officers and boards of directors and issuing new senior preferred stock and common stock warrants.

Kathryn Lloyd Gustafson

See Also Federal Home Loan Mortgage (Freddie Mac); Great Depression (1929–1939); Market Capitalism; New Deal; Roosevelt, Franklin Delano; Securities and Exchange Commission (SEC); Servicemen's Readjustment Act of 1944 (GI Bill)

Further Reading

Alford, Rob. 2003. "What Are the Origins of Freddie Mac and Fannie Mae?" History News Network, George Mason University, December 8. Accessed December 20, 2013. http://hnn.us/article/1849.

Fannie Mae. N.d. "Company Overview." Accessed December 20, 2013. http://www.fanniemae.com/portal/about-us/company-overview/about-fm.html.

Federal Housing Finance Agency, Office of the Inspector General. N.d. "History of the Government Sponsored Enterprises." http://fhfaoig.gov/LearnMore/History.

Hagerty, James R. 2012. "Assessing Fannie's Past and Future." *Wall Street Journal*, September 3. http://online.wsj.com/news/articles/SB10000872396390444772804577622012226706948.

Kelsie, Brandlee. 2011. "Promoting Homeownership in the United States: The Rise and Fall of Fannie Mae and Freddie Mac." University of Iowa College of Law, Center for International Finance and Development. Accessed December 20, 2013. http://ebook.law.uiowa.edu/ebook/content/promoting-homeownership-us-rise-and-fall-fannie-mae-and-freddie-mac.

Pickert, Kate. 2008. "A Brief History of Fannie Mae and Freddie Mac." *Time Business and Money*, July 14. http://content.time.com/time/business/article/0,8599,1822766,00.html.

Resources for Teachers

federalreserveeducation.org. N.d. "What You Should Know about Home Equity Lines of Credit." Accessed December 20, 2013. http://www.federalreserveeducation.org/resources/detail.cfm?r_id=3046cdb8-7e43-46e5-80b7-fd7f5d2dc139.

Hollander, Barbara Gottfried. 2013. "Pop Goes the Housing Bubble." econedlink. http://www.econedlink.org/lessons/index.php?lid=1100&type=educator.

Federal Reserve Act of 1913

Popular call for a central U.S. bank began after Americans experienced the severe inflation of Continental currency during the American Revolution. It was not until 1791 that Treasury Secretary Alexander Hamilton helped Congress establish the First Bank of the United States in Philadelphia. The 20-year charter was not renewed when it expired, as some Americans were uncomfortable with the idea of a large, powerful bank. Public opinion later shifted and Congress created the Second Bank of the United States in 1816. Congress did not renew this charter when it expired in 1836, however, as Andrew Jackson (elected president in 1828) led the fight against central bank power.

The United States suffered a severe depression in 1893 and again in 1907 after severe banking panics and bank runs arose from a liquidity crisis. New York financier J. P.

Morgan stepped in both times, using his vast resources and wealth to stabilize the American economy. Many Americans realized the need for reform of the banking system. However, debate between the conservative "money trust" financiers of New York City and the "progressives" continued over the necessity of a nation's central bank. The progressive solution, endorsed by William Jennings Bryan, suggested public control of a central bank, while conservatives like Senator Nelson Aldrich of Rhode Island advocated a banker-controlled plan.

In May 1908, Congress passed the Aldrich-Vreeland Act, establishing the bipartisan National Monetary Commission to study central banking and monetary reform. In November 1910, Aldrich and others, such as Paul Warburg, Frank Vanderlip, Harry P. Davison, Benjamin Strong, and A. Piat Andrew, traveled to Jekyll Island off the coast of Georgia to create a U.S. banking and currency reform plan known as the Aldrich plan.

The American public elected Democrat Woodrow Wilson in 1912 before the Aldrich Plan could be enacted into law. Yet it became the foundation for the Federal Reserve Bill along with another bill Senator Robert Latham Owen proposed, known as the Glass-Owen Bill. H. Parker Wills, an economics professor from Washington and Lee, and Virginia Democrat representative Carter Glass worked to create this version of a central banking plan. Glass was later to chair the House Committee on Banking and Finance.

After much deliberation and revision, the 30-section Federal Reserve Act passed the House with 298 yeas to 60 nays, and the Senate with 43 yeas to 25 nays. The Democrats supported the act, while the banker Republicans opposed it. Bankers were concerned because only one of seven members of the board could represent the banking community. On December 23, 1913, President Woodrow Wilson signed the Federal Reserve Act into law.

The Federal Reserve Act called for a central bank that could make decisions for the best interest of the country without political or private pressure, a compromise of public and private interests. A second compromise was for at least 8 but no more than 12 private regional Federal Reserve banks, each with its own branches, board of directors, and district boundaries.

The Federal Reserve System required a seven-member Board of Governors consisting of officials appointed by the president and confirmed by the Senate. They would serve 10-year staggered terms to govern the central bank. Two board members would be the Secretary of the Treasury and the Comptroller of the Currency. This was later changed in 1922 to become eight members, before a final settlement of seven was again restated in the Banking Act of 1935. The permanent member requirement was later also eliminated and terms were extended to 14 years.

The act encouraged diversity, as the president was to take due regard for a fair representation of the different commercial, industrial, and geographic divisions of the country when selecting the five remaining board members, none of whom should be selected from any one Federal Reserve district. In addition, two of the members had to have banking or finance experience. The experience requirement was also later dropped.

The president would select the governor and vice governor of the board—later called the chair and vice chair of the board—each serving four-year terms. Federal Reserve

Bank assessments would pay the salaries of the board members and they were required to submit an annual report to Congress. In addition, the act specified a 12-member Federal Advisory Committee and a single U.S. currency of the Federal Reserve Note.

Membership was mandatory for all national or federally chartered banks, and an option for state-chartered banks. All nationally chartered banks were now required to purchase nontransferable stock in their regional Federal Reserve banks, and keep a specific amount of reserves with their respective bank. Member banks would now be subject to supervision, were limited to earning no more than a 6 percent dividend on their stock, and may have discounted loans.

The act was also later changed to create the Federal Open Market Committee (FOMC), consisting of the seven board members and five representatives from the Federal Reserve Banks, one of which is always from the New York Federal Reserve. They direct all open-market operations of the Federal Reserve banks.

In the 1970s, the act was amended again to promote the goals of maximum employment, stable prices, and moderate long-term interest rates. The chair was now required to report at semiannual hearings to inform Congress of policy objectives and plans concerning monetary policy, economic development, and future prospects.

Today, the Federal Reserve continues to conduct the nation's monetary policy; supervise and regulate member banks; maintain the stability of the financial system and contain systemic risk that may arise in financial markets; and provide financial services to depository institutions, the U.S. government, and foreign official institutions.

Kathryn Lloyd Gustafson

See Also Banking Act of 1933 (Glass-Steagall Act); Bernanke, Ben; Federal Reserve System; Greenspan, Alan; *McCulloch v. Maryland, 17 U.S. 316* (*1819*); Volcker, Paul

Further Reading

Board of Governors of the Federal Reserve System. 2013. "Federal Reserve Act." http://www.federalreserve.gov/aboutthefed/fract.htm.

Federal Reserve. N.d. "History of the Federal Reserve." http://www.federalreserveeducation.org/about-the-fed/history/.

Flaherty, Edward. N.d. "A Brief History of Central Banking in the United States." Accessed June 16, 2013. http://www.let.rug.nl/usa/essays/general/a-brief-history-of-central-banking/.

Johnson, Roger T. 2010. "Historical Beginnings hellip; The Federal Reserve." Accessed June 16, 2013. http://www.bos.frb.org/about/pubs/begin.pdf.

Smale, Pauline H. 1995. "Board of Governors of the Federal Reserve System: History, Membership, and Current Issues." Congressional Research Service. Accessed June 16, 2013. http://llsdc.org/attachments/wysiwyg/544/CRS-95-292-1995.pdf.

Sprague, O.M.W. 1914. "The Federal Reserve Act of 1913." *The Quarterly Journal of Economics* 28: 213–54.

Resources for Teachers

The Federal Reserve. 2005. "The Federal Reserve System Purposes and Functions." http://www.federalreserve.gov/pf/pdf/pf_1.pdf#page=4.

Whitehouse, Michael A. 1989. "Paul Warburg's Crusade to Establish a Central Bank in the United States." http://www.minneapolisfed.org/publications_papers/pub_display.cfm?id=3815.

Federal Reserve System

Financial panics were frequent occurrences during the nineteenth and early twentieth centuries. These panics led to banking failures and businesses frequently going out of business. The monetary system of the day was highly disruptive to the economy. Banks were often unstable and not able to consistently provide the intermediation services and liquidity necessary for an economy to grow. The financial crisis of 1907 caused Congress to pass the Federal Reserve Act. Established by Congress, the Act became law when it was signed by President Woodrow Wilson on December 23, 1913.

The idea of a central bank in the United States was a hotly debated political issue at the time of the Act's passage. As a result, the Federal Reserve Act of 1913 included a political compromise. As a compromise, while the act established a central bank for the nation, many of the responsibilities of a central bank were to be conducted by a network of regional banks.

The Fed had two key purposes: to create a more stable central banking system and to provide the U.S. economy with a stable monetary system. As time has passed, the monetary and banking system duties and responsibilities of the Fed have expanded several times. Today's Federal Reserve System has four major themes: overseeing the nation's monetary policy; supervising and regulating the nation's banks; creating a stable banking system; and providing banking services to the nation's banks, i.e., serving as the banks' bank. Federal Reserve Board economists are known for their innovative research on many economic and finance topics and issues. They are known for their high-quality research at conferences, published articles in journals, and presentations to many political representatives.

Even though the Fed was created by an act of Congress and the signature of the president, the Federal Reserve System was established as an independent central bank. The decisions of the Fed are not subject to any approval or rejection by either Congress or any agency of the executive branch, including the president. However, the Fed must still conduct its business within the framework of government and its overall financial and policy goals. The chair of the Federal Reserve Board of Governors does report to Congress. This independence of decision making has often been the subject of debate within both Congress and the executive branch.

Since 1913, several laws have been enacted to refine, revise, or expand the responsibilities of the Federal Reserve System. First was the Banking Act of 1935, followed by the Employment Act of 1946, and the Bank Holding Company Act of 1956. The last half of the twentieth century saw further revisions of the Fed with the International Banking Act of 1978; Depository Institutions Deregulation and Monetary Control Act of 1980; Financial Institutions Reform, Recovery, and Enforcement Act of 1989; Federal Deposit Insurance Corporation Act of 1991; and Gramm-Leach-Bliley Act of 1999.

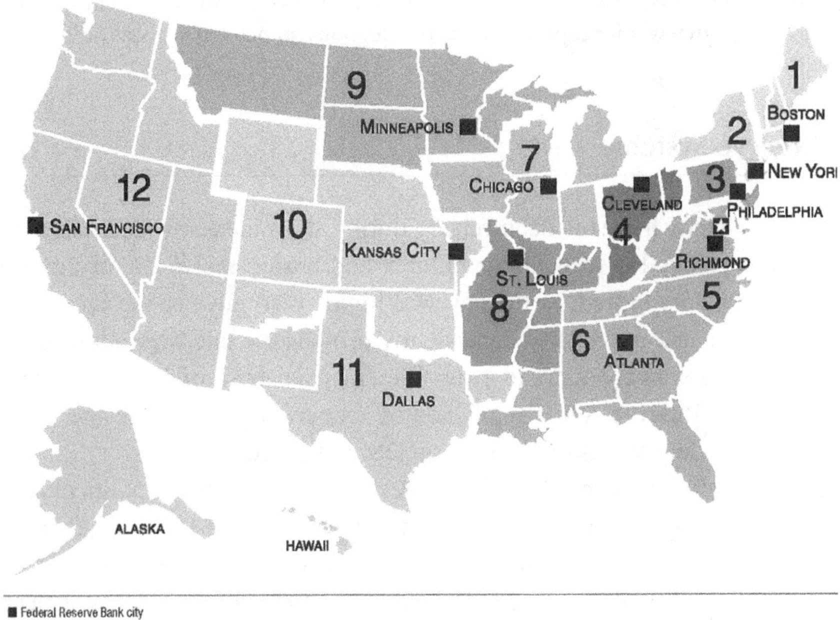

Federal Reserve Regional Banks. The Federal Reserve System is a network of twelve regional banks and their branches. Each regional bank is responsible for a specific geographic region, or district.

1 Boston
2 New York
3 Philadelphia
4 Cleveland
5 Richmond
6 Atlanta
7 Chicago
8 St. Louis
9 Minneapolis
10 Kansas City
11 Dallas
12 San Francisco

(Board of Governors of the Federal Reserve System, 99th Annual Report, 2012, http://www.federalreserve.gov/publications/annual-report/, page 2.)

Board of Governors

The Board of Governors of the Federal Reserve System has seven members. The members are appointed by the president and confirmed by the Senate. Each board member is appointed for a 14-year term. The seven terms are staggered so that one term will expire on January 31 during even-numbered years (i.e., 2000, 2002, 2004, etc.). A board member is appointed for only one 14-year term. They cannot be reappointed. New members appointed to complete a former member's term may be appointed to their own 14-year term.

Current members of the board are eligible to serve as the chair and vice chair of the board. A selection by the president for chair or vice chair may be double-appointed to the board and to chair or vice chair at the same time. They are also appointed by the president and confirmed by the Senate. Each position serves a four-year term and may be reappointed.

The district banks are the operational extensions of the central banking system. These banks are responsible for the duties of a central bank. These duties include maintaining a national payment system, distributing the nation's money supply, and serving as a regulator and supervisor of banks and as the banker for the U.S. Treasury Department. Each regional bank also serves its region with various district duties. The district banks also report to Congress.

Each district bank has its own board of directors. The district boards are made up of nine members from outside the bank, representing business, agriculture, labor, banking, and labor sectors of the district bank. Each district board of directors employs a president and first vice president to serve as chief executive of the district bank.

Federal Open Market Committee (FOMC)

A major component of the Federal Reserve System is the Federal Open Market Committee (FOMC). The FOMC members are members of the Board of Governors, and presidents of four district banks on a rotating basis, excluding the New York district bank. The Federal Reserve Bank of New York president is a continuous member of the FOMC. The FOMC is responsible for the open market operations of the Fed. This monetary policy tool is used by the Fed to influence interest rates and money supply.

David A. Dieterle

See Also Bernanke, Ben; Greenspan, Alan; Monetary Policy; United States Treasury; Volcker, Paul

Further Reading

Federal Reserve System. 2011. *21st Century Guide to the Federal Reserve System: Purposes and Functions; Detailed Look at the Structure, Responsibilities, and Operations of the Fed, Monetary Policy, America's Central Bank.* Washington, DC: U.S. Government Printing Office.

Greider, William. 1989. *Secrets of the Temple.* New York: Simon & Schuster.

Hafer, Rik W. 2005. *The Federal Reserve System: An Encyclopedia.* Santa Barbara, CA: Greenwood.

Sources for Teachers and Researchers

EconEdLink. N.d. "Focus on Economic Data: The Federal Reserve and Monetary Policy, May 1, 2013." http://www.econedlink.org/lessons/index.php?lid=1165&type=educator.

The Federal Reserve Board. N.d. "Purposes and Functions." http://www.federalreserve.gov/pf/pf.htm.

The Federal Reserve Board. N.d. "The Twelve Federal Reserve Districts." http://www.federalreserve.gov/otherfrb.htm.

Federal Reserve Education. N.d. "federalreserveeducation.org." http://www.federalreserveeducation.org/.

Federal Trade Commission

The Federal Trade Commission (FTC) is an independent agency within the U.S. government that regulates competition between businesses and protects consumers from unethical business transactions. The Federal Trade Commission serves and protects consumers from unfair business practices by preventing industries from forming anticompetitive trusts.

The forerunner to the FTC was the Bureau of Corporations, created on February 14, 1903, by then President Theodore Roosevelt as a promise under his Square Deal. The Bureau of Corporations was created as an investigatory agency under the Department of Commerce and Labor. The Bureau examined industries' business practices, specifically those businesses that engaged in interstate commerce. The reports the bureau created were useful when examining antitrust cases. Up until this time period, trusts had become a major problem in the United States. Trusts are companies or organizations that work together to limit competition from other similar companies or organizations. In 1890, Congress passed the Sherman Antitrust Act, which made these trusts illegal. With the Sherman Antitrust Act, if the federal government felt a company was limiting competition, then an investigation would take place. The act was not fully enforced until the creation of the Bureau of Corporations. The Federal Trade Commission replaced the Bureau of Corporations in 1915.

According to its Web site, the FTC's mission is to prevent business practices that are deceptive, unfair, or anticompetitive, and to enhance informed consumer choice and public understanding of the competitive process without burdening legitimate business activity. They also have three main goals. The first goal is to protect consumers by preventing unfair business practices and deception from taking place. The second goal is to maintain competition by preventing trusts from forming, creating a lack of competition in the marketplace. The third goal is to advance their performance through maintaining organizational, individual, and management excellence.

In order to fulfill its mission and meet its goals, the FTC has created a variety of agencies and bureaus to oversee specific components of their organization. This list includes the Office of Public Affairs, Office of Congressional Relations, Office of the Executive Director, Office of the General Counsel, Office of Equal Employment Opportunity, Office of International Affairs, Office of the Secretary, Office of Administrative Law Judges, Office of Policy Planning, Office of Inspector General, Bureau of Competition, Bureau of Economics, and Bureau of Consumer Protection.

The Bureau of Consumer Protection enforces a variety of consumer protection laws enacted by Congress, as well as trade regulation rules issued by the FTC. Its actions include individual company and industrywide investigations, administrative and federal court litigation, rule-making proceedings, and consumer and business education. In addition, the bureau contributes to the commission's ongoing efforts to inform Congress and other government entities of the impact that proposed actions could have on consumers.

The Office of Congressional Relations works with members of Congress. The office informs FTC staff of Capitol Hill issues and policies and helps provide information on legislation of interest to the commission. It also coordinates the preparation of both congressional testimony and responses to congressional inquiries concerning FTC policies and programs.

The Office of Equal Employment Opportunity investigates complaints of discrimination based on race, color, national origin, religion, disability, sex, reprisal, sexual orientation, genetic information, and parental status.

The Office of International Affairs' main role with the FTC is to work with competition and consumer protection agencies around the world to promote cooperation and convergence toward best practices.

The Bureau of Competition is considered the antitrust arm of the FTC. Its job is to prevent anticompetitive business practices and stop business mergers that are anticompetitive. By doing this, the FTC promotes consumers' freedom to choose goods and services in an open marketplace at a price and quality that fit their needs. This is also good for other, similar businesses, as it guarantees opportunity for businesses by ensuring a level playing field among competitors.

The Bureau of Economics helps the FTC by providing economic analysis and support to consumer protection and antitrust investigations and rules. It also analyzes the impact of government regulation on competition and consumers and provides the government with economic analysis of market processes related to antitrust, consumer protection, and regulation.

In addition, the FTC has regional offices that cover seven geographic areas. The regional offices work with the Bureaus of Competition and Consumer Protection to conduct investigations and litigation; provide advice to state and local officials on the competitive implications of proposed actions; recommend cases; provide local outreach services to consumers and businesspersons; and coordinate activities with local, state, and regional authorities.

Ekaterini Chrisopoulos-Vergos

See Also Clayton Antitrust Act of 1914; Sherman Antitrust Act of 1890

Further Reading

Federal Trade Commission. N.d. www.ftc.gov.

Resources for Teachers

admongo.gov. N.d. "Teachers." www.admongo.gov/teachers.aspx.

Bonner, Patricia. 2007. "Deceptive Advertising: Crossing the Line." econedlink. www.econedlink.org/lessons/index.php?lid=663&type=educator.

Scholastic. N.d. "Admongo.gov, Advertising Literacy Lessons for Grades 5 and 6." Accessed April 25, 2013. www.scholastic.com/admongo/.

Federal Trade Commission Act of 1914

Even though the year was only 1914, the government aimed to maintain a competitive marketplace while serving as the protector of the unsuspecting consumer to unfair business practices. The passage of the Federal Trade Commission Act of 1914 created the Federal Trade Commission (FTC). The FTC was created with the mission to police the marketplace for noncompetitive business practices that would take advantage of the consumer. This stance by the FTC included enforcement and policing business practices on one end, and educating the consumer to be aware of these practices.

The FTC was granted the power to place "cease and desist" orders on companies as a way to enforce and prevent unfair business and trade practices. While creating the Federal Trade Commission, the act also gave Congress additional authority. The act established the Federal Trade Commission as the only federal agency with authority over and responsibilities to both the producer and consumer. It was to prevent the continuation of unfair, deceptive, or illegal business practices on the producer side, and serve as a form of marketplace police to protect the consumer and respond to consumer complaints from such practices.

The balancing act for the FTC was to oversee both sides of the market without interrupting or distorting the market or negatively influencing legal business activity with unintended consequences of its policies. A goal of the FTC from the beginning was to promote competition through the prevention of illegal business practices. Implementation of these policies without upsetting the balance of the marketplace was tricky and delicate. Often the FTC was seen as overstepping its bounds and being more of the problem than the solution.

Another goal of the FTC was to provide an authority for educating consumers to be watchful of the unfair business practices the FTC was also enforcing. This involved serving as marketplace police but also being the marketplace educator of the consumer. Through the FTC, consumers were educated on how to suspect unfair business practices and what business practices the FTC considered noncompetitive so the consumer could report their activity, and on when they were being victims of unscrupulous, unfair, or illegal business activity.

The Sherman Antitrust Act was signed in 1890 as a first step to attack and break up the business trusts such as Standard Oil. When President Woodrow Wilson signed the Federal Trade Commission Act on September 26, 1914, business trusts were still very active in the U.S. business environment. One objective of the FTC was to continue to pursue and break up the business trusts as they were currently structured. The Federal Trade Commission Act was considered by some as a follow-up to the 1890 Sherman Antitrust Act as consumer protection.

While working to break up the trusts, the FTC had two mandates relative to the consumer. One, protect the consumer and two, educate the consumer. The FTC was assigned to serve in the consumers' place to lodge complaints against unfair or illegal business practices. Once a consumer complaint was filed, it was the FTC's responsibility to investigate, and if necessary prosecute the offending business. The FTC is very active in its law enforcement against businesses and on behalf of the consumer.

A third goal of the FTC is to research, collect data, and serve as a clearinghouse of consumer protection information for Congress and other national governments that have companies doing business in the United States, state governments, consumers, and businesses. In this capacity, the FTC also conducts seminars and workshops, conferences, and educational programs for both businesses and consumers.

The Federal Trade Commission itself is comprised of five members appointed for seven-year terms by the president. The Federal Trade Commission has several internal departments, including the Bureau of Consumer Protection and the Bureau of Competition and Economics. The FTC also has seven regional offices across the United States and an office of general counsel. Its headquarters are in Washington, D.C.

David A. Dieterle

See Also Federal Trade Commission; Sherman Antitrust Act of 1890

Further Reading

Cornell University Law Information Institute. N.d. "5 USC § 41: Federal Trade Commission Established; Membership; Vacancies; Seal." http://www.law.cornell.edu/uscode/text/15/41.

Federal Trade Commission. N.d. "About the FTC." http://www.ftc.gov/ftc/about.shtm.

Federal Trade Commission. N.d. "Federal Trade Commission: A History." http://www.ftc.gov/ftc/history/ftchistory.shtm.

Resources for Teachers

Center for the Advancement of Capitalism. N.d. "The Federal Trade Commission Act of 1914 (As Amended Thru 1996)." http://www.capitalismcenter.org/Advocacy/antitrust/other_resources/FTC_Act.htm.

Federal Trade Commission. N.d. "Consumer Information." http://www.consumer.ftc.gov/.

Page, Brian. 2013. "Mobile Phones Matter." econedlink. http://www.econedlink.org/lessons/index.php?lid=1150&type=educator.

Financial Reform Act of 2010 (Dodd-Frank Act)

The Financial Reform Act was an effort to reform financial regulation and avoid a financial crisis similar to the crisis of 2008. President Barack Obama signed the act into law on July 21, 2010. The law is also known as the Dodd-Frank Wall Street Reform and Consumer Protection Act, or simply "Dodd-Frank," in reference to the significant work of Senator Christopher J. Dodd (D–CT) and Representative Barney Frank (D–MA) to create and pass the bill through their respective chambers of Congress. Dodd-Frank is one of the most extensive financial reforms since the Banking Act of 1933 (Glass-Steagall Act), which was created after numerous bank failures due to excessive speculative investment ventures.

Specifically, it ends the possibility of taxpayers being businesses asked to write a bailout check to failing. Dodd-Frank, also known for its massive length, establishes new agencies and reorganizes the roles and responsibilities of others to preempt future large-scale financial woes.

The act established the Financial Stability Oversight Council, consisting of a chair—the Secretary of the Treasury—as well as 10 federal financial regulators, an independent member, and five nonvoting members (OFR, FIO, state banking insurance, and securities regulators). The council's purpose is to identify risks for U.S. financial stability from financial and nonfinancial organizations, promote market discipline, and respond to emergency risks to the U.S. financial system.

The Orderly Liquidation Authority and Fund monitors companies deemed "too big to fail" and assists in the liquidation of failing companies to prevent widespread economic problems. The tough new capital and leverage requirements make it undesirable to be too big.

The new Office of Financial Research, headed through presidential appointment and Senate confirmation, works within the Department of Treasury to support the council's work collecting financial data and conducting economic analysis. It monitors emerging risks to the economy and makes information public in reports and testimony to Congress. The director reports to and testifies before the Senate Committee on Banking, Housing, and Urban Affairs and the House Committee on Financial Services of the House of Representatives.

The Federal Insurance Office, working within the Department of Treasury, serves to monitor the insurance industry for gaps in regulation that could cause systemic risk, gaps in access to affordable insurance for underserved communities, and in other insurance matters.

The act also creates the "Volcker Rule," named for former chair of the Federal Reserve and proposer of the rule Paul Volcker. The Volcker Rule restricts the trading that financial companies can do with their own accounts and limits their ability to take excessive risks. It restricts owning, investing, or sponsoring hedge funds, private equity funds, or proprietary trading for their own profit. Some have considered the Volcker Rule as a semireturn to the banking regulations under the Glass-Steagall regulations, while others claim that the Volcker Rule did not go far enough.

The new Consumer Financial Protection Bureau, housed and funded within the Federal Reserve, consolidates the functions of many different agencies. It works to write rules, supervise companies, and enforce federal consumer financial protection laws. It also serves to promote financial education and monitor financial markets for new risks to consumers. In addition, it works to enforce laws that outlaw discrimination and other unfair treatment in consumer finance. The president appoints its director (who is confirmed by the Senate) and it has an independent budget paid for by the Federal Reserve.

New rules for the Federal Reserve allow it to provide system-wide economic support (but not for individual firms) and establish uniform standards and supervision for the management of risk. It also creates a vice chair for supervision—a member of the Board of Governors—to develop policy recommendations regarding supervision and regulation for the board reporting to Congress semiannually.

The act requires the Securities and Exchange Commission (SEC) or the Commodity Futures Trading Commission (CFTC) to regulate credit rating agencies to avoid overrating risky derivatives like credit default swaps.

To streamline bank regulation and oversight, the act eliminates the Office of Thrift Supervision.

Kathryn Lloyd Gustafson

See Also Banking Act of 1933 (Glass-Steagall Act); Bernanke, Ben; Federal Reserve System; Securities and Exchange Commission (SEC); United States Treasury; Volcker, Paul

Further Reading

Brost, Kirstin. N.d. "Summary: Restoring American Financial Stability." Senate Committee on Banking, Housing, and Urban Affairs, Chairman Chris Dodd (D–CT). www.banking.senate.gov/public/_files/FinancialReformSummary231510FINAL.pdf.

Dennis, Brady. 2010. "Congress Passes Financial Reform Bill." *Washington Post*, July 16. www.washingtonpost.com/wp-dyn/content/article/2010/07/15/AR2010071500464.html.

The Economist. 2012. "The Dodd-Frank Act Too Big Not to Fail." *The Economist*, February 18. www.economist.com/node/21547784.

Frank, Barney, and Christopher J. Dodd. 2010. "Dodd-Frank Wall Street Reform and Consumer Protection Act." H.R. 4173, July 21. www.sec.gov/about/laws/wallstreetreform-cpa.pdf.

Jackson, Jill. 2010. "Wall Street Reform: A Summary of What's in the Bill." *CBS News*, June 25. www.cbsnews.com/8301-503544_162-20008835-503544.html.

Rowlan, Karda. 2010. "Historic Wall Street Reform Bill Signed." *Washington Times*, July 21. www.washingtontimes.com/news/2010/jul/21/obama-signs-financial-reform-law/.

Resources for Teachers

federalreserveeducation.org. N.d. "The Fed Today." www.federalreserveeducation.org/resources/fedtoday/FedTodayAll.pdf.

federalreserveeducation.org. N.d. "Page One Economics: Financial Regulation; A Primer on the Dodd-Frank Act." www.federalreserveeducation.org/resources/detail.cfm?r_id=e0b3c476-481b-4e6a-a72b-930942fa89cf.

Fiscal Policy

Fiscal policy is a government's intentional use of spending and tax policy to influence the economy. Fiscal policy is the responsibility of the federal and state governments. Government's involvement in an economy using the tools of fiscal policy was first suggested by John Maynard Keynes in his 1936 classic, *The General Theory on Interest, Money, and Employment*. Keynes suggested the use of fiscal policy during two economic periods. One was during economic recessions when government should serve as a third partner in a market economy and stimulate demand, increasing incentives of individuals and businesses to consume and invest. The second period was during times when an economy is "overheating" (demand was outstripping supply) and government should implement fiscal policy to slow down the economy.

The primary tools of fiscal policy are government spending and taxes. Which tool to use is determined by the incentives government would like to promote and the economic problem that needs to be solved. To address a lack of consumer spending, government would likely implement a reduction in taxes to stimulate consumer spending and business investment. If the government would like to decrease unemployment, it would increase its spending on public structures such as roads, bridges, dams, and schools. This was a popular use of fiscal policy by President Franklin Roosevelt. Many of his New Deal initiatives involved government spending on the public's infrastructure.

Fiscal policy is most influencing during times of recessions or when economic expansions are too fast for the economy to absorb. During times of recession, government can implement fiscal policies using one or both tools. A government could increase its spending, making it possible for more people to be employed, resulting in a household having more money to buy goods and services. A second option for the government would be to cut taxes, increasing the amount of a person's take-home pay to spend on goods and services.

However, if the economy is growing too fast, that threatens inflation. The government can decrease government spending, leaving fewer opportunities for jobs and thereby decreasing individuals' ability to buy goods and services. If the government chooses to use taxes as the fiscal policy tool, it would increase taxes, leaving individuals with less money to buy goods and services.

The main problems of fiscal policy deal with time lags between identification, implementation, and the time between identifying and the effects of a fiscal policy solution impacting the economy. The first time lag is in recognizing that an economic problem needs to be addressed. This leads to the time lag created by the political process in approving a fiscal policy solution, or the implementation time lag. As a result of fiscal policy being determined through the political process and with different economic philosophies of fiscal policy represented in the Congress or a state legislature, this lag can often be significant. Once a need for a fiscal policy solution is identified, a proposed solution needs to pass through the legislative process in a prompt enough time frame to be effective. This implementation lag time may lead to a fiscal policy solution being implemented at a time after the crisis that required it has passed.

The time taken during the implementation lag leads to a third lag: the impact or effect lag. Beyond recognizing the problem and implementing a solution, and the solution impacting the economy, this lag may make the fiscal policy solution worsen the economic crisis or create a new economic problem.

As part of fiscal policy responsibility, Congress has instituted automatic stabilizers for an economy. These are programs that automatically go into effect when the economy warrants. Two programs that automatically impact the economy without actions from either Congress or the president are unemployment benefits and the progressive tax structure for income taxes.

David A. Dieterle

See Also Keynes, John Maynard; New Deal; Roosevelt, Franklin Delano

Further Reading

Hansen, Bent. 2008. *The Economic Theory of Fiscal Policy*. London: Routledge.

Kopcke, Richard W., Geoffrey M. B. Tootell, and Robert K. Triest. 2005. *The Macroeconomics of Fiscal Policy*. Cambridge, MA: MIT Press.

Resources for Teachers

Foundation for Teaching Economics. N.d. "Fiscal Policy." http://www.fte.org/teacher-resources/lesson-plans/rslessons/fiscal-policy/.

Herman-Ellison, Lisa C. 2007. "Fiscal and Monetary Policy Process." econedlink. http://www.econedlink.org/lessons/index.php?lid=352&type=educator.

Free Rider

A free rider is anyone who benefits from a public good or service without paying for it. In economic terms, free riders are considered beneficiaries of a market failure. Economists view the free riders as beneficiaries of market failure because of the fact that in many instances, no one can be excluded from using the public good and everyone can enjoy the good without taking it away from someone else.

The free rider problem stems from the use of public goods and services. Things such as street lights, police services, and national defense can all be considered public goods and services. At one time or another, everyone will need the use of these goods and services, but the problem lies in the fact that not everyone who benefits from their use actually contributes to paying for their cost. Unlike private goods and services, which can only be used by the person who purchased them, public goods and services are available to everyone, and one person using those goods and services does not stop another person from enjoying those same goods and services at the same time.

For example, streetlights that illuminate a neighborhood at night are a public good used by everyone who lives in or visits the neighborhood. Everyone within the neighborhood benefits from having the streetlights, regardless of whether they live in the neighborhood or are just visiting. Yet only those who live in the neighborhood have paid the taxes to provide the streetlights. Everyone else within the boundaries of the neighborhood benefitting from the streetlights is a free rider as they have not paid for the streetlight.

No one can stop people from using the streetlights, regardless of who pays the taxes that supply them. One person using the streetlight does not mean that others in the neighborhood cannot. If the electrical company tried to get money from residents on the street based on their consumption of the benefit provided by the streetlights, they would be unable to see who used the most and who used the least.

All public goods have a free rider problem, including national public goods such as national defense. The military defends the nation in times of need, and everyone in the nation enjoys the benefits of this defense. The military receives its pay from the government, which in turn taxes citizens in order to pay for these costs. The free rider problem occurs when those who do not pay taxes enjoy the benefits of national defense alongside those whose taxes go toward funding the cost of this protection.

Ekaterini Chrisopoulos-Vergos

See Also Externalities; Market Failure; Public Goods

Further Reading

O'Neill, Ben. 2007. "Solving the 'Problem' of Free Riding." Auburn, AL: Ludwig von Mises Institute. http://mises.org/daily/2769.

Tuck, Richard. 2008. *Free Riding*. Cambridge, MA: The President and Fellows of Harvard College.

Wolf, Sebastian. 2004. *Obstacles to Strong Democracy: Prisoner's Dilemma and Free Rider Effect-Seminar Paper*. GRIN. Accessed May 21, 2013. http://www.grin.com/search?searchstring=Obstacles+to+Strong+Democracy%3A+Prisoner%E2%80%99s+Dilemma+and+Free+Rider+Effect-+Seminar+Paper&product=ebook&source_type=document.

Resources for Teachers

Kehler, Abbejean. 2007. "The Mystery of Is It Mine or Ours?" econedlink. http://www.econedlink.org/lessons/index.php?lid=462&type=educator.

Niederjohn, Scott. 2006. "No Fireworks on the 4th of July." econedlink. http://www.econedlink.org/lessons/index.php?lid=626&type=educator.

VanFossen, P. 2010. *Market Structures and Market Failures. Econ Alive! The Power to Choose.* Madison, WI: Teachers Curriculum Institute.

Friedman, Milton

Born: July 31, 1912, in Brooklyn, New York; Died: November 16, 2006, in San Francisco, California; American; monetary policy, price theory, public policy, monetary history, Nobel Prize (1976); Major Works: *A Theory of the Consumption Function* (1957), *Capitalism and Freedom* (1962), *A Monetary History of the United States, 1867–1960* (1971).

Milton Friedman is considered one of the most influential economists of the twentieth century for his ability to explain and defend the merits of free markets and individual freedom. Friedman was also considered the embodiment of the Chicago school of economics with an emphasis on monetary policy, free markets, and less government intervention. Friedman was instrumental in the economic policies of President Ronald Reagan and Prime Minister Margaret Thatcher. Milton Friedman won the Nobel Prize in Economics in 1976, and President Reagan honored him with the Presidential Medal of Freedom in 1988. Friedman died in 2006.

Milton Friedman was born in Brooklyn, New York, on July 31, 1912. Growing up in New Jersey in the home of immigrant Hungarian parents, young Friedman graduated from the public high school when he was 15, a month before his sixteenth birthday. He was destined for college, but the untimely death of his father during his senior year narrowed his college direction to Rutgers University. Financing his own education with the help of a small scholarship, Friedman graduated from Rutgers University in 1932. Originally a mathematics major planning on becoming an actuary, he became interested in economics. Friedman graduated from Rutgers with a double major in mathematics and economics.

Encouraged to pursue graduate work in economics, Friedman accepted a scholarship to the University of Chicago. His early experiences there framed his economics and research philosophies. During this time at the University of Chicago, he met the woman who would become his wife and lifelong working partner, Rose Director. After one year at the

University of Chicago, Friedman received a fellowship to Columbia University. Even though he returned to the University of Chicago after only one year at Columbia, he received his PhD in economics from Columbia in 1946.

In 1935, Friedman was recruited by his friend W. Allen Wallis to join him on the National Resources Committee in Washington, D.C. Friedman's role on the committee was to continue earlier work on a consumer budget study. It was this work on the consumer budget study that became the basis for one of the two key components of his later groundbreaking work, *A Theory of the Consumption Function*.

In 1937, Friedman accepted a position with the National Bureau of Economic Research (NBER). At NBER, he worked with Simon Kuznets, publishing *Incomes from Independent Professional Practice*. Kuznets and Friedman introduced the concepts of permanent and transitory income. They also initiated a debate among Washington bureaucrats by asserting that the incomes of physicians were higher than dentists due to the monopoly power of physicians. For Friedman, this study also provided the second key component of his later work on the consumption function.

Friedman continued his work in Washington during World War II. From 1941 to 1943, he directed his efforts toward tax policy at the U.S. Treasury. In 1943, he joined his friend Wallis again, this time at Columbia University, applying his mathematical and statistical expertise on military tactics, design, and metals. After one year at the University of Minnesota, in 1946, Friedman returned to the University of Chicago. He would remain at the University of Chicago until his retirement from active teaching in 1977. Another close friend, Arthur Burns, who was directing NBER, persuaded Friedman to rejoin NBER. Friedman remained with NBER till 1981.

In 1953, Friedman wrote "The Methodology of Positive Economics." He argued that the validity of economic theories should be based on the ability to predict human behavior. He followed this in 1957 with his classic *A Theory of the Consumption Function*. Friedman's case was that it was necessary to think of individuals making rational spending and saving decisions over a lifetime. The basis was a return to his earlier work with Kuznets and the permanent income hypothesis. His thesis in *A Theory of the Consumption Function* was also a return to classical economic thinking, which had been replaced in the middle of the twentieth century by the economic philosophies of John Maynard Keynes.

Friedman's launching of the Money and Banking Workshop at the University of Chicago set the academic and research foundation for his next target in economic research: monetary policy. The research and publications that originated from the workshop highlighted the Chicago school of economics' emphasis on the role of monetary policy as the key determinant to inflation and business cycles.

Friedman's work explaining the role of the money supply and monetary policy on an economy earned him an international reputation. His monetary policy theories were highlighted in 1969 with *The Optimum Quantity of Money and Other Essays*. The workshop provided the environment for many contributors and researchers to generate significant work on monetary policy. Through his work with the workshop and NBER, he began a collaboration with economic historian Anna J. Schwartz. In 1971, they wrote the classic *A Monetary History of the United States, 1867–1960*.

Another groundbreaking accomplishment in economic theory for Milton Friedman came when he suggested that the popular inflation-unemployment rate trade-off was not necessarily a long-run trade-off, as most assumed. In 1967, while he acknowledged a short-run trade-off, he asserted that government intervention to keep inflation high to promote low unemployment would eventually fail, with ultimately both unemployment and inflation rising. This argument would be proven correct in the 1970s, and the ensuing period that became known as stagflation.

In 1976, Friedman was awarded the Nobel Prize in Economics for his work on consumption, monetary history, and stabilization policy. In 1986, he received the Japanese government's Grand Cordon of the First Class Order of the Sacred Treasure. In 1988, he received both the Presidential Medal of Freedom from President Reagan and the National Medal of Science.

After his retirement from active teaching, he became involved in public affairs and public policy. He assisted presidential candidates Barry Goldwater, Richard Nixon, and Ronald Reagan as an economic adviser during their campaigns. He would later serve as an economic adviser to Presidents Nixon and Reagan. He also began writing columns for the popular news magazine *Newsweek* promoting the virtues of individual freedom and markets unfettered by government intervention.

In 1981, he served on President Reagan's Economic Policy Advisory Board. Friedman is given significant credit for the economic philosophies of President Reagan and Prime Minister Margaret Thatcher in the 1980s and later decades of the twentieth century. Friedman was viewed as the opposition to the popular theories of John Maynard Keynes that dominated economic thought and political economic policy after World War II through the 1970s.

Friedman's popularity with the general public reached its pinnacle in 1980 with the release of the popular 10-part series *Free to Choose*. Coauthored with his wife, Rose, the series was accompanied by a book of the same name. The book was a nonfiction best seller in 1980, a rare occurrence for one with the high academic stature of Milton Friedman. Since its release, the series and book have been translated into 14 languages; the series can be seen in many foreign countries.

Friedman concluded his career at the University of Chicago as the Paul Snowden Russell Distinguished Service Professor Emeritus of Economics. He also served the Hoover Institution at Stanford University as a senior research fellow.

Milton Friedman died on November 16, 2006, in San Francisco, California.

David A. Dieterle

See Also Burns, Arthur; Keynes, John Maynard; Kuznets, Simon

Selected Works by Milton Friedman

Friedman, Milton. 1991. *Money Mischief: Episodes in Monetary History*. Reprint ed. Orlando, FL: Harcourt Brace.

Friedman, Milton. 1976. *Price Theory*. Piscataway, NJ: Aldine.

Friedman, Milton. 1969. *The Optimum Quantity of Money and Other Essays*. New York: Macmillan.

Friedman, Milton. 1966. *Essays in Positive Economics*. Chicago: University of Chicago Press.

Friedman, Milton. 1962. *Capitalism and Freedom*. Chicago: University of Chicago Press.

Friedman, Milton. 1957. *A Theory of the Consumption Function*. Princeton, NJ: Princeton University Press.

Friedman, Milton, and Rose Friedman. 1984. *The Tyranny of the Status Quo*. Orlando, FL: Harcourt.

Friedman, Milton, and Rose Friedman. 1980. *Free to Choose: A Personal Statement*. Orlando, FL: Harcourt.

Friedman, Milton, Leonard J. Savage, and Gary Becker. 2007. *Milton Friedman on Economics: Selected Papers*. Chicago: University of Chicago Press.

Friedman, Milton, and Anna Jacobson Schwartz. 1971. *A Monetary History of the United States, 1867–1960*. Princeton, NJ: Princeton University Press.

Selected Works about Milton Friedman

Ebenstein, Lanny. 2012. *The Indispensable Milton Friedman: Essays on Politics and Economics*. Washington, DC: Regnery.

Ebenstein, Lanny. 2007. *Milton Friedman: A Biography*. Basingstoke, UK: Palgrave Macmillan.

Friedman, Milton. N.d. "Autobiography." Nobelprize.org. http://nobelprize.org/nobel_prizes/economics/laureates/1976/friedman-autobio.html.

Friedman, Milton, and Rose Friedman. 1998. *Two Lucky People: Memoirs*. Chicago: University of Chicago Press.

Lindbeck, Assar, ed. 1992. *Nobel Lectures, Economics 1969–1980*. Singapore: World Scientific.

G

Galbraith, John Kenneth

Born: October 15, 1908, in Dunwich Township, Ontario, Canada; Died: April 29, 2006, in Cambridge, Massachusetts; American; general economics, economic policy; Major Works: *American Capitalism: The Concept of Countervailing Power* (1952), *The Great Crash of 1929* (1954), *The Affluent Society* (1958).

John Kenneth Galbraith was quite possibly the most widely read economist of the mid-twentieth century. He authored over 30 books. His best-known work, *The Affluent Society*, published in 1958, became a popular read for the general population as well as for academics. Galbraith is credited with coining terms that are now part of the economics and political lexicon, including "conventional wisdom," "countervailing power," and, of course, "the affluent society." Galbraith was known for addressing the economics topics and issues of the day as part of everyday life and not as an esoteric science. Galbraith died in 2006.

John Kenneth Galbraith was born on October 15, 1908, in Ontario, Canada, and raised on a small farm in Dunwich Township, Ontario. Of Scottish descent, his father was a farmer and schoolteacher who had a major influence on young Galbraith's early views of politics and his liberal philosophy. He attended Ontario Agricultural College (OAC), taking courses to be a farmer. While at OAC, he became more interested in the economics of farming than in farming itself. He completed his undergraduate work at the University of Toronto and went on to complete his master's and doctorate in agricultural economics at the University of California, Berkeley, in 1934.

Galbraith's writing notoriety started early in his academic career while at the University of California, Berkeley. This early success led him to Harvard, where he joined the faculty as an instructor in 1934. In 1937, he received a fellowship to attend Cambridge University and study under John Maynard Keynes. During the Depression, the theories of Keynes were dominating both the economic and political landscapes. This single year under Keynes was to be the turning point in Galbraith's career. Yet he admitted that his economic philosophy was also influenced by Thorstein Veblen.

Returning to Harvard from Cambridge, he remained at Harvard only one more year. In 1939, Galbraith joined the economics faculty at Princeton University. He also became an American citizen. However, with the outbreak of World War II, Galbraith joined President Roosevelt's administration, becoming an administrator in the Office of Price Administration. As administrator of wage and price controls, he gained a contentious reputation with industry. He resigned his post in 1943.

After holding various positions both in and out of government, including a brief term as a writer for *Fortune* magazine, which introduced the United States to both John

Maynard Keynes and his U.S. protégé, John Kenneth Galbraith, he returned to Harvard in 1949. This began what was to become his period of famous lectures and even more famous writings.

In 1952, Galbraith wrote *American Capitalism: The Concept of Countervailing Power*. In *American Capitalism*, he submitted the idea that U.S. economic power was concentrated between corporations on one side and unions on the other. These countervailing forces kept the U.S. economy in equilibrium. Also in 1952, Galbraith wrote *A Theory of Price Control*. In 1954, Galbraith wrote *The Great Crash of 1929*, suggesting that the same errors made in 1929 were being made in 1955. He went so far as to testify to the U.S. Senate that another "crash" was likely to occur.

His influence reached its zenith in 1958, when *The Affluent Society* was published. With *The Affluent Society*, Galbraith became a global success. He suggested that U.S. businesses had overproduced, leading consumers to overspend without thought to solving the social issues of the day. He went on to predict inflationary and recessionary dynamics with the overemphasis on private goods and with public goods being the trade-off.

One area where Galbraith was ahead of his time was in thinking about economic progress and its impact on the environment. He blamed advertising for frivolous spending at the expense of addressing environmental concerns as well as the social benefits to society. Along with several other writers of the 1950s, Galbraith began to change the public views of an economic system that would best suit a postwar United States.

Beyond his work in the Roosevelt administration, Galbraith also had a significant influence in the later political arena. An avowed political liberal, he was influential in shaping the ideas and views of the Democratic Party in the 1950s and 1960s. He advised presidential candidate Adlai E. Stevenson and eventual president John F. Kennedy on the Keynesian view of how to best deal with the economy. He was also instrumental in devising and promoting President Lyndon Johnson's Great Society program. During this period, he was also a speechwriter for Roosevelt, Kennedy, and Johnson. Galbraith served as ambassador to India under President Kennedy.

Galbraith was not without his critics. As popular as he was with the general public, the economic academic community regarded his writings as often too simplistic to be highly regarded. Others considered his blatant liberal political views as interfering with his economic objectivity. One area where his ideas were later disputed was advertising. As he submitted in *The Affluent Society*, he blamed advertising as the cause of an overly consumption-oriented economy. This notion was later countered by Nobel laureates Gary Becker and George J. Stigler using mathematical proofs that advertising was indeed informative to the consumer and not leading them to undesired consumption.

In 1967, Galbraith called for a new class of policy decision makers in *The New Industrial State*. In 1973, Galbraith wrote *Economics and the Public Purpose*. He called for socialism, an increase in central planning, increasing tax progressivity, and more public housing and medical care, along with nationalizing some corporations that serve the federal government. In 2004, at the age of 95, Galbraith published *The Economics of Innocent Fraud*, a short book that questioned much of standard economic wisdom.

John Kenneth Galbraith received many awards, the most prestigious of which was the Medal of Freedom, which he received twice, first in 1946 from President Harry Truman and again in 2000 from President Bill Clinton. In 2001, Galbraith received India's Padma Vibhushan, its second-highest civilian award. In Canada, he received the Officer of the Order of Canada in 1997, and in Dutton, Ontario, the library was renamed the John Kenneth Galbraith Reference Library. In 2010, he was (posthumously) the first economist to have his popular works included in the Library of America series.

John Kenneth Galbraith died on April 29, 2006, in Cambridge, Massachusetts.

David A. Dieterle

See Also Keynes, John Maynard

Selected Works by John Kenneth Galbraith

Galbraith, John Kenneth. 1996. *The Good Society*. New York: Houghton Mifflin.

Galbraith, John Kenneth. 1981. *A Life in Our Times*. Boston: Houghton Mifflin.

Galbraith, John Kenneth. 1967. *The New Industrial State*. Boston: Houghton Mifflin.

Galbraith, John Kenneth. 1964. *The Scotch*. New York: Houghton Mifflin.

Galbraith, John Kenneth. 1958. *The Affluent Society*. Boston: Houghton Mifflin.

Galbraith, John Kenneth. 1954. *The Great Crash of 1929*. New York: Houghton Mifflin.

Galbraith, John Kenneth. 1952. *American Capitalism: The Concept of Countervailing Power*. Boston: Houghton Mifflin.

Galbraith, John Kenneth. 1952. *A Theory of Price Control*. Cambridge, MA: Harvard University Press.

Selected Works about John Kenneth Galbraith

Parker, Richard. 2005. *John Kenneth Galbraith: His Life, His Politics, His Economics*. New York: Farrar Straus Giroux.

Stanfield, J. R. 1996. *John Kenneth Galbraith*. London: Macmillan.

Stanfield, J. R., and J. B. Stanfield. 2004. *Interviews with John Kenneth Galbraith*. Jackson: University Press of Mississippi.

George, Henry

Born: September 2, 1839, in Philadelphia, Pennsylvania; Died: October 29, 1897, in New York City; American; political economy, editor, publisher, social reformer; Major Work: *Progress and Poverty: An Inquiry into the Cause of Industrial Depressions and of Increase of Want with Increase of Wealth: The Remedy (1886)*.

Henry George was a political economist who promoted the reforms of taxation and trade to benefit society as a whole. He developed his philosophy from his life experience without formal education or class privilege. His ideas were embraced by vast numbers of followers worldwide and are taught in "Georgist" schools of economics today. George argued that taxes and the government banking system favored the few at the expense of the masses and demanded social justice for citizens without regard to race and sex. He believed he had found a method of spreading wealth and dedicated his life to sharing it with the world. George died in 1897.

Henry George was born on September 2, 1839, in Philadelphia, Pennsylvania, the son of Richard S. H. George and Catherine Pratt Valliance George. The second of 10 children, he quit school at 15 to work in an office and aboard a ship bound for India and Australia. He later wrote about seeing small numbers of wealthy Indians compared to the majority of citizens. Upon his return home, George learned to set type. When the printing business declined, he was hired to work aboard a ship sailing to California. When he arrived on the West Coast, he worked as a typesetter before joining his cousin's mining store in British Columbia on the Frazer River.

In 1858, his enthusiasm for gold prospecting waned and he returned to San Francisco. After struggling financially, he found a job as a newspaper printer and writer. A speaker he heard on the topic of protectionism challenged his thinking about the negative impact of protectionism on individual prosperity. The editor of two small newspapers, George began to promote the benefits of free trade. The tariffs supported by protectionists kept prices for goods high. He saw that tariffs enriched a few at the expense of the majority. George found growing support for his viewpoint and was encouraged to run for a state office. He lost the election but was gaining a following for his ideas.

His writing promoted free trade, and then another idea stirred his conscience: land use reform. The common folks, barely eking out a living, outnumbered the few land speculators who were enriched by railroad and other developments. The seed of his best-known work, *Progress and Poverty*, began with a magazine article published on September 18, 1877.

A year and a half later, in 1879, George completed his first book and self-published the first 500 copies. The thesis of the book was that it was immoral to charge and collect rents on raw land that individuals had not created. George submitted that what nature had provided could not be owned by individuals. People would own only what they themselves produced. George concluded that poverty was caused by the private ownership of land, which resulted in wealth for a small minority. He observed that land values depended on someone's need for the land and believed that this policy threatened democracy.

A single tax on land, not on improvements to land, was the only tax morally justified in George's view. He believed that all other taxes should be abolished and that since landowners did nothing to create the value of the land they owned, they should not extract increasingly higher rent from laborers. He concluded that the land's value was created by the need of someone to use it. Common working men found a hero in Henry George, and they rallied around him. Additional volumes of his book were printed, and eventually sales surpassed all other volumes except for the Bible. At 42 years old, George became world famous, and was a popular public speaker on the topic of political economy. Europeans and Australians invited him to speak.

Renowned European economist Alfred Marshall debated George, who was considered a leader inspiring great societal changes beyond the United States. Proponents of land reform arose, empowered by the Henry George movement. He was warmly welcomed by the British and the Irish working classes and social reformers. The well-known scientist

Alfred Russell Wallace touted the significance of *Progress and Poverty*. George's public policy influences were popular as far away as Australia and New Zealand.

Politicians and union leaders desired his affiliation. The United Labor Party, a sector of Democrats who opposed the Tammany Hall political machine, supported his candidacy for mayor of New York City in 1886. They presented a petition signed by over 30,000 New Yorkers that helped convince George to run. He lost to Democrat Abram Stevens Hewitt and beat Republican Theodore Roosevelt.

Although George was maligned as a socialist and a communist, he participated in political campaigns to spread his message and appeal for broadened support of his ideology. As editor of the New York–based paper *The Standard*, George continued to educate the populace about the morality of his brand of economics. He published *The Condition of Labor*; *The Science of Political Economy*; and *Protection or Free Trade*, which became a part of the Congressional Record of 1890. He used every opportunity to spread his message by traveling and debating.

In George's final campaign for mayor of New York, in 1897, he represented his former affiliation, renamed the Party of Thomas Jefferson. He was in poor health but decided to press on. The campaign would allow him to influence more people to consider his views on economic practices, which he was convinced would alleviate the suffering of the impoverished.

Henry George's ideas are still discussed and debated today. In many cities, Henry George Schools of Social Science exist to continue teaching his philosophy of economics. Because he was one of the common folk with no formal education and no influential family, and because of his moral basis to fight for equality, justice, and fairness, the appeal of his policies endures.

Henry George died days before the mayoral election, on October 29, 1897, in New York City.

Cynthia Blitz Law

See Also Command Economy; Democratic Socialism; Economic Systems; Welfare State

Selected Works by Henry George

George, Henry. 1912. *The Land Question*. New York: Doubleday, Page.

George, Henry. 1891. *The Condition of Labor: An Open Letter to Pope Leo XIII*. New York: United States Book.

George, Henry. 1886. *Progress and Poverty: An Inquiry into the Cause of Industrial Depressions and of Increase of Want with Increase of Wealth: The Remedy*. New York: D. Appleton.

George, Henry. 1886. *Protection or Free Trade*. New York: Doubleday, Page.

George, Henry, Francis Amasa Walker, William Saunders, and Francis George Shaw. 1911. *Social Problems, A Perplexed Philosopher*. New York: Doubleday, Page.

Selected Works about Henry George

Cottler, Joseph. 1936. *Champions of Democracy*. Boston: Little, Brown.

Formaini, Robert L. 2005. "Henry George Antiprotectionist Giant of American Economics." *Economic Insights* 10, no. 2: 1–4.

George de Mille, Agnes. N.d. "Who Was Henry George?" Accessed March 30, 2011. http://www.progress.org/books/george.htm.

"Labour Land Campaign." N.d. Australian School of Social Science. Accessed March 30, 2011. http://www.labourland.org/lvt/what_is_lvt.php.

Post, Louis. 2002. *The Prophet of San Francisco.* Honolulu, HI: University Press of the Pacific, 1904. Reprinted by the Minerva Group.

Gibbons v. Ogden, 22 U.S. 1 (1824)

A Supreme Court Case That Gives the Federal Government the Ability to Maintain Uniform and Equal Rule of Law within the Whole of the United States

Economic Concepts

Barter; commodities; creative destruction; entrepreneur; free enterprise; monopoly; rule of law; property rights

Economic Impact

The Supreme Court addressed the monopoly in transportation issue. In addition, it addressed the issue of states' responsibility versus the authority of the federal government to make laws regarding business and commerce, specifically interstate transportation. As on many occasions throughout history, this case was also a case of creative destruction, as technology was changing the face of an industry, in this case the transportation industry. Creative destruction is an economic concept allowing old methodologies of manufacturing, production, or distribution to be replaced with new methodologies.

Economic Summary

In the late 1700s, the introduction of steam to drive boats spurred a rush of innovation. A race began to build a better engine that would be designed to make a profitable industry from this new power source. Among the many entrepreneurs and inventors in this race, Robert Fulton, in 1807, was the first to make steamboating a commercial success. Between 1807 and 1814, the *North River Steamboat* (also known as the *Clermont*) operated as a commercial transportation vessel on the North River (now known as the Hudson River). This commercial success was due in part to his partner, the former chancellor of New York, Robert R. Livingston (1746–1813), who negotiated the legal details with the legislature that gave it exclusive right to operate steamboats on waters within the state of New York—in other words, a monopoly.

Fulton and Livingston sold franchises to rivals who wanted a part of the industry. Aaron Ogden bought a license from them in 1815. Ogden's business associate, Thomas Gibbons, began an operation of steamboats between Elizabethtown, New Jersey, and New York City. In 1818, Gibbons began an independent steamboat line, much to Ogden's annoyance.

To stop Gibbons, Ogden sued him in a New York court and won. Gibbons appealed to the United States Supreme Court. The greatest questions in this case were how to interpret the commerce clause and the boundaries to the supremacy clause of the U.S. Constitution. Finally, in an era of invention and growth of industry, what is the responsibility of the state and federal government to make laws regarding business, industry, and commerce? The Court addressed these questions, and Chief Justice John Marshal clarified commerce and supremacy.

Case Summary

Robert R. Livingston was one of the committee of five who wrote the Declaration of Independence. As the chancellor of New York, he held the highest judicial position in the state and swore in George Washington as the first president of the United States. With this political clout, it was not a stretch for Livingston to secure for his partner, Robert Fulton, the exclusive authority to navigate the waters of New York with steam-powered engines. This created a legal monopoly of navigation by steam of all waterways in and around New York.

Establishing rule of law and property rights in a free enterprise system is fundamental. Early in the history of the United States, the Articles of Confederation allowed such laws and rights to be maintained by state legislatures. In the federal system established by the U.S. Constitution, states granting legal monopolies for commerce between states was brought into question. *Gibbons v. Ogden* solved the dilemma of who was the legitimate authority to regulate interstate commerce. Thomas Gibbons was a former Tory (colonist who was loyal to the British King during the Revolutionary War), lawyer, businessman, and Mayor of Savannah, Georgia. Gibbons left Georgia for New Jersey in 1801, where he joined into business with Aaron Ogden. Aaron Ogden was a former Revolutionary War hero and governor of New Jersey who, after a license fee, secured from Livingston and Fulton a franchise to operate a steamboat business between Elizabethtown, New Jersey, and New York City.

By 1818, Gibbons and Ogden were at odds with one another. Gibbons started his own steamboat business with a license obtained from Congress under a 1793 law that pertained to the regulation of trade along the coastline. Gibbons partnered with Commodore Cornelius Vanderbilt to operate a steamboat from New Jersey to New York. Ogden sued Gibbons in a New York State court to stop him. The state court held that securing navigational rights to waterways was a concurrent power, not one expressly given in the Constitution to the federal government. Gibbons' lawyer, Daniel Webster, argued that the Constitution did in fact give the power to regulate trade between the states explicitly to the federal government and that this state law conflicted with the U.S. Constitution.

The New York court ruled in favor of Ogden, perpetually enjoining Gibbons from navigating the waters of the state of New York with steamboats the *Stoudinger* and the *Bellona*. Gibbons appealed this case to the Supreme Court.

The Supreme Court heard arguments in February 1824. Fulton and Livingston were deceased by this time, while Ogden was heading to debtors' prison and Gibbons was determined to succeed. The appellant maintained that the laws allowing a state to regulate interstate commerce were in opposition to the U.S. Constitution.

The state of New York disagreed, and contended that New York was the legitimate authority in such business matters. New York defined commerce as traffic and the buying and selling of commodities. Chief Justice Marshall defined commerce differently. The Court included navigation and the power to regulate the vessels of one state into the port of another state to engage in buying or selling or barter. This was the definition the writers of the Constitution had intended when they expressed this power in Article I, Section 8. Consequently, New York argued that regulation of the coastal waters surrounding the state was a concurrent power.

The Supreme Court disagreed with this as well. Chief Justice Marshall's opinion stated that concurrent powers were such that by their practical operations, they needed to reside in different levels of government. For example, the power to lay and collect taxes is essential to maintaining government function at any level and therefore is concurrent. By contrast, the power to regulate commerce is appropriate in the hands of the federal government for the purpose of maintaining a more perfect union and securing domestic tranquility within the nation. However, the Court did recognize that there would be gray areas where states may pass laws that interfere with or are contrary to an act of Congress.

The framers of the Constitution foresaw this collision of powers and provided for it in Article VI of the U.S. Constitution, declaring the supremacy not only of the Constitution, but also of the laws made in pursuance of it. Finally, New York laws only pertained to vessels with steam engines, not sails. The Supreme Court expressed the opinion that steam-propelled vessels were entitled to the same privileges and protections that vessels using sails were. The rule of law includes a level playing field for innovation in a free enterprise economy. Hence, requiring only steam-powered vessels to obtain a license from private citizens who possessed exclusive legal monopolies on certain technologies was construed as a hindrance.

This case established the federal government as the legitimate authority to determine regulation of commerce among the states and the U.S. Constitution as the supreme law of the land. On March 2, 1824, a unanimous opinion of the court reversed and annulled the decree of the Court of New York, ruling in favor of Gibbons. This case illustrates the supremacy clause of the Constitution, which gives the federal government the ability to maintain uniform and equal rule of law within the whole of the United States.

Kathleen C. Simmons

See Also Contracts; Private Property

Related Cases

Ware v. Hylton, 3 U.S. 199 (1796)

Martin v. Hunter's Lessee, 14 U.S. 304 (1816)

Cohens v. Virginia, 19 U.S. 264 (1821)

Further Reading

Cox, Thomas H. 2009. *Gibbons v. Ogden, Law, and Society in the Early Republic*. Athens: Ohio University Press.

Johnson, Herbert Alan. 2010. *Gibbons v. Ogden: John Marshall, Steamboats, and the Commerce Clause*. Lawrence: University Press of Kansas.

Resources for Teachers

Levinson, Isabel Simone. 1999. *Gibbons v. Ogden: Controlling Trade between States*. Berkeley Heights, NJ: Enslow Publishers.

OYEZ, ITT Chicago, Kent School of Law. N.d. "*Gibbons v. Ogden*." http://www.oyez.org/cases/1792-1850/1824/1824_0.

www.ourgovernments.gov. N.d. "*Gibbons v. Ogden* (1824)." http://www.ourdocuments.gov/doc.php?flash=true&doc=24#.

Glass-Steagall Act (See Banking Act of 1933)

Government Failure

When markets fail to provide the right amount of a good or service or provide too much of a bad thing, i.e., an externality—in other words, when a market failure occurs—citizens expect the government to step in and be the remedy. Consumers expect government to supply the desirable quantity of a good or service or protect the consumer/citizen from harm or economic hardship through the efforts of others. Often, government will interfere with those markets with success. However, there are times when a government will interfere with a market and the outcome expected by government's intervention is not the outcome achieved. These consequences are known as government failures. Even though one may automatically think of a government failure at the national level, government failures occur at the state and local levels of government as well.

Government failures occur for many reasons. Some government failures are the result of the influence and political self-interest of special interest groups, the self-interest of political and civil servants to preserve programs or jobs, or government intervention that results in overregulation at the expense of consumers. Government actions often lead to creating disincentives or avoidance activity by businesses or consumers, or a government action falls victim to the law of unintended consequences.

When government failures occur, several consequences develop. One consequence is when the economic costs of a government decision outweigh the economic benefits realized. Since many times components of the economic costs and economic benefits of an activity are estimated and fairly subjective, this often leads to disagreements as to whether a government action was a failure, a success, or some of both. Certainly, trade policies of a government to protect an industry or special interest group would be an example of this type of government failure. On the one side, consumers would view the protectionist policy of the sugar tariff as a government failure since it makes consumers pay a higher price for sugar and other food items. For the consumer, the economic costs outweigh the economic benefits. Yet the corn industry views this government action quite differently, as it receives significant economic benefits from higher corn prices, and relative to the production of corn-based ethanol versus sugar-based ethanol.

Another type of government failure is when a government action to change behavior does not produce the desired change of action. For example, a government may act to curtail pollution through fines and penalties. While the governmental unit may impose the fine or penalty on a polluting company, if the fine or penalty is not severe enough to alter the company's behavior regarding its polluting activity, the company will be inclined to pay the fine and continue polluting. While the government may collect the fine, it did not accomplish the purpose of the fine by altering the company's polluting activity. If the fines and penalties are too heavy, the penalized company may close its facility and move elsewhere. While the closed or moved company would certainly not pollute anymore, the negative economic impact on the locale would most definitely be a heavy and unwanted consequence of the government action.

There are times when government failure occurs from the fact that the regulations being imposed are outdated. During these times, it is up to the government to update or eliminate its policies. There are times when this occurs through the government itself taking action, as the federal government did in deregulating the airline industry and eliminating the Civil Aeronautics Board. At other times, the courts imposed actions on the government to take, as with the communications industry and the federal government giving monopoly power to AT&T (see 1994 Supreme Court case *MCI Telecommunications Corp. v. American Telephone and Telegraph Co.*). This type of government failure is also seen at the local level as communities grow, or shrink, and current local policies either inhibit growth or prevent a community from addressing a changing demographic or geographic disparity. Many Midwest communities, such as Detroit, Michigan, or Dayton, Ohio, experience this type of government failure as they try to transform themselves for the future economy.

Interestingly, there have also been times in history when government action can be seen as a government failure through government interfering and regulating a market that did not exist. The famous Yak Fat Caper of the Interstate Commerce Commission (ICC) is one example. While it could be considered a government failure, there were no serious consequences to the action outside of some embarrassing moments for the ICC.

David A. Dieterle

See Also Market Capitalism; *MCI Telecommunications Corp. v. American Telephone and Telegraph Co., 512 U.S. 218 (1994)*; Protectionism

Further Reading

Economics Online. N.d. "Government Failure." http://www.economicsonline.co.uk/Market_failures/Government_failure.html.

IJReview. N.d. "Unintended Consequences: 14 Big Government Programs That Failed to Achieve Their Goals." http://www.ijreview.com/2013/01/33536-biggest-government-failures-of-the-last-century/.

Lee, Dwight R., and J. R. Clark. 2013. "Market Failures, Government Solutions, and Moral Perceptions." *Cato Journal* 33, no. 2 (Spring/Summer 2013): 287–97. http://object.cato.org/sites/cato.org/files/serials/files/cato-journal/2013/5/cj33n2-10.pdf.

Resources for Teachers

Focus: Understanding Economics in Civics and Government. N.d. "Lesson 13: Government Failure; Using Public Choice Theory to Analyze Political Decisions." http://civics.councilforeconed.org/lesson.php?lid=13.

Master Resource. 2009. Hertzmark, Donald. "Rent Seeking, Crony Capitalism, and U.S. Energy Politics: Who Wins from the Racket?" August 5. http://www.masterresource.org/2009/08/rent-seeking-crony-capitalism-and-us-energy-politics-who-wins-from-the-racket/.

Great Depression (1929–1939)

The Great Depression is arguably the most traumatic economic event in the history of the United States. It was a period of global economic stagnation that lasted a decade. One of its main effects was that more Americans began to accept the idea that the government should be more involved in the economy.

The 1920s were a time of economic expansion in the United States. However, the economy began to weaken in 1929, and a succession of events sent the nation into a plunge: on October 29, now known as Black Tuesday, stock market prices plummeted. In 1930, a drought began that ruined the crops of farmers throughout most of the United States. This was the era that became known as the Dust Bowl. Farmers were often deeply in debt and, when their crops failed, they could not pay back their loans to the banks, which in turn caused the banks to go out of business. Even more severe damage was caused to the banking system when depositors began to panic and pull all their savings out of the banks, causing a steady string of bank failures from 1930 through 1933. Additionally, President Hoover signed the Tariff Act of 1930, usually known as the Smoot-Hawley Tariff (after the congressmen who wrote it), which raised taxes on imported goods. This tariff, along with similar policies passed by other nations in response to it, caused a sharp drop in international trade that worsened the situation.

In past recessions, Americans had generally presumed that the national government should not intervene in an economic crisis. But the 1930s brought a change of mind-set. The president of the United States, Herbert Hoover, was known as "The Engineer"—that is, as a brilliant man who could understand the nation and fix its problems. Accordingly, he worked with a favorable Congress to enact a string of government actions to keep wages from falling and to ensure public confidence in the economy. He made large corporations promise not to decrease wages (a promise that they kept), initiated construction of public works such as the Boulder Dam (now called the Hoover Dam), and signed the above-mentioned tariff into law. He refused to increase government debt, so he paid for the increased spending by raising corporate taxes and income taxes for wealthy Americans. These actions did not improve the economy. Instead, unemployment skyrocketed, reaching 25 percent by 1932 (see www.stlouisfed.org/great-depression/pdf/GD_g-lesson_4.pdf). Hoover was defeated for reelection by Franklin Delano Roosevelt, and a great many members of Congress were elected who were favorable to Roosevelt's view of governing and his view of government involvement in the economy.

Though Hoover had believed in a more active government than had past presidents, his approach was quite conservative compared to Roosevelt's. President Roosevelt had adopted the new writings and philosophy of the British economist John Maynard Keynes

(1883–1946). Keynes's economic views promoted an even greater participation of government in the economy. Immediately upon taking office, Roosevelt launched what he called the New Deal. With the goals of relief, recovery, and reform, the New Deal increased government spending, provided government jobs for people who were unemployed, abolished the gold standard (a version of which was reinstated after World War II), increased prices for farm crops by cutting production, established Social Security, reformed the banking industry, and made many other government interventions in the name of jump-starting the economy. The results were mixed. A hesitant recovery began in 1933, but was interrupted by another recession in 1937. The outbreak of World War II in 1939 ended mass unemployment as European nations relied on American production to supply their war efforts, and the United States itself prepared for conflict.

The lessons to be drawn from the period are not entirely clear. Some economists blame too much government spending for the length and severity of the Depression. Others say there was not enough spending by government. Still others blame labor policies that were intended to keep wages high.

The idea from the Great Depression that has drawn the support of most macroeconomists has focused on proper monetary policy in times of deep recession or depression. The most important lesson learned and the most significant factor in the crisis was the Federal Reserve Board's failed contractionary monetary policy of increasing interest rates, which led to a collapse of the money supply. This collapse brought on thousands of bank failures, kept unemployment at historically high levels, and the Federal Reserve deserves the blame for not instituting expansionary monetary policy. Instead, it neglected to pump enough new money into the economy. For this reason, the Federal Reserve System is now seen as the main force for combating recessions. At the time, the disaster of the 1930s ushered in a change in mind-set regarding the relationship of the government to the economy. The popularity of the New Deal programs of President Roosevelt during the Great Depression shows Americans had an increased tolerance in the early and mid-twentieth century for a larger, more activist government.

Stephen H. Day

See Also Bernanke, Ben; Contractionary Monetary Policy; Expansionary Fiscal Policy; Federal Reserve System; Friedman, Milton; Keynes, John Maynard; Keynesian Economics; New Deal; Roosevelt, Franklin Delano

Further Reading

Egan, Timothy. 2006. *The Worst Hard Time: The Untold Story of Those Who Survived the Great American Dust Bowl.* Boston: Mariner Books.

The Great Depression. N.d. "Lesson 4: Dealing with the Great Depression." N.d. http://www.stlouisfed.org/great-depression/pdf/GD_g-lesson_4.pdf.

Johnson, Paul. 2006. *Modern Times: The World from the Twenties to the Nineties.* New York: Harper Perennial.

Shlaes, Amity. 2009. *The Forgotten Man: A New History of the Great Depression.* New York: Harper Collins.

Resources for Teachers

edtechTeacher. N.d. "The Great Depression." Best of History Web sites. Accessed April 15, 2013. www.besthistorysites.net/index.php/american-history/1900/great-depression.

Federal Reserve Bank of St. Louis. N.d. "The Great Depression Lesson Plans." www.stlouisfed.org/great-depression/curriculum.html.

OwlTeacher. N.d. "Unit 17: The Great Depression." Accessed April 15, 2013. www.owlteacher.com/the-great-depression.html.

Great Society

There are moments in history when time stands still. In those moments, anyone living old enough to remember has etched in their memory exactly where they were and what they were doing. The day President John F. Kennedy was assassinated, November 22, 1963, was one of those days. History took another turn with that fateful event. With the assassination of President Kennedy, Lyndon Baines Johnson became president of the United States. The new president began to institute his agenda for a new day in civil rights, urban renewal, and lifting the general welfare of the citizens. The Great Society is commonly seen as the most far-reaching agenda of domestic legislation since the New Deal. The genesis of this new legislation lay in speeches President Johnson gave in 1964 at Ohio University and the University of Michigan.

The 1964 election was a definite choice in different approaches to government's participation and involvement in the U.S. economy. President Johnson's Great Society initiatives and Barry Goldwater's promise to reduce the size and reach of the federal government in the 1964 presidential election were definitively ideological and pragmatic polar opposites. The voters' choice was clear. Johnson won 46 states, capturing 61 percent of the popular vote. Johnson was secure with such a margin of victory; he had a mandate and the support of the American people. In his 1965 State of the Union address, he proposed his plans for a Great Society. With a cooperative Congress, his plans moved quickly, and many new government programs were legislated. Roosevelt introduced society to the New Deal; Johnson introduced it to the Great Society. First, however, was completing the legacy of President Kennedy with the passing of the Civil Rights Act in 1964.

As expected, many aspects of U.S. life were impacted by the programs launched by Johnson in the name of the Great Society. Foremost was the Economic Opportunity Act of 1964. The act created two new agencies to address the economic and social needs of those in poverty. The Job Corps and Volunteers in Service to America (VISTA) were created to fight poverty at home. The Job Corps was initiated as a program to help young people ages 16 to 24 receive vocational training. VISTA had the look of President Kennedy's Peace Corps, only with a domestic agenda, as young people were trained and placed in the poverty-stricken urban and rural areas of the United States to assist with uplifting the living standards regarding the most basic human needs. The Economic Opportunity Act of 1964 also made loans available to farmers, small businesses, and community programs to fight poverty.

A second major area of American life impacted by the Great Society was the entire educational spectrum from primary to secondary to higher education. At the preschool level, Head Start was launched as a preschool summer program for low-income children to prepare them for school in areas such as basic early childhood education, the importance of parental involvement, health, hygiene, and nutrition. In 1965, the Elementary and Secondary Education Act funded federal programs for the first time in the elementary and secondary education. The Higher Education Act provided financial assistance to those wishing to pursue a college education. The private sector had the Job Corps; education now had the National Teacher Corps through the Higher Education Act.

The United States was changing from an urban to suburban society in the 1960s. The civil rights movement was having an impact on the nation's urban areas. A third area addressed by the Great Society was urban renewal and conservation. Johnson created the Department of Housing and Urban Development (HUD) with the signing of the Housing and Urban Development Act of 1965. This act greatly increased federal funding in urban areas for public housing and addressed the needs of blighted urban areas. On the conservation side, Johnson increased federal funding to regulate water and air quality with the Highway Beautification Act.

Access to health care was another endeavor of the Great Society, especially for two specific groups, low-income families and senior citizens. For many, these two groups were one and the same. For the low-income population, the Great Society provided Medicaid, and for senior citizens, Medicare. Both Medicaid and Medicare made medical care both accessible and affordable for both these groups. In the case of Medicare, all evidence through the years has shown that it has positively impacted the standard of living of senior citizens.

The architect for much of Johnson's Great Society was Republican John Gardner. Gardner was selected by Johnson to lead the Department of Health, Education, and Welfare. President Johnson had the vision and ideas for the Great Society. John Gardner, as head of Health, Education, and Welfare, had the implementation know-how.

Many of the programs started during the Johnson Administration as part of the Great Society are still operational federal programs. Programs such as Medicare and Medicaid, Head Start, and the Elementary and Secondary Education Acts are government programs that are part of the American fabric. Of course, many of these programs, as with any government program, have their critics, who believe government is overreaching into these areas of our life. But their impact on American life since the mid-1960s cannot be denied.

Maura Donnelly
David A. Dieterle

See Also Entitlements; New Deal

Further Reading

Andrew, John A. 1998. *Lyndon Johnson and the Great Society*. Chicago: I. R. Dee.

DeWisconsin, Henry. 2010. *Great Society: A Dark Comedy.* Bloomington, IN: AuthorHouse.

Helsing, Jeffrey W. 2000. *Johnson's War/Johnson's Great Society: The Guns and Butter Trap.* Westport, CT: Praeger.

Milkis, Sidney M., and Jerome M. Mileur, eds. 2005. *The Great Society and the High Tide of Liberalism*. Amherst: University of Massachusetts Press.

Resources for Teachers

Discovery Education. N.d. "Lesson Plan Library: Lyndon B. Johnson." Accessed December 10, 2013. http://www.discoveryeducation.com/teachers/free-lesson-plans/lyndon-b-johnson.cfm.

LBJ Presidential Library. N.d. "LBJ's Great Society Lesson Plan & Documents." http://www.lbjlibrary.org/assets/uploads/education/GreatSociety_LessonPlan.pdf.

Stanford History Education Group. N.d. "Great Society Lesson Plan; Central Historical Question: Was the Great Society Successful?" Accessed December 10, 2013. http://sheg.stanford.edu/upload/Lessons/Unit%2012_Cold%20War%20Culture%20and%20Civil%20Rights/Great%20Society%20Lesson%20Plan1.pdf.

Greenspan, Alan

Born: March 6, 1926, in New York City; American; monetary policy, chairman of the Federal Reserve System, 1987–2006; Major Work: *The Age of Turbulence: Adventures in a New World* (2007).

Alan Greenspan served an unprecedented five terms as chairman of the Federal Reserve System (the Fed). While chairman, he experienced the stock market crash of 1987, fallout from the savings and loan (S&L) scandal, a record increase in the market, followed by the bursting of the dot-com and housing bubbles. He is a fiscal conservative, believing in free market economics. He believes in creative destruction—that is, allowing some companies to fail, freeing resources for newer companies.

Alan Greenspan was born in Washington Heights, in New York City, on March 6, 1926. He received training at the Juilliard School in 1943 (clarinet) before enrolling at New York University (NYU) in 1944, receiving his bachelor of science (1948) and master of arts (1950) degrees. His pursuit of a PhD from NYU was interrupted by his work experience, but he would earn the degree in 1977.

Greenspan began his career in 1950 with the National Industrial Conference Board. He would gain political attention for his research of the Defense Department's use of metal, twice published in the *Business Record*. In 1953, he formed a partnership with William Townsend called the Townsend-Greenspan Company. During this time he met Objectivist and author Ayn Rand. He was greatly influenced by her views. He would write several articles in the 1960s for Rand's *The Objectivist Newsletter*, and she would include essays by him in her collection called *Capitalism: The Unknown Ideal*.

Greenspan's first political post was in 1967, as a volunteer economic and domestic policy adviser for Richard Nixon's 1968 presidential campaign. He served on the Commission on an All-Volunteer Armed Force, which worked to abolish the draft in 1970. Just before President Nixon resigned in 1974, Greenspan became chairman of the Council of Economic Advisers, serving as an economic adviser to the president. He remained on the council through Gerald Ford's administration, helping to devise policies to fight inflation and unemployment. In 1980, he helped Ronald Reagan's campaign. He served on the Economic Policy Board and later worked to overhaul Social Security.

President Reagan appointed Greenspan chairman of the Fed in 1987. He inherited a national situation that had seen vast increases in the stock market and a tripling of the federal deficit under Reagan, plus an increase in inflation, measured by the consumer price index (CPI). When he increased interest rates in September 1987, the stock market experienced its largest single-day drop (508 points) on Black Monday, October 19. The Fed responded by buying billions of dollars of treasury securities (increasing liquidity), encouraging lending by the Fed's member banks. The markets began to stabilize by November and growth resumed in the first quarter of 1988.

Greenspan continued his role as chairman of the Fed into the George H. W. Bush administration, though his relationship with the president was more strained under a difficult economy. Greenspan worked with the Resolution Trust Corporation to resolve issues with the S&L scandals of the late 1980s, which resulted in the federal government being saddled with about $87 billion in losses, less than expected. The recession continued into the 1990s despite the Fed lowering interest rates. The administration wanted rates cut lower, but Greenspan believed that the short-term benefit would quickly lead to a long-term inflation problem. Bush reappointed Greenspan as chairman of the Fed in 1991.

Under President Clinton, Greenspan encouraged passage of a 1993 budget that would begin to reverse the trend of steadily rising national debt. Greenspan believed that this was necessary to encourage businesses to invest more and allowed the Fed to lower rates to sustain long-term growth. Following pressure by Congress to allow more transparency, Greenspan agreed to announce immediate moves of the Federal Open Market Committee. The Fed raised interest rates a quarter point in 1994 as a preemptive strike against inflation, the first increase in five years. The stock market would grow amid the dot-com boom of the late 1990s and Greenspan warned of irrational exuberance in investing. He believed the boom would not last long. Clinton reappointed Greenspan in 1996 and 2000 under a strong economy. As the dot-com bubble was bursting in 2000, Greenspan believed that the growing surplus of the federal budget should be used to pay down the national debt and that "triggers" should be implemented to prevent a reversal in the surplus.

Under George W. Bush, following the terrorist attacks on 9/11 and in response to recession, the Fed cut interest rates several times to stimulate the economy. Greenspan disagreed with the president's plans to continue to cut taxes to stimulate the economy, figuring it was more important to control the deficit, and was displeased with the president's unwillingness to veto spending bills.

Greenspan is often criticized for politicizing the Fed. Despite being a libertarian Republican, he often praised both parties when they acted in a fiscally conservative manner. He also received criticism for the economic downturn of the 2000s, with many claiming his monetary policy was too lax. Since finishing his record fifth term as Fed chairman, Greenspan has accepted some fault for the problems related to the economy that could be linked to the Fed.

Joseph Lee Hauser

See Also Burns, Arthur; Volcker, Paul

Selected Works by Alan Greenspan

Greenspan, Alan. 2007. *The Age of Turbulence: Adventures in a New World.* New York: Penguin Press.

Greenspan, Alan. 2004. *A History of the Federal Reserve, 1913–1951.* Vol. 1. Chicago: University of Chicago Press.

Selected Works about Alan Greenspan

Kahaner, Larry. 2000. *The Quotations of Chairman Greenspan: Words from the Man Who Can Shake the World.* Holbrook, MA: Adams Media.

Martin, Justin. 2001. *Greenspan: The Man behind the Money.* Cambridge, MA: Perseus Books.

Sheehan, Frederick. 2010. *Panderer to Power: The Untold Story of How Alan Greenspan Enriched Wall Street and Left a Legacy of Recession.* New York: McGraw-Hill.

Woodward, Bob. 2000. *Maestro: Greenspan's Fed and the American Boom.* New York: Simon & Schuster.

Gross Domestic Product (GDP)

Gross Domestic Product (GDP) is the main measurement of the size of a nation's economy. It represents the market value of all final goods and services produced within a country in a given year. It is an important economic indicator that measures the total economic output of a country. In general, a growing Gross Domestic Product is considered a sign of positive economic health.

In the United States, the job of calculating GDP falls to the Bureau of Economic Analysis (BEA), within the Department of Commerce. The bureau publishes its findings quarterly, and its comprehensive report is closely watched by the chief architects of both fiscal and monetary policy, as well as by the business sector. The economists who measure GDP can do so through an income method, a value-added approach, and an expenditure method. In the income approach, GDP is measured as the sum of the incomes earned and the costs incurred in production. In the value-added approach, economists add the "value added" at each stage of the production process (equivalent to the total sales minus the value of the intermediate inputs).

The expenditure method is the most common of the methods of calculating GDP. GDP is calculated by adding together the final value of goods and services in the four main sectors of the economy: household consumption (C), business investment (I), government purchases (G), and the net of exports minus imports (NX); GDP = C + I + G + (NX).

For the calculation, only "final" products are calculated: those goods or services at the last stage before consumption, rather than intermediate goods, which are inputs in the production process. If intermediate goods were included in the GDP calculation, it would overstate the value of production by counting products several times before they reached their final form in the market. So economists rely on the final value of goods and services only. The calculation results in a figure known as nominal, or "current dollar," GDP, which reflects the output of the economy in current prices, demonstrating the purchasing power of dollars in the year they are spent.

Nominal GDP does not take inflation into account so it is impossible to know, when comparing nominal GDP from year to year, how much of the growth is a result of inflation and how much is an increase in real output. To compensate for the effects of inflation, the Bureau of Economic Analysis also calculates real GDP, which shows the value of an economy's output in constant dollars. Real GDP allows economists to compare GDP from year to year to show the rate of growth. For example, the report of the Commerce Department for the second quarter of 2013 showed that real GDP increased at a rate of 2.5 percent. This means that even accounting for inflation of the dollar, there was growth in the overall size of the U.S. economy from the first quarter of the year to the second quarter. Each GDP report also explains the reasons for the growth or decline by identifying the segment(s) of the economy that changed the most, such as business investment, consumer spending, or government expenditures. Real GDP is the best measurement for showing economic growth over time.

It is also important to note that GDP includes only those goods produced within the United States. It includes the output of foreign companies producing within the United States, but does not include the output of U.S. companies producing in foreign countries.

Economists can also adjust the GDP for population, which allows them to compare the economies of individual countries. Per capita GDP takes population into account by counting GDP "per person," rather than the total amount for the country as a whole. This calculation involves taking a country's real gross domestic product and dividing it by the population. This calculation is often used to determine a nation's standard of living. It is the most accurate measurement when comparing the GDPs of various countries because it averages it out over the number of people living in that country. China's GDP may seem significant at over 8 trillion (2012), but when dividing that up over the substantial number of people living in China, it averages to a per capita GDP of $6,188. When compared to the total GDP of the United Kingdom, which is $2 trillion, China's GDP might appear larger, but upon calculating the UK's per capita rate of $38,000, it is considerably lower (see http://data.worldbank.org/).

While GDP is a widely accepted calculation for determining a country's economic health, there are limitations to GDP as an economic indicator. For instance, GDP does not take all productive activity into account. Economic activity that is not completed in the market, such as a homeowner's work on his or her personal home or an unpaid volunteer's work, is not included in the calculation. It also does not include leisure time, which is indicative of the overall well-being and satisfaction within a nation. Thus, GDP is understated. GDP also does not include the underground, or black market, economy—such as the activities of gamblers, smugglers, or drug dealers—in its calculations. Additionally, GDP does not take into account improvements in product quality over time. It does not consider the by-products of increased production, such as environmental harm. The calculation also does not tell us about how the output is actually distributed, so even per capita GDP fails to indicate the size of the gap between the wealthy and the poor.

It is commonly noted that as per capita GDP increases, so too do other factors associated with a higher standard of living, including the literacy rate and life expectancy. The infant mortality rate also tends to decrease as GDP increases.

GDP varies throughout the phases of the business cycle. It increases during periods of growth, stops increasing at the peak of economic growth, decreases during periods of contraction, and stops decreasing at the trough. If GDP falls for more than six months (two consecutive quarters), economists define that as a recession. Periods of depression tend to be identified with an even more substantial plunge in real GDP.

Michelle D. Holowicki

See Also Bureau of Economic Analysis; Department of Commerce; Economic Growth, Measures of

Further Reading

Bureau of Economic Analysis. N.d. "National Economic Accounts: Gross Domestic Product." www.bea.gov/national/index.htm#gdp.

Federal Reserve Bank of St. Louis (FRED). N.d. "Gross Domestic Product (GDP)." research.stlouisfed.org/fred2/series/GDP.

World Bank. N.d. "Data." http://data.worldbank.org/.

The World Bank. N.d. "GDP (current US $)." http://data.worldbank.org/indicator/NY.GDP.MKTP.CD.

Resources for Teachers

Council for Economic Education. N.d. "What Does the Nation Consume?" Accessed December 15, 2013. www.councilforeconed.org/lesson-resources/lessons/sample-lessons/Focus_Middle_School_Econ_Sample_Lesson.pdf.

federalreserveeducation.org. N.d. "GDP and Pizza." Accessed December 15, 2013. www.federalreserveeducation.org/resources/detail.cfm?r_id=6c32381f-b058-48c9-84f8-3034f9e74a57.

Group of Eight (G8)

The Group of Seven was officially formed in 1975. Previously known as the Group of Five (G5), the countries included were France, Germany, Japan, the United Kingdom, and the United States. Moving forward, the Group of Five added two more countries, which automatically changed its name, and adopted the new name the Group of Seven (G7), which consists of the following countries: France, Germany, Japan, the United Kingdom, the United States, Canada, and Italy. They are the seven wealthiest developed nations by global net wealth on the planet. The G8 represents more than 63 percent of net global wealth. Russia joined in 1998 to expand to the Group of Eight (G8). In 1999, a group of 20 nations (G20 or Group of 20) formed to address issues regarding the international financial system as the global economy expanded.

The G8 Summit has consistently dealt with macroeconomic management, international trade, and relations with developing countries. Questions of East to West economic relations, energy, and terrorism have also been of recurrent concern. From this initial foundation, the summit agenda has broadened considerably to include microeconomic issues such as employment and the information highway, transnational issues such as the environment, crime and drugs, and a host of political-security issues ranging from human rights through regional security to arms control. The summit also provides the international community with help in prioritizing and defining new issues and providing guidance to established international organizations.

The G8 is made up of finance ministers from the eight nations and central bankers. The G8 consists of annual meetings that are held three to four times a year involving the ministers who are also known as Sherpas. There are 6 to 10 meetings between senior officials. Presidents of the G8 countries also meet among themselves. There is no official legal status to the G8 and it does not have a permanent home like other similar organizations, i.e., the World Bank, the International Monetary Fund, and the United Nations.

The G8's meetings are geared toward discussing the main issue of economic interdependence. A form of international financial system has evolved from this interdependence. The discussions of the ministers and central bankers on such issues as national currencies, national financial systems, and global financial stability have led the G8 countries to formulate joint positions and led to a pseudoform of international financial system.

The G8 also meets during various times to discuss issues of energy, terrorism, economic development, drug-related money laundering, nuclear safety, and transnational organized crime. In order for the topics to be moved forward, leaders have created their own study groups to help them on particular issues that require urgent response. The G8 Summit gives leaders of the eight nations an opportunity to discuss complex issues as well as an opportunity to know each other on a personal level and to share success with each other in terms of the similarities in their developed nations.

Each calendar year, the responsibility of hosting the G8 rotates through the member states in the following order: France, United States, United Kingdom, Russia, Germany, Japan, Italy, and Canada. The holder of the presidency sets the agenda, hosts the summit for that year, and determines which ministerial meetings will take place.

The G8 also influences international communities by setting the necessary trade and energy standards to be adhered to by the international communities. During the G8 Summits, compliance is high when it comes to these topics.

Bernard P. Kanjoma

See Also European (Economic) Community; International Monetary Fund (IMF); World Bank; World Trade Organization (WTO)

Further Reading

Baker, Andrew. 2006. *The Group of Seven: Finance Ministries, Central Banks and Global Financial Governance*. Abington, UK: Routledge.

Global Research. N.d. "Deepening European Banking Crisis: G8 Holds Emergency Meeting." Accessed November 10, 2013. http://www.globalresearch.ca/deepening-european-banking-crisis-G8-holds-emergency-meeting.

Resources for Teachers

G8 Information Centre, University of Toronto. "What Is the G8?" 2012. Accessed November 10, 2013. http://www.g8.utoronto.ca/what_is_g8.html.

University of Illinois at Chicago. N.d. "Sea Island Summit: High School Lessons for Teaching About the G-8." Accessed May 21, 2014. http://dosfan.lib.uic.edu/ERC/g8usa/G8high_Lesson1.pdf.

Hayek, Friedrich von

Born: May 8, 1899, in Vienna, Austria; Died: March 23, 1992, in Freiburg, Germany; Austrian, naturalized English citizen; economic theorist, trade cycle theory, monetary theory, credit policy, Nobel Prize (1974); Major Works: *Profits, Interest and Investment* (1939), *The Pure Theory of Capital* (1941), *The Road to Serfdom* (1944), *The Constitution of Liberty* (1960).

Friedrich von Hayek was one of the most influential economists of the twentieth century. He not only made many important theoretical contributions in his field, but blazed new paths in political theory, history, philosophy, and theoretical psychology as well. His acceptance of the Nobel Prize in Economics in 1974 was for his penetrating work during the 1920s and 1930s in the area of business and trade cycle theory and the effects of monetary and credit policy. Hayek's prodigious output and legacy have helped to revive interest and respect in Austrian and neo-Austrian economics. Hayek died in 1992.

Friedrich August von Hayek was born May 8, 1899, in Vienna, Austria, the eldest of three sons of August von Hayek and Felicitas Hayek, née von Juraschek. Not only was Hayek's father a medical doctor and later a professor of botany at the University of Vienna, but his brothers Heinz and Erich were later to become Austrian professors as well, of anatomy and chemistry, respectively. In 1917, at the age of 19, Hayek served in an Austro-Hungarian artillery battery on the Italian front during World War I. After the war, Hayek entered the University of Vienna, receiving his doctorate in law in 1921 and a second doctorate in political economy in 1923. At university, Hayek attended the *Privatseminars* of Ludwig von Mises, later leading to a lifelong friendship and association. After attending New York University as a postgraduate research student in 1923–1924, Hayek returned to Vienna and joined Mises at the temporary Abrechnungsamt, or Office of Accounts, as a legal consultant. In 1927, with Hayek as its first director, he and Mises founded the Austrian Institute for Business Cycle Research in Vienna.

In 1928, invited to a London Conference on Economic Statistics, Hayek met John Maynard Keynes for the first time. They would later become friends, as well as fierce intellectual critics of each other's economic positions.

In 1929 Hayek was appointed to his first academic post as a privatdozent in economics and statistics at the University of Vienna and authored his first book, entitled *Geldtheorie und Konjunkturtheorie*, published in 1933 in English as *Monetary Theory and the Trade Cycle*. Seeing a connection between business cycles and capital and monetary theory, Hayek saw the market as an unplanned, spontaneous order that coordinates the activities of all factors of production.

Lionel Robbins invited Hayek to speak at the London School of Economics in 1931, leading to Hayek's publication of *Prices and Production*, which explained in greater detail his theory of underconsumption. Artificial increases in the money supply by central banks led Hayek to conclude that distortions between short- and long-term interest rates could create only "mal-investment." That same year, Hayek assumed the Tooke Chair as professor of economic science at the London School of Economics, a position that he held for 19 years. Between 1931 and 1937, Hayek was engaged in a number of anti-Keynesian critiques and essays, culminating in his 1938 work entitled *Collectivist Planning: Critical Studies on the Possibilities of Socialism*. He never, however, waged nor planned a full-scale refutation of *The General Theory of Employment, Interest and Money*, something he regretted later in life. In 1938, he became a naturalized British citizen.

During these years, von Hayek's most significant works included: *Profits, Interest and Investment* (1939); *The Pure Theory of Capital* (1941), which delved into the complex nature of capital as it relates to economic booms and slumps; *The Road to Serfdom* (1944); and *Individualism and Economic Order* (1948). There was no work that took Hayek and the publishing industry more by surprise than *The Road to Serfdom*. Its unlikely success put Hayek back into the spotlight, warning his readers how the "ideal" of planning popular in Great Britain at the time could quickly turn into a totalitarian nightmare. Originally intended for a British audience, the condensed *Reader's Digest* version gained him an audience in the United States and established him as the world's most celebrated classical liberal economist. In 1947, following the devastation of World War II, Hayek, anxious to revive classical liberalism in Europe, convened the first meeting of like intellectuals at Mont Pèlerin in the Swiss Alps, known later as the Mont Pèlerin Society.

In 1950, Hayek was appointed professor of social and moral science and member of the Committee on Social Thought at the University of Chicago. Over the next 12 years, Hayek produced some of his best and most diverse writings. These included *John Stuart Mill and Harriet Taylor: Their Friendship and Subsequent Marriage* (1951), *The Counter-Revolution of Science: Studies on the Abuse of Reason and The Sensory Order* (1952), *Capitalism and the Historians* (1954), and *The Constitution of Liberty* (1960), published on the 100th anniversary of the publication of John Stuart Mill's *On Liberty*. In this work, Hayek developed his view of the proper role of government, and his famous essay, "Why I Am Not a Conservative," was placed in the postscript.

In 1962, after 31 years out of his native Austria, Hayek left the University of Chicago and assumed a professorship at Freiburg University. In 1967, he published *Studies in Philosophy, Politics, and Economics*, dedicated to the philosopher Karl Popper. This work, unlike earlier studies, highlighted Hayek's outstanding breadth of intellectual knowledge. Though fighting ill health and irrelevance, Hayek published the first volume of his trilogy *Law, Legislation and Liberty: Rules of Order* in 1973.

In 1974, reinvigorated after being awarded the Nobel Prize, along with Swedish economist Gunner Myrdal, he completed the final two volumes of *Law, Legislation and Liberty*, subtitled *The Mirage of Social Justice* (1976) and *The Political Order of a Free People* (1979). By the late 1970s, as inflation ravaged the industrialized world and standard Keynesian prescriptions appeared to be ineffective, Hayek again found himself in great demand after 30 years, speaking extensively about free-market solutions to packed lecture halls throughout the world. Approaching the age of 90, Hayek wrote his final book, *The Fatal Conceit: The Errors of Socialism* (1988). This strong critique of socialism would nearly coincide with the dissolution in 1989 of the former Soviet superstructure that was based on a collectivist foundation.

Friedrich von Hayek died on March 23, 1992, in Freiburg, Germany, at the age of 93.

Joseph A. Weglarz

See Also Keynes, John Maynard; Mises, Ludwig von

Selected Works by Friedrich von Hayek

Hayek, Friedrich von. 1988. *The Fatal Conceit: The Errors of Socialism.* Chicago: University of Chicago Press.

Hayek, Friedrich von. 1960. *The Constitution of Liberty.* London: Routledge.

Hayek, Friedrich von. 1944. *The Road to Serfdom.* Chicago: University of Chicago Press.

Hayek, Friedrich von. 1941. *The Pure Theory of Capital.* London: Jarrold and Sons.

Hayek, Friedrich von. 1939. *Profits, Interest and Investment and Other Essays on the Theory of Industrial Fluctuations.* London: Routledge.

Selected Works about Friedrich von Hayek

Caldwell, Bruce. 2004. *An Intellectual Biography of F. A. Hayek.* Chicago: University of Chicago Press.

Ebenstein, Alan. 2003. *Hayek's Journey.* New York: Palgrave Macmillan.

Ebenstein, Alan. 2001. *Friedrich Hayek: A Biography.* New York: St. Martin's Press.

Hayek, F. A. 1994. *Hayek on Hayek: An Autobiographical Dialogue.* Edited by Stephen Kresge and Leif Wenar. Chicago: University of Chicago Press.

Heller, Walter

Born: August 27, 1915, in Buffalo, New York; Died: June 15, 1987, in Seattle, Washington; American; Keynesian, Council of Economic Advisers (1961–1964); Major Work: *Monetary vs. Fiscal Policy* (with Milton Friedman) (1968).

Walter Heller is best known from his time working on the Council of Economic Advisers under Presidents Kennedy and Lyndon Johnson from 1961 to 1964. He also was influential in the reconstruction of the West German economy after World War II while working as a tax adviser to the U.S. military government in Germany in 1947 and 1948. Heller returned to an earlier post with the University of Minnesota's Economics Department and retired a year before his death. He died in 1987.

Walter Wolfgang Heller was born on August 27, 1915, in Buffalo, New York, to German immigrant parents. He moved with his family first to Washington State, before settling in Milwaukee at age six. He received his BA in economics from Oberlin College in Ohio in 1935. He would complete an MA degree in 1938 and a PhD in 1941 from the University of Wisconsin while studying finance and taxation. He focused on state income tax laws for his dissertation, which he studied by touring 31 states, the District of Columbia, and Canada over the course of a year.

Heller would spend the next almost 20 years varying his work experience between government work and the education field, while becoming an expert on taxation. Between 1941 and 1945, he worked in tax research as a senior analyst in the Department of the Treasury. From 1945 until 1960, he was an associate professor at the University of Minnesota, missing time on occasion to perform various government jobs. In 1947, he spent a year in Germany as chief of finance for the U.S. military government, and would spend another year in Germany in 1951 studying German fiscal problems.

Heller's work in the 1950s would acquaint him more with the U.S. government. During Eisenhower's administration, Heller appeared before Congress on several occasions to encourage more federal spending on education and other programs, while also encouraging Congress to raise taxes. In 1952, he began to consult the United Nations on issues of encouraging growth and development of underdeveloped countries. From 1955 to 1960, he was an economic adviser and consultant to the governor of Minnesota and the Department of Taxation. In a 1957 article, he criticized the Committee for Economic Development's plan to create flexible tax rates and expenditures to adjust for inflation and deflation; he believed the plan failed to adequately consider short-run economic forecasts. In 1960, he assisted the nation of Jordan in reforming its taxation and fiscal policies.

Heller was sought out by President-elect Kennedy in 1960 to become the chairman of the Council of Economic Advisers. One of the main tasks for Heller would be to implement strategies to help the country get out of a slight recession that it had been in for about six months, though Heller linked the problem to a recession that the nation had not fully recovered from that was from 1957–1958. Kennedy's main focus was to use the Employment Act of 1946, which stated that the federal government should enact fiscal policy to maintain high employment and also created the Council of Economic Advisers, to its fullest potential.

Heller viewed the problem of recession as not being recovered until the nation's Gross National Product rose above previous levels, not just bouncing back to what it was before. To do this, he was not concerned with a balanced budget, but rather wanted to see more economic growth and unemployment down to around 4 percent, as opposed to the 7 percent in March 1961. One way he would attack this problem would be through adjusting tax rates to eliminate loopholes and tax advantages for certain groups, and lowering the tax range from 20 to 91 percent to 14 to 60 percent.

While working with Kennedy, Heller believed it was important to use forecasting tools to estimate how the economy was going to work. He also believed in the federal government's power to correct small problems with inflation and unemployment as needed through spending more. He supported cutting taxes in 1962 to pick up the lagging economy, a measure that was supported by Kennedy, who promised to enact it when it was necessary. The actual cut in taxes did not occur until February 1964, after Kennedy's assassination.

Heller maintained his position initially as Lyndon Johnson finished Kennedy's term, but he would resign by the end of 1964. Early in the year, Heller realized that cutting taxes was leading to higher inflation and reversed his position, calling for a tax increase, especially as U.S. involvement in Vietnam increased. Johnson did not take his advice. His decision to leave his post, however, is attributed more to his own personal circumstances and not his disagreement with Johnson. He returned to teaching at the University of Minnesota.

One of Heller's most well-known books is *Monetary vs. Fiscal Policy*, a record of his debate with Milton Friedman at New York University in 1968, which was a friendly give-and-take between a supporter of monetary policy and the Keynesian. Heller also contributed to the *Wall Street Journal* and *Time* magazine. His ideas about the use of tax cuts to stimulate the economy would be embraced by Republicans in the 1980s, specifically by Ronald Reagan and "supply-side economists." He has been called an "educator of presidents."

Walter Heller died in Seattle on June 15, 1987, at the age of 71, due to a heart attack.

Joseph Lee Hauser

See Also Keynes, John Maynard

Selected Works by Walter Heller

Heller, Walter. 1976. *The Economy: Old Myths and New Realities*. New York: Norton.

Heller, Walter, ed. 1968. *Perspectives on Economic Growth*. New York: Random House.

Heller, Walter. 1966. *New Dimensions of Political Economy*. Cambridge, MA: Harvard University Press.

Heller, Walter W., and Milton Friedman. 1969. *Monetary vs. Fiscal Policy*. New York: Norton.

Selected Works about Walter Heller

"Heller, Walter W(olfgang)." *Current Biography Yearbook, 1961 Edition*. Edited by Charles Moritz. 1962. New York: H. W. Wilson.

Kilborn, Peter T. "Walter Heller, 71, Economic Adviser in 60's, Dead." *New York Times*, June 7, 1987. http://www.nytimes.com/1987/06/17/obituaries/walter-heller-71-economic-adviser-in-60-s-dead.html?pagewanted=all&src=pm.

Stein, Herbert. 1969. *The Fiscal Revolution in America*. Chicago: University of Chicago Press.

Helvering v. Davis, 301 U.S. 619 (1937)

A Supreme Court Case Upholding Social Security

Economic Concepts

Taxes; entitlements

Economic Impact

This case upheld the constitutionality of the Social Security Act of 1935. In upholding the Social Security Act, the case also expanded the role of the federal government into economic areas previously reserved for states, and local and private entities.

Economic Summary

The case of *Helvering v. Davis* must be viewed through the lens of the Great Depression. The devastation of this extreme market collapse brought social as well as economic and political changes to the fabric of American life. President Roosevelt offered the nation a "New Deal." Congress passed the Social Security Act of 1935, which provided income to elderly, blind, unemployed, widowed, or orphaned, as well as other state health initiatives. Funds were appropriated that originated from employee income taxes as well as employer excise taxes. As shareholder of a corporation subject to these taxes, Davis opposed them, claiming that they were in conflict with the Tenth Amendment to the Constitution. Whether or not Social Security is the best remedy for business cycle ailments in a free market economy remains to be seen, but the constitutionality of the issue was resolved. A new approach to government involvement in the economy began. This case set the stage for cooperative federalism and a new era in government involvement in the economy.

Case Summary

Historically, Boston is not a stranger to citizens who stand up to defend their property from governments eager to tax. George P. Davis may be a footnote in history, but his stand as a citizen to defend his property from what he believed was an unconstitutional tax is reminiscent of the Sons of Liberty dumping tea. In 1936, Davis owned a small number of stock shares in Edison Electric Illuminating Company in Boston, Massachusetts. Although he lacked large amounts of wealth, what assets he did possess he tended with diligence. At a time when many Americans sought governmental assistance to deal with the desperate consequences of the Great Depression, Davis was focused on keeping his equities clear of government encroachment.

In January 1937, Davis knew that Edison Electric was preparing to accommodate the employers' share of the payroll tax to fulfill its responsibility to the Social Security Act of 1935. This additional expenditure would diminish the company's bottom line and his equity. His objection to this tax was based on the Tenth Amendment to the Constitution. It was his opinion that taking care of the elderly in a financial capacity was the domain of the state, and therefore a federal excise tax was beyond the scope of the national government's powers.

Meanwhile, back in Washington, D.C., Congress and President Franklin Roosevelt were fighting to keep New Deal legislation alive. The president's landslide reelection signaled public support for Roosevelt's new economic policies. However, the Supreme Court, insulated from the necessity to respond to public opinion, continued to rule legislative reforms unconstitutional. In 1935, the Court declared the National Industrial Recovery Act and the Frazier-Lemke Farm Bankruptcy Act void. In 1936, the Court struck down the Agricultural Adjustment Act, stating on the same judicial principle that the federal government had overstepped its constitutional boundaries as set by the Framers.

Regardless of these setbacks, President Roosevelt proposed that Congress pass legislation that would give it the power to provide direct aid to states for the "general welfare." The 74th Congress passed the Social Security Act in an effort to assist indigent elderly, abandoned wives and children, and people suffering from the effects of extremely high unemployment and health issues at an individual and public level. The plan included augmenting incomes and matching state monies with equal or greater federal assistance to alleviate hardships and stimulate a stagnant economy.

In summary Social Security Act looked like this: Title I covered grants for old-age assistance. Title II set up an account within the National Treasury to handle the monthly payments to qualified recipients. Title III spelled out details of the unemployment compensation. Title IV granted state aid to children who were abandoned or orphaned. Title V gave assistance to states for the health and welfare of crippled children. Title VI provided states money to set up public health facilities and train workers. Title VII established a three member Social Security Board, appointed by the president and confirmed by the Senate to carry out the spirit of the law. Title VIII explained the Employee Income Tax and the Employer Excise Tax. It also detailed several jobs that are exempt from these taxes. Title IX explained the payroll exemption for employers with less than eight employees, or who employ their family. Title X granted assistance to blind people. Title XI defined all the terms of the act and includes Alaska, Hawaii, and Washington, D.C. It also defined the separability of the act whereby if any one part is found invalid it doesn't invalidate the other parts.

Until the Great Depression, with the exception of veterans' benefits, most of the aforesaid economic programs were the prerogative of state, local, or private endeavors. In 1936, the judiciary under the leadership of Chief Justice Charles Hughes adhered to a strict constitution doctrine (James Madison's idea of limiting federal usurpation of state powers). However, these were extraordinary times, and President Roosevelt devised a plan whereby he proposed to Congress adding one justice to the Supreme Court for every justice currently serving who had reached the age of 70. Increasing the Court from 9 to 15 would swing the balance in the favor of the president. This proposal was met with bipartisan suspicion and indignation.

In the meantime, George Davis filed suit in district court to stop Edison Electric from paying the employer payroll tax and void the act. The government intervened on Edison's behalf, and Guy Helvering, commissioner of the Internal Revenue Department, took the case. The district court upheld the tax, and Davis appealed. The Federal Court of Appeals for the First Circuit reversed the district court, and Helvering requested that the Supreme Court take the case in order to establish the validity of the tax. The Court granted certiorari (request for a lower court to send the records of the case to the Supreme Court) and heard the case in May of 1937.

In *Helvering v. Davis*, it was the responsibility of the Supreme Court to determine whether Social Security taxes were valid exercises of the taxing power in Article I, Section 8; whether providing the benefits was valid under the general welfare clause; and if Titles II and VIII of the Social Security Act were a valid use of the taxing power granted Congress in the Constitution. Title II established the parameters for the payment of benefits for old-age assistance. Title VIII describes an income tax on employees and an excise tax on the employers that will fund the old-age assistance. Both taxes are with respect to income from wages for workers and having people in their employment and are measured by wages. Both taxes are paid to the U.S. Treasury and into the general revenue. No funds are earmarked. There are penalties for nonpayment. The federal government argued that the nation could not solve current complex issues facing the economy if it remained in 1789. Flexible interpretation of the Constitution allows the nation to progress and provide for the general welfare. New to the previous discussions advocating old-age assistance was the clarification by the government that these were indeed true taxes, and therefore valid exercises of Congress's power to tax. In addition, it concluded that the desperate situation of the elderly at this time was a problem too big for private charity or the state, and therefore needed to be addressed by the federal government to fulfill its obligation to promote the general welfare.

The respondent countered with the argument that if these taxes were truly intended to raise general revenue, taxing the lowest wage earners and stopping at an income of only $3,000 seemed counterintuitive. In addition, leaving out several categories of wage earners—for example, agricultural and domestic workers, government workers, and those who worked for charitable organizations—segregated the laborers who would be eligible to receive benefits. Furthermore, the Tenth Amendment clearly reserves the power of the states to cover what is not expressly given to the federal government or denied to the states. Therefore, the respondents concluded, this was an unconstitutional power grab by Congress in violation of states' rights.

In a 7–2 vote, the Hughes Court broke from its previous conservative judicial philosophy. The Court disagreed with the respondent that Title II violated the Tenth Amendment. Congress is charged with maintaining the general welfare, and what defines that is apt to fluctuate with current events. More importantly, the Depression of the 1930s had created a national situation that demanded a national solution, and the wisdom of Congress, which heard testimony and reviewed evidence, should be deferred to. Justice Cardozo wrote the majority opinion and Justice McReynolds and Justice Butler dissented.

Whether or not the Court acquiesced to Roosevelt's political arm-twisting due to the court-packing initiative is open to debate. Regardless, the decision ushered in the era of cooperative federalism, in which national, state, and local governments interacted collectively to solve problems. New Deal programs increased the flow of federal money to the states for a variety of purposes. These matching funds or grants of large sums of money often pulled states away from their priorities and made the national agenda more of a reality. This new relationship between federal and state government ushered in with the New Deal and Social Security Act can be viewed through either a lens of coercion or one of cooperation. It remains to be seen if one lens is more accurate, or if indeed either has merit.

Kathleen C. Simmons

See Also Banking Act of 1933 (Glass-Steagall Act); Constitution of the United States (see Appendix); Entitlements; Great Depression (1929–1939); New Deal; Roosevelt, Franklin Delano; Social Security Act of 1935; Taxes

Related Cases

United States v. Butler, 297 U.S. 1 (1936) (Struck down the Agricultural Adjustment Act as unconstitutional)

Steward Machine Co. v. Davis, 301 U.S. 548 (1937) (Upheld the validity of Title IX [the taxing of employers to fund the unemployment part] of the Social Security Act of 1935)

Further Readings

Downey, Kirstin. 2009. *The Woman behind the New Deal: The Life of Frances Perkins, FDR's Secretary of Labor and His Moral Conscience.* New York: Nan Talese.

Legal Information Institute, Cornell University Law School. N.d. "42 USC Chapter 7: Social Security." http://www.law.cornell.edu/uscode/text/42/chapter-7.

Legal Information Institute, Cornell University Law School. N.d. "*Helvering v. Davis* (No. 910) 89 F.2d 393, reversed; CARDOZO, J., Opinion of the Court." http://www.law.cornell.edu/supct/html/historics/USSC_CR_0301_0619_ZO.html.

Levy, Robert A., and William H. Mellor. 2008. "Promoting the General Welfare." In *The Dirty Dozen: How Twelve Supreme Court Cases Radically Expanded Government and Eroded Freedom*, 19–36. New York: Sentinel.

OCLC Wildcat. 2003. "Seidman's Legislative History of Federal Income Tax Laws, 1938–1861." http://www.worldcat.org/title/seidmans-legislative-history-of-federal-income-tax-laws-1938-1861/oclc/51059052/viewport.

Resources for Teachers

Legal Information Institute, Cornell University Law School. N.d. "*Helvering v. Davis* (No. 910) 89 F.2d 393, reversed: Syllabus." http://www.law.cornell.edu/supct/html/historics/USSC_CR_0301_0619_ZS.html.

OYEZ, ITT Chicago, Kent College of Law. N.d. "*United States v. Butler*." http://www.oyez.org/cases/1901-1939/1935/1935_401.

www.ourgovernments.gov. N.d. "Social Security Act (1935)." http://www.ourdocuments.gov/doc.php?flash=old&doc=68.

Steward Machine Co. v. Davis, 301 U.S. 548 (1937) upheld the validity of Title IX [illegible] of employers so that the unemployment part of the Social Security Act of 1935.

Further Readings

[illegible]

Legal Information Institute, Cornell University Law School. [illegible] "Social Security." [illegible]

Legal Information Institute. [illegible]

[illegible]

[illegible]

Readings for Teachers

[illegible]

[illegible]

[illegible]

I

Immigration Reform and Control Act of 1986

President Ronald Reagan signed the Immigration Reform and Control Act into law on November 6, 1986. The Act was an effort to revise the previous Immigration and Nationality Act. It was also known as the Simpson-Mazzoli Act, named for Senator Allan Simpson, Republican Senator from Wyoming, and Romano Mazzoli, a Democratic Representative from Kentucky who spearheaded the effort through Congress.

The Act revised or changed in several ways the way in which the United States dealt with immigrants. For one, employers now had to prove the immigrant status of their employees. The act also made it against the law to hire illegal immigrants, except those illegal immigrants who were seasonal workers. There was a grandfather clause for the illegal immigrants who had been in the United States before January of 1982.

The focus of the Act was on several areas of immigration. Several aspects revolved around the employer-employee relationship regarding immigrants. The new Act put the burden on the employer to know the immigration status of new hires: it forced employers to affirm the immigration status of all employees, and it put the responsibility on the employer to ensure that no illegal immigrants were hired. Not knowing an individual was an illegal immigrant at the time of hire was not an excuse for evading the Act.

The Immigration Reform and Control Act did provide several exceptions. One, immigrants who were working in seasonal agricultural industries were considered legal and allowed to work. Another exception was for those immigrants who had been in the United States prior to 1982. They were legalized if they could prove they had been law abiding citizens and not been found guilty of breaking any laws and could pass a basic citizenship test on U.S. government and U.S. history, and prove they could speak and understand basic English.

The Immigration Reform and Control Act changed illegal immigrants' impact on the economy, and more specifically on the labor market. Since the act put the responsibility of proving that employees were not illegal immigrants on the employer, and since hiring illegal immigrants, knowingly or not, was against the law, employers became much more skeptical of hiring anyone who appeared they may be an illegal immigrant. This was especially applicable to the Hispanic population. One tactic to which employers turned was the use of subcontractors for hiring. Using subcontractors moved the liability from the employer to the subcontractor. Also, for contract work, the employer could pay a lower wage.

David A. Dieterle

See Also Reagan, Ronald

Further Reading

Social Security. "SI 00501.440 Immigration Reform and Control Act of 1986." N.d. http://policy.ssa.gov/poms.nsf/lnx/0500501440.

U.S. Citizenships and Immigration Services. "Immigration Reform and Control Act of 1986 (IRCA)." N.d. http://www.uscis.gov/tools/glossary/immigration-reform-and-control-act-1986-irca.

Resources for Teachers

Marshall, Tom. "Pathways to America: Teaching about Immigration Changes." *New York Times Learning Network*, May 21, 2013. http://learning.blogs.nytimes.com/2013/05/21/pathways-to-america-teaching-about-immigration-changes/?_r=0.

Tenement Museum. "The Lower Eastside Tenement Museum, Virtual Tour." N.d. Accessed May 21, 2013. http://www.tenement.org/Virtual_Tour/index_virtual.html.

U.S. Citizenship and Immigration Services. "Lesson Plan and Activities." N.d. http://www.uscis.gov/citizenship/teachers/lesson-plans-and-activities.

Indian Gaming Regulatory Act of 1988

Gaming has been a pastime ever since playing cards and dice were invented. The Indian Gaming Regulatory Act was passed by Congress and signed in 1988 by President Ronald Reagan as a reaction to a Supreme Court case the previous year. In 1987, the Supreme Court ruled in favor of the Native Americans when the Court decided the states had no regulatory jurisdiction over the gaming privileges and rights of Indians on their land.

Indian nations were considered sovereign nations, like any other nation on the globe. Striking the balance between maintaining their sovereignty and being part of the United States was often a thin line. As nations, they had the right and power to conduct their own governmental activities, including regulating their own gaming activity. The Indian nations had been conducting gaming activity and self-regulating long before the states tried to usurp that power from them.

States were responsible for the regulation and control over their gaming regulations. Many states depended on the revenue generated by gaming licenses to provide such control. The conflict between Indians' gaming rights had economic impacts on a state's ability to regulate this popular recreational activity. Some of the Indian gaming activity had become quite sizable and generated significant business operations. As the size of the Indian gaming activity grew, the states wanted more control to regulate that activity, limit it, or even forbid it.

When the Supreme Court ruled in *California v. Cabazon* in the Indians' favor, the states did an about-face and joined with the federal government to pass the Indian Gaming Regulatory Act in an attempt to retain some regulatory control over the gaming of the Indians.

The Indian Gaming Regulatory Act of 1988 recognized the sovereignty of the Native American nations to regulate gaming on their lands. In addition, a National Indian Gaming Commission, the Interior Department, and Congress, along with the states, would negotiate with the Indians to establish gaming contracts. As a result of the Act, states are obligated to negotiate the contracts regarding the regulations Indians would abide by. If a state refused, the Indians could sue or request mediation in a federal court. If the state continued to disobey the federal act or any decisions by a mediator or court, the Department of Interior would impose regulations and procedures on both the Indians and the states.

In an interesting post–Indian Gaming Regulatory Act twist, the states changed their positions and went on the attack and lobbied for the right to tax, regulate, and control the gaming operations of the Indian nations. In an even more interesting twist, the states were now claiming that their sovereignty was being violated by Congress and the conditions of the act. The states were claiming an unconstitutional federal invasion of their power by Congress, forcing the states into agreements to which they may not wish to be party.

The Indian nations themselves have accepted the conditions of the Indian Gaming Regulatory Act to protect the future of Indian gaming and the significant revenues and business success that follows. Since the passage of the act, the economic impact on Native Americans has been significant. As of 2013, 420 gaming establishments were in operation by 240 Native American tribes, generating in excess of $27 billion in revenues nationally. The revenues generated were used to support tribal governments and their programs, the welfare of the tribes' members, charitable organizations, and the economic development of both the tribes and the local communities.

There have been positive outcomes for Indians as a result of the act. Both household income and tribal government revenues have increased, revenue to the areas of the gaming activity has increased, employment among the tribal communities has increased, and the gaming revenue has generated nongaming investments by the Indian nations. Political influence has also increased as the Indian nations' gaming and nongaming businesses have grown.

Given the growth and size of the gaming businesses, a dark side of the business operations has also emerged. Depending on the contracts of the Indian tribes relative to the gaming activity, an increase in the drop-out rate of Indian students in high schools and disincentives to pursue postsecondary education has occurred, as young Native Americans see their future in the gaming industry. Local communities surrounding the gaming activity have also expressed concerns regarding the trade-offs of gaming patrons spending on gaming activity as opposed to other, more necessary expenses. While the gaming industry as a whole continues to be researched, no direct conclusions have been reached to support either position regarding the economic damage to the local communities' citizens.

Besides the regulatory components of the act, a National Indian Gaming Commission was created as an independent agency of the federal government. The commission consists of three members, a chair and two commissioners. The president appoints the chair, with confirmation by the Senate. The two commissioners are appointed by the Secretary of the Interior. Through terms of the act, two of the three sitting commissioners must belong to an Indian tribe, and no more than two can be members of the same political party. The commission is headquartered in Washington, D.C., with offices in Portland, Oregon, Sacramento, Phoenix, St. Paul, Tulsa, and Oklahoma City.

David A. Dieterle

See Also Reagan, Ronald; Supreme Court

Further Reading

Indian Gaming. N.d. "Industry Overview." Accessed December 15, 2013. http://www.indiangaming.com/industry/.

Indianz.com. 2013. "Opinion: Looking at 25 Years of Indian Gaming Regulatory Act." Accessed December 15, 2013. http://www.indianz.com/IndianGaming/2013/027042.asp.

National Indian Gaming Association. N.d. "Indian Gaming Regulatory Act History & Facts." Accessed December 15, 2013. http://www.indiangaming.org/info/pr/presskit/STATES.pdf.

National Indian Gaming Commission. N.d. "About Us." Accessed December 15, 2013. http://www.nigc.gov/About_Us.aspx.

Resources for Teachers

Education World. N.d. "Celebrate Native Americans in the Classroom." Accessed December 15, 2013. http://www.educationworld.com/a_special/native_americans.shtml.

Federal Reserve Bank of Boston. 2000. "Communities and Banking: The Political Economy of Indian Gaming; The New England Experience." Accessed December 15, 2013. http://www.bostonfed.org/commdev/c&b/2000/winter00.pdf.

Scholastic. N.d. "Teachers: Classroom Activity; Native American Games." Accessed December 15, 2013. http://teacher.scholastic.com/lessonrepro/lessonplans/ect/nativegames.htm.

Inflation

Inflation is the rate at which the price of goods and services rises over time. When the inflation rate increases, the purchasing power of currency decreases, since consumers must spend more on goods and services across the economy. When the inflation rate decreases, the purchasing power of currency increases, since consumers can spend less on most goods and services across the economy. The three main causes of inflation are an increase in the cost of the productive resources used to produce goods and services (cost-push inflation), an increase in the demand for goods and services by consumers (demand-pull inflation), and monetary expansion.

A leading cause of inflation is called demand-pull inflation. Demand-pull inflation occurs when there is more demand for goods and services than there is supply available. Demand-pull inflation is a result of low unemployment rates, more money in the pockets of consumers, and increased government purchases, leading to higher demand for goods and services. These scenarios create excess demand and "pull" the price of the goods and services upward. As more and more people seek to purchase a limited supply of these items, the price continues to increase. An extension of demand-pull inflation is that businesses, in an effort to increase the quantity supplied, are willing to pay more for raw materials as well as more for employees to come in and work overtime. This increased cost for businesses to increase the quantity supplied is also passed off to consumers in the form of the consumer paying more for the end product.

A second cause of inflation is cost-push inflation, which is the opposite of demand-pull inflation. Cost-push inflation occurs when the cost to produce goods and services increases which "pushes" up the price of the finished product. This increased cost is passed on to consumers and causes inflation. The increased cost to produce these goods and services may be because of increases in commodity prices, higher employee wages, or an increase in the price of raw materials such as oil.

Monetary expansion is the third cause of inflation. Monetary expansion occurs when expansionary monetary policy and expansionary fiscal policy are used to increase the money supply. Expansionary monetary policy is a tool of a central bank (Federal Reserve System); it increases the quantity of money in an economy, freeing funds so that banks can lend at lower interest rates. When expansionary fiscal policy is used, the government spends more and taxes less. If expansionary monetary and expansionary fiscal policies are continued too long, the two can combine to create inflation. This is when economists refer to inflation as "too many dollars chasing too few goods."

A consequence of inflation is a decline, or depreciation, in the value of the domestic currency relative to foreign currencies. When the value of currency declines relative to foreign currencies, consumers must spend more on imported goods and services.

Deflation

It is important in a discussion of inflation to include the opposite of inflation: deflation. Deflation is a term used to describe a drop in prices across the economy as a result of long-term decrease in demand for goods and services. The main cause of deflation is a decrease in the money supply. Deflation is described as a decline in price levels of goods and services across the economy due to lessened demand from the government, consumers, and businesses.

In order to combat deflation, a combination of tools may be used. Initially, the general thought among economists is to decrease the supply of money, which then results in lower demand for goods and services. John Maynard Keynes, a noted economist and founder of Keynesian economics, theorized that aggregate demand is the key factor in determining the health of the economy. If aggregate demand decreases, as it does during deflation, this is a sign that consumers have stopped purchasing goods and services, and a surplus of goods may become available. Low aggregate demand may be the result of the government enforcing too strict contractionary fiscal policy tools to counter inflation. Or the Federal Reserve may use contractionary monetary policy to decrease the money supply beyond what is necessary. The Great Depression was a consequence of a too-tight contractionary monetary policy.

Whenever there is a low supply of money, price levels have to drop, as there is not enough money to support the quantity of goods and services that businesses produce. Prices are forced to fall as businesses try to encourage consumers to make purchases. In addition to selling products at lower rates, a business may decide at this point to lay off workers to make up for lost revenues, decrease its employees' wages, or halt production of goods and services entirely. However, this hurts the economy more, since lost wages and high unemployment stifle the purchasing power of consumers.

Finally, it is important to note that a reduction in inflation, or disinflation, is not the same as deflation. With disinflation, the general increase in prices continues, just at a slower pace. Deflation is a decrease in the general price level in absolute terms.

Inflation is measured through the use of the Consumer Price Index (CPI), the Producer Price Index (PPI), Personal Consumption Expenditures (PCE), or the money supply. The CPI is a report developed by the Bureau of Labor Statistics. It measures the average change over time in the prices paid by consumers for a market basket of goods and services. The number reported by the CPI is an indicator of how well the economy is performing.

Ekaterini Chrisopoulos-Vergos

See Also Bernanke, Ben; Bureau of Labor Statistics; Contractionary Fiscal Policy; Contractionary Monetary Policy; Deflation; Demand-Pull Inflation; Expansionary Fiscal Policy; Expansionary Monetary Policy; Federal Reserve System; Great Depression (1929–1939); Greenspan, Alan; Volcker, Paul

Further Reading

Agarwal, Prateek. 2011. "Causes of Inflation: Demand-Pull Inflation." *Intelligent Economist*, http://www.intelligenteconomist.com/causes-of-inflation-demand-pull-inflation/.

Amadeo, Kimberly. N.d. "Causes of Economic Inflation." *US Economy News Articles and Statistics*. http://useconomy.about.com/od/inflationfaq/f/Causes-Of-Inflation.htm.

Bernanke, Ben S. 2002. "Speech, Bernanke: Deflation." Board of Governors of the Federal Reserve System, November 21. http://www.federalreserve.gov/boarddocs/speeches/2002/20021121/default.htm

Wu, Tao. 2004. "Understanding Deflation." Federal Reserve Bank of San Francisco, April. http://www.frbsf.org/economic-research/publications/economic-letter/2004/april/understanding-deflation/.

Resources for Teachers

European Central Bank. N.d. "Inflation Island: How Inflation Affects the Economy." http://www.ecb.europa.eu/ecb/educational/inflationisland/html/index.en.html.

Federal Reserve Bank of St. Louis. N.d. "The Great Inflation: A Historical Overview and Lessons Learned (Page One Economics Classroom Edition)." Econlowdown. http://www.stlouisfed.org/education_resources/the-great-inflation-a-historical-overview-and-lessons-learned-page-one-economics-classroom-edition/.

Florian, Tim. 2008. "What Causes Inflation?" econedlink.nhttp://www.econedlink.org/lessons/index.php?lid=615&type=educator.

Inflation, Measures of

Inflation is the general rise of prices in an economy and the number one issue in many economies. Inflation reduces the real value of an economy. It depreciates the value of a currency, reducing the confidence of holding the currency. Very high inflation, or hyperinflation, can destroy an economy and be a catalyst to civil and political unrest.

There are two key measures of inflation: the Consumer Price Index (CPI) and the Producer Price Index (PPI). Each measure provides a separate picture of the economy. When taken together, these three key measures provide a broad measure of an economy's price level. Other measures that economists study for inflation indicators include personal consumption expenditures, import prices, unit labor costs, and the GDP deflator.

Consumer Price Index (CPI)

The most watched and most popular measure of inflation is the Consumer Price Index (CPI). The CPI data are collected, analyzed, and presented by the Bureau of Labor Statistics, an agency of the Department of Labor. The CPI is reported monthly, and unlike the GDP measure, there are no monthly revisions. There are, however, annual revisions that can revert back five years. There are many versions of the CPI for different geographical areas. While the CPI is used to determine the "cost of living" index to determine increases in Social Security and other government entitlement programs, the best use of the CPI is to view price trends and to measure retail prices over time.

The Bureau of Labor Statistics (BLS) constructs a market basket of goods and services. The BLS surveys over 20,000 retail outlets in over 85 urban areas. It collects prices on 80,000 goods and services, from medical and dental services to computers, beer, and rental housing. The data collected on 200 categories of goods and services are divided into eight major categories, each weighted to reflect its impact on a household.

1) Housing, which includes shelter, utilities, household furnishings, and operations, is weighted at 42.2 percent.
2) Transportation is the second most weighted category, at 17.4 percent. This category includes new vehicles, motor fuel, maintenance and repair, and used cars and trucks. It also includes the use of public transportation.
3) Food and beverages are a third category, and account for 15 percent.
4) Medical care is weighted at 6.2 percent.
5) Just below medical care is education and communication, at 6 percent.
6) Recreation is 5.6 percent of the market basket.
7) Apparel is weighting at 3.8 percent.
8) Other goods and services, such as tobacco and smoking products, are 3.5 percent.

The CPI is an index and therefore uses a base year on which to measure growth over time, usually the period of one year. The current CPI base year is the timeframe from 1982 to 1984, which has a value of 100. Each month, the CPI is calculated and measured against the base year (1982–1984) along with the previous year. So if in a current year, the CPI is calculated at 150, the general price level of the market basket of goods and services has risen 150 percent of the 1982–1984 price level (150/100 = 1.5 × 100 = 150%). So based on the CPI, if an item cost $1.00 in 1982, it would cost $1.50 today. Of course, the CPI is only an average, so some items may have fallen in price, while others may have risen more than 50 percent. If the following year the measured CPI is 155, the annual inflation rate would be 25 percent (155 – 150 = 5/150 = .033 × 100 = 3.3%).

The BLS computes several measures of CPI. One measure is CPI-W, which measures the price index for wage earners and clerical workers. A second measure for urban professionals, including the self-employed, managers, and technical workers, is the CPI-U. The BLS measures the price index for 14 specific geographic areas as well. The BLS also takes into account seasonal factors, such as specific growing seasons, that impact a product's price, oranges for example.

The BLS press releases also identify a CPI in two versions: "headline inflation" and "core inflation." Headline inflation is the inflation measure using all items in all categories, as described above. Core inflation, however, is the CPI measure minus the food and energy categories. The core inflation measure was an invention of the high inflation 1970s to minimize the high prices of the two volatile categories of food costs and energy costs.

Producer Price Index (PPI)

Beginning in 1902, the Producer Price Index (PPI) is the oldest of the government's measures. It is the first monthly measure announced by the Bureau of Labor Statistics. The PPI measures changes in prices that businesses pay for the intermediate goods they use in producing goods and services. The PPI is announced by the BLS monthly, often several weeks after the month being measured. It is updated four months after the initial release, and annually in February from the January measure.

The Department of Labor requests prices on approximately 100,000 products from approximately 30,000 companies nationally. The weighting of each product is based on its value to the economy. The products are re-weighted every five years based on changes in the economy. Imported goods are excluded from the PPI, as are services. Like the CPI, a baseline for the PPI is established. The PPI baseline year is 1982.

The PPI is actually a combination of indexes. The PPI measures the price level of three separate goods in production; commodity prices, intermediate goods, and finished goods just prior to being sent for retail. Commodities are the natural resources used in the production process. Intermediate goods are the manmade goods used in the production of final goods and services, such as machinery. Finished goods are the final product ready to be sold to consumers. This last measure is the one most publicized in the news and of interest to investors and businesses. The finished goods measure is determined by the other two and makes them a leading indicator of finished goods prices. Since the PPI measures these early prices and costs in the production process, it is a leading indicator of future retail inflation, as businesses are inclined to pass along cost increases to consumers.

The PPI for crude goods measures the cost of raw materials, such as agricultural products; oil and copper are examples of commodities. These product prices are often based on the supply of the product, making them subject to significant changes in variables such as weather, labor costs, or political uprisings. The PPI for intermediate goods includes the price changes in items just before final production, such as automobile parts, cotton, flour, or machine parts. These two components make up approximately 40 percent of the total PPI measure.

The PPI for finished goods includes prices in 11 categories, including automobiles, groceries, fuels, and clothing. This component is similar to the CPI components. The components for the finished goods PPI are comprised of approximately 75 percent finished consumer goods (20 percent finished consumer foods and 55 percent finished consumer goods) with 25 percent finished capital equipment. As with CPI, a core PPI of finished goods is measured removing food and energy costs. This removes the volatility of weather and geopolitical situations in the inflation predictors.

Economists and investors are especially interested in price changes as they occur from crude products to intermediate products to finished products. Price changes through this process are key signals of what sectors of an economy are experiencing inflation. Knowing where the inflation is originating allows economists and investors to know which stage inflation is present and which sectors and businesses can predictably have inflation in the future.

Economists will often claim that there is no relation between the producer price index and the consumer price index. Experience during the 1970s and 1980s does not often support that claim; measures during the end of the twentieth century were not as consistent. Most economists agree that the two measures will ultimately converge in the long term.

David A. Dieterle

See Also Bureau of Labor Statistics; Deflation; Department of Labor; Economic Growth, Measures of; Inflation

Further Reading

Baumohl, Bernard. 2008. *The Secrets of Economic Indicators*. 2nd ed. Philadelphia: Wharton School Publishing.

Bureau of Labor Statistics. N.d. "Consumer Price Index." www.bls.gov/cpi.

Bureau of Labor Statistics. N.d. "Producer Price Index." www.bls.gov/ppi.

Resources for Teachers

Federal Reserve Bank of Atlanta. N.d. "Inflation Resources." http://www.frbatlanta.org/edresources/classroomeconomist/inflation_resources.cfm.

Ferrarini, Tawni. N.d. "Overview-Consumer Price Index." Common Sense Economics. http://www.commonsenseeconomics.com/documents/student/CPI01_Student.pdf.

Florian, Tim. 2008. "What Causes Inflation?" econedlink. http://www.econedlink.org/lessons/index.php?lid=615&type=educator.

Foundation for Teaching Economics. N.d. "Inflation and Unemployment." http://www.fte.org/teacher-resources/lesson-plans/rslessons/inflation-and-unemployment/

Foundation for Teaching Economics. N.d. "Lesson 9: Money and Inflation." http://www.fte.org/teacher-resources/lesson-plans/efllessons/lesson-9-money-and-inflation/.

Internal Revenue Service (IRS)

History

In 1862, during the Civil War, Congress passed and President Abraham Lincoln signed a bill establishing the position of commissioner for Internal Revenue. The commissioner was charged with collecting income taxes to help pay for the Union's war expenses. The income tax was repealed a decade later. In 1894, the income tax was again instituted, and a year later, it was again ruled unconstitutional by the Supreme Court. The income tax did not become legal until the passing and ratification of the U.S. Constitution's 16th

Amendment in 1913. The 16th Amendment made income tax a legal form of revenue collection for the federal government to authorize.

The first income tax, levied in 1913, was 1 percent on a person's net income above $3,000, and 6 percent on incomes above $500,000. The income tax increased to 77 percent in 1918 to finance World War I, but dropped to 24 percent in 1929, after the war. The federal government was also a victim of the Great Depression, and again raised the income tax rate. Congress began payroll withholding and quarterly tax payments to raise revenue during World War II.

The Bureau of Internal Revenue had become a government agency of patronage. During the 1950s, the Bureau of Internal Revenue was restructured and became the Internal Revenue Service, the IRS. The commissioner of the IRS and chief counsel were appointed by the president with confirmation from the Senate.

The IRS was significantly restructured again in 1998, with the Restructuring and Reform Act. The essence of the restructuring was to create an organization focusing on its consumer needs as if it were a business in the private sector. One significant change to the IRS through the act was the way in which it interfaced with taxpayers. Along with the modernizing of the IRS as a federal institution, the IRS developed a system of taxpayers' rights. The new IRS was charged with assisting taxpayers with the preparation of their tax returns, helping with submission and compliance. The aim was for the agency to be more than just a tax collector to the public. For those who did not comply, the IRS was to enforce the laws and policies of U.S. government.

The IRS Today

Headquartered in Washington, D.C., the Internal Revenue Service is the largest bureau of the U.S. Department of Treasury. The IRS is responsible for assessing and collecting tax revenue for the federal government. The IRS collects not only personal income taxes but also corporate income taxes, estate taxes, gift taxes, excise taxes, and employment taxes for the Social Security Administration. The Internal Revenue Service today is considered by many to be one of the most efficient tax administrators in the world, processing over 220 million tax returns, based on 2004 IRS data. According to the 2012 *IRS Data Book*, the IRS spends only 48 cents per $100 collected.

At the same time, many others have labeled the IRS as the most mistrusted and unpopular federal agency of them all. As the federal government's tax collector, it often finds itself in the middle of or as a topic of political debates over how the government is funded, or the roles and enforcement of IRS policies. When the IRS Restructuring and Reform Act was passed in 1998, and a more comprehensive IRS philosophy with the expansion of taxpayers' rights was instituted, it was hoped the perceptions and dealings between the IRS and the public would be less antagonizing.

IRS Enforcement

Even though the Internal Revenue Service depends on taxpayers to voluntarily provide information regarding their financial records and earnings, the IRS is charged with upholding the tax laws and policies of the U.S. government. The Internal Revenue Service has several options at its disposal to force compliance of tax laws and policies, including audit, confiscation, criminal investigation, and prosecution. The IRS has the power to confiscate and auction one's personal and real property, such as cars and homes. The money raised from an IRS auction is used to recoup the tax liability and accrued interest created by the individual's negligence in paying taxes.

Criminal Investigations (CI) is the enforcement section of the IRS. It is the agency responsible for enforcing the Internal Revenue Code and is charged with investigating and prosecuting violators of the code. Special agents of the CI investigate money laundering, tax crimes, and crimes related to the illegal sources of income, as well as Bank Secrecy Act laws. The CI is considered one of the most effective law enforcement agencies in the federal government.

Individuals can also participate in IRS enforcement through the IRS Informant Award. As a type of reward or bounty, the IRS will award up to 30 percent of the original tax owed to an individual who is a whistleblower and reports to the IRS those who have not paid their taxes.

The CI agency of the IRS is not without its critics. Complaints of power overreach are not uncommon for the agency. This criticism has escalated with the addition of CI's oversight of drug and narcotic financial investigations.

IRS and Its Critics

Reform of the Internal Revenue Service and taxes in general is a constant debate from the highest-level politicians to the friendly confines of the local pub. There are those who would like to reduce the tax collection process to a postcard-sized tax return and eliminate the IRS completely. There are those who suggest that the IRS is not large enough, and should be expanded to accommodate and adequately regulate the tax policies of a growing economy with greater personal and corporate wealth, and a global economy offering newer ways to avoid taxes through technology.

In recent years, the debate has taken on technological focus with the inclusion of the online filing process for tax returns. Critics of the IRS charge that the agency's power and ability to invade the private space of individuals has increased with the advent of online filing of tax returns.

David A. Dieterle

See Also Taxes; United States Treasury

Further Reading

ALLGOV-Everything Our Government Really Does. N.d. "Internal Revenue Service (IRS)." Accessed June 3, 2014. http://www.allgov.com/departments/department-of-the-treasury/internal-revenue-service-irs?agencyid=7262.

Internal Revenue Service. N.d. "About." http://www.irs.gov/uac/About-IRS.

Internal Revenue Service. N.d. "Brief History of the IRS." http://www.irs.gov/uac/Brief-History-of-IRS.

Internal Revenue Service. N.d. "Today's IRS Organization." http://www.irs.gov/uac/Today's-IRS-Organization.

Resources for Teachers

IRS. N.d. "Publication 2181(Rev.5-2013) Catalog Number 24585I—Department of the Treasury Internal Revenue Service. http://www.irs.gov/pub/irs-pdf/p2181.pdf.

IRS. N.d. "Understanding Taxes: The Quick and Simple Way to Understand Your Taxes." http://apps.irs.gov/app/understandingTaxes/.

Smith, Melissa. 2008. "Tax Time Scavenger Hunt." econedlink, July 30. http://www.econedlink.org/lessons/index.php?lid=748&type=educator.

International Monetary Fund (IMF)

The International Monetary Fund (IMF) was part of the Bretton Woods Agreement following World War II. The IMF was officially founded in July 1944 in the city of Bretton Woods, New Hampshire. The architects of the IMF were John Maynard Keynes (1883–1946), a British economist, and Harry Dexter White (1892–1948), an American delegate. Their goal was to build a framework for multilateral international economic cooperation that would avoid a repetition of the disastrous economic policies that had contributed to the Great Depression of the 1930s and the global conflict that followed. The agreement led to the formation of the International Monetary Fund (IMF) and the International Bank for Reconstruction and Development (IBRD). The IMF began operations on March 1, 1947, with the goal to "foster global growth and economic stability." Each member is charged a fee or quota as the price of membership. By December 1945, the International Monetary Fund had 29 member countries, and by the end of 1946, it had 39 members. France was the first country to borrow from the International Monetary Fund.

The IMF provides policy advice and financing to member nations in economic difficulties, and also works with developing nations to help them achieve macroeconomic stability and reduce poverty. The IMF promotes international monetary cooperation and exchange rate stability, facilitates the balanced growth of international trade, and provides loans to help member nations that are having balance of payments difficulties. A nation has balance of payments problems when it does not have enough money to pay for the goods and services imported into the country, or the value of the nation's currency has dropped so low that other nations refuse to accept it as payment for those imports. The IMF also tracks global economic trends and performance, and alerts member countries when it sees a potential for balance of payments problems on the horizon. The IMF can also provide a forum for policy dialogue, and advise governments on how to tackle economic difficulties.

The International Monetary Fund provides loans to its members under different programs for the short, medium, and long term. The size of the quota varies with the size of the nation's economy and the importance of its currency in world trade and payments. Decisions made by the IMF are determined by vote, with the weight of each nation's vote proportional to its quota. For example, this gives the high-income countries of the world a voting advantage that is disproportionate to their population. The United States alone controls 17 percent of the total votes, and the six other largest industrial economies (Canada, Italy, France, Germany, Japan, and the United Kingdom) control almost 45 percent. Various votes on IMF policy require a "super majority" of 85 percent.

The IMF has its own currency, called a special drawing right (SDR). SDRs are based on a country's quota and are part of a nation's international reserves. If a country lacks reserves, it cannot pay for its imports, nor can it pay the interest and principal it owes on its international borrowings. Some of the IMF requirements for lending money require the borrower to make fundamental changes in the relationship between government and markets in order to quality for IMF funds. These requirements are known as IMF conditionality. Currently, the IMF is an organization made up of 188 countries and headed by Christine Lagarde, a French labor lawyer and politician.

Bernard P. Kanjoma

See Also Bretton Woods Agreement; Keynes, John Maynard

Further Reading

Gerber, James. 2011. *International Economics*. San Diego: Person Education.

International Monetary Fund. N.d. "International Monetary Fund." http://www.imf.org /external/.

Resources for Teachers

International Monetary Fund. N.d. "EconEd Online-Lesson Plans." http://www.imf.org /external/np/exr/center/econed/≤ssonplans.

International Monetary Fund. N.d. "EconEd Online-Student Interactives." http://www.imf.org /external/np/exr/center/econed/∞teractives.

Interstate Commerce Act of 1887

The Interstate Commerce Act of 1887 was originally designed to legislate and regulate the monopolistic behavior of the railroad industry. The Interstate Commerce Commission (ICC) was created to oversee and enforce the implementation of the act. The main purpose of the act was to force the railroads to offer "reasonable and just" rates to their customers and publicize those rates. The act prohibited price discrimination between the rate differences of short- and long-haul rates, a common practice of the railroads at the time. It was the first federal law to regulate a private industry.

The Interstate Commerce Act of 1887 was a national reaction to concern over the increasing size and power of companies in the United States. No industry was gaining more power as quickly as the railroads. At the end of the nineteenth century, the railroads had become the main form of transportation for both people and freight. As a result, the rates they charged for both had a significant impact on trade, commerce, and the movement of people.

Competition both within the railroad industry and from other modes of transportation was minimal. It was no secret that the railroad companies were forming cartels and colluding to control rates. It was also clear that this collusion was creating rates that were extraordinarily high relative to what market rates would be without the collusion. Another policy adopted by the railroads that moved the government to take action was the practice of charging a higher per-mile rate for short hauls versus long hauls. This put small businesses at a distinct disadvantage.

States attempted to limit these practices by the railroads by passing their own legislation, but the interstate aspect of the railroad industry made enforcement difficult. Then, in 1886, the Supreme Court ruled in *Wabash, St. Louis & Pacific Railway Company v. Illinois* that state laws were unconstitutional, as they violated the commerce clause of the Constitution, which gave the federal government the power to legislate commerce between states. The federal government that had up to this point avoided getting involved was now forced to act. So in 1887, the Interstate Commerce Act was passed by Congress and signed into law by President Grover Cleveland on February 4 the same year.

The act forced the railroads to publish its rates, thereby eliminating the practice of price discrimination, which helped to increase competition. The increase in competition changed the revenue stream of railroad companies, which diminished their financial allure to investors and stockholders.

The act established the Interstate Commerce Commission (ICC) to oversee its enforcement. It was the first independent agency established by the federal government for the express purpose of regulating a private industry. The role of the ICC was to preside over complaints lodged against the railroad companies, issue cease-and-desist orders against practices that the ICC deemed unfair, and contest any unfair practices of the railroads. The ICC scope of enforcement was limited to railroads that operated across state lines.

Several amendments were made to the Interstate Commerce Act early in the twentieth century. From 1903 through 1910, amendments increased the scope of the ICC to include bridges, ferries, oil pipelines, cable, telephone, and telegraph companies. The Motor Carrier Act was passed by Congress in 1935 to include the trucking industry and bus lines.

Congress began to deregulate the railroad industry through the 1970s and 1980s. The Railroad Revitalization and Regulatory Reform Act of 1976 removed pricing barriers for the railroad industry. Through the 1980s, ICC authority was reduced further as the railroad and trucking industries were further deregulated. In 1995, the ICC was abolished by Congress and its functions moved to the new Surface Transportation Board.

David A. Dieterle

See Also Market Capitalism; Regulated Monopolies; Supreme Court

Further Reading

Gartner, Karl Knox. 1921. *Commentaries on the Interstate Commerce Act.* New York: The Traffic Publishing Co.

NOLO Law for ALL. N.d. "Interstate Commerce Act of 1887." http://www.nolo.com/legal-encyclopedia/content/interstate-commerce-act.html.

PBS. N.d. "Interstate Commerce Act." *American Experience.* http://www.pbs.org/wgbh/americanexperience/features/general-article/streamliners-commerce/.

Resources for Teachers

Bill of Rights Institute. N.d. "Americapedia: Interstate Commerce Act (1887)." https://billofrightsinstitute.org/resources/educator-resources/americapedia/americapedia-documents/interstate-commerce-act/.

National Archives. N.d. "Search the National Archives Website." http://search.archives.gov/query.html?qt=Interstate+Commerce+Act&submit=GO&col=1arch&col=social&qc=1arch&qc=social.

Teaching Future Historians. N.d. "Is There Such a Thing as Too Much Profit? The Interstate Commerce Act of 1887: Excerpts from a Debate in the House." http://dig.lib.niu.edu/teachers/ica-debate.html.

J

Juilliard v. Greenman, 110 U.S. 421 (1884)

A Supreme Court Case Upholding the Legal Tender Acts in Peacetime

Economic Concepts

U.S. legal tender notes; fiat money; specie money; greenbacks; continentals; cheap money

Economic Impact

This case upheld the constitutionality of the Legal Tender Act in peacetime, making paper currency legal without regard to national emergency.

Economic Summary

The Legal Tender cases were a series of cases filed during and after the Civil War, culminating in *Juilliard v. Greenman*. The Civil War brought an economic urgency to the Union. In 1862, Congress passed the Legal Tender Act, allowing U.S. notes to be printed to help finance the war debt. Paper money depreciates in terms of gold and silver, which were used prior to its issuance. Cheap money chases out expensive money, and old debts were soon paid with controversial paper. During Reconstruction, these cases challenged the authority of Congress to print paper money. Beginning with *Hepburn v. Griswold* in 1870, the Supreme Court said paper currency was unconstitutional, and ending in 1884, with the *Juilliard* case stating the opposite interpretation. Article I, Section 8, of the Constitution grants Congress the power to coin money, but gold and silver are the metals mentioned. Whether the framers could have fathomed "plastic" as a method of payment is open to speculation; however, some argue that if their prohibition on paper money had been implemented, the American economy would have been sent into disarray at best, and at worst, would have ceased to exist. This case settled once and for all the constitutional disputes between paper money and a currency limited to gold and silver.

Case Summary

Augustus D. Juilliard was a Frenchman who made his wealth in New York textiles. His skills as a businessman proved beneficial to the arts, as upon his death in 1919, he bequeathed a large amount of money to establish the Juilliard School of Music. In all these endeavors he was a winner, but in the Supreme Court he was a loser. This is not to say that the United States did not benefit from his loss.

Juilliard v. Greenman was a case that grew out of fear and hard times. There was a fear of cheap money (money without intrinsic value or backed by gold or silver) combined with insecurities about government. American political stability had been tested by the Civil War, the assassination of the president, and a financial panic in 1873 that was referred to as the "great depression" until the depression of the 1930s took the title. This sad constellation of events did very little to encourage trust in the federal government's greenbacks (the first noninterest-bearing notes printed by the government to pay for the war debt).

In 1879, Juilliard sued Thomas S. Greenman of Connecticut to secure payment of a private debt. Greenman had purchased 100 bales of cotton from Juilliard, who expected a payment of $5,122.90 upon delivery. Greenman paid $22.90 in gold and silver coin and offered U.S. paper notes (paper money issued by the U.S. government without intrinsic value or backed by gold or silver), also known as greenbacks (because the back is printed in green) for the remainder of the bill. Juilliard refused the paper currency. Greenman took the $5,000 note and the $100 note into court to prove his intent to pay, whereupon the plaintiff demurred (made an objection or delay) on the grounds that the defendant's response to being sued was to produce the same evidence that had caused the action and therefore was without legal significance. The Circuit Court of the United States for the Southern District of New York disagreed, and ruled in favor of the defendant.

Juilliard filed a writ of error (a directive to a trial court to send the records of a case to the appellate court to be examined for potential procedure errors) to the Supreme Court with two assertions. First, the act passed by Congress on May 31, 1878, allowing U.S. bank notes to be paid out and reissued did not make those notes legal tender (a currency that is recognized by law as legal and must be accepted in payment of debts). Secondly, to construe that this act did make the notes legal tender is unconstitutional because Congress does not have the power to make such a law. The case was submitted to the Supreme Court in January 1884.

Julliard's legal representative argued that the Constitution had intended for gold and silver to be the monetary base of the new country. James Madison and other framers remembered the debacle of the continentals (bills of credit that states had issued that depreciated and lost their value) during the Revolutionary War under the Articles of Confederation and had every intention of correcting that mistake in the new Constitution. The plaintiff claimed that Article I, Section 8 of the Constitution established the federal government as sole possessor of the power to coin money. However, wartime measures revisited the U.S. Treasury in 1861, bringing back a reliance on greenbacks, which were very similar to continentals. The legal tender clauses of the acts passed in 1861, 1862, and 1863 were wartime measures enacted to preserve the Union. They were police powers that could not be justified as constitutional without the context of an extreme emergency, which did not exist in 1879, and therefore were void in peacetime. Furthermore, they concluded, printing paper money and declaring it legal tender by statute gave the Congress the ability to change the Constitution without abiding by Article V (the constitutional requirement that amendments have a two-thirds vote of both houses of Congress to propose an amendment and three-fourths of the states to ratify such proposals).

The defense stated that the defendant had followed the full faith and credit of the government. It argued forcibly that Congress had the power to make notes issued by legislative statute into legal tender without contradicting the Constitution; Article I, Section 8, Clause 18, grants Congress the power to do what is necessary and proper to ensure the functioning of the government. The defense found no error of procedure and viewed the Court's decision as necessary to establish the constitutionality of the acts in question. The responsibility of the Supreme Court in *Juilliard v. Greenman* was to determine whether or not acts of Congress issuing paper currency considered legal tender for private and public use during wartime could be considered legal tender during peacetime as well.

The Supreme Court decided this case on March 3, 1884. Justice Gray wrote the majority opinion. All the judges agreed that this case could not be separated in principle from the previous legal tender cases of *Dooley v. Smith* (1871), *Railroad Co. v. Johnson*, and *Maryland v. Railroad Co.*, which established the power of Congress to make notes of the U.S. legal tender in payment of private debts. However, Justice Field dissented for the same reasons that he had in the previous cases. Justice Gray revisited John Marshall's opinion in *McCulloch v. Maryland*, where the powers of the government are limited but not to the point where the government cannot execute its duties set forth in the Constitution. Therefore, Congress has the power to make all necessary and proper laws that are conducive toward those legitimate ends. The rule of interpretation thus laid down is what is deferred to in this case. There are no enumerated powers granting the establishment of banks or creating corporations, as these are among the powers implied in the Constitution. The Court affirmed the ruling and upheld once and for all the constitutionality of paper currency as legal tender.

When the framers left out the phrase "and emit bills" from the prohibited powers of Congress, they left it up to future generations to determine whether the power to issue paper money was best for the nation. If they found it important enough to eliminate titles of nobility, certainly they did not overlook a prohibition on printing paper currency. The men at the Philadelphia convention may not have foreseen plastic money, but they included flexibility into the Constitution to provide for a means of exchange that can adapt to it whatever the future may bring.

Kathleen C. Simmons

See Also Bureau of Engraving and Printing; Constitution of the United States (see Appendix); Money; Supreme Court; United States Mint

Related Cases

Hepburn v. Griswold, 75 U.S. 603 (1869) (Ruled that U.S. bank notes as legal tender were not constitutional for all debts)

Dooley v. Smith, 80 U.S. 604 (1871) (Overruled *Hepburn v. Griswold* and upheld constitutionality of U.S. bank notes as legal tender)

Railroad Company v. Johnson, 82 U.S. 195 (1872) (Affirmed constitutionality of U.S. bank notes as legal tender)

Maryland v. Railroad Company, 89 U.S. 105 (1874) (Upheld constitutionality of U.S. bank notes as legal tender when specified in a contract)

Further Readings

Legal Information Institute, Cornell University Law School. N.d. "The Legal-Tender Cases, *Juilliard v. Greenman*, 110 U.S. 421 (4 S.Ct. 122, 28 L.Ed. 204)." http://www.law.cornell.edu/supremecourt/text/110/421.

Supreme Court of the United States. N.d. "*Juillard v. Greenman*, 1884." http://www.supremecourt.gov/search.aspx?Search=juilliard+v.+greenman+1884&type=Site.

Resources for Teachers

federalreserveeducation.org. N.d. "Benjamin Franklin and the Birth of a Paper Money Economy Lesson." http://www.federalreserveeducation.org/resources/detail.cfm?r_id=9da90c90-1bf7-4491-ae3a-a516706d5ba5.

The Online Library of Liberty. N.d. "Lesson VI: The Value of Paper Money; Simon Newcomb, The ABC of Finance [1877]." http://oll.libertyfund.org/?option=com_staticxt&staticfile=show.php%3Ftitle=307&chapter=140189&layout=html&Itemid=27.

U.S. Department of the Treasury. N.d. "About 1800–1899." http://www.treasury.gov/about/history/Pages/1800-1899.aspx.

K

Kahn, Alfred

Born: October 17, 1917, in Paterson, New Jersey; Died: December 27, 2010, in Ithaca, New York; American; regulation and deregulation; Major Work: *The Economics of Regulation: Principles and Institutions* (1970).

Alfred Kahn led the U.S. economy of the late twentieth century into the era of deregulation. Kahn's career was highlighted by his efforts to deregulate those U.S. industries whose regulations he considered anticonsumer. Appointed by President Jimmy Carter to head the Civil Aeronautics Board, Kahn was instrumental in deregulating the airline industry. Kahn's deregulation of the airline industry transformed air travel into a form of mass transportation with discount prices affordable by almost everyone. Kahn was known for continually extolling the virtues of simpler wording to explain the law or economics. He died in 2010.

Alfred Edward Kahn was born on October 17, 1917, in Paterson, New Jersey. The son of Russian Jewish immigrants, Kahn graduated from New York University when most his age (18) were graduating from high school. He continued his graduate studies in economics, beginning at New York University and ending at Yale, where he earned his doctorate in 1942. Kahn began his career in public service at the U.S. Justice Department, Antitrust Division. He served in the army during World War II.

Following World War II, he served as chair of the Economics Department at Ripon College before moving on to Cornell in 1947. He also chaired the department at Cornell. He eventually became dean of the College of Arts and Sciences and a member of the Cornell board of trustees.

Kahn authored many books and articles in his academic career. His classic work was *The Economics of Regulation: Principles and Institutions*. *The Economics of Regulation* was a two-volume set in which he brought economics to the forefront of exploring the costs and benefits of regulation. Many of his works focused on the deregulation of industries.

Kahn reentered public service in 1974, when he chaired the New York Public Service Commission. Alfred Kahn was responsible for utility companies charging different rates for different times or seasons. Using marginal analysis theory, utilities changed their rate charge practices to charge higher rates during peak times when costs were higher. This created incentives for customers to pursue alternatives and use power during off-peak times when rates were lower. As a result, the utilities earned revenues based on costs and consumers saved by using the utilities during lower-cost, and consequently lower-priced, periods. Kahn is also credited with the telephone industry eliminating free telephone directory assistance. He also served the private sector as an expert on regulations and deregulation in the electricity, transportation, telecommunications, and utility industries.

His recognition as a public servant reached national status when he joined the Carter administration as President Carter's economic adviser on inflation in 1978. With inflation rates as high as ever in the United States, President Carter appointed Kahn to head his Council on Wage and Price Stability. Tagged the "inflation czar," Kahn called the job thankless, and in 1980, he resigned after only 15 months in the position. He had even lamented that the only reason he was not fired was that no one else would take the job.

President Carter appointed Kahn as head of the Civil Aeronautics Board (CAB) in 1977. At the time of his appointment, the airlines industry was highly regulated, from prices and routes down to the meals that would be served on a flight. This structure of the airline industry was viewed as very much a benefit to the airlines at a cost to consumers. Kahn went to work putting his economics and experience in deregulation to work on the industry. During 1977 and 1978, Kahn and the CAB deregulated the airline industry, freeing up routes, carriers, and prices. Under Kahn's leadership, the CAB did such a good job of deregulating the airline industry that it ceased to exist in 1978. Kahn has been labeled the "father of the airline deregulation," a label he did not cherish.

While Kahn took his work very seriously, he was noted for the quick quip or quote. He once used the word "depression" when describing a potential scenario for the U.S. economy. Being ever the economist and not the politician, he was admonished for using the "d" word. So when the same topic came up again, he changed the "d" word to "banana." However, after objections from the banana industry, addressing the same issue a third time he changed "banana" to "kumquat." He was also known for sarcastically asking if an economic or law statement could be made more complicated. This attitude played directly into his continual efforts to have legal and economic policies explained in simple, understandable language.

In 1980, Kahn returned to Cornell, continuing his role as dean of Cornell's College of Arts and Sciences. He was also the Robert Julius Thorne Professor Emeritus of Political Economy. In 1997, he received the L. Welch Pogue Award for Lifetime Achievement in Aviation.

Alfred Kahn died on December 27, 2010, in Ithaca, New York.

David A. Dieterle

See Also Galbraith, John Kenneth; Samuelson, Paul

Selected Works by Alfred Kahn

Kahn, Alfred. 2004. *Lessons from Deregulation: Telecommunications and Airlines after the Crunch*. Washington, DC: Brookings Institution Press.

Kahn, Alfred. 2002. *Whom the Gods Would Destroy, or How Not to Deregulate*. Washington, DC: American Enterprise Institute for Public Policy Research.

Kahn, Alfred. 1998. *Letting Go: Deregulating the Process of Deregulation; Temptation of the Kleptocrats and the Political Economy of Regulatory Disingenuousness*. East Lansing: Michigan State University Institute of Public Utilities.

Kahn, Alfred. 1993. *Great Britain in the World Economy*. Surrey, UK: Ashgate.

Kahn, Alfred. 1970. *The Economics of Regulation: Principles and Institutions*. Cambridge, MA: MIT Press.

Selected Works about Alfred Kahn

"Alfred Kahn, Father of 1970s Airline Deregulation, Dies at 93." 2010. *Bloomberg News*, December 28. http://www.bloomberg.com/news/2010-12-28/alfred-kahn-who-oversaw-airline-industry-break-up-for-carter-dies-at-93.html.

Cornell University Cornell Chronicle. 2010. "Economist Alfred Kahn, 'Father of Airline Deregulation' and Former Presidential Adviser, Dies at 93." December 27. http://news.cornell.edu/stories/Dec10/KahnObit.html.

McCraw, Thomas K. 1984. *Prophets of Regulation: Charles Francis Adams, Louis D. Brandeis, James M. Landis, Alfred E. Kahn*. Cambridge, MA: Harvard University Press.

Russell, George. 1986. "Flying among the Merger Clouds" *Time*, September 29. http://www.time.com/time/magazine/article/0,9171,962408-3,00.html.

Kellogg Co. v. National Biscuit Co., 305 U.S. 111 (1938)

A Supreme Court Case on Trademarks and Patents

Economic Concepts

Trademarks; patents; copyrights; intellectual property rights; innovation; trade; trade laws

Economic Impacts

Trademarks and patents protect innovation with time limits and standards that guard against long-term monopolies and unfair trade practices.

Economic Summary

Imitation may be the highest form of flattery, but in a competitive market it can rob an innovator of his or her profit and stifle his or her motivation to create. Legal protections for property that someone has invented, thought of, discovered, or created are commonly known as intellectual property rights. Trademark and patent rights are included in this category. Although these rights do not ensure the profitable success of the inventor or originator, they do offer an incentive for entrepreneurs to keep innovating. Some might argue that Americans' ability to innovate and think creatively has been one of the key factors in the nation becoming an economic world leader. In the *Kellogg* case, the courts clarified judicial precedents for intellectual property rights in the United States. The rule of law as applied to intellectual property helps safeguard against unfair trade practices as well as motivating productivity.

Case Summary

The biscuit war in Battle Creek, Michigan, was more than just a pillow fight. At the turn of the nineteenth century, America was waking up to a new breakfast. Persuading people to leave bacon and eggs and start their day with what seemed more like chicken feed was not a simple task. Innovations in the process of manufacturing different cereals followed research concerning the healthiness of grain-based diets. Dr. John Harvey Kellogg was a physician and innovator in manufacturing of grains. Working with his brother W. K. Kellogg, they created a flake of wheat and repeated the process with corn. After much experimentation, wheat and corn flakes were boxed and marketed as the secret to a healthy diet.

Meanwhile, several other cereal entrepreneurs were adding their recipes to this new food industry. As early as 1877, Henry Seymour had applied for the first registered trademark for a breakfast cereal, using a traditionally dressed Quaker man as the company symbol and calling it Quaker Oats. W. C. Post was busy inventing Grape Nuts, a cereal named for the smell of grapes while being produced and the nut-like texture of the finished product, thought it contained neither grapes nor nuts. In 1893, Henry Perky and his partner William Henry Ford patented a machine that shredded wheat, resulting in a pillow-shaped biscuit predictably called "Shredded Wheat." Link these trailblazers with the pasteurization of milk, and what was once in a trough was now in Americans' breakfast bowls. The nation transitioned to a cold, fast breakfast that came out of a cardboard advertising Mecca known as the cereal box. This set the stage for a competition that would see battle in the courts as well as on the grocery shelves.

By definition, cereal is any edible grain. However, to get from edible to appetizing took innovation. To get from factories to breakfast tables took marketing. The process was fueled by cereal-industry competition and guided by the rule of law concerning fair trade practices, patents and trademarks. In the *Kellogg Co. v. National Biscuit Co.* case, two major competitors and a pillow-shaped bundle of shredded wheat created case law that started with a skirmish and grew into an international brawl.

Henry Perky was a lawyer turned inventor who intended to sell machines. John Kellogg was a man of medicine. The two men knew each other and both believed in the benefits of grains in the diet. However, John Kellogg turned toward religion and his brother C. W. Kellogg took the reigns of the business and purchased the rights to Cornflakes, starting the Kellogg Toasted Corn Flakes Company in 1906. Meanwhile, Perky struggled with his mental health and eventually sold his patents and the Shredded Wheat Company in 1881 to the National Biscuit Company (the name was changed to Nabisco in 1971). However, the biscuit design patent was invalidated one year prior to its expiration date in 1908. The National Biscuit Co. and the Kellogg Company continued to parallel each other during the vertical climb toward the top of the cereal market, the former exclusively connected with Shredded Wheat biscuits and the latter with Corn Flakes. When the 20-year exclusivity to produce shredded wheat had expired due to patent time limits, the gloves came off.

Soon, Kellogg Co. began producing biscuit-shaped shredded wheat cereal under the Kellogg signature. In 1935, the National Biscuit Co. sued Kellogg, claiming that Kellogg had violated unfair competition practices by deceiving the public into thinking that shredded wheat was a Kellogg product and by copying National Biscuit's product. Kellogg countered that the patent was in the public domain, as was the pillow shape.

National Biscuit Co. retorted that when Kellogg depicted the shredded wheat biscuits in a bowl with milk poured over them, it was too closely associated with National Biscuit Co.'s cereal box, and consequently misled the consumer into purchasing a Kellogg product thinking it was a National Biscuit Co. product.

The Federal District Court in Delaware ruled in favor of Kellogg Co., stating that the term "shredded wheat" is free for all to use, and cereal bowls and milk flow naturally from that free domain. In 1937, National Biscuit Co. appealed its case to the Federal Circuit Court of Appeals, which reversed the decision of the District Court and ordered Kellogg to stop using the term "shredded wheat," to stop selling its product in the shape of a pillow-shaped biscuit, and to pay damages in line with its subsequent fraud. A small percent of the shredded wheat cereal sold by Kellogg to hotels and restaurants was not labeled sufficiently and this influenced the court to believe that there was evidence to support deception. Kellogg Co. appealed to the U.S. Supreme Court, but certiorari (request for a lower court to send the records of the case to the Supreme Court) was denied.

At the same time, court battles were taking place between the Canadian-held sister companies of both parties. However, over the northern border, the decision was different. Canadian opinion held that there was no right to a patent that was public domain, as was the case with shredded wheat. Furthermore, the biscuit shape was a description of what happens when anyone bakes wheat that has been shredded. Hence, descriptions are not exclusive property. This international court mirrored the opinions of the U.S. Federal District Court; it handed down a ruling in favor of the Kellogg Company of Canada in May 1938.

Meanwhile, back in the United States, Kellogg continued to sell shredded wheat in a box with the biscuit image, clearly favoring a different interpretation of the U.S. Federal Appellate Court's opinion. National Biscuit Company requested clarification of the Supreme Court's orders to halt sales. Afterwards, the decision from Canada became available and Kellogg resubmitted a request to the Supreme Court to hear its appeal again, taking into consideration the ruling of the British Privy Council (one of Canada's vestige appellate courts from British colonialism abolished in 1949) in *Canadian Shredded Wheat Co., Ltd., v. Kellogg Company of Canada, Ltd.*, 55 R.P.C. 125. The Supreme Court granted certiorari and heard *Kellogg Co. v. National Biscuit Co.* in October 1938.

National Biscuit Co. did not claim the exclusive right to produce shredded wheat, but it did claim the right to the trade name "Shredded Wheat" and the right to the biscuit design. Kellogg Company claimed that "shredded wheat" was a generic term used to describe the product that the company had the right to make. The Court found no doctrine of secondary meaning (legal protection of an otherwise not protected trademark that arises when advertising and time make that mark signify a particular product). The National Biscuit Company needed to show that people thought of it alone when seeing the words or the shape. It failed to do so. Instead, it made clear that the words or shape brought to the mind of consumers a basic product that could have been made by any cereal company. Therefore, the only obligation Kellogg owed was to clearly identify itself to the consumer, which it made a point to do by having W. K. Kellogg's own signature on every box as a trademark. On November 14, 1938, the Supreme Court ruled in favor of the Kellogg Company; Justice Brandeis wrote the opinion.

The framers of the Constitution knew how important it was to protect the intellectual property rights of authors and inventors in order to ensure innovation in science and the arts. Article I, Section 8 of the Constitution includes among the enumerated powers of Congress the power to secure, for limited times, the exclusive right of those who create. The significance of this power is evident in the myriad of patents, copyrights, and trademarks filed in the United States annually. In the Kellogg case, the courts established a point of reference for the laws for intellectual property rights in industrial America. It helped define what was in the public domain and to what degree the functionality of a product could influence control over its economic use. Setting rules for intellectual property is one more weapon in the battle against unfair trade practices.

Kathleen C. Simmons

See Also Constitution of the United States (see Appendix); Private Property; Supreme Court

Related Cases

Singer Mfg. Co. v. June Mfg. Co., 163 U.S. 169 (1896) (It is self-evident that on the expiration of a patent the monopoly granted by it ceases to exist, and the right to make the thing formerly covered by the patent becomes public property)

Holzapfel's Compositions Co. v. Rahtjen's American Composition Co., 183 U.S. 1 (1901) (Unknowingly used a trademark but without intention to defraud or unfair gain; Court agreed they did not gain and ruled no lost profits to be paid)

Saxlehner v. Wagner, 216 U.S. 375 (1910)

Further Readings

Justia, U.S. Supreme Court Center. N.d. "*Kellogg Co. v. National Biscuit Co.*, 305 U.S. 111 (1938)." http://supreme.justia.com/cases/federal/us/305/111/.

Legal Information Institute, Cornell University Law School. N.d. "*Kellogg Co. v. National Biscuit Co.* 305 U.S. 111 (59 S.Ct. 109, 83 L.Ed. 73), Nos. 2, 56, Opinion, Justice Brandeis." http://www.law.cornell.edu/supremecourt/text/305/111#writing-type-1-BRANDEIS.

U.S. Patent and Trademark Office. 2005. "General Information Concerning Patents." http://www.uspto.gov/web/offices/pac/doc/general/index.html.

U.S. Small Business Administration. N.d. "Protecting Your Ideas." http://www.sba.gov/starting_business/startup/ideas.html.

Resources for Teachers

The Breakfast Bowl. N.d. "Cereal and the Economy." Accessed December 1, 2013. http://breakfastbowl.blogspot.com/2008/12/cereal-and-economy.html.

Topher's Castle. N.d. "Topher's Breakfast Cereal Character Guide Analysis of the Cereal Industry." Accessed December 1, 2013. http://www.lavasurfer.com/cereal-analysis.html.

Tasteful Inventions. N.d. "Perky Shredded Wheat." Accessed June 5, 2014. http://tasteful-inventions.blogspot.com/2008/08/perky-shredded-wheat.html.

Kelo v. City of New London, Connecticut, 545 U.S. 469 (2005)

A Supreme Court Case on Private Property Rights and Role of Eminent Domain

Economic Concepts

Eminent domain; public goods; private property

Economic Impact

A governmental entity can claim eminent domain in the name of economic development.

Economic Summary

In the United States, it is customary to think that home ownership is secure. Private property rights give good reason to trust in this assurance. Following the decision in *Kelo v. New London*, the question of how secure individuals are in their right to ownership of private property has been brought into question. In this case, the government's power to take private property through eminent domain was granted to a private corporation, which in turn condemned individuals' homes and leased the property to private businesses with the intended purpose of economic revitalization for the area at large.

The Supreme Court's responsibility in this case was to determine whether the reason private property was taken from individuals was within the meaning of the Fifth Amendment to the U.S. Constitution. In a close vote, the Court indicated that indeed the city did not violate the takings clause of the Fifth Amendment.

The majority opinion interpreted economic development as a traditional and accepted function of government. Quoting precedent cases, the majority of justices embraced an acquiescence to local government, the ability to have pragmatic knowledge of what was appropriate to area economies rather that courts having such insight. However, much can be inferred from the minority opinion as well. Justice Sandra Day O'Connor gives a foreshadowing of why this case was destined to have such a lasting imprint on the American free enterprise system and its underlying premise of private property and rule of law. She warned that the ghost of condemnation would haunt all property, and not much would prevent a government entity from replacing a single home, farm, or small business with a larger, more prosperous and tax-generating strip mall or manufacturing plant. It is one thing to give property to a railroad or utility that will be used by the public, but to give it to another private entity to create jobs and pay higher amounts of taxes is another thing altogether (see Justice O'Connor's dissenting opinion at http://www.law.cornell.edu/supct/html/04-108.ZD.html).

Case Summary

New London is a city in Connecticut midway between Boston and New York. It was once the second-largest whaling port in the world, and currently hosts the United States Coast Guard Academy. New London experienced significant economic decline during the 1980s and 1990s. During this time, the government closed the Naval Undersea Warfare Center, a submarine industry that employed a large number of the area's working population. In 1990, a state agency declared New London a distressed municipality.

In 1998, a pharmaceutical company announced the development of a global waterfront research facility within the area of New London. In 2000, acting through the New London Development Corporation (NLDC), a nonprofit private entity, New London adopted a wide-ranging redevelopment plan. The plan focused on a 90-acre development area adjacent to the new global waterfront research facility. The NLDC purchased the majority of the land from property owners. However, 15 property owners did not want to sell. Therefore, by means of the authority granted by the City of New London and state law, NLDC used the power of eminent domain (the ability to take private property for public use) to acquire the remaining property.

The NLDC began the process of taking these properties through condemnation (the process of taking private property through the power of eminent domain), which is generally understood to be for public use, such as building a school, road, utility, etc. The power of eminent domain allows governmental entities to take properties from homeowners as long as the homeowners are granted due process and just compensation. The Fifth Amendment to the U.S. Constitution, as well as the Connecticut State constitution, authorizes the power of eminent domain. Condemnation is not unusual where the property being taken is deteriorated or in poor condition. This was not the case in New London. Instead, these maintained homes were to be taken by NLDC, a private entity, for the benefit of private developers in an effort to create jobs and increase tax revenue for the city of New London. The NLDC would own the land within the development area and contract leases with private developers, which would be required to comply with the development plan that had been approved by city and state governments. In summary, it was a situation in which the government's power to take private property was in the hands of a private corporation, which then leased this property to private businesses for them to carry out a plan with the intention of benefiting the public at large.

Susette Kelo was among the owners whose property was condemned by the NLDC. These property owners sued New London in state court to stop the city from seizing their property. The petitioners alleged that the taking of their properties violated the public use requirement of the Fifth Amendment. They argued that an economic redevelopment project does not qualify as public use because private parties will own most of the condemned property. The Connecticut Supreme Court held that economic development was a valid "public use" because the local legislature, when granting the power of eminent domain, determined the "taking" was reasonably necessary to implement a plan that increased tax revenue and created jobs, and would improve the neighboring economy. The Connecticut Supreme Court upheld the legislature's rationale and ruled in favor of New London. The homeowner petitioners appealed to the Supreme Court and were granted certiorari (a request by the Supreme Court to the lower court for the files of the case to be sent up for review).

The petitioners claimed the decision by the Connecticut Supreme Court to uphold the NLDC's use of eminent domain as public use could not include the development of land for private economic purposes. Furthermore, the petitioner argued that because the character of these takings would not produce immediate public benefit, the Court should establish a more inquiring test that entailed some degree of realistic assurance that the condemned properties would actually be put to public use. This could be demonstrated through contracts or state guarantees among other things.

In 2004, *Kelo v. City of New London* was argued in the U.S. Supreme Court. In 2005, the Rehnquist Court returned a 5–4 opinion delivered by Justice John Paul Stevens in favor of New London. The majority held that the city's taking of private property to sell for private development qualified as a "public use" within the meaning of the takings clause of the Fifth Amendment. The Court held that New London was not taking the land to benefit a certain group of private individuals, but rather to benefit the community as a whole. As long as a clear economic development plan was followed, the process did not violate the Constitution. The majority opinion stated that this expansive interpretation of public use as public purpose was inferred in the Fifth Amendment and did not require a literal interpretation. The majority opinion explained that among other things, promoting economic development is a time-honored and accepted function of government.

In the minority opinion, Justice Sandra Day O'Connor stated that the Fifth Amendment's takings clause was violated in the New London case. She said there was no interpretation except the literal application of the words "public use." In addition, the minority opinion expressed the belief that taking a private citizen's property to sell to private investors was not for "public use" but rather corporate profit. In Justice O'Connor's opinion, by ruling in favor of New London, the citizen lost any effectual check on the eminent domain power. Which begs the question: How secure are we in our homes?

Kathleen C. Simmons

See Also Private Property; Public Goods; Taxes

Related Cases

Berman v. Parker, 348 U.S. 26 (1954) (Re: Washington, D.C., blighted areas; landowners in Washington, D.C., challenged the constitutionality of taking from one businessman for the benefit of another businessman; the Court found that a legitimate public purpose had been established by Congress in the case of D.C. in creating the entire redevelopment plan, which made it constitutional)

Hawaii Housing Authority v. Midkiff, 467 U.S. 229 (1984) (The land oligopolies in Hawaii were broken up and land ownership redistributed; this was deemed legitimate due to the original property ownership stemming from a royalty ownership prior to statehood that was not beneficial to the area as a whole)

Further Reading

Legal Information Institute, Cornell University Law School. N.d. http://www.law.cornell.edu/supct/html/04-108.ZS.html.

OYEZ, ITT Chicago, Kent School of Law. N.d. http://www.oyez.org/cases/2000-2009/2004/2004_04_108#chicago. (Audio of oral arguments and majority opinion of the case)

OYEZ, ITT Chicago, Kent School of Law. N.d. "Transcript of Majority Opinion and Oral Arguments of the Case." http://www.oyez.org/cases/2000-2009/2004/2004_04_108#chicago.

Supreme Court of the United States. No. 04-108, *Susette Kelo, et al., Petitioners v. City of New London, Connecticut, et al.* N.d. "Proceedings and Orders." http://www.supremecourt.gov/Search.aspx?FileName=/docketfiles/04-108.htm.

The Supreme Court of the United States, Susette Kelo, et al. Petitioners v. No. 04-108 City of New London, Connecticut, et al. http://www.supremecourt.gov/oral_arguments/argument_transcripts/04-108.pdf. (Transcripts of oral arguments of the case)

Resources for Teachers

Benedict, Jeff. 2009. *Little Pink House: A True Story of Defiance and Courage.* New York: Grand Central Publishing.

Bill of Rights Institute. 2005. "*Kelo v. New London* (2005)." http://billofrightsinstitute.org/resources/educator-resources/lessons-plans/landmark-cases-and-the-constitution/kelo-v-new-london-2005/.

Justice John Paul Stevens (Ret.). 2011. Albritton Lecture, "*Kelo*, Popularity and Substantive Due Process." The University of Alabama School of Law, Tuscaloosa, Alabama, November 16. http://www.supremecourt.gov/publicinfo/speeches/1.pdf.

Keynes, John Maynard

Born: June 5, 1883, in Cambridge, England; Died: April 21, 1946, in Firle, Sussex, England; English; macroeconomic theory; Major Works: *The Economic Consequences of the Peace* (1919), *Treatise on Probability* (1921), *Tract on Monetary Reform* (1929), *The General Theory of Employment, Interest and Money* (1936).

John Maynard Keynes, Baron Keynes of Tilton in the County of Sussex, was an English economist who impacted both political theory and modern economics. Keynesian economics promotes a mixed economy dominated by the private sector but with a large role for government and the public sector. Keynesian economics argues that at the macroeconomic level, the private sector is at times inefficient in its allocation of resources. When this occurs, the public sector needs to be actively involved in the fiscal and monetary policies to create stability of the business cycle. Keynes followed a legacy of successful nonconformists within his family and is revered as the father of macroeconomics. Keynes died in 1946.

John Maynard Keyes was born in Cambridge, England, on June 5, 1883. His father was a lecturer and the university's chief administrative official. His mother was an accomplished author, Cambridge's first woman councilor and also its mayor. After enjoying an elite education at Eton College, Keynes completed his postsecondary studies at King's College in Cambridge, earning his degree in mathematics in 1905. He spent additional time studying under Alfred Marshall and Arthur Pigou and received a master's of arts in economics.

Keynes's early career started as a civil servant in London; he had placed second on an examination, which cost him his preferred job in the Treasury Department. He was appointed to a position in foreign affairs to the Royal Commission on Indian Currency and

Finance, a bureau that extended advice on the administration of India, one of England's dominions at the time. Keynes accepted this foreign affairs job and learned how a government department operates. He soon developed an interest in Indian affairs and currency; Keynes gained the attention of numerous government officials because he was able to apply economic theory to practical problems. His experience helped him write his first book in economics, *Indian Currency and Finance* (1913), a description of the Indian monetary system.

In 1908, Keynes returned to Cambridge to teach economics. Tired of the slow-moving departments of the Indian Office, his attentions turned to writing. He composed an essay based on his experiences in government entitled "Recent Economic Events in India" (1919), which was his first major article in print. In addition to being a journalist and lecturer, Keynes was part of the acclaimed Bloomsbury Group of literary greats, including Virginia Woolf and Bertrand Russell. In 1911, Keynes was given the prestigious honor of editor of *The Economic Journal*. This was a significant accomplishment, especially due to the fact that he had few publications at this time.

World War I put a hefty burden on the British economy, and in 1915, Keynes was offered a job at the British Treasury. He gladly accepted this offer to actively participate in the war effort. Keynes served as the treasury's chief representative at the Paris Peace Conference of 1919, since his division had done much of the work on the preliminary reparations and war debts; however, its result was quite unfavorable to him. After returning to England, he resigned from this post and turned to writing a book. By the fall of 1919, Keynes had published *The Economic Consequences of the Peace*, which became an international best seller and a close foreshadowing of the immediate future. He predicted that the treaty's terms were too harsh and were aimed to cripple Germany instead of punishing them. Keynes's contention was that the provisions in the treaty would hamper Germany's postwar economy, Germany would eventually repudiate the treaty, and a rearming of Europe would ensue. Just as Keynes had suggested, the German economy experienced hyperinflation in 1923, and only a fraction of the reparations were ever received.

After 1929, the entire world was in an economic free fall when Keynes decided to take on the task of explaining and determining new ways to control trade cycles. This resulted in two books, *Tract on Monetary Reform* (1929) and *The General Theory of Employment, Interest and Money* (1936). Through these books, Keynes proclaimed that there needed to be both national and international programs that would lead to a cohesive monetary policy. He believed that a national budget should be used as a primary instrument in planning the national economy. Keynes asserted that policies were needed to regulate the ups and downs of the trade cycle. He firmly believed that it was the responsibility of government to regulate the levels of employment and investment. Keynes's response to a depression or recession was government actions designed to encourage spending and discourage saving; a key component of his ideas is that the government's central bank should lower interest rates when prices are too high and raise interest rates when prices fall.

Keynes made other important contributions to economics, one focused on the disorganization caused by World War I and the other on the deterioration in the balance of trade between Europe and the United States. He continued to help the British government and became an unofficial adviser to Germany. Keynes worked with Roosevelt and other writers of the New Deal, contributing directly to its implementation. By the time World War II began, Keynes was a famous and accredited expert on economics. He assumed a primary role in establishing the Bretton Woods system, which would eventually lay foundations for the International Monetary Fund and the World Bank. He strongly supported William Beveridge's proposal for an expansion of Britain's social services, which led to the United Kingdom's National Health Service. Keynes occupied a seat in the House of Lords as a member of the Liberal Party and supported equal opportunities for women in business.

John Maynard Keynes suffered from several heart attacks before losing his life on April 21, 1946, in Firle, Sussex, England, due to heart failure. He was cremated and his ashes were scattered on the Downs above Tilton.

Samantha Lohr

See Also Fiscal Policy; Galbraith, John Kenneth; Great Depression (1929–1939); Keynesian Economics; New Deal; Public Goods; Samuelson, Paul

Selected Works by John Maynard Keynes

Keynes, John Maynard. 1940. *How to Pay for the War*. New York: Harcourt, Brace.

Keynes, John Maynard. 1936. *The General Theory of Employment, Interest and Money*. New York: Macmillan.

Keynes, John Maynard. 1931. *Essays in Persuasion*. New York: Macmillan.

Keynes, John Maynard. 1929. *Tract on Monetary Reform*. London: Macmillan.

Keynes, John Maynard. 1926. *The End of Laissez-Faire*. London: L & Virginia Woolf.

Keynes, John Maynard. 1922. *A Revision of the Treaty*. London: Macmillan.

Keynes, John Maynard. 1921. *Treatise on Probability*. London: Macmillan.

Keynes, John Maynard. 1919. *The Economic Consequences of the Peace*. New York: Harcourt, Brace & Howe.

Keynes, John Maynard. 1913. *Indian Currency and Finance*. London: Royal Economic Society.

Selected Works about John Maynard Keynes

Maynardkeynes.org. N.d. "John Maynard Keynes." Accessed March 23, 2011. http://www.maynardkeynes.org/.

Minsky, Hyman P. 1975. *John Maynard Keynes*. Columbia Essays on the Great Economists. New York: Columbia University Press.

Skidelsky, Robert. 2009. *Keynes: The Return of the Master*. New York: Public Affairs.

Skidelsky, Robert. 1994. *John Maynard Keynes*. Vol. 2, *The Economist as Savior, 1920–1937*. New York: Viking Adult.

Skidelsky, Robert. 1980. *John Maynard Keynes: 1883–1946: Economist, Philosopher, Statesman*. New York: Macmillan.

Skidelsky, Robert. 2001. *John Maynard Keynes*. Vol. 3, *Fighting for Freedom, 1937–1946*. New York: Viking Adult.

Skidelsky, Robert. 1986. *John Maynard Keynes*. Vol. 1, *Hopes Betrayed, 1883–1920*. New York: Viking Adult.

Keynesian Economics

Keynesian economics is the economic philosophy of John Maynard Keynes (1883–1946). Keynes has been considered by many as one of the most influential persons of the twentieth century due to his ideas about a more expansive role for government as a means of influencing an economy. The central theme of Keynesian economics is that government can serve a useful role in leveling out the peaks and troughs of a business cycle through the use of taxes or government spending to eliminate the extremes of the business cycle. Keynes is credited with the "invention" of what is now called fiscal policy.

A Keynesian economist believes in several ideas that are at the core of Keynes's economic philosophy. The key belief is that aggregate demand (total spending by consumers) has significant impact on an economy's output and inflation, and that it is influenced by many different economic decisions. Keynesians also believe prices are "sticky" downward, do not go down as fast as they rise, and do not respond predictably to conventional (classical) economic supply and demand models. This notion was quite unconventional at the time Keynes suggested it in 1936 with the publication of *The General Theory of Employment, Interest and Money*. Keynes also believed wages, like prices, were "sticky" downward.

Keynesians believe the wide variations of the business cycle negatively impact an economy and government involvement can improve a market economy. Keynesians are most noted for the belief that active government action can be used to stabilize the business cycle, minimizing recessions and downturns while also compressing excessive growth to stabilize an economy and avoid bouts of excessive demand-pull inflation (a concept proposed by Keynes). Finally, early on, Keynesian economists were more concerned with curing unemployment than inflation.

Over the years, Keynesians have debated and often changed their views on what essentially defined Keynesian economics. Most economists today question whether government can ever have enough knowledge to be able to act as a fine-tuning instrument of the economy. This general agreement is based on the understanding that there are three policy lags that prevent governments from being successful. One is the recognition lag between the time a policy is needed and the time that government realizes a policy is needed. The second lag is the implementation lag between when a policy is needed and when the new policy takes action. The final lag is the impact lag between when a policy is passed and when it becomes effective. Each of these lags can be several months long, meaning that the time between recognition and impact could be quite long. These lags suggest that by the time a policy's impact is felt, the economy could in fact be in a very different position. The policy could be exactly what not to do and exacerbate a bad economic environment. Even though there is agreement that the lags exist, Keynesians today still believe government is the correct tool to stabilize an economy.

An additional concept added to the economic vocabulary and thinking promoted by the Keynesian position is the idea of a multiplier effect of fiscal policy on an economy.

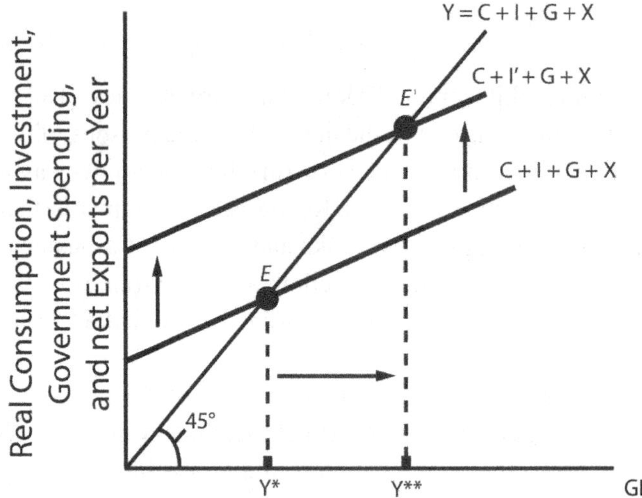

According to Keynes, government spending will increase GDP (Y* to Y**)

Keynesians believe government spending has a ripple effect throughout an entire economy, not just at the point of infusion. This ripple, or multiplier, effect suggests an impact on economic growth. For example, a million dollars injected into the economy by government that actually increases economic growth by 2 million dollars has a multiplier of two. The increase could be as little as 10 percent, but the Keynesian economic model suggests that any multiple increase is a reflection of a multiplier effect on an economy.

Role of Monetary Policy

Another discussion between the Keynesians that has been debated over the years has been the role of monetary policy. Most, though not all, Keynesians believe that there is a role for monetary policy in stabilization, albeit a more minor role than fiscal policy. Monetarists focus on one of two metrics; the money supply or interest rates. Keynesians who hold a belief for monetary policy generally focus on interest rates as their key monetary policy metric. Keynesians hold that low interest rates spur investment. Therefore, during times when expansionary monetary policy is the prescription, low interest rates will expand the money supply and spur investment and economic growth (GDP = C + I + G + X) (C=Consumption, I=Investment, G=Government, X=Net, Exports). History has shown this to be a valuable metric while an economy is either in a downturn or recession. Once an economy achieves full employment, however, history has shown this to be an activist position for inflation.

Keynesian theory is differentiated from other economic philosophies because of three distinct views. One, Keynesians view unemployment as a function of aggregate demand, an economy's total demand for goods and services. Two, they advocate government being active to stabilize an economy and reduce the ultimate peaks or lows of the business cycle. This belief is the most distinguishing viewpoint of the Keynesians and the most important viewpoint for Keynesians to hold. Third, Keynesians generally believe that limiting unemployment is more important than limiting inflation, and is the key macroeconomic goal that will lead to economic growth. This view, however, is much less universal, and many Keynesians today lean toward a more monetarist, low-inflation-first position, stressing low interest rates as the key monetarist goal.

Critics of Keynesian Economics

Every economic philosophy has its critics and Keynesian economics is no exception. The criticisms of Keynesian economics were especially loud during the 1970s, when inflation and unemployment were both present in the economy. During this decade, several events were occurring in the economy that the Keynesians position could not defend. Keynesians believed that in the long run, unemployment and inflation could not occur at the same time and were therefore trade-off goals. Keynesians held the view that government stabilization policies would cure unemployment during economic contractions or halt inflation during periods of economic expansion in the short run, but did not have to be concerned about both simultaneously. A. W. Phillips (1914–1975) solidified this unemployment-inflation trade-off with his Phillips curve. Phillips showed that policies to achieve gains in reducing unemployment were met with only slight increases in inflation in the short run. In support of short-run over long-run policies, Keynes famously remarked, "[I]n the long run we are all dead." This position could not adequately explain the wage-price spiral and stagflation of the 1970s.

A second criticism of Keynes was the Keynesian monetarist view of focusing on interest rates instead of the money supply as the more advantageous short-run monetary tool to control the money supply. To the critics, this view was especially flawed during the 1970s, as Arthur Burns and the Federal Reserve kept interest rates artificially low during a time of economic growth. Keynesianism's critics attribute this action as a major reason for the high inflation rates of the mid to late 1970s.

David A. Dieterle

See Also Galbraith, John Kenneth; Gross Domestic Products (GDP) Keynes, John Maynard; Monetary Policy; New Deal; Phillips, A. W. H.; Samuelson, Paul

Further Reading

Arnon, Arie, Jimmy Weinblatt, and Warren Young, eds. 2011. *Perspectives on Keynesian Economics*. Verlag: Springer.

Blinder, Alan S. N.d. "Keynesian Economics." Library of Economics and Liberty, the Concise Encyclopedia of Economics. http://www.econlib.org/library/Enc/KeynesianEconomics.html.

Holt, Richard P. F., and Steven Pressman. 2001. *A New Guide to Post-Keynesian Economics*. London: Routledge.

Keynes, John Maynard. 1936. *General Theory of Employment, Interest and Money*. London: Macmillan.

Resources for Teachers

Foundation for Teaching Economics. N.d. "The Economic Way of Thinking." http://www.fte.org/teacher-resources/lesson-plans/rslessons/the-economic-way-of-thinking/.

Jesperson, Jesper, and Mogens Ove Madsen, eds. 2013. *Teaching Post Keynesian Economics.* Northampton, MA: Edward Elgar.

Khan Academy. N.d. "Keynesian Economics." Accessed June 3, 2014. https://www.khanacademy.org/economics-finance-domain/macroeconomics/aggregate-supply-demand-topic/keynesian-thinking/v/keynesian-economics.

Klein, Lawrence

Born: September 14, 1920, in Omaha, Nebraska; Died: October 20, 2013, in Gladwyne, Pennsylvania; American; econometrics, Nobel Prize (1980); Major Works: *The Keynesian Revolution* (1947), *Economic Fluctuations in the United States, 1921–1941* (1950), *Econometric Model of the United States, 1929–1952* (with Arthur Stanley Goldberger) (1955), *The Economies of Supply and Demand* (1983).

Lawrence Klein is the leading figure in the mathematization of economics. Using the newly created power of computers, Klein pushed economics into ever more difficult calculations in an attempt to properly represent the complexity of the economy. His work was useful in predicting the effects of government policies in a time when macroeconomists were confident about the possibility of "steering" the economy through fiscal policy. He was awarded the Nobel Prize in 1980.

Lawrence Robert Klein was born in 1920 in Omaha, Nebraska. The Great Depression began when he was nine years old and continued throughout his teenage years. Klein studied mathematics at Los Angeles City College and economics at the University of California, Berkeley. He went on to earn his PhD in economics from the Massachusetts Institute of Technology in 1944, where he studied under Paul Samuelson. He then joined the research faculty at the University of Chicago. While in Chicago, he briefly joined the Communist Party, evidently not from sincere Marxist beliefs, but because the local Communist Party insisted that he join if he was to deliver lectures to them on Marxist theory.

World War II was coming to an end at this time, and a common belief among economists was that the influx of soldiers returning from the war would create mass unemployment and perhaps sink the United States into another bout of the Great Depression. Klein drew up a mathematical model of the economy that contradicted this theory. Rather, wrote Klein, the purchasing power of the returning soldiers, coupled with unsatisfied consumer demand during the war years, would create an economic boom. He turned out to be correct, and this early example of the predictive powers of his models earned him fame among economists. He also established himself in the Keynesian tradition, not just because of his 1947 book *The Keynesian Revolution*, but because his early analysis focused on total demand rather than supply or the level of money.

Klein taught at the University of Michigan from 1950 to 1954, but was denied tenure due to an unforeseen problem. His previous membership in the Communist Party had caught the attention of the House Un-American Activities Committee. Subsequently,

Michigan denied him promotion and tenure. He then fled to England, to the University of Oxford. In 1958, he returned to the United States for a post at the University of Pennsylvania, where he remained for more than 50 years.

With the advent of computers, Klein deepened his use of models by starting a project called LINK, in which he attempted to create econometric models that included all the countries in the world. He also created the Brookings model and the Wharton econometric forecasting model. For these and other innovations, he earned the John Bates Clark Medal in 1959 from the American Economic Association and the Nobel Prize in Economics in 1980. Furthermore, he served as president of the Econometric Society, the Environmental Economics Association, and the American Economics Association. In 1976, Klein joined Jimmy Carter's economic task force during the presidential election, though he declined to take a job with the administration itself. In 1984, he joined W. P. Carey and Co. as director and chairman of the economic policy committee.

Klein did not remain dogmatically attached to Keynesian ideas. With the growing popularity of supply-side economics and monetarism in the early 1980s, he included the ideas of these challenges to Keynes in his models, noting that there are many important components to managing an economy. Nevertheless, his tendency to recommend government intervention as a key part of stabilizing the economy kept him firmly within the Keynesian tradition. The application of ultra-complex math has been criticized by some who think that no quantitative model is central to the scientific side of economics, allowing economists to explain the movements of society in more detailed terms. Economics remains a thoroughly math-oriented field of study thanks in part to Lawrence Klein's technical genius.

Lawrence Klein died on October 20, 2013, in Gladwyne, Pennsylvania.

Stephen H. Day

See Also Economic Systems; Keynes, John Maynard; Keynesian Economics; Marxism

Selected Works by Lawrence Klein

Bodkin, Robert G., Lawrence R. Klein, and Kanta Marwah. 1991. *A History of Macroeconomic Model Building*. Northampton, MA: Edward Elgar.

Klein, Lawrence. 1983. *The Economics of Supply and Demand.* Baltimore: Johns Hopkins University Press.

Klein, Lawrence. 1950. *Economic Fluctuations in the United States, 1921–1941*. Hoboken, NJ: Wiley.

Klein, Lawrence. 1947. *The Keynesian Revolution.* New York: Macmillan.

Klein, Lawrence R., and Arthur Stanley Goldberger. 1955. *Econometric Model of the United States, 1929–1952*. Amsterdam: North-Holland.

Selected Works about Lawrence Klein

Breit, William, and Barry T. Hirsch, eds. 2004. *Lives of the Laureates*. Cambridge, MA: MIT Press.

Klein, Lawrence. 2001. "Keynesianism Again: Interview with Lawrence Klein." *Challenge 44*, no. 3 (May 1): 6–16.

Kuznets, Simon

Born: April 30, 1901, in Pinsk, Russia; Died: July 8, 1985, in Cambridge, Massachusetts; American; national income accounting, Nobel Prize (1971); Major Works: *National Income and Capital Formation* (1937), *Modern Economic Growth: Rate, Structure, and Spread* (1966), *Economic Growth of Nations: Total Output and Production Structure* (1971).

Simon Kuznets was a pivotal leader in transforming the field of economics from a largely speculative study to an empirical science. Economics was once viewed as a subsection of moral philosophy, and Kuznets was influential in establishing it as an independent academic discipline. Kuznets was instrumental in devising classifications and subcategories for national income accounting to more accurately measure a nation's economic growth. He won the Nobel Prize in Economics in 1971. Kuznets died in 1985.

Simon Smith Kuznets was born in Pinsk, Russia, on April 30, 1901. His education began as a child in Kharkov, where he completed his primary schooling and gymnasium. Following his education, he served for a short time in the Ukrainian government's Bureau of Labor Statistics, and then emigrated to the United States in 1922. In the United States, Kuznets soon returned to his studies and distinguished himself with degrees from Columbia University, earning his BA in 1923, his MA in 1924, and his PhD in 1926.

Throughout his career, Kuznets held a number of important academic and government positions. From 1930 to 1954, he was professor of economics and statistics at the University of Pennsylvania. In 1954, he became a professor of economics at Johns Hopkins University, where he remained until 1960, when he left for Harvard. He was at Harvard until 1971. He was a member of the research staff at the National Bureau of Economic Research (NBER) from 1927 to 1961. During his career, he authored over 200 papers and 31 books.

As an officer of the government, Kuznets made significant changes in the way government operations were carried out. From 1932 to 1943, he served in the Department of Commerce, where he began his work in transforming the way the government collects economic statistics. He also served on the Bureau of Planning and Statistics of the War Production Board during World War II and was instrumental in establishing the Conference on Research in Income and Wealth in 1936. In 1947, he established its international counterpart, the International Association for Income and Wealth. He also advised the governments of China, Japan, India, Korea, Taiwan, and Israel on how to set up their economic statistical gathering operations.

During his life, Kuznets made major contributions to many fields, most notably national income accounting. He was also influential in the fields of economic demography, the distribution of income, and the role of capital in economic growth. He had a significant impact on how government uses statistics to analyze economic growth and consumption.

The idea of measuring a nation's macroeconomy was introduced by John Maynard Keynes. A nation's economic growth can be measured in terms of its Gross Domestic Product (GDP) or in terms of its Gross Domestic Income (GDI). The measure known as GDP is the final value of purchases of all the goods and services produced in an economy during a given period of time, usually one year. The measure adds all the purchases of household consumption, business investment spending, and government spending with net exports. The second approach, GDI, measures total incomes earned by summing wages and salaries, rents, profits, interest, and other income.

The United States was in the midst of the Great Depression and policy makers were forced to use fragmentary and sketchy economic data to inform their policy decisions. President Roosevelt had to rely on incomplete stock indices, train freight statistics, and steel output levels. There was no clear picture by which policy makers could understand the economy as a whole. Kuznets was instrumental in breaking down into classifications and subcategories the U.S. national product and income accounts. These classifications allowed policy makers to get a bird's-eye view of the economy.

The U.S. national accounts to measure economic growth have become the foundation of modern macroeconomic analysis, allowing policy makers, economists, and the business community to analyze the impact of different plans, the impact of price shocks, and the impact of monetary policy on the economy as a whole and on specific parts of final demand, incomes, industries, and regions. The significance of Kuznets's work on national income accounts may be best portrayed by the fact that the U.S. Department of Commerce cited the development of national income accounting and product accounts as its "achievement of the century."

The result of these comprehensive standards developed and implemented by Kuznets shows that since their implementation, economic fluctuations have been less severe. Recurring problems like bank runs, financial panics, and depressions have become far less painful than they were before World War II. The economy still has cyclical ups and downs, but the ability to measure the economy has resulted in a far more stable economic environment. Postwar prosperity in the United States is due in great part to the comprehensive data provided by the national accounts.

Simon Kuznets died on July 8, 1985, in Cambridge, Massachusetts.

John E. Trupiano

See Also Friedman, Milton; Keynes, John Maynard

Selected Works by Simon Kuznets

Epstein, Lillian, Elizabeth Jenks, and Simon Kuznets. 1946. *National Product since 1869.* New York: National Bureau of Economic Research.

Friedman, Milton, and Simon Kuznets. 1945. *Income from Independent Professional Practice.* New York: National Bureau of Economic Research.

Kuznets, Simon. 1971. *Economic Growth of Nations: Total Output and Production Structure.* Cambridge, MA: Belknap Press of Harvard University Press.

Kuznets, Simon. 1969. *Economic Growth and Structure: Selected Essays.* New York: Oxford & IBH.

Kuznets, Simon. 1966. *Modern Economic Growth: Rate, Structure, and Spread.* New Haven, CT: Yale University Press.

Kuznets, Simon. 1937. *National Income and Capital Formation.* New York: National Bureau of Economic Research.

Selected Works about Simon Kuznets

Fogel, Robert W. 2001. *Simon S. Kuznets 1901–1985: A Biographical Memoir*. Washington, DC: National Academy Press.

Kuznets, Simon. 1971. "Autobiography." Nobelprize.org. http://www.nobelprize.org/nobel_prizes/economics/laureates/1971/kuznets.html.

Lundberg, Erik. 1971. "Simon Kuznets' Contribution to Economics." *The Swedish Journal of Economics* 73, no. 4 (December): 444–59.

L

Labor Force

The labor force is made up of those at least 16 years of age who are willing and able to work. It excludes those incapable of working and those not looking for work, as well as those in the armed forces or those who are institutionalized. The labor force is directly affected by the economy and economic conditions.

During the Great Depression, the unemployment rate was as high as 25 percent, as millions of people were out of work. Yet they continued to seek employment, and so were counted as part of the labor force. Many workers had given up and stopped looking for work. They were labeled "discouraged workers," and because they stopped looking for employment they were not counted as part of the labor force. The involvement of the United States in World War II increased the demand for workers, stimulated the economy, and increased the size of the labor force as many people began looking for employment again.

One significant impact on the United States labor force was the baby boom generation coming of age. In the 1970s, there was a marked increase in the labor force as the baby boomers entered the workforce. In the 2000s, the United States experienced a reversal and decline in the labor force with the aging of the baby boomer population. As the baby boomers retire, there will be significant effects on the labor force and a marked decrease in the growth of the labor force. It is estimated by the year 2020, those 55 years of age and older will account for less than 25 percent of the labor force (see Toossi, 2006).

The number of women in the labor force has also fluctuated over the years. In the 1950s, the percentage of women in the labor force was significantly low. Men had returned from World War II and as a result, women went back into the home after working in factories producing war-related goods. Women's labor participation rates increased steadily in the 1970s and 1980s and led to a growth in gross domestic product (GDP). Women's labor force rates had leveled off by the end of the 1990s and fluctuated around 59 to 60 percent. It is anticipated that in the future, this rate will continue to decline and will be lower than that of men.

Those aged 24 to 54 have the highest labor participation rates (see Toossi, 2006) (this measures the labor force as a percentage of the total population at least 16 years of age), and are considered prime-aged workers. This group generally has labor force rates of 80 percent or higher and it is expected that this trend will continue in the future.

The increasing ethnic and racial diversity of the United States is expected to account for increases of these groups within the labor force. In the future, Asians and Hispanics are expected to increase the population, as well as the labor force and labor participation rate. Both Asians and Hispanics have high labor participation rates that will add to the labor force in the coming years. Blacks will also continue to add to the labor force with higher birth rates and high participation rates among women.

The Bureau of Labor Statistics (BLS) publishes labor force projections every two years assuming full employment at 5 percent unemployment (or 95 percent employment). These reports estimate labor force participation rates based on the age, race/ethnicity, and gender of the population. Demographics and changes within the population affect the labor force as well as the types of unemployment the economy is experiencing. It appears that changes within the labor force are a direct result of a changing population. The BLS also analyzes the growth rate of the civilian noninstitutional population, which seems to have maintained a steady growth rate of around 1 percent.

In the 1980s, the term "discouraged worker" was redefined as someone who has stopped looking for work because he or she did not believe a job was available. Discouraged workers are not counted in the nation's unemployment rate, and if they were, unemployment rates would be slightly higher than the published rates provided by the BLS. Age, gender, and race play a factor in how long a person remains a discouraged worker before he or she tries to look for a job to reenter the workforce.

The business cycle and cyclical changes within the economy also impact the labor force. As the economy expands, the labor force increases, and as the economy declines, the labor force decreases.

Today, the labor force is still an indicator of economic health and growth. In the future, the labor force participation rate is expected to decrease due to the retirement of the baby boomers, lower fertility rates, and a decrease in immigrants.

Angela M. LoPiccolo

See Also Bureau of Labor Statistics; Cyclical Unemployment; Discouraged Workers; Gross Domestic Product (GDP); Unemployment

Further Reading

Castilo, Monica D. 1998. "Persons outside the Labor Force Who Want a Job." *Monthly Labor Review* 121: 34–42.

Fullerton, Jr., Howard N. 1999. "Labor Force Participation: 75 Years of Change, 1950–98 and 1995–2025." *Monthly Labor Review* 122: 3–12.

Toossi, Mitra. 2011. "A Behavioral Model for Projecting the Labor Force Participation Rate." *Monthly Labor Review* 134: 25–42.

Toossi, Mitra. 2006. "A New Look at Long-Term Labor Force Projections to 2050." *Monthly Labor Review* 129: 19–39.

Toossi, Mitra. 2012. "Projections of the Labor Force to 2050: A Visual Essay." *Monthly Labor Review* 135: 3–16.

Teacher Resources

Bureau of Labor Statistics. N.d. "Databases, Tables, & Calculators by Subject." http://www.bls.gov/data/.

Federal Reserve Bank of St. Louis. N.d. "Barbie in the Labor Force." http://www.stlouisfed.org/education_resources/barbie-in-the-labor-force/.

Foundation for Teaching Economics. N.d. "The Job Jungle: A Labor Market Game." http://www.fte.org/teacher-resources/lesson-plans/efllessons/the-job-jungle-a-labor-market-game/.

Laffer, Arthur

Born: August 14, 1940, in Youngstown, Ohio; American; fiscal policy, political economy; Major Works: *Foundations of Supply-Side Economics* (with Victor A. Canto, Douglas H. Joines, Marc A. Miles, and Robert I. Webb) (1983), *End of Prosperity: How Higher Taxes Will Doom the Economy—If We Let It Happen* (with Stephen Moore and Peter J. Tanous) (2008), *Return to Prosperity* (with Stephen Moore) (2010).

Arthur Laffer is one of the few economists whose work became a namesake and foundation for a whole school of economic thought. The supply-side philosophy of economics laid the foundation for what was to become the Reaganomics of the 1980s. Supply-side economics underscored that lower tax rates would generate higher tax revenues. With this thesis, Laffer influenced the business, government, and academic worlds. Laffer served the United States in several positions, including consultant to Treasury Secretaries William Simon and George Shultz, chief economist for the Office of Management and Budget for George Shultz, and consultant to President Reagan's Economic Policy Advisory Board. Laffer was a founding member of the Congressional Policy Advisory Board. Arthur Laffer held academic positions at Pepperdine University, the University of Southern California, and the University of Chicago.

Arthur Betz Laffer was born on August 14, 1940, in Youngstown, Ohio. After receiving his BA in economics from Yale in 1963, he earned an MBA from Stanford University in 1965 and a PhD from Stanford in 1972. In 1967, he began his academic career, joining the faculty at the University of Chicago. In 1976, Laffer left Chicago for the University of Southern California, where he was the Charles B. Thornton Professor of Business Economics. In 1984, he joined the faculty of Pepperdine University, where he remained until 1987.

Laffer's career in the political arena began in 1970, when he served as chief economist for the Office of Management and Budget under U.S. Secretary of the Treasury George Shultz, a colleague of his at the University of Chicago. From 1972 to 1977, he served as a consultant to Treasury Secretary George Shultz, as well as to U.S. Secretary of Treasury William Simon and Defense Secretary Ronald Rumsfeld. From 1981 to 1989, Arthur Laffer's economic-political influence heightened when he served on President Reagan's Economic Policy Advisory Board. His association with President Reagan began in 1980 as a member of then presidential candidate Ronald Reagan's Executive Advisory Committee. During the 1980s, he was also a consultant to UK prime minister Margaret Thatcher.

Using the Laffer curve illustration as a teaching tool in his classes, Laffer showed that at some level of tax rates, government would generate less revenue by creating disincentives to be productive through labor and more incentives to barter, participate in an underground economy, or just enjoy leisure. Consequently, these disincentives would reduce tax revenues.

While this relationship between tax rates and tax revenues has become known as the Laffer curve, Laffer himself never made any claim that the tax rates–tax revenues relationship was an original insight. He credited Ibn Khaldun and John Maynard Keynes as early architects. In the mid-1770s, both Adam Smith and David Ricardo had made similar arguments.

Acceptance of the Laffer curve premise has not been universal. While there has been some research to identify tax rate ranges at which the tax rate–tax revenue relationship turns negative, there is also significant criticism of Laffer's illustration. Nobel laureates John Kenneth Galbraith and Paul Krugman both criticized Laffer's approach on the basis of equity and fairness. Others have criticized Laffer's description as too simplistic, while others attacked the theory, claiming that the economy and consequently tax revenues would not totally be eliminated at a tax rate of 100 percent. Regardless of the criticisms, supply-side economics was the basis for the Kemp-Roth Tax Cut of 1981 and both the Economic Growth and Tax Relief Reconciliation Act of 2001 and Jobs and Growth Tax Relief Reconciliation Act of 2003 (the "Bush tax cuts").

Arthur Laffer has authored several books and many articles on business economics and the political economy. In 1971, Laffer authored *Private Short-Term Capital Flows*. In 1983, Laffer—with Victor Canto, Douglas Joines, Marc Miles, and Robert Webb—laid the foundations for supply-side economics with *Foundations of Supply-Side Economics: Theory and Evidence*. As an author, Laffer is noted more for his recent works: *End of Prosperity: How Higher Taxes Will Doom the Economy—If We Let It Happen* (2008) with Stephen Moore and Peter Tanous, and *Return to Prosperity* (2010) with Stephen Moore.

Laffer has received many awards and honors during his career. In 1999, he was recognized as one of "The Century's Greatest Minds" for the Laffer curve. He received several Graham and Dodd Awards from the Financial Analyst Federation, the National Association of Investment Clubs Distinguished Service Award, and the Adam Smith Award.

David A. Dieterle

See Also Galbraith, John Kenneth; Hayek, Friedrich von; Keynes, John Maynard; Smith, Adam

Selected Works by Arthur Laffer

Canto, Victor A., Douglas H. Joines, Arthur B. Laffer, Marc A. Miles, and Robert I. Webb. 1983. *Foundations of Supply Side Economics: Theory and Evidence*. New York: Academic Press.

Laffer, Arthur. 2004. "The Laffer Curve: Past, Present, and Future by Arthur B. Laffer." Heritage Foundation, June 1. http://www.heritage.org/research/reports/2004/06/the-laffer-curve-past-present-and-future.

Laffer, Arthur. 1986. "The Ellipse: An Explication of the Laffer Curve in a Two-Factor Model." In *The Financial Analyst's Guide to Fiscal Policy*, edited by Victor A. Canto, Charles W. Kadlec, and Arthur B. Laffer, 1–35. New York: Greenwood Press.

Laffer, Arthur B., and Stephen Moore. 2010. *Return to Prosperity: How America Can Regain Its Superpower Status*. New York: Threshold Editions.

Laffer, Arthur B., Stephen Moore, and Peter J. Tanous. 2008. *End of Prosperity: How Higher Taxes Will Doom the Economy—If We Let It Happen*. New York: Threshold Editions.

Selected Works about Arthur Laffer

CNBC. N.d. "Dr. Arthur Laffer." *CNBC*. http://www.cnbc.com/id/24732335.

Laffer Center for Supply-Side Economics. N.d. "Arthur Laffer." Accessed June 3, 2014. http://www.laffercenter.com/the-laffer-center-2/.

Tennessee's Business. N.d. "We Are All Keynesians Now." Jones College of Business, Middle Tennessee State University. http://frank.mtsu.edu/~berc/tnbiz/stimulus/laffer.html.

Wiggin, Addison, and Kate Incontrera. 2008. *I.O.U.S.A: One Nation. Under Stress. In Debt.* Hoboken, NJ: Wiley.

Laffer Curve

Supply-side economists often use the Laffer curve, named after the economist Arthur Laffer (1940–), to illustrate the effects of tax rates on tax revenue. The Laffer curve shows the relationship between the tax rate set by the government and the total tax revenue that the government collects. The total revenue depends on both the tax rate and the health of the economy. The Laffer curve illustrates that high tax rates may not bring in much revenue if these high tax rates cause economic activity to decrease.

Suppose the government imposes a tax on the wages of workers. If the tax rate is zero, the government will collect no revenue. However, with no taxation, the economy will prosper. As the government raises the tax rates, it starts to collect some revenue. According to Laffer, as the tax rate increases, government revenue will also increase to a certain point, known as the revenue maximizing point.

Even though higher tax rates do discourage some people from working as many hours as possible, the net effect of a higher tax rate and a slightly lower tax base is an increase in revenue to a certain point. However, any point along the curve to the right of the revenue maximizing point illustrates the negative effects of increased taxation. Once the tax rate surpasses the revenue maximizing point, the decrease in workers' efforts is so large that the higher tax rate actually decreases total tax revenue. Another effect of the higher tax rates is on companies and their unwillingness to invest and increase production due to more spending on taxation. In effect, the high rates of taxation will eventually discourage so many people from working and businesses from investing that the tax revenues will fall sharply. In the most extreme case, at a 100 percent tax rate, no one would want to work and the government would collect no revenue.

Biography of Laffer

Arthur Laffer studied economics at Yale and Stanford, earning a PhD in 1972. He was chief economist for the Office of Management and Budget, and advised President Ronald Reagan on economic issues. He made an unsuccessful run for the U.S. Senate in 1986. Several years later, he founded an economics consulting firm with a longtime partner, Victor A. Canto.

Laffer is a conservative economist, best known for his supply-side theories of economics. His theories were in favor among Republicans in the 1970s and 1980s, an era that saw

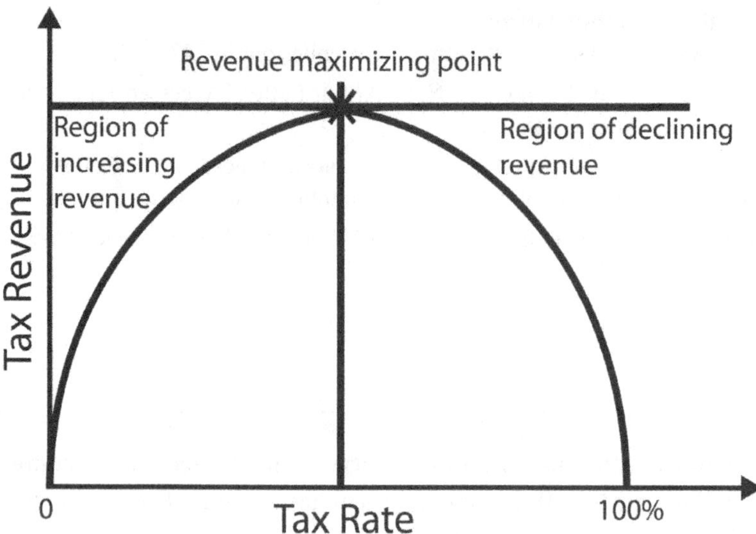

Arthur Laffer proposed with the Laffer Curve high tax rates will result in lower government revenue

a major drop in top marginal income tax rates, from 70 percent in 1980 to 28 percent by 1990. The most noteworthy use of Laffer's theory was under the presidency of Ronald Reagan in the 1980s.

Laffer Curve in Practice

Arthur Laffer's theory has not been widely accepted by economists, even though the relationship between tax rates and tax revenues he proposed appeared logical in theory. One major issue that economists point to is the ability to actually find the extreme levels of tax rates Laffer suggests (i.e., the highest point on the curve in which tax revenues begin to decline as tax rates increase). From 1945 to 1960, the top marginal income tax rates were in the 90 percent range. And from 1965 to 1980, they were lowered but still remained high in the 70 percent range.

By 1980, Arthur Laffer's curve had caught the attention of presidential candidate Ronald Reagan. An integral component of candidate Reagan's platform was cutting tax rates, à la the Laffer curve. Candidate Reagan campaigned on the issue that the current high income tax rates discouraged employment. His remedy was to follow the ideas of Laffer and lower tax rates to provide incentives for employment, and by extension increase human dignity and government revenues. Between Laffer's economic focus and Reagan's political focus on increasing the incentives by which individuals would participate in the labor force and the supply side of the economy, the theory became the basis for what would become supply-side economics.

Even though debates continue over the economic theories of the 1980s and the Laffer curve, the general consensus is that the implementation of major income tax cuts is favorable overall. To evaluate Laffer's theory would be impossible since one would need to rerun history without the tax cuts to see if tax revenues would have been higher or lower.

However, most economists agree that a relationship between tax rates and government revenues exists, and likely additional government revenues are generated when tax rate cuts occur for those in the highest tax brackets. The Laffer curve also creates a standard measurement of tax rates throughout the world and can be used by nations to increase or decrease their income tax rates accordingly.

Tracy L. Ripley

See Also Laffer, Arthur; Reagan, Ronald; Supply-Side Economics; Taxes

Further Reading

Mankiw, N. Gregory. 2011. *Principles of Microeconomics.* Cincinnati, OH: South-Western Cengage Learning.

O'Sullivan, Arthur, and Steven M. Sheffrin. 2007. *Economics Principles in Action.* Upper Saddle River, NJ: Pearson: Prentice Hall.

Resources for Teachers

Cochran, John P. 2013. "Coolidge and the Laffer Curve." Ludwig von Mises Institute. http://mises.org/daily/6381/.

Laffer, Arthur. 2004. "The Laffer Curve: Past, Present, and Future." The Heritage Foundation. http://www.heritage.org/research/reports/2004/06/the-laffer-curve-past-present-and-future.

Leahy-Smith Act (See America Invents Act)

Lechmere, Inc. v. National Labor Relations Board, 502 U.S. 527 (1992)

A Supreme Court Case on Private Property Rights and Rights of Union Organizers to Access Employees

Economic Concepts

Property rights; labor union; labor; markets; competition

Economic Impact

This case protected an employer's private property rights while employees were engaged in their right to join a union.

Economic Summary

Private property is fundamental in a free enterprise economy. *Lechmere, Inc. v. NLRB* is about balancing the private property rights of employers with the rights of their employees in the process of deciding to join a union. In a capitalist system, when private property rights are secure, competition is defined by peaceful means and guided by the rule of law. To maintain this balance, Congress passed the National Labor Relations Act in 1935. Section 7 established an employee's right to join a union and take part in collective bargaining, as well as an administrative board to enforce all requirements thereof. Congress deferred any ambiguity within the act to the board for final resolve. In the *Lechmere* case, the Supreme Court changed this default setting from the rule of deference to Court-based adjudication favoring the protection of private property rights.

Case Summary

In the United States, property rights are considered human rights. In the Declaration of Independence, Thomas Jefferson referenced this thought as a person's right to life and freedom, and to be secure in their property. *Lechmere, Inc. v. NLRB* (National Labor Relations Board) was concerned with balancing the private property rights of employers with rights of their employees in the process of deciding to join a labor union. This balancing act is key if there is to be equity on both sides of the bargaining table. Nonetheless, there remains inequality in a free market economy. In the view of Adam Smith, a few owners could combine much easier to gain an advantage in bargaining power in the marketplace over the multitude of workers. The result is inequality of bargaining power. This delicate balance is critical in perpetuating a healthy marketplace for both owners and laborers.

The Cohen family started Lechmere, Inc., in 1913 in the Boston area. One of the first large discount stores, it grew rapidly in the 1950s and 1960s. In the late 1980s, it opened a retail store in a shopping mall in Newington, Connecticut. The company owned part of the parking lot and 4 of the 46 feet of grassy barrier between the parking lot and the Berlin Turnpike. The store had over 200 employees, most of which parked there. Lechmere maintained a no-soliciting policy that pertained to everyone from the Salvation Army bell ringers to Girl Scouts.

In June 1987, the United Food and Commercial Workers International Union (UFCW) began a campaign to organize the workers at Lechmere. While the history of the UFCW began in 1979, the history of the retail industry organizing in the United States began much earlier. In the late nineteenth century, retail employees earned perhaps $10 per week and 80-plus-hour workweeks were not uncommon. Toward the turn of the century, the Retail Clerks National Protective Union joined with the American Federation of Labor, later to become the UFCW. The UFCW struggled for better working conditions with fair hours and equal pay. It was the first to establish the principle of overtime pay for anything over 63 hours worked in a week.

The UFCW's campaign to organize Lechmere's retail store in Newington included using strategies to communicate with employees meeting times and union information. The parking lot allowed the union organizers within four feet of the employees' vehicles. It also allowed nonemployee organizers to picket in the grassy area with signs indicating union meetings. Furthermore, union organizers recorded license plates of workers to obtain addresses for mailing information. The nonemployee organizers placed ads in *The Courant*, a local newspaper. From the union's point of view, all of these attempts were lacking.

Union organizers circulated handbills in the parking lot to reach employees more directly. Lechmere company representatives asked them to leave; when they returned, Lechmere called the police to enforce the no soliciting rule. In response, the UFCW filed an unfair labor practice charge with the NLRB, claiming that Lechmere violated Section 7 of the NLRA, which establishes an employee's right to join a union and participate in collective bargaining activities. The board joined the union as correspondent in an appeal to an administrative law judge who held that the co-petitioners could not be banned from the parking lot. Lechmere appealed to the U.S. Court of Appeals for the First Circuit. The appellate court affirmed the board's ruling, and Lechmere appealed to the Supreme Court and was granted a hearing on certiorari (a request by the Supreme Court to the lower court for the files of the case to be sent up for review).

The *Lechmere* case was argued in the Supreme Court in November 1991. The petitioner stated that the question was whether an employer could prohibit nonemployee union organizers from trespassing on its private property in an attempt to organize its employees when other reasonable ways to reach them were available. Stopping this trespass did not constitute unfair labor practice; rather, it was a consistent policy that applied to everyone. Furthermore, Lechmere argued that it was not access on which union organizers based their unfair plea, but instead how effectively their persuasion was through the various means they had available to reach the employees. Robert Joy, attorney for Lechmere, cited *NLRB v. Babcock & Wilcox Co.* (1956) as the precedent that held that an employer may indeed exclude the union to preserve private property rights when reasonable means were available.

The NLRB countered that Congress had charged it with implementing the policy legislated in the National Labor Relations Act, and as such, it would know the best interpretation. The respondents used the *Babcock* case as well. They claimed that it established that some circumstances might warrant the right of the union to distribute literature on private property and although in *Babcock* those circumstances did not exist, in *Lechmere* they did. In addition, Michael Dreeben, attorney for the NLRB, argued that *Hudgens v. National Labor Relations Board* (1976) set an additional precedent. In the *Hudgens* case, the employer prohibited the trespass during a lawful strike by employees of a shoe company. There could be scores of circumstances to consider when determining whether or not the employer's property rights and the employee's rights under Section 7 of the NLRA were balanced. *Babcock* established that they should be considered; *Hudgens* established that it was the primary responsibility of the board to make those interpretations. Furthermore, it was argued that the board historically and consistently used the criterion in each case whereby rights were balanced with the least amount of damage of one so as to maintain the other.

The Supreme Court decided the case on January 27, 1992, in a 6–3 decision in favor of Lechmere, Inc. Justice Clarence Thomas wrote for the majority. He reasoned that private property rights could not be denied the owners where there were alternatives short of trespass to communicate effectively. In this case, there were signs held in petition, mailings, phone calls, home visits, and newspaper ads. The majority opinion stated that because the union had failed to establish the existence of any special impediments that frustrated access to Lechmere's employees, the board erred in concluding that Lechmere committed an unfair labor practice by barring the nonemployee organizers from its property. This defense of private property reversed the judgment of the First Circuit and denied enforcement of the NLRB's order.

The opposite view was expressed in the dissenting opinion. Justice White wrote the opinion and was joined by Justice Blackmun. They agreed that the Court should follow a policy of deferment, keeping the role of the judiciary narrow. It was their opinion that the board had made its decision on reasonable information and rational logic. Justice Stevens wrote a separate dissent. The current interpretation of the *Babcock* decision, Stevens wrote, is open to question. The majority opinion errors in establishing inflexible judicial rules where Congress has delegated authority to the NLRB to deal with ambiguous matters such as the issue of Section 7 and private property rights. Again, Justice Stevens deferred to the judgment of the board.

Between 1935 and 1992, much changed in the bargaining power between owners and employees. Government intervention in the affairs of the market weighed heavily on the side of labor unions and collective bargaining. In an effort to swing the pendulum back toward equilibrium, the *Lechmere* case placed a heavier burden on the board to supply evidence that the employees' statutory rights supersede the owner's fundamental natural right to control access to its private property. It is also a reminder that Congress cannot defer to a bureaucratic agency that which is not clearly articulated, in view of the fact that the judiciary has the final word.

Kathleen C. Simmons

See Also Contracts; Market Capitalism; National Labor Relations Act of 1935 (Wagner Act); National Labor Relations Board (NLRB); Private Property; Supreme Court

Related Cases

NLRB v. Babcock & Wilcox Co., 351 U.S. 105 (1956) (Union organizers sued for the right to distribute literature in a company parking lot; upheld due to the difficulty of circumstances)

Central Hardware Co. v. NLRB, 407 U.S. 539 (1972)

Hudgens v. National Labor Relations Board, 424 U.S. 507 (1976) (During a lawful union strike, employees were barred from picketing on the employer's private property)

Further Readings

Legal Information Institute, Cornell University Law School. N.d. "*Lechmere Inc., Petitioner v. National Labor Relations Board*, 502 U.S. 527 (112 S.Ct. 841, 117 L.Ed.2d 79) No. 90-970. Opinion, Justice Thomas." http://www.law.cornell.edu/supremecourt/text/502/527#writing-type-1-THOMAS.

Legal Information Institute, Cornell University Law School. N.d. "*Lechmere Inc., Petitioner v. National Labor Relations Board*, 502 U.S. 527 (112 S.Ct. 841, 117 L.Ed.2d 79) No. 90-970. Dissent, Justices White and Blackmun." http://www.law.cornell.edu/supremecourt/text/502/527#writing-type-16-WHITEBLACKMUN.

Legal Information Institute, Cornell University Law School. N.d. "*Lechmere Inc., Petitioner v. National Labor Relations Board*, 502 U.S. 527 (112 S.Ct. 841, 117 L.Ed.2d 79) No. 90-970. Dissent, Justice Stevens." http://www.law.cornell.edu/supremecourt/text/502/527#writing-type-16-STEVENS.

OYEZ, ITT Chicago, Kent College of Law. N.d. "*Lechmere Inc. v. NLRB*." http://www.oyez.org/cases/1990-1999/1991/1991_90_970.

Resources for Teachers

Foundation for Teaching Economics. N.d. "Lesson 4: Property Rights." http://www.fte.org/teacher-resources/lesson-plans/edsulessons/lesson-4-property-rights/.

Kehler, Abbejean. 2007. "The Mystery of Is It Mine or Ours?" econedlink. http://www.econedlink.org/lessons/index.php?lid=462&type=educator.

OYEZ, ITT Chicago, Kent College of Law. N.d. "*Lechmere, Inc., v. NLRB*," http://www.oyez.org/cases/1990-1999/1991/1991_90_970.

Lenin, Vladimir

Born: April 22, 1870, in Simbursk, Russia; Died: January 21, 1924, in Gorki Leninskiye, Russia; first head of the Soviet state; Major Works: *Imperialism* (1916), *The Highest Stage of Capitalism* (1916).

Vladimir Ilyich Ulyanov was born on April 22, 1870, in Simbursk (now called Ulyanovsk), Russia. It was not until 1901 that he adopted the surname "Lenin" while doing some underground party work. Lenin's parents were educated, which caused school to play a central role in Lenin's upbringing. In 1887, shortly after the death of his father, Lenin's older brother, Aleksandr, was arrested and executed for being part of a group that had tried to assassinate Emperor Alexandr III. The responsibility of being head of the household then fell upon Lenin's young shoulders. Many years later, his wife said that it was this event that caused Lenin to become a revolutionary who fought against the system that had been responsible for his brother's execution.

In 1887, Lenin enrolled at Kazan University to study law, but was soon expelled for taking part in a student demonstration. After leaving Kazan University, Lenin went to live with his sister, Anna, and immersed himself in a host of radical literature. The German philosopher Marx captured a great deal of Lenin's attention. Marx's book *Das Kapital* had a huge impact on Lenin's thinking; in 1889, Lenin declared himself a Marxist. Lenin finally managed to finish his law degree in 1892 and moved to Samara to pursue his career as a lawyer. His clients in Samara were mainly Russian peasants, and they helped him better understand the problems of the poor. Lenin saw that the rich abused the poor; he believed that everybody should be equal. He wanted a government that truly represented the people. In the mid-1880s, Lenin left Samara to pursue revolutionary politics with other Marxists. In December 1885, Lenin and other Marxist leaders were found, arrested, and sent to live in exile in Siberia for three years. When Lenin left Siberia, he returned to St. Petersburg to continue leading the revolutionary movement.

In 1904, Russia went to war with Japan. After a number of defeats that impacted Russia's domestic budget, citizens began to speak out about their displeasure with the country's political system. It was around this time that a separate subgroup called the Mensheviks formed under the Marxists. The Mensheviks argued against Lenin, who believed that a real and complete revolution must be led by the proletariat. He formed his own group, called the Bolsheviks, which managed to win a majority on the central committee. The Mensheviks protested that the Bolsheviks paved the way for a one-man dictatorship. Lenin split from the Marxists after his disagreement with the Mensheviks and went into a self-induced exile during the beginning of World War I. In 1916, he fled to

Switzerland, where he wrote *Imperialism* and *The Highest Stage of Capitalism*, which depicted war as the natural result of international capitalism.

In 1917, Russia dispatched its tsars in what became known as the Bolshevik Revolution. Lenin returned to Russia around 1917 as well. From the moment Lenin returned to Russia, he began making plans to secure victory and power for the Bolsheviks. Lenin knew the current leaders' hesitation in pulling the country out of World War I could be easily exploited. After nearly four years of massive losses, the troops were ready to come home to Russia. Lenin used that to his advantage, demanding that Russia exit the war immediately. With this position, Lenin received support from Russia's armed forces, which became a significant asset for him when he sought to seize power. On June 9, 1917, the Bolsheviks encouraged all citizens and soldiers to fill the streets of the capital and to openly demand an immediate end to the war. In June, Lenin found his chance to set the stage for an armed protest against the government. The minister of war, Alexander Kerensky, sent troops out for an offensive along the Austrian front. The offensive failed and the losses weakened Kerensky politically. The stage was set for a revolution.

In October 1917, Lenin led what is now known as the October Revolution, which eventually led to him becoming the leader of Russia. Three years of civil war followed. Determined to win, Lenin proved himself strong enough to secure power. He launched the Red Terror, a campaign used to eliminate opposition in the civilian population. Lenin came out victorious in Russia's bloody civil war, despite the magnitude of the opposition. However, the Russia Lenin dreamed of leading, free of class conflict and truly representative of all citizens, was not actualized, as the country was still reeling from the horrendous civil war. Furthermore, extricating Russia from World War I was extremely expensive. Famine and poverty was rife. In August 1918, Lenin was nearly assassinated, supposedly by Fanny Kaplan. He survived, but was severely wounded and his health was never the same. In 1921, Lenin faced the same kind of peasant uprising upon which he himself had risen to power. To ease the tension, that same year Lenin introduced the New Economic Policy, which allowed workers to sell their grain on the open market. This policy helped the economy somewhat, but Lenin's dreams of Russian glory were never realized.

Lenin suffered a stroke in May 1922, and a second stroke in December of the same year. On March 10, 1923, Lenin had yet another stroke, this one rendering him mute. Nearly 10 months later, on January 21, 1924, he died at age 51 in a village now known as Gorki Leninskiye. In honor of Russia's great leader, Lenin's corpse was embalmed and placed in a mausoleum in Moscow's Red Square, where it remains today for public viewing.

Shima Sadaghiyani

See Also Economic Systems; Marx, Karl; Marxism; Stalin, Joseph

Further Reading

Remnick, David. 1994. *Lenin's Tomb: The Last Days of the Soviet Empire*. New York: Vintage.

Service, Robert. 2000. *Lenin: A Biography*. London: Macmillan.

Trotsky, Leon. 1971. *On Lenin: Notes towards a Biography*. Translated by Tamara Deutscher. London: Harrap.

Resources for Teachers

Huffman, Anne. 2009. "Lemonade and Cookies." econedlink. http://www.econedlink.org/lessons/index.php?lid=350&type=educator.

Lochner v. New York, 198 U.S. 45 (1905)

A Supreme Court Case on Minimum Working Hours

Economic Concepts

Labor movement; contracts; employer; employee; labor unions; labor; derived demand; resource market; public welfare

Economic Impact

An individual right to liberty of contracts is protected from police powers of the state unless the public welfare and safety are threatened.

Economic Summary

The Fourteenth Amendment to the U.S. Constitution, as interpreted in 1905 by the Fuller Court (1903–1905), prohibits states from interfering with most employment contracts. The right to buy and sell labor is a fundamental freedom that in a federal system of governing is protected from arbitrary statutes and acts of state legislatures. Unless there is a reasonable threat to public welfare or realistic concern for public health and safety, regulation of wages between employer and employee cannot be interfered with using the police power of the state. So whether you shoe horses or bake biscuits, your right to buy and sell your labor is exactly that: your right to be protected from arbitrary, unfair, and discriminatory treatment by state legislatures.

Case Summary

The *Lochner* case is about making "dough," figuratively and literally. How much "dough" could a baker make if a baker could make dough, without being limited? It sounds simple; however, the case is not just about bread and wages, it is also an important lesson in federalism and the labor movement, and established a new era in constitutional law regarding the due process clause of the Fifth and Fourteenth Amendments known as the Lochner era.

The United States was the first country to adopt a federal system of government. The framers of the Constitution designed the U.S. model of federalism wherein the national and state governments share power and derive all their authority from the people. The national government is sovereign over the states with defined powers as stated in Article I, Section 8 of the Constitution. Powers not specifically given to the federal government or denied to the states are reserved to the states (as per the Tenth Amendment). However, many powers are shared, such as the power to regulate the health and safety of the people. Setting wage limits and working guidelines for industries are not powers mentioned in the

Constitution, nor are they denied. Therefore, they are left for legislatures to act upon and courts to interpret. The *Lochner* case is an example of this interpretation.

The period between 1870 and the turn of the century in American history is known as the Gilded Age (a term coined by Mark Twain that captured the attitude of less-than-accurate expectations of immigrants toward America at that time). This era was marked by industrial growth, enormous poverty, and the rise of the labor movement. New York was flooded with immigrants from Europe, many believing in the promise of a better life. Conditions did not match these expectations; a few found prosperity, but the reality for the masses was long hours of labor for little pay and crowded unsanitary living conditions. Thousands of workers searched for employment, saturating the labor market. During this era there were few regulations on hours, wages, age, or gender of workers, working conditions, and so forth. Industries often employed fewer workers—frequently women and children because they did not agitate as much as men—at low wages for long hours in unsafe conditions. These circumstances gave rise to labor unions, which organized and pursued an agenda that they felt would improve the lives of the working poor.

In 1894, the New York Press published a series of "muckraking" (a term coined by Theodore Roosevelt to describe writers who exposed the weaknesses of the capitalist system during the Gilded Age) articles on the baking industry. The articles exposed an unhealthy state of affairs, unsafe working conditions, and filthy kitchens. Within months, the public outcry resulted in state officials crafting legislation that significantly changed the baking industry and gave the labor movement a victory. The Bakeshop Act of 1895 pertained specifically to biscuit, bread, and cake bakeries, as well as confectionery establishments. The law restricted the maximum number of hours a person could work in a bakery to 10 hours per day, and not to exceed 60 hours in a week. In addition, it made requirements of building conditions, employee lodging (many journeyman bakers lived in the kitchens where they cooked), ventilation, and overall cleanliness. Within a decade of the state of New York enacting this law, the national government, under the leadership of President Theodore Roosevelt, passed the Pure Food and Drug Act of 1906 to deal with similar public health and safety issues.

Joseph Lochner owned a bakery in Utica, New York, in 1904, and was issued a citation for violating Section 110 of Article 8, Chapter 415, of the law known as the labor law of the State of New York or the Bakeshop Act of 1895 because one of his workers had exceeded the 60-hour rule. He paid a $25 fine. Lochner was given a second citation for the same violation. This time the fee was $50, or 50 days in jail. He asserted that he had been denied his due process, as was his right in the Fourteenth Amendment to the Constitution. His misdemeanor was heard in the county court of Oneida County, where he demurred (made an objection or delay) on several grounds, mainly that what he did was not a crime. The court disagreed and found him guilty. Lochner argued that a person had a liberty of contract with regard to carrying out his business. It was his general right to negotiate with persons to buy and sell their labor and to be free to exercise their right of contract. This right is protected by the due process clause of the Constitution and subject only to legitimate police power of the state. Lochner contended that in this case, there were no reasonable grounds for the state to deny him of this right.

Joseph Lochner appealed his case to the New York Appellate Court and to ultimately the New York Supreme Court, which upheld the ruling of the lower court finding in favor of the state of New York. A writ of error (a writ issued by an appellate court directing the court of record to send a trial record to the appellate court to be looked at for potential errors) brought Lochner to the U.S. Supreme Court, which serves as the final word on policy matters that challenge the delicate balance between federal versus state power and individual rights.

The Supreme Court's responsibility in this case was to determine if the U.S. Constitution prohibited states from restricting the rights of individuals and businesses to negotiate labor and employment contracts. The Court used judicial review to scrutinize the balance between the interests being served by the government statute and the infringement of individual rights. Justice Peckman in writing the opinion of the court held there was no reasonable governmental interest that justified this encroachment on individual liberty. The Court claimed the singling out of bakery workers was arbitrary and discriminatory. These workers were in no less peril for their health and well-being as were lawyers and others who toiled many hours in their occupations. In his dissent, Justice Harlan stated that it was the burden of the appellant (Lochner) to prove that the New York law was indeed beyond a question plainly not reasonable and was in excess of legislative authority, which he claimed Lochner did not do. In his separate dissent, Justice Holmes cited Sunday laws (laws designed to restrict or ban some or all Sunday shopping for religious standards) and usury laws (the practice of making unethical monetary loans with excessive interest rates) as early examples of state laws that may regulate life in such a way as to interfere with the liberty to contract, but nevertheless remained laws.

In March 1905, the Supreme Court voted to reverse the lower court's verdict. The Fuller Court determined the outcome in favor of individual freedom and against the power of the state to enact legislation restricting free enterprise. The Lochner era is characterized by this new interpretation of the due process clause to have a substantive content. Using this lens, the Constitution protected minorities and individuals from arbitrary control by government with regard to fundamental rights that are inherent within their personal freedom. However, this interpretation would end with *West Coast Hotel Co. v. Parrish* (1937).

The Lochner era was an outcome of the industrial revolution. Today, however, interpretation of substantive due process with an emphasis on minority rights and protection from government encroachment of private conduct remains well established, though still controversial.

Kathleen C. Simmons

See Also Contracts; Supreme Court

Related Cases

Holden v. Hardy, 169 U.S. 366 (1898) (Utah state eight-hour maximum working day law for miners was upheld; Peckham dissented in this case)

Muller v. Oregon, 208 U.S. 412 (1908) (Oregon state law restricting women to maximum 10-hour work days in a mechanical establishment or factory or laundry upheld due to the prevailing opinion about women's work capabilities)

Adkins v. Children's Hospital, 261, U.S. 525 (1923) (Found that a Washington, D.C., law regarding a minimum wage established for women and children was unconstitutional and overreached the legitimate police power of the state)

West Coast Hotel Co. v. Parrish, 300 U.S. 379 (1937) (Minimum wage for women in Washington State upheld)

Further Readings

Legal Information Institute, Cornell University Law School. N.d. "*Lochner v. New York* (No. 292), Syllabus, Supreme Court of the United States, 198 U.S. 45." http://www.law.cornell.edu/supct/html/historics/USSC_CR_0198_0045_ZS.html.

Legal Information Institute, Cornell University Law School. N.d. "*Lochner v. New York* (No. 292), Syllabus, Supreme Court of the United States, 198 U.S. 45, Opinion Justice Peckham." http://www.law.cornell.edu/supct/html/historics/USSC_CR_0198_0045_ZO.html.

Legal Information Institute, Cornell University Law School. N.d. "*Lochner v. New York* (No. 292), Syllabus, Supreme Court of the United States, 198 U.S. 45, Dissenting Opinion Justice Harlan." http://www.law.cornell.edu/supct/html/historics/USSC_CR_0198_0045_ZD.html.

Legal Information Institute, Cornell University Law School. N.d. "*Lochner v. New York* (No. 292), Syllabus, Supreme Court of the United States, 198 U.S. 45, Dissenting Opinion Justice Holmes." http://www.law.cornell.edu/supct/html/historics/USSC_CR_0198_0045_ZD1.html.

Resources for Teachers

Foundation for Teaching Economics. N.d. "Lesson 5: Labor Markets." http://www.fte.org/teacher-resources/lesson-plans/efllessons/lesson-5-labor-markets/.

Library of Congress. N.d. "Labor-Lesson Plans." http://www.loc.gov/teachers/classroommaterials/themes/labor/lessonplans.html.

OYEZ, ITT Chicago, Kent College of Law. N.d. "*Lochner v. New York*." http://www.oyez.org/cases/1901-1939/1904/1904_292.

Majority Rule

Majority rule is a mechanism of government associated mostly with democratic societies. It is a principle based on the suggestion that everyone is equal, demonstrated through votes—that is, one person, one vote. Political decisions and outcomes are based on which proposal receives more than half of the votes of those present. In other words, those whose views lie in the majority—more than 50 percent—should prevail.

The philosophical foundation of the majority mechanism is partly based upon the Jeffersonian notion that there is more intelligence and wisdom in a number of persons united than in a single individual, and that the number of the legislators is more important than their quality. Although presented as an argument for the First Amendment of the U.S. Constitution, the principle that truth and wisdom will prevail over falsehood and ignorance in a free and open marketplace of ideas explains the Founding Fathers' preference for the majority rule mechanism. The Founding Fathers believed that the American people and their elected representatives would be able to marginalize fanatical ideas, and that the decisions of Congress would reflect the majority preference of a centrist, more balanced resolution.

Despite this philosophy, in early American history, some leaders were suspicious of the idea of giving power to the majority, fearing that the collective decisions made by non-elite actors would harm the interest of the politically and financially privileged. Some were also afraid of a tyranny of the minority, where power would be concentrated in the hands of the few. To resolve this, the Founding Fathers wanted to create a republic (a government in which power is exercised by elected representatives) rather than a government in which the people could rule directly.

Some have argued that majority rule disallows the possibility of minority interests realizing any gain; that in the majority rule mechanism, there is nothing to prevent the majority from expropriating the minority, or from tyrannizing it in other ways by imposing the majority's preferences on the minority. According to James Madison, the prevention of tyranny rests with the federalization of the United States. By balancing power between the state and federal governments, the possibility of a total majority takeover of the United States is essentially foreclosed. For Madison, the main danger that remained was that the majority poor citizenry would vote for a confiscatory legislation at the expense of the rich minority. Again, however, this is avoided by the Jeffersonian belief that political representatives, in the interest of keeping their positions, will vote in accordance with the balanced interests of their constituents.

Regarding the notion of a tyranny of the minority, economist and social scientist Mancur Olson argued in *The Logic of Collective Action: Public Goods and the Theory of Groups* (1971) that narrow, well-organized, and more resourceful minorities are more likely to assert their interests over those of the majority. Olson argues that when the benefits of political action (e.g., lobbying) are spread over fewer agents, there is a stronger individual incentive to contribute to that political activity. Lobby groups or those with narrow interests, especially those who can reward active participation to their group goals, might therefore be able to thwart the political process of the majority rule mechanism.

Majority rule implies that for all issues, a prevailing side with 50 percent or more of the votes will exist. In reality, this scenario is rarely realized, as arguments around an issue can have many sides. In addition, to realize the support of 50 percent or more takes considerable time and resources to convince politicians. The reliance on resources to sway votes gives a disadvantage to those positions that lack organizational, grassroots, and financial support, and is counterintuitive to the principle of equally weighted votes.

In this case, when there is no majority, governments relax the majority rule principle and allow a plurality: the position with the most votes wins, not necessarily requiring a 50 percent majority.

Nevena Trajkov

See Also Olson, Mancur

Further Readings

Olson, Mancur. 1971. *The Logic of Collective Action: Public Goods and the Theory of Groups*. Cambridge, MA: Harvard University Press.

Tocqueville, Alexis de. 1838. "Chapter XV-Power of the Majority in the United States, and Its Consequences." In *Democracy in America*, 201–15. London: Saunders and Otley.

Wayne, S., G. C. Mackenzie, and R. Cole. 2006. *Conflict and Consensus in American Politics*. Belmont, CA: Wadsworth.

Resources for Teachers

Learning to Give. N.d. "Majority Rules, but (The)." http://learningtogive.org/lessons/unit47/lesson2.html.

Parliamentary Education Office (PEO). N.d. "Parliamentary Lesson Plans: Representation; Majority Rule." http://www.peo.gov.au/teachers/parliamentary-lesson-plans/majority-rule.html.

Mankiw, Gregory

Born: March 2, 1958, in Trenton, New Jersey; American; macroeconomics, public policy economics; Major Works: *Principles of Economics* (1st ed., 2000), *Intermediate Macroeconomics* (2010), *Macroeconomics and the Financial System* (with Laurence Ball) (2010).

N. Gregory Mankiw is one of the major contributors to new Keynesian economic theory. New Keynesian economic theory was developed by new classical economic theorists in response to the criticisms of the traditional Keynesian model. Through his writings and textbooks, Mankiw is considered one of the key interpreters of the neo-Keynesian theory to the general public. He also is a major contributor to the current macroeconomic policy debate and its development.

Mankiw was born in Trenton, New Jersey, on March 2, 1958, of Ukrainian parents. He holds a BA in economics from Princeton University and a PhD in economics from the Massachusetts Institute of Technology. Mankiw has been influenced throughout his career by many famous economists of differing viewpoints, including John Maynard Keynes, Arthur Pigou, Stanley Fischer, and Milton Friedman.

Mankiw's research interests include the U.S. economy, entitlements, international trade policy, price adjustment, consumer behavior, financial markets, monetary and fiscal policy, and economic growth. Mankiw's interest and study of economics has led him to author several textbooks, write a daily blog, and receive many honors. He is Robert M. Beren Professor of Economics at Harvard University. His teaching includes the very popular "Principles of Economics" course. He is also a visiting research fellow at the American Enterprise Institute. From 2003 to 2005, he was chairman of President George W. Bush's Council of Economic Advisers. He also maintains a blog that is read widely across the country and the world (http://gregmankiw.blogspot.com).

Mankiw has authored several of the most popular textbooks used in high school and college economics courses, including *Principles of Economics*, in its sixth edition; *Intermediate Macroeconomics*, in its seventh edition; and his newest text, with Laurence M. Ball, *Macroeconomics and the Financial System*, in its second edition. His academic papers are published in such journals as *American Economic Review*, *Journal of Political Economy*, and the *Quarterly Journal of Economics*. He is a frequent contributor to the *New York Times*, reflecting the views of the new Keynesian economics.

Mankiw's contributions to new Keynesian economics highlight the disagreement with new classical economics regarding the adjustment of wages and prices. Classical and monetarist theory says that in the short run, changes in the money supply affect employment and production levels. New classical economics theorizes that wages and prices are flexible, allowing markets to clear and regain their equilibrium (rebalancing demand and supply). New classical thinkers Robert Lucas Jr., Thomas J. Sargent, and Robert Barro criticized Keynesian theory (*The General Theory of Employment, Interest and Money*), saying that the Keynesian model does not explain the sluggish nature of wage and price changes to obtain equal demand and supply (market-clearing mechanism).

Through his writings and textbooks, Mankiw is one of the leading authors to interpret and explain the new Keynesian theory for the general public's understanding. Mankiw's writings are a response to the criticisms levied by the new classical economists regarding the initial market-clearing mechanism (prices determined by equal demand and supply) first proposed by John Maynard Keynes. The new Keynesian economics suggest that markets do not clear (where demand and supply are equal) quickly and that economic fluctuations are explained through models where wages and prices are not as mobile or flexible as the new classical economists contend. This new Keynesian model includes involuntary unemployment along with the important role of monetary policy to adjust supply-and-demand conditions when markets do not clear (which is assumed in the new classical thinking).

In the 1990s, a combination view emerged between the new classical and new Keynesian theorists. Mankiw's textbooks reflect this consensus view of a dynamic economy with inflexible components and market imperfections in the short run, but ultimately a dynamic economy that adjusts in the long run.

Mankiw's awards include the Wolf Balleisen Memorial Prize in 1980 and the Galbraith Teaching Prize in 1991.

Martha Rowland Blenman

See Also Friedman, Milton; Keynes, John Maynard

Selected Works by Gregory Mankiw

Ball, Laurence, and Gregory Mankiw. 2010. *Macroeconomics and the Financial System*. 2nd ed. New York: Worth.

Mankiw, Gregory. 2010. *Intermediate Macroeconomics*. 7th ed. New York: Worth.

Mankiw, Gregory. 2011. *Principles of Economics*. 6th ed. Boston: South-Western.

Mankiw, N. Gregory, and David Romer, eds. 1991. *New Keynesian Economics*. 2 vols. Cambridge, MA: MIT Press.

Selected Works about Gregory Mankiw

"Gregory Mankiw." N.d. Harvard University Department of Economics. http://www.economics.harvard.edu/faculty/mankiw.

Mankiw, Greg. "Greg Mankiw's Blog: Random Observations for Students of Economics." Accessed May 11, 2012. http://gregmankiw.blogspot.com/index.html.

Market Capitalism

Capitalism is an economic system that emphasizes the private ownership of the factors of production, competition, and markets where the interaction of buyer and seller is free and unregulated. Capitalism can also be referred to as the free enterprise system or a market economy.

Capitalism existed long before the term was used. Ancient European trade routes were utilized for years to exchange goods. In some cases, merchants became wealthy as a result of trade and the expansion of trade networks.

Capitalism can be traced back to the European system of trade called mercantilism. From the 1400s to the 1700s, European nations sought to gain money by exporting more than they imported. The mercantilist system was nationalist in nature and existed for the sole benefit of the mother country. Countries with overseas colonies were also used for trading purposes and were unable to trade freely with other nations. The mother country would extract raw materials from its colonies and then produce the final goods that would be sold to the colonies.

Adam Smith (1723–1790) attacked mercantilism and promoted the benefits of free trade when he wrote *An Inquiry into the Nature and Causes of the Wealth of Nations* (1776). *The Wealth of Nations* emphasized that the government should not interfere in economic affairs of individuals and businesses. Smith spoke of laissez-faire trade, a system in which the government should not interfere in trade nor should it impose trade restrictions, such as tariffs. This idea of free trade was a new and radical economic philosophy in the 1700s. The writings of Adam Smith would be later adopted by much of the world as the mercantilist system was abandoned and a new economic philosophy changed the world.

Karl Marx (1818–1883) was critical of capitalism; he believed it gave an advantage to business owners at the expense of workers. He stated that at some point, the system of capitalism would be overthrown by the working class, or proletariat. His beliefs led to the creation of communism and were published in books such as the *Communist Manifesto* (1848). Marx believed that someday capitalism would be overthrown in favor of socialism and communism.

Max Weber (1864–1920) is also linked to capitalism and wrote about the subject in his major work, *The Protestant Ethic and the Spirit of Capitalism* (1930). In the book, he discusses how the Protestant work ethic contributed to the development of capitalism.

The Industrial Revolution also contributed to the growth of capitalism. As new technology was created, so were new products. For example, Britain's textile industry boomed as the result of the spinning jenny, invented in 1764, and the water frame, invented in 1768. This revolution led to the faster production of new goods but also led to low wages and long hours for workers. As countries industrialized, new problems and challenges developed, such as unfair competition, child labor, and a larger gap between the rich and the poor.

As a result of the Great Depression in the 1930s, economist John Maynard Keynes (1883–1946) developed a new theory of government intervention to stabilize a capitalist economy. In his book *The General Theory of Employment, Interest and Money* (1936), Keynes promoted government's increased role in society in response to the severe economic crisis.

A distinct feature of capitalism is open markets that are naturally regulated by supply and demand and the unfettered interaction of buyers and sellers. In this system, individual choice is the basis for a capitalist economy where consumers choose which goods and services to consume to satisfy their economic wants. Producers produce goods to satisfy economic wants and to make a profit. In this system, there is little government involvement, as the factors of production are privately owned and not regulated or owned by the government.

In market capitalism incentives play the key role. In an economy that has an environment with the appropriate incentives for producers and consumers, both gain. Market capitalism sets the appropriate incentives for individuals as producers to be successful and earn profits. Competition helps create the proper incentives for a market economy.

For the consumer, competition can drive down prices and lead to high quality goods and services. Private businesses can also be created that are free from government control. Furthermore, this type of market is characterized by specialization as businesses produce the goods and services that they are suited for or that they can produce most efficiently, or at a low opportunity cost. The circular flow model details how interactions occur in a market economy.

After the fall of communism in the Soviet Union, more countries turned to capitalist economic systems. This transition was not easy and resulted in economic struggles for many former communist nations. Economic powerhouses such as China have mixed economies that contain some capitalist elements. Most economies today are in fact mixed economies, and are not truly capitalist in nature.

Angela M. LoPiccolo

See Also Economic Systems; Keynes, John Maynard; Keynesian Economics; Marx, Karl; Mercantilism; Smith, Adam

Further Reading

Appleby, Joyce. 2010. *The Relentless Revolution: A History of Capitalism*. New York: W. W. Norton.

Bassiry, G. R., and Marc Jones. 1993. "Adam Smith and the Ethics of Contemporary Capitalism." *Journal of Business Ethics* 12: 621–27.

Collins, Randall. 1980. "Weber's Last Theory of Capitalism: A Systematization." *American Sociological Review* 46: 925–42.

Keynes, John Maynard. 1936. *The General Theory of Employment, Interest and Money*. New York: Macmillan.

Marx, Karl, and Frederick Engels. 2010. *The Communist Manifesto*. London: Arcturus.

Smith, Adam. 1776. *An Inquiry into the Nature and Causes of the Wealth of Nations*. London: J. J. Tourneisen and J. L. Legrand.

Weber, Maximillian. 1930. *The Protestant Ethic and the Spirit of Capitalism*. London: Allen & Unwin.

Resources for Teachers

Foundation for Teaching Economics. N.d. "Is Capitalism Good for the Poor?" http://www.fte.org/teacher-resources/lesson-plans/is-capitalism-good-for-the-poor/.

Herman-Ellison, Lisa C. 2007. "Comparative Economic Systems." econedlink. http://www.econedlink.org/lessons/index.php?lid=322&type=educator.

Market Failure

An economic condition is considered a market failure when an economic variable exists that makes a specific economic interaction unfeasible, unproductive, or unresponsive to society. The term "market failure" encompasses a need for an outside agent, usually government, to become involved with a specific economic transaction. A market failure can be the result of the market price being too high for the transaction to be commercially feasible, a market not producing enough of a specific economic good, or the market interaction causing externalities (costs external to the transaction). Market failure can also be the result of too little information on the part of the buyer.

The three key sources of market failure are externalities, public goods, and imperfect information. Markets are most efficient when all the costs and benefits of a decision are internalized and borne solely by the buyer and seller. Externalities exist when the benefits or costs are not totally internalized and impact a third party not involved in the original decision. A market transaction fails to include external costs or external benefits. An outside agent such as a government is necessary to address the external costs or benefits of the transaction, or too much of some goods would be produced and not enough of others.

A negative externality results when the costs of a transaction spill over to someone other than those who were party to the original transaction. Pollution is a negative externality, as it is a transaction cost borne outside the original transaction that created the pollution. To correct for a negative externality such as pollution, the government institutes policies to alter the behavior of those involved and internalize as much as possible the transaction costs or reduce the size of the externality. Government may do this by imposing a tax or fine on the transaction, or it may provide an incentive to change behavior with a tax credit or subsidy.

If there is a positive externality, someone outside the original transaction benefits from the action. To expand a positive externality, the government can subsidize the good.

A public good is also an example of a market failure. Public goods are nonexclusive, which means that everyone can use a good and no one can be excluded from its benefit. They are also nonrival, which means that consumption by one person does not reduce the usefulness of a good to others. The classic example of a public good is national defense.

Another example of market failure is imperfect information, which results in buyers and sellers having different amounts of information about a good. In this case, buyers depend on the firm's reputation and personal experience, and it is possible that they will pay more for a good or service than necessary.

A natural monopoly is the result of market failure. A natural monopoly can set prices higher than its costs and does not allow for competing businesses to be created. In some cases, though, it is more practical to have a government-operated or government-regulated natural monopoly in some industries, such as utilities. In these industries, there are relatively large fixed costs accompanied with low marginal costs. To have different companies competing for an undifferentiated commodity would be a gross misallocation of resources. The companies in these industries need to be very large to achieve the economies of scale necessary for the product to be priced so the consumer can afford it and the producer is willing to produce it and achieve a profit to stay in business. Market failure can also lead to government failure, which occurs when government intervention makes a situation worse. In some cases, this is because governments do not have information to correct the problem. It may also be due to government intervention being more complicated than anticipated, and may make the problem worse.

When examining market failure, one should apply the double market failure test. The problem should be identified and the possible resolutions to correcting the market failure should also be considered. Potential solutions depend on the nature of the problem as well as the potential effect or anticipated results of the proposed resolution.

When looking at correcting a market failure, the transaction cost must also be considered. The transaction cost affects how an externality is dealt with and if the costs become too high the desire to resolve the problem will disappear. The government may determine how to implement a resolution to a market failure based on this approach.

Market failure will continue to focus on goods and services that affect a large number of users and will only disappear when the costs of operating the price system are zero, which is impossible to achieve. Issues such as clean air and clean water will continue to be addressed by the government.

Angela M. LoPiccolo

See Also Externalities; Free Rider; Public Goods

Further Reading

Colander, David C. 2010. *Economics*. New York: McGraw-Hill/Irwin.

Foldvary, Fred, and Daniel B. Klein. 2001. "Technology and Market Failure." *Regulation* 24: 9–11.

Yao, Dennis A. 1988. "Beyond the Reach of the Invisible Hand: Impediments to Economic Activity, Market Failures, and Profitability." *Strategic Management Journal* 9: 59–70.

Zerbe Jr., Richard O., and Howard McCurdy. 2000. "The End of Market Failure." *Regulation* 23: 10–14.

Zerbe Jr., Richard O., and Howard E. McCurdy. 1999. "The Failure of Market Failure." *Journal of Policy Analysis and Management* 18: 558–78.

Resources for Teachers

Federal Reserve Bank of St. Louis. N.d. "Externalities: The Economic Lowdown Podcast Series." http://www.stlouisfed.org/education_resources/economic-lowdown-podcast-series/externalities/.

McREL. N.d. "Not in My Backyard!" http://www2.mcrel.org/compendium/activityDetail.asp?activityID=68.

Marx, Karl

Born: May 5, 1818, in Trier, Prussia (Germany); Died: March 14, 1883, in London, England; German; economic philosophy; Major Works: *The Communist Manifesto* (with Friedrich Engels) (1848), *Capital: A Critique of Political Economy* (1867).

Karl Marx used the study of economics to write harsh and systematic criticisms of capitalism, and by extension, the governments and societies that foster it. He proposed a completely new world order called communism, characterized by a stateless society and an equal distribution of resources. Marx's writings covered political philosophy, history, and economics. Marx died in 1883.

Karl Heinrich Marx was born on May 5, 1818, in Trier, Prussia (present-day Germany). Marx's father, a lawyer and descendant of Jewish rabbis, had disavowed Judaism and converted to Lutheranism. Marx later rejected religion of any type, coining the famous dictum, "Religion is the opium of the masses."

Marx studied law to please his father. However, he was more interested in philosophy, transferring to the University of Berlin and changing his studies to philosophy. He earned his doctorate in 1841. Upon graduation, Marx found a job in Cologne as a journalist for the Socialist newspaper *Die Rheinische Zeitung*. Prussia—and indeed most of Europe—was not tolerant of dissident ideas, and Marx soon found himself expelled from Prussia. He spent most of the next decade moving from country to country, repeatedly exiled for his radical beliefs. In 1848, Marx penned his seminal work *The Communist Manifesto* in Brussels, Belgium. It was intended as an outline of doctrine for the small international communist movement.

The Communist Manifesto (or in the original German, *Manifest der Kommunistische Partei*) begins with a sweeping statement that the history of the existing society is a history of class struggles. Marx described human history as characterized by conflicts between the oppressed and the oppressors of social classes. To Marx, any and every idea, institution, religion, or belief served to support the accumulation of wealth of the dominant social class.

Marx identified capitalism as the economic system that replaced feudalism. He credited capitalism with immense powers of production, and he described a shrinking, globalizing world that brings industrial workers—the proletariat—into closer association with one another as they crowd into cities to seek jobs. However, he also noted several "contradictions" within capitalism that would eventually spell doom for the system.

Marx submitted that shrinking profits force the capitalist bourgeoisie either to seek new markets for their products or to exploit their workers with increasing cruelty. Even though these techniques restore profits, the frenzy of exploitation causes overproduction, followed by financial panics, recessions, and reduced profits. Eventually, the cycle begins all over again. According to Marx, capitalism also results in an increasing concentration of the proletariat into factories. This competition among workers reduces wages to the bare level of subsistence. This idea is similar to David Ricardo's iron law of wages. As workers become more like one another, they are more likely to band together to fight for a bigger share of the profits, even while resources are monopolized under fewer and fewer capitalists. The final result of this unstable equilibrium will be a revolution of the proletariat. Marx then predicts that the proletariat will overthrow the bourgeoisie and usher in a new social and political order. A brief period of socialism with the proletariat acting as the ruling class will exist, in which the government reorganizes society to achieve total equality. Once realized, the government will become irrelevant and wither away, making way for a classless state called communism.

Marx was the intellectual giant of the early communist movement. As such, he was under constant pressure by his colleagues to write a full-length work that would show the economic necessity of the ideas enshrined in *The Communist Manifesto*.

Marx lived his years in poverty, supported mainly by his friend and cowriter, Friedrich Engels. Engels encouraged Marx to expand his work. In 1867, Marx published a more thorough analysis of capitalism, *Capital: A Critique of Political Economy*. He used many of the tools of economic analysis that were created by classical economists such as Adam Smith and David Ricardo. He begins with the concept of value and how commodities become valuable. For Marx, items are valuable according to the amount of labor that it takes to produce them. By adding capital resources to the production process, capitalists can reduce labor to that of a simple tool from which still more value, or surplus value, is obtained. His economic analysis merged the political and historical theories he described in *The Communist Manifesto*.

Soon after Marx's death, the impact of his ideas gained such influence that he has been called the most important thinker of the second millennium. His writings inspired revolutions in Russia, China, Cuba, North Korea, Vietnam, and Cambodia. By 1950, about a third of the world lived under a political system based on Marxist thought. Perhaps more importantly, Marxian methods have been introduced into every social science discipline. Marx's work taught later social researchers to use class analysis, which in turn opened the door for others to think in terms of oppressed cross sections of society. Ironically, Marxian analysis is used least in the field of economics. Marx's ideas continue to challenge a world still coming to terms with the implications of capitalism.

Karl Marx died on March 14, 1883, in London, England.

Stephen H. Day

See Also Command Economy; Economic Systems; Smith, Adam; Welfare State

Selected Works by Karl Marx

Marx, Karl. 1909. *Capital*. Vol. 3 (1894, published posthumously by Friedrich Engels). Chicago: Charles H. Kerr.

Marx, Karl. 1907. *Capital*. Vol. 2 (1885, published posthumously by Friedrich Engels). Chicago: Charles H. Kerr.

Marx, Karl. 1906. *Capital: A Critique of Political Economy*. Vol. 1 (1867). Chicago: Charles H. Kerr.

Marx, Karl, and Friedrich Engels. N.d. *The Communist Manifesto*, 1848. Accessed December 23, 2010. http://www.marxists.org/archive/marx/works/1848/communist-manifesto/index.htm.

Selected Works about Karl Marx

Berlin, Isaiah. 1995. *Karl Marx*. London: Fontana Press.

Berlin, Isaiah. 1978. *Karl Marx: His Life and Environment*. Oxford: Oxford University Press.

Engels, Frederick. N.d. "Marx-Engels Biography: Karl Marx." Marx and Engels Internet Archive. Accessed March 15, 2011. http://www.marxists.org/archive/marx/bio/marx/eng-1869.htm.

Wheen, Francis. 2008. *Marx's Das Kapital: A Biography*. New York: Grove Press.

Marxism

Marxism is the economic and political theory and practice introduced by the German political philosophers Karl Marx (1818–1883) and Friedrich Engels (1820–1895). Marxian economics holds that actions and human institutions are economically determined and class struggle is the basic agency of historical change. This class struggle will result in capitalism ultimately being overtaken by communism.

Karl Heinrich Marx was born on May 5, 1818, and died in March 1883. Marx is known most as a revolutionary socialist. His class struggle theory has influenced much of economic thought. Marx published *The Communist Manifesto* (1848) and *Capital*, or *Das Kapital* (1867), two key publications of the Marxist movement.

Friedrich Engels was born on November 28, 1820, and died on August 5, 1895. He was a German social scientist, philosopher, author, and was also known as the father of Marxist theory. He is the publisher of *The Condition of the Working Class in England* (1844). This book was written based on his personal observations and his research. When Karl Marx died, Engels continued working on *Das Kapital* book volumes.

The writings of Marx and Engels's contribution to Marxism economics had a significant impact and influence in their fight for Marxism economics. *The Communist Manifesto* has been recognized as one of the world's most influential political manuscripts. The book was held dearly and championed by the Communist League as it laid out its purposes and program. *The Communist Manifesto* presents an analytical approach to the problems with capitalism and the resulting class struggle. The book contains Marx and Engels's theories about the nature of society and politics in their own words. The book briefly describes their ideas about how capitalist society would soon be replaced by a classless society, i.e., socialism, then advancing to communism. It does not offer a prediction of communism's potential future forms.

In *Das Kapital*, Marx submits that the true worth and value of an economy is based on the value of its labor. Labor, therefore, is the definitive source of a company's profit. Marx further claims that the value of the labor exceeds a company's profit, leading to the surplus value of labor or exploitation of the laborer. As a result, Marx argues that capitalism's excessive surplus value of labor leads to capitalists abusing the laborer. This abuse of the laborer will lead to an uprising of the laborer over the capitalist in a revolution that he and Engels describe in *The Communist Manifesto*.

According to Marxian economic theory, social relations form the basis of society, including the forces and relations of production. The components of the production process can be understood as the employer-employee working relationship and conditions, the division of labor, and property relations into which people enter to produce the necessities of life.

These relations make an impact on society's other relationships and ideas, which translate into a societal superstructure. The superstructure of a society includes culture, institutions, political power structures, roles, and rituals. Along with the location also known as a state, the economic system creates the base. Forces that are applied by people in the process of production (materials, resources, tools, and techniques, and the human body and brain) are defined by this concept, including management and engineering functions. In addition, human knowledge can be defined as a productive force.

Bernard P. Kanjoma

See Also Command Economy; Democratic Socialism; Economic Systems; Fascism; Lenin, Vladimir; Marx, Karl; Stalin, Joseph; Welfare State

Further Reading

Marx, Karl, and Frederick Engels. 1848. "Manifesto of the Communist Party." https://www.marxists.org/archive/marx/works/download/pdf/Manifesto.pdf.

Marxists Internet Archive. N.d. "Beginners Guide to Marxism." https://www.marxists.org/subject/students/index.htm.

Sowell, Thomas. 1985. *Marxism Philosophy and Economics*. New York: William Morrow & Company.

Woods, Alan. 2013. "The Ideas of Karl Marx." *In Defence of Marxism*. http://www.marxist.com/karl-marx-130-years.htm.

Resources for Teachers

Cross Curricular Connections. 2008. "Car Shopping." econedlink. http://www.econedlink.org/lessons/index.php?lid=176&type=educator.

EDvantage. N.d. "Economics: History of Economic Thought; Karl Marx." http://www.theedvantage.org/economics/history-economic-thought/marx-karl.

Foundation for Teaching Economics. N.d. "Lesson 4: How Incentives Affect Innovation." http://www.fte.org/teacher-resources/lesson-plans/is-capitalism-good-for-the-poor/lesson-4-how-incentives-affect-innovation/.

Mr. Donn's Social Studies Site. N.d. "Karl Marx & Marxism:Lesson Plans, Games, Activities." Accessed June 3, 2014. http://sociology.mrdonn.org/marxism.html.

McCulloch v. Maryland, 17 U.S. 316 (1819)

A Supreme Court Case Regarding the Federal Government's Authority to Establish a National Bank

Economic Concepts

Central bank; national bank; taxation; debt

Economic Impact

This case confirmed that the federal government had the authority to establish a national bank.

Economic Summary

In 1790, Alexander Hamilton, the first U.S. Secretary of the Treasury, was adamant regarding the importance of a central bank to the stability of property within a nation. The First Bank of the United States was started to help facilitate the management of Revolutionary War debt. The Second National Bank was established with the intention of serving the nation's commercial and banking needs.

Unlike the power to create post offices, the power to create banks is not stated in the Constitution. However, the powers to lay and collect taxes, borrow money, regulate commerce, declare war, and raise and support armies and navies are listed in the Constitution.

These powers include a considerable portion of the industry of the nation. The United States did not create a bank simply to be in the banking business but rather as a means to carry out its expressed duties. The architects of the Constitution intended there to be inherent powers in the government, in addition to those necessary and proper to carry out the government's responsibilities.

Case Summary

In 1811, the U.S. Congress lacked the one vote necessary to continue the First Bank of the United States. Consequently, in 1816, after the War of 1812, Congress set up the Second National Bank to assist in dealing with the economic consequences of yet another war debt on the nation. The Second Bank functioned as a clearinghouse; it held large quantities of state banks' notes in reserve and could discipline banks with the threat of redeeming those notes if there was any concern regarding unregulated currency (the overissuing of notes). In effect, this procedure functioned as an early bank regulator.

The Second National Bank was similar in structure to the First Bank, in that the government held one-fifth of the shares, but it had more than double the capital. The Second National Bank opened in Philadelphia and added branches in other states, one of which was in Baltimore, Maryland. In reaction to the branch bank opening in the state of Maryland, the General Assembly of Maryland enacted a tax on all banks or branches thereof, within its boundaries that were not chartered by the legislature of the state of Maryland. This tax was based on the transactions of bank notes. Any bank not chartered by the authority of the state was required to use special stamped paper for its bank notes and, in effect, pay 2 percent of the value of the notes as a tax, or pay a general tax of $15,000 a year. Many states, particularly in the West and South, attempted to keep branches of the national bank out of their states by passing similar state laws. The power to tax the federal bank notes held the potential to close the national bank's doors within the state of Maryland.

James McCulloch, a cashier for the Baltimore branch of the Second National Bank, refused to pay it. A representative of the State of Maryland took the bank deposits (totaling over $2,000) from the Baltimore branch of the Second National Bank in response to the bank's failure to pay the tax or follow Maryland law. McCulloch was then sued for violating the Maryland Act.

James McCulloch admitted in Baltimore County Court that he was not complying with the Maryland rule to pay the tax or the annual lump sum. The county court found in favor of Maryland. The case was appealed to the Court of Appeals of the State of Maryland, which affirmed the county court's ruling. This was the culmination of a huge dispute between the federal and state governments that the Supreme Court was required to remedy.

The case was taken by writ of error (in this case a command by the U.S. Supreme Court for the records of a case, in order that some alleged error in the proceedings of that case might be corrected) to the U.S. Supreme Court. The petitioner, James McCulloch, was more than a federal bureaucrat; he was essentially the power of the federal government. The respondent was the state of Maryland.

The case was heard on February 22, 1819, in front of a seven-member court led by Chief Justice John Marshall. The Supreme Court heard oral arguments and narrowed the case to two fundamental questions. First, can the national government create a bank? This was not an unfamiliar issue. Since the opening of the First National Bank, there had been an ongoing debate in Congress as to whether or not this was within the constitutional powers of the federal government. Although there was no enumerated power granted to Congress to incorporate a bank, there was the implied power that the Court felt was inherent within the government to perform the other responsibilities and expectations the people had of the government. In addition, the power granted in the U.S. Constitution to Congress to make laws that are necessary to carry out the execution of the enumerated and expressed powers is clearly stated in the Constitution. The end result must be the legitimate accomplishment of the role of government. Chief Justice Marshall expressed the opinion of the Court that it was in fact within the power of Congress to create a bank.

Therefore, a second question followed: If it is constitutional for the government to create a bank, can a state tax that entity if it is within the boundaries of the state? The Court's retort to Maryland's claim that the Constitution was enacted by independent states and therefore subordinates to the states was that this claim was inaccurate. It expressed the thought that the Constitution was ratified by three-fourths of the states. The Constitution's reference to "We the People" is a collective response to accepting the legality of the Union. Legitimizing the Union as stated in the Constitution as the superior law of the land relegated the previous sovereignty of the states, which created it, subordinate. Therefore, although limited in its powers, the Constitution is supreme over state laws and the states cannot apply taxes that would possibly destroy federal legislative law.

For that reason, the Maryland's state tax on the U.S. Bank was found to be unconstitutional. In a unanimous decision on March 6, 1819, the Marshall Court reversed the judgment of the lower court. This landmark case by the Supreme Court established the precedent of supremacy of the federal government over the states.

Kathleen C. Simmons

See Also Federal Reserve Act of 1913; Federal Reserve System; Taxes

Related Cases

Bank of the United States v. Deveaux, 9 U.S. 61 (1809)

Briscoe v. Bank of Kentucky, 36 U.S. 259 (1837)

Veazy Bank v. Fenno, 75 U.S. 533 (1869)

Juilliard v. Greenman, 110 U.S. 421 (1884)

Further Reading

Internet Archive; FedFlix. 1977. "*McCulloch v. Maryland* (1977), Judicial Conference of the United States." http://archive.org/details/gov.ntis.AVA02154VNB1.

Legal Information Institute. Cornell University Law School. N.d. "*McCulloch v. Maryland* 100 U.S. 1." http://www.law.cornell.edu/supct/html/historics/USSC_CR_0017_0316_ZO.html.

Legal Information Institute, Cornell University Law School. N.d. "Syllabus: *McCulloch v. Maryland* 100 U.S. 1." http://www.law.cornell.edu/supct/html/historics/USSC_CR_0017_0316_ZS.html.

www.ourdocuments.gov. N.d. "100 Milestone Documents: *McCulloch v. Maryland* (1819)." http://www.ourdocuments.gov/doc.php?flash=true&doc=21.

www.ourdocuments.gov. N.d. "Transcript of *McCulloch v. Maryland* (1819)." http://www.ourdocuments.gov/doc.php?doc=21&page=transcript.

Resources for Teachers

Leonore Annenberg Institute for Civics. 2009. "Equal Justice Under Law, a Lesson by Linda Weber for Sunnylands Seminars." http://www.annenbergclassroom.org/files/documents/lessonplans/equaljusticeunderlawlessonplan.pdf.

OYEZ, U.S. Supreme Court Media, ITT Chicago, Kent College of Law. N.d. "*McCulloch v. Maryland*." http://www.oyez.org/cases/1792-1850/1819/1819_0.

MCI Telecommunications Corp. v. American Telephone and Telegraph Co., 512 U.S. 218 (1994)

A Supreme Court Case Acknowledging Technology as a Market Structure Change Agent

Economic Concepts

Competition; economies of scale; government regulation; infrastructure market power; market prices; monopoly; price discrimination

Economic Impact

The case acknowledged that improved technology had the ability to make a current regulated monopoly an obsolete market structure for an industry. In this case, the industry impacted was the long-distance communications industry and the regulated monopoly power that had been granted to American Telephone and Telegraph (AT&T).

Economic Summary

In 1913, AT&T's company structure was that of a conglomerate of multiple Bell Companies. It had made an agreement with Congress giving it a phone service monopoly. In 1934, Congress passed the Federal Communications Act, with the goal of securing an economical and well-functioning system of national and global communications infrastructure. In the almost 80-year history of the act, the progression of technology and business acumen paralleled the growth of government regulation. The Federal Communications Commission (FCC) had extensive oversight in technologies such as wireless, satellite, and microwave communications. The FCC employed various techniques to maintain fair trade practices, i.e., competition, reasonable rates, and prevention of price discrimination.

The *MCI Telecommunications Corp. v. American Telephone and Telegraph Co.* case, however, limited the discretionary ability and power of the commission's power, referring the authority of intent back to Congress. The result of this decision was the Telecommunications Act of 1996, allowing economies of scale to work within the industry and decreased regulation of the communications industry.

Case Summary

Historically, the evolution of the communications industry in the United States has faced many legal challenges. After Alexander Graham Bell patented his new telephone device in 1876, the communications industry began a worldwide expansion. Early in the twentieth century, the Bell companies evolved through reorganization and acquisition into the American Telephone and Telegraph Company, or AT&T.

In 1913, Congress had given AT&T a phone service monopoly. In 1935, the Federal Communications Act established the FCC. The courts gave the FCC wide room to regulate the communications industry. Congress has continually tried to update and amend commission policy and power to keep pace with technological changes and public interest.

In1967, a fledgling business, Microwave Communications of America, Inc. (MCI), applied to the FCC for appropriate licenses as a common carrier (a company that transports goods for the general public, in this case communications). It was granted a license by the FCC to tap into the private line (a permanent communication channel between two or more places) to advance communications. Microwaves, fiber optics, satellites, and a myriad of other associated innovations culminated in opening of the long-distance market in the 1990s. At the time of *MCI v. AT&T*, there were 481 nondominant carriers adding to the global communications infrastructure, all in direct competition with AT&T. The commission recognized the benefits of greater competition, and in staying with the intent and goals of the 1934 act, enacted regulations that would enhance competition.

In 1980, the commission studied the market and distinguished between dominant carriers (those with market power) and nondominant carriers, the former being AT&T and the latter being all others. In the original act, Section 203(a) stated that carriers were required to file with the FCC the amount of the tariffs they charged customers to provide prices to assure reasonable pricing for the public in a monopolistic market. The prices then could not be changed without prior indication. Section 203(b) gave the commission the power to modify any of the requirements of the previous section.

Consequently, after a market review in the 1980s, the commission submitted new rules. Initially, filing tariffs seemed necessary to ensure that all customers had sufficient information about the price of services offered. Filing tariffs set prices at the rates posted. However, as technology allowed more competition to enter the market, this admirable intention did more harm than good. Posting prices facilitated parallel pricing and price stifling, leaning to the advantage of dominant carriers. If rates were not filed, prices could be negotiable, which was more to the advantage of newly emerging nondominant carriers. The FCC viewed "detariffing" (the release of carriers from this filing stipulation) as a significant step in encouraging price competition. Therefore, the FCC changed the rules, requiring only dominant carriers to file tariffs whereas it was optional for nondominant carriers. Later, the commission made nonfiling tariffs or "detariffing" mandatory for all nondominant carriers. Hence, only AT&T had to file their tariffs. In 1985, MCI transitioned into a greater share of the communications market and challenged this new interpretation of Section 203 in the United States Court of Appeals for the District of Columbia. The D.C. court struck down this new rule disagreeing with the commission's interpretation of Section 203 of the Communications Act.

The commission considered the court's interpretation and reissued the policy convinced they were right. MCI did not file tariffs and AT&T sued. The appeals court ruled that the FCC had violated Sections 203(a) and (b) of the Communications Act. MCI and the federal government, together with the FCC, petitioned for certiorari (a writ to the lower court to send the case to the Supreme Court for review). The Supreme Court granted their petitions and heard the case in March 1994. The question before the Court was whether the FCC had overstepped the authority Congress had granted to it by eliminating rate filing requirements for nondominant carriers of long-distance services.

The petitioners claimed that since 1980, the commission had held that it had authority to lift the rate-filing requirement. Furthermore, it stated that Section 203(a) and (b) had given the FCC the authority over formalities of rate filing such as information regarding rate filing, printing, and posting place for public inspection, et cetera, all of which were to be determined by regulations required by the commission. Hence, the modification to reduce the requirement to file rates by nondominant carriers of long-distance services was a formality legitimately within the authority of the commission. In addition, the rate filing had not been lifted for international calls or a number of the local exchange carriers that did most of the interstate access services. Rather, it only eliminated the mandatory requirement for 40 percent of the long-distance market not served by AT&T. It was clear to the commission that Congress's intent was to enable it to change the rules when the circumstances required, in effect allowing the government regulation to adapt to a rapidly changing technological and economic marketplace. The plaintiff cited the fact that AT&T no longer held a monopoly over long-distance services as evidence of this special situation. This discretionary power is owed through substantial deference.

The respondent disagreed. AT&T claimed that the FCC had overstepped the authority granted by Congress in the Communications Act. In the respondent's view, Congress had intended rate filing as a means to secure equal rates for customers of like situations. This would eliminate price differences because all carriers' rates would be public so customers would know what they were and could request that rate. AT&T claimed that MCI and other nondominant carriers were charging lower rates than those set forth in the tariff and negotiating discounts of 5 and 10 percent below their valid rates. Thus, it argued that the FCC had the authority to modify but not obliterate that rule. The fact that there is competition in the long-distance market is significant but does not eliminate the need for the rate-filing requirements because price differences occur even in competitive markets. Furthermore it cited the *Maislin Industries, U.S., Inc. v. Primary Steel, Inc.*, 497 U.S., 1990, case, which established that filing rates prevent price discrimination and unequal rates were the opposite of what the Communications Act was designed to prohibit.

The Rehnquist Court concurred. Justice Scalia penned the majority opinion and in summary said that rate filings were essential to the rate regulation of the communications industry as expressed in the Communications Act. It was not the intent of Congress to leave this core characteristic at the discretion of the commission. The term "modify" did not mean "to do away with." If the rate filings were to be eliminated, it must be by an act of Congress to change the authority of the commission to have that discretionary power. Justice Stevens, joined by Justice Blackmun and Justice Souter, dissented. They argued the commission's authority was expansive for the specific job of dealing with special circumstances that would legitimately call for different regulatory treatment. Justice Stevens stated rather than guess what Congress meant when it attempted to regulate an almost completely monopolized industry, the Court should acquiesce to the very solid, experience-tested and well-explained judgment of the FCC. On June 17, 1994, the majority opinion of the Court affirmed the decision of the Federal Appeals Court.

Kathleen C. Simmons

See Also Clayton Antitrust Act of 1914; Sherman Antitrust Act of 1890

Related Cases

Permian Basin Area Rate Cases, 390 U.S. 747 (1968)

Maislin Industries, U.S., Inc. v. Primary Steel, Inc., 497 U.S. 116 (1990)

Further Reading

Cornell University Law School, Legal Information Institute. N.d. "*MCI Telecommunications Corporation, Petitioner, v. American Telephone and Telegraph Company*; *United States, et al., Petitioners v. American Telephone and Telegraph et al.*" http://www.law.cornell.edu/supremecourt/text/512/218.

Wagner, Frank D., Reporter of Decisions. 1998. *United States Reports, Volume 512: Cases Adjudged in the Supreme Court at October Term, 1993*. June 13–September 30, 1994. Washington, DC: U.S. Government Printing Office. http://www.supremecourt.gov/opinions/boundvolumes/512bv.pdf.

Resources for Teachers

Cornell University Law School, Legal Information Institute. N.d. "*Supreme Court of the United States, Syllabus, MCI Telecommunications Corp. v. American Telephone & Telegraph Co.*" http://www.law.cornell.edu/supct/html/93-356.ZS.html.

OYEZ, U.S. Supreme Court Media, ITT Chicago, Kent College of Law. N.d. "*MCI Telecommunications Corp. v. American Telephone & Telegraph Co.*" http://www.oyez.org/cases/1990-1999/1993/1993_93_356.

Meltzer, Allan

Born: February 6, 1928, in Boston, Massachusetts; American; monetary policy; Major Works: *Money and the Economy: Issues in Monetary Analysis* (with K. Brunner) (1997), *A History of the Federal Reserve* (Vol. 1, 2003), *A History of the Federal Reserve* (Vol. 2, 2009).

Allan Meltzer is an economist and a professor of political economy at Carnegie Mellon University. He is the author of volumes 1 and 2 of *A History of the Federal Reserve* (2003 and 2009), and several other books. He has published more than 350 peer-reviewed academic papers and many newspaper articles. Meltzer held various key administrative positions such as the consultant on economic policy for Congress, the U.S. Treasury, the Federal Reserve, and the World Bank. He was the cofounder and cochair of the Shadow Open Market Committee from 1973 to 1999, and the director of many economic institutions, including the Commonwealth Foundation, the Global Economic Action Institute, and the Pittsburgh Economic Club. From 1999 to 2000, he served as the chairman of the International Financial Institution Advisory Commission. Meltzer has won quite a few prestigious awards and honors throughout his career.

Allan H. Meltzer was born February 6, 1928, in Boston, Massachusetts. He received his BA from Duke University in 1948. He then earned his MA and PhD in economics from the University of California, Los Angeles, in 1955 and 1958, respectively. In 1957, he started his academic career as an assistant professor at the Carnegie Institute of Technology, Graduate School of Industrial Administration. In 1964, Meltzer was promoted to full professorship and still teaches at the Carnegie Institute of Technology. Throughout his career, Meltzer has been a visiting professor at Ivy League institutions within the United States and abroad, teaching political economics and monetary policy. Along with his academic career, Meltzer has held many key administrative positions at the Graduate School of Industrial Administration at the Carnegie Institute of Technology. From 1966 to 1969, Meltzer became the chairman of the PhD committee, and from 1972 to 1973, he was acting dean. In 1981–1982 and 1990–1991, he was the chairman of the Dean Search Committee. From 1981 to 2000, Meltzer was a member of the finance committee of the board of trustees. Since 1975, Meltzer has written numerous newspaper articles in the *Los Angeles Times*, *Wall Street Journal*, and other respected newspapers. He has written more than 23 books and monographs and has published more than 350 peer-reviewed academic papers.

Allan Meltzer has won a great many awards, such as the Irving Kristol Award from the American Enterprise Institute (2003), History Makers Award for Education from the John Heinz History Association (2003), Alice Hanson Jones Award for the best book on North American Economic History (2004), and the David Horowitz Award from the Bank of Israel and the Israeli Bankers Association (2004), just to name a few.

The Federal Reserve is one of the most powerful economic institutions in the world. Yet prior to the publication of Meltzer's colossal books, *A History of Federal Reserve* (2003 and 2009), not much was known about the institution. Allan Meltzer's book is one of the most thorough analyses and revealing histories of the Federal Reserve ever published. Volume 1 covers the history of the Federal Reserve from its origination in 1913 through the Treasury-Federal Reserve Accord of 1951. Volume 2 was published in two parts in 2009. One part of Volume 2 covered the Federal Reserve's history from 1951 to 1986.

The documents and notes of the Minutes of the Federal Reserve meetings, which the book is based on, were not publicly available until the 1970s. Meltzer analyzed what the Federal Reserve did during its key turning points in history through careful review and analysis of the Minutes' notes, correspondence, and other internal documents. In the first volume, for instance, Meltzer explains the reasons behind the Federal Reserve's passive policies in the years that lead to the Great Depression. He brilliantly shows what actions of the Federal Reserve helped produce the sizable recession of 1937 and 1938. In addition, Meltzer examines the Federal Reserve's influence on international affairs, and its impact on the origination of the International Monetary Fund (IMF) and the World Bank.

The second volume of the book, published in two parts in 2009, covers the Federal Reserve's history from 1951 to 1986, when the great inflation in the United States ended. The second volume manifests the evolution and development of the Federal Reserve, from the Treasury to the most powerful financial and economical institution in the United States, during one of the most rapidly changing eras of the United States' history. Meltzer critically examines the gradual change of the Federal Reserve from a passive financial institute to a proactive economic think tank of the mid-1980s. The second volume of *A History of Federal Reserve* (2009) ends with a prologue briefly discussing the 2007–2009 financial and economic crises and the need for financial regulations. Academicians and policy makers alike benefit greatly from the rich and detailed history that Meltzer reveals.

In his masterpiece, *A History of the Federal Reserve*, Meltzer provides not only a detailed history of the Federal Reserve but also a history of monetary policy and its political economy for more than seven decades, starting in 1913. His effort to recognize trends and lessons learned from 1913 to 1987 is the best that has ever been made in understanding monetary policy and its economic and political consequences in the United States. Meltzer's insights magnify the limitations of a central bank's monetary policy. He shows that in the United States, a failure to provide a consistent and transparent lender-of-last-resort policy during the history of the Federal Reserve has been the origin of many avoidable economic fluctuations. Meltzer brilliantly shows how the personalities of key policy makers and their ideas and politics have influenced the United States' monetary policy over time.

Elham Mahmoudi

See Also Burns, Arthur; Greenspan, Alan; Volcker, Paul

Selected Works by Allan Meltzer

Brunner, Karl, and Allan H. Meltzer. 1997. *Money and the Economy: Issues in Monetary Analysis*. Cambridge: Cambridge University Press.

Meltzer, Allan H. 2009. *A History of the Federal Reserve*. Vol. 2. Chicago: University of Chicago Press.

Meltzer, Allan H. 2003. *A History of the Federal Reserve*. Vol. 1, 1913–1951. Chicago: University of Chicago Press.

Selected Works about Allan Meltzer

Carnegie Mellon Tepper School of Business. n.d. Meltzer Research. Accessed May 25, 2011. http://www2.tepper.cmu.edu/afs/andrew/gsia/meltzer.

Politico's The Arena. N.d. "Arena Profile: Allan Meltzer." Accessed May 25, 2011. http://www.politico.com/arena/bio/allan_meltzer.html.

Menominee Tribe v. United States, 391 U.S. 404 (1968)

A Supreme Court Case on Property Rights and Rule of Law Assessing the Hunting and Fishing Rights Granted through a Previous Federal Government Treaty

Economic Concepts

Common-pool resources; property rights

Economic Impact

The court decision maintained the integrity and importance of the rule of law and property rights in the U.S. economy by upholding the U.S. government's previous obligations. This decision also altered the impacted states' ability to collect hunting and fishing fees, i.e., state revenues.

Economic Summary

In 1961, Congress enacted the Menominee Termination Act. The act terminated the Menominee Tribe of Indians' traditional hunting and fishing rights in Wisconsin. The Indians felt this act violated their property rights as given to them in an earlier Wolf River Treaty. The court case centered on the Menominee Indians' property rights as they related to Wisconsin's water and land common-pool resources (i.e Wisconsin's public waters and lands). Also in question was whether the U.S. government would be subject to rule of law and if property rights which the government had earlier granted would be upheld. A secondary economic relevance would be the precedence set for states to collect hunting and fishing fees, i.e., generate state revenue, from the hunting and fishing activity of the states' Indian population.

Case Summary

The Supreme Court's responsibility in *Menominee Tribe v. Untied States* was to determine if the Menominee Termination Act, enacted by Congress in 1961, terminated hunting and fishing rights granted in the Wolf River Treaty of 1854. In this treaty, the hunting and fishing rights within the territory described as the Menominee Indian Reservation were not specifically stated, but legally implied, and would therefore constitute property rights and require just compensation. With federal recognition, the Menominee tribe had a flourishing economy. It ran a lucrative timber industry and hospital, utilities, and education systems. It paid Bureau of Indian Affairs (BIA) salaries and had other such examples of infrastructure and economic success. In terms of overall economic well-being, the Menominee tribe was categorized as prosperous within the Indian tribes of the United States.

In 1954, Congress began the process of ending recognition, and by 1961, Congress had terminated the Menominee tribe's federal recognition completely through the Menominee Termination Act. With this act, the government terminated the tribe's right to govern itself, receive federal support for healthcare, education and fire and police protection, as well as tribal rights to lands. Consequently, the Menominee tribal reservation boundaries became Menominee County, Wisconsin. In preparation for this termination, the Menominee tribe incorporated the boundaries of the Indian reservation and set up a charter that enabled the tribal council to remain the governing entity. However, the tribe lost the utility, education, and hospital systems and much revenue from the timber industry. As a county, it had no tax base to support basic infrastructure. The tribe was also under the laws and jurisdiction of the state of Wisconsin. Within a few years of the termination, the Menominee tribe was categorized among the poorest within the Indian tribes of the United States. The Menominee considered the traditional rights to hunt and fish the territory as essential to economic survival.

The Menominee Indian tribe had lived in the area that became the states of Wisconsin, Michigan, and Illinois for thousands of years. Through a series of treaties made with the U.S. government in the 1800s, the area of land they inhabited was reduced from millions of acres to just over a couple of hundred thousand acres in the area of northern Wisconsin. The current land area is referred to as an Indian reservation. Although the definition of "Indian" in the United States is complicated, the United States establishes the legal status of an Indian tribe according to laws and acts passed by the U.S. Congress.

The Menominee tribe was federally recognized as one of over 500 tribes in the United States and therefore granted self-governing powers much like a state, excluding such powers as making war and coining money. The termination by the act in 1961 changed the social, political, and economic aspects of the tribe by removing federal assistance and placing the tribe under state authority. In addition, the termination forced a restructuring of the tribe as a corporate organization.

In 1962, tribal members Joseph Sanapaw, William Grignon, and Francis Basina were charged with violating state hunting and fishing regulations by hunting deer with headlights or flashlights, a process known as "deer shining." They admitted this act in court, but claimed that the Wolf River Treaty signed in May 1854 secured their right to hunt and fish. The state trial court agreed and acquitted the three. The state appealed to the Wisconsin Supreme Court, which agreed that although the Wolf River Treaty did not specifically mention hunting and fishing rights, it certainly implied them, and upheld that claim. Following that determination, the court held that the Menominee tribe no longer had hunting and fishing rights due to the Termination Act by the federal government ending its treaty rights as well as its Indian recognition.

The Supreme Court would not grant certiorari (a writ to the lower court to send the case to them for review) at this point; therefore, the tribal members appealed to the Federal Court of Claims to recover compensation from their loss of hunting and fishing rights. Retaining their rights to hunt and fish within the territory established by the Wolf River Treaty as the Menominee Indian reservation was the essential goal. Acknowledgment of the current economic hardships faced by the tribe and pursuit of just compensation for the loss of formerly granted rights were secondary aims.

The Court of Claims held that the Menominee Termination Act did not end the tribe or its membership, but abolished federal trusteeship of the tribe. The tribe had a right to claims of the Wolf River Treaty, and therefore, the court denied the right to compensation but upheld the tribe's right to fish and hunt not subject to state jurisdiction. The opposite rulings by the Wisconsin State Supreme Court and the Federal Claims Court brought the issue to the U.S. Supreme Court.

This case is unusual in that both the Menominee (the appellee) and the United States (the appellant) argued that the decision of the Court of Claims should be affirmed. In this case, the Supreme Court invited the state of Wisconsin to participate in the court hearings as an amicus curiae (one who is not a party to the case, but believes the court's decision may have a relevant impact on its interest). When Congress ended federal recognition of the Menominee tribe in 1961, the hunting and fishing rights that were implied in the Wolf River Treaty of 1854 were terminated. Therefore, the state of Wisconsin argued that the Court of Claims ruling should be reversed. Consequently, the state of Wisconsin contended that the tribe should be given just compensation for that taking. However, the Menominee argument focused on the hunting and fishing rights within the current incorporated boundaries of the terminated Menominee Indian reservation. The tribe considered these rights guaranteed to them by the Wolf River Treaty regardless of federal government ending recognition of the tribe in 1961 or not. The Federal Claims Court was in agreement with the Menominee.

The Supreme Court, led by Chief Justice Earl Warren, heard arguments on January 22, 1968, and again on April 26, 1968, deciding the case on May 27, 1968. The Supreme Court held that the tribe retained its hunting and fishing rights under the Wolf River Treaty of 1854, as the fishing and hunting rights were implied in the treaty. In addition, the Court stated that these rights were not abolished by the Termination Act, but rather would necessitate specific congressional statutes, and without these plain and simple statements by Congress, these rights could not be taken away. However, in his dissenting opinion, Justice Stewart acknowledged the hunting and fishing rights given to the Menominee tribe in the Wolf River Treaty, but agreed with the state of Wisconsin that Congress nullified those rights with the Termination Act. Justice Steward, joined by Justice Black, therefore would have reversed the decision of the Federal Claims Court, letting the ruling of the Wisconsin State Supreme Court stand. Of the hundreds of treaties signed by the U.S. government with the Native Americans, less than 1 percent were honored. This decision placed the Wolf River Treaty in that small percentage. However, the greater impact was in expanding the rule of law for a portion of the population with very little history of secured property rights, thereby stretching the tent of American promise over a wider group of "we the people."

Kathleen C. Simmons

See Also Private Property; Public Goods; Taxes

Related Cases

United States v. Creek Nation, 295 U.S. 103 (1935)

Shoshone Tribe v. United States, 299 U.S. 476 (1937)

United States v. Klamath Indians, 304 U.S. 119 (1938)

Further Reading

Cornell University Law School, Legal Information Institute. N.d. "*Menominee Tribe of Indians, Petitioner, v. United States*." http://www.law.cornell.edu/supremecourt/text/391/404.

OYEZ, U.S. Supreme Court Media, ITT Chicago, Kent College of Law. N.d. "*Menominee Tribe v. United States*." http://www.oyez.org/cases/1960-1969/1967/1967_187.

Resources for Teachers

Indian Land Tenure Foundation, Lessons of Our California Land. N.d. "Grades: 9th–12th; Standard Three: Contemporary Land Issues." http://www.landlessons.org/Mono9-12Standard3Lesson1.

Justia.com, U.S. Supreme Court Center. 1968. "*Menominee Tribe of Indians v. United States*, 391 U.S. 404 (1968)." http://supreme.justia.com/cases/federal/us/391/404/.

Mercantilism

Mercantilism refers to the preferred economic system in Europe between the sixteenth and eighteenth centuries, in which governments regulated their nations' economies through commercial trade. The practice was heavily used, especially in British colonies.

The governments in mercantilist economies sought to regulate their nations' economies by controlling trade. They believed that their economic strength was dependent on maximizing exports and minimizing imports through the heavy use of tariffs. The reason that maximizing exports was at the heart of mercantilism was the belief that gold was the key to strength in the economy, and that if one country had more gold than another, that country was seen as the strongest. Taking full advantage of exports guaranteed that gold would always be coming into the nation, and limiting the amount of imports through high tariffs ensured that the gold in the nation did not leave its boundaries.

Known as the bullion system, accumulating gold was necessary for a nation to be strong. Some nations, like Great Britain, passed specific laws, like the Navigation Acts, restricting other nations from trading with Great Britain and its colonies in order to maximize their gold stores. Beginning in 1651, the Navigation Acts were intended to restrict trade from the Americas. In all, four Navigation Acts were passed, and these acts declared that only English or English ships could carry cargo between ports; that only certain goods, like tobacco and furs, could not be shipped to foreign nations; that Parliament would pay bounties to Americans who produced raw goods while raising protectionist tariffs on the same goods produced in other nations; and finally, that Americans could not compete with English manufacturers in large-scale manufacturing. The Navigation Acts ensured that any bullion available in the colonies remained with the British, and only the British.

Also, during the Napoleonic Wars, the French wore down their opponents by not allowing them to export goods and only allowing imported goods. Forcing those countries to use up their gold by making them purchase foreign goods was seen as a far worse fate than allowing a country to starve.

Mercantilism, though, could only benefit a nation for so long. In his classic book *An Inquiry into the Nature and Causes of the Wealth of Nations* (1776), Adam Smith

(1723–1790), an economist and theorist, argued that mercantilism was not the best way for nations to maintain their power and add wealth. Smith made three important arguments against mercantilism. He stated that trade benefits all nations involved. Second, he argued that when nations specialize in the production of goods and services, it improves growth and efficiency. His third argument stated that although mercantilist policies benefited both the government and the commercial class, few others in the nation would see any gains from the practice. Through trade, all people in a nation could see an economic benefit.

For example, although the British used a mercantilist system, they could not adhere only to domestic production of goods and services to maintain their wealth. A black market for imported goods began, and the government could do little to stop it. Also, with the production gains from the Industrial Revolution, it was not deemed profitable to maintain an export-only nation. Soon, Great Britain eliminated mercantilist policies and adopted a free-trade stance, with many other nations following suit.

Later, in the twentieth century, British economist John Maynard Keynes (1883–1946) argued that the way to increase national wealth was for a nation to maintain a positive balance of trade, which caused increased demand. Anyone asking for protective tariffs on imports was considered a mercantilist.

After World War I, several nations passed protectionist policies to support their industries. For example, the United States saw the passage of the Tariff Act of 1930, also known as the Smoot-Hawley or Hawley-Smoot Tariff Act. The Tariff Act was passed to protect products in the United States by imposing massive tariffs on imported goods. At first, the policy seemed promising, as employment and production by various industries increased. However, many other nations retaliated against the Tariff Act of 1930 by placing huge tariffs on imported goods themselves. The global economy, which was in a recession by this time, began to take an even deeper downward turn as import and export levels fell across the world, leading to lessening of each nation's gross domestic product (GDP). Many economists feel that the Tariff Act worsened the global recession, fueling the Great Depression.

After the end of World War II and the economic chaos that followed, a series of agreements were passed to stop mercantilist policies from taking effect again. The General Agreement on Tariffs and Trade (GATT) was passed in 1947 to guarantee a reduction in tariffs and trade barriers across the world. Furthermore, other organizations, such as the World Trade Organization (WTO) and the General Agreement on Trade in Services (GATS), were enacted to enforce international trade rules.

Arguably, some mercantilist policies and ideas still exist today. Some economists and politicians consider any country whose trade policies are heavily weighted toward exports with minimal imports the "new mercantilists" of today's modern global economy.

Ekaterini Chrisopoulos-Vergos

See Also Gross Domestic Product (GDP); Keynes, John Maynard; Market Capitalism; Smith, Adam; Tariff Act of 1930 (Smoot-Hawley Tariff Act); World Trade Organization (WTO)

Further Reading

Free Exchange Economics. 2013. "What Was Mercantilism?" *The Economist*, August 23. Accessed October 7, 2013. http://www.economist.com/blogs/freeexchange/2013/08/economic-history.

LaHaye, L. N.d. "Mercantilism." *The Concise Encyclopedia of Economics*. http://www.econlib.org/library/Enc/Mercantilism.html.

Smith, Adam. 1776. *An Inquiry into the Nature and Causes of the Wealth of Nations*. London: J. J. Tourneisen and J. L. Legrand.

SparkNotes. N.d. "Mercantilism." Accessed October 7, 2013. http://www.sparknotes.com/testprep/books/sat2/history/chapter5section4.rhtml.

Resources for Teachers

CECHE, Big Ideas. N.d. "Mercantilism Simulation." Accessed October 7, 2013. https://sites.google.com/a/caldwellschools.com/cechs-big-ideas/home/9th-grade/explorer/world-history-world-geography/mercantilism-simulation.

Council for Economic Education. N.d. "Focus: Middle School World History-Lesson 22, Mercantilists and the Midas Touch." http://msh.councilforeconed.org/lessons.php?lid=68381.

Zucker, James. 2010. "Mercantilism Game." Lesson Corner. http://www.lessoncorner.com/l/jzucker/MercantilismGame.

Mint Act (See Coinage Act of 1792)

Mirrlees, James

Born: July 5, 1936, in Minnigaff, Scotland; Scottish; political economy, asymmetric information in economics, Nobel Prize (1996); Major Works: "Optimal Taxation and Public Production I: Production Efficiency" (1971), "Optimal Taxation and Public Production II: Tax Rules" (1971), *Economic Policy and Nonrational Behaviour* (1987), *Welfare, Incentives, and Taxation* (2006).

James Mirrlees is a Scottish economist. With William Vickrey, he was awarded the Nobel Prize in Economics in 1996 for his work on asymmetric information and incentives. Through his research on marginal income tax rates, Mirrlees was an early proponent of the flat tax, suggesting that all taxpayers pay the same marginal tax rate of 20 percent for optimal income tax rate efficiency. He also suggested that high-income earners should pay no tax, which later became a variation of supply-side economics. His work with Peter Diamond became known as the Diamond-Mirrlees efficiency theorem. In 1998, he was knighted for his contributions in the areas of political economy and economics.

James Alexander Mirrlees was born on July 5, 1936, in Minnigaff, Scotland. Graduating from Douglas Ewart High School in Newton Stewart as a brilliant math student in 1954, Mirrlees enrolled in Edinburgh University with the intention of preparing to be a math professor. His time at Edinburgh was influential in two ways: he again excelled in the math classroom and through his cousin he was introduced to the world of philosophy. This philosophical influence was an important part of Mirrlees's later work in economics. Graduating from Edinburgh in three years, in 1957 he ventured to Cambridge University to pursue a second undergraduate degree in mathematics at Trinity College. With an interest in underdeveloped countries, Mirrlees pursued a degree in economics.

Mirrlees's professional career began while at Cambridge, where he served as a research assistant to future Nobel laureate Nicholas Kaldor. Also studying under the likes of Frank Kahn and future laureate Joan Robinson, his academic credentials grew. In 1963, Mirrlees received his PhD in economics from Cambridge.

At the urging of Amartya Sen, Mirrlees went to India in 1962–1963 as an adviser to the India Project as part of the Massachusetts Institute of Technology (MIT) Center for International Studies. After a summer at MIT, he and his wife moved to New Delhi, India. Returning to Cambridge in 1963, Mirrlees became a lecturer of economics at Cambridge University's Trinity College. In 1968, he left Cambridge to become the Edgeworth Professor of Economics at the University of Oxford. In 1995, he returned to the University of Cambridge as a professor of political economy. During his professorships at Oxford and Cambridge, he was an adviser to the Pakistan Institute of Development Economics, and a visiting professor at MIT on three different occasions, in 1968, 1970, and 1976. He also served University of California, Berkeley, and Yale University in the same capacity, in 1986 and 1989, respectively.

While at Oxford, his most significant research interests took form. Mirrlees investigated problems generated by incomplete or asymmetrical information in economic transactions. One study of special significance, with William Vickrey, discussed the effects of asymmetrical information on the savings rate of an economy. Mirrlees also devoted much of his research to discovering the optimal marginal tax rate. Besides the academic and economic significance of the study, his research in this area became the basis for Mirrlees's Nobel Prize in Economics in 1996.

Mirrlees was also influential in the study of optimum income tax rates. As an adviser to the British Labour Party in the 1960s and 1970s, he assumed that high tax rates were most beneficial for the poor. However, his research led him, much to his own surprise and others', to the thesis that all taxpayers should pay a top marginal income tax rate of only 20 percent; i.e., they should pay a flat tax rate. Mirrlees took his income tax thesis one step further and suggested that the highest-income earners pay no income tax. He thought that a tax cut would incentivize high-income earners to work more, thus generating more wealth for the whole society. Mirrlees's additional tax research on consumption taxes with coauthor Peter Diamond concluded that small economies would be better off taxing consumption and not imports through tariffs.

Mirrlees's research efforts also included studies of moral hazard, or the situation in which individuals (or companies) will take excessive risks, even beyond the risks they would take if granted immunity for the outcomes. For example, knowing that an insurance company will provide coverage for losses creates an environment of moral hazard. Mirrlees created a mathematical model for such environments, showing that the optimal condition in which insurance markets will not become conducive to moral hazard. He showed that a combination of incentives and disincentives could align the insured's behavior with those who are uninsured and vice versa.

Once retired from the University of Cambridge, James Mirrlees became an emeritus professor of political economy at the University of Cambridge and a Trinity College fellow. He also divides his academic endeavors between the University of Melbourne, the

Chinese University of Hong Kong, and the University of Macau. James Mirrlees was the lead reviewer of the UK tax system for the Institute of Fiscal Studies. He also is a member of Scotland's Council of Economic Advisers.

David A. Dieterle

See Also Taxes; Vickrey, William

Selected Works by James Mirrlees

Diamond, Peter A., and James A. Mirrlees. 1971. "Optimal Taxation and Public Production I: Production Efficiency." *American Economic Review* 61, no. 1: 8–27.

Diamond, Peter A., and James A. Mirrlees. 1971. "Optimal Taxation and Public Production II: Tax Rules." *American Economic Review* 61, no. 3, Pt. 1: 261–78.

Mirrlees, James. 2006. *Welfare, Incentives, and Taxation*. Oxford: Oxford University Press.

Mirrlees, James. 1987. *Economic Policy and Nonrational Behaviour*. Berkeley, CA: Institute of Business and Economic Research.

Mirrlees, James. 1971. "An Exploration in the Theory of Optimum Income Taxation." *Review of Economic Studies* 38, no. 2: 175–208.

Selected Works about James Mirrlees

Institute for Fiscal Studies, ed. 2010. *Dimensions of Tax Design: The Mirrlees Review*. Oxford: Oxford University Press.

Institute for New Economic Thinking. N.d. "Sir James Alexander Mirrlees." Accessed October 25, 2013. http://ineteconomics.org/people/sir-james-alexander-mirrlees-fba.

"James Mirrlees—Mathematics and Real Economics." 2010. Inaugural Conference at King's, Institute for New Economic Thinking, King's College Cambridge, England, April 23. Accessed October 25, 2012. http://www.youtube.com/watch?v=-39znKX8kC8.

"James A. Mirrlees." 2008. In *The Concise Encyclopedia of Economics*. Edited by David R. Henderson. The Library of Economics and Liberty. http://www.econlib.org/library/Enc/bios/Mirrlees.html.

Mirrlees, James A. 1996. "Autobiography." Nobelprize.org. http://www.nobelprize.org/nobel_prizes/economics/laureates/1996/mirrlees-autobio.html.

Mises, Ludwig von

Born: September 29, 1881, in Lemberg, Austro-Hungarian Empire; Died: October 10, 1973, in New York City; American, naturalized U.S. citizen; trade cycle theory, monetary policy, credit policy analyst, economic epistemology; Major Works: *Theorie des Geldes und der Umlaufsmittel* (1912), translated as *The Theory of Money and Credit* (1934); *Die Gemeinwirtshaft* (1922), translated as *Socialism* (1936); *Nationalökonomie* (1940); *Human Action: A Treatise on Economics* (1949); *Theory and History* (1957).

Ludwig von Mises was one of the most influential Austrian economists of the twentieth century. He was not only the driving force and influence behind many contemporary Austrian-born economists, including Friedrich August von Hayek, Gottfried Haberler,

Alfred Schütz, and Fritz Machlup, but also made important contributions in the areas of epistemology, history, political philosophy, trade cycle theory, and the economic effects of monetary and fiscal policy. Mises's output and influence laid the groundwork for a significant revival in Austrian and neo-Austrian economics. Mises died in 1973.

Ludwig von Mises was born on September 29, 1881, in the city of Lemberg, a part of the Austro-Hungarian Empire, to Arthur von Mises and Adele Landau. Mises attended the Akademische Gymnasium in Vienna from 1892 until 1900, studying classics, classical languages, and the liberal arts. After a one-year military obligation with an artillery regiment near Vienna and the initial phase of his academic studies completed at the University of Vienna, Mises returned to his studies in 1903. It was in this year that he attended the lectures of Friedrich von Wieser and read *The Principles of Economics* by Carl Menger, the acknowledged founder of the Austrian School. He was also greatly influenced by the lectures (1905) and guidance of Finance Minister Eugen von Böhm-Bawerk, a second-generation Austrian economist who wrote *Capital and Interest*, a two-volume treatise on economics and the history of economic thought. Mises would attend his seminar until 1913. After obtaining a doctor of laws degree in 1906 and with the assistance of Böhm-Bawerk, Mises began work on a monetary treatise that was published in 1912 under the title *Theorie des Geldes und der Unlaufsmittel*, translated in 1934 as *The Theory of Money and Credit*.

This path-breaking work on monetary theory brought Mises significant recognition by integrating the theory of money and banking into the framework of Menger's theory of value and price. No longer was money simply seen as a *numéraire* or measure of value, nor as a historical accident, but rather as a natural commodity that has an integrative effect on the economic system. Unable to obtain a full professorship at an Austrian university, Mises taught in an unsalaried position as a *privatdozent* at the University of Vienna in 1913 and was given the title of associate professor in 1918. After a short stint as a lawyer in Vienna, he obtained a full-time position in 1909 at the Austrian Chamber of Commerce as a *konzipist*, or analyst, remaining there for the next 25 years. It was at this post that Mises conducted his famous *Privatseminar* that met regularly in his *Kammer* office throughout the 1920s.

During World War I, Mises saw action as a first lieutenant on the Eastern Front, but was called back to Vienna after sustaining injuries and contracting typhoid fever in 1917. He later worked in the economics division of the Department of War in Vienna for the remainder of hostilities. From 1918 to 1920, he was director of the *Abrechnungsamt*, an office designed to reconcile various settlement questions arising from the Treaty of St. Germain. It was in this capacity that he first met and hired the man who would become his lifelong friend and colleague, the Nobel Prize–winning economist Friedrich August von Hayek, as an assistant. His reflections on the political situation in Europe after the war prompted his *Nation, Staat und Wirtschaft* (1919), later translated as *Nation, State and Economy* (1983). The book contained an in-depth analysis of the various causes of the war, personal reminiscences, and observations about the economic challenges and political pressures facing a post–World War I Austria. It was followed in 1922 by another path-breaking work, *Die Gemeinwirtschaft*, translated in 1936 as *Socialism: An Economic and Sociological Analysis*. Mises not only laid out a cogent argument for the impossibility of socialist economic calculation but also now became a leading critic of all forms of socialism.

In 1926, Mises was instrumental in establishing the *Österreiches Konjunkturforschungsinstitut*, or the Austrian Institute for Business Cycle Research, with Hayek as one of its major contributors. A successful private association from its inception, it became an important intellectual outlet for Austrian economic research on business cycle theory, predicting with great accuracy the banking crisis in Austria in 1931. In addition, his 1927 work *Liberalismus*, translated as *The Free and Prosperous Commonwealth* in 1962, signaled to his contemporaries his adherence to and advocacy of the free-market economy. In 1934, Mises joined the faculty of the Graduate Institute of International Studies in Geneva, Switzerland, as a professor of international economic relations.

In 1940, forced to leave his post because of the Nazi threat, Mises sought refuge in the United States, settling in New York City and obtaining U.S. citizenship in 1946. Unable to obtain a salaried teaching position at an American university, Mises accepted the position of visiting professor at the Graduate School of Business Administration at New York University, where he remained from 1945 to 1969. Sponsored largely by the William Volcker Fund, Mises was able to reinstitute his seminars, continue his writing and research, and attract a new generation of students and scholars, as he had earlier in Vienna.

Mises's most important work was *Human Action: A Treatise on Economics* (1949). This comprehensive 889-page treatise on economics grew out of his earlier work, *Nationalökonomie* (1940), and firmly established him as the primary spokesman for classical liberal thought in the United States. This work would later become a cornerstone document in the revival of the Austrian School, especially in the works of Murray N. Rothbard. During this period he also published *Bureaucracy* (1944), *Omnipotent Government* (1944), *Planning for Freedom and Other Essays and Addresses* (1952), and *The Anti-Capitalist Mentality* (1956). In his last two significant works, *Theory and History* (1957) and *The Ultimate Foundation of Economic Science* (1962), Mises presented the epistemological case for capitalism.

Mises was the recipient of the William Volcker Fund Distinguished Service Award (1956), the Austrian Medal of Honor (1962), an honorary doctorate from New York University (1963), and an honorary doctorate in political science from the University of Freiburg (1964), and was a distinguished fellow of the American Economic Association (1969).

Ludwig von Mises died on October 10, 1973, in New York City, at the age of 92.

Joseph A. Weglarz

See Also Classical Economics; Economic Systems; Hayek, Friedrich von; Market Capitalism

Selected Works by Ludwig von Mises

Mises, Ludwig von. 1978. *On the Manipulation of Money and Credit: Three Treatises on Trade-Cycle Theory*. Translated by Bettina Bien Greaves. Edited by Percy L. Greaves Jr. New York: Free Market Books.

Mises, Ludwig von. 1969. *The Historical Setting of the Austrian School of Economics*. New Rochelle, NY: Arlington House.

Mises, Ludwig von. 1962. *The Ultimate Foundation of Economic Science*. New York: Van Nostrand.

Mises, Ludwig von. 1957. *Theory and History*. New Haven, CT: Yale University Press.

Mises, Ludwig von. 1949. *Human Action: A Treatise on Economics*. New Haven, CT: Yale University Press.

Mises, Ludwig von. 1947. *Planned Chaos*. Auburn, AL: Ludwig von Mises Institute.

Mises, Ludwig von. 1936. *Socialism: An Economic and Sociological Analysis*. London: Jonathan Cape.

Mises, Ludwig von. 1934. *The Theory of Money and Credit*. London: Jonathan Cape.

Mises, Ludwig von. 1929. *A Critique of Interventionism*. Stuttgart, Germany: Gustav Fischer Verlag.

Mises, Ludwig von. 1927. *Liberalism: In the Classic Tradition*. 3rd ed. Translated by Ralph Raico. San Francisco: Cobden Press.

Selected Works about Ludwig von Mises

Butler, Eamonn. 1988. *Ludwig von Mises: Fountainhead of the Modern Microeconomics Revolution*. Aldershot, UK: Gower.

Greaves, Bettina Bien. 1969. *The Works of Ludwig von Mises*. Irvington-on-Hudson, NY: Foundation for Economic Education.

Hayek, Friedrich von, ed. 1971. *Toward Liberty: Essays in Honor of Ludwig von Mises on the Occasion of His 90th Birthday*. Menlo Park, CA: Institute for Humane Studies.

Hülsmann, Jörg Guido. 2007. *Mises: The Last Knight of Liberalism*. Auburn, AL: Ludwig von Mises Institute.

Kirzner, Israel M. 2001. *Ludwig von Mises*. Wilmington, DE: ISI Books.

Moss, Laurence S. 1974. *The Economics of Ludwig von Mises: Towards a Critical Appraisal*. Kansas City, MO: Sheed and Ward, Institute for Humane Studies Series in Economic Theory.

Sennholz, Mary, ed. 1956. *On Freedom and Free Enterprise: Essays in Honor of Ludwig von Mises*. Princeton, NJ: Van Nostrand.

Monetary Policy

Monetary policy is the policy of determining the quantity of money liquidity in an economy. Liquidity in an economy is measured by the amount of cash, credit, and cash complements, such as money market mutual funds, available for purchasing goods and services. Monetary policy is the responsibility of a nation's central banking authority. An economy's central banking authority is the central regulatory agency responsible for regulating a nation's banking system. This central agency could take the form of a central bank, a currency board, or other central regulatory agency.

Universally, the goal of monetary policy is stable prices. In the United States, monetary policy was formalized with the Federal Reserve Act in 1913. The United States' central bank, the Federal Reserve System, has the added goal of achieving low unemployment. Central banks use monetary policy to influence interest rates; i.e., the price of money. Monetary policy also determines the quantity of money in an economic system along with the rate of money supply's growth or reduction.

Central banks influence employment, economic growth, and the general level of prices. Using monetary policy tools, central banks influence the quantity of money, credit, and interest rates used to purchase goods, services, and productive resources. Central banks have three main tools to effectively implement monetary policy. First, a central bank can lower or raise the discount rate. The discount rate is the short-term interest rate the central bank charges its depository institutional customers, who borrow from the central bank mostly in overnight loans. A second tool for monetary policy is to alter the reserve requirement of banks. The reserve requirement is the amount of money reserves the banks, under the central bank's jurisdiction, are required to maintain in their vaults at the end of each business day.

The third and primary tool is buying and selling government securities (bills, notes, bonds) on the open market to influence nominal interest rates by influencing the fed funds rate. The fed funds rate is the overnight interest rate the banking industry charges each other for overnight loans. In the United States, the open market operations are a weekly event of the Domestic Trading Desk at the Federal Reserve Bank of New York and the Federal Open Market Committee (FOMC) of the Federal Reserve System. In the open market operations, dealers and brokers bid for the U.S. securities, and the distribution of the securities is based on a competitive market, not by selection of the central bank.

In the United States, the central authority responsible for regulating the nation's banks and using monetary policy to determine the monetary size of the economy is the Federal Reserve System. Monetary policy is the function of the Federal Reserve System to influence the economy. Implementing the three tools of monetary policy, the Federal Reserve System can control both the quantity of money and the amount of credit in an economy.

Using the tools of monetary policy, expansionary monetary policy is when an economy is lagging and near the bottom of the business cycle. To stimulate and expand the economy, the central banking authority could lower the discount rate, reduce the reserve requirement, or buy U.S. securities to expand the quantity of money in the economy. Contractionary monetary policy is prescribed when the economy is accelerating, with excessive demand by consumers resulting in inflation (higher general price level); to contract and be restrictive, slowing down the economy, the central banking authority can raise the discount rate, increase the reserve requirement, or sell U.S. securities to contract the quantity of money in the economy.

Critics of Monetary Policy

Not everyone is a supporter of monetary policy. Critics of monetary policy make claims that an economy is at risk the more influence monetary policy has on the economy. If the central banking authority uses monetary policy too freely ("loose monetary policy"), an economy's inflationary pressures are greater. Conversely, if monetary policy is too strict ("tight monetary policy"), the economy has deflationary pressures that keep prices, wages, and investment values declining. Critics suggest the banking authority cannot accurately predict with precision and timing the monetary policy's proper positioning within an economy at any given point in time.

A second criticism of monetary policy is timing. Critics make the claim that monetary policy has an implementation lag that makes monetary policy ineffective. They suggest that by the time any decisions regarding monetary policy are implemented, the economy would have moved on, and the current economic condition would not be the same as when the monetary policy decision was made.

David A. Dieterle

See Also Central Banking; Federal Reserve System; Inflation; Inflation, Measures of

Further Reading

The Economist. N.d. "Monetary Policy." http://www.economist.com/topics/monetary-policy.

Federal Reserve Bank of San Francisco. "What Is the Fed: Monetary Policy." http://www.frbsf.org/education/teacher-resources/what-is-the-fed/monetary-policy.

Friedman, Milton. 1968. "The Role of Monetary Policy." *American Economic Review* LVIII, no. 1: 1–17.

Tobin, James. N.d. "Monetary Policy." http://www.econlib.org/library/Enc/MonetaryPolicy.html.

Resources for Teachers

Federal Reserve Bank of San Francisco. N.d. "Education Highlights: Workshop on Teaching Monetary Policy for Professors." http://www.frbsf.org/education/.

Federal Reserve Bank of San Francisco. 2002. "Dr. Econ: What Is the Difference between Fiscal and Monetary Policy?" http://www.frbsf.org/education/publications/doctor-econ/2002/march/fiscal-monetary-policy.

federalreserveeducation.org. N.d. "Monetary Policy Basics." http://www.federalreserveeducation.org/about-the-fed/structure-and-functions/monetary-policy/.

Herman-Ellison, Lisa C. 2007. "Fiscal and Monetary Policy Process." econedlink. http://www.econedlink.org/lessons/index.php?lid=352&type=educator.

Money

Most people would refer to money as the coins and bills in their wallet or the paycheck one receives from their job. Economists define money in terms of its three uses. Money is anything that serves as a medium of exchange, a unit of account, and a store of value. Money also has distinct characteristics that make it common throughout the world.

Money as a Medium of Exchange

Money as a medium of exchange is anything that is used to determine value during the exchange of goods and services. Without the use of money, people acquire goods and services through the barter system. This type of exchange would require a great deal of time and energy. First, one would have to find someone who wanted to barter for the items that one has, and second, the two parties would have to agree to the value of each item or service. This type of exchange only works well in small, traditional economies.

With the use of money as a medium of exchange, one only needs to find someone that is willing to pay the amount that a good or service is worth. Because money makes exchanges so much easier, people have been using it for thousands of years.

Money as a Unit of Account

The use of money as a unit of account provides a means for comparing the values of goods and services. With the use of money, one can compare the cost of an item offered at different locations because the price is expressed in the same common way in every location. For example, in the United States, the value of a good or service is expressed in dollars and cents. Other countries have their own forms of money that serve as units of account, such as the Japanese yen or the British pound.

Money as a Store of Value

When money is serving as a store of value, it means that the currency keeps its value if one decides to hold on to it instead of spending it. The money will still be valuable and will be recognized as a medium of exchange weeks, months, or even years into the future.

Money serves as a good store of value, with one important exception. Sometimes economies experience a period of rapid inflation. If an economy should experience inflation, the saved money would lose its value, or buying power, at the rate of inflation. For example, if the United States experiences 10 percent inflation during a year and one has stored money for that same year, when one uses that money it will have 10 percent less buying power. Therefore, when an economy experiences inflation, money does not function well as a store of value.

Common Characteristics of Money

The coins and paper that are used as money in the United States today were not always used as currency. In the past, societies have used a wide range of objects as currency. Cattle, salt, furs, precious stones, gold, and silver have all served as currency at various times in various places. Even teeth, rice, shells, and olive oil have been used in nations as currency. Although all of these items were used successfully in the past, none of these items would function very well in our economies of today. Each of these items lacks at least one of the six common characteristics that economies use to judge how well an item serves as currency. These six characteristics are durability, portability, divisibility, uniformity, limited supply, and acceptability.

Durability

Objects used as money must withstand the physical wear and tear that comes with being used over and over again. If money wears out or is destroyed too easily, it cannot be trusted to serve as a store of value. Unlike salt, rice, or olive oil, coins last for many years. Also, when paper bills wear out, the U.S. government can easily replace them with new bills.

Portability

Currency needs to be easily transferred from one person to another. It must be able to be carried as people go about their daily business; therefore, it must be lightweight and small. Paper money and coins are very portable, which is why they are used as the primary means of currency throughout the world.

Divisibility

In order for money to be useful, is must be easily divided into smaller denominations or units of value. When money is divisible, people only have to use as much of it as necessary for any exchange. Most currencies around the world consist of various denominations, such as 10-cent coins, 50-cent coins, $1 bills, $10 bills, and so on.

Uniformity

Any two units of money must be exactly the same in terms of what they will buy. In other words, people must be able to count and measure money accurately. A $1 bill in the United States must always buy $1 worth of goods or services in order for the currency to work accurately.

Limited Supply

Supply creates the value of items; currency must also be in limited supply in order to have value. If leaves were used as currency and your nation was filled with trees, the currency would be in too great an abundance to have any value. Therefore, in the United States as well as most other nations, the government controls the supply of money in circulation.

In the United States, the Federal Reserve System is the government-run entity that controls the money supply. It is able to monitor, distribute, and limit the amount of money available at all times. This system helps to keep the amount of money is circulation in limited supply, which in turns helps to maintain the value of the currency.

Acceptability

Finally, everyone in an economy must be able to exchange the objects that serve as the money (dollars and coins) for goods and services in said society. When one person uses a certain currency, it must be able to be reused by the receiver of the currency in that person's next transaction throughout the entire society.

In the United States, we expect that other people in the country will continue to accept the paper and coins that are issued by the government in exchange for purchases of goods and services. The use of the money issued and accepted throughout a nation makes an economy flow more easily and with a common currency language.

Tracy L. Ripley

See Also Bureau of Engraving and Printing; Deflation; Federal Reserve System; Inflation; Inflation, Measures of; *Juilliard v. Greenman, 110 U.S. 421 (1884)*; Monetary Policy; United States Mint; United States Treasury

Further Reading

Bastiat, Frederic. 1853. *Essays on the Political Economy: Part III. Government and What Is Money?* London: W. and F. G. Cash, 5, Bishopsgate Without. https://mises.org/journals/qjae/pdf/QJAE5_3_7.pdf.

Federal Reserve Bank of San Francisco. 2001. "What Are the Money and Foreign Exchange Markets? What Forces Influence Supply and Demand in These Markets?" June. http://www.frbsf.org/education/publications/doctor-econ/2001/june/money-market-foreign-exchange.

O'Sullivan, Arthur, and Steven M. Sheffrin. 2007. *Economics Principles in Action.* Upper Saddle River, NJ: Pearson Prentice Hall.

Resources for Teachers

Federal Reserve Bank of Atlanta. N.d. "Education Resources: Lessons and Activities." http://www.frbatlanta.org/edresources/lessons_activities.cfm.

Foundation for Teaching Economics. N.d. "Money and the Banking System: The Mechanics." http://www.fte.org/teacher-resources/lesson-plans/rslessons/money-and-the-banking-system-the-mechanics/.

United States Mint. N.d. "Lesson Plans for Grades K-12." http://www.usmint.gov/kids/teachers/lessonPlans/.

N

National Bank Act of 1863

A national or central bank is not an institution that has always been part of the United States. Alexander Hamilton attempted the first national bank, the First Bank of the United States, in 1791. It eventually failed, but the Second Bank of the United States was established in 1816 when signed into law by President James Madison. It, too, failed when its charter expired in 1836, and it was not renewed by Congress. The National Bank Act of 1863, with its revisions in 1864 and 1865, was to try again to create a national banking system.

Prior to these national banking initiatives, banks were state chartered. To have state-chartered banks, without federal oversight, was the predominant formula of the banking industry until the mid-nineteenth century. As the dates would suggest, the origination of a national bank was a response to the Civil War. As the nation divided and the Civil War ensued, state-chartered banks were not benefiting the war effort for the Union. The National Bank Act of 1863 created national charters for banks, and the National Bank Act of 1864 revised the original 1863 act. These two national bank initiatives were the predecessor to the Federal Reserve Act in 1913.

President Abraham Lincoln desired to apply some national influence on and control over the banking industry, but was not interested in forming a central bank. The National Bank Act had three goals to benefit the Union. First was to create a system of national banks under the influence of the federal government. The second goal was to establish a new national currency to help finance the Civil War. Finally, also to help finance the Union's Civil War effort, the National Bank Act would establish a secondary market so the federal government could sell war bonds and treasury securities. None of these goals were very popular with Congress at the time. The National Bank Act of 1863 and 1864 had great difficulty getting passed through Congress.

A mechanism for creating the national currency and the national banking system was set out in the National Bank Act of 1863. The federal government would sell government securities to banks, and these holdings would be the backing of a national currency. At the same time, the 1863 act levied a heavy tax on the currency of state banks, the goal being to drive the state bank–backed currencies out of the system. The plan failed and was in part the reason for the follow-up 1864 act.

The first goal of the National Bank Act of 1863 was to permit the establishment of national banks. Essentially the same as the private and state banks that currently existed, the national banks would be chartered by the federal government. National charters were good for 20 years, subject to renewal at that time. This gave the federal government regulatory control, which was quite different from the banking control by the states. Nationally chartered banks had higher reserve requirements and were required to hold more capital. They were also forbidden to make real estate loans, nor were they able to make large loans to individuals that exceeded 10 percent of the bank's capital holdings.

Secondly, the National Bank Act of 1863 and 1864 set out to establish a national currency. Today a common currency is taken for granted, but in the mid-nineteenth century there were as many as 200 different currencies in circulation throughout the states of the Union. Quite obviously, a common national currency would make interstate and national transactions much easier. This was accomplished through the national banks, as they were required to accept each other's banknotes at a value set by the federal government. The printing of these new national banknotes was the oversight responsibility of the newly created Comptroller of the Currency office. This new office, as set out in the 1863 Banking Act, would be an office of the Department of Treasury. The comptroller would also have the responsibility for inspecting the national banks to ensure they were adhering to the capital requirements and values for the new national banknotes, or currency.

The final goal of the National Bank Act was to aid in the Civil War financing for the Union army. To this end, each nationally chartered bank was required to maintain a large deposit of U.S. Treasury securities with the Comptroller, collateral for offering national banknotes. In return, the bank received the new national banknotes with a value of up to 90 percent of the market value of the bonds on which they were backed. A nationally chartered bank could only make loans up to the value of the securities they had on deposit with the Comptroller. If a bank wished to increase its loaning capability, it needed to increase its holdings of securities with the Comptroller. This form of reserve banking created a secondary market for bonds, but more importantly at the time, and to achieve its goal, provided funds to the Union without extensive borrowing. The first nationally chartered bank was the First National Bank of Philadelphia, but this was not the first to be in business. That honor went to the fifteenth chartered national bank, the First National Bank of Davenport, Iowa.

A third revision in 1865 levied a 10 percent tax on state, i.e., not federally issued, currency. The intent was to drive state currencies, and essentially state banks, out of existence. While the tax succeeded in eliminating state currencies, state-chartered banks invented the demand deposit or checking account. Many state-chartered banks converted to national charters. But they did not go away. With the invention of the checking account, their numbers actually grew, and they again became the dominant face of the banking industry.

As the Civil War ended, so did national banking. With the lack of a central banking mechanism to oversee monetary policy, the economy often suffered extreme peaks and troughs in the business cycle. By 1865, the number of national banks had grown to over 1,500, over 80 percent of the total number of national and state-chartered banks (see Flaherty, http://www.let.rug.nl/usa/essays/general/a-brief-history-of-central-banking/).

David A. Dieterle

See Also Central Banking; Federal Reserve System; Money

Further Reading

American History from Revolution to Reconstruction. N.d. "National Bank Acts of 1863 and 1864." http://www.let.rug.nl/usa/essays/general/a-brief-history-of-central-banking/national-banking-acts-of-1863-and-1864.php.

Flaherty, Edward. N.d. "A Brief History of Central Banking in the United States." *American History from Revolution to Reconstruction.* Accessed June 3, 2014. http://www.let.rug.nl/usa/essays/general/a-brief-history-of-central-banking/.

National Bank History of the United States. N.d. http://www.nationalbankhistory.com/.

Resources for Teachers

The Federal Reserve Bank of Minneapolis. N.d. "A History of Central Banking in the United States." http://www.minneapolisfed.org/community_education/student/centralbankhistory/bank.cfm.

federalreserveeducation.org. N.d. "History of the Federal Reserve." http://www.federalreserveeducation.org/about-the-fed/history/.

Kornegay, Julie. N.d. "Money and Banking in American History 1833–1933; SMART Board Lesson Plan." http://www.frbatlanta.org/edresources/classroomeconomist/12history_centralBanking/history_centralBanking_Instructions.pdf.

National Bureau of Economic Research (NBER)

The National Bureau of Economic Research (NBER) was officially founded in 1920. It is a nonprofit private research entity that promotes better understanding of the economy, and it is the largest economic research organization in the United States. The NBER's target audiences are policy makers and academic and business professionals. Over the years, the NBER has examined important macroeconomic issues such as business cycles, economic growth, demand for money, and national income accounting.

Today, the NBER is the top economic research organization in the United States. NBER researchers are well respected in the field and are among the leading scholars of economics and business in the world. NBER researchers have included 22 Nobel Prize winners in economics, 13 previous chairs of the President's Council of Economic Advisers, and many business and economic professors at leading research universities across the United States. Five guiding principles of the bureau in dealing with major issues related to economic policies are: 1) analyzing and defining economics facts and their relationships, 2) analyzing quantitative measures of data, 3) pursuing a scientific approach to all economic problems, 4) publishing the findings with utmost regard to impartiality, and 5) refraining from making policy recommendations.

Although the founders of the bureau had very different opinions on economic and social policies, they all believed strongly that social programs should be based on objective knowledge of facts and reliable quantitative and scientific research approaches. The main question was how to obtain objective knowledge and ensure that the public would accept its objectivity. This question was raised in 1916, when Malcolm C. Rorty, an engineer and statistician, discussed the idea with Nahum I. Stone, an economist. Although the two men had very different views on social and economic policies, they agreed that it would represent significant progress to have an independent organization dedicated to finding facts on controversial economic issues. They concluded that in order to earn the public's confidence, the organization should include a group of well-known and well-respected economists from different schools of thought, should follow a thorough quantitative economic research method, and should include representatives of all important organized interests, such as financial, industrial, labor, and so on, in the country.

The start of World War I in 1917 delayed the establishment of the National Bureau of Economic Research until 1920. In January 1920, with enough funding in sight, the bureau was legally formed. It has never had any specific theories or policies to advance; neither has it had any obligations toward any other entities. This freedom of action and impartiality in findings has been essential for the bureau to earn the public's trust. In order to assure that all research is conducted using a scientific approach, the board of directors has been responsible for reviewing the design, findings, and presentation of the data in each study. Publication of the findings depends on a favorable vote from the majority on the board.

NBER's headquarters are located in Cambridge, Massachusetts. The organization's board of directors consists of economists from the top leading research universities and research organizations in the United States. In addition, it employs research associates and research fellows, with fewer than 50 employees as support staff. Wesley Mitchell was the first director of research at the bureau. He set the standards high and led a very productive research staff during his 25 years of service.

The bureau's first study was about the distribution, size, industrial composition, and growth and fluctuation of the national income. Because today's economic life is centered on either making or spending money, the resulting framework could be used as a basis for many other unanswered questions—questions regarding the magnitude, process, and consequences of aggregate changes in distribution of the nation's income. It took less than two years for the bureau to complete the national income study. The results were published in two volumes. But more importantly, through this work, the bureau successfully established its reputation as a thorough and reliable research organization among public and professional individuals and organizations.

Studying the national income was just a starting point in developing deeper knowledge of the economy. While finishing an initial examination of the national income, the bureau had already started investigating the geographical distribution of the income, comparing it among different states. Furthermore, in 1921, the bureau started another related study on annual savings. Later, in 1930, Simon Kuznets, a student of Mitchell's and one of the bureau's staff, started leading a series of studies on the nation's income, savings, and expenditures. This important study extended over the next three decades and was considered the initial step in estimating the Gross National Product (GNP) and other related statistics.

In 1921, the board's executive committee approved Mitchell's proposal to study business cycles. In 1927, with the bureau's help, Mitchell published the first part of his proposal series. The study was titled *Business Cycles: The Problem and Its Setting*. The title was the same as the first part of the study done in 1913, but the later work included many new ideas and materials.

Over the years, the bureau has completed many important studies on various subjects such as the fluctuations of savings, cyclical changes in productivity, and cyclical changes in employment. The bureau's founders established a culture of strict action. Although it is difficult to focus on important economic issues while paying attention to their symptoms, it is not impossible. The founders' stringent principle of scientific and empirical analysis and impartiality guided the bureaus' work from one generation to another. NBER has earned the trust and respect of government, business, and academic professionals. Today, the bureau's budget is more than $6 million, and there are more than 100 research associates located in the United States and abroad who conduct important domestic and international economic studies (see www.nber.org).

Elham Mahmoudi

See Also Bureau of Economic Analysis; Bureau of Labor Statistics; Department of Commerce; United States Census Bureau

Further Reading

Burns, Arthur F., and Wesley C. Mitchell. 1946. *Measuring Business Cycles*. Washington, DC: NBER Books.

Fabricant, Solomon. 1927. "Toward a Firmer Basis of Economic Policy: The Founding of the National Bureau of Economic Research." www.nber.org/nberhistory/sfabricantrev.pdf.

Mitchell, Wesley. 1927. *Business Cycles: The Problem and Its Setting*. New York: Bureau of Economic Research.

Resources for Teachers

Chauvet, Marcelle. N.d. "Real Time Analysis of the U.S. Business Cycle." Federal Reserve Bank of Atlanta, Center for Quantitative Research. www.frbatlanta.org/cqer/researchcq/chauvet_real_time_analysis.cfm.

National Bureau of Economic Research. 2010. "Business Cycle Dating Committee, National Bureau of Economic Research." www.nber.org/cycles/sept2010.html.

National Deficit vs. Debt

The deficit refers to when a government spends more than it takes in over a given period of time, usually one year. The national debt is the accumulation of government deficits over time. The publicly held debt consists of the U.S. Treasury securities held by individuals, financial intuitions, and foreign governments. Another portion of the debt is called the intragovernmental debt, which consists of the Treasury bonds held by agencies of the federal government, including the Social Security Trust Fund. Since the 1930s, there has not been a consistent plan to pay down the national debt, and any decreases are a result of inflation and economic growth.

Deficit

Deficit spending occurs when a government spends more than it collects in revenue in a given year. These annual deficits contribute to the national debt, the total amount that a nation owes. Many things can contribute to deficit spending, such as national emergencies including wartime, maintaining infrastructure and public goods, stabilizing the economy during a recession or depression, and government programs such as Social Security, Medicare, and Medicaid.

To cover the deficit, the government must sell Treasury bonds, which are bonds that pay a fixed interest rate and mature in 10 years. These bonds generally have low interest rates, but are the safest since they are backed by the full faith and credit of the U.S. government. When these bonds mature, they pay the face value plus interest. Commonly, these bonds can be purchased through auction and sometimes at less than face value.

Debt

The debt of the United States can be traced back to the Continental Congress, which borrowed money in order to finance the Revolutionary War. When the U.S. Constitution went into effect in 1789, the United States was already $75 million in debt. The nation's first Secretary of the Treasury, Alexander Hamilton, authorized the Treasury to borrow money so it could pay interest on the national debt and also authorized Treasury bonds to be issued for the first time. Tariffs and taxes were also used by Hamilton to pay down the national debt.

The nation was completely debt free under President Andrew Jackson's administration (although a series of economic crises ensued after he left the White House). The United States next went into debt as a result of the Civil War, when the federal government borrowed $2.8 billion, or 30 percent of the Gross Domestic Product (GDP) (Gramm and McMillin, 2013). The public debt increased from $65 million to $2.76 billion by 1866 (Phillips, 2013).

The Great Depression resulted in a large increase in the national debt, which reached 43 percent of GDP in 1934 (or $40 billion) (Phillips, 2013). The U.S. debt was high after World War II, at about 130 percent of GDP (Gordon, 2011). The post–World War II economic boom created a high demand for U.S. goods and services, a demand that remained high through the 1950s. During this same period, government spending was cut immensely. An economic boom and decreased government spending helped bring down the debt to GDP ratio.

In the 1970s, the debt to GDP ratio was 39 percent (Gordon, 2011), the lowest since the Great Depression. In the 1980s, a recession increased the debt to GDP ratio again. As the U.S. economy entered the 1990s, the debt was 58 percent of GDP (Gordon, 2011). As the economic boom of the 1990s continued, the federal government achieved a budget surplus for the first time in 30 years. In 2003, however, the debt to GDP ratio again rose to over 61 percent as a result of a recession (Gordon, 2011). The Great Recession was also a significant contributor to an increase in the debt to GDP ratio. In 2009, it reached over 84 percent and continued until it reached 100 percent (Gordon, 2011). To avoid increasing debt and a potential debt crisis, a nation must grow faster than the interest rate paid on its debt or it risks no gains in economic growth.

There are many implications of a rising national debt. Economic conditions can be affected in the form of higher interest rates and increased income taxes, as well as the depreciation of the dollar.

A key issue that contributes to the national debt is government spending. Congress has struggled to establish policies on limiting the size of the nation's debt. In 1985, Congress established sequestration, which means that if it went over its deficit ceiling or spending caps, the budget would be subjected to automatic spending cuts. The Budget Enforcement Act of 1990 introduced a pay-as-you-go concept for the nation's budget. Any spending increases would have to be offset by tax increases.

Another issue confronting Congress and the national debt is what Congress must do when the debt ceiling is reached. The debt ceiling is a legal limit set by Congress determining how much the federal government can exceed its current debt obligations. The amount of additional debt the federal government increases can only be changed by a vote of Congress. Consequently when the debt ceiling is reached, Congress must decide to either increase the debt ceiling (allow the debt to increase) or shut down the government. Congress has acted to increase the debt ceiling 77 times since 1962.

Currently, the U.S. federal debt exceeds 100 percent of GDP and continues to increase. U.S. taxpayers now and in the future bear the burden of paying the interest and principal of the debt, if surpluses can be achieved. The government has options to decrease the national debt that include cutting federal spending and increasing taxes. These options have costs and benefits that must be weighed to determine what is best for the future of the U.S. economy.

Angela M. LoPiccolo

See Also Entitlements; Fiscal Policy; Gross Domestic Product (GDP); U.S. Treasury Bills, Notes, and Bonds

Further Reading

Gordon, John Steele. 2009. "A Short History of the National Debt." *Wall Street Journal*, February 18. http://online.wsj.com/article/SB123491373049303821.html.

Gordon, John Steele. 2011. "A Short Primer on the National Debt." *Wall Street Journal*, August 29. http://online.wsj.com/article/SB10001424053111903480904576510660976229354.html.

Gramm, Phil, and Steve McMillin. 2013. "The Debt Problem Hasn't Vanished." *Wall Street Journal*, May 21. http://online.wsj.com/article/SB10001424127887324787004578494864042754582.html.

Phillips, Matt. 2013. "The Long Story of U.S. Debt, from 1790 to 2011, in 1 Little Chart." *The Atlantic*, November 13. http://www.theatlantic.com/business/archive/2012/11/the-long-story-of-us-debt-from-1790-to-2011-in-1-little-chart/265185/.

Schiller, Brad. 2013. "A History of the National Debt." *Washington Times*, February 19. http://www.washingtontimes.com/news/2013/feb/19/a-history-of-the-national-debt/.

Resources for Teachers

Council for Economic Education. N.d. "Teaching Debt, Budget & Deficit through History, Civics & Economics Courses." http://www.councilforeconed.org/resource/teaching-debt-budget-deficit-through-history-civics-economics-courses/.

Marketplace.Org. "Budget Hero." N.d. Accessed May 11, 2013. http://www.marketplace.org/topics/economy/budget-hero9.

U.S. Debt Clock. N.d. Accessed May 11, 2013. http://www.usdebtclock.org/.

Yopp, Marty. 2000. "The Role of Government: The National Debt vs. the Deficit." econedlink. http://www.econedlink.org/lessons/index.php?lid=184&type=educator.

National Labor Relations Act of 1935 (Wagner Act)

The National Labor Relations Act (NLRA) of 1935 (29 U.S.C. §§ 151–169) affected labor laws in the United States by protecting the rights of employees in the private sector to organize themselves into labor unions. President Franklin D. Roosevelt signed the act into law on July 5, 1935. The unofficial name of the act, the Wagner Act, recognizes the efforts of New York senator Robert F. Wagner (1927–1949) in leading Congress to pass the legislation as a response to the Supreme Court striking down the National Industrial Recovery Act as unconstitutional.

A combination of worldwide labor movements against exploitive employers and governments and economic conditions in the aftermath of the Great Depression provided the impetus for Congress to propose a bill that would protect the rights of workers in the United States. In the 1930s, organized labor wanted legal support from employers who spied on, interrogated, disciplined, discharged, and blacklisted union members. Workers organized themselves militantly, and between 1933 and 1934, numerous strikes occurred across the United States, some with violent confrontations between workers trying to form unions and the powers defending antiunion employers, including the police.

Recognizing that other world governments were violently replaced with communist ideology at the hands of a disillusioned labor sector in difficult economic conditions, Democrats sought to keep the communist movement out of the United States. In addition, as outlined in Section 1 of the Act, members of Congress believed that industrial peace was essential to a functioning economy, and that suffering employees could hinder full economic production.

As stated in the NLRA Act of 1935, the goal of the NLRA is to remedy

> the inequality of bargaining power between employees who do not possess full freedom of association or actual liberty of contract and employers who are organized in the corporate or other forms of ownership association substantially burdens and affects the flow of commerce, and tends to aggravate recurrent business depressions, by depressing wage rates and the purchasing power of wage earners in industry and by preventing the stabilization of competitive wage rates and working conditions within and between industries.

The passage of the NLRA gave employees the freedom to organize and form a legally protected bargaining unit, or trade union, meant to collectively bargain terms and conditions of employment. As a last resort, if there is an impasse with the employer on reaching an agreement, the act gives legal protection for unions to take collective action against the employer, including the organization of a strike.

In the decade that followed the passing of the Wagner Act, House and Senate Republicans repeatedly attempted to repeal or amend it, worried that its provisions contradicted the principles of a capitalist society, would hinder maximum growth and profit across industry markets, and would indirectly promote socialist/Marxist ideology in the United States. Republicans were so concerned about the promotion of this ideology that they encouraged businesses and employers not to comply, and to file an injunction in federal court to negate the act. All efforts by House and Senate Republicans either failed to pass in one or both chambers, or were vetoed by the president.

The provisions of the Wagner Act are not applicable to government workers at any level of administration (federal, state, or local). In addition, because the Railway Labor Act covers workers in the railway and airline industries, they are also exempt from coverage under the Wagner Act. Other employees not covered by the act are agricultural employees, domestic workers, supervisors, independent contractors, and close relatives of individual employers. Employees whose religious beliefs prevent their joining and contributing to unions are also exempt from any requirement to associate or financially support them (Section 19).

Section 3 of the NLRA established the National Labor Recovery Board (NLRB), whose primary duties are to oversee the unionization process of employees, as well as to provide legal and financial support to unions seeking to prosecute an employer for violations. In this capacity, the NLRB can lead investigations, collect evidence, issue subpoenas, and call on witnesses to testify and provide evidence.

Section 7 of the act explicitly addresses the rights of unions in the collective bargaining processes. This section states that employees have the right to self-organize, and to join or assist a labor organization. The bargaining unit can bargain for the collective group through representatives of its own choosing (as outlined in Section 9), and can also participate in activities that would provide mutual aid or protection for employees. Section 7 also outlines that each bargaining unit is allowed only one representative, that employees are allowed to discuss wages with each other to ensure fair pay, that the union is allowed to promote itself to employees, and that employers are compelled to bargain in good faith with the representatives for the employee unit.

Section 8 of the act outlines what would be considered unfair labor practices by employers. These include interfering with, restraining, or coercing employees in terms of exercising their rights guaranteed in Section 7 of the NLRA, interfering in either the formation of the labor organization or in the collections of financial contributions to support it, influencing employment or promotion on condition of discouraging or exemplifying nonsupport for unions, discriminating against employees who file charges or testify against the employer in union initiated cases, and refusing to bargain with the representative for the collective unit.

The NLRA also outlines what would be considered unfair practices of labor organizations against employees and employers. These include threats to job loss or punishment for lack of support toward the union or choosing not to be a member; refusing to process a grievance because an employee criticized the union or its officials; firing employees who left the union; misconduct during pickets including threats, assault, or preventing nonstrikers from accessing the employer's premise; and striking over issues unrelated to employment terms and conditions.

Nevena Trajkov

See Also Great Depression (1929–1939); National Labor Relations Board (NLRB); New Deal

Further Reading

Cornell University Law School, Legal Information Institute. N.d. "National Labor Relations Act (NLRA)." http://www.law.cornell.edu/wex/national_labor_relations_act_nlra.

National Labor Relations Board. N.d. "National Labor Relations Act." http://www.nlrb.gov/national-labor-relations-act.

Society for Human Resources Management. N.d. "Federal Statutes, Regulations and Guidance." Accessed April 15, 2013. http://www.shrm.org/LegalIssues/FederalResources/FederalStatutesRegulationsandGuidance/Pages/NationalLaborRelationsAct(NLRA)of1947.aspx.

U.S. National Archives and Records Administration. N.d. "National Labor Relations Act (1935)." http://www.ourdocuments.gov/doc.php?doc=67.

Resources for Teachers

Kohler, Thomas C. N.d. "National Labor Relations Act (1935)." eNotes: Study Smarter. Accessed April 15, 2013. http://www.enotes.com/national-labor-relations-act-1935-reference/national-labor-relations-act-1935.

Tubach, Linda. N.d. *Case Study: A National Labor Relations Board Union Representation Election at Get-Well Community Hospital.* http://laborstudies.org/pdfs/NLRBUnionElection.pdf.

National Labor Relations Board (NLRB)

In 1935, the National Labor Relations Act created the National Labor Relations Board (NLRB) for the purpose of improving working conditions by overseeing and protecting the rights of workers to organize. The act set out a framework from which nongovernmental employees could bargain for better wages and working conditions or decertify a current labor union if they so choose.

The National Labor Relations Act covers an array of labor rights for employees. Under the act, employees are protected to form a labor union or organization, decertify a labor union or organization, and to engage in collective bargaining with their employer. The act also protects employees if they do not wish to bargain collectively, or if they wish to bargain collectively without the representation of a labor union. The National Labor Relations Act provides employees the right to collective bargaining for better working conditions, including wages. Under the act, employers are forbidden from interfering with their employees' right to form a union, join a union, or participate in union activities. However, it also protects employees who do not wish to participate in such activity.

The National Labor Relations Board is headquartered in Washington, D.C. There are also 30-plus regional offices across the United States. The NLRB is made up of five members. The board members are appointed for five-year terms by the president of the United

States with consent of the Senate. The members are staggered so that one term expires each year. There is a general counsel for the board who is also appointed by the president. The general counsel's term is four years. The general counsel's responsibility is to prosecute unfair labor practices. A division of judges hears the unfair labor practice cases and rules upon their status.

Any employee or employer who feels his or her rights have been violated can file an unfair labor practice charge with the NLRB. The general counsel investigates and determines if a case exists to be heard. When it is determined that a charge has merit, the case is heard before one of 40 administrative law judges. Once the decision is determined, the board encourages the parties involved in the case to comply with the judge's decision. However, the party found in the wrong has the due process to appeal the decision to the board. When the party does not comply, it is the responsibility of the general counsel to prosecute and seek legal enforcement in the U.S. Court of Appeals.

J. Warren Madden was the first chair of the National Labor Relations Board. Madden created five separate divisions with the NLRB. Of the five divisions, the economic division was created to address three tasks. First, the economic division collects economic data to support the NLRB's position in court cases. Secondly, the division researches labor relations to support the board's decision and policy-making efforts. Finally, its members write papers and conduct research on labor relations history, collective bargaining, and case studies regarding labor disputes to serve as experts in the area of labor relations.

As with most new, far-reaching federal legislation, the National Labor Relations Act faced several constitutional issues. Fearing the composition of the Supreme Court would make it inclined to rule against the NLRB, Madden delayed court challenges until he felt the Court would be sympathetic to the NLRB. His tactics appear to have been successful. In 1937, the Supreme Court upheld the constitutionality of the National Labor Relations Act in *National Labor Relations Board v. Jones & Laughlin Steel Corporation*. The Supreme Court further endorsed the NLRB's rulings in 19 cases, and only denied 2 cases.

Interestingly, the American Federation of Labor (AFL) was the NLRB's most ardent rival in court. The AFL accused Madden of pitting the AFL against its ardent union competitor, the Congress of Industrial Organizations (CIO). The two labor organizations would later merge to create the powerful AFL-CIO labor union.

In 1938, after prompting from the AFL, an investigation of the NLRB by the House of Un-American Activities Committee confirmed that Madden had hired at least one member of the Communist Party of the United States. A 1940 House of Representatives Special Committee investigation was led by an antilabor representative, Howard W. Smith from Virginia. The committee's efforts led to major restructuring of the NLRB and expansion of the board from the original three members to the current five. The two investigations damaged the NLRB's reputation with both the public and Congress. While President Roosevelt supported the National Labor Relations Board, the reputational damage of the investigations has been connected with the eventual passage of the Taft-Hartley Act of 1947.

David A. Dieterle

See Also Labor Force; National Labor Relations Act of 1935 (Wagner Act); Roosevelt, Franklin Delano; Supreme Court

Further Reading

Gross, James A. 1974. *The Making of the National Labor Relations Board: A Study in Economics*. Albany, NY: The State University of New York Press.

National Labor Relations Board, ed. 2007. *Decisions and Orders of the National Labor Relations Board*. Volume 352. Washington, DC: Government Printing Office.

National Labor Relations Board. N.d. "What We Do." http://www.nlrb.gov/what-we-do.

Resources for Teachers

Carmack, Carmen. 2008. "Who Is Working?" econedlink. http://www.econedlink.org/lessons/index.php?lid=474&type=educator.

The Harlan Institute. N.d. "*Lesson Plan: National Labor Relations Board v. Noel Canning Corporation*." http://harlaninstitute.org/contests/virtual-supreme-court/virtual-supreme-court-lesson-plan-national-labor-relations-board-v-canning/.

National Labor Relations Board. N.d. "Home." http://www.nlrb.gov/.

New Deal

In 1932, the United States' economy was mired in the depths of the Great Depression. The unemployment rate had leapt to about 25 percent, and production had collapsed. In the presidential election of 1932, voters turned to the charismatic President Franklin D. Roosevelt, who promised "a new deal for the American people."

The New Deal was the name given to a broad array of government programs intended to combat the Great Depression. It represented a move away from a philosophy of a small government with a limited role in the economy, and a shift toward confidence in direct action by a large, powerful federal government in keeping with the new economic philosophy of John Maynard Keynes. New Deal programs created the framework for the contemporary American welfare state, and provided a rallying point for those who saw a larger federal government as a force for the protection of liberty and prosperity.

The New Deal began immediately with the inauguration of Roosevelt as president in March 1933, and with the seating of many new congressional representatives who were sympathetic to the president's ideas. This first phase of the New Deal lasted until 1935. Most of the programs can be put into one of three categories: relief, recovery, or reform. Relief programs attempted to provide jobs for people so that they could meet immediate needs; recovery programs were to help damaged sectors of the economy get moving in the right direction again; and reform programs were an attempt to prevent future crises. Significantly, the New Deal abolished the gold standard, meaning that people could no longer demand payment of contracts in gold rather than paper money. This was one of the New Deal's many efforts to shore up the banking system, which had been devastated by panics.

The new laws, loans, and public spending poured money into the economy and caused substantial budget deficits. But production increased, and the unemployment rate dropped, though it remained above 20 percent. Importantly, the New Deal legislation was broadly popular. But it was not popular with everyone. Conservatives were troubled by the unprecedented and unrelenting expansion of government power. Others of opposite political persuasion thought that the New Deal had not gone far enough to redistribute wealth, and offered Roosevelt a bruising political challenge from the left. Roosevelt dealt with these threats by giving up on winning conservative support and moving to adopt policies that increased government intervention still further, therefore winning more liberal backing and short-circuiting some truly radical strains of thought from the left.

This shift marked what has been called the Second New Deal, which lasted from 1935 to 1938. Roosevelt launched a verbal assault on the "entrenched greed" of the "money classes," and followed this rhetoric with ambitious and populist government programs, like increased taxes on the wealthy. The Second New Deal included the Works Progress Administration (WPA), in which the federal government directly hired several million unemployed Americans for tasks ranging from raking leaves to building airports, and the Social Security Act, which provided welfare payments to vulnerable people and guaranteed pensions for retirees. Roosevelt won the 1936 election by a landslide.

Nevertheless, Roosevelt's policies continued to encounter difficulties, both in the political and economic realms. Starting in 1935, the Supreme Court had declared several aspects of New Deal legislation unconstitutional. Congress had proceeded by amending and moderating these laws in order to pass the scrutiny of the Court. But the New Deal reforms were always in danger of being struck down by wary justices. Roosevelt decided to alter this situation by simply changing the makeup of the Supreme Court, adding more justices of his own choosing in order to gain favorable rulings. In this, he made a political miscalculation—Congress did not support him, and he alienated much of the Democrat voting base, therefore slowing the pace and scope of the Second New Deal. To make the matter worse, late 1937 brought a sudden and sharp recession-within-a-depression, and the unemployment rate, which had sunk to 14 percent, shot back up to 20 percent. Dismayed voters elected a more conservative Congress in 1938.

By 1939, Roosevelt had to be content to simply maintain the New Deal programs that he and the Congress had already implemented. By this time, a new crisis was looming—World War II. But New Deal programs stayed in place even as the nation whirred to life in preparation for global war.

The economic impact of the New Deal is not entirely obvious. Though the economy certainly turned around and began to recover with the onset of the New Deal, after six years the unemployment rate still stood at 17 percent. Some economists claim that the New Deal did not spend enough money to boost the economy. Others claim that it spent too much, and that the money was wasted. It is likely that some programs were harmful to the economy and others were helpful. The Agricultural Adjustment Act of 1936 that paid farmers to produce fewer crops probably falls into the former category. But most economists agree that the abolition of the gold standard aided recovery by expanding the money supply and halting bank runs, therefore allowing the economy to begin its long, slow recovery.

The political legacy of the New Deal is clearer. Its popularity created a new political coalition that solidified the identity of the Democratic Party. It laid the foundation of the United States welfare state and instituted programs and government agencies that still exist to this day, most notably Social Security. The New Deal greatly increased the size and scope of the federal government in American life, reflecting a growing belief that a powerful national government could in fact be an agent in securing peoples' economic well-being.

Stephen H. Day

See Also Entitlements; Great Depression (1929–1939); Keynes, John Maynard; Keynesian Economics; Roosevelt, Franklin Delano; Social Security Act of 1935; Supreme Court

Further Reading

Kennedy, David. 1999. *Freedom from Fear.* New York: Oxford University Press.

Leuchtenburg, Anthony. 2009. *Franklin D. Roosevelt and the New Deal: 1932–1940.* New York: Harper Perennial.

Rauchway, Eric. 2008. *The Great Depression and the New Deal: A Very Short Introduction.* New York: Oxford University Press.

Resources for Teachers

New Deal Network. N.d. "Links: K-12 Projects, Lesson Plans and Webquests." Accessed December 1, 2013. http://newdeal.feri.org/classrm/b.htm.

PBS. N.d. "The Dust Bowl Experience: The Great Plow Up; Economics of the Dust Bowl." http://www.pbs.org/kenburns/dustbowl/educators/lesson-plans/#deal.

PBS. N.d. "Lesson Plan 1: The Role of Government and the New Deal." The American Experience, http://www.pbs.org/wgbh/americanexperience/features/teachers-resources/1930s-teachers-resource/.

North American Free Trade Agreement (NAFTA)

On January 1, 1994, trade in North America took a significant step toward more open trade and globalization. The North American Free Trade Agreement (NAFTA) created a trilateral trade bloc between the United States, Canada, and Mexico. NAFTA became the third-largest trade bloc in the world, behind the Trans-Pacific Partnership and the United States–European trade bloc. NAFTA impacts over 460 million people and is the largest in land size. The International Monetary Fund estimated NAFTA's 2010 nominal GDP at over $17 trillion. NAFTA has three headquarters: Washington, D.C.; Ottawa, Canada; and Mexico City, Mexico.

The roots of NAFTA are grounded in the Canada–United States Free Trade Agreement. Discussions of a trilateral trade bloc for North America go back to 1986, during the George H. W. Bush presidency. After lengthy negotiations, Bush, Mexican President Carlos Salina de Gortari, and Canadian Prime Minister Brian Mulroney signed the North American Free Trade Agreement in San Antonio, Texas, on December 17, 1992. However,

NAFTA would not become an official trade bloc until each nation's government's legislature or parliament had approved the Agreement.

Approval by the three governments was not a foregone conclusion, especially in Canada and the United States. Canadians were never very pleased with NAFTA's predecessor, the Canada–United States Free Trade Agreement. In the 1986 Canadian election, more people voted against free trade than for it. But it was completed as the two separate parties opposing free trade split the votes, leaving the free trade proponents with the ability to pass NAFTA. Yet the Canadian story was not quite finished. In the United States, NAFTA had many supporters, but there was a very vocal anti-NAFTA contingent led by labor unions and environmental groups. When President George H. W. Bush lost his reelection bid to Bill Clinton, the future of NAFTA in the United States became in doubt as well. Bill Clinton's major support came from labor unions and groups opposed to NAFTA. His election made it a real possibility that NAFTA might lose support.

Back in Canada, the political landscape had also changed against NAFTA approval. Prime Minister Brian Mulroney had been replaced by the more conservative Kim Campbell. But in the 1993 election, Canadians chose Liberal Jean Chrétien as their new prime minister. Between new U.S. president, Democrat Bill Clinton, and Chrétien, the newly elected Canadian prime minister, NAFTA's survival was in serious doubt. However, President Clinton and Prime Minister Chrétien negotiated two new addenda to NAFTA. One was the North American Agreement on Environmental Cooperation, to protect the environment and force companies doing business in Mexico to adhere to environmental standards as if they were in the United States. The second addendum was the North American Agreement on Labor Cooperation, aimed at protecting U.S. labor, especially union labor, with the right to join a union and the right to collective bargaining. With these two addenda added, both Canada and the United States approved NAFTA, and on January 1, 1994, the economic landscape of North America took on a whole new, globalized look.

With NAFTA as the trade law of North America, the aim was to break down the trade and investment barriers between Canada, the United States, and Mexico. Since virtually all trade between the United States and Canada was already free of barriers, when NAFTA took effect on January 4, 1994, the first noticeable effect was the elimination of U.S. tariffs on approximately one-half of the United States' imports from Mexico, and the Mexican tariffs being removed from approximately one-third of Mexico's imports from the United States. The window for total elimination of U.S. and Mexican tariffs was 10 years, or 2004, with the exception of some U.S. agricultural products, for which the timeframe was set at 15 years. NAFTA also addressed the sensitive issue of protecting intellectual property and removing all nontariff barriers to trade.

With the elimination of many, if not all, of the tariffs between the United States, Canada, and Mexico, trade between the nations definitely increased for many products, from durable goods such as automobiles and televisions to agricultural products such as corn and meats. Imports and exports increased across all the borders.

Has the North American Free Trade Agreement been a positive or negative for the U.S. economy? Judging by the pure amount of trade between the three nations, NAFTA has been very successful. Regarding environmental or labor issues that were of concern prior to NAFTA, the success or failure depends on which side of the issue one is speaking. Some jobs have been lost in the U.S. labor market, but others have been created. Environmental groups would argue environmental standards have not been upheld and the United States has exported its environmental issues to Mexico. Certainly, NAFTA has changed the way business is conducted in the three nations. The age of globalization makes it very likely that NAFTA will continue to set the rules of trade and investment between the United States, Canada, and Mexico.

David A. Dieterle

See Also Labor Force; Market Capitalism; Protectionism

Further Reading

CBP.gov. N.d. "NAFTA: A Guide to Customs Procedures." http://www.cbp.gov/trade/nafta/a-guide-to-customs-procedures/.

MacArthur, John R. 2000. *The Selling of "Free Trade:" NAFTA, Washington, and the Subversion of American Democracy*. Berkeley: University of California Press.

NAFTA Secretariat. N.d. "Welcome." https://www.nafta-sec-alena.org/Default.aspx?tabid=85&language=en-US.

Resources for Teachers

Aberdeen, Stan. N.d. "How to Teach the North American Free Trade Agreement." eHow. Accessed July 16, 2013. http://www.ehow.com/how_7349013_teach-north-american-trade-agreement.html.

Lesson Planet. N.d. "NAFTA Teacher Resources: Find NAFTA Educational Ideas and Activities." Accessed July 16, 2013. http://www.lessonplanet.com/lesson-plans/nafta.

Luksetich, William. 2007. "NAFTA: Are Jobs Being Sucked out of the United States?" econedlink. Accessed July http://www.econedlink.org/lessons/index.php?lid=50&type=student. 16, 2013.

Office of Management and Budget (OMB)

The Office of Management and Budget (OMB) is an office of the executive branch of the U.S. government. The main function of the OMB is to serve the president of the United States. As the largest of the agencies of the executive branch, it has wide-ranging duties, responsibilities, and influence with the president as well as other offices and agencies of the executive branch of government. The OMB helps the president set priorities as well as assist in seeing that the president's agenda is implemented.

As its name would suggest, the major responsibility of the OMB is to assist the president with the development of a budget and to manage its operations. The OMB is an extension of the president's influence throughout government regarding budgetary creation and execution. The OMB works with all aspects of the government during the budget process. The OMB serves the president in carrying out presidential decisions and policies regarding a wide variety of topics and issues ranging from the economy to national security.

As its number one priority and responsibility to the president, developing a budget is a multilevel, multifaceted task for the OMB. There are five different offices of the OMB responsible for the development, review, and execution of the executive budget. These are called regional management offices, or RMOs. First, the RMOs help the president frame the spending side of the budget. These plans are then compared against the funding proposals of the many offices and agencies of the federal government. From this study of the proposals and the president's spending plan, the budgetary funding priorities are established.

Once this process is concluded and the budget is in place for execution, the RMOs are then responsible for the implementation and continuing guidance of the budget to see that its funding and management priorities are met. On a continuing basis, the RMOs evaluate, assess, and analyze the operations and implementations of the government's programs. The OMB also monitors congressional appropriations and other legislation regarding government spending.

A second area in which the OMB serves the president is in the management of the president's office and the executive office. The OMB evaluates the operational policies of the executive office regarding financial and information management, assesses the efficiency and effectiveness of the office, and assesses the systems and processes in place for the federal government's purchasing of goods and services for the efficient operation of the federal government. In assessing the executive office's efficiency, the OMB reviews all regulations and policies as they pertain to the different executive offices and departments that report to the president.

The OMB is responsible for seeing that the executive offices are not only efficient but also carrying out the priorities of the president. An important consideration for the president is that the OMB has carefully and thoughtfully assessed the economic impact and economic consequences of the president's priorities, policies, and decisions. The OMB works closely with the legislature to be certain there is coordination between the president's agenda and that of the Congress.

The OMB also serves the president with legislative proposals and implementation of bills. When the president prepares a bill for Congress, the OMB reviews the bill prior to its being sent to Congress. The OMB is charged with reviewing the bill with all the executive agencies that might be affected by it to ascertain their views on the proposed legislation. Once the OMB has comprehensively reviewed the bill with the appropriate agencies, the OMB "clears" the bill to be sent to Congress. Any concerns or disagreements with a proposed bill are clarified during the clearing process. Once a president's bill is sent to Congress, the OMB is responsible for submitting statements of administration policy (SAPs). Once a bill is passed, the president then calls on the OMB once again to solicit views from the impacted agencies prior to the president's signing or vetoing legislation.

When the president requests counsel on economic issues, the president leans on the Office of Economic Policy (EP) of the OMB, the Council of Economic Advisors (CEA), and the Department of Treasury. The Office of Economic Policy assists with developing the president's budget, and assists RMOs with their budgeting preparation and policy proposals, as well as creating economic models for gathering economic data on tax policy, labor, education, credit, and insurance.

The OMB is headed by a director. The director's main role is the management and oversight of a management agenda for all of the federal government, from IT to financial management to human resources. There are five main management offices of the OMB. The five offices are the Office of Federal Financial Management (OFFM), the Office of Federal Procurement Policy (OFPP), the Office of E-Government and Information Technology, the Office of Performance and Personnel Management (OPPM), and the Office of Information and Regulatory Affairs (OIRA). Several other departments within the OMB include general counsel, economic policy, legislative affairs, and legislative reference, communications, and management and operations. All five of the management offices are self-contained and include administration and policy management, as well as evaluation and assessment of the policies for which they are responsible. Each management office works closely with the RMOs to ensure that the policies for which they are responsible are being implemented appropriately and in keeping with the agenda and policies of the president. Noted former OMB directors include George Shultz, David Stockman, Casper Weinberger, and Alice Rivlin.

David A. Dieterle

See Also Congressional Budget Office; Rivlin, Alice; Shultz, George

Further Reading

Office of Management and Budget. N.d. "The Mission and Structure of the Office of Management and Budget." http://www.whitehouse.gov/omb/organization_mission/.

Walser, George H. 1986. *Office of Management and Budget: Evolving Roles and Future Issues, with an Overview*. Vol. 4. Washington, DC: Government Printing Office.

Resources for Teachers

LessonPlanet. N.d. "Government Teacher Resources." http://www.lessonplanet.com/search?keywords=government&type_ids%5B%5D=357917&gclid=CPT6hNa1kLsCFSdp7AodKXAA1A.

Stegon, David. 2012. "FedScoop interview: OMB PortfolioStat Lead Andrew McMahon." fedscoop. http://fedscoop.com/fedscoop-interview-omb-portfoliostat-lead-andrew-mcmahon/§hash.qdmtGo4n.dpufhttp://fedscoop.com/fedscoop-interview-omb-portfoliostat-lead-andrew-mcmahon/.

Okun, Arthur

Born: November 28, 1928, in Jersey City, New Jersey; Died: March 23, 1980, in Washington, D.C.; American; neo-Keynesian, econometrics; Major Work: *Equality and Efficiency: The Big Tradeoff* (1975).

Arthur Okun is an American economist most noted for the economic law that bears his name. While a senior economist at the Council of Economic Advisers (CEA), Okun discovered the relationship between economic growth and changes in unemployment. He asserted that each point change in the unemployment rate equated to a change in real economic growth as measured by the gross national product (GNP) of between 2 and 3 percent. This inverse relationship applied with changes to either the unemployment rate or economic growth. A rise in one would create a decrease in the other and vice versa. Okun died in 1980.

Arthur Melvin Okun was born on November 28, 1928, in Jersey City, New Jersey. He received his BA and PhD degrees from Columbia University. He began his academic career when he accepted an offer to join the economics faculty at Yale University.

Early in his career, Okun began public service when he became a member of President Kennedy's Council of Economic Advisers (CEA). Okun joined the CEA as an adviser in 1962 and served as a member until 1969. In 1968 and 1969, during President Johnson's administration, he chaired the CEA. While a senior economist there, Okun discovered a relationship between economic growth and changes in unemployment.

Based on data collected between World War II and 1960, when President Kennedy was elected, Okun provided Kennedy with the data necessary for him to make Keynesian-style tax cuts to boost a sagging economy. Okun asserted that a 1 percent decrease in the unemployment rate would create an approximately 3 percent increase in economic growth, measured as real gross national product (GNP). Conversely, a change in real GNP would create an opposite percentage change in the unemployment rate. The evidence of the relationship convinced Kennedy to enact the tax cuts. The validity of this relationship has been proven over time and is now known as Okun's Law.

As robust as Okun's Law may be, Okun himself applied boundaries. One, the relationship applied only to the U.S. economy. Two, he asserted that its precision was accurate only when the unemployment rate was between a certain range of 3 to 7 percent. He was also careful to acknowledge that there are many variables that cause economic growth. Okun was quick to point out that correlation between the two variables did not equate to causation. This correlation-causation has also been amended over time as Okun's Law proves predictably strong.

Over time, Okun's boundaries have been revised. Okun's Law has been applied to other economies, most notably those of industrialized nations. Economists now assert that there is at least some causation to economic growth through lower unemployment. It has also been converted to the relationship between the unemployment rate and Gross Domestic Product (GDP). This relationship fell to approximately a 2 percent growth in GDP for every 1 percent reduction in the unemployment rate.

As a stagnant economy continues to plague politicians and economists, research is beginning to question the modern reliability of Okun Law's predictability. As the global economy develops and grows along with new technologies changing productivity variables, the economic growth–unemployment rate relationship and the ratios promoted by Okun face further research and scrutiny.

A second field in which Okun is noted is his work on wealth transfer. Using taxes as the transfer mechanism, he makes his case in *Equality and Efficiency: The Big Tradeoff* (1975). He admits both the inefficiency of such an action and the lack of incentives on both the poor and rich. For the inefficiency, he uses the analogy of a leaky faucet. Such things as administrative costs and lack of incentives provide shortcomings for the tax revenues to be completely transferred. He further acknowledges a complete lack of incentives on both the poor and rich. The poor lose the incentive to work by receiving the transfer of wealth and the rich have no incentive to work since a significant portion of their marginal dollar earned will be taxed away.

Fellow CEA member James Tobin labeled Okun's Law as one of the most reliable regularities in macroeconomics. Arthur Okun also served as a Brookings Institution fellow from 1969 to 1980.

Arthur Okun died on March 23, 1980, in Washington, D.C., of heart failure.

David A. Dieterle

See Also Keynes, John Maynard

Selected Works by Arthur Okun

Okun, Arthur M. 1981. *Prices and Quantities: A Macroeconomic Analysis*. Washington, DC: Brookings Institution Press.

Okun, Arthur M. 1975. *Equality and Efficiency: The Big Tradeoff*. Washington, DC: Brookings Institution Press.

Okun, Arthur M. 1970. *The Political Economy of Prosperity*. Washington, DC: Brookings Institution Press.

Okun, Arthur M. 1962. "Potential GNP: Its Measurement and Significance." Cowles Foundation Paper 190. New Haven, CT: Cowles Foundation.

Selected Works about Arthur Okun

Abel, Andrew B., Ben S. Bernanke, and Dean Croushore. 2008. *Macroeconomics*. 6th ed. Boston: Pearson.

"Arthur M. Okun." 2008. In *The Concise Encyclopedia of Economics*. Edited by David R. Henderson. The Library of Economics and Liberty. http://www.econlib.org/library/Enc/bios/Okun.html.

Daly, Mary, Bart Hobijn, and Joyce Kwok. 2009. "Labor Supply Responses to Changes in Wealth and Credit." Federal Reserve Bank of San Francisco Economic Letter, 2009-05. January 30. http://www.frbsf.org/publications/economics/letter/2009/el2009-05.html.

Pechman, Joseph A., ed. 1983. *Economics for Policymaking: Selected Essays of Arthur M. Okun*. Cambridge, MA: MIT Press.

Olson, Mancur

Born: January 22, 1932, in Grand Forks, North Dakota; Died: February 19, 1998, in College Park, Maryland; American; group dynamics, public goods, labor; Major Works: *The Logic of Collective Action: Public Goods and the Theory of Groups* (1965), *The Rise and Decline of Nations: Economic Growth, Stagflation, and Social Rigidities* (1984), *Power and Prosperity: Outgrowing Communist and Capitalist Dictatorships* (2000).

Mancur Olson is best known for his work introducing the concept of the free-rider problem with public goods. He is remembered as an outstanding economic thinker with a keen ability to integrate ideas from sociology and political science into economic theory and made lasting contributions to how we study and understand our world. Olson died in 1998.

Mancur Lloyd Olson Jr. was born on January 22, 1932, in Grand Forks, North Dakota. He studied as an undergraduate at North Dakota Agricultural College. From there he was awarded a Rhodes Scholarship and attended University College, Oxford. Upon returning to the United States, he performed his doctoral work at Harvard University, where he completed his widely recognized thesis, "The Logic of Collective Action" (1965). After finishing his doctoral work, Olson was hired at Princeton University in its economics department, and later worked in the government for two years under the Johnson administration in the Department of Health, Education, and Welfare. After his stint in the government, Olson returned to academia at the University of Maryland, where he spent the rest of his career.

Olson was a leader and pioneer in the study of group dynamics within a nation. An important concept that was first developed by Olson is known as the free-rider problem. Free riders are people who join a group and expect to gain the benefits that the collective action of the group yields, but are not willing to incur the costs associated with the work of the group. In his book *The Logic of Collective Action*, Olson shows that individuals can and will act in a self-interested manner that works contrary to the goals of collective action. For example, in a perfectly competitive market where there are many producers of a single identical good, it is in the collective interest of the producers to organize and raise the price of the product as high as possible in order to ensure higher profits for all. This is unlikely to happen because a single firm may well consider that it is in its self-interest not to join the price-setting collective action. If one producer refuses to join the group and sells at below market price, it will gain the majority of market share. This explains how sometimes the individual self-interest of a firm can be opposed to the interest of collective action.

Another example of problems that can result from the dissymmetry between individuals and groups is that of people who seek benefits from collective actions, such as in the case of unions. All workers benefit from the higher wages and better working conditions that result from the collective bargaining actions of the union, including workers who are not members of the union. Since there is a cost associated with joining the union, the nonjoiners gain the benefits of membership without paying their dues. Nevertheless, people still do join unions, likely because they recognize that if too many people attempted to free ride, there would not be enough members to achieve their goals. One solution addressing the free-rider problem in the case of unions has been to pass legislation requiring membership, or to use selective incentives individuals will want, such as insurance, but can obtain only through membership.

Olson does not address the issue of mandatory union membership from the perspective of rights, as some of its critics do. He likens it to paying taxes or a military draft, not something we have constitutional protections from. Olson thinks the more relevant consideration is how important a society considers the benefits of strong unions to be.

In his second book, *The Rise and Decline of Nations* (1984), Olson makes the counterintuitive claim that long-term political stability can have a negative impact on economic growth. He supports his claim by showing how small interest groups become entrenched within a political system, achieving successful lobbying efforts that result in inefficiencies for the rest of the economy. As opposed to larger interest groups, where the free-rider principle is at work, smaller groups have the incentive to work and successfully lobby for their interests. Their success secures certain political benefits for their groups, which stifle innovation and growth, limiting long-term growth. Olson called this idea institutional sclerosis. For example, after World War II, Japan and Great Britain exhibited surprisingly fast economic growth that could be attributed in part to the clearing away of the old institutions that resulted from the war.

Olson was also concerned with the role of the government in fostering or blocking economic growth. While many had argued that the government was merely extracting benefits from citizens, Olson showed that even governments have an interest in ensuring at least minimal prosperity for their citizens. Olson's view was that government is not perfect, but it can do some things right if given proper incentives.

Mancur Olson died on February 19, 1998, in College Park, Maryland.

John E. Trupiano

See Also Keynes, John Maynard; Keynesian Economics

Selected Works by Mancur Olson

Olson, Mancur. 2000. *Power and Prosperity: Outgrowing Communist and Capitalist Dictatorships*. New York: Basic Books.

Olson, Mancur. 1984. *The Rise and Decline of Nations: Economic Growth, Stagflation, and Social Rigidities*. New Haven, CT: Yale University Press.

Olson, Mancur. 1965. *The Logic of Collective Action: Public Goods and the Theory of Groups*. Cambridge, MA: President and Fellows of Harvard College.

Selected Works about Mancur Olson

Dixit, Avinash. 1999. "Mancur Olson—Social Scientist." *The Economic Journal* 109, no. 456: F443–52.

Heckelman, Jac C. 2010. *Collective Choice: Essays in Honor of Mancur Olson*. Heidelberg, DE: Springer-Verlag.

McLean, Iain. 2000. "The Divided Legacy of Mancur Olson." *British Journal of Political Science* 30, no. 4: 651–68.

McLean, Iain. 1998. "Obituary: Professor Mancur Olson." *The Independent*, March 2. http://www.independent.co.uk/news/obituaries/obituary-professor-mancur-olson-1147952.html.

Rowley, Charles K. 2004. *The Encyclopedia of Public Choice*. New York: Kluwer Academic.

Ostrom, Elinor

Born: August 7, 1933, in Los Angeles, California; Died: June 12, 2012, in Bloomington, Indiana; American; economic governance of common-pool resources, individual choice theory, Nobel Prize (2009); Major Works: *Governing the Commons: The Evolution of Institutions for Collective Action* (1990), *Rules, Games, and Common-Pool Resources* (with Roy Gardner and Jimmy Walker) (1994), *Working Together: Collective Action, the Commons, and Multiple Methods in Practice* (with Amy R. Poteete and Marco A. Janssen) (2010).

Elinor Ostrom's research involved local public and private stakeholders at multiple levels managing common-pool resources. Her work was acknowledged by the Nobel Committee in 2009. Along with Oliver Williamson, Ostrom was awarded the Nobel Prize in Economics in 2009. She was the first woman to receive this honor. Ostrom died in 2012.

Elinor Awan Ostrom was born on August 7, 1933. Growing up, her parents fed her from their vegetable garden and orchard, taught her to knit, and enrolled her in the nearby public school. She was a competitive swimmer and an accomplished member of her high school debate team. Following the majority of her peers at Beverly Hills High School, she decided she was going to be the first in her family to attend college. Holding jobs as a secretary, an assistant personnel manager, and graduate assistant, she acquired the funds she needed to attend the University of California, Los Angeles (UCLA). While at UCLA she earned her undergraduate degree in political science in 1954 (finishing with honors in three years by attending year-round), her master's in 1962, and her PhD in 1965.

She wrote her dissertation on management of the groundwater industry in Southern California. In what was to become the introduction to her life's work, she studied the West Basin in Los Angeles County. This was her first common-pool resource problem. Because

Garrett Hardin's classic article "The Tragedy of the Commons" had not yet been published, she was in a position to approach problems of the commons in her own way.

Ostrom was affiliated with Indiana University, Bloomington, beginning in 1965 as a professor and cofounder of the Workshop in Political Theory and Policy Analyses. Her distinguished career included the position of Arthur F. Bentley Distinguished Professor of Political Science and Senior Research Director of the Workshop at Indiana University. She was also the founding director of the Center for the Study of Institutional Diversity at Arizona State University, Tempe. Her topics in commons research were as diverse as forests, irrigation, and police departments.

For over a dozen years, Elinor Ostrom researched law enforcement delivery systems in six metropolitan areas. She concluded that large departments of 100 officers were no more efficient than small to medium cadres of 25 to 50 officers. Her long-term study included traffic, patrol, emergency response, and criminal investigators. She produced strong, empirical evidence that large, centralized institutions were not always more efficient than community organizations.

Based on her research, Ostrom concluded that it was indeed realistic to put the management of common resources in the hands of individuals and small groups without private property rights or centralized authority. Her findings defied popular assumptions that powerless, reasonable people were stuck in no-win situations in terms of commons management. She concluded that regime regulations or efforts to privatize to prevent waste and ruin of the commons often were not the best alternative. The empirical evidence indicated that multiple small governments operate effectively even though they lose some advantages gained from the opportunities presented by economies of scale.

In contrast to prevailing wisdom, Ostrom found that individuals and small parties could write their own rules and self-monitor to obtain maximum benefit from resources they shared in common. The widely held belief was that privatization was not the most favorable solution in many situations. She asserted that chaos and inefficiency were not certain outcomes without property rights, as many traditional policy makers proclaimed. She warned that broken trust within public and private partnerships had more lasting detrimental effects on achieving efficient use of the commons. Ostrom contended that a complex system of large and small public bodies along with private individuals operating at all levels was the most beneficial strategy for optimizing the use of common-pool resources.

Along with her husband, Vincent Ostrom (also an Arthur F. Bentley Professor at Indiana University), in 1973, Ostrom founded the Workshop in Political Theory and Policy Analyses. The focus of the workshop was to encourage collaboration among social scientists. Researchers from multiple disciplines developed common methodologies for collecting, testing, and sharing data. The workshop schedules regular meetings for scientists worldwide with similar research interests.

Elinor Ostrom has many accolades to her credit. Most notable was being awarded the Nobel Prize in Economics in 2009. In addition to being a Nobel laureate, she was honored with the John J. Carty Award for the Advancement of Science by the National Academy of Science in 2004 and the Johan Skytte Prize in Political Science in 1999. She was recognized as an honorary fellow for the International Institute of Social Studies in 2002, and received the James Madison Award given by the American Political Science Association in 2005 and the William H. Riker Prize in Political Science in 2008. She served as president of the American Political Science Association and the Public Choice Society.

Cynthia Blitz Law

See Also Market Failures; Public Goods

Selected Works by Elinor Ostrom

Ostrom, Elinor. 1990. *Governing the Commons: The Evolution of Institutions for Collective Action*. Cambridge, MA: Cambridge University Press.

Ostrom, Elinor, Roy Gardner, and Jimmy Walker. 1994. *Rules, Games, and Common-Pool Resources*. Ann Arbor: University of Michigan Press.

Poteete, Amy R., Marco A. Janssen, and Elinor Ostrom. 2010. *Working Together: Collective Action, the Commons, and Multiple Methods in Practice*. Princeton, NJ: Princeton University Press.

Selected Works about Elinor Ostrom

Aligica, Paul Dragos. 2003. "Rethinking Institutional Analysis: Interviews with Vincent and Elinor Ostrom." Arlington, VA: Mercatus Center, George Mason University.

Droste, Nils. 2010. *Regime Effectiveness of Climate Protection: Adapting Elinor Ostrom's Institutional Design Principles*. Norderstadt, DE: GRIN Verlag.

Nobelprize.org. 2009. "Elinor Ostrom—Biographical." http://nobelprize.org/nobel_prizes/economics/laureates/2009/ostrom.html.

P

Phillips, A. W. H.

Born: November 18, 1914, in Dannevirke, New Zealand; Died: March 4, 1975, in Auckland, New Zealand; New Zealander; economic growth, Phillips curve; Major Works: "A Simple Model of Employment, Money and Prices in a Growing Economy" (1961), "Employment, Inflation and Growth" (1962).

A. W. H. Phillips was a leading twentieth-century New Zealand economist who spent most of his academic career at the London School of Economics (LSE). Phillips was noted for his work on the relationship between the level of unemployment and the rate of wage inflation, illustrated by what would become known as the Phillips curve. Using his engineering knowledge, Phillips also designed and built the MONIAC hydraulic economics computer in 1949. Phillips was appointed to the prestigious Tooke Professorship in Economics at the London School of Economics in 1958, and to a research professorship at the Australian National University in 1967. Phillips died in 1975.

Alban William Housego "A. W." "Bill" Phillips was born on November 18, 1914, in Dannevirke, New Zealand. Having a father who experimented with technology, he had an adventurous youth traveling through Australia (where he ran an outback movie theater) and South East Asia. At the age of 15, he left school to become an apprentice engineer for the Public Works Department. For the next 10 years, he worked at various jobs in New Zealand, Australia, and Britain. However, his civilian life was interrupted by World War II, which he joined. He later was captured and held as a Japanese prisoner of war. During the war, Phillips was an armaments officer in Singapore and was awarded an MBE (Military Division) for outstanding courage while under attack.

With his fascination with the interactions of sectors across the economy and his engineering training, in 1949 he developed a hydraulic model of the macroeconomy the MONIAC (Monetary National Income Analogue Computer). It was initially known as the "Phillips Machine." The model consisted of flows of water from one container to another, representing monetary flows—e.g., from consumption to income and thence, via an accelerator mechanism, to investment. "Leakages" to imports were included, and multiple models were built to represent multiple countries—interlinked by pipes. It was very well received, and Phillips was soon offered a teaching position at the LSE.

Having worked on modeling the national economic processes of the British economy with his MONIAC, he published his own work on the relationship between inflation and unemployment, illustrated by the "Phillips curve" in 1958. The curve has been described as the most influential and productive macroeconomic idea in the postwar era. Phillips observed that there is a trade-off between a strong economy and low inflation. In years when the unemployment rate was high, wages tended to be stable, or possibly fall. Conversely, when unemployment was low, wages rose rapidly, leading to inflationary pressures.

Following this publication, two other notable economists, Paul Samuelson and Robert Solow, wrote an influential article describing the possibilities suggested by the Phillips curve in the context of the United States. Although the Phillips curve has changed substantially over time, it remains an important feature of macroeconomic analysis of economic fluctuations; e.g., while it has been observed that there is a stable short-run trade-off between unemployment and inflation, this has not been observed in the long run.

He made several other notable contributions to economics, particularly relating to stabilization policy. He asserted that not only is it crucial to have the right policies, but these policies also must be implemented at the right time. The right policy implemented at the wrong time can make the economy worse. However, the subtlety and wisdom of Phillips's stabilization exercises were largely overlooked, as both monetarists and the Phillips curve Keynesians competed for policy influence. With a profound distaste for such policy manipulation, he gradually abandoned macroeconomics for Chinese economic studies.

After the 1968 student riots in London, Phillips returned to Australia for a position at Australian National University and later at University of Auckland, which allowed him to devote half his time to Chinese studies. He became one of the first Western economists to turn his attention to Chinese developments with the anticipation of the rise of the Chinese economy despite its then perilous state. Although he did not become an academic until 1950 at the age of 36, his contributions have been significant and lasting.

A. W. H. Phillips died on March 4, 1975, in Auckland, New Zealand.

Ninee Shoua Yang

See Also Contractionary Fiscal Policy; Expansionary Fiscal Policy; Fiscal Policy; Keynes, John Maynard; Samuelson, Paul

Selected Works by A. W. H. Phillips

Phillips, A. W. H. 1962. "Employment, Inflation and Growth." *Economica* 29: 1–16.

Phillips, A. W. H. 1961. "A Simple Model of Employment, Money and Prices in a Growing Economy." *Economica* 28: 360–70.

Phillips, A. W. H. 1958. "The Relation between Unemployment and the Rate of Change of Money Wage Rates in the United Kingdom, 1861–1957." *Economica* 25: 283–99.

Phillips, A. W. H. 1957. "Stabilisation Policy and the Time Form of Lagged Response." *The Economic Journal* 67: 265–77.

Phillips, A. W. H. 1954. "Stabilisation Policy in a Closed Economy." *The Economic Journal* 64: 290–323.

Phillips, A. W. H. 1950. "Mechanical Models in Economic Dynamics." *Economica* 17: 283–305.

Selected Works about A. W. H. Phillips

Bollard, Alan E. 2011. "Man, Money and Machines: The Contributions of A. W. Phillips." *Economica* 78: 1–9.

Gordon, Robert J. 2011. "The History of the Phillips Curve: Consensus and Bifurcation." *Economica* 78: 10–50.

Hally, Mike. 2005. *Electronic Brains: Stories from the Dawn of the Computer Age*. Washington, DC: Joseph Henry Press.

Laidler, David. 2000. "Phillips in Retrospect." A review essay on *A. W. H. Phillips: Collected Works in Contemporary Perspective*. Edited by Robert Leeson. Cambridge: Cambridge University Press. Available at http://economics.uwo.ca/faculty/laidler/workingpapers/phillips.pdf.

Leeson, Robert. 1995. *The Life and Legacy of A. W. H. Phillips*. Perth, AU: Murdoch University.

Phillips, A. W. H., and A. R. Bergstrom. 1978. *Stability and Inflation: A Volume of Essays to Honour the Memory of A. W. H. Phillips*. Hoboken, NJ: Wiley.

"Phillips Curve." 2008. In *The Concise Encyclopedia of Economics*. Edited by David R. Henderson. The Library of Economics and Liberty. http://www.econlib.org/library/Enc/PhillipsCurve.html.

Pollock v. Farmers' Loan & Trust Company, 157 U.S. 429 (1895)

The Supreme Court Case Disallowed Congress's Power to Tax All Forms of Income

Economic Concepts

Ability to pay principle of taxation; benefits received principle of taxation; business cycle; capital; consumption taxes; direct tax; duties; income tax; indirect tax; sales tax; tariffs; progressive tax; regressive tax; unemployment rate

Economic Impact

This case confirmed Congress's inability to impose a national income tax on all forms of income. It led to the U.S. Constitution's Sixteenth Amendment, allowing a national income tax.

Economic Summary

The power of Congress to tax is a very extensive power. The Constitution provides for it with one exception and two qualifications. Congress cannot tax exports, and it must impose direct taxes by the rule of apportionment, and indirect taxes by the rule of uniformity. Most revenue the federal government acquired was through tariffs, duties, and other consumption taxes, (i.e., sales taxes).

The Supreme Court's responsibility in *Pollock v. Farmers' Loan & Trust* was to settle the issue of whether or not a tax on income earned from property violated Article I, Section 2, Clause 3 of the U.S. Constitution. This article requires that direct taxes imposed by the national government be apportioned among the states on the basis of population.

The Economic Panic of 1893 resulted in the United States experiencing a financial contraction in the business cycle, characterized by high unemployment rates and difficult access to capital. In response, Congress passed the Wilson-Gorman Tariff Act of 1894. Believing this income tax violated the Constitution, Charles Pollock sued the Farmers' Loan & Trust Company in 1895. The Supreme Court reversed its previous ruling in *Springer v. United States* (102 U.S. 586, October 1880) and agreed in part with Pollock. Afterwards, it became difficult for Congress to impose a national income tax that applied to all forms of income until the 1913 ratification of the U.S. Constitution's Sixteenth Amendment.

Case Summary

Corporations cannot spend shareholders profits in ways that are illegal. Charles Pollock believed that Farmers' Loan & Trust Company was going to do that very thing if it took his share of the net profits to pay what he alleged was an unconstitutional tax. Charles Pollock was not rich by the standards of the day, nor was he poor. He owned 10 shares in the Farmers' Loan & Trust Company of Massachusetts with a value of over $5,000, which would be close to $140,300 in 2013 dollars (based on inflation calculator, Bureau of Labor Statistics, 2013). Pollock's investment was not great, but the significance of his objection was not small.

Charles Pollock could not sue Congress. Therefore, he sued the corporation he was employed with in a federal circuit court, enjoining it from paying the tax and reporting the shareholders' income to the Internal Revenue officer. Other stockholders of Farmers' Loan & Trust, many of whom did not think they should pay 2 percent of their net profit to the federal government, shared in this litigation. Pollock argued that the tax was unconstitutional. He lost and appealed his case to the Supreme Court.

At the turn of the twentieth century, the time of *Pollock v. Farmers' Loan & Trust Company*, the nation was divided on political principles. Against the opposition of Republicans, Congress passed an emergency revenue bill, the Internal Revenue Act of 1862 and 1864, to implement a temporary income tax on the wealthy to help finance the Civil War. Prior to this time, most of the revenue the federal government acquired was from tariffs, duties, and other consumption taxes (i.e., sales taxes). In *Springer v. U.S.* (1864), the Supreme Court upheld the constitutionality of the income tax. This tax was allowed to expire, as it had been mainly an emergency measure.

In 1892, Grover Cleveland became the first Democratic president elected since the Civil War. Only months after his inauguration, the nation experienced the economic panic of 1893. The economy went into a contraction phase of the business cycle characterized by high unemployment, bank panics, and a severe difficulty in obtaining capital. President Cleveland and Congress responded by lowering tariffs and duties. In addition, in 1893, Congress and President Cleveland reimplemented the income tax by enacting the Wilson-Gorman Tariff Act.

The act stipulated that every citizen would pay a 2 percent tax on income from property, rents, interest dividends, salaries, and so forth over the amount of $4,000. This income included sales of bonds, notes, and agricultural products. In addition, any person of lawful age having an income of at least $3,500 would be required to submit a list or record of their income to the Internal Revenue collector. Investment and banking institutions must submit that payment of tax on behalf of the investors whose interest and rent were the subject of taxation. Farmers' Loan & Trust Company, a corporation of the state of New York, held a fiduciary responsibility to its clients that required it to report the income and pay the 2 percent tax. The capital stock of the corporation was worth 1 million dollars. There were 40,000 shares of stock at a par value of 25 dollars per share (see the transcript of syllabus of the case; see Further Reading). Additional assets of the corporation included property and a host of New York City municipal bonds.

The Supreme Court took the *Pollock v. Farmers' Loan & Trust* case to settle an issue with regard to whether or not a tax on income earned from property violated Article I, Section 2, Clause 3 of the Constitution, which requires that direct taxes imposed by the national government be apportioned among the states on the basis of population. Pollock argued that income derived from property was a direct tax and as such was not collected per apportionment, as was the constitutional requirement. In addition, the federal government could not tax municipal bonds any more than state governments could tax federal bonds.

When writing the opinion of the Court, Chief Justice Fuller made great effort to construe what the framers of the Constitution intended by "direct" and "indirect" taxes. It was his conclusion that even with the readings of Adam Smith at their disposal, it could not be determined. The issue of apportionment and taxation was a compromise by the convention to keep the negotiations going. It was clear that the states could not tax imports, and commerce was to be regulated by the federal government. Actual apportionment within a state, however, was left to the state. Furthermore, Fuller concurred with the argument that municipal bonds were not eligible for taxation, thereby finding sections of the Wilson-Gorman Tariff Act in violation of the Constitution. The Court held that imposing taxes on personal income derived from real estate investments and personal property such as stocks and bonds was a direct tax and had not been apportioned properly among the states.

Justice White's dissenting opinion was ardent. Joined by Justice Harlan, White expressed concern that precedent had been established whereby no legal power could obstruct or control the collection of taxes. If there were a mechanism to do this, the very existence of the government might hang on the authority of an antagonistic judiciary. White stated that as long as Pollock had recourse to legal remedy after his taxes were paid, he had no grounds for a case prior to payment. In addition, White argued that to ponder the intent of the framers of the Constitution was to ignore the opinions of William Paterson, who was a contributor at the Constitutional Convention. Justice Paterson later sat on the Supreme Court and clearly stated that the power to tax was extensive. Justice Harlan added in a short dissent that the framers' interpretation of direct and indirect taxation was clear and vested in the United States' plenary powers of taxation with the exception of exports (see the transcript of Justice Harlan's dissenting opinion; see Further Reading).

Nonetheless, Chief Justice Fuller agreed that the framers of the Constitution had aimed at compromise with the rule of apportionment, but added that if the federal government is allowed to call a direct tax indirect, the power boundary is broken and the safeguard of private rights and private property could disappear as well (see the transcript of Chief

Justice Fuller's majority opinion; see Further Reading). The Supreme Court ruled that the Circuit Court finding was to be reversed and the case remanded with directions to enter a decree in favor of Pollock.

Kathleen C. Simmons

See Also Private Property; Taxes; U.S. Treasury Bills, Notes, and Bonds

Related Cases

Hylton v. United States, 3 Dall. 171, (1796)

Springer v. United States, 102 U.S. 586, (1880)

Further Reading

Legal Information Institute, Cornell University Law School. N.d. "*Pollock v. Farmers Loan and Trust Co.*" http://www.law.cornell.edu/supct/html/historics/USSC_CR_0157_0429_ZS.html. (Syllabus of the case)

Legal Information Institute, Cornell University Law School. N.d. "*Pollock v. Farmers Loan and Trust Co.*" http://www.law.cornell.edu/supremecourt/text/157/429#writing-USSC_CR_0157_0429_ZO. (Transcript of Chief Justice Fuller's majority opinion)

Legal Information Institute, Cornell University Law School. N.d. "*Pollock v. Farmers Loan and Trust Co.*" http://www.law.cornell.edu/supremecourt/text/157/429#writing-USSC_CR_0157_0429_ZX. (Transcript of Justice Field's separate opinion)

Legal Information Institute, Cornell University Law School. N.d. "*Pollock v. Farmers Loan and Trust Co.*" http://www.law.cornell.edu/supremecourt/text/157/429#writing-USSC_CR_0157_0429_ZD. (Transcript of Justice White's dissenting opinion)

Legal Information Institute, Cornell University Law School. N.d. "*Pollock v. Farmers Loan and Trust Co.*" http://www.law.cornell.edu/supremecourt/text/157/429#writing-USSC_CR_0157_0429_ZD_1. (Transcript of Justice Harlan's dissenting opinion)

OYEZ ITT Chicago, Kent School of Law. N.d. "*Pollock v. Farmers Loan and Trust Co.*" http://www.oyez.org/cases/1851-1900/1894/1894_893/. (Facts of the case)

Resources for Teachers

Currie, David P. 1990. *The Constitution in the Supreme Court: The Second Century, 1888–1986*. Vol. 2. Chicago: University of Chicago Press.

The Federal Reserve Bank of Minneapolis. N.d. "Consumer Price Index (Estimate) 1800." Handbook of Labor Statistics, U.S. Department of Labor, Bureau of Labor Statistics. http://www.minneapolisfed.org/community_education/teacher/calc/hist1800.cfm">http://www.minneapolisfed.org/community_education/teacher/calc/hist1800.cfm.

Joseph, Richard J. 2004. *The Origins of the American Income Tax: The Revenue Act of 1894 and Its Aftermath*. Syracuse, NY: Syracuse University Press.

Private Property

The origins of private property may lie deeply, perhaps genetically, ingrained in human nature. The first hominids who found a useful rock or stick, or crafted a tool, or settled in a place, almost certainly asserted ownership, and then had to defend it. As societies formed, rules were adopted to protect citizens' rights and possessions. As people(s) began to trade, possession inherently acknowledged ownership.

In 350 BCE, Plato and Aristotle argued over whether property should be owned privately or collectively (by the state). More than 2,000 years later, the debate continued, as capitalism, fundamentally dependent on private property rights, waged ideological war with socialism and communism, which espoused collective ownership of the means of production, for the economic future of the world. It is also worth noting that, in the fairly recent past, the world was torn over whether property could even include human beings!

While public property is owned by the state (government), economists recognize private property as that which assumes ownership or the exclusive right over a productive resource by entities other than the government, including not only material things but also the product of one's labor, such as original ideas, symbols, methods, writings, and so forth. These rights can generally be traded or transferred through legal contracts.

Free-market (capitalist) advocates such as Milton Friedman (1912–2006) and Friedrich von Hayek (1899–1992) believed that private property, and the exclusive right to profit from it, is absolutely essential for the efficient allocation of resources to achieve the greatest economic benefits to society. When individuals are allowed to directly own productive resources and to employ them to create things of value for others, the potential to earn profits will serve as a very powerful incentive to protect, maintain, and even improve upon those assets. Those resources will then be employed in innovative and productive ways to generate profit for the owners by serving others, producing useful new goods or services, and solving problems in an economy. Conversely, when property is owned collectively, or when individuals cannot earn personal profit from employing them productively, there is no direct or enduring incentive for them to do so. Then, resources tend to be underutilized, poorly maintained, or even abused.

In every society, there is common property such as streets, parks, and waterways; natural resources; and intangible things like (clean) air and even peace and quiet. What if one person's right over property or use of it infringes on the rights, or diminishes the well-being, of others, perhaps the whole of society? Think of a factory polluting the surrounding air or water. Those outside the direct market who must bear costs associated with others' consumption or production of a good are said to suffer negative externalities. Those who likewise receive benefits enjoy positive externalities. When the public good is served, government may actually seize private property (after fairly compensating the owners) for purposes like constructing dams, bridges, parks, and so on, through the process of eminent domain. Even nations with developed legal systems and effective enforcement mechanisms struggle with issues and conflicts where property rights are not clearly defined.

When there are no clearly established private property rights, productive assets tend to be overutilized, depleted, or even destroyed by users who gain direct personal benefit from utilizing the common resource before others do, but who do not share in the cost of maintaining it. The "tragedy of the commons" is exemplified by the plight of the Atlantic cod fishing industry in the 1980s, as fishermen competed vigorously to catch clearly depleting stocks of cod before other fishermen took them. This rule of capture, asserting clear private ownership only upon capture of the common good, led to more and more overfishing as the price of cod rose, reflecting its dramatically escalating scarcity. Despite recognition that continued fishing would diminish the fish population below levels necessary to effectively reproduce and sustain a stable population, thus destroying the entire industry and thus their own livelihood, individual fishermen were perversely incentivized (through higher prices and the rule of capture) to actually increase fishing until the fish stocks went commercially extinct.

Market failure occurs whenever resources are not efficiently allocated toward their most productive uses. This is not to say that alternative solutions are apparent. But establishing and enforcing clear property rights, especially for common resources, continues to pose significant challenges to all economic systems to this day.

Steven J. Eschrich

See Also Externalities; Friedman, Milton; Hayek, Friedrich von; Public Goods

Further Readings

Friedman, Thomas. 2009. "(No) Drill, Baby, Drill," *New York Times*, April 12. http://www.nytimes.com/2009/04/12/opinion/12friedman.html?_r=0.

Lai, Lawrence W. C. 2011. *The Ideas of Ronald H. Coase: Market Failure and Planning by Contract for Sustainable Development.* New York: Routledge.

Mises, Ludwig von. 1998. *Human Action: A Treatise on Economics.* Auburn, AL: The Ludwig von Mises Institute.

Ostrom, Elinor. 1990. *Governing the Commons: The Evolution of Institutions for Collective Action.* Cambridge: Cambridge University Press.

Resources for Teachers

EconWorks. 2013. "Lesson 4: Property Rights in a Market Economy, Grades 9–12." http://econworks.org/portfolio/14-greatest-hits-for-teaching-high-school-economics/.

Foundation for Teaching Economics. N.d. "Lesson 2: Property Rights and the Rule of Law." http://www.fte.org/teacher-resources/lesson-plans/is-capitalism-good-for-the-poor/lesson-2-property-rights-and-the-rule-of-law/.

Foundation for Teaching Economics. N.d. "Lesson 4: Property Rights." http://www.fte.org/teacher-resources/lesson-plans/edsulessons/lesson-4-property-rights/.

Prohibition

Prohibition, the banning of the manufacturing, sale, and transportation of alcoholic beverages, became national policy in the United States with the ratification of the Eighteenth Amendment in 1919. The act, however, did not outlaw the consumption of alcohol. Congress passed the Volstead Act, also known as the National Prohibition Act, in 1920 in order to further define the parameters of the amendment as well as to give the national and state governments the tools necessary to carry out the law. The act also created a special agency inside the U.S. Treasury Department known as the Prohibition Bureau to enforce it. Many wealthy Americans and private businesses were able to purchase and store large supplies of alcoholic beverages before the law went into effect.

The origins of the movement actually began before the American Revolution at local levels but began to receive more national attention during the 1800s. The average American in the early 1800s consumed almost seven gallons of pure alcohol a year (Burns, 2011), more than three times what Americans drink today. Alcohol abuse challenged the stability of many families during this time, especially when considering the limited legal rights and financial dependence of women. Growing from the roots of abolitionists and Protestant Church reform, supporters first urged moderation and then later full prohibition via legislation. Temperance activist Neal Dow led Maine to become the first of many states to pass Prohibition laws during the mid-1800s. This created momentum for the creation of a national Prohibition law. Groups such as the American Temperance Society and the Woman's Christian Temperance Union (WCTU), led by Francis Willard, argued that alcoholic beverages were the cause of many of the social ills of the time period. Alcohol was blamed for contributing to such immoral behavior as gambling, domestic violence, and prostitution. Business interests also supported the movement because they felt it would improve productivity and reduce absenteeism. The Anti-Saloon League, founded in 1893, worked to create political support for Prohibition under the leadership of Wayne B. Wheeler. The Anti-Saloon League quickly became an incredibly successful lobbying group drawing diverse groups of Americans from all walks of life, including Republicans, Democrats, suffragists, and Populists, to create a constitutional amendment supporting Prohibition.

The movement gained further momentum during the Progressive Era, when many middle-class reformers saw the prohibition of alcoholic beverages as a means to improve the moral behavior and economic condition of the urban poor and working classes. World War I became the final impetus for the passage of a constitutional amendment banning the production, sale, and transportation of alcohol. Anti-German sentiments gave force to the Progressive arguments that poor, urban areas inhabited by immigrants were hotbeds of immorality and disloyalty. The powerful Anti-Saloon League helped to promote the idea that beer and brewers were viewed as a German plot to sap America's will to fight the war.

In 1913, the federal government ratified the Sixteenth Amendment making income tax a major form of revenue for the federal government. Consequently, they were no longer dependent on liquor taxes as a major revenue source. This left a clear road for the Eighteenth Amendment to pass through both houses of Congress and have state ratification in just 13 months.

Prohibition was an unpopular law from the start, creating black markets and a significant underground economy. Many Americans made liquor at home and others visited underground bars known as speakeasies, which were numerous in most large cities across the United Sates. Loopholes in the law allowed people to obtain alcohol through unconventional, black market, and nonmarket economic means. Farmers, physicians, pharmacists, and even religious leaders could all use exceptions to the law to obtain and distribute alcohol to the greater public. "Bootlegging" was a term used to describe the illegal production, sale, and distribution of alcohol during Prohibition. Bootleggers also smuggled alcohol into the United States from Canada, the Caribbean, and Europe.

Bootlegging, black market, and underground economic activity led to a rise in organized crime and corruption in the United States. Organized crime had existed throughout U.S. history, but grew to unprecedented levels during Prohibition, as the illegal distribution and sale of alcohol became quite lucrative. Gangsters such as Al Capone built criminal empires with the money made from black market operations, bootlegging alcohol, and speakeasies. Al Capone was able to monopolize Chicago's illegal activity by murdering his competition and anyone else who stood in his way. At the height of his operations, Capone had built a multimillion dollar operation from his black market operations (http://www.history.com/topics/al-capone). Capone was never convicted of murder, but was found guilty of tax evasion and sentenced to 11 years in the famous Alcatraz Federal Penitentiary.

Problems enforcing the amendment were apparent from the start. Federal, state, and local governments were in charge of policing an action that many, if not most, Americans felt was a natural part of society. Complicating matters was the issue of resources allotted to the Prohibition Bureau. Only 1,500 federal agents were assigned to the bureau, which made it impossible to patrol the nation's thousands of miles of coast and international borders, much less find and shut down illegal stills and underground bars. Al Capone alone employed 1,000 men to protect his liquor trade.

Prohibition supporters believed that it would stimulate local economies. They believed people would purchase household goods and luxury items like soft drinks, movies, or real estate as they looked for other forms of recreation. The reality was the closing of many entertainment industries and restaurants due to slow sales without alcohol. Many also lost jobs within and related to the brewing, distilling, and saloon industry.

The movement to end Prohibition began shortly after it became national policy. It quickly became apparent that the costs of enforcing the Eighteenth Amendment far exceeded the benefits.

The Great Depression furthered the cause of those who wanted to repeal the Eighteenth Amendment. They argued that many jobs could be created by allowing the sale and manufacturing of alcohol, which would also increase government revenues through excise taxes. Opponents successfully used these arguments and others to fight for the passage and ratification of the Twenty-First Amendment in 1933, which repealed the Eighteenth Amendment. Several states went on to pass their own statewide prohibition laws, which were not fully repealed until 1966.

Jeremy Robinson
Kathryn Lloyd Gustafson

See Also Constitution of the United States (see Appendix); Market Capitalism

Further Reading

Burns, Ken, and Lynn Novick. 2011. "Prohibition." *PBS.* http://www.pbs.org/kenburns/prohibition/.

Hampson, Rick. 2010. "Dry America's Not-So-Sober Reality: It's Shrinking Fast." *USA Today.* June 30. http://usatoday30.usatoday.com/news/nation/2010-06-30-dry-counties_N.htm.

Hanson, David J. 2013. "Repeal of Prohibition." http://www2.potsdam.edu/hansondj/Controversies/1131637220.html#.Upo4KsuA2M9.

History.com. N.d. "Al Capone." Accessed June 3, 2014. http://www.history.com/topics/al-capone.

History.com. 2013. "Prohibition." Accessed June 3, 2014. http://www.history.com/topics/prohibition.

Hoyt, Alia. 2008. "How Prohibition Worked." *How Stuff Works*, January 8. http://history.howstuffworks.com/historical-events/prohibition.htm.

Minson, Douglas C. 2012. "The Joy of Drinking: Prohibition, Legislating Morality, and Celebrating Repeal Day." *The Imaginative Conservative*, December. http://www.theimaginative-conservative.org/2012/12/celebrating-repeal-day-prohibition.htm.

Okrent, Daniel. 2010. "Wayne B. Wheeler: The Man Who Turned off the Taps." *Smithsonian.com*, May. http://www.smithsonianmag.com/history-archaeology/Wayne-B-Wheeler-The-Man-Who-Turned-Off-the-Taps.html.

Resources for Teachers

History.com. N.d. "18th and 21st Amendments." Accessed June 3, 2014. http://www.history.com/topics/18th-and-21st-amendments.

History.com. N.d. This Day in History: "December 5, 1933; Prohibition Ends." Accessed June 3, 2014. http://www.history.com/this-day-in-history/prohibition-ends.

The U.S. National Archives and Records Administration. N.d. "Teaching with Documents: The Volstead Act and Related Prohibition Documents." http://www.archives.gov/education/lessons/volstead-act/.

Protectionism

Protectionism is the act of a government to discourage the importing of a good or service by a company in another country. Protectionist measures can also be applied to encourage domestic production to favor the domestic industry and create a market that discourages foreign competition. Protectionism by a country can be either transparent or nontransparent. The three main forms of protectionism are tariffs, quotas, and subsidies. These are called transparent types of protectionism. All three are overt means of a government to protect an industry.

Tariffs are a tax on a country's imports. Since tariffs generate revenue, they can have several uses, depending on the country imposing the tariff. Developed nations use tariffs for protective purposes. Tariffs are not as much of a protectionist measure for less developed countries (LDCs). For an LDC a tariff is usually their main source of tax revenue. Since income, consumption levels, and property values are small relative to the size of the economy, imports remain the main source of generating tax revenue.

Quotas are another form of protection limiting the number of imports. Quotas are not a tax and therefore do not generate tax revenue. As a result, they are almost exclusively instituted by developed countries to protect a domestic industry. The United States used quotas in the 1970s to protect the U.S. automobile industry from the early introduction of Japanese imports. Another form of quota is the voluntary export restraint (VER). This type of quota, as the name suggests, is the exporting nation voluntarily limiting an export to an importing nation. President Ronald Reagan used this type of protection for the automobile industry by persuading Japan to voluntarily restrict its exporting of automobiles to the United States.

Tariffs and quotas are considered transparent protective barriers. Transparent protective measures are an overt act of the domestic government and clearly visible to everyone. More invisible types of barriers are nontransparent, such as patents, copyrights, certain manufacturing rules, licenses, or fees.

Governments institute protectionism measures for several reasons. An industry might be protected because it is considered important to a nation's national defense. In addition, if an industry is young and developing, it may lobby government to be protected from the competition of more mature foreign industries or companies. A government may institute a tariff or quota to protect a specific labor group.

The politics of protectionism can be quite sensitive. A government may institute a tariff or quota in retaliation for the imposition of a similar protected measure by another country. Retaliation is a downside to protectionism. This was evident in the United States in the 1930s, when the rest of the world responded to the passage of the Smoot-Hawley Tariff Act. When a government decides to impose a tariff, quota, or some other form of protectionism, it must take into consideration the possibility of retaliations.

The benefits of tariffs and quotas can be identified by the reason for the protective measure or the specific industry or labor group being protected, but the costs are more expansive as they are spread out among a wide number of people. This idea of narrowly focused beneficiaries against the very broad base of those paying the costs is the theory behind Mancur Olson's *The Logic of Collective Action*. Market costs of protectionism include an inefficiency of production, additional costs to domestic businesses, and increased prices to consumers. While import substitution policies of developing nations have the intent to promote domestic production, they cut off developing nations from outside trade and new technologies.

The enactment of subsidies is also a form of protectionism. Direct subsidies to producers often lead to overproduction or restricting imports from a market. These types of subsidies are implemented especially in the agricultural industry. In a global economy, the benefits and costs of subsidies are often hard to identify. While some subsidies may benefit consumers with lower prices, the lower prices hurt producers in developing countries. Yet in some developing countries, the lower world prices raise their standard of living. Economists usually measure the benefits and costs of subsidies based on a nation-by-nation study.

David A. Dieterle

See Also Olson, Mancur; Tariff Act of 1930 (Smoot-Hawley Tariff Act)

Further Reading

Bhagwati, Jagdish. 1988. *Protectionism*. Cambridge, MA: MIT Press.

Olson, Mancur. 1971. *The Logic of Collective Action: Public Goods and the Theory of Groups*. Cambridge, MA: Harvard University Press.

Resources for Teachers

The Economics Classroom. N.d. "Protectionist Tariffs." http://www.econclassroom.com/?p=4466.

"Lesson 16: Protectionism vs. Globalization." N.d. Foundation for Teaching Economics. http://www.fte.org/teacher-resources/lesson-plans/efiahlessons/protectionism-vs-globalization/.

Public Goods

Public goods are goods and services provided by a government, as opposed to goods offered by private businesses or organizations. Public goods are often defined because of market imperfections where the private market does not supply the quantity of a good society deems appropriate, such as education. Examples of public goods include national defense, interstate highways, state and city parks, public state universities, public schools and education, public libraries, and fire and police protection. Public goods are deemed to be public goods because a society has deemed the good or service to be a valuable benefit to society.

To be considered a public good, two key characteristics need to be fulfilled: shared consumption and nonexclusion principles. Shared consumption has also been known as nonrival consumption. Shared consumption means more than one person can receive the benefit of the good or service at the same time. Everyone benefits from the Internet or local police protection at the same time without that benefit being diminished by anyone. Likewise, many people can enjoy a public park on a sunny day without reducing the enjoyment of the others.

While shared consumption is a necessary criterion for a public good, shared consumption does not automatically mean a good or service is public. Golf courses definitely satisfy shared consumption since many golfers can be enjoying a golf course at the same time. However, golf courses are both a public good and a private good. While there are many public golf courses, there are also many private golf courses. The same can be said for elementary schools, colleges and universities, or campgrounds.

The second main criterion is the nonexclusion principle. The nonexclusion principle for a good is that a person cannot be excluded from the benefits of the good or service, whether or not he or she has paid to support the good or service. This nonexclusion principle best exemplifies a public good. Conversely, a private good's key criterion is that the purchaser of the good has the right to decide who consumes the good. He or she can exclude others from its use. When a person buys a cup of coffee, car, or new pair of shoes he or she decides who benefits from the good. The buyer has the right to exclude another from benefiting from the purchase. A public good, however, does not permit such exclusive-use decisions.

The best example of the nonexclusion principle is national defense. It does not matter if a person pays taxes to support the military. If the military becomes involved in a war or military conflict to protect its citizens, it does not protect only those who paid taxes. It protects everyone, taxpayers and nontaxpayers alike. A public good where everyone can benefit presents governments who provide public goods with a key problem: the free rider problem.

Public Goods

	Excludable	Non-Excludable
Rival	Private Goods (Groceries, Clothes, TVs)	Common Goods (Fisheries, Oceans, School Cafeteria)
Non-Rival	Club Goods (Parks, Golf Courses, Movie Theaters)	Public Goods (National defense, police, fire, roads)

Free Rider Problem

The free rider problem is an inherent problem for every government that offers a public good. The government (regardless of whether it is federal, state, or local) is constantly confronted with how to deal with free riders and minimize the free rider issue. One key solution to the free rider issue is to increase the exclusivity of the public good. This has been accomplished through the use of tolls for roads and bridges, fees for parks, or licenses for many professional and recreational activities.

A second problem for a public good is when ownership and property rights are not well defined. When ownership of a resource, such as the ocean, cannot be well defined, there is a tendency to overuse the good without consideration of the costs of use. This imbalance of excess use without concern for costs leads to negative externalities such as pollution. This type of public good problem is called the "tragedy of the commons." Ownership is based on rule of capture, which results in the overuse of the good. This free rider problem has been confronted throughout history with preserving different types of fish or buffalo herds. This form of free rider problem is addressed through improved property rights. Defining property ownership and property rights to a property such as a body of water is a problem for government. While no solution has been found to be perfect, this issue has been addressed through establishing quotas or increasing fees for use.

Critics of public goods suggest that governments and societies are often too quick to designate a good or service a good that should be available to all (i.e., a public good). Critics point out that many of these goods could have been satisfactorily distributed in the marketplace as private goods. Some historically public goods have indeed over time been transferred, at least in part, to the private sector. In some parts of the country, fire protection has actually been transformed into a more private good, where those who do not pay the fee do not receive fire protection.

Funding of Public Goods

Public goods are funded through taxes, fees, fines, and licenses. The type of funding a public good receives is often determined by the characteristics of the public good. For national defense, for example, where it is clearly shared consumption and excluding someone would be virtually impossible, taxes is the revenue choice. Education is another example of funding through taxes because consumption is shared and one cannot be excluded from benefiting. If the public good is an activity (see Club Goods on p. 288) where the nonrival principle does not hold and someone can be excluded, then fees or licenses are used as an incentive to participate and fund the activity. States often require fishing and hunting licenses to participate in those activities. A fee is often charged to enter national and state parks. One cannot drive a car without a driver's license and a license plate.

Public Goods and the Global Economy

An increasing concern as the global economy grows and expands is the role of institutions in providing an amount of certainty and order to the global economic environment. It has been argued that this lack of general international rules leads to financial crises. At issue regarding a free rider problem is the use of international public goods to define how countries choose (or not) to participate in the global economy. Global public goods can include capital flows to developing countries, international money settlements for international debts, and last-resort lending. A lack of international rules and institutions creates incentives for some nations to be free riders in solving these international issues, creating a fragile global economy. Some countries choose not to pay, but participate in the international marketplace and international institutions such as the World Bank and International Monetary Fund. These countries that do not pay participating fees to the World Bank or International Monetary Fund receive emergency financial assistance from either or both organizations. These nations are essentially free riders in the global economy.

David A. Dieterle

See Also Externalities; International Monetary Fund (IMF); Private Property; Taxes; World Bank

Further Reading

Alesina, Alberto, Reza Baqir, and William Easterly. 1999. "Public Goods and Ethnic Divisions." *Quarterly Journal of Economics* 114, no. 4: 1243–84. http://qje.oxfordjournals.org/content/114/4/1243.abstract.

Cowen, Tyler. N.d. "Public Goods." The Concise Encyclopedia of Economics. Library of Economics and Liberty. http://www.econlib.org/library/Enc/PublicGoods.html.

Gerber, James. 2014. "Chapter 2: International Economic Institutions Since World War II." In *International Economics*, 6th ed., 29–32. New York: Pearson Education.

Holcomb, Paul. 1997. "A Theory of the Theory of Public Goods." *Review of Austrian Economics* 10, no. 1: 1–22. http://mises.org/journals/rae/pdf/rae10_1_1.pdf.

Johnson, Dr. Paul M. N.d. "Public Goods." *A Glossary of Political Economy Terms*. http://www.auburn.edu/~johnspm/gloss/public_goods.

Resources for Teachers

Council for Economic Education Technology Staff. 2012. "Goods and Services: Some Are Private, Some Are Not." econedlink. http://www.econedlink.org/lessons/economic-lesson-search.php?type=educator&cid=175.

Econport. N.d. "Public Goods Experiment Teaching Model." Accessed December 2, 2013. http://www.econport.org/content/teaching/modules/PublicGoods.html.

Foundation for Teaching Economics. N.d. "Property Rights and 'Green' Incentives." http://www.fte.org/teacher-resources/lesson-plans/eelessons/property-rights-and-green-incentives/.

R

Reagan, Ronald

Born: February 6, 1911, in Tampico, Illinois; Died: June 5, 2004, in California; 40th President of the United States (1981–1989); Major Works: *Where's the Rest of Me?* (1965); *The Creative Society* (1968); *Abortion and the Conscience of the Nation* (1984); *Speaking My Mind* (1989); *An American Life* (1990).

Ronald Wilson Reagan was born in Tampico, Illinois, on February 6, 1911, to John Edward Reagan and Nellie Wilson Reagan. The family lived in a series of small towns, finally settling down in Dixon, Illinois, in 1920 when his father opened a shoe store. Reagan attended Dixon High School, where he was an avid athlete, student body president, and actor in a number of school plays. In 1928, he graduated from Dixon High School and enrolled in Eureka College in Illinois on an athletic scholarship. He played football, ran track, and was captain of the swim team. He also served as student council president and acted in several school productions. Reagan graduated from Eureka College in 1932 with majors in economics and sociology. His first job was as a radio sports announcer at radio station WOC in Davenport, Iowa. In 1937, Reagan signed a seven-year contract with Warner Brothers Studios. Over the next three decades, he appeared in over 50 films, including *Knute Rockne, All American* (1940) and *Kings Row* (1942). During World War II, after being disqualified from army combat because of his poor eyesight, Reagan spent his time in the military making training films, leaving the army as a captain.

From 1947 to 1952, Reagan served as president of the Screen Actors Guild. In 1954, he became host of the weekly television drama series *The General Electric Theater*. Part of his job as host was to tour the United States as a public relations representative for General Electric. During this time, his political views shifted from liberal to conservative. He began to lead probusiness discussions and spoke out against excessive government regulation, which would become the central themes of his future political career.

Reagan stepped into the political spotlight in 1964, when he gave a televised speech for Republican presidential candidate Barry Goldwater. In 1966, Ronald Reagan was elected governor of California, defeating Democratic incumbent Edmund Brown Sr. by almost 1 million votes. He was reelected for a second term in 1970. In 1968 and 1976, Reagan made unsuccessful bids for the Republican nomination for president. In 1980, he finally succeeded. He defeated Democratic incumbent President Jimmy Carter, becoming at 69 the oldest person to be elected president.

On March 30, 1981, Reagan was leaving the Washington Hilton Hotel with several of his advisers when they heard shots. Quick-thinking Secret Service agents pushed Reagan into his limousine, discovering that Reagan had been shot. The bullet pierced Reagan's lung and narrowly missed his heart. Within several weeks of the shooting, President Reagan was back at work.

Reagan's domestic agenda included advanced policies that reduced social programs and restrictions on businesses. As presidential nominee, Reagan was a proponent of a fairly new economic theory, supply-side economics. Tax cuts were the key tool of supply-side economics, as popularized by economist Arthur Laffer (1940–). Reagan used supply-side tax cuts to stimulate the U.S. economy. He increased military spending, instigated reductions in certain social programs, and implemented measures to deregulate business. Even though the nation's economy was starting to recover from a severe recession by 1983, Reagan's critics complained that he had increased the deficit and hurt the middle class. In 1981, Reagan also made history by appointing Sandra Day O'Connor as the first woman justice on the U.S. Supreme Court.

President Reagan was reelected in November 1984, soundly defeating Democratic challenger Walter Mondale. Reagan carried 49 of the 50 states and received 525 of 538 electoral votes, the largest number ever won by an American presidential candidate. Reagan's second term was tarnished by the Iran-Contra affair. The Iran-Contra affair was a complex "arms-for-hostages" deal with Iran. Reagan authorized the sale of arms to Iran in exchange for U.S. hostages in Lebanon. The money gained from the sale was then illegally diverted to anticommunist insurgencies in Central America. The Reagan administration initially denied it, but later announced that it was a mistake.

Though Reagan faced many foreign affairs conflicts, his most pressing was the Cold War. Reagan started massively building up the nation's weapons and troops. He also implemented the "Reagan Doctrine," which provided aid to anticommunist movements in Africa, Asia, and Latin America. In 1983, Reagan planned the Strategic Defense Initiative, in an aim to develop space-based weapons to protect the United States from attacks by Soviet nuclear missiles. In the Middle East, Reagan sent 800 U.S. Marines to Lebanon as part of an international peacekeeping force in June 1982. One year later, in October 1983, suicide bombers attacked barracks in Beirut, killing 241 Americans. That same month, Reagan ordered U.S. forces to invade the Caribbean island of Grenada after Marxist rebels overthrew its government. In addition to problems in Lebanon and Grenada, Reagan's administration had to deal with the ongoing combative relationship between the United States and Libyan leader Muammar al-Gaddafi. In 1987, the United States and Russia signed a historic agreement to eliminate intermediate-range nuclear missiles. Also in 1987, Reagan spoke at Germany's Berlin Wall (which was a symbol of communism) and famously challenged Gorbachev to tear it down. The people of Germany ended up tearing the wall down in 1989, ending Soviet domination of East Germany and leading to the creation of a reunified Germany.

After leaving the White House in January 1989, Reagan returned to his home in Los Angeles, California. In 1991, the Ronald Reagan Presidential Library and Museum opened in Simi Valley, California. In 1994, Reagan revealed that he had Alzheimers.

Ronald Reagan died on June 5, 2004, in Los Angeles, California. He was later buried on the grounds of his presidential library in California.

Shima Sadaghiyani

See Also Laffer, Arthur; Laffer Curve; Market Capitalism; Supply-Side Economics

Further Reading

Morris, Edmund. 1999. *Dutch: A Memoir of Ronald Reagan.* New York: Random House.

Noonan, Peggy. 2001. *When Character Was King: A Story of Ronald Reagan.* New York: Random House.

Reagan, Ronald. 1990. *An American Life: The Autobiography.* New York: Simon & Schuster.

Resources for Teachers

Biography.com. N.d. "Ronald Reagan: Biography." Accessed May 21, 2013. http://www.biography.com/people/ronald-reagan-9453198.

The Ronald Reagan Presidential Foundation & Library. N.d. "Lesson Plans and Resources." Accessed May 21, 2013. http://www.reaganfoundation.org/lesson-plans-overview.aspx.

Ronald Wilson Reagan, 1911–2004. N.d. Accessed May 21, 2013. http://www.ronaldreagan.com/.

TeachingAmericanHistory.org. N.d. "Documents." Accessed May 21, 2013. http://teachingamericanhistory.org/library/reagan/.

Regulated Monopolies

A monopoly market structure is best defined as a market situation in which a single supplier makes up the entire industry for a good or a service with no close substitutes. The problem that arises with monopoly markets is that the monopolistic firm, left to its own accord, will most likely choose to price its product or service much higher than the socially optimal price, and produce at an output level that is much lower than the socially optimal output. By restricting output and charging a higher price, the monopolist is attempting to ensure maximum profits for the firm. However, this act by the monopolist firm comes at the cost to society of less overall consumer surplus or welfare.

The idea of a monopoly in an industry goes against competition, one of the foundations of the market economic system that is widely practiced throughout the world. In 1890, the United States Congress passed the Sherman Antitrust Act. This act has had the same basic objective for over a century: to regulate business operations through the court system in accordance with these laws, thus ensuring that competitive markets prevail.

Unfortunately, in some industries, due to the wide range of output and economies of scale, it makes sense for only one firm to participate in that market. Such markets are called natural monopolies, which are monopolies that arise because a single firm can supply a good or a service to an entire market at a smaller cost than could two or more firms. Some examples of markets that have become known as natural monopolies include utilities such as gas, electric, and water providers.

Despite the fact that these natural monopoly industries do make more sense in terms of efficient production, they still exhibit the characteristics of a monopoly market structure in that they have an incentive to price their products high and keep output at lower than socially optimal levels. To ensure that the socially optimal levels are met, these natural monopolies often require some form of government regulation. In regulating these markets, the government regulators face the dilemma of how much the governing body should regulate the firm. This can be best answered in analyzing a graph of a natural monopoly.

A monopoly cost curves graph displays the demand, costs, and revenue for a market that could be classified as a natural monopoly. For example, the market for electricity will be analyzed through the use of the graph. Just as all firms in all market structures do, the electricity firm will operate at the profit-maximizing point, which is where marginal costs (MC) intersect marginal revenue (MR). At this profit-maximizing point, we can see that the electric firm would desire to have an output value at Qm, or the quantity associated with the profit-maximizing point. The electric firm will charge Pm, or the price associated with the profit-maximizing point. The issue that arises with the electric company's profit-maximizing price and quantity is that those price and quantity values are not socially optimal.

It would be ideal for society if the firm operated at the allocatively efficient point on the graph, which is where price equals marginal costs, or P = MC. When a firm is allocatively efficient, it means that the right amount of the good or service is being provided to the right amount of people. In the graph referenced above, the allocatively efficient point is where P = MC yields a production quantity of Qso, or quantity socially optimal. It is now clear in the graph that the socially optimal quantity is much more than the quantity that the firm would like to produce at the profit-maximizing point.

This discrepancy is why a governing body must step in and regulate the monopoly. In regulating this market, the government has two options. The government can set a price ceiling at the allocatively efficient spot. This would result in Pso, price socially optimal, and Qso, quantity socially optimal, which would solve the problem of underallocation; however, with a price ceiling at that point, the firm is charging a price that is below its average total costs, or ATC, and so the firm that once was making significant abnormal profit is now operating at a loss, which might cause the firm to shut down all-together.

What most governments have done in the past to resolve this issue is to set the price ceiling at a fair return price, or a price that equals the firm's ATC. This fair return price will allow for the firm to break even. With the regulation at the fair return price, the amount of output is at Qfr, or quantity fair return, which is not at the socially optimal quantity but close to it, and much greater than the profit-maximizing quantity of Qm. Also, this fair return price, Pfr, is not as low as the socially optimal price, but again is much lower than the profit-maximizing price, Pm, that the firm would like to charge.

In answering the question of how much a governing body should regulate a natural monopoly firm, the rational response seems to be to regulate to the extent to which the quantity of output produced is as close to the socially optimal quantity as possible, while still establishing a price that allows the firm to receive a fair return or break even.

Emily N. Manoogian

See Also Clayton Antitrust Act of 1914; Kahn, Alfred; Market Failure; Sherman Antitrust Act of 1890; Tennessee Valley Authority (TVA)

Further Readings

Kahn, Alfred. 1988. *The Economics of Regulation, Principles and Institutions*. Boston: Massachusetts Institute of Technology.

Posner, Richard. 1975. "The Social Costs of Monopoly Power and Regulation." *Journal of Political Economy* 83, no. 4 (August): 807–28.

Sherman, Roger. 1990. *The Regulation of Monopoly*. Cambridge: Cambridge University Press.

Resources for Teachers

EconWorks. N.d. "Regulating Monopoly." http://econworks.org/course/regulating-monopoly/.

EDvantage. N.d. "Monopoly." http://www.theedvantage.org/economics/monopoly.

Pass, Andrew. 2008. "The Choice Is Us: Monopolies." econedlink. http://www.econedlink.org/lessons/index.php?lid=686&type=afterschool.

Reich, Robert

Born: June 24, 1946, in Scranton, Pennsylvania; American; political economy; Major Works: *The Next American Frontier* (1983), *The Work of Nations: Preparing Ourselves for 21st-Century Capitalism* (1991), *Supercapitalism: The Transformation of Business, Democracy, and Everyday Life* (2007).

Robert Reich is a political economist, author, professor, and political commentator. He is currently Chancellor's Professor of Public Policy at the Richard and Rhoda Goldman School of Public Policy at the University of California, Berkeley. He has served in the administrations of Presidents Ford and Carter and was the secretary of labor under President Clinton from 1993 to 1997. Reich also worked on then President-elect Obama's transition advisory board. He has written extensively on industrial policy and contributes regularly to National Public Radio, several forms of social media, and television programs.

Robert Bernard Reich was born in Scranton, Pennsylvania, on June 24, 1946. He began his life with Fairbanks disease, or multiple epiphyseal dysplasia, a rare congenital disorder that can stunt growth. As an adult, he is 4 feet and 10½ inches tall. Reich earned his AB summa cum laude from Dartmouth College in 1968 and his MA from Oxford University in 1970, where he was a Rhodes Scholar. He continued on to earn his JD from Yale University in 1972, where he was an editor of the *Yale Law Journal*. He married Clare Dalton in 1973. After graduating, Reich clerked for a federal judge, and then went to work for his former law school professor Robert H. Bork, who was then U.S. solicitor general in the Ford administration. He was the policy-planning director for the Federal Trade Commission from 1976 to 1981. Reich next became a professor of business and public policy at the John F. Kennedy School of Government at Harvard University from 1981 to 1993. He served as President Clinton's secretary of labor from 1993 to 1996, when he left to spend more time with his teenage sons.

Reich made many lasting changes in his role as the secretary of labor with the Clinton administration. He implemented the Family and Medical Leave Act; headed the administration's successful effort to increase the minimum wage; secured worker pensions;

started job-training programs, one-stop career centers, and school-to-work initiatives; and led a national fight against U.S. sweatshops and illegal child labor around the world. In 2008, *Time* magazine named him one of the 10 most successful cabinet secretaries of the century.

Reich explores industrial policy, the practice of using government intervention as a solution to a troubled American economy, throughout many of his published works. While teaching at Harvard, Reich authored many works, including *The Next American Frontier* and *The Work of Nations: Preparing Ourselves for 21st-Century Capitalism*. In *American Frontier*, Reich promotes industrial policy, or more governmental power, over more conservative Keynesian thought. He also discusses the failure of "paper entrepreneurialism" to promote the American economy. He writes that business managers are maneuvering company assets and production figures to achieve profit instead of advancing production. He also advocates moving from simple product manufacturing to a skilled and flexible labor force. He argues that government promotion of human capital, tax incentives, and loans for companies that train the unemployed, and the elimination of tax incentives for industries planning mergers, would promote a positive influence on the American economy in light of foreign competition.

Reich promotes the global market and individual education in *The Work of Nations*. He advises the United States to open its doors to global trade and invest in education, or human capital, for unskilled American workers. In his book *Locked in the Cabinet*, Reich candidly writes of his years serving as the labor secretary in the Clinton White House. Reich clearly illustrates his frustrations in trying to represent the common worker within the Washington bureaucracy and his ultimate decision to return to teaching. In *Supercapitalism: The Transformation of Business, Democracy, and Everyday Life*, Reich advises corporations to make quality products and services with an underlying theme of corporate social responsibility.

Reich has had a significant partnership with the Democratic Party. He served as a summer intern for Senator Robert Kennedy in 1968, coordinated Eugene McCarthy's 1968 presidential campaign, and worked as an adviser to Democratic presidential candidates Walter Mondale (1984) and Michael Dukakis (1988). He was a member of the governing board of Common Cause in Washington, D.C. (1981 to 1985), a member of the board of directors for Business Enterprise Trust (1989 to 1993), and trustee for Dartmouth College from 1989 to 1993.

He also founded the periodical *American Prospect* and served as the host of the PBS television programs *Made in America* and *At the Grass Roots*. He continues to cohost the television series *The Long and the Short of It* and regularly contributes to National Public Radio, the *New York Times*, *The New Yorker*, the *Los Angeles Times*, the *Boston Globe*, the *Washington Post*, the *Observer*, and *Business Week*.

Reich was the contributing editor of *The New Republic* from 1982 to 1992 and chair of the editorial board of *American Prospect* in 1990. His book *The Next American Frontier* won the Louis Brownlow Book Award from the National Academy of Public Administration in 1983. In 2002, he unsuccessfully ran for governor of Massachusetts. In 2003, the former Czech president awarded Reich the Vaclav Havel Foundation VIZE 97 Prize for his work in economics and politics. He continues to work as a political commentator on television programs such as *Hardball with Chris Matthews*, *This Week with George Stephanopoulos*, CNBC's *The Kudlow Report*, and APM's *Marketplace*.

Kathryn Lloyd Gustafson

See Also Keynes, John Maynard; Labor Force

Selected Works by Robert Reich

Reich, Robert. 2007. *Supercapitalism: The Transformation of Business, Democracy, and Everyday Life*. New York: Knopf.

Reich, Robert. 1997. *Locked in the Cabinet*. New York: Knopf.

Reich, Robert. 1991. *The Work of Nations: Preparing Ourselves for 21st-Century Capitalism*. New York: Knopf.

Reich, Robert. 1983. *The Next American Frontier*. New York: Times Books.

Selected Works about Robert Reich

CNBC. N.d. "Robert Reich Profile." http://www.cnbc.com/id/24730820/.

Kelly, Michael. 2004. *Things Worth Fighting For: Collected Writings*. New York: Penguin Press.

Leibovich, Mark. 2002. "The True Measure of a Man." *Washington Post*, March 14, C-1.

Politico's The Arena. N.d. "Arena Profile: Robert B. Reich." http://www.politico.com/arena/bio/robert_b_reich.html.

Reich, Robert. 2011. "Robert Reich." Accessed September 15. http://www.robertreich.org.

Rivlin, Alice

Born: March 4, 1931, in Philadelphia, Pennsylvania; American; fiscal policy, monetary policy; Major Works: *Systematic Thinking for Social Actions* (1971), *Reviving the American Dream: The Economy, the States and the Federal Government* (1993).

Alice Rivlin is an economist who has devoted her career to public service for the American people. She served as the first director of the Congressional Budget Office (February 1975 to August 1983) during the Carter and Reagan administrations. She was also the 30th director of the Office of Management and Budget (October 1994 to April 1996) during the Clinton administration. She then became the vice chair of the Federal Reserve from June 1996 through July 1999. President Barack Obama appointed Rivlin to his National Commission on Fiscal Responsibility and Reform in 2010. She has also worked for the Brookings Institution throughout her career. She is currently a visiting professor at the Georgetown Public Policy Institute in addition to her work on the National Commission of Fiscal Responsibility and Reform.

Alice Mitchell Rivlin was born on March 4, 1931, in Philadelphia, Pennsylvania. She began her studies at Bryn Mawr College with a focus on history. After she took a first-year summer course in economics with Reuben Zubrow at Indiana University, she decided that economics would be more useful. She graduated in 1952, writing her senior thesis on the economic integration of Western Europe, including the European monetary union. She then moved to Paris, where she held a junior position working on the Marshall Plan. She was later rejected from the public administration program at Harvard because she was of marriageable age and consequently was considered a poor student risk. She then applied to the economics program at Radcliffe College (part of Harvard University), where she earned her PhD in economics in 1958. She is married to economist Sidney G. Winter, who is a professor at the University of Pennsylvania. She is a frequent contributor to newspapers, television, and radio, and has written numerous books.

Instead of an academic career, Rivlin ultimately focused on policy work instead, as she saw this as an avenue to improving people's lives. In her book *Systemic Thinking for Social Actions*, Rivlin examines how systemic analysis has positively contributed to social action programs like education, health, manpower training, and income maintenance, and where it falls short due to inadequate data or methods. Rivlin ultimately endorses widespread implementation of social experimentation and acceptability of the federal government with the requirement of comprehensive, reliable performance measures.

In *Reviving the American Dream*, Rivlin discusses how to foster faster growth rates in average incomes over the long run. She states that this is necessary to restore confidence in the United States as a place where people who work hard can expect to do better than their parents did. Specifically, Rivlin proposes a common tax for states to be collected on a uniform basis and rate across the country and shared by the states on a formula basis. She advocates that this policy would encourage interstate commerce and ultimately promote growth. She also writes that state tax policy should shift away from tax breaks and move toward improving services, as this would encourage an aggressive effort for states to improve their infrastructure and their education systems to attract business.

Rivlin was at the forefront of the representation of women within the profession of economics. Rivlin recounts that her years as a graduate student at Harvard in the 1950s were not always smooth. She taught mixed-gender economics classes but initially was assigned only women tutees. When wanting to allow a swap of students with a male colleague for a research project, a senior tutor objected to the switch on the grounds that a female tutor would make male students feel second class. In addition, Rivlin did not teach introductory economics in the spring of her second year due to the birth of her child. The man who picked up the class in the spring announced that since a woman could not adequately teach economics, all work and grades previously given would not count. Fortunately, the department chair intervened and Rivlin's students were able to keep their prior grades. She has maintained that she has never worried about being the only woman (or one of the few) in her government positions, as people eventually realized she was competent and not self-conscious about her gender.

Rivlin is also the director of Brookings Institution's Greater Washington Research Project. President Lyndon Johnson appointed Rivlin to serve as assistant secretary for planning and evaluation at the U.S. Department of Health, Education, and Welfare (1968–1969). She was the founding director of the Congressional Budget Office (CBO) during 1975–1983, where she was known to criticize Reaganomics. In 1983, she won a MacArthur Foundation "genius" award. She was a senior fellow for economic studies at the Brookings

Institution from 1983 to 1993. Under President Clinton, she served as deputy director of the Office of Management and Budget and then as the first female director from 1994 to 1996.

From 1996 to 1999, she served as a governor of the Federal Reserve (Fed) and the Fed's vice chair. She was also chair of the District of Columbia Financial Responsibility and Management Assistance Authority from 1998 to 2000, where she helped rescue the District of Columbia from bankruptcy. She has taught at Harvard University, George Mason University, and the New School Universities. She has served as president of the American Economic Association and is currently a member of the board of directors of the New York Stock Exchange. She is the author or coauthor of 16 books, and numerous articles and papers.

Kathryn Lloyd Gustafson

See Also Bernanke, Ben; Burns, Arthur; Volcker, Paul

Selected Works by Alice Rivlin

Rivlin, Alice. 1993. *Reviving the American Dream: The Economy, the States and the Federal Government.* Washington, DC: Brookings Institution Press.

Rivlin, Alice. 1971. *Systematic Thinking for Social Actions.* Washington, DC: Brookings Institution Press.

Selected Works about Alice Rivlin

Edison, Hali J. 1998. "An Interview with Alice Rivlin." American Economic Association. http://www.aeaweb.org/committees/cswep/awards/rivlin.php.

Levy, David. 1997. "Interview with Alice Rivlin." *The Region: Minneapolis Fed Magazine,* June 1. http://www.minneapolisfed.org/publications_papers/pub_display.cfm?id=3638.

Woodward, Bob. 1994. *The Agenda: Inside the Clinton White House.* New York: Simon & Schuster.

Romer, Christina

Born: December 25, 1958, in Alton, Illinois; American; economic history, monetary policy, fiscal policy; Major Works: *Reducing Inflation: Motivation and Strategy* (coedited with David H. Romer) (1997), "Do Tax Cuts Starve the Beast?: The Effect of Tax Changes on Government Spending" (with David H. Romer) (2009), "The Macroeconomic Effects of Tax Changes" (with David H. Romer) (2010).

Christina Romer has been a Class of 1957 Garff B. Wilson Professor of Economics at the University of California, Berkeley, since 1997. She has also been a codirector of the Program in Monetary Economics at the National Bureau of Economic Research from 2010 to the present, as well as from 2003 to 2008, with programs in monetary economics, economic fluctuations and growth, and the development of the American economy. She served as the chair of the Council of Economic Advisers for Barack Obama from January 2009 to September 2010 during one of the worst economic crises in American history.

She is regarded as a premier Great Depression academic and has published numerous articles collaborating with her husband, economist David Romer, the Herman Royer Professor in Political Economy at the University of California, Berkeley.

Christina Duckworth Romer was born on December 25, 1958, in Alton, Illinois. She graduated with a bachelor's degree in economics from the College of William and Mary in 1981 and earned her PhD from the Massachusetts Institute of Technology (MIT) in 1985. She was an assistant professor of economics and public affairs at the Woodrow Wilson School at Princeton University until 1988, when she moved to the University of California, Berkeley. It was during her time at MIT that she met and married her husband and fellow notable economist, David H. Romer. In 2009, Christina Romer was chair of the Council of Economic Advisers in the Obama administration. She worked with economist Jared Bernstein to coauthor the administration's plan for recovery from the 2008 recession.

Romer's early work with pre–World War II Gross National Product figures cast doubt on Nobel laureate Simon Kuznets's prior calculations, which supported the idea that government economic policy shortened U.S. recessions while lengthening expansions. Romer noted that pre–World War II recessions were longer than postwar downturns, but that the severity of economic fluctuations on both sides of the Great Depression are roughly equal; thus, the perceived stabilization of the postwar economy due to government policy was not strongly supported by the data.

Romer's work also illustrated that fiscal or monetary policy error can add to economic downturns. Specifically, Romer has argued that fiscal policy stimulus packages (change in taxes and spending) have not helped the U.S. economy recover from previous recessions. She explains that during the New Deal, for example, taxes were raised as quickly as government spending increased, giving fiscal policy just a minor role in the recovery. Romer writes that it was accidental monetary policy (the devaluation of the dollar and introduction of European capital) that helped the United States into recovery from the Great Depression.

Romer also analyzed the forecasting ability of the Federal Open Market Committee (FOMC) and compared it to that of the Federal Reserve (Fed) staff. She ultimately determined that the FOMC added very little extra value to the forecasting data. She writes that while monetary policy making has improved since World War II, the FOMC could have made better decisions if it had fully used the forecasting expertise of the Fed staff economists. The FOMC, as a representative for the American people, should use its comparative advantage in making value judgments about which outcome or path is best given the situation.

Romer's work often shows that simply looking at correlation can mislead one to infer causation. In her work, she uses additional data and details from history to achieve a fuller picture of causation. In 2009, Romer researched the history of tax changes. She isolated the tax change decisions that would test her hypothesis that cutting taxes would ultimately shrink the size of government. Her conclusion indicates that tax cuts are usually associated with increases in government spending and that tax increases cause the economy to contract. In "Do Tax Cuts Starve the Beast?," Romer and her husband wrote that their research results "provide no support for the hypothesis that tax cuts restrain government spending; indeed, the point estimates suggest that tax cuts may increase spending. The results also indicate that the main effect of tax cuts on the government budget is to require subsequent legislated tax increases" (2009, 139).

Romer's numerous published articles and commitment to her profession are notable. She resigned from the White House Council of Economic Advisers in September 2010 to allow her son to spend his high school years in one place. She remains active within the economics community, working with an impressive number of organizations. She was vice president of the American Economic Association in 2006 and active on other committees for this group starting in 2001. She was an academic consultant (December 1991 and September 2006) and later visiting scholar for the board of governors of the Federal Reserve System from 1991 to 1993, and in 2004. She served on the program and nominating committees for the Economic History Association and on the editorial boards of the *American Economic Journal: Macroeconomics* (2007–2008), *Review of Economics and Statistics* (1994–2002), and the *Journal of Economic History* (1994–1997). She has received numerous grants from the National Science Foundation and the Social Science Research Council. She also held training seminars on the Great Depression for the International Monetary Fund in 2002, 2003, and 2005. In addition, her fellowships include the John Simon Guggenheim Memorial Foundation Fellowship (1998–1999), the Alfred P. Sloan Research Fellowship (1989–1991), the National Bureau of Economic Research Olin Fellowship (1987–1988), the Alfred P. Sloan Doctoral Dissertation Fellowship (1984–1985), and the American Academy of Arts and Sciences Hellman Fellowship (2004). She also earned an honorary doctor of public service from the College of William and Mary in 2010 and a Distinguished Teaching Award from the University of California, Berkeley, in 1994.

Kathryn Lloyd Gustafson

See Also Kuznets, Simon

Selected Works by Christina Romer

Romer, Christina D. 2009. "Lessons from the Great Depression for 2009." Paper presented at the Brookings Institution, Washington, DC, March 9. http://www.brookings.edu/~/media/Files/events/2009/0309_lessons/20090309_romer.pdf.

Romer, Christina D., and David H. Romer. 2010. "The Macroeconomic Effects of Tax Changes: Estimates Based on a New Measure of Fiscal Shocks." *American Economic Review* (June): 763–801.

Romer, Christina D., and David H. Romer. 2009. "Do Tax Cuts Starve the Beast?: The Effect of Tax Changes on Government Spending." *Brookings Papers on Economic Activity* 1: 139–200.

Romer, Christina D., and David H. Romer, eds. 1997. *Reducing Inflation: Motivation and Strategy*. Chicago: University of Chicago Press for NBER.

Selected Works about Christina Romer

"Christina Romer." University of California, Berkeley. http://elsa.berkeley.edu/~cromer/index.shtml.

Clement, Douglass. 2008. "Interview with Christina and David Romer." *The Region: Minneapolis Fed Magazine*, June 25. http://www.minneapolisfed.org/pubs/region/08-09/romers.pdf.

Rampell, Catherine. 2008. "The New Team—Christina D. Romer." *New York Times*, November 25. http://www.nytimes.com/2008/11/25/us/politics/25web-romer.html.

Roosevelt, Franklin Delano

Born: January 30, 1882, in Hyde Park, New York; Died: April 2, 1945, in Warm Springs, Georgia; 32nd President of the United States, 1932–1944; Only U.S. president to be elected for four consecutive terms.

Franklin Delano Roosevelt was born January 30, 1882, in Hyde Park, New York. Roosevelt was an only child, raised in an environment of privilege. Private tutors educated him until the age of 14, when, in 1896, he attended Groton School for Boys in Massachusetts. After graduating from Groton in 1900, Roosevelt graduated from Harvard in three years. During his last year at Harvard, Roosevelt met and became engaged to Eleanor Roosevelt (1884–1962) (his fifth cousin and the niece of his idol, Theodore Roosevelt). Eleanor and Franklin Roosevelt were married on March 17, 1905. Roosevelt then went on to study law at Columbia. He passed the bar exam in 1907, though he did not get his degree. For the next three years, Roosevelt practiced corporate law in New York.

In 1910, at the age of 28, Roosevelt was invited to run for the New York State Senate. He ran, and was elected as a Democrat in a heavily Republican district. As a state senator, Roosevelt opposed elements of the Democratic political machine in New York. While he angered Democratic Party leaders, he gained national attention. It was during this time that Roosevelt formed an alliance with political consultant Louis Howe (1871–1936). Louis Howe would end up shaping Roosevelt's political career for the next 20 years. Roosevelt was reelected in 1912 and served as chair of the Agricultural Committee. During the 1912 National Democratic Convention, Roosevelt supported presidential candidate Woodrow Wilson. After Wilson won, Roosevelt was rewarded with an appointment as assistant secretary of the Navy. Roosevelt specialized in business operations and founded the U.S. Naval Rescue.

In 1914, Roosevelt lost a race for a U.S. Senate seat in New York. He was soundly defeated, but learned that national stature could not defeat a well-organized political organization. In 1920, Roosevelt accepted a nomination for vice president on the ticket with James M. Cox. They were defeated, but Roosevelt once again gained experience and national exposure.

Roosevelt was diagnosed with polio in 1921 while he vacationed in Campobello Island, New Brunswick. Despite efforts, he never regained the use of his legs. He later established the March of Dimes foundation at Warm Springs, Georgia. The March of Dimes would be the program eventually responsible for finding an effective polio vaccine. Roosevelt thought having polio spelled the end of his political career, but Eleanor Roosevelt and Louis Howe encouraged him to keep moving forward. He spent the next few years improving his physical and political appearance. He taught himself to walk short distances in braces and was never, in his entire political career, seen or photographed in public with his wheelchair. Al Smith urged Roosevelt to run for governor of New York in 1928, so he began to repair his relationship with the Democratic political machine. He was narrowly elected. While Roosevelt was governor, he established many new progressive programs.

By 1930, the Great Depression had begun, and when Republicans began to get blamed, Roosevelt saw his chance to win the presidency. Roosevelt had adopted the new economic policies of British economist John Maynard Keynes (1883–1946), who promoted the direct involvement of government to stimulate a failing economy. Roosevelt began to campaign on the platform that the government should help reform and recover the economy. Roosevelt defeated Hoover in November 1932. When Roosevelt took office in 1933, the Great Depression was at its height. Thirteen million Americans were unemployed, and hundreds of banks were closed due to the turbulent economic times.

During the first 100 days of his presidency, Roosevelt made sweeping changes in an attempt to better the nation's economic state. First, Roosevelt temporarily closed all the banks. He formed a "Brains Trust" of economic advisers. These advisers designed the alphabet agencies: the Agricultural Adjustments Act (to support farm prices), the Civilian Conservation Corps (to employ young men), and the National Recovery Administration, to name a few. Other agencies insured bank deposits, regulated the stock market, and provided relief for the unemployed. By 1936, the economy showed some signs of improvement, most notably that unemployment had dropped from 25 percent to 14 percent.

As the first U.S. president to embrace the ideas of Keynesian economics, Roosevelt faced criticism for increased government intervention in the economy he promoted. Many of his critics thought he was moving the nation toward socialism. The Supreme Court declared several of Roosevelt's New Deal programs unconstitutional. Roosevelt responded by proposing to pack the courts with justices more favorable to his reforms. This idea was rejected by Congress. By 1938, the negative press, the continued sluggishness of the economy, and unexpected Republican victories in midterm elections halted Roosevelt's ability to pass more reforms.

Since World War I, America had adopted an isolationist policy in foreign affairs. In Europe and Asia conflicts raged, and Roosevelt sought ways to assist China in its war with Japan. Roosevelt also declared that France and Great Britain were America's "first line of defense" against Nazi Germany.

With World War II looming, Roosevelt won an unprecedented third presidential term in 1940. In March 1941, Roosevelt signed the Lend-Lease Bill to aid nations at war with Germany and Italy. On December 7, Japan bombed Pearl Harbor, and Roosevelt delivered his "day of infamy" speech. He asked for a formal declaration of war against Germany the same day. In 1942, Roosevelt created a "grand alliance" of Allied powers through "the Declaration of the United Nations." In 1944, Roosevelt was reelected as president for his fourth and final term.

In February 1945, Roosevelt attended the Yalta Conference with British Prime Minister Winston Churchill and Soviet General Secretary Joseph Stalin to discuss postwar recovery. Coming into Yalta, the Allied leaders knew that victory in Europe was certain, but were less sure of an end to the war in the Pacific. As a result, the United States and Great Britain saw it as a major strategic approach to have the Soviet Union enter the Pacific war under specific conditions discussed and agreed upon by Stalin: in exchange for Soviet participation in Pacific war, the Soviets would have a sphere of influence in Manchuria after Japan's surrender. The future of Eastern Europe was also discussed at the Yalta conference. Specifically, France was to be included in postwar governing of Germany, Germany would handle its own reparations, and the Soviets would pledge free elections in all territories liberated from Germany. The initial reactions to Yalta were celebratory. However, after Roosevelt's death in April 1945, Truman's new administration clashed with the Soviets over influence in Eastern Europe. Americans, alarmed by the perceived lack of cooperation from the Soviets, began to criticize Roosevelt's diplomacy at the Yalta negotiations.

Franklin Delano Roosevelt died on April 2, 1945, in Warm Springs, Georgia, and was buried in Hyde Park, New York; however, his legacy lives to this day. His responses to the challenges he faced (the Great Depression and the rise of Germany and Japan among them) made him a defining figure in American history. Under FDR, the federal government assumed new and more powerful roles in the United States' economy. For example, the New Deal plan instigated to deal with the Great Depression crippling the nation enhanced the capacity of the presidency to meet new responsibilities. Also, after World War II, FDR hoped for a more secure world, so the United States would become a major part of a postwar United Nations. Roosevelt reshaped the presidency by building a bond between himself and citizens and establishing one of the roles of the president as being a caretaker of the people.

Shima Sadaghiyani

See Also Great Depression (1929–1939); Keynes, John Maynard; Keynesian Economics; New Deal

Further Reading

Black, Conrad. 2003. *Franklin Delano Roosevelt: Champion of Freedom*. New York: Public Affairs.

Brinkley, Alan. 2009. *Franklin Delano Roosevelt*. New York: Oxford University Press.

Hiltzik, Michael. 2011. *The New Deal: A Modern History*. New York: Free Press.

Smith, Jean Edward. 2007. *FDR*. New York: Random House.

Resources for Teachers

EDsitement. N.d. "Lesson 1: FDR's Fireside Chats: The Power of Words." http://edsitement.neh.gov/lesson-plan/fdrs-fireside-chats-power-words.

Franklin D. Roosevelt Presidential Library and Museum. N.d. "Curriculum Guides." http://www.fdrlibrary.marist.edu/education/resources/curriculumguides.html.

National Archives. N.d. "Teachers: Teaching with Documents; FDR's Fireside Chat on the Purposes and Foundations of the Recovery Program." http://www.archives.gov/education/lessons/fdr-fireside/.

S

Samuelson, Paul

Born: May 15, 1915, in Gary, Indiana; Died: December 13, 2009, in Belmont, Massachusetts; American; macroeconomics, author, Nobel Prize (1970); Major Work: *Economics: An Introductory Analysis* (first published 1948).

Paul Samuelson is probably one of the most referenced and decorated of contemporary economists. Economic historians have referred to him as the "father of modern economics," and the *New York Times* once referred to him as the foremost academic economist of the twentieth century. He authored the best-selling college economics textbook of all time, *Economics: An Introductory Analysis*. In 1970, Paul Samuelson was the first U.S. economist to receive the Nobel Prize in Economics. He died in 2009.

Paul Anthony Samuelson was born on May 15, 1915, in Gary, Indiana. He received his bachelor of arts degree in 1935 from the University of Chicago. He went on to Harvard University, where he was awarded his PhD in 1941. His early economic influences at Harvard were noted economists Wassily Leontief, Joseph Schumpeter, and Alvin Hansen. At the age of 21, while a doctoral student at Harvard, Samuelson wrote his first published article, "A Note on the Measurement of Utility."

In 1940, Samuelson accepted a position as assistant professor at the Massachusetts Institute of Technology (MIT), where he would remain till his retirement. Paul Samuelson was more than the author, and later coauthor, of the most widely used economics college textbook in history. During his tenure at MIT, Samuelson worked in the fields of international trade, welfare economics, consumer theory, applying nonlinear dynamics to economic analysis, and public-private choice allocation. In each of these areas, Samuelson has been credited for adding to the body of economic knowledge. In terms of economic philosophy, Professor Samuelson referred to himself as a "right wing . . . New Deal economist," i.e., a Keynesian.

In 1938, he introduced a way to measure consumer choices and satisfaction-witnessing consumer behavior. This became known as the revealed preference theory. In 1941, with economist Wolfgang Stolper, he developed the Stolper-Samuelson theorem in trade theory. This theorem proposed that under certain conditions, when a resource is scarce, trade will lower real wages, and thus protectionism will raise real wages. Stolper and Samuelson would submit that trade between developed and developing countries lowers the wages of the unskilled labor in the developed country that is competing with the lower unskilled wages in the developing country. The Stolper-Samuelson theorem was influential in the later international trade models.

Another area of economics in which Samuelson was recognized was public finance where he is credited for his efforts in resource allocation between public and private goods and services.

One thing that set Samuelson apart from other economists of his time was his use and application of mathematical analysis. In 1947, Samuelson published *Foundations of Economic Analysis*. Samuelson illustrated the importance of mathematics to the science of economics. In 1948, he published the first edition of what was to become the bestselling, most widely used economics textbook in history, *Economics: An Introductory Analysis*. Since the first edition in 1948, "Samuelson" has been translated into over 40 languages. Many consider it the most influential economics textbook since World War II. The Keynesian approach Samuelson presents had a great influence on the embrace of John Maynard Keynes's theories in the United States.

From 1941 to 1945, during World War II, Paul Samuelson served on the National Resources Planning Board, the War Production Board, and the Office of War Mobilization and Reconstruction. Following the war, he served in various government positions till 1960. From 1960 to 1961, he was a member of the National Task Force on Economic Education. Samuelson served as an adviser to Presidents John F. Kennedy and Lyndon B. Johnson, and was a consultant to the U.S. Treasury, the Bureau of the Budget, the Council of Economic Advisers, and the Federal Reserve Bank. Samuelson wrote a weekly column for *Newsweek* magazine along with Chicago school economist Milton Friedman, where they represented opposing sides: Samuelson took the Keynesian perspective, and Friedman represented the monetarist perspective.

Paul Samuelson was the first economist to introduce the idea of "cost-push" inflation. Cost-push inflation is the inflation caused by general rise in resource prices, which includes wages. As the cost of resources increases, price increases follow. In 1960, Samuelson was particularly sensitive to, and expressed concern about, the fact that even during periods when full employment had not yet been reached, the future effects of the high employment were visible in the economy.

Along with his Nobel Prize in 1970, Paul Samuelson was the honoree of the David A. Wells Prize in 1940 from Harvard University and the John Bates Clark Medal given by the American Economic Association in 1947. Paul Samuelson was a member of the editorial board of the Econometric Society and was its president in 1951. He was elected president of the International Economic Association in 1965.

Paul Samuelson described himself as a "generalist" whose true interests were in teaching and research. Samuelson is not the only economist in the family. His nephew is Harvard professor and former presidential economic adviser Larry Summers.

Paul Samuelson died on December 13, 2009, at the age of 94.

Dave Leapard

See Also Keynes, John Maynard; Keynesian Economics; Summers, Lawrence

Selected Works by Paul Samuelson

Samuelson, Paul. 1948. *Economics: An Introductory Analysis*. New York: McGraw-Hill.

Samuelson, Paul, and William A. Barnett, eds. 2007. *Inside the Economist's Mind: Conversations with Eminent Economists*. Malden, MA: Blackwell.

Samuelson, Paul, Robert L. Bishop, and John R. Coleman, eds. 1955. *Readings in Economics*. New York: McGraw-Hill.

Samuelson, Paul, Robert Dorfman, and Robert Solow.1958. *Linear Programming and Economic Analysis*. Santa Monica, CA: RAND Corporation.

Selected Works about Paul Samuelson

Brown, Edgar Cary, and Robert Solow.1983. *Paul Samuelson and Modern Economic Theory*. New York: McGraw-Hill.

Nobelprize.org. 1970. "Paul A. Samuelson: Biography." http://www.nobelprize.org/nobel_prizes/economics/laureates/1970/samuelson-bio.html.

Szenberg, Michael, Aron A. Gottesman, and Lall Ramrattan. 2005. *Paul A. Samuelson: On Being an Economist*. New York: Jorge Pinto Books.

Weinstein, Michael M. 2009. "Paul Samuelson, Economist, Dies at 94." *New York Times*, December 14. http://www.nytimes.com/2009/12/14/business/economy/14samuelson.html.

Wong, Stanley. 1978. *The Foundations of Paul Samuelson's Revealed Preference Theory: A Study by the Method of Rational Reconstruction*. Oxford: Routledge & Kegan Paul.

Schwartz, Anna

Born: November 11, 1915, in New York City; Died: June 21, 2012, in New York City; American; economic and financial history, banking policy, monetary policy, international economic policy, financial policy; Major Works: *The Growth and Fluctuation of the British Economy, 1790–1850: An Historical, Statistical, and Theoretical Study of Britain's Economic Development* (with A. D. Gayer and W. W. Rostow) (1953, 2nd ed., 1975), *A Monetary History of the United States, 1867–1960* (with Milton Friedman) (1963).

Anna Schwartz worked as an economist at the National Bureau of Economic Research since 1941. She has been praised for her contributions to economic history and her use of this insight to interpret current day events. She is best known for her collaboration with Nobel laureate Milton Friedman in their book *A Monetary History of the United States, 1867–1960*, which outlines the importance of the quantity of money—not interest rates—in influencing monetary policy and the economy as a whole. In addition, they critique the actions of the Federal Reserve during the banking panics of the 1930s. Collaboration skills, empirical rigor, and longevity of research defined a woman who significantly contributed to economics scholarship. Schwartz died in 2012.

Anna Jacobson Schwartz was born on November 11, 1915, in New York City. At age 18, she graduated from Barnard College, where she was elected to Phi Beta Kappa. One year later, she earned her master's degree in economics from Columbia University. Schwartz then married and started her family (including four children) all while continuing to work as a professional economist. She ultimately earned her PhD from Columbia in 1964.

In 1936, Schwartz worked briefly for the U.S. Department of Agriculture and then at the Columbia University Social Science Research Council. In 1941, she began her work in statistical research at NBER, which she has continued till her retirement. Eleven years later she began teaching at Brooklyn College and then Baruch College for a short time along with her work at the National Bureau. In 1967, she became an adjunct professor of economics for City University of New York, Graduate Division at Hunter College, for several years. In 1969, she was adjunct at New York University, Graduate School of Arts and Sciences. She served on the editorial boards of the *American Economic Review* (1972–1978), the *Journal of Money, Credit, and Banking* (1974–1975, 1984–2012), the *Journal of Monetary Economics* (1975–2012), and the *Journal of Financial Services Research* (1993–2012). Schwartz served as the president of the Western Economic Association from 1987 to 1988. She also was an honorary visiting professor of the City University Business School in London from 1984 to 2002.

Schwartz began her academic collaboration with Milton Friedman in 1948 at the suggestion of Arthur Burns. She had recently completed work on another collaboration project with Arthur D. Gayer and Walt Rostow, *The Growth and Fluctuation of the British Economy, 1790–1850*. Many have remarked that neither Friedman nor Schwartz could have completed *Monetary History* without the other. Notably, this collaboration was carried out between New York City, where Schwartz worked and lived, and Chicago, where Friedman worked and lived. The two did meet in New York or talk on the phone occasionally, but most correspondence, editing, and other writing activity for this work was carried out using the postal mail service.

Schwartz and Friedman stated that their inspiration for *Monetary History* arose from the NBER program to study the cyclical behavior of different economic processes like transportation, inventory management, and consumption. This work illuminated the importance of fluctuations in the growth rate of the money stock and the business cycle and criticized the ineptness of the Federal Reserve during the Great Depression. Many note that this work's greatest effect has been to focus monetary policy on the goal of price stability.

Schwartz was a founding member of the Shadow Open Market Committee, created in 1973 to act as a watchdog over Federal Reserve policy. She published numerous articles and publications over the course of her career—many in collaboration with Michael Bordo.

Schwartz continued her work at the National Bureau of Economic Research and as adjunct professor of economics at the Graduate School of the City University of New York until her death. She earned numerous honorary doctorates from prestigious schools such as Williams College, Loyola University, Emory University, Rutgers University, and London City University, to name a few. She was the distinguished fellow of the American Economic Association in 1993, the honorary fellow of the Institute of Economic Affairs in 1997, and a fellow of the Academy of Arts and Sciences in 2007.

Anna Schwartz died on June 21, 2012, in Manhattan, New York City.

Kathryn Lloyd Gustafson

See Also Burns, Arthur; Federal Reserve System; Friedman, Milton

Selected Works by Anna Schwartz

Gayer, A. D., W. W. Rostow, and Anna Schwartz. 1975. *The Growth and Fluctuation of the British Economy, 1790–1850*. 2 vols. 2nd ed. Sussex, UK: Harvester Press.

Schwartz, Anna, and Milton Friedman. 1963. *A Monetary History of the United States, 1867–1960*. Princeton, NJ: Princeton University Press for NBER.

Selected Works about Anna Schwartz

Feldstein, Martin. 2000. "Anna Schwartz at the National Bureau of Economic Research." *Journal of Financial Services Research* 18, no. 2/3: 115–17. http://www.nber.org/feldstein/schwartz.html.

Ferguson, Tim. 2012. "Anna Schwartz, Monetary Historian, RIP." *Forbes*, June 21. http://www.forbes.com/sites/timferguson/2012/06/21/anna-schwartz-monetary-historian-rip.

Fettig, David. 1993. "Interview with Anna J. Schwartz." Federal Reserve Bank of Minneapolis. September 1. http://www.minneapolisfed.org/publications_papers/pub_display.cfm?id=3724.

Matthews, Steve, and Vivien Lou Chen. 2012. "Anna Schwartz, Economist Milton Friedman's Co-Author, Dies at 96." *Bloomberg.com*, June 22. http://www.bloomberg.com/news/2012-06-21/anna-schwartz-economist-milton-friedman-s-co-author-dies-at-96.html.

Securities and Exchange Commission (SEC)

As the twentieth century began, the world was changing rapidly. Transportation, communication, and investing were only a few of the areas in which significant global changes were occurring. The inventions of the day were bringing the possibilities of many people from all walks of life investing in these new inventions through the stock markets and striking it rich. Regulating this investing frenzy was not encouraged or promoted by the federal government or anyone else. The stock market crash of 1929 and the significant loss of money by both the investors and investees changed the environment of one from emphasizing the positives of investing in the stock market to focusing on only the negatives. Confidence in the markets was lost. Confidence in the economy was lost. The Great Depression was beginning.

In the mid-1930s, most acknowledged that for any economic progress to occur confidence in the banking industry and capital markets had to be restored. In 1933, Congress passed the Securities Act, and followed it up with the Securities Exchange Act in 1934. Both acts were designed to clean up the market exchange between the buyer and seller. They enforced the dissemination of more information to investors and created rules by which investor transactions would occur. By cleaning up the rules of the investing game and opening the channels of information for investors, the government was anticipating a restoration of confidence and activity in the capital markets to boost the depressed economy. Added to the rules and information changes, the Securities Exchange Act of 1934 also created the Securities and Exchange Commission to oversee and enforce the implementation of the new rules.

The objectives of the new laws were twofold. One, they required companies that now wanted to offer securities on the stock market to openly provide the public information on their businesses, what securities they were selling, and quite possibly most important, what risks were involved in investing in their companies. The second requirement of the new laws was directed at the stock brokers and stock dealers, and those who sold the securities to the investing public. The new laws stipulated that they were to be more concerned with the interests and honest dealings with the public investors than with the companies doing the selling. Both objectives were quite broad in nature, but it was the charge of the new Securities and Exchange Commission to do the enforcing.

As both banking and stock market investing grew, they became different in one very important aspect. With the creation of the Federal Deposit Insurance Corporation (FDIC), bank deposits became an insured savings tool for the general public. This insurance feature did not extend to the stock market and stock investing, which made the role of the SEC as the capital markets enforcer that much more important for the consumer. The Securities and Exchange Commission was the capital markets' police force. The SEC was charged with protecting consumers from tactics such as accounting fraud, providing inaccurate and misleading information about either the company or its securities offerings, and insider trading.

While the SEC was established to enforce the new laws, its primary responsibility was to protect the investors in capital markets goods and services. Investors are its main source of information about potential unlawful activity by companies and the capital markets industry, including the stock market. To assist investors, the SEC provides educational information on many topics, issues, and activities within the capital markets industry. The material is designed to educate, inform, and alert the consumers about capital markets goods and services of possible illegal activity in which they may have been unknowing participants.

President Franklin D. Roosevelt appointed Joseph Kennedy, father of future President John F. Kennedy, as the first chair of the Securities and Exchange Commission. The commission is made up of five commissioners, all appointed by the president. One is elected chair. The commissioners serve five-year terms, staggered to maintain consistency. Nonpartisanship is maintained, as a maximum of three can be from the same political party. The SEC is a dynamic commission working closely with Congress, the Federal Reserve, and the Treasury Department to maintain regulations and policies that are up to date and applicable to the current financial, economic, and investing environment.

The SEC is comprised of five separate divisions and 23 offices. The five divisions are the Division of Corporation Finance, Division of Economic and Risk Analysis, Division of Investment Management, Division of Enforcement, and Division of Trading and Markets. The offices of the SEC include the Office of the General Counsel, Office of the Chief Accountant, Office of Compliance Inspections and Examinations, Office of Credit Ratings, Office of International Affairs, Office of Investor Education and Advocacy, Office of the Chief Operating Officer, Office of Human Resources, Office of Information Technology, Office of Legislative Affairs and Intergovernmental Relations, Office of Public Affairs, Office of the Secretary, Office of Equal Employment Opportunity, Office of the Inspector General, and Office of Administrative Law Judges. All, including the SEC, are headquartered in Washington, D.C.

The role of the Securities and Exchange Commission has become much more important, and has expanded in the years since its inception in 1934. Stock market investing took on a glamour that attracted many people from varied walks of life. The average citizen saw the stock market as the saving and investing mechanism for the first home, college fund, and retirement. The global economy attracted foreign investors, and the SEC broadened its outlook to incorporate global financial and capital markets. The role, responsibilities, and regulation of the Securities and Exchange Commission have grown and become more complex.

David A. Dieterle

See Also Federal Deposit Insurance Corporation (FDIC); Federal Reserve System; Great Depression (1929–1939); Roosevelt, Franklin Delano; United States Treasury

Further Reading

RooseveltInstitute.org. 2010. "Next New Deal: The Blog of the Roosevelt Institute." August 6. "Securities and Exchange Act." http://www.nextnewdeal.net/securities-and-exchange-act.

Securities and Exchange Commission Historical Society. N.d. "The Mechanics of Legislation: Congress, the SEC, and Financial Regulation." http://www.sechistorical.org/.

U.S. Securities and Exchange Commission. N.d. http://www.sec.gov/.

Resources for Teachers

Federal Resources for Educational Excellence. N.d. "Agency Resources: Securities and Exchange Commission: 2 Resources." http://free1.ed.gov/subjects.cfm?agency_id=108.

Investor.gov. N.d. "In the Classroom." http://www.investor.gov/classroom#.Uqprg_RDuSo.

Securities and Exchange Commission Historical Society. N.d. "Timeline." http://www.sechistorical.org/museum/timeline/.

Seminole Tribe of Florida v. Florida, 517 U.S. 44 (1996)

A Supreme Court Case That Determined the Extent of an Indian Nation's Economic Autonomy

Economic Concepts

Economic sustainability; gaming; property tax; market economy; profits

Economic Impact

This case's economic impact on the Native American economy lay in the transition from a traditional economic system to a market-based system. The Supreme Court addressed a confrontation between tribal sovereignty, states' rights, and federal supremacy powers. It determined the economic future and direction of Native Americans throughout the United States.

Economic Summary

The Seminole tribes struggled through economic challenges as their way of living changed from their traditional economy to a market-based economy. The Indian gaming industry was an evolution of ideas starting with bingo and graduating to class III high-stakes gambling (high stakes games such as casinos, racetracks, etc.). The revenue from these businesses and other associated enterprises allowed the Seminole Indian tribes to support health facilities, schools, roads and other such infrastructure, and distribute dividends from the profits throughout the entire remaining tribe members. With this case, the Supreme Court determined the extent of an Indian nation's economic autonomy.

Case Summary

The Seminole are a blend of various Southeastern Indians who relocated to what is now the state of Florida. After the Civil War, the U.S. Congress passed several acts that relocated the Indians to reservations. The Seminole tribe of Florida's reservations included Hollywood, Big Cypress, and Brighton, all located in southern Florida near Lake Okeechobee and the Everglades.

Much of the background of this case centers on the tribe's economic evolution and the federal Indian policy of the early twentieth century. In the 1930s, Congress recognized hundreds of Indian tribes on lands held in trust by the federal government. As wards of the state, the federal government provided economic support and granted tribal sovereignty. After World War II, Congress reversed its Indian policy. In 1953, Public Law 280 was passed, which gave the states control over criminal and limited civil issues within Indian territory. In addition, in an effort to encourage the Native Americans to assimilate into American society, Congress terminated the legal status of over 100 tribes throughout the United States, which eliminated a great deal of their revenue. Most reservations during this time were geographically isolated from the economic resources necessary to grow prosperous communities.

The 1976 Supreme Court decision in *Bryan v. Itasca County* paved the way for alternative economic initiatives within Indian reservations. Members of the Minnesota Chippewa tribe, the Bryans, sued Itasca County, Minnesota, claiming that states did not have the right to assess a tax on Native American property located on Indian reservations. The state of Minnesota claimed that Public Law 280 gave the states an inherent power to tax Indian property on reservations. The Supreme Court ruled in favor of the Bryans. The Court held that Congress, through the Indian Commerce Clause, had that power and the states could only share in that if Congress specifically granted that authority to them.

In the 1970s, the Seminole tribe built a bingo hall. The state of Florida allowed bingo two days a week for charitable organizations, with maximum jackpots of $100. In 1979, the tribe opened the bingo hall six days a week, with increased jackpots. The state of Florida shut it down because it violated Florida laws. An important political precedent was whether or not the Seminole tribe had the right to sue the state or whether the Eleventh Amendment to the U.S. Constitution (giving the states sovereign immunity whereby they cannot be sued in federal court without their consent) provided Florida with immunity.

In *Seminole Tribe of Florida v. Butterworth* (1981), a federal court ruled in favor of the Seminole tribe, affirming Indian sovereignty, federal supremacy, and the states' obligation to negotiate in good faith with the Indian tribes regarding gaming. In 1987, in *California v. Cabazon Band of Mission Indians*, the Supreme Court again confirmed that

Indian gaming was to be regulated exclusively by Congress and not state governments. In 1988, President Reagan signed the Indian Gaming Regulatory Act (IGRA), which established a federal commission to oversee the regulation of Indian gambling. Central to the IGRA was the duty of state officials to negotiate with the Indian tribes and enter compacts that balanced states' rights, Indian sovereignty, and federal power. By 1991, 121 Indian tribes in 23 states had entered into 137 compacts pursuant to the IRGA.

In 1991, the Seminole Indians sued the state of Florida and its governor, alleging that they had failed to negotiate in good faith toward a tribe-state compact. The state of Florida moved to dismiss the suit on the grounds that the Eleventh Amendment to the Constitution prohibited states from being sued without their consent. The district court denied this motion and Florida appealed to the Eleventh Circuit Court. They reversed the district court's decision regarding the state of Florida's Eleventh Amendment rights and remanded the case (sent it back to the lower court) with instructions to dismiss the petitioner's suit.

The Seminole tribe was granted certiorari (a request by the Supreme Court to the lower court for the files of the case to be sent up for review) by the Supreme Court in 1995. The question was whether or not the Seminole tribe could sue the state of Florida. Florida repeated its Eleventh Amendment argument. The plaintiff supported its argument by pointing to *Ex parte Young*, a 1908 Supreme Court case that affirmed that officials representing a state could be sued when the litigation involved possible abridgment of constitutional rights. In oral arguments, the attorney for the Seminoles made it clear that the state needed to adhere to the duty required in the IRGA or there was no need for the state to be a part of this regulatory function. For the tribe, a single regulator, the federal government, was preferable to dealing with two regulators, state and federal. Florida's response questioned the obligation to negotiate if the only remedy was to agree with the federal government. Florida argued that negotiation choice is actually no choice, using the example that tribal gambling was illegal in Florida, but even so was happening on Indian reservations. Therefore they would rather yield to the federal government than have Florida write regulations that could be overruled by the federal government nonetheless.

Chief Justice Rehnquist delivered the opinion of the Court, in which he stated that Congress does not have the authority under the commerce clause to subject states to suit in federal court, nor does *Ex parte Young* allow a suit against state officials, except in a particular circumstance that was not at issue in this case. In a 5–4 vote, the Supreme Court affirmed the Eleventh Circuit Court's dismissal of the petitioner's suit. Furthermore, Chief Justice Rehnquist wrote that even if Congress intended to abrogate the states' sovereign immunity, the Indian commerce clause does not grant Congress that power. Therefore, the courts cannot grant jurisdiction over a state that does not consent to be sued. In the dissenting opinion, both Souter and Stevens penned different perspectives yet agreed that Congress could not abrogate state sovereign immunity. However, they did not agree that a state official and a state were the same thing. The federal government can sue a state in order to require the state to follow federal mandates, this being a political safeguard of federalism.

Kathleen C Simmons

See Also Economic Systems; Indian Gaming Regulatory Act of 1988; Taxes

Related Cases

Ex Parte Young, 209 U.S. 123 (1908)

Bryan v. Itasca County, 426 U.S. 373 (1976)

Seminole Tribe of Florida v. Butterworth, 658 U.S. 310 (1981)

California v. Cabazon Band of Mission Indians, 480 U.S. 202 (1987)

Further Reading

Cornell University Law School, Legal Information Institute. N.d. "*Seminole Tribe of Florida v. Florida.*" http://www.law.cornell.edu/supct/html/historics/USSC_DN_1995_0041_ZS.html. (Summary of the case)

Cornell University Law School, Legal Information Institute. N.d. "*Seminole Tribe of Florida v. Florida.*" http://www.law.cornell.edu/supct/html/historics/USSC_DN_1995_0041_ZO.html. (Transcript of Chief Justice Rehnquist's majority opinion)

Cornell University Law School, Legal Information Institute. N.d. "*Seminole Tribe of Florida v. Florida.*" http://www.law.cornell.edu/supct/html/historics/USSC_DN_1995_0041_ZD.html. (Transcript of Justice Stevens's dissenting opinion)

Cornell University Law School, Legal Information Institute. N.d. "*Seminole Tribe of Florida v. Florida.*" http://www.law.cornell.edu/supct/html/historics/USSC_DN_1995_0041_ZD1.html. (Transcript of Justice Souter's dissenting opinion)

OYEZ, U.S. Supreme Court Media, ITT Chicago, Kent College of Law. N.d. "*Seminole Tribe of Florida v. Florida.*" http://www.oyez.org/cases/1990-1999/1995/1995_94_12/. (Facts of the case)

Teaching Materials

Certiorari to the United States Court of Appeals for the Eleventh Circuit No. 94-12. http://caselaw.lp.findlaw.com/scripts/getcase.pl?court=US&vol=000&invol=U10198.

FindLaw for Legal Professions. N.d. *Seminole Tribe of Florida v. Florida, ___ U.S. ___ 1996.*

Indian Treaties Vol. V: Florida Indians Based on Charles J. Kappler. 1991. Edited by Larry S. Watson. Yuma, AZ: Histree Co.

Justia.com, U.S. Law. N.d. "658 F.2d 310: *Seminole Tribe of Florida, an Organized Tribe of Indians, as Recognized under and by the Laws of the United States, Plaintiff-Appellee, v. Robert Butterworth, the Duly Elected Sheriff of Broward County, Florida, Defendant-Appellant.*" http://law.justia.com/cases/federal/appellate-courts/F2/658/310/50773/.

Seminole Tribe of Florida v. Florida, ___ U.S. ___ (1996)

Seminole Tribe of Florida, Petitioner v. Florida et al.

Schultz, David Andrew. 2004. *Encyclopedia of Public Administration and Public Policy*. New York: Facts on File.

Servicemen's Readjustment Act of 1944 (GI Bill)

As World War II came to a close, there was a need to help returning servicemen acclimate back to civilian life. President Franklin Roosevelt and Congress were keenly aware of the civil unrest following World War I, when no benefits were made available to returning military. The Servicemen's Readjustment Act, or the GI Bill, as it became known, offered a wide range of benefits for the returning GIs. "GI" was an acronym used in the military to identify "general issue" military items. It later became a label for those serving in the military as well as returning veterans. The Servicemen's Readjustment Act became popularly known as the GI Bill, or GI Bill of Rights, acknowledging those who would be receiving the benefits.

As part of President Franklin Roosevelt's overall plan to use the federal government to achieve economic ends, he originally proposed a comprehensive plan to provide a wide range of benefits only to military personnel who met a means-tested criteria to be considered poor. Under the congressional leadership of Senator Earnest McFarland, Democrat from Arizona, and Representative Edith Nourse Rodgers, Republican from Massachusetts, who offered their own version of a GI bill, Roosevelt's means-tested plan was ignored. The final bill presented in both Houses of Congress was directed to all returning military who had been on active duty for longer than 90 days. As long as the veteran had served longer than 90 days and received an honorable discharge, he would qualify for the bill's benefits. The Servicemen's Readjustment Act was signed into law by President Franklin Roosevelt on June 2, 1944.

The new GI Bill included benefits ranging from loans to start a business, tuition reimbursements for those who wanted to return to school and either finish high school or attend a postsecondary school, living expenses including one year of unemployment compensation, and below-market interest mortgage loans to buy homes without a down payment. Because the U.S. economy had such massive pent-up demand for consumer goods and services following World War II, finding a job was not very difficult for the majority of veterans who wanted to enter the labor force immediately after the war. This made the no-down-payment, low-interest mortgages a very attractive benefit for many veterans, as postwar families moved from the cities to suburbia. The other major benefit claimed by veterans was the tuition benefit. If a veteran did not return to the labor force, he most likely used the GI Bill and the tuition benefit to enter college or vocational postsecondary education.

Most economists consider the GI Bill a major economic success for the United States. The tuition benefit alone quickly elevated the level of human capital in the United States to levels never before realized or considered by most economists. When the original GI Bill ended in 1956, the number of new college graduates provided a generation with new skills and knowledge to challenge the problems of a post–World War II world. This vast new human capital made the United States the world leader in moving the world forward. Between the pent-up demand for goods and services and the rapid growth of human capital as a result of the GI Bill, the United States' post–World War II economy experienced an era of significant economic growth and rise in the standard of living for most U.S. citizens.

While the GI Bill proved to be the catalyst for economic growth and a higher standard of living in the United States, what may be considered its most significant contribution to the nation's lifestyle was the foundation it established for the future treatment of returning military veterans. Since 1944 and the first GI Bill, veteran benefit programs have been established to assist all honorably discharged veterans, whether they served during wartime or as peacekeepers.

The use of subsequent GI Bills, especially for education, continued through the Korean War and Vietnam War. Offspring of the original 1944 Servicemen's Readjustment Act included the Veterans' Readjustment Act of 1952 following the Korean War. The Veterans' Readjustment Benefits Act of 1966 was signed into law by President Lyndon Johnson. It was the first veterans' benefit bill to include veterans who served during peacetime.

Like the 1944 bill, these bills also had their critics. Many veterans did not think the bills provided enough benefits. An increase adjustment was made in 1972 with the signing of the Readjustment Assistance Act, which designated increases each year up to 1977.

However, in 1973, the rules of the game changed, and so did the incentives of the GI Bill. In 1973, the United States switched from a conscription military to an all-volunteer military. The Veterans Educational Assistance Program (VEAP) and the Montgomery GI Bill (MGIB) were signed into law not to be veterans' benefits as much as to be incentives for joining the military. The VEAP is a voluntary program for military personnel to set aside part of their current pay for future use toward their education. A second educational benefit program is the MGIB. The MGIB is open to all current service personnel and veterans. The MGIB-SR is available to members of the National Guard as well as the U.S. Navy, Coast Guard, Marine Corps, Air Force, and Army Reserves.

Regardless of the adjustments and revisions of any future GI bills, the Servicemen's Readjustment Act of 1944 clearly had an impact on the U.S. economy that was as significant as any legislation before it or since.

David A. Dieterle

See Also Great Depression (1929–1939); New Deal; Roosevelt, Franklin Delano

Further Reading

Humes, Edward. 2006. *Over Here: How the G.I. Bill Transformed the American Dream*. Orlando, FL: Harcourt.

Military.com. N.d. "Home." Accessed December 2, 2013. http://www.military.com/education/gi-bill/learn-to-use-your-gi-bill.html.

Suberman, Stella. 2012. *The GI Bill Boys: A Memoir*. Knoxville: University of Tennessee Press.

Resources for Teachers

Missouri Department of Elementary and Secondary Education. N.d. "Lesson Plan Template: When Dreams Came True: A Case Study of the GI Bill." dese.mo.gov/divcareered/documents/vet-edGIBillLesson.pdf.

Tennessee4me. N.d. "G.I. Bill of Rights." Accessed December 2, 2013. www.tn4me.org/tpsapage.cfm/sa_id/21/era_id/8.

United States Department of Veteran Affairs. N.d. "Home." Accessed December 2, 2013. www.gibill.va.gov/.

Sherman Antitrust Act of 1890

Named for Senator John Sherman, Ohio Republican, the Sherman Antitrust Act forbids certain business practices that would diminish the competitiveness of a market. The act gave the federal government the right to investigate and bring federal suits against businesses if the federal government deemed a business practice in violation of the act. The act focused primarily on monopoly behavior by businesses and the collusion of companies through cartels. It was the first federal act to interfere in a private market, sharply limiting or making illegal monopolies and cartels. Even though the act was signed July 2, 1890, by President Benjamin Harrison, it was not until 1901, under President Theodore Roosevelt, that the act was first enforced to limit the monopoly and cartel behavior of businesses.

There were three key sections to the Sherman Antitrust Act. The first was directed at defining noncompetitive behavior by businesses. This section deemed illegal any organizational structure or contract that led to restraint of trade among either the states or with another country. The second section defined which market results would constitute noncompetitive behavior. Violation of the act was a felony. The third section extended the reach of the act to include U.S. territories and the District of Columbia.

The spirit of the act was to protect consumers from the uncompetitive behavior of businesses that have either monopoly power in their market or companies that have banded together to exert cartel market behavior. Monopoly or cartel collusion creates market disadvantages for consumers. Monopoly and cartel power of a market allows the monopoly company, or companies that make up the cartel, to impose two disadvantages to consumers. First, they have the ability to withhold market information from the consumer. This allows them greater market power than would otherwise be the case under purely market conditions. This leads to the second disadvantage to consumers. Companies are allowed to charge a price higher than that likely under pure market conditions and control the quantity produced for the market. The Sherman Antitrust Act was legislated to diffuse and balance the market between the business and the consumer.

The act was an effort by the federal government to keep businesses from restricting market competition and trade so they could raise prices. To that end, however, the federal government clearly distinguished between purposeful monopolies and businesses that found themselves in a monopoly position purely as the result of business success. The focus of the act was on deterring and punishing those that deliberately created either monopoly power in a market or the collusion of several companies to create the market result of monopoly power.

One of the major issues at the time of the Sherman Antitrust Act was whether Congress had the authority to pass a law with such broad market limitations. Congress asserted its power to do so by way of the Constitution and its role in regulating interstate commerce. Several Supreme Court case decisions solidified the Sherman Antitrust Act as law. The act was meant to protect the competitive nature of a market, not interfere with it. Prominent Supreme Court cases confirming the Sherman Antitrust Act as law included *Addyston Pipe and Steel Company v. United States* (1899) and *Standard Oil Co. of New Jersey v. United States* (1911).

The term "trust" in the name of the act references a type of business structure that was popular at the time of the legislation. Although not a popular form of business today, at the end of the nineteenth century and early twentieth century, C. T. Dodd of Standard Oil

Company of Ohio invented the trust agreement, allowing Standard Oil to circumvent an Ohio law regarding companies owning stock (ownership) in other companies. This new business structure allowed Standard Oil to construct a vertically integrated company that eventually had such large market share that it enjoyed monopoly power. It was this intentional type of business activity that led to the 1890 Sherman Antitrust Act.

David A. Dieterle

See Also Market Capitalism; Regulated Monopolies; *Standard Oil Co. of New Jersey v. United States, 221 U.S. 1 (1911)*; Supreme Court

Further Reading

Cefrey, Holly. 2004. *The Sherman Antitrust Act: Getting Big Business under Control*. New York: The Rosen Publishing Group.

Letwin, William. 1965. *Law and Economic Policy in America: The Evolution of the Sherman Antitrust Act*. Chicago: University of Chicago Press.

Thornton, William Wheeler. 1913. *A Treatise on the Sherman Anti-Trust Act*. Cincinnati, OH: W. H. Anderson Co.

Resources for Teachers

Street Law. N.d. "Lesson 1: Why Do We Have Antitrust Laws?" Accessed December 15, 2013. http://www.fairfightfilm.org/lessons/lesson1.pdf.

Teaching American History. 1890. "The Sherman Anti-Trust Act." http://teachingamericanhistory.org/library/document/the-sherman-anti-trust-act/.

Worth, Richard. 2011. *Sherman Antitrust Act*. Singapore: Marshall Cavendish Corporation.

Shultz, George

Born: December 13, 1920, in New York City; American; economist, public administration, public policy; Major Works: *Guidelines, Informal Controls and the Market Place* (Studies in Business) (1966), *Turmoil and Triumph: My Years as Secretary of State* (1993), *Putting Our House in Order: A Guide to Social Security and Health Care Reform* (2008).

George Shultz served in several executive positions in the United States. He also worked as an economist, researcher, and political adviser, and he influenced American conservative policies for more than 50 years.

George Pratt Shultz was born on December 13, 1920, in New York City. He attended Princeton University, and directly after graduation, he joined the U.S. Marine Corps. He served during World War II and rose to the rank of captain. After the war, he enrolled at the Massachusetts Institute of Technology (MIT), earning a PhD in industrial economics.

After his graduation from MIT, Shultz rose quickly to power and influence. He became a professor of economics at MIT, and shortly thereafter served as an economic adviser to President Dwight Eisenhower. He returned briefly to MIT before moving to the University of Chicago in 1957, becoming dean of the university's Graduate School of Business in

1962. Chicago was the center for free-market ideas and for the new monetarist theories of Milton Friedman. Such ideas ran counter to the Keynesianism that was popular at the time and prepared Shultz for his later career as a Republican policy maker.

In 1969, Shultz was appointed to the administration of President Richard Nixon, first as secretary of labor, then as director of the Office of Management and Budget. Upon taking office, Shultz and the Nixon administration faced two major economic problems: the imminent failure of the gold standard and the threat of inflation.

After World War II, the Bretton Woods Conference had created a world monetary system in which the United States set a value for the dollar tied to the price of gold; other countries set the value of their money according to the dollar. As the demand for gold fluctuated, the United States was having trouble keeping up its end of the deal, and it became apparent to the administration that the Bretton Woods gold standard had to end. But there was a problem with this.

Going off the gold standard was likely to make the dollar less valuable, which would, in turn, make inflation worse. Inflation was high when Shultz took office, and though it had been declining (falling from 6% to 5% in 1970), administration officials feared that it would go back up when the gold standard ended.

A tempting option presented itself: wage and price controls. John Connally, the Secretary of the Treasury, recommended that Nixon simply mandate a 90-day freeze in wages and prices if Congress would allow it. George Shultz claimed to have opposed the idea—he noted later that "it's always much easier to get into something like that than to get out of it"—yet the freeze continued anyway.

Though the price freeze was initially popular, it ultimately failed to tame inflation, which would continue to be a problem until the early 1980s. Shultz later summarized that wage and price controls, even when instituted by the talents of Shultz, Richard Nixon, John Connally, Dick Cheney, and Don Rumsfeld, would not work. During Shultz's years in public life, he considered wage and price controls an ineffective public policy.

Shultz replaced Connally as Secretary of the Treasury in 1972, but he resigned from this office shortly before President Nixon himself resigned in the face of the Watergate scandal. Shultz spent the next eight years as a private citizen, working as president of Bechtel Corporation, the largest engineering company in the United States. As president, Shultz oversaw several major projects in the areas of hydroelectric power, steel factories, deep-water ports, and other heavy industries.

In 1982, Shultz was called back to Washington, D.C., by the administration of Ronald Reagan, this time to serve as secretary of state. In this capacity, he was in charge of foreign relations for the United States at a time when the Cold War was the central concern of American foreign policy. Shultz supported an increased nuclear presence in Europe in order to put pressure on the Soviet Union, even though an expansion of nuclear arms was extremely controversial. However, he also encouraged a dialogue with the Soviet leader, Mikhail Gorbachev.

While Shultz retired from government service in 1989, he did not retire completely. He remained active influencing policy in many capacities: as a scholar at the Hoover Institute, a board member of several companies, cochair of California's Economic Recovery

Council, and adviser to President George W. Bush, as well as serving on other policy-influencing organizations.

Stephen H. Day

See Also Contractionary Fiscal Policy; Expansionary Fiscal Policy; Fiscal Policy; Friedman, Milton; Reich, Robert; Romer, Christina

Selected Works by George Shultz

Shultz, George. 1993. *Turmoil and Triumph: My Years as Secretary of State*. New York: Scribner.

Shultz, George, ed. 1966. *Guidelines, Informal Controls and the Market Place*. Studies in Business. Chicago: University of Chicago Press.

Shultz, George P., and John B. Shoven. 2008. *Putting Our House in Order: A Guide to Social Security and Health Care Reform*. New York: Norton.

Selected Works about George Shultz

Manweller, Matthew, ed. 2012. *Chronology of the U.S. Presidency*. Santa Barbara, CA: ABC-CLIO.

Norris, Lloyd. 2011. "George Shultz on Politics and Budgets." *New York Times*, September 16. http://economix.blogs.nytimes.com/2011/09/16/george-shultz-on-politics-and-budgets/.

PBS.org. 2000. "Interview with George Shultz." *Commanding Heights*, October 2. http://www.pbs.org/wgbh/commandingheights/shared/minitextlo/int_georgeshultz.html.

Simons, Henry

Born: October 9, 1899, in Virden, Illinois; Died: June 19, 1946, in Chicago, Illinois; American; monetary theory, taxation; Major Works: *A Positive Program for Laissez Faire: Some Proposals for a Liberal Economic Policy* (1934), *Personal Income Taxation: The Definition of Income as a Problem of Fiscal Policy* (1938).

Henry Simons was an American economist who spent his teaching career at the University of Chicago. Simons is best known for defending free-enterprise solutions to revive the U.S. economy after the Great Depression. He proposed a modified laissez-faire role of government to protect and defend the free-market economy. Simons opposed monopoly power, and advocated clear monetary policy rules and price stability. He developed a definition of income for taxation purposes. He is remembered as an invaluable early contributor to the Chicago school theories of antitrust and monetary policy, and as an influential teacher responsible for teaching many famous Chicago economists, including Milton Friedman and George Stigler. Simons died in 1946.

Henry Calvert Simons was born on October 9, 1899, in Virden, Illinois. His parents greatly valued higher education and sent him to the University of Michigan. In 1920, he received his bachelor's degree from the University of Michigan and continued additional study at the University of Michigan and Columbia University. In 1921, he continued graduate work at the University of Iowa and taught there until 1927. He transferred to the University of Chicago to study with Frank H. Knight, who interested him in the Department of Economics. Simons completed his graduate work in economics at Chicago but never finished his dissertation to receive a PhD. He spent his entire career teaching and researching at the University of Chicago, first as a lecturer. In 1942, he was named an associate professor.

In 1934, Simons published his most famous work, *A Positive Program for Laissez Faire*, as University of Chicago Press Pamphlet No. 15. This work was published as the Great Depression was ending. Simons wanted to see a strong resurgence of private market activity and was unhappy with some of the policies being promoted, which relied on what he considered excessive and unnecessary government intervention. In this pamphlet, he outlined his major policy beliefs, and continued throughout his career to expand, revise, and defend them. His positions addressed many economic issues. Simons promoted reforming the monetary system, a position later made famous by Milton Friedman. He promoted eliminating all monopoly power in a market that included large oligopoly corporations, applying antitrust laws to labor unions, instituting a federal incorporation law to limit corporate size, and government ownership of low-cost technology firms. He also addressed tax system reform, including income tax equity. On international trade, Simons would abolish all tariffs. Simons was not an enthusiast of advertising and marketing, and would limit their use.

Simons believed in a laissez-faire economic philosophy, but also believed that government had an important, though limited, role to play. The government should protect the free-market forces as they operated to determine prices. For example, he wanted government to actively pursue antitrust activities against any type of monopoly—large corporations as well as labor unions. He was absolutely against any group obtaining an unfair amount of power, which would interfere with the efficient operation of a free-market economy. He did think that government could own and operate natural monopolies for reasons of low-cost production.

In addition to promoting conditions that encouraged competition, Simons believed in a role for government in establishing sound economic conditions using monetary policy necessary to protect the free markets. He believed that there should be clear monetary policy rules to determine the supply of money or price-level stability. However, any monetary policy must allow for flexible prices and wages. He understood how the phases of the business cycle could be influenced by monetary policy and also recognized the importance of complementary fiscal and monetary actions.

Simons agreed with Irving Fisher, who recommended that banks establish a 100 percent reserve requirement rule for funds held on deposit. He believed that too much short-term borrowing or excessive speculation would contribute to financial instability, and that there was danger in allowing the development of too much private credit. He felt the organization of the current central banking system needed to be thoroughly evaluated, but believed some sort of central monetary control was needed. The ideas in his 1936 article "Rules versus Authorities in Monetary Policy" influenced the later works of Milton Friedman on monetary policy, and Hyman Minsky's theory of financial crises.

The ideas explained in *Personal Income Taxation* in 1938 discussed the concepts of progressive taxation. Simons felt strongly that other forms could also address the social goal of reducing inequality. Along with Robert M. Haig, Simons developed the Haig-Simons definition of income used for tax purposes: the sum of consumption plus the change in the value of assets owned. Debate on the U.S. federal tax system still relies on ideas proposed and clarified by Simons.

His life was cut short by an accidental overdose of sleeping pills. Henry Simons died in Chicago, Illinois, on June 19, 1946.

Jean Kujawa

See Also Friedman, Milton; Taxes

Selected Works by Henry Simons

Simons, Henry. 1950. *Federal Tax Reform*. Chicago: University of Chicago Press.

Simons, Henry. 1948. *Economic Policy for a Free Society*. Chicago: University of Chicago Press.

Simons, Henry. 1938. *Personal Income Taxation*: *The Definition of Income as a Problem of Fiscal Policy*. Chicago: University of Chicago Press.

Simons, Henry. 1936. "Rules versus Authorities in Monetary Policy." *Journal of Political Economy* 44, no. 1: 1–30.

Simons, Henry. 1934. *A Positive Program for Laissez Faire: Some Proposals for a Liberal Economic Policy*. Public Policy Pamphlet, no. 15. Chicago: University of Chicago Press.

Selected Works about Henry Simons

Director, Aaron. 1946. "Simons on Taxation." *University of Chicago Law Review* 14: 15–20.

Friedman, Milton. 1967. "The Monetary Theory and Policy of Henry Simons." *Journal of Law and Economics* 10: 1–13.

"Guide to the Henry C. Simons Papers 1925–1962." Special Collections Research Center, University of Chicago Library. http://www.lib.uchicago.edu/e/scrc/findingaids/view.php?eadid=ICU.SPCL.SIMONS&q=citation.

Kasper, Sherryl D. 2002. *The Revival of* Laissez-Faire *in Twentieth Century Macroeconomics: A Case Study of Its Pioneers*. London: Edward Elgar.

Stigler, George. 1974. "Henry Calvert Simons." *Journal of Law and Economics* 17: 1–5.

Smith, Adam

Baptized: June 5, 1723 (exact birthdate unknown), in Kirkcaldy, Scotland; Died: July 17, 1790, in Edinburgh, Scotland; Scottish; moral philosophy, political economy (economic theory); Major Works: *The Theory of Moral Sentiments* (1759), *An Inquiry into the Nature and Causes of the Wealth of Nations* (1776).

Adam Smith is considered the father of modern economics. The theories contained in his seminal book *The Wealth of Nations* include division of labor, the importance of competition, the idea of the "invisible hand," and arguments for free trade. These concepts form much of the foundation of modern economic thought. Though Adam Smith is considered the founder of free-market economics, other ideas that he held, such as the labor theory of value, were used by later writers to form the foundation for socialism. For his part, Smith was a quintessential Enlightenment thinker. He believed in natural rights, natural law, and limited government. Theology had little place in his writings. He viewed the world, human society, and hence the economy as being governed by natural law that if left on its own would work smoothly, like a grand machine. Smith died in 1790.

Adam Smith was born in Kirkcaldy, Scotland, in 1723. His father, a lawyer and customs official, died shortly before his birth. He was raised by his mother, Margaret Douglas, with whom he had a close lifelong relationship. At the age of seven, he was enrolled at the reputable Burgh School of Kirkcaldy, where he studied classics and mathematics. He studied moral philosophy at Glasgow University and Oxford University. Upon graduating he sought an academic career, eventually becoming the professor of moral philosophy at Glasgow. He held this position for 13 years, during which time he assembled his lecture notes into a book entitled *The Theory of Moral Sentiments*, published in 1759. In *The Theory of Moral Sentiments*, Smith argues that human morality originates through a natural desire to identify with the emotions of others.

Smith quit his position at Glasgow when he was offered a lucrative job as tutor to a Scottish duke. Though this job lasted only about two years, it provided Smith with a pension on which he could live for the next decade without having to worry about other employment.

The Wealth of Nations begins with the observation that "division of labor," or specialization, is essential for increasing the production of wealth. Division of labor occurs because human beings have a tendency to "truck, barter, and exchange one thing for another," that is, to trade. This causes people to become dependent on one another. Smith's fundamental insight is his explanation as to how this complex interdependence is organized: trade and division of labor occur because of individual self-interest, not from kindness or the designs of politicians. When each individual acts as he or she sees best, within the constraints of the law and in a competitive business environment, the economy organizes itself naturally, as if guided by an "invisible hand."

Trade was a controversial issue in the British Empire in Smith's time, and *The Wealth of Nations* was a powerful weapon for those who favored free trade. The book explained that division of labor was limited by the extent of the resources available to a market and that a greater division of labor, and therefore greater wealth, could be obtained by expanding the market through global trade. It also sharply criticized the ideas of mercantilism, which held that a country should attempt to accumulate gold by encouraging exports and discouraging imports. By showing the importance of trade, Smith gained great popularity among merchants, whose work had previously been considered distasteful.

While Smith's work legitimized the work of traders and capitalists, it asserted that an item receives its value from the work of the laborers who made it, called the labor theory of value. It assumes that there is a natural price for a certain commodity that is made up of the amount of work that went into producing it. However, this natural price is difficult to know, since the circumstances of the world can cause the actual price for which the item is sold to change. Smith explains that the sale price will gravitate to the natural labor price, even if they are not always exactly the same. In this analysis of value, Smith recognizes the importance of supply and demand (which had been described by earlier economic thinkers) but defers to the labor theory of value.

The labor theory has been rejected by economists, who now see value as something subjective and price as being determined by supply and demand. It gained adherents, however, in David Ricardo and Karl Marx. Marx built his entire economic philosophy on the labor theory and drew other parts of socialist thought from elements of Smith's macroeconomic observations. Later economists used Smith's work in a different way, applying his concepts of supply and demand, competition, spontaneous order, market price, and voluntary trade to all areas of economic thought, eclipsing the indefensible-labor theory and turning economics into the versatile social science that it is today.

Adam Smith died on July 17, 1790, in Edinburgh, Scotland. His gravesite in Edinburgh has become a shrine and symbol of free markets, capitalism, and the strength and power of individual freedom.

Stephen H. Day

See Also Classical Economics; Market Capitalism; Private Property

Selected Works by Adam Smith

Smith, Adam. 1776. *An Inquiry into the Nature and Causes of the Wealth of Nations*. London: J. J. Tourneisen and J. L. Legrand.

Smith, Adam. 1759. *The Theory of Moral Sentiments*. London: A. Millar, A. Kincaid, and J. Bell.

Selected Works about Adam Smith

Buchan, James. 2006. *The Authentic Adam Smith: His Life and Ideas*. New York: Norton.

Colander, David, and A. W. Coats, eds. 1989. *The Spread of Economic Ideas*. Cambridge: Cambridge University Press.

McKenna, Stephen. 2006. *Adam Smith: The Rhetoric of Propriety*. Albany: State University of New York Press.

Muller, Jerry Z. 1993. *Adam Smith in His Time and Ours: Designing the Decent Society*. Princeton, NJ: Princeton University Press.

Otteson, James R., and John Meadowcroft. 2011. *Adam Smith*. New York: Continuum International.

Phillipson, Nicholas. 2010. *Adam Smith: An Enlightened Life*. New Haven, CT: Yale University Press.

Rae, John. 2010. *Life of Adam Smith*. Charleston, SC: Nabu Press.

Shapiro, Michael J. 2002. *Reading "Adam Smith": Desire, History and Value*. Lanham, MD: Rowman & Littlefield.

Smoot-Hawley Tariff Act (See Tariff Act of 1930)

Social Security Act of 1935

During the Great Depression, many saw the fabric of American life being threatened as the unemployment rate reached extraordinary levels. Children were being abandoned in the streets or left as orphans, wives and mothers and their children were being abandoned by husbands and fathers who could not support them or left the home to go look for work and never return. The elderly, handicapped, and blind were being left to the care of families, churches, or states.

The Social Security Act was signed into law on August 14, 1935, by President Franklin D. Roosevelt. The intent of the act was to establish a system to benefit older workers who had accidents while on the job or became unemployed, and to support handicapped and single mothers with children. The original act also provided benefits for the blind and the physically handicapped. President Roosevelt was the first president to publicly support federal efforts to help the elderly.

Prior to the Social Security Act, the social safety net for older citizens was considered the province of local or state governments, or a social organization such as the family or the church. The Great Depression's extremely high unemployment rate made the status quo inadequate. A national discussion followed on how to bring a broad-based social safety net to those most affected by the Great Depression—the elderly and the infirm. There was significant national discussion of the issue; a national social safety net, as it was being discussed, was not supported by everyone. Many thought such a federal plan was an attack on personal freedom and personal space. Businesses, knowing that the cost of any government-sponsored and government-administered pension plan would fall on them, sought protection in the form of exemptions from the plan. Despite the array and diverse public debate of the topic, on August 15, 1935, President Roosevelt signed into law the new federal government–directed retirement program, the Social Security System.

The new Social Security Act had many moving parts. First, it provided universal support to the elderly. It established a national account within the Treasury to administer payments to those who qualified, including the blind. The act provided aid to states for children abandoned during the Depression and orphans. It also provided states with funds to provide for the health and well-being of crippled children. Partnering with the states again, the federal government provided funds to set up public health facilities and the personnel training so that facilities and health care would be adequately and professionally administered. Quite possibly the most unique aspect of the new law was that the system would be financed by both employers and employees. Finally, the act specified who would be exempt from the law (family employed and businesses of less than eight employees), established a Social Security Board to oversee the new program, and set forth the legal terminology defining geographical inclusion (Alaska, Hawaii, and Washington, D.C.) and separation of the many parts of the new program. The only hurdle left for the new Social Security System to withstand were the court challenges sure to follow.

The Supreme Court ruled twice sustaining the Social Security Act's constitutionality. Two years after the act became law, the Supreme Court ruled in *Steward Machine Company v. Davis* to uphold the act. In a 5–4 ruling, the Court claimed national funding to relieve the strains of such a national crisis as the Depression indeed promoted the general welfare. The second Supreme Court ruling sustaining the Social Security Act was also in 1937, on the same day as the *Steward Machine Company v. Davis* case. *Helvering v. Davis* sustained the constitutionality of the federal government's right to impose a tax to fund the new program.

With the support of the Supreme Court, implementation of the act began in earnest. Yet implementation of the new program brought with it new complex administrative problems for the federal government. Key among them were registering citizens so they could receive the program's benefits, setting up the intricate system of taxing and receiving the contributions from both employers and employees, and, of course, the system of disbursing benefits to the recipients. In more recent times, the major challenge is the funding of Social Security in the long run.

David A. Dieterle

See Also Entitlements; Great Depression (1929–1939); *Helvering Davis, 301 U.S. 619 (1937)*; New Deal; Public Goods; Roosevelt, Franklin Delano; Supreme Court; Taxes

Further Reading

Segal, Elizabeth A. 2010. *Social Welfare Policy and Social Programs: A Values Perspective*. Belmont, CA: Brooks/Cole Cengage Learning.

Social Security. N.d. "The Social Security Act of 1935." http://www.ssa.gov/history/35act.html.

www.documents.gov. N.d. "Social Security Act (1935)." http://www.ourdocuments.gov/doc.php?doc=68.

Resources for Teachers

EDSITEment. N.d. "Lesson 2: The Social Security Act." http://edsitement.neh.gov/lesson-plan/social-security-act.

IRS: Understanding Taxes, Teachers. N.d. "Theme 2: Taxes in U.S. History Lesson 4: The Social Security Act of 1935." http://apps.irs.gov/app/understandingTaxes/teacher/whys_thm02_les04.jsp.

Understanding Fiscal Responsibility. N.d. "The History of Social Security." http://teachufr.org/admin/the-history-of-social-security-2/.

Sowell, Thomas

Born: June 30, 1930, in Gastonia, North Carolina; American; political economy, economics, author; Major Works: *Race and Economics* (1975), *Inside American Education* (1993), *Basic Economics* (2007), *The Housing Boom and Bust* (2009).

Thomas Sowell is an economist, author, professor, and syndicated columnist. He currently serves as the Rose and Milton Friedman Senior Fellow on Public Policy at the Hoover Institution of Stanford University. He has served as faculty at various institutions, including Cornell University and University of California, Los Angeles. He has written extensively about politics, education, ethnic relations, and child development, and is the author of 40 books and numerous articles. He has a syndicated column that appears in numerous newspapers around the United States.

Thomas Sowell was born on June 30, 1930, in Gastonia, North Carolina. At the age of nine, he moved to Harlem, New York, with his family. He dropped out of high school as a teenager and began working various jobs. Sowell was drafted into the U.S. Marine Corps during the Korean War and served as a photographer. After his service, he attended classes at Howard University in Washington, D.C., receiving high marks and earning him acceptance into Harvard University on recommendations from professors. At Harvard, much of Sowell's study was on the German philosopher Karl Marx, on whom he wrote his senior thesis. He received his bachelor's degree in economics in 1958. Sowell received his master's degree from Columbia University in 1959. In 1968, Sowell obtained his doctorate degree from the University of Chicago, studying under George Stigler and Milton Friedman.

Sowell's economic career began when he became a labor economist for the U.S. Department of Labor from 1960 to 1961. He taught at Howard University and Rutgers before accepting a position as an economic analyst at AT&T from 1964 to 1965.

From 1965 to 1970, Sowell was on the faculty at Cornell and Brandeis University. Sowell was affiliated with the Urban Institute from 1972 to 1974. He served on the faculty at the University of California, Los Angeles, and has served as a senior fellow at the Hoover Institution since 1980. When Ronald Reagan was elected president in 1980, he offered Sowell a cabinet position to bring an African American conservative voice to his administration, but Sowell declined. He served on the White House Economic Advisory Board for a one-meeting stint for Reagan, but quit because of the difficulty in traveling to Washington, D.C., from California.

Sowell's writings span a range of topics, including economics, political ideology, race relations, affirmative action, education, and child development. Known for his conservative and libertarian viewpoint, Sowell's writings have drawn criticism from liberal counterparts. Sowell's position on race and income is the theme of his 1975 publication, *Race and Economics*. In this book, he analyzed the relationship between blacks and wealth, drawing on factors from slavery and contrast to other ethnicities, as well as criticizing government policies directed toward blacks.

Also a strong critic of affirmative action, Sowell's 1990 book *Preferential Policies: An International Perspective* criticized the use of quotas in college admissions and employment. He asserted that such policies led to degraded standards and did not allow individuals to reach their full potential. His 2004 publication *Affirmative Action around the World: An Empirical Study* compares the policy in recent U.S. history to policies of other nations. His concluding arguments are that affirmative action policies have negligible effects on their intended groups and lower incentives for achievement. His work received critical acclaim with other economists agreeing and arguing that affirmative action had gone too far beyond its purpose.

Aside from his writing on economics and policy, Sowell has taken to writing on child development and education. In his book *The Einstein Syndrome: Bright Children Who Talk Late* investigates the phenomenon of late-talking children, a follow-up to his earlier book *Late-Talking Children*. The research in his book argues that these children are misdiagnosed as autistic or as having another disorder, but instead they are developing other areas of the brain and not using functions of the brain for language development. In Sowell's book *Inside American Education*, he is highly critical of the American educational system. He argues that the standards, practices, and programs used in the educational institutions lack credibility, and calls for reform.

Sowell detailed his life story in his book *A Personal Odyssey*, published in 2001. He writes about his childhood and stages of life, as well as his education, from growing up poor in the South, moving to Harlem, and eventually to Harvard. He also accounts for the vast differences of wealth that he has experienced in his life in this personal story.

In addition to Sowell's books, he is a regularly syndicated columnist, writing for the mass media. His column focuses on issues in the economy, affirmative action, government policy, and social issues, with a free-market viewpoint. It appears in over 150 newspapers in the United States and has been featured in *Newsweek*, *Forbes*, and the *Wall Street Journal*. His conservative opinions often draw criticism from liberals. Some of his essays were published in his work *Ever Wonder Why?: And Other Controversial Essays* in 2006.

Sowell was a recipient of the Francis Boyer Award, given by the American Enterprise Institute in 1990. He was awarded the National Humanities Medal in 2002 and the Bradley Prize in 2003.

Sowell serves as Rose and Milton Friedman Senior Fellow on Public Policy at the Hoover Institution of Stanford University.

Sara Standen

See Also Classical Economics; Friedman, Milton; Labor Force

Selected Works by Thomas Sowell

Sowell, Thomas. 2011. *Basic Economics: A Common Sense Guide to the Economy*. 4th ed. New York: Basic Books.

Sowell, Thomas. 2009. *The Housing Boom and Bust*. New York: Basic Books.

Sowell, Thomas. 2004. *Affirmative Action around the World: An Empirical Study*. New Haven, CT: Yale University Press.

Sowell, Thomas. 1993. *Inside American Education: The Decline, the Deception, the Dogmas*. New York: Free Press.

Sowell, Thomas. 1990. *Preferential Policies: An International Perspective*. New York: Morrow.

Sowell, Thomas. 1975. *Race and Economics*. New York: McKay.

Selected Works about Thomas Sowell

Quartey, Kojo A. 2003. *A Critical Analysis of the Contributions of Notable Black Economists*. Burlington, VT: Ashgate.

Sowell, Thomas. 2000. *A Personal Odyssey*. New York: Free Press.

"Thomas Sowell." N.d. Accessed July 16, 2012. http://tsowell.com.

Stalin, Joseph

Born: December 18, 1879, in Gori, Russia; Died: March 5, 1953, in Kuntsevo, Russia; Russian; Ruled the Soviet Union from 1929–1953.

Iosif Vissarionovich Dzhugashvili (he later changed his name to Stalin) was born December 18, 1879, in the village of Gori, Georgia (a country that was part of the Russian empire). A bout of childhood smallpox left his face scarred and his left arm slightly deformed. The village children treated him cruelly and made him feel inferior as they made fun of his deformed face and arm. Stalin grew to have a need for greatness and respect and had a cruel streak toward those who crossed him. In 1888, Stalin's mother enrolled him in church school in Gori so he could become a priest. In 1894, he graduated top of his class and went on to Tiflis Theological Seminary in the village of Tbilisi on a scholarship. A year later, he came into contact with a secret organization, the Georgian Social Democratic organization, which supported Georgian independence from Russia. It was this organization that introduced Stalin to the writings of Marx and Lenin, and Stalin officially joined it in 1898. Stalin then left the seminary in 1899 and stayed in Tbilisi to focus on the revolutionary movement. He was arrested not long after, in 1902, for joining the Social Democratic Labor Party, and was exiled to Siberia. He escaped after only a month in exile and returned to Gori. It was around this time that he adopted the name Stalin, meaning "steel" in Russian.

In the years after 1905, the radicals retreated underground, and Stalin finally met Lenin at a party conference after writing an anti-Menshevik creed that attracted Lenin's attention. Stalin also helped the revolutionaries in banditry, for the revolutionaries were forced to turn to crime as a way to get money. Stalin was in the city of Baku in Azerbaijan when he was arrested in March 1908. He was sent to Siberia for two more years but escaped within a year. He was re-arrested and sent to Siberia yet again, but this time he had to stay and serve his full sentence. Stalin was never politically inactive; he corresponded with Lenin throughout the duration of his stay.

In February 1917, the Russian Revolution began, and the tsar abdicated the throne. Stalin immersed himself in Marxism. Although he was never a strong speaker like Lenin, Stalin was extremely proficient at doing the mundane tasks of the revolution, like handing out pamphlets. In 1922, Stalin was appointed the general secretary of the Communist Party. This appointment gave him control over all other party member appointments. He abused this power, however, and he made shrewd appointments that only strengthened his power as secretary.

After Lenin's death in 1924, Stalin set out to take Lenin's place. His success was partly due to his political genius, and partly due to the way Stalin always found it easy to bend and twist things to his advantage. His rivals were gifted idealists and Marxist men to the core. Stalin, however, never truly understood the core principles of Marxism and was always willing to change them so they favored him. When Stalin took control of Russia, paranoia set in. His reign of terror began. Stalin had people arrested during the night and, with public trials, executed them in the morning; he wanted to teach a lesson to all "opposition." Also, potential rivals were killed off under the notion that they were aligning with capitalist nations.

In the late 1920s and the 1930s, Stalin began industrializing Russia rapidly. In the beginning, this was hugely successful, but soon turned destructive. The heavy machinery and industry caused the death toll to skyrocket and heavily impacted the environment and national budget; an idea that was originally fruitful turned sour in Stalin's hands. In 1939, Stalin signed the nonaggression pact with Hitler, never thinking that the German forces would double-cross him. This naiveté caused the Russian forces to be unprepared when the Nazis struck in June 1941. The "purges" of the 1920s and 1930s that Stalin had ordered did nothing to help the Soviet Army against the Nazis, and the Soviets suffered massive losses.

Stalin had been suspicious of the West ever since the Soviet Union threw off the tsar. In 1945, this suspicion deepened when the Allies refused to open a second front against Germany in World War II. Even after the war was over, Stalin was obsessed with the fear that the United States would invade Russia. Stalin made a "buffer zone" between Western Europe and Russia so that no one could pass into Russia unnoticed. Stalin also ordered an economic blockade of the new Soviet-controlled German city of Berlin. He went as far as building a wall around the Soviet-controlled part of Berlin. In 1989, the Allies forced the Soviets to back down and memorably tore down the wall, ending the blockade. East and West Germany reunified into a single state in 1990.

Stalin's health began to deteriorate in the early 1950s, and he died on March 5, 1953, of a stroke at the age of 74. His successor, Nikita Khrushchev (1956), rekindled the popularity that Stalin had lost with Russia's younger generation. Although Stalin had left a legacy of death and terror, he managed to turn Russia into a world superpower to be revered and feared.

Shima Sadaghiyani

See Also Command Economy; Lenin, Vladimir; Marx, Karl; Marxism

Further Reading

Montefiore, Simon Sebag. 2004. *Stalin: The Court of the Red Tsar*. London: Weidenfelt and Nicolson.

Volkogonov, Dmitri. 1998. *The Rise and Fall of the Soviet Empire: Political Leaders from Lenin to Gorbachev*. New York: HarperCollins.

Volkogonov, Dmitri. 1991. "Stalin: Triumph and Tragedy." Translated by Harold Shukman. *New York,* 127, no. 131: 76–77.

Resources for Teachers

Scholastic Teacher. N.d. "Joseph Stalin by Jeffrey Zuehlke." http://www.scholastic.com/teachers/book/joseph-stalin@rt/cleanup.

Teller, Gus. N.d. "The Rise of Stalin." Lesson Plan. http://filebox.vt.edu/users/ateller/portfolio/intasc8/stalinlp.html.

Standard Oil Co. of New Jersey v. United States, 221 U.S. 1 (1911)

A Supreme Court Case Upholding the Sherman Antitrust Act

Economic Concepts

Monopoly; government regulation; competition; Sherman Antitrust Act; market capitalism

Economic Impact

This case ordered the dissolution of the Standard Oil Company monopoly into separate firms due to unreasonable restraint of trade.

Economic Summary

The Standard Oil Company was the largest and richest trust in the United States at the beginning of the twentieth century. By 1904, it owned a Leviathan's share of all the oil production in the United States and had interests in other markets as well. Through a process of acquisition, Standard Oil ingested all market competition. Through vertical integration, Standard Oil controlled aspects of oil production from drilling to refining, and finally retail sales to customers. John D. Rockefeller, along with the other trustees, implemented product standardization that greatly enhanced sales by streamlining production, reducing costs, and undercutting competition. However, when power is unchecked or not limited by competition, that power has the potential to become corrupt.

A monopoly exists when one company has all the power to control the market. Standard Oil monopolized the petroleum industry. This market dominance was contrary to the principles of free enterprise, in which competition is fundamental. In this case, there were no viable substitutes and prices could be set and supply could be minimized. Congress passed the Sherman Antitrust Act in 1890 to deal with monopolies that threatened consumers. The Supreme Court used the Sherman Antitrust Act to check the power of monopolies and restore the principles of the market.

Case Summary

John D. Rockefeller came from modest beginnings, but his aptitude for mathematics and business helped him become one of the richest men in the world. His relationship with Standard Oil began as a partnership between himself, as an expert on running a corporation, and Samuel Andrews, who knew the petroleum industry. Competition in the fledgling oil industry was fierce. However, Rockefeller had a plan. He gathered a few partners: S. V. Harkness provided financial assets, H. M. Flagler had the power to get the railroads to cut their rates so the company could ship oil at a cheaper cost than competitors, and his older brother William Rockefeller provided a refinery. These partners formed a group of trustees that ran the company for shareholders. Through a series of acquisition strategies, the company carved out a solid foothold in the oil industry. This foothold led to a stronghold and finally a stranglehold.

During an early skirmish in the battle for total control of the oil industry, Standard Oil fought the Pennsylvania Railroad. Standard Oil had had the foresight to invest in various means of transport for its oil. It turned to new methods such as the pipeline and the railroad tank car. In addition, anticipating the competition, Standard Oil developed its own ships, docking facilities, barrel-making plants, warehouses, and everything else connected to the manufacture, distribution, and sale of its product. Because the company did not need to rely on other businesses, the railroad eventually capitulated to Standard Oil and the monopoly was near perfect.

However, the government was slowly catching up with legislation that prohibited companies from owning the stock of another company. This made the reorganization of Standard Oil necessary. A new business arrangement emerged in the early 1880s whereby shareholders assigned their shares to trustees who held the decision-making power of the company. These new organizations became known as trusts, but soon the technical term was less important than its reputation. Many Americans believed trusts suppressed competition and led to collusion and price setting.

Meanwhile, journalist Ida Tarbell published a series of articles systematically chronicling the misdeeds of John Rockefeller and Standard Oil. *McClure's* magazine ran the 19 articles from1902 until 1904. Later they were compiled in a book, *The History of the Standard Oil Company* (1904). Tarbell's own father was one of the small refineries forced out of business by Standard Oil. This condemnation added to the political pressure for government to do something about these trusts.

President Theodore Roosevelt, known as the "trust-buster," encouraged the commissioner of corporations to study Standard Oil's undertakings. By 1900, Standard Oil had morphed into a holding company based in New Jersey in an effort to keep a step ahead of antitrust laws. Rockefeller had retired from active control of the company to focus on his philanthropic endeavors. At the conclusion of the government's investigation of Standard Oil was confirmation that the trust participated in unfair competition practices and had violated the Sherman Antitrust Act. In 1909, the U.S. Department of Justice sued Standard Oil in the Circuit Court of the United States for the Eastern District of Missouri. The circuit court ruled against Standard Oil. Standard Oil of New Jersey plus 33 other holding companies, along with Rockefeller and the other trustees, appealed the case to the Supreme Court. The Court agreed to hear the case in 1910 and arguments were heard the next year.

A corporation is a legal entity. Its creation gives legal protection to individual owners from the consequences of company actions. In the Standard Oil case, the responsibility of the Supreme Court was to determine if the Sherman Antitrust Act had been violated. The government claimed Standard Oil was an unreasonable monopoly. Standard Oil would get cheaper shipping rates and other companies would be charged higher rates regardless of distance traveled or weight, resulting in an unreasonable advantage over their competitors. In addition, Standard raised prices where there was no competition and its customers had no other choices. Furthermore, it would use fake companies that did not appear to be owned by Standard Oil to drop the prices of their product when competition was plentiful, starting a price war that their competition would not win.

In response to these allegations, Standard Oil disagreed upon the construction and application of most all sections of the Sherman Act, but particularly the first and second sections referencing "contract in restraint of trade." The words were vague and unclear. The company argued that the framers did not have the dismemberment of companies in mind when they included the commerce clause in Article I of the Constitution. Standard Oil produced a laundry list of underappreciated contributions. Through its better quality of goods and uniform standards, Standard Oil improved the daily lives of citizens by providing kerosene to heat and light their homes. Furthermore, in an effort to be more efficient, the company used the refinery by-products and created new uses such as paraffin wax, lubricating oils, and heating oil. In addition, it improved the environment by recycling the sludge into fertilizer for farmers instead of dumping it into the ocean. The bottom line was simply that if left alone, the market regulates itself. Standard Oil reinvested its profits into expansion, innovation, and efficiency, resulting in a benefit for the general welfare.

Chief Justice White wrote the opinion of the Court. He expressed the necessity to clarify words and terms that had meaning from English common law. Terms such as "freedom to contract" had changed over time in response to the injurious consequences of monopolies. He concluded that Congress has the right to set definitions of what a trust is as well as to prohibit restraint of trade. This is in accordance with Article I of the Constitution. However, White briefly stated concerns about the lower courts' decree in that modifications should be made in accordance to what amount of harm or danger it may have on the public. Oil was a vital resource to people all over America and any disruption in that market could have negative effects on the general welfare. The Court affirmed the lower court's decree with the modification that the dissolution should not affect the safety of the public. Consequently, the breakup of Standard Oil mirrored somewhat the breakup of AT&T, where the former spawned baby Standards and the latter baby Bells.

The penalty for being found guilty of conspiring to set prices and practicing unfair labor practices increased the fortune of John Rockefeller. The worth of his stock went up and his spinoff companies became more valuable than the original.

In the case of Standard Oil, the dissenting opinion of Justice Harlan clearly expressed the idea that the Court had no business interpreting what Congress meant when it passed regulatory legislation. Nor did it have any business discussing the merits of policy passed by Congress. Harlan asserted for the minority that only Congress can make laws and only it should make clear what it intended that law to mean.

The Sherman Act lacked specificity in wording that for years gave Congress the benefit of appearing to be tough on monopolies, but made it difficult for the courts to enforce. This case made Standard Oil synonymous with "trust-busting." It propelled Congress to clarify the antitrust legislation, and three years later pass the Clayton Antitrust Act of 1914.

Kathleen C. Simmons

See Also Clayton Antitrust Act of 1914; Constitution of the United States (see Appendix); Market Capitalism; Sherman Antitrust Act of 1890; Supreme Court

Related Cases

United States v. E.C. Knight Co., 156 U.S. 1 (1895) (Antitrust case that upheld Congress's commerce power)

United States v. Joint Traffic Association, 171 U.S. 505 (1898) (Antitrust case that upheld the Sherman Act)

Hopkins v. United States, 171 U.S. 578 (1898)

Anderson v. United States, 171 U.S. 604 (1898)

Montague & Co. v. Lowrey, 193 U.S. 38 (1904)

Further Readings

Legal Information Institute, Cornell University Law School. N.d. "*Standard Oil Co. of New Jersey v. United States* () 100 U.S. 1, 173 Fed. Rep. 177, modified and affirmed." http://www.law.cornell.edu/supct/html/historics/USSC_CR_0221_0001_ZS.html.

Legal Information Institute. Cornell University Law School. N.d. "*Standard Oil Co. of New Jersey v. United States* () 100 U.S. 1, 173 Fed. Rep. 177, modified and affirmed. WHITE, C.J., Opinion of the Court." http://www.law.cornell.edu/supct/html/historics/USSC_CR_0221_0001_ZO.html.

Legal Information Institute, Cornell University Law School. N.d. "*Standard Oil Co. of New Jersey v. United States* () 100 U.S. 1, 173 Fed. Rep. 177, modified and affirmed HARLAN, J., Concurring in Part, Dissenting in Part." http://www.law.cornell.edu/supct/html/historics/USSC_CR_0221_0001_ZX.html.

Resources for Teachers

American Experience 25 Years. N.d. "The Rockefellers." http://www.pbs.org/wgbh/americanexperience/features/primary-resources/rockefellers-mcclures/.

OYEZ, ITT Chicago, Kent College of Law. "*Standard Oil Co. of NJ v. United States.*" N.d. http://www.oyez.org/cases/1901-1939/1909/1909_398#chicago. (Facts of the case)

Tarbell, Ida. 1904. *The History of the Standard Oil Company.* Boston: McClure, Phillips.

State Capitalism

State capitalism dates back to the East India Company and its relationship with the British government. Throughout history, young rising international powers have relied on the state for early economic growth. For example, the United States after the Revolutionary War and Japan after World War II relied on the state to protect their economies.

State capitalism has taken on a new look in the modern era. No longer do nations begin businesses with the idea of converting them to private businesses. Modern state capitalism involves businesses owned or backed by the government with the behavior of a private sector multinational company. Today's modern state business develops into a full-fledged business model owned and operated by the state yet participating in the private global marketplace. The state-owned or state-partnered business model has become an influential economic structure in nations around the globe. The Europeans and Asians have incorporated state capitalism to create industrial centers and welfare states.

State capitalism has its proponents and practitioners in both the developed world and the developing world. As of 2013, France owned 85 percent of Europe's largest energy company, and Germany owned 32 percent of its largest telecommunications company. In Asia, Japan owns 50 percent of the Japan Tobacco Company (*Economist* Staff, 2012, 5). The rich, developed nations of the Organization for Economic Co-operation and Development (OECD) state-owned businesses have an employment of over 6 million people and total value of almost $2 trillion (*Economist* Staff, 2012, 5).

Modern state capitalism came of age with three global events. One was the growth of Singapore as an Asian economic powerhouse. A second was the transformation of China when it embraced globalization and instituted economic incentives with Chinese special economic zones, then welcomed foreign private companies to China. This new, more twenty-first century form of state capitalism created in Asia was described as capitalism with "Asian values" (*Economist* Staff, 2012, 5). Asian values were defined as a combination of family values with authoritarianism state oversight. Deng Xiaoping, who led China into the era of state capitalism, promoted its economic transformation. He required China's new government-led enterprises to embrace the business model of the Western world. Importantly, he supported and sponsored large amounts of investment in research and development.

A third global event leading to the rise of modern state capitalism was the fall of the Soviet Union. Even though it was initially seen as a victory for personal freedom, liberty, and economic capitalism, soon former Communist leaders and oligarchs literally stole massive amounts of the commanding heights and economic base. This economic theft left the new countries of the former Soviet Union severely in debt as they attempted to transform themselves from command economies to capitalist economies. This disarray led to a return to state-owned enterprises under Russian president Vladimir Putin. Putin promoted and endorsed an all-encompassing combination of private businesses comprising a private sector with a strong presence of state capitalism enterprises.

Modern state capitalism is different from the state capitalism of history. China's state-capitalistic companies are global companies with business operations around the globe. The Chinese government focuses its state-owned industries in countries where they can have a significant economic impact. The Chinese new modern economic position is that state capitalism is a viable, long-term business model and not just a bridge from a command economy to a market economy.

The new view of state capitalism has supporters in many emerging and transitional nations, such as Brazil and South Africa. As emerging nations strive to compete and participate in the global economy, state capitalism is a very appealing model for growth. With government support, the young economic nation gains instant credibility and clout as if it were a mature privately held company.

State capitalism has strident supporters as well as critics. Supporters of state capitalism strongly promote it as a business model that can provide both growth and stability. State capitalism promotes a strong link between government and business.

State capitalism's critics are many. They believe state capitalism as an economic model is more a danger than a solution. One concern the critics often cite is that state-capitalist governments are often unpredictable. Regardless of the business sector the state-owned business is operating, if the government backing the business is not stable, the likelihood of a stable business greatly lessens. Another concern is the government protection and favoritism provided to government entities, making domestic competition unlikely. When the government supports and subsidizes one set of companies, the other companies in the sector are hurt. Supporters of market capitalism point to the resources used by state-owned enterprises that could have been used by privately owned enterprises. Finally, critics of state capitalism refer to the imbalance of the global trading community when a state-owned business enjoys government support regarding trade policy and foreign exchange policies, which creates an uneven trading environment.

David A. Dieterle
Kerry Hritz

See Also Democratic Socialism; Lenin, Vladimir; Market Capitalism; Smith, Adam

Further Reading

Dean, Jason, Andrew Browne, and Shai Oster. 2010. "China's 'State Capitalism' Sparks a Global Backlash." *Wall Street Journal Business*, November 16. Accessed December 2, 2013. http://online.wsj.com/news/articles/SB10001424052748703514904575602731006315198.

The Economist Staff. 2012. "Special Report: State Capitalism; The Visible Hand." *The Economist*, January 21, 3–18.

Kurlantzick, Joshua. 2012. "The Rise of Innovative State Capitalism." *Bloomberg BusinessWeek Global Economics*, June 28. http://www.businessweek.com/articles/2012-06-28/the-rise-of-innovative-state-capitalism.

Resources for Teachers

Baker, Matt. 2012. "Socialism vs. Capitalism Lesson Plan." http://www.beaconhillacademy.org/lessons/socialism-vs-capitalism-lesson-plan.html.

Foundation for Teaching Economics. N.d. "Classroom Activity: Lesson 1, Part 2; Will the Real Capitalism Please Stand Up?" http://www.fte.org/teacher-resources/lesson-plans/is-capitalism-good-for-the-poor/will-the-real-capitalism-please-stand-up/.

Steelworkers Strike of 1919

The Great Steelworkers Strike occurred in 1919 in an effort to form a union and push for better wages and working conditions, an eight-hour workday, and collective bargaining.

This strike was the most significant since the Homestead Strike of 1892. The Homestead Strike was the result of Henry Clay Frick's desire to decrease workers' wages due to the declining price of steel. Andrew Carnegie, who owned the plant, was in agreement with Frick and hoped to break the Amalgamated Association of Iron and Steel Workers union. Frick brought in the Pinkertons, which led to bloodshed and eventually the end of the strike when federal troops were called in. The strike was a major defeat for labor and devastated the unions until 1919, when labor rose up once again.

World War I played an influential role in the plight of labor and steelworkers leading up to the Great Strike of 1919. The war increased the demand for steel and for workers; wages temporarily increased because a shortage of labor existed, as fewer immigrants were coming to the United States from Europe due to wartime travel restrictions. Employers responded with modest wage increases, but that was not enough to combat the long hours and poor working conditions that steelworkers faced. Many hoped there would be more cooperation between workers and employers once the war ended; that did not come to pass, however.

With President Woodrow Wilson preoccupied with postwar peace, labor's interests were pushed aside as a period of big business supremacy was ushered in. Also, due to postwar inflation, there was a massive rise in the cost of living and the economy began to stagnate. Workers wanted to establish a basic standard of living based on hours, wages, and working conditions, and they hoped to maintain the wages they had received during the war.

In the post–World War I era, labor also had to contend with the aftereffects of the 1917 Bolshevik Revolution in Russia. Americans feared communism and its spread, and the socialist ideas with which it was associated. Labor unions were quickly equated with socialism, anarchism, and communism.

In August 1918, several trade unions met in an effort to form a National Committee Organizing Iron and Steel. William Z. Foster, a radical and Communist, played a large role in organizing the strike, and knew he needed widespread support. The problem was that not everyone agreed on how to pursue a strike. There was also much opposition to the organization of workers into unions and employers sought to prevent these groups from meeting. Workers were supported by the American Federation of Labor, which brought the conditions to the attention of Judge Elbert H. Gary, chairman of U.S. Steel's board of directors. When nothing came of this, union leaders began to organize and set a date for a strike. Once again, an effort to meet was declined as members of U.S. Steel stated that it would not discuss anything related to the workplace with union workers. The steel companies had the advantage: they could easily fire workers who participated in a strike and replace them.

President Woodrow Wilson hoped for a solution and urged the leaders of the strike to postpone the strike until a meeting of the industries could take place. Samuel Gompers wanted to follow the request of the president, but others did not because they feared radicals would have carried out the strike anyway. Foster, on the other hand, pressed ahead with the September 22 strike date.

The strike commenced on September 22 with approximately 275,000–300,000 steelworkers (or half the labor force) leaving their jobs. Workers pressed for collective bargaining rights and a shorter workday and workweek. Workers did not want to work seven days per week or keep the 24-hour shifts that some were forced to work. They also wanted overtime pay and the reinstatement of those fired for their participation in union activities.

Within a week the strike spread to about 365,000 workers total. Some steelworkers did not participate in the strike due to its suspected link to communism and radicalism and because they feared losing their jobs.

The role of the media heavily influenced public opinion, as they presented a one-sided view of the strike. Newspapers ran headlines that drew much attention to the strike and some of this attention was negative as it pointed to socialism and radicalism, labels that labor unions had previously been given. The deliberate agitation of the striking workers made things look much worse than they were, including making the workers appear to be lawless individuals. Newspapers used every opportunity to point to the strikes as radical, red, or Bolshevik in nature.

The Great Steel Strike ended on January 8, 1920, with little progress made by labor. The demands of collective bargaining, better working conditions, and hours were never addressed. If workers managed to avoid being blacklisted, they returned to their jobs and the same working conditions they had fought to change. Many were left waiting for the next big labor movement, which did not occur until the 1930s.

Later, with the formation of the Congress of Industrial Organizations (CIO), labor would once again rise up to fight the steel industry and push for the demands workers had fought for in 1919. The CIO, formed in 1938 by John L. Lewis, aimed to organize skilled and unskilled workers into industrial unions.

Labor would later have some support and successes during President Franklin D. Roosevelt's New Deal programs with the National Labor Relations Act in 1935. Also known as the Wagner Act, it permitted collective bargaining and the organization of trade unions.

Angela M. LoPiccolo

See Also National Labor Relations Act of 1935 (Wagner Act); New Deal; Roosevelt, Franklin Delano

Further Reading

Asher, Robert. 1978. "Painful Memories of the Historical Consciousness of Steelworkers and the Steel Strike of 1919." *Pennsylvania History* 45: 61–86.

Howenstine, Jr., E. Jay. 1944. "The High Cost-of-Living Problem after World War I." *Southern Economic Journal* 10: 222–34.

Marcus, Irwin M. 1996. "The Johnstown Steel Strike of 1919: The Struggle for Unionism and Civil Liberties." *Pennsylvania History* 63: 96–118.

Murray, Robert K. 1951. "Communism and the Great Steel Strike of 1919." *The Mississippi Valley Historical Review* 38: 445–66.

Newell, Stephanie E. 1997. "The Transformation of U.S. Steel 1945–1985: Perspectives from the Corporation and the Union." *Journal of Management History* 3: 166–92.

Resources for Teachers

Brody, David. 1965. *Labor in Crisis: The Steel Strike of 1919*. Philadelphia: Lippincott.

Foster, William Z. 1920. *The Great Steel Strike and Its Lessons*. New York: B. W. Huebsch.

"History of U.S. Steel. 2012." N.d. Accessed December 2, 2013. http://www.ussteel.com/uss/portal/home/aboutus/history.

Summers, Lawrence

Born: November 30, 1954, in New Haven, Connecticut; American; public finance, labor economics, finance economics; Major Work: *Understanding Unemployment* (1990).

Lawrence "Larry" H. Summers began his economic political career as a domestic policy economist on the Council of Economic Advisers under President Reagan in 1982–1983. During the 1980s, Larry Summers wrote or coauthored over 50 papers on debt, savings, taxes, stocks, the overall economy, and more. In 1987, he was awarded the Alan T. Waterman Award from the National Science Foundation. This award, along with its $500,000 research grant, is awarded every year to honor an exceptional young scientist or engineer from the United States whose work demonstrates originality, innovation, and a significant impact within his or her field.

Lawrence Henry Summers was born on November 30, 1954, in New Haven, Connecticut, into a family of economics professors. His parents, Robert and Anita Summers, were both economics professors at the University of Pennsylvania, and two of his uncles—Paul Samuelson of the Massachusetts Institute of Technology (MIT) and Kenneth Arrow of Stanford University—were Nobel laureates. Summers spent most of his childhood in Penn Valley, a suburb of Philadelphia. Encouraged in early childhood to take part in family discussions of economic theory and current events, Summers followed his love of the topic and attended MIT, where he received his bachelor's of science in economics in 1975. He taught economics for three years at MIT and was named an assistant professor in 1979 and associate professor in 1982. As a graduate student, Summers attended Harvard University and received his PhD in economics in 1982. Summers went on to teach at Harvard and became one of its youngest tenured professors at the age of 28, returning to serve as the Charles W. Eliot University Professor.

In the 1990s, Summers wrote or coauthored over 50 papers and five books, including *Understanding Unemployment* (1990). He left Harvard in 1991 and became the chief economist of the World Bank (1991–1993). Later, he became the U.S. Deputy Secretary of the Treasury (1995–1999), and then the Secretary of the Treasury (1999–2001). During his tenure as Treasury Secretary, the U.S. economy experienced an unprecedented period of sustained economic growth. As a result, he is considered an expert on domestic economics and a leading authority on international finance. It was during his work with the Clinton administration that he recommended the deregulation of the derivatives contracts within the financial industry. Specifically, he endorsed the Gramm-Leach-Bliley Act, which removed the separation between investment and commercial banks, repealing the Banking Act of 1933, also known as the Glass-Steagall Act.

Summers is not without his critics; some claim that he ignored the 1990s stock bubble and later the housing bubble. He left the political limelight to become president of Harvard University from 2001 to 2006. While there, he wrote and edited a number of works, including papers for the Brookings Institution and the *Harvard Business Review*, and cowrote a paper with Henry Kissinger for the Council on Foreign Relations. While at Harvard, he quarreled with a number of the faculty and resigned under pressure. After taking a year off, he returned as a professor of economics in Harvard's Kennedy School of Government.

Summers was an adviser to Barack Obama's presidential campaign and was later named director of the National Economic Council in 2009. As in President Clinton's administration, Summers held significant influence over economic policies in President Obama's administration. He frequently writes for a variety of news publications including the *Washington Post*, *Financial Times*, *Boston Globe*, and *Wall Street Journal*.

In 1993, Summers was awarded the John Bates Clark Medal for being an outstanding young American economist.

Carol Lynn Nute

See Also Arrow, Kenneth; Contractionary Fiscal Policy; Expansionary Fiscal Policy; Fiscal Policy; Samuelson, Paul; Taxes

Selected Works by Lawrence Summers

Summers, Lawrence. 1994. *Investing in All the People: Educating Women in Developing Countries*. Washington, DC: World Bank Publications.

Summers, Lawrence. 1990. *Understanding Unemployment*. Cambridge, MA: MIT Press.

Summers, Lawrence, ed. 1987–1990. *Tax Policy and the Economy*. Cambridge, MA: MIT Press.

Summers, Lawrence H., and Lawrence H. Goulder. 1987. *A General Equilibrium Analysis*. Cambridge, MA: National Bureau of Economic Research.

Summers, Lawrence H., and Lawrence H. Goulder. 1987, 1990. *Tax Policy, Asset Prices, and Growth: Understanding Unemployment*. Cambridge, MA: National Bureau of Economic Research.

Summers, Lawrence H., Timothy J. Hatton, and Alan M. Taylor. 2007. *The New Comparative Economic History: Essays in Honor of Jeffrey G. Williamson*. Cambridge, MA: MIT Press.

Summers, Lawrence H., and Henry Kissinger. 1994, 2004. *Renewing the Atlantic Partnership: Report of an Independent Task Force*. Washington, DC: World Bank Publications.

Summers, Lawrence H., C. K. Prahalad, and Rosabeth Moss Kanter. 2004. *Harvard Business Review on Leadership in a Changed World*. Cambridge, MA: Harvard Business School Press.

Selected Works about Lawrence Summers

Bradley, Richard. 2005. *Harvard Rules: Lawrence Summers and the Battle for the World's Most Powerful School*. New York: HarperCollins.

Harvard Kennedy School. N.d. "Lawrence H. Summers." http://www.hks.harvard.edu/about/faculty-staff-directory/lawrence-summers.

Kinsley, Michael. 2008. *Creative Capitalism: A Conversation with Bill Gates, Warren Buffett, and Other Economic Leaders*. New York: Simon & Schuster.

New York Times. 2013. "Lawrence Summers: News about Lawrence Summers, Including Commentary and Archival Articles Published in the *New York Times*." http://topics.nytimes.com/top/reference/timestopics/people/s/lawrence_h_summers/index.html.

MIT News. "Economist Lawrence Summers, MIT '75, Named Harvard President." March 12, 2001. http://web.mit.edu/newsoffice/2001/summers.html.

Supply-Side Economics

Proponents of supply-side economics posit that bolstering an economy's ability to supply more goods is the most effective way to stimulate economic growth. Based on insights derived from the Nobel Prize–winning economists Robert Mundell, Milton Friedman, and James Buchanan with economist Arthur Laffer, the supply siders developed a new program based on tight money to stop inflation and cuts in marginal tax rates to stimulate growth during the stagflation years of the late 1970s. Supply-side theorists advocated income tax reduction in order to increase private investment in corporations, facilities, and equipment.

Many people refer to supply-side economics as "Reaganomics" because of the "trickle-down" policy espoused by Ronald Reagan as a candidate for president of the United States when he ran against standing President Jimmy Carter. During the 1980s, then newly elected President Reagan popularized the idea that tax cuts for investors and

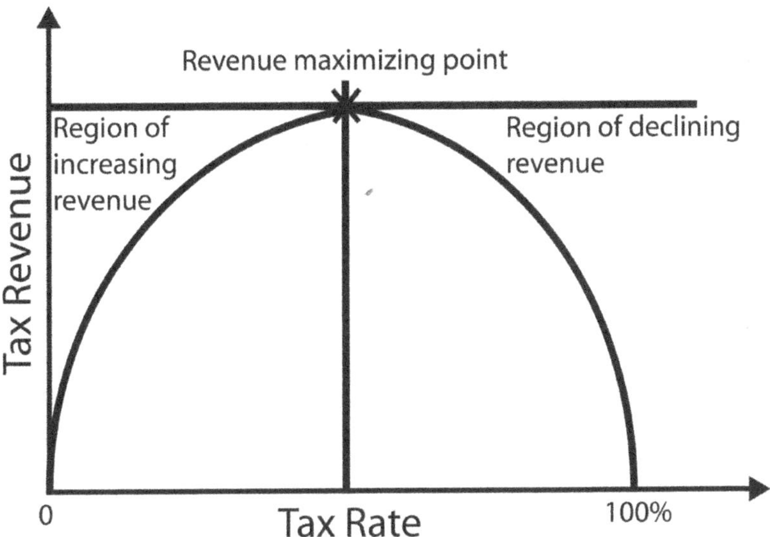

Arthur Laffer proposed with the Laffer curve high tax rates will result in lower government revenue

entrepreneurs would provide incentives to save, invest, and produce the economic benefits that would trickle down to the overall economy.

A basic economic principle is that aggregate demand and aggregate supply intersect to determine overall output and price levels. The supply siders contend that an increase in supply will increase output and lower prices. Supply siders often go further and claim that demand is largely irrelevant, since overproduction and underproduction are not sustainable phenomena. They argue that when companies temporarily "overproduce," excess inventory will be created, prices will subsequently fall, and consumers will increase their purchases to offset the excess supply.

In general, supply-side theory has three pillars: tax policy, regulatory policy, and monetary policy. Since the single idea behind all three pillars is that production is most important in determining economic growth, supply siders are often contrasted with Keynesians, who believe that consumers and their demand for goods and services are key economic drivers.

Supply siders argue for lower marginal income tax rates in order to tempt workers to choose work over leisure. Certain supply siders might even argue that the government would not lose total tax revenue because lower rates would be offset by a higher tax revenue base as a result of greater employment and productivity. This relationship between marginal tax rates and tax revenues was promoted by economist Arthur Laffer with his famous Laffer curve.

In regard to regulatory policy, supply siders prefer a smaller government and less intervention in the free market. This is logical because supply siders do not support that induced demand promoted by Keynesian economic theory can either rescue a recession or have a sustainable impact on growth. Unlike the Keynesian supposition that monetary policy is an important tool for tweaking the economy and dealing with business cycles, supply siders do not think that monetary policy can create economic value. They are concerned that the Fed might either create too much inflationary liquidity with expansionary monetary policy, or alternately, might not sufficiently "grease the wheels" of commerce with enough liquidity due to a tight monetary policy. Since neither outcome is desirable, strict supply siders fear that any action by the Fed may inadvertently stifle growth.

Since supply siders view monetary policy not as a tool that can create economic value but rather as a variable to be controlled, they advocate a stable monetary policy or a policy of gentle inflation tied to economic growth. This principle is the key to understanding why supply siders often advocate a return to the gold standard. The idea is not that gold is particularly special, but rather that gold is the most obvious candidate as a stable "store of value." Supply siders argue that if the United States were to peg the dollar to gold, the currency would be more stable, and fewer disruptive outcomes would result from currency fluctuations.

Since supply-side economics implies a reduced role for government and a less progressive tax policy, the supply-side philosophy reappears during most political campaigns. Supply-side economics has become the economic philosophy synonymous with tax cuts regardless of economic conditions.

Maura Donnelly

See Also Buchanan, James; Contractionary Fiscal Policy; Contractionary Monetary Policy; Expansionary Fiscal Policy; Expansionary Monetary Policy; Friedman, Milton; Hayek, Friedrich von; Keynesian Economics; Laffer, Arthur; Laffer Curve; Reagan, Ronald

Further Reading

Bartlett, Bruce R. 1981. *Reaganomics: Supply-Side Economics in Action.* New York: Arlington House.

Feldstein, Martin S. 1986. *Supply-Side Economics: Old Truths and New Claims.* Washington, DC: National Bureau of Economic Research.

Raboy, David G. 1982. *Essays in Supply-Side Economics.* Washington, DC: Institute for Research on the Economics of Taxation.

Resources for Teachers

Galles, Gary. N.d. "Supply-Side Economics in One Lesson." Foundation for Economic Education. http://www.fee.org/the_freeman/detail/supply-side-economics-in-one-lesson#axzz2li4Yte2s.

Teaching Economics as If People Mattered. N.d. "Born on Third Base." http://www.teachingeconomics.org/content/index.php?topic=thirdbase.

Supreme Court

The Supreme Court of the United States was established under Article III, Section 1 of the U.S. Constitution when it was ratified in 1789. It is a part of the judicial branch of the government. The role of the Supreme Court is to interpret the laws created by the legislative branch of the government. The rulings by the Supreme Court are considered final. These rulings set a precedent for all other rulings similar to them.

When Congress first met on March 4, 1789, one of the first items of business was how to organize and establish the court system. Article III, Section 1 of the Constitution establishes the need for a court system and asks for a Supreme Court, stating, "The judicial Power of the United States shall be vested in one supreme Court and in such inferior Courts as the Congress may from time to time ordain and establish." The Constitution allowed Congress to decide how the court system should be organized. To do this, Congress passed the Judiciary Act of 1789. This act created 13 district courts in major cities, three circuit courts, and a Supreme Court comprised of a chief justice and five associate justices. It also set up a lower federal court system.

The Supreme Court is the highest court in the United States and considered the court of last resort. The Supreme Court gets a great deal of power due to judicial review. In 1803, the case of *Marbury v. Madison* established the principle of judicial review, allowing the Supreme Court to declare any laws that went against the Constitution as invalid. This gave the Supreme Court much more influence, as it now could oversee the executive and legislative branches to ensure what they were doing was constitutional. Since the Supreme Court uses the Constitution as its guiding document, the decisions made by the court are said to stand the test of changing.

Over time, the number of justices that serve on the Supreme Court has increased from six to nine, with one serving as chief justice. Supreme Court justices are chosen by the president and confirmed by the Senate. According to the Constitution, the justices "shall serve their offices during good behavior." This has been interpreted as justices serving for life terms, until they decide to retire or resign, or are impeached from their position. Congress cannot change the salaries of a justice during his or her term in office. This is done so as not to influence the justices in their decisions by increasing or decreasing their pay.

Under Article III, Section II of the Constitution, the Supreme Court has original jurisdiction in cases that involve more than one state and cases involving ambassadors, ministers, and consuls. It also has jurisdiction in cases that involve treaties and events that happen on the open sea. The Supreme Court has appellate jurisdiction over cases that deal with constitutional or federal law. The Court receives over 10,000 petitions for a writ of certiorari on a yearly basis. A petition for writ of certiorari is a document that a losing party files with the Supreme Court asking the Supreme Court to review the decision of a lower court. It includes a list of the parties, a statement of the facts of the case, the legal questions presented for review, and arguments as to why the Court should grant the writ. Of these 10,000 petitions, the Court agrees to hear oral arguments on 75 to 80 cases yearly. The Supreme Court hears these cases during yearly terms while it is in session from the first Monday in October until the first Monday in October the following year.

In order for a case to be heard, there must be a quorum of six justices present. The justices review the decisions of the lower courts and the history of the case prior to listening to oral arguments from the petitioner and the respondent. Justices can also participate in cases by listening to audio recordings of the arguments and reading transcripts from the cases. Justices make a decision by voting on how they feel the case should be decided, either upholding the decision of the lower courts or reversing the decision. A decision is reached when five of the nine justices have voted for or against the decision of the lower court.

The Supreme Court justices have other responsibilities in addition to hearing cases and making decisions based on precedent and the Constitution. Whenever they make a decision, they may also decide to write their opinions on the cases. These opinions may be concurring with the majority opinion or dissenting from it. Also, the Supreme Court justices are responsible for overseeing one or more of the 13 federal circuit courts and handling emergency applications from these courts.

The Supreme Court plays a vital role in how the U.S. government functions. With the power to oversee the actions of both the executive and legislative branches, the Court sets appropriate limits on the government and ensures that all Americans can enjoy the freedoms promised to them through the Constitution and proper due process of law.

Ekaterini Chrisopoulos-Vergos

See Also Constitution of the United States (see Appendix); *see* individual Supreme Court cases

Further Reading

About the Supreme Court. "USCourts.gov." N.d. http://www.uscourts.gov/educational-resources/get-informed/supreme-court/about-supreme-court.aspx.

"Definition: Certiorari, Petition for Writ of Certiorari." N.d. *Tech Law Journal*. http://www.techlawjournal.com/glossary/legal/certiorari.htm.

Supreme Court of the United States. N.d. "Supreme Court of the United States: The Court as an Institution." http://www.supremecourt.gov/about/institution.aspx.

Supreme Court of the United States. N.d. "The Supreme Court of the United States: History." http://www.judiciary.senate.gov/nominations/SupremeCourt/SupremeCourtHistory.cfm.

Resources for Teachers

The Supreme Court Historical Society. N.d. "How the Court Works: The Chief Justice's Role." The Supreme Court Historical Society. Accessed October 25, 2013. http://www.supremecourthistory.org/how-the-court-works/how-the-court-work/the-chief-justices-role/.

T

Tariff Act of 1930 (Smoot-Hawley Tariff Act)

In 1930, when the United States had begun to slip into a depression, one of the strategies that the federal government attempted to use to help the economy get back on its feet was to pass the Tariff Act of 1930 (Smoot-Hawley Tariff Act). Consumer spending was on the decline and many workers had lost their jobs. Congress hoped the passing of this act would protect American workers from foreign competition.

History of the Smoot-Hawley Tariff Act

During the 1920s, the agriculture industry lobbied Congress for protection from the intense competition of the European farmers as it recovered from World War I. Also during this time period, overproduction had drastically reduced agricultural prices. In 1922, the Fordney-McCumber Act was passed by Congress to impose strict protectionist tariffs, raising the average tariff 40 percent.

In 1928, Republican presidential candidate Herbert Hoover campaigned on a platform of increasing tariffs on agricultural products. Once elected president, he was influenced to broaden the tariffs to many other products. By 1929, when the U.S. economy began to slip into the greatest depression of all time, and in response to the stock market crash, protectionism was gaining strength. President Hoover signed the Tariff Act of 1930 on June 17, despite the objections of over 1,000 economists who had signed a petition against the legislation. The legislation became known as the Smoot-Hawley Tariff Act for the legislation's chief sponsors, Senator Reed Smoot of Utah and House Representative Willis Hawley of Oregon. Senator Smoot was chairman of the Senate's Finance Committee, and Representative Hawley was chairman of the House Ways and Means Committee. The Smoot-Hawley Tariff Act was the last legislative act in which the United States imposed definitive tariff rates.

Effects of the Smoot-Hawley Tariff Act

The Smoot-Hawley Tariff Act raised the average tariff on all imported products to 50 percent and started a trade war between the United States and its trading partners around the world. Other nations responded by raising tariffs against American-made goods. The trade war that resulted decreased international trade and deepened the worldwide depression of the 1930s. Most economists blame the Smoot-Hawley Act for increasing American unemployment. The trade war had closed foreign markets to American goods and reduced international demand for all goods.

In retaliation, more than two dozen countries also passed tariff legislation to counter Smoot-Hawley. The world economy was already very fragile and global trade had been on the decline. The act further added to Wall Street losing confidence in the economy. It was also the beginning of U.S. isolationism. Between 1929 and 1932, total U.S. trade (exports and imports) fell by approximately two-thirds. World trade fell by a similar margin, feeling the repercussions of Smoot-Hawley's impact and those of the retaliatory tariffs of other nations.

Response to the Smoot-Hawley Tariff Act

President Franklin D. Roosevelt signed the Reciprocal Trade Agreements Act in 1934. This legislation liberalized trade policies, reduced tariff rates from the Smoot-Hawley levels, and began the reconciliation with foreign governments to reestablish global trade. It has been suggested that the Smoot-Hawley Tariff Act caused the Great Depression to be deeper and last longer. The act may have also been an influence for the rise of political extremism and fascism throughout Europe.

Trade wars still break out between the United States and other nations, but most disputes center on a few products instead of all imports, which is what happened with the Smoot-Hawley Tariff Act. Recent conflicts have included the Beef War of 1999 and the Steel Tariff of 2002.

European countries launched the Beef War by banning the import of American beef from cows raised with hormones. The United States responded by imposing tariffs on European clothing and specific foods, including certain cheeses, meats, and mustards.

The Steel Tariff dispute began when the United States introduced temporary tariffs on imported steel to help American steel producers recover from bankruptcy. Angry European nations sued and threatened to retaliate. An international panel ruled these tariffs illegal in 2003.

Reasons for Tariffs

Why does a country impose trade barriers, such as what was done with the Smoot-Hawley Tariff Act? There are three main arguments that support protectionism: protecting workers' jobs, protecting infant industries, and safeguarding national security. Tariffs would also be initiated in retaliation against another country's tariffs on domestic goods. This was the case when other nations instituted tariffs in retaliation to the Smoot-Hawley Act.

The argument for protecting workers' jobs, which is why the Smoot-Hawley Act was passed in the 1930s, is that it shelters workers in industries that would be hurt by foreign competition. If the United States reduces tariffs on certain imports, domestic manufacturers may not be able to compete. They would have to close their factories and lay off workers.

In an ideal world, the laid-off workers would take new jobs in other industries. In practice, however, retraining and relocation can be difficult. Many workers do not have the skills to work in other industries, and obtaining such skills takes time and money. In addition, industry and political leaders often do not want to shut down existing industries and lose jobs in their home regions.

The same theory is true regarding tariffs protecting infant industries from foreign competition until they have had a chance to acquire the ability to produce goods efficiently and at a competitive price. Once the infant industry has had time to become competitive on a global scale, the tariff can be eliminated or reduced.

Two main difficulties with implementing tariffs to protect infant industries exist. First, the start-up industry lacks the incentive to become more efficient and competitive since it is secured by the tariff from true global competition. Secondly, once an industry is given tariff protection, it is difficult to take the protection away. The tariff can prevent the infant industry from ever really growing up.

Safeguarding national security is the final argument in favor of tariffs. Even supporters of free trade agree that some industries need to be protected and produced within the United States, or at least receive government assistance in order to reduce dependence on other nations in times of crisis.

Tracy L. Ripley

See Also Fascism; Protectionism; Roosevelt, Franklin Delano; Taxes

Further Reading

Beaudreau, Bernard. 2005. *Making Sense of Smoot-Hawley: Technology and Tariffs*. Lincoln, NE: iUniverse.

O'Sullivan, Arthur, and Steven M. Sheffrin. 2007. *Economics Principles in Action.* New York: Pearson Prentice Hall.

Sherden, William A. 2011. *Best Laid Plans: The Tyranny of Unintended Consequences and How to Avoid Them.* Santa Barbara, CA: ABC-CLIO/Greenwood Publishing Group.

Resources for Teachers

Foundation for Economic Education. N.d. "The Smoot-Hawley Tariff and the Great Depression." http://www.fee.org/the_freeman/detail/the-smoot-hawley-tariff-and-the-great-epression #axzz2li4Yte2s.

Foundation for Teaching Economics. N.d. "Lesson 16: Protectionism vs. Globalization." http://www.fte.org/teacher-resources/lesson-plans/efiahlessons/protectionism-vs-globalization/.

Taxes

Governments at all levels (federal, state, local) need revenue to provide the public goods and services. While some describe all government revenue as taxes, others describe government revenue as taxes, fines, fees, and licenses. Taxes are also a major topic of public debate and discussion. This is especially true regarding what should be the sources of government revenue and how much a government should tax.

Components of a Tax

All taxes have three things in common. All taxes have a tax base (i.e., what is being taxed). The source of all taxes is either current wealth (income), accumulated wealth (property), or consumption (sales). Current wealth is defined as income and is associated with income taxes. Property taxes, estate taxes, capital gains taxes, or personal property taxes are examples of taxes where accumulated property is the source. Consumption is the source of sales taxes.

A second component of every tax is the tax rate. There are two types of tax rates: ad valorem or flat rate. Ad valorem is a Latin phrase translated to mean "by value." A tax whose amount is determined as a percentage of the base's value is an ad valorem tax. A flat rate is a per-unit rate such as an excise or unit tax.

Finally, every tax has a tax structure, also known as a tax system. The term "system" is relative to the accumulated effect of all taxes of an economic system. In addition, this same distinction is used to define the "structure" of a tax. There are three tax structures. A tax is classified as either progressive, proportional, or regressive.

Taxes are often identified by their structure. If the burden of the tax increases as one's income increases, the tax structure is progressive. A progressive tax system is one in which those with higher incomes pay a higher percentage of income as taxes. If the tax burden is equal to all regardless of one's income, it is proportional. If the tax is more of a burden on lower incomes, it is regressive. A regressive tax system is one in which the percentage of tax increases for those with lower incomes.

Then, of course, if the tax has the same burden on all income levels, it is proportional. A proportional tax system is one in which all income levels pay the same proportion of taxes. So while an individual tax will be regressive, progressive, or proportional, the goal of most tax systems (in a market economy) is for the system to be proportional. At the end of the day, a tax system can only be of one system: i.e., it is either a progressive tax, a proportional tax, or a regressive tax.

While taxes are often the main topic of many discussions and debates from the dinner table to the halls of state and national capitols, much has been written about the relationship between taxes and tax revenues, taxes and standards of living, and taxes and public goods. One example of these theories is the correlation between tax rates and tax revenues. This theory promotes that tax rates will raise to a point that consumers will begin to find ways to avoid taxes, participating in nontaxable activities such as black markets, getting paid in cash, bartering goods and services, and other measures. This relationship is exhibited in the theory attributed to economist Arthur Laffer.

Types of Taxes

Federal Taxes

At the federal level, the primary tax base for generating revenue is current wealth with the personal and business income taxes. But the federal government also relies on accumulated wealth with an estate tax and current wealth with a business tax and capital gains tax on investment earnings. The federal government generates revenue on the consumption base with excise taxes such as those imposed through utilities and telephone or communications usage.

The most used tax rate at the federal level is the ad valorem ("by value") or percentage rate. Most of those who pay federal income tax are familiar with the personal income tax schedules seen every year before "Tax Day," April 15. Federal business and investment

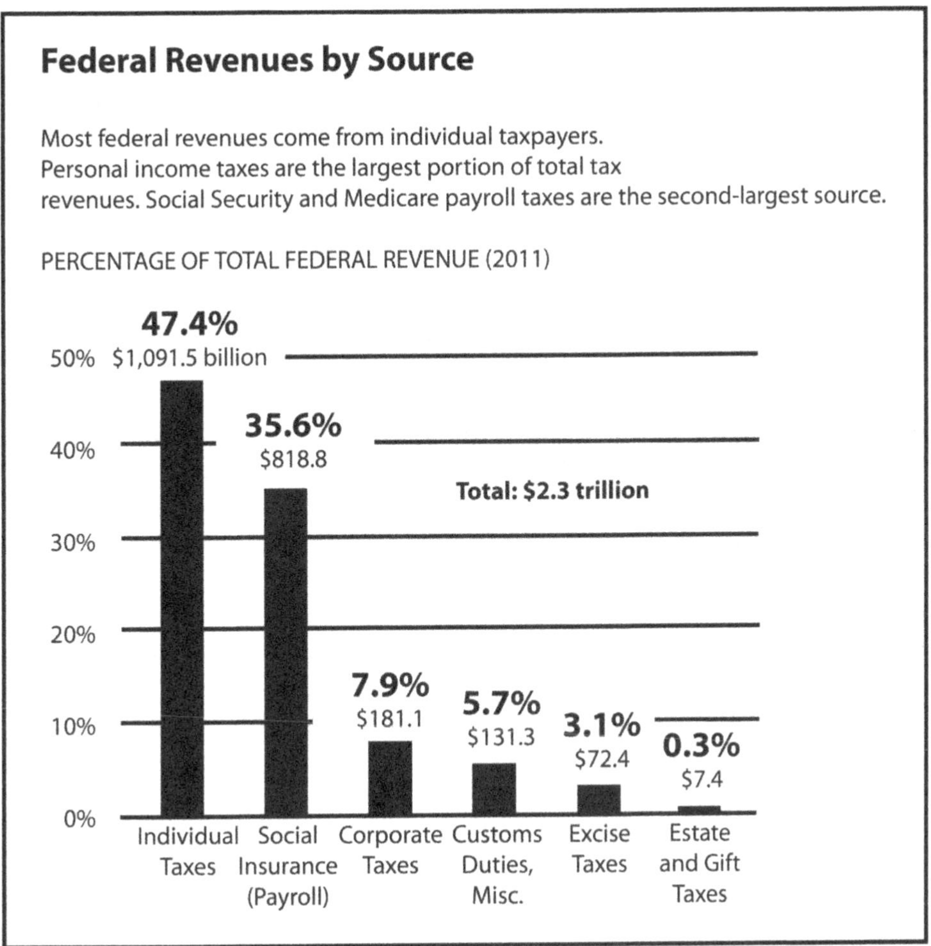

(Source: http://www.heritage.org/federalbudget/federal-revenue-sources)

taxes use ad valorem tax rates. Political debates on taxes are often on what level of tax rate is appropriate and fair for a particular tax base. The estate tax is also determined on an ad valorem rate. The excise or unit tax rate is also used to raise federal tax revenue. Many utility or telephone bills include a federal excise tax to tax our use of these services. Historically, the federal government has tried to tax consumption of specific goods, such as luxury cars or yachts, with mixed success.

The federal tax structure is designed to be progressive so that those whose income and wealth are greater pay a larger percentage of their income in taxes. The progressivity of the federal tax structure is tempered by the use of tax deductions, tax credits, and income or wealth thresholds and limitations. Instituting deductions, credits, and limitations is an attempt to bring the tax structure into a more proportional range. This is why the federal tax schedules for personal income taxes range from 0 to 39 percent. Tax schedules have historically been as high as 95 percent on the wealthiest individuals. This also accounts for only estates over $2 million being subject to the federal estate taxes.

State Taxes

Each state has its own unique range of taxes and tax component combinations. Generally, most states strive for a proportional tax structure, even though in some states the main source of revenue is a regressive sales tax. States often neutralize the regressive sales tax by exempting the most used goods and services by everyone such as food and prescription drugs. A state may also provide some tax credits on one's personal income taxes, based on income, to alleviate the burden of the sales tax on a family or household's total income. Many states also impose what are often referred to as "sin" taxes. "Sin" taxes are taxes levied on consumption goods considered hazardous to one's health, such as alcohol, cigarettes, and other smoking items. These are often excise or unit taxes (specific amount per unit of good).

Many states also apply a tax on the current wealth base of income. However, some states are eliminating this tax base in favor of a broader consumption or sales tax. Most states also have some form of business income tax or accumulated wealth tax on business inventories. Accumulated wealth is also taxed in several states through a personal property tax and business taxes. In these states, individuals pay a tax on the value of personal items such as automobiles.

A personal property tax levied by a state is an ad valorem tax rate because the amount of tax levied is based on the value of the personal property being taxed. An automobile valued at $10,000 will have a lower personal property tax than one valued at $20,000. State sales taxes are ad valorem, as the amount of tax is a percentage of the sale.

Local Taxes

The most widely used tax base on the local level is accumulated wealth, with the property tax on real estate. The prominence of the real estate property tax at the local level dates back to agrarian communities, and the emphasis on property ownership as a statement of wealth. The real estate property tax is used by local governments to fund and operate everything from the local library and public schools to the local community college and the upkeep for roads and local police and fire protection. Virtually no one is exempt from paying some local real estate property tax. Real estate property taxes are paid directly through ownership of a home or property, or indirectly through rental payments on an apartment.

Larger local governmental units, especially large cities and counties, have also added taxes on consumption, with local sales taxes and excise taxes on certain goods like alcohol and cigarettes. Another tax base added by large governmental units is on current wealth, with personal and business income taxes. Many large cities now levy a personal income tax on individuals who either live or work within their city limits.

The tax structure of local taxes is very mixed. Property taxes today in many locales are regressive in structure, since they no longer adequately reflect the relative wealth of the owner. Income taxes in larger cities tend to be proportional, while taxes on consumption are regressive, even when certain tax credits are applied to neutralize the regressive structure of sales tax.

Criteria of a Good Tax

While some may consider the term "good tax" an oxymoron, there is little debate that taxes are necessary for the functioning and delivering of public goods and services. Regardless of one's views on taxes, there are several criteria that determine when a levied tax is considered a good tax.

A tax is considered a good tax if the following criteria are met:

- Horizontal equity: people in same economic circumstances should pay the same taxes;
- Vertical equity: people with a higher ability to pay should pay a higher percentage;
- Stability: regardless of the state of the economy, the tax can produce the same level of revenue;
- Sufficiency: tax revenues should be able to fund government programs now and in the future;
- Simplicity: low administrative costs, in that the costs of administrating the tax are both efficient and low; and
- Neutrality: the implementation of the tax does not change either the willingness and ability of the producers to stay in the market or the willingness and ability of consumers to leave the market of the particular good or service being taxed.

Incidence of a Tax

Tax incidence is sometimes considered a component of a tax like the base, rate, and structure. Other economists consider tax incidence a criteria for a good tax. Tax incidence refers to the question of who pays. A goal of a sales tax is to tax the consumer, since it is a consumption tax. The incidence of the sales tax is clearly on the consumer and is properly allocated, because the consumer does indeed pay the sales tax. A tax where the incidence is not so clear is the corporate tax. The corporate tax incidence is a topic of considerable debate. While the corporate income tax is calculated based on corporate income, does the corporation really pay the tax? Is the tax liability passed on to consumers in the form of higher prices? Do the employees pay with lower wages? Do the stockholders receive lower dividends, essentially paying the tax? Tax incidence is almost always a debate among economists, in terms of who is really paying the taxes. One thing is certain: people pay taxes, regardless of their business, personal, or social structure.

David A. Dieterle

See Also Laffer, Arthur; Laffer Curve; Private Property; Public Goods

Further Reading

Bartlett, Donald L., and James B. Steele. 1994. *America: Who Really Pays the Taxes?* New York: Touchstone.

Internal Revenue Service. N.d. www.irs.gov.

La Bell, Laura. 2011. *How Taxation Works*. New York: The Rosen Publishing Group.

Miller, Roger Leroy. 2014. *Economics Today*. 17th ed. Upper Saddle River, NJ: Pearson Education, Inc.

Murphy, Liam, and Thomas Nagel. 2002. *The Myth of Ownership: Taxes and Justice*. New York: Oxford University Press.

Steuerle, C. Eugene. 1992. *The Tax Decade: How Taxes Came to Dominate the Public Agenda*. Washington, DC: Urban Institute Press.

Resources for Teachers

Cross-Curricular Connections. 2009. "Tic Tac Taxes." econedlink. http://www.econedlink.org/lessons/index.php?lid=370&type=educator.

IRS. N.d. "Understanding Taxes: Teacher." http://apps.irs.gov/app/understandingTaxes/teacher/index.jsp.

Lesson Corner. N.d. "Taxes Lesson Plans." http://www.lessoncorner.com/Social_Studies/Economics/Taxes.

Telecommunications Reform Act of 1996

The Telecommunications Reform Act of 1996 was the first major overhaul of telecommunications law since the Communications Act of 1934. The Communications Act of 1934 created the Federal Communications Commission (FCC) to regulate and oversee the telegraph, telephone, and radio sectors of the communications industry. Its oversight was later expanded to include the new cable television and satellite sectors of the communications industry along with issuing broadcast licenses. The FCC was also given the enforcement responsibilities to regulate communications signals and had the ability to fine broadcasting companies that violated the rules and regulations of the FCC.

The FCC added censorship to its list of duties as it took on a more dynamic role in the communications industry. It became the communications censor as it judged content appropriate or inappropriate on the radio and television stations. The communications industry changed in the 1980s, when the Bell telephone monopoly was ordered to disband. Yet the FCC was not disbanded.

The Telecommunications Reform Act of 1996 changed the way we work, live, and learn. Immediately effective once signed by President Bill Clinton electronically on February 8, 1996, it made major changes in laws affecting cable TV and telecommunications. It was the first piece of legislation to address Internet access. The 335-page law specifies how local telephone carriers can compete, how and under what circumstances local exchange carriers (LEC) can provide long-distance services, and the deregulation of cable TV rates.

The White House Web site suggested that telecommunications reform had to simultaneously encourage competition and promote private investment while providing parents with control technologies to oversee the viewing habits of children. The reform was also aimed at improving universal access and media protections regarding the right of free speech. The Telecommunications Reform Act was aimed at preparing the U.S. economy for the fast-growing and expanding information society.

In order to promote access, the act called for schools, libraries, and hospitals to be connected to the information superhighway by the year 2000. This goal had to allow for family autonomy. Thus, the act included a provision that new televisions be built with a "V-chip." A V-chip is a device that allows parents control over what their children watch on television. A new ratings system was also established for television stations to display on-screen during programs.

In order to protect a diversity of viewpoints and voices among the media, the act limited the number of stations one entity can own to stations that reach up to 35 percent of all national TV viewers, and kept existing rules that forbid one company from owning two TV stations in a local market, or a newspaper and TV station in the same market, or a newspaper and cable in the same market. The act also maintains the ownership ban of a cable company and a broadcast company in the same market.

The White House Web site suggests that in order to promote competition, the act "breaks down the Berlin Walls of regulation that previously kept telephone companies from competing with one another, while keeping safeguards in place to ensure competition and serve the public interest."

Despite the changes brought about by the act, there were many disgruntled interest groups, including consumers, policy makers, and businesses. When the act was passed in 1996, many Internet and communications goods and products we take for granted today did not exist. The swift development of the Internet and Internet products has created issues in today's communications industry that are not addressed by the act. The issues that critics of the act would like to see addressed deal with Internet broadband and bandwidth issues, such as broadband classifications and Internet piracy.

As the world becomes more connected through the Internet and Web-based news and information become the norm, there is a growing concern that the current regulations pertaining to ownership of newspapers and radio stations should be reexamined. There are First Amendment concerns regarding the communications decency elements of the act. The Telecommunications Reform Act of 1996 remains the latest word on the fast-changing and growing communications sector of the American economy.

Maura Donnelly

See Also Constitution of the United States (see Appendix); Market Capitalism; Private Property; Public Goods

Further Reading

Brock, Gerald W. 1994. *Telecommunication Policy for the Information Age: From Monopoly to Competition.* Cambridge, MA: President and Fellows of Harvard College.

Goldfarb, Charles B. 2006. *Telecommunications Act: Competition, Innovation, and Reform.* New York: Nova Science Publishers.

Shelley, Gary B. 2004. *Business Data Communications: Introductory Concepts and Techniques.* 4th ed. Stamford, CT: Cengage Learning.

Resources for Teachers

Council for Economic Education Technology Staff. 2012. "Goods and Services: Some Are Private, Some Are Not." econedlink. http://www.econedlink.org/lessons/index.php?lid=978&type=educator.

Tennessee Valley Authority (TVA)

The Tennessee Valley Authority (TVA) was established in 1933. The TVA was established to deliver low-cost electricity to the Tennessee Valley and manage the region's natural resources. The Tennessee Valley Authority includes all or parts of the states of Tennessee, Georgia, Alabama, Kentucky, Virginia, Mississippi, and North Carolina, encompassing 80,000 square miles and serving over 9 million people. The TVA has grown to be the largest provider of power by a public entity in the United States. Originally funded as part of Roosevelt's New Deal, the Tennessee Valley Authority is now totally financed through power delivery sales.

History of the Tennessee Valley Authority

On May 18, 1933, Congress passed and President Franklin D. Roosevelt signed the Tennessee Valley Authority Act. A novel business structure in 1933, the TVA Act created a government agency with the characteristics of a private business.

As part of President Roosevelt's New Deal recovery programs, the TVA built dams in the Tennessee River to turn the river's power into electricity. The TVA aimed to create much more than just electricity. It was also intended to enrich the land; to create fish-filled lakes that would, in turn, increase tourism; and to provide jobs for the residents of the Tennessee Valley. Although the TVA achieved some of the goals, it was not well received by everyone. Farmers whose lands were permanently flooded by the backwaters the dams created were unhappy. Also, some business leaders considered the government-sponsored agency an unfair competitor in the electric industry. They argued that the TVA could charge extremely low rates with which private industries could not compete.

The Tennessee Valley was a microcosm of the Great Depression. The valley's farmland had been depleted. Farmers had smaller-than-normal crop yields, and thus smaller incomes than normal. Timber lands had been laid bare. The one resource remaining was the rivers in the region. One role of the TVA was to build dams to generate electricity, flood control, and better navigation of the rivers. As Roosevelt's New Deal job creation unfolded, the TVA was a prime component. The TVA was an educational unit teaching farmers how to use fertilizers and improve crop yields. Jobs were created to plant trees for forests, re-create wildlife and fish habitat, and operate the dams to generate electricity. These many efforts attracted new industry and more jobs to the region.

By the 1950s, 650 miles of navigation had been channeled through the Tennessee River. The TVA was the largest supplier of electricity in the United States. By 1959, the TVA had become a self-financing public-private corporation. By the 1960s, the Tennessee Valley had seen significant economic growth in agriculture and industry. The TVA continued to grow and adapt as the region grew. Through private financing and growth, electricity costs were some of the lowest in the nation.

Additional change came to the TVA during the 1990s. The TVA was forced to reduce operating costs and workforce and delay its nuclear plant plans while increasing power generation. As the twenty-first century began, the TVA focused on combining environmental issues and economic development in the region. In 2004, the TVA corporate structure was changed by Congress to a nine-member part-time board, replacing the full-time three-member board. The TVA returned to building a nuclear plant in 2007 with the approval of the Watts Bar Nuclear Unit 2. The TVA supported new environmental policies with lower carbon emission standards in 2008. The TVA worked closely with the regional leaders to improve the region's environment.

Present-Day TVA

The Tennessee Valley Authority continued to improve its business model. The TVA's vision for the future focused on cleaner air, increased nuclear production, and improved efficiency in power delivery. The Bellefonte nuclear plant was approved for completion by 2020.

In regards to improving the environment, beyond the continuation of the nuclear plant construction, the TVA began working with the EPA to disconnect 59 coal-fired plants by 2017. Since 1977, the TVA has spent $5.3 billion on clean air technology, reaching new heights in the reduction of sulfur dioxide and nitrogen oxide emissions.

Tracy L. Ripley

See Also Environmental Protection Agency (EPA); New Deal; Public Goods; Roosevelt, Franklin Delano

Further Reading

Culvahouse, Tim, ed. 2007. *The Tennessee Valley Authority: Design and Persuasion.* New York: Princeton Architectural Press.

Nash, Gary B. 1997. *American Odyssey.* New York: Glencoe/McGraw-Hill.

Tennessee Valley Authority. N.d. "Tennessee Valley Authority." www.tva.com.

Resources for Teachers

Classroom. N.d. "Lesson Plans for 'TVA: Electricity for All.'" http://newdeal.feri.org/classrm/classtva.htm.

teachinghistory.org. N.d. "Tennessee Valley Authority." http://teachinghistory.org/history-content/national-resources/23637.

Thatcher, Margaret

Born: October 13, 1925, in Grantham, England; Died: April 8, 2013, in London, England; Prime Minister of the United Kingdom, 1979–1990; Awarded the Presidential Medal of Freedom in 1991; Major Works: *The Downing Street Years* (1993), *The Path to Power* (1995).

Margaret Thatcher made her mark in British politics and economics. The first woman to lead a major Western democracy, she was the British prime minister for more than 11 years. Thatcher reshaped almost every part of British politics and helped create a school of conservative, conviction-led politics. She left office in 1990 after winning three consecutive general elections, and died on April 8, 2013, in London, England.

Thatcher was born in Grantham, England, on October 13, 1925. Her parents were Methodists, and her childhood was based on an ethos of self-help, charitable work, and truthfulness. It was this upbringing that helped her to become the powerful politician and speaker that she was known to be. Her father was a local councilor in Grantham and would often come home and talk to Thatcher about the issues that had arisen in his work. Thatcher went on to study chemistry at Oxford under future Nobel Prize winner Dorothy Hodge, an experience that would greatly influence her outlook in politics. While at Oxford, she rose to become president of the Student Conservative Association, clearly demonstrating her interest in politics.

In 1951, Thatcher left chemistry behind and ran as the conservative candidate for the labor safe seat of Dartmouth. She failed to win the seat twice, but nevertheless gained national publicity. Her experience standing for election in Dartmouth also helped shape her political style; she was known to speak with poise and confidence on issues that mattered to voters.

In the 1950s, Thatcher studied to become a lawyer, and in 1959, she was elected to serve in England's Parliament as MP for Finchley. During the late 1960s, she established her place among senior figures of the Conservative Party as a shadow minister. In 1970, Thatcher achieved a cabinet position in Ted Heath's government as education secretary, which was not an easy position to gain or hold. Facing a bleak economy, she imposed a series of harsh budget cuts, the most notorious being the removal of a program left over from the days of the Great Depression that guaranteed a daily pint of milk to schoolchildren between the ages of 7 and 11. The abolition of this program gave Thatcher the nickname "milk snatcher," which haunted her for the rest of her career. The early 1970s also saw student radicalism at its peak, and Thatcher's speeches were often disrupted by protesters. In 1975, Thatcher was elected as the Conservative Party leader and became the first woman to lead a British political party. In 1976, she earned her iconic nickname, "Iron Lady." It was given to her by the Soviets for her uncompromising speeches against them. However, while she did not soften her criticisms of the Soviet system, when Gorbachev became the new leader of the Soviet Union, Thatcher pronounced him someone whom she could "do business with."

In the 1974 general election, no party had a majority. The Conservative Party won the popular vote, but the Labour Party took the most seats. Heath tried to negotiate a coalition with the Liberal Party but failed, and subsequently resigned. The Labour Party, lead by Wilson, had established itself as the minority government. By the end of 1975, there had been some economic growth, but inflation was still high. In 1976, Wilson resigned and was replaced by Callaghan. During the winter of 1978–1979, public opinion was against the Labour government. "The Winter of Discontent," as it was dubbed, was characterized by widespread strikes by trade unions in response to the ongoing pay caps imposed by Callaghan's Labour Party in an effort to control inflation. The government's inability to control the strikes helped the conservatives (led by Thatcher) win a Parliamentary majority in the 1979 general election. The very next day, Thatcher took office, becoming the first female prime minister of the United Kingdom.

During Thatcher's first term as Prime Minister, from 1979 to 1983, her government pledged to check and reverse Britain's economic decline. Although the key economic goal during the first Thatcher government was controlling inflation, Thatcher took steps toward privatization through less government intervention in the economy, less government spending, and lower taxes. Thatcher's privatization was associated with marked improvements in performance (especially in labor productivity). Regulation was also expanded to compensate for loss of direct government control. At first, however, the measures she took were painful and produced no noticeable change in the economy. She did cut the abhorred direct taxes; however, she increased indirect taxes to make up for this loss of income. By the end of Thatcher's first term, more than 3 million British citizens were unemployed. Thatcher's reelection was only made certain by the British victory in the Falklands War. The British response to the Argentine invasion of the Falkland Islands in 1982 displayed the firm and careful touch for which Thatcher was known. When diplomacy failed, Great Britain's military action was quick and successful. The Falklands were back under British control in 1982. By fighting for the islands in a calm and efficient manner, Thatcher not only ensured her reelection but also increased public confidence in her.

In 1984, during Thatcher's second term (1983–1987), the government found itself dealing with a yearlong miners' strike. In 1986, the Irish Republican Army tried to assassinate Thatcher by bombing her hotel in Brighton during the Conservative Party Conference. She survived unharmed, but some of her closest colleagues were injured or killed. Thatcher proceeded to negotiate the Anglo-Irish Agreement of 1985 to improve security and cooperation between Britain and Ireland. In 1985, Thatcher's reforms aimed at curbing the influence of the trade unions defeated the miners' union, proving that the reforms would endure. Thatcher, however, faced heavy criticism from within her own party for her decision to allow U.S. warplanes to fly from Britain's bases to attack Libya in 1986. But the economy continued to improve during the period from 1983 to 1987. With the strong economy, in June 1987, the Conservative government was reelected and Thatcher returned as prime minister for a third term.

Thatcher's third and final term was her most ambitious one. In 1988, she took measures to reform the education system by introducing a national curriculum. She also introduced a new tax system for local government, commonly known as the poll tax, which replaced the property tax. All of these measures, however, were controversial and stirred up heavy criticism. It did not help that the previously booming economy started to decline, and the public was made aware of a division within the government over different styles of management. Thatcher found herself at odds with her foreign secretary on everything involving European integration.

In 1990, many of her cabinet ministers had already begun to desert her by the time Michael Heseltine launched a challenge to her party leadership. Although Thatcher won the first ballot, she did not win by a wide enough margin to secure an outright victory. She resigned on November 28, 1990, and was succeeded by her chancellor, John Major.

After 1990, Thatcher remained an internationally recognized political figure, though the Conservative Party distanced itself from her. She wrote two memoirs, *The Downing Street Years* (1993) and *The Path to Power* (1995). She began touring and lectured around the world. In 1991, Thatcher received the Presidential Medal of Freedom from U.S. president George Bush.

Thatcher remains an intensely controversial figure in Britain. Critics claim that she was harsh and uncaring, pointing to her treatment of the coal miners in the 1980s, the withdrawal of free milk for children, and the controversial poll tax, while defenders point to how much Britain's economy grew and changed under her administration. Both critics and supporters recognize her time in government as a period of significant change in British political history.

Margaret Thatcher died of a stroke on April 8, 2013, in London, England, at the age of 87.

Shima Sadaghiyani

See Also Hayek, Friedrich von; Market Capitalism; Reagan, Ronald

Further Reading

Campbell, John. 2012. *The Iron Lady: Margaret Thatcher: Grocer's Daughter to Iron Lady*. New York: Vintage Books.

Thatcher, Margaret. 1993. *The Downing Street Years*. London: HarperCollins.

Thatcher, Margaret. 1995. *The Path to Power*. London: HarperCollins.

Young, Hugo. 1989. *The Iron Lady: A Biography of Margaret Thatcher*. New York: Farrar Strauss Giroux.

Theory of Public Choice

The theory of public choice (or public choice theory) is rooted in the application of economic principles used by economists to understand and predict people's actions in the marketplace. In addition, it also deals with understanding government or political behavior in collective decision-making situations. The theory states that no matter which role one plays in the collective decision-making process—voter, elected official, or interest group—people are largely motivated by self-interest.

Public choice theory dates to the 1950s, and evolved throughout the early 1970s. The founders of the theory of public choice include Anthony Downs, James Buchanan, Duncan Black, Kenneth Joseph Arrow, Gordon Tullock, Mancur Olsen, and William A. Niskanen.

Modern public choice theory begins with Anthony Downs, who is known for the idea that voters are not always aware of current political issues. He believes that the vote of one person generally does not decide an election. Therefore, most informed voters reason that their votes will be canceled out by those of uninformed voters, making their time investment in becoming informed a waste. The informed voter then rationalizes a zero-sum game in being knowledgeable about the issues. As a result, since most voters are easily influenced, politicians do what they can to get votes and win an election. Downs also believes that some people vote simply to preserve the democratic practice and that people vote based on their pocketbooks or how well-off they are, or are promised to be (Pressman, 2004).

James Buchanan is considered to be a founder of public choice theory, and earned a Nobel Prize in Economic Sciences in 1986. He is famous for referring to the theory as "politics without romance" (Buchanan, 2003), meaning that there are many self-interested factors that influence the decision making of politicians and bureaucrats.

In 1962, James Buchanan and Gordon Tullock wrote *The Calculus of Consent: Logical Foundations of Constitutional Democracy*, which describes how economists view the organization of the political society. They examine how government officials, politicians, and bureaucrats use their self-interest when making decisions on behalf of the public. Both men also look to the Constitution as a basis for how the government works and how it can be regulated. In this work, they also emphasize voting and how majority rule is necessary when approaching public issues. In the end, if everyone is aware of the rules in democratic society, even self-interested politicians are not dangerous to society as a whole because the Constitution itself places limitations on certain things such as the powers of the government. These ideas have evolved into a theory called constitutional economics.

Mancur Olson, the author of *The Logic of Collective Action: Public Goods and the Theory of Groups* (1965), is known for the idea that public choice is heavily influenced by interest groups who seek to redistribute wealth. Despite this, these groups often struggle to gain support from those who would benefit the most from their work. Interest groups, or lobbyists, fight for specific causes or reforms for citizens and are rewarded by getting politicians to listen to their concerns. For example, an interest group might be pushing for a higher minimum wage, and might ask a particular congressperson or senator to help introduce a bill on the issue.

The theory of public choice applies economic principles to understanding and predicting the decision-making actions of legislators. Legislators, elected to carry out the best interests of their constituents, make decisions on behalf of many others, not just themselves. Legislators may also engage in pork-barrel politics or logrolling in an effort to trade votes on one issue to gain something in another area. Pork-barrel politics involves a politician promising something to his or her constituents in an effort to gain their support. He or she might promise more spending for local public schools, to be tough on crime, or to build a new public park in an effort to gain their votes. Logrolling involves politicians supporting the bill of another politician in an effort to gain support for a bill that is important to them. Some criticize politicians for these practices, but they are used by politicians to gain things for the districts they represent. In this case, the constituents would be pleased with their legislators because they are bringing things to their local city or town.

Another element emphasized in the theory of public choice is government failure and the idea that sometimes government intervention in the marketplace can do more harm than good. For example, a government of a country decides to take over its health care system in an effort to streamline it and make it more affordable for citizens, but instead makes the health care system worse off. When a government intervenes in the economy, its goal is to put something in place that the people will view favorably. Perhaps this new health care reform policy is what people favor, but at the same time it puts more power in the hands of the government, and too much government involvement can cause the government to fail.

Today, the theory of public choice still focuses on collective decision making and its impact on the political world. Political parties are increasingly working toward appealing to the median voter, and voters seek to weigh the costs and benefits of policies when voting for a particular political party.

Angela M. LoPiccolo

See Also Arrow, Kenneth; Buchanan, James; Olson, Mancur; Tullock, Gordon

Further Reading

Arrow, Kenneth J. 1963. *Social Choice and Individual Values*. 2nd ed. New York: Wiley.

Black, Duncan. 1958. *The Theory of Committees and Elections*. Dordrecht, NL: Kluwer Academic.

Buchanan, James M. 2003. "Public Choice: Politics without Romance." *Policy* 19, no. 3: 13–18.

Downs, Anthony. 1957. *An Economic Theory of Democracy*. New York: Harper and Row.

Lee, Dwight R. 1913. "Politics, Ideology, and the Power of Public Choice." *Virginia Law Review* 74: 191–98.

McDowell, George R. 1978. "An Analytical Framework for Extension Community Development Programming in Local Government." *Agricultural and Applied Economics Association* 60: 416–24.

Niskanen, Jr., William A. 1971. *Bureaucracy and Representative Government*. Chicago: Aldine Transaction.

Olson, Mancur. 1965. *The Logic of Collective Action: Public Goods and the Theory of Groups*. Cambridge: Harvard University Press.

Pennington, Mark. 2000. *Planning and the Political Market: Public Choice and the Politics of Government Failure*. New Brunswick, NJ: The Althlone Press.

Pressman, Steven. 2004. "What Is Wrong with Public Choice." *Journal of Post Keynesian Economics* 27: 3–18.

Shughart, William F., and Robert D. Tollison. 2005. "Public Choice in the New Century." *Public Choice* 124: 1–18.

Shughart, William F., and Robert D. Tollison. 2005. "The Unfinished Business of Public Choice." *Public Choice* 124: 237–47.

Tullock, Gordon, Arthur Seldon, and Gordon L. Brady. 2002. *Government Failure: A Primer in Public Choice*. Washington, DC: Cato Institute.

Resources for Teachers

Buchanan, James M., and Robert D. Tollison, eds. 1984. *The Theory of Public Choice—II*. Ann Arbor: University of Michigan Press.

Buchanan, James M., and Gordon Tullock. 1962. *The Calculus of Consent: Logical Foundations of Constitutional Democracy*. Ann Arbor: University of Michigan Press.

Shaw, Jane S. 2008. "Public Choice Theory." *The Concise Encyclopedia of Economics*. http://www.econlib.org/library/Enc1/PublicChoiceTheory.html.

Tobin, James

Born: March 5, 1918, in Champaign, Illinois; Died: March 11, 2002, in New Haven, Connecticut; American; macroeconomics, monetary policy, neo-Keynesian economics, portfolio theory, Nobel Prize (1981); Major Works: *Essays in Economics* (vols. 1–4, 1987–1996), *Full Employment and Growth* (1996).

James Tobin was an American economist who spent his long career explaining and developing John Maynard Keynes's *General Theory of Employment, Interest and Money*, leaving a legacy as an essential neo-Keynesian. Tobin was a strong advocate of government intervention in the economy to avoid recessions and stabilize output. He made numerous significant economic contributions, including his portfolio theory, which won him the 1981 Nobel Prize in Economics. Other notable contributions by Tobin included the Tobin's q, the Tobin tax, and the Tobin model. Tobin died in 2002.

James Tobin was born on March 5, 1918, in Champaign, Illinois. His father was the publicity director for the University of Illinois athletics department, and Tobin attended University High School, run by the University of Illinois College of Education. Tobin graduated summa cum laude in economics from Harvard University in 1939 and stayed to complete his MA degree in 1940. His doctoral studies were interrupted by work at the Office of Price Administration and Civilian Supply and the War Production Board in Washington, D.C., prior to World War II. Following the attack on Pearl Harbor, Tobin enlisted in the U.S. Navy. After serving on the destroyer USS *Kearny* for four years, he returned to Harvard and finished his PhD in 1947. He remained at Harvard as a junior fellow until 1950.

In 1950, Tobin began his career at Yale University, becoming a full professor in 1955, and in 1957, receiving the honor of becoming the Sterling Professor of Economics. He formally retired in 1988, but stayed at Yale to continue working on his theories.

Tobin became interested in the subject of economics for two reasons: he enjoyed the intellectual challenge, and he wanted to use economics for comprehending world events. Tobin saw economics as a means to prevent human misery from reoccurring. Tobin's fundamental concern was how economic policies affected people's lives. He believed that the federal government could use fiscal and monetary measures to benefit society. At Harvard as a young freshman, he quickly became a convert to the new theories of Keynes. He spent the remainder of his life explaining and developing theoretical supports to Keynesian economics. He wrote extensively as a pioneer in the development of macroeconomics.

Besides his treasured teaching at Yale in New Haven, Tobin also served as director of the Cowles Foundation for Research in Economics from 1955 to 1961, and again from 1964 to 1965. Tobin occasionally left his professorial post at Yale, commonly as a visiting professor at another academic institution or as a consultant, but one significant departure from academics was serving on the Council of Economic Advisers at the express request of newly elected President John F. Kennedy from 1961 to 1962. That Council produced the *Economic Report of 1962*, dubbed by the media as the "new economics." Tobin himself described this report as a comprehensive account of the theories and practices for economic growth.

Tobin was author or editor of 16 books and over 400 articles concerning economics. The topics ranged from econometrics to macroeconomics, monetary theory, monetary policy, fiscal policy, public finance, and portfolio theory and asset markets. Tobin is remembered for his work in financial analysis, especially the portfolio theory, which explained that investors should balance portfolios with both low- and high-risk assets to minimize risk. Tobin described his portfolio theory as not putting all of one's investment eggs in a single basket.

It was accepted monetary policy that interest rates could influence capital investment. Tobin felt, however, that there was another important consideration. He developed Tobin's q, a measure to predict whether there will be an increase or decrease in capital investment. The q was a mathematical ratio between the market value of an asset and the cost to replace it. If the ratio is greater than one, new investment will be profitable. If less than one, new investment in similar equipment will not be profitable. Tobin suggests that at this point companies tend not to invest in new plants and equipment, but decide instead to purchase existing companies.

Another of Tobin's ideas is the Tobin tax. The Tobin tax is a small tax on currency transactions in international markets to reduce short-term currency speculation. He felt that such a tax would help stabilize exchange markets without being a burden on free trade. Today, his tax idea is often proposed as a way to raise revenue. He also developed a regression to analyze spending decisions called the Tobin model, an econometric model investigating dependent variables within a model.

Tobin served in many professional associations and received numerous awards beyond the Nobel Prize in 1981. He was awarded the John Bates Clark Medal in 1966 and was president of the American Economic Association in 1971. Tobin will be remembered through his prolific research and publications as one of the most influential macroeconomists of the twentieth century, especially in his lifelong contributions in explaining and elaborating on the theories of Keynes.

James Tobin died on March 11, 2002, in New Haven, Connecticut.

Jean Kujawa

See Also Contractionary Fiscal Policy; Expansionary Fiscal Policy; Fiscal Policy; Heller, Walter; Keynes, John Maynard; Okun, Arthur; Taxes

Selected Works by James Tobin

Tobin, James. 2003. *World Finance and Economic Stability: Selected Essays of James Tobin.* London: Edward Elgar.

Tobin, James. 1996. *Full Employment and Growth.* London: Edward Elgar.

Tobin, James. 1987–1996. *Essays in Economics.* Vols. 1–4. New Haven, CT: Yale University Press.

Tobin, James. 1979. *Asset Accumulation and Economic Activity: Reflections on Contemporary Macroeconomic Theory.* New Haven, CT: Yale University Press.

Tobin, James. 1969. "A General Equilibrium Approach to Monetary Theory." *Journal of Money, Credit, and Banking* 1, no. 1: 15–29.

Tobin, James. 1958. "Liquidity Preference as Behavior towards Risk." *Review of Economic Studies* 25, no. 1: 65–86.

Tobin, James, and Stephen S. Golub. 1998. *Money, Credit, and Capital.* New York: Irwin/McGraw-Hill.

Selected Works about James Tobin

Breit, William, and Roger Spencer, eds. 1986. *Lives of the Laureates, Seven Nobel Economists.* "James Tobin." Cambridge, MA: MIT Press.

Nobelprize.org. 2012. "James Tobin—Autobiography." July 15. http://www.nobelprize.org /nobel_prizes/economics/laureates/1981/tobin-autobio.html.

Nobelprize.org. 2012. "James Tobin—Prize Lecture: Money and Finance in the Macro-Economic Process." July 8. http://www.nobelprize.org/nobel_prizes/economics/laureates/1981 /tobin-lecture.html.

Trade-Offs

The title line from the popular song *You Can't Always Get What You Want* by the Rolling Stones (a British rock band of the 1960s) announces the basic dictum of economics. Anyone exposed to this song was, perhaps unknowingly, being introduced to the prime economic concept of trade-offs. While the resources available to produce economic goods and services are limited, the desire to obtain the goods and services is limitless. Economic wants are unlimited yet the ability to produce goods and services is limited. Therefore, it is up to an economic system to make choices and decide the trade-offs of an economy. When decisions are made to allocate resources to a set of goods and services, the same decision is also claiming that society is not going to allocate those resources to other goods and services. There is a trade-off between what to produce and what not to produce.

A trade-off describes what you sacrifice to get something else. Scarcity forces people and societies to make choices. And choices always involve a trade-off. Trade-offs are part of everyone's daily life. Whether it is how we spend our income or what we do with our time, one's resources are never enough. Every time we make a decision we are going to give up the possibility of having something else or doing something with that resource. Every trade-off also has a cost and a benefit that must be considered.

Every choice has a cost, called the "opportunity cost." Opportunity cost refers to the cost of not choosing what was given up. For example, one might choose to read this entry instead of making a sandwich. The trade-off is giving up time needed to make the sandwich for the chance to read. Opportunity cost refers to what was given up. In this example, the opportunity to eat was relinquished. Most decisions are not all or nothing decisions. They are made incrementally, or at the margin. This is known as "marginal analysis."

Our world is one of trade-offs and opportunity costs at all levels of life. Since all decisions involve a trade-off and opportunity cost, trade-offs are made by individuals, families, companies, governmental agencies at all levels, and more and more, globally. All these entities have limited resources and therefore must give up something with each decision. Not all decisions are made in the same way. Companies make decisions via their leadership or stockholders. Government decisions are made by voters or those who are voted into office. Consumers make decisions in the marketplace. Not all trade-offs are identical. One consumer may choose a hamburger over French fries, while another consumer may choose a hamburger over a soda.

Another type of trade-off made by economic systems is between the social goals of an economy. One society may decide that economic security is more important than economic freedom. Yet another economic system may choose economic freedom over economic security. While both may be worthwhile, an economic system and society must make a decision as to which is more important. Societal and economic system decisions, and their trade-offs, are made by political leaders, voters when they vote, or maybe consumers when they vote with their money in the marketplace.

Individuals face similar dilemmas. All of the choices that individuals make in the marketplace involve a trade-off of another good or service. In a market economy, the decisions and trade-offs of consumers determine which goods and services will be produced and which will not. As a result, the market economy decisions of consumers determine which businesses will be successful and which will fail. Any situation that involves losing one quality or aspect of something in return for gaining another quality or aspect can be considered a trade-off. Everyone, everywhere, has been forced into making decisions with trade-offs. The decision to read this entry has taken away the time to spend doing something else. The term may reference a decision made with full comprehension of both the up side and the down side of a particular choice; it can also be used in an evolutionary context, in which case the selection process acts as the "decision maker."

This concept does not apply only to decisions involving money. Every time you are asked, "Would you like fries with that?" or your Amazon checkout reminds you that there is free shipping on orders over $25, you are being asked to practice marginalism and make trade-offs that will afford you the greatest satisfaction for your buying power. Producers, in an attempt to maximize profits, will seasonally adjust the size of the workforce and the items produced. If you want to lifeguard in the winter or eat a mince pie in July, you are likely to be disappointed. At times like that, it is a good idea to remember the wisdom of the Rolling Stones.

Maura Donnelly

See Also Private Property; Public Goods; Taxes

Further Reading

Smith, Estellie. 2000. *Trade and Trade-Offs: Using Resources, Making Choices, and Taking Risks.* Lake Zurich, IL: Waveland Press.

Weber, Elke U., with Jonathan Baron and Graham Loomes, eds. 2001. *Conflict and Tradeoffs in Decision Making.* Cambridge: Cambridge University Press.

Winter, Harold. 2013. *Trade-Offs: An Introduction to Economic Reasoning and Social Issues.* 2nd ed. Chicago: University of Chicago Press.

Resources for Teachers

EcEdWeb Economics Lesson. N.d. "Give and Take." http://ecedweb.unomaha.edu/lessons/giveandtake.htm#.

Foundation for Teaching Economics. N.d. "Trade Offs and Opportunity Cost." http://www.fte.org/teacher-resources/lesson-plans/rslessons/trade-offs-and-opportunity-cost/.

Page, Brian. 2013. "Mobile Phones Matter." econedlink. http://www.econedlink.org/lessons/index.php?lid=1150&type=educator.

Transaction Costs

Transaction costs are the costs associated with an economic exchange. All decisions involve costs, but those costs related to buying or selling in a market are the transaction costs. The costs that accompany buying or selling in a market typically fall into three broad categories, and do not include the actual market price involved in the trade. These categories are generally sorted into search and information costs, bargaining costs, and policing or enforcement costs. Search and information costs are incurred when a party is trying to determine what goods are available in the market and which seller has the lowest price. Bargaining costs are those costs that are encountered when trying to come to an agreement with the other party, as negotiations take place and the terms of agreement or contract are drawn up. The policing or enforcement costs include making sure that the other party sticks to the contract and following through with appropriate legal action if not.

Transaction costs, sometimes known as frictional costs or coordination costs, are a critical factor in determining whether an exchange will take place. They include the time and effort it takes to search for the best supplier of a product or service, the cost of reaching an agreement and carrying out a market transaction, and the cost of monitoring and enforcing the implementation of that contract. These costs differ from ordinary production costs because they are measured in time, effort, and frustration. This is more difficult to measure because transaction costs are not as easily identifiable as standard production costs like labor and capital. Therefore, these costs are not reflected in economic measurements like Gross Domestic Product (GDP). According to some estimates, these costs might amount to as much as a third of total GDP, were they included.

Transactions are most likely to occur when the costs of the agreement or trade are small in comparison to the benefit of the exchange. However, transactions do not always occur in a market. The chief reason for this is because markets sometimes break down, or fail to perform properly, particularly when the transaction costs are too high. This explains the creation of firms. Firms exist to keep transaction costs to a minimum. Firms sometimes find it beneficial to provide a service "in house" rather than contact an outside firm for the same service. The determination of whether to produce within a firm or not is derived from a consideration of the transaction costs.

According to economist Oliver E. Williamson, among the things to be considered in a transaction are the frequency, specificity, and uncertainty surrounding a transaction. Williamson popularized his theory about the determinants of transaction costs in a 1995 publication called "Transaction-Cost Economics." He received a Nobel Prize for Economics in 1999 for his contributions to the field. Most credit Williamson for extending the reasoning of Ronald Coase, who did not coin the term "transaction cost," but used the concept to describe when certain economic tasks would be performed by firms rather than in a market.

Coase received the Nobel Prize in Economics in 1991 for his 1937 work entitled "The Nature of the Firm," which outlined the significance of transaction costs. Coase showed that organizations are created to reduce market transaction costs. He explained that the operations of doing business are often extremely costly in both time and money. Thus, sometimes the additional costs of using a market can lead to a more efficient production process within a firm. This is even more likely to happen when property rights are not preserved, in which case markets might work poorly or not at all.

Transaction costs are also faced in decision-making processes by political groups, whether domestic, regional, or international. Any group that makes decisions by some form of voting endures transaction costs, the highest of which are sustained by groups needing unanimous collective decisions. Consensus of this type is the most burdensome in terms of cost because it takes the longest to achieve. Transaction costs are low in a dictatorship, where only one person makes the decisions, but this rarely makes the majority happy. Thus, a simple majority is probably the best mechanism for both minimizing transaction costs and letting the majority prevail. Interestingly, in politics, there does not seem to be as much of a drive to minimize transaction costs as there is in the economic sector. The more local the group, the more likely a transaction-cost minimizing mechanism is to be adopted, whereas at a regional or international level, unanimity or a supermajority is often favored.

Michelle D. Holowicki

See Also Coase, Ronald; Private Property; Public Goods

Further Reading

Dixit, Avinash. 1996. *The Making of Economic Policy: A Transaction-Cost Politics Perspective.* Boston: The MIT Press.

Groenewegen, John, ed. 1996. *Transaction Cost Economics and Beyond.* Norwell, MA: Kluwer Academic.

Schwartz, Pedro. "Ronald Coase, the Unexpected Economist." Library of Economics and Liberty, October 7. http://www.econlib.org/library/Columns/y2013/SchwartzCoase.html.

Williamson, Oliver. 2013. "Transaction-Cost Economics: The Governance of Contractual Relations." *Journal of Law and Economics* 22, no. 2 (1979): 233–61.

Williamson, Oliver E., and Scott E. Masten. 1999. *The Economics of Transaction Costs.* Northampton, MA: Edward Elgar Publishing.

Resources for Teachers

Foundation for Teaching Economics. N.d. "Lesson 2: Bridges and Barriers to Trade, Activity; The Euro—Currency Exchange and Transaction Costs." http://www.fte.org/teacher-resources/lesson-plans/tradelessons/the-euro-currency-exchange-and-transaction-costs/.

Foundation for Teaching Economics. N.d. "Lesson 5: Transaction Costs—Life in a Soviet Household." http://www.fte.org/teacher-resources/lesson-plans/edsulessons/lesson-5-transaction-costs/.

LessonPlanet. N.d. "23 Transaction Costs Teacher Resources." http://www.lessonplanet.com/search?keywords=transaction+costs&type_ids%5B%5D=357918&button=.

Tullock, Gordon

Born: February 13, 1922, in Rockford, Illinois; American; public choice theory, rent seeking theory; Major Works: *The Calculus of Consent: Logical Foundations of Constitutional*

Democracy (with James Buchanan) (1962), *The Social Dilemma: The Economics of War and Revolution* (1974), *The Economics of Special Privilege and Rent Seeking* (1989).

Gordon Tullock is considered a leader and forward thinker among twenty-first-century classical economists. His contributions in the field of classical economics are impressive and often understated. Tullock's interdisciplinary study of behavioral economics and political theory helped initiate a new focus in economics. His ideas launched a new journal, *Public Choice*, and inspired additional study and research by a new group of economists who became known as the Public Choice Society.

Gordon Tullock was born on February 13, 1922, in Rockford, Illinois. He attended public schools in Rockford before enrolling at the University of Chicago in 1940. He completed the initial two-year program in only a year. He took only one economics course, which was taught by Henry Simons. His progress was interrupted in 1943, however, when he was drafted into the U.S. Army. Tullock was deployed for a brief stint to Europe before being reassigned as a clerk. As the war came to a close, Tullock's unit was demobilized and he was sent home.

Upon returning home, Tullock continued his studies at the University of Chicago where he earned his law degree in 1947. Following a brief experiment in law, where Tullock experienced moderate success in the courtroom, he accepted a position as an officer with the Foreign Service. The Foreign Service took him to Asia for a decade and from 1947 until 1956, he held positions in China, Hong Kong, and Korea. During this time, he also pursued Chinese studies at Yale and Cornell. During this turbulent time in Asia, Tullock learned a substantial amount about the government and its inner workings. Tullock resigned from the Foreign Service upon his return to the United States in 1956.

Tullock served as research director for the Princeton Panel, a subsidiary of the Gallup organization. By this time, Tullock had already published in several journals. In 1958–1959, he secured a postdoctoral fellowship at the Thomas Jefferson Center for Political Economics at the University of Virginia, where he met future Nobel laureate James Buchanan, another classical economist who would be influential in his life. Tullock's seminal paper on applying theory and analysis to majority voting propelled Tullock into a new realm of critical thinkers.

With the publication of *The Calculus of Consent* with Buchanan in 1962, Tullock combined the behavioral economics of choice with political theory. This type of unconventional combination of ideas sparked several other efforts as well. In 1966, Tullock launched a journal called *Papers in Non-Market Decision Making*, which would later be known as *Public Choice*. The journal later inspired a series of monthly meetings, which became a group known as the Public Choice Society. Tullock served the society as its president. Tullock first introduced the idea of rent seeking during this time. Rent seeking is the manipulation of information through lobbying or other means to redistribute existing wealth, as opposed to creating new wealth.

Tullock spent over five decades in university settings. He went from the University of Virginia to Rice University and then to Virginia Polytechnic Institute, now known as Virginia Tech. Along with colleague Charles Goetz, he launched what would be known as the Center for Study of Public Choice in 1968, and was reunited with Buchanan. Tullock's law background provided the basis from which to build a strong foundation in the field. Public choice theory combined economics with political science.

By the 1970s, Blacksburg, Virginia, had become the geographical home of the Center for the Study of Public Choice. An administrative shake-up in Blacksburg during the latter part of the 1970s caused the center to be relocated to George Mason University in 1983. The move for Tullock brought him closer to the epicenter of his universe—Washington, D.C., a place where economics and politics collided.

Tullock accepted a position as the Karl Eller Professor of Economics and Political Science with the University of Arizona in 1987. Tullock brought new energy to the economics faculty in Tucson, which focused on experimental economics, a field of great interest to Tullock. He spent 12 years at the University of Arizona before returning to George Mason University in 1999.

Tullock served his academic communities by publishing journals, articles, and books, and by serving the scholarly community in a variety of other capacities. Tullock was recognized as a distinguished fellow from the American Economic Association in 1998.

Gordon Tullock retired from George Mason University in 2008.

William S. Chappell

See Also Buchanan, James; Simons, Henry; Theory of Public Choice

Selected Works by Gordon Tullock

Tullock, Gordon. 2005. *Public Goods, Redistribution and Rent Seeking*. Northampton, MA: Edward Elgar Publishing.

Tullock, Gordon. 1989. *The Economics of Special Privilege and Rent Seeking*. Boston: Kluwer Academic.

Tullock, Gordon. 1974. *The Social Dilemma: The Economics of War and Revolution*. Blacksburg, VA: University Publications.

Tullock, Gordon, and James Buchanan. 1962. *The Calculus of Consent: Logical Foundations of Constitutional Democracy*. Ann Arbor: University of Michigan Press.

Tullock, Gordon, Arthur Seldon, and Gordon L. Brady. 2002. *Government Failure: A Primer in Public Choice*. Washington, DC: Cato Institute.

Selected Works about Gordon Tullock

George Mason University. "Gordon Tullock." http://economics.gmu.edu/people/gtullockemeritus.

Mercatus Center. N.d. "Gordon Tullock." http://mercatus.org/gordon-tullock.

Rowley, Charles K., and Daniel Houser. 2012. "Life and Times of Gordon Tullock." *Public Choice* 152, nos. 1–2 (July): 3–27.

Tyson, Laura

Born: June 28, 1947, in Bayonne, New Jersey; American; macroeconomics, industrial competitiveness, trade, public policy; Major Works: *The Yugoslav Economic System and*

Its Performance in the 1970s (1980), *Economic Adjustment in Eastern Europe* (1985), *Who's Bashing Whom: Trade-Conflict in High Technology Industries* (1992).

Laura Tyson is an American economist and the S. K. and Angela Chan Professor of Global Management at the Haas School of Business at the University of California, Berkeley. She is an expert in trade and international competitiveness. In addition, she is a member of President Barack Obama's Council of Jobs and Competitiveness, Obama's Economic Recovery Advisory Board (PERAB), and former secretary of state Hillary Clinton's Foreign Affairs Policy Board. She was the first female chair of the Council of Economic Advisers (1993–1995) and then served as part of the President's National Economic Council (1995–1996) during the Clinton administration. She has published books and numerous articles on industrial competitiveness and trade.

Laura D'Andrea Tyson was born on June 28, 1947, in Bayonne, New Jersey. Her father was a World War II GI veteran who became an accountant, and her mother was a housewife. Tyson majored in economics at Smith College, graduating summa cum laude in 1969. She earned her PhD in economics from the Massachusetts Institute of Technology in 1974. Tyson worked as a professor of economics at Princeton University for three years before she moved to the University of California, Berkeley, in 1977. She served as the dean of Berkeley's Haas School of Business from 1998 to 2001 and as the first female dean of the London Business School from 2002 to 2006. She was the only woman to head a major U.S. business school (Berkeley) and she was the first woman to lead a top-10 international business school (London).

Tyson also founded the London Business School's Center for Women in Business. While working in London, the United Kingdom's Department of Trade and Industry appointed Tyson chair of a task force on nonexecutive directors, which authored a recommendation for the recruitment and development of nonexecutive directors. Tyson has since returned to the University of California, Berkeley.

As part of the Obama and Clinton teams, Tyson greatly influenced domestic and international monetary policy. As chair of the Council of Economic Advisers, she provided guidance and analysis on all economic policy concerns, the economic forecasts, and the annual *Economic Report of the President*.

Tyson has published many books and articles on trade, industrial competitiveness, and transitions of European countries to market systems. Her studies include worldwide trends in gender gaps for women in education, economics, politics, and health.

Her academic work centers on globalization, trade liberalization, the impact of high technology, and domestic economics. She regularly promotes the benefits of globalization for domestic economies. Some, however, fear as a member of the Berkeley faculty she may favor protectionist and antiglobalization measures, which are popular ideologies at Berkeley. Tyson advocates concern for these ideas, such as global warming and environmental impact, yet promotes the ethical responsibility to these issues of the businesses involved.

In addition to her work at Berkeley, where she has received the Distinguished Teaching Award, Tyson is also a senior adviser at the McKinsey Global Institute, the Credit Suisse Research Institute, and the Rock Creek Group. She continues to write opinion columns for many sources such as the *New York Times*, *BusinessWeek*, and the *Financial Times*. Tyson is a member of the World Economic Forum's Global Agenda Council; the National Academies' Board on Science, Technology and Economic Policy; and the National Academies Committee on Research Universities, to name a few. She serves on the boards of directors and advisory boards of many companies, such as Morgan Stanley, AT&T, Newman's Own, and the Peter G. Peterson Institute of International Economics.

Kathryn Lloyd Gustafson

See Also Contractionary Fiscal Policy; Expansionary Fiscal Policy; Fiscal Policy; Summers, Lawrence

Selected Works by Laura Tyson

Tyson, Laura. 1992. *Who's Bashing Whom: Trade Conflict in High-Technology Industries*. Washington, DC: Institute for International Economics.

Tyson, Laura. 1985. *Economic Adjustment in Eastern Europe*. RAND Report. San Diego: RAND.

Tyson, Laura. 1980. *The Yugoslav Economic System and Its Performance in the 1970s*. Berkeley: Institute of International Studies, University of California.

Selected Works about Laura Tyson

Cicarelli, James and Julianne Cicarelli, eds. 2003. "Laura D'Andrea Tyson (1947–)." In *Distinguished Women Economists*, 202–5. Westport, CT: Praeger.

Greenslade, Nick. 2006. "The First Lady of Business." *The Observer*, May 20. http://www.guardian.co.uk/business/2006/may/21/theobserver.observerbusiness3.

The White House. N.d. "President's Economic Recovery Advisory Board." http://www.whitehouse.gov/administration/eop/perab/members/tyson.

U

Unemployment

Unemployment is the working state of someone who is willing and able to work but not working currently. It is measured in several different ways by several different organizations, some private and some public. The most widely accepted and quoted measure, the unemployment rate, is the responsibility of the Bureau of Labor Statistics (BLS), an agency of the Department of Labor.

Economists study unemployment as one barometer to achieving a major economic goal—high employment. The BLS collects data on a variety of employment and unemployment conditions. The BLS also determines the size of the labor force, which is a variable in determining the unemployment rate. It establishes the definition of an unemployed worker. An individual is classified as unemployed if he or she is over 16 years of age and does not currently have a job, but is able to work and actively pursuing employment. No measure of unemployment is precise. All measures of unemployment and methods of collecting data have some flaws along with their benefits. Unemployment rates and other unemployment and employment metrics give economists portions of the labor picture. It is up to economists, policy makers, and the public to take these aggregate measures in total to create an accurate picture of an economy's capacity for labor.

There are four categories of unemployment recognized by economists: frictional, cyclical, structural, and seasonal.

Frictional Unemployment

Frictional unemployment is a type of unemployment that occurs when a person is between jobs. Frictional unemployment is considered only temporary, since typically, as soon as the unemployment occurs the person begins to search for employment almost immediately.

There are many causes of frictional unemployment. People may decide to leave their jobs on their own accord. Their reasons for leaving may include low pay, little or no opportunity for growth and furthering education, and a difficult work environment or undesired location. Another cause is the fact that some people may overlook certain jobs because they feel as if those jobs are below their skill level, or may simply believe that an available position is "below" them. Likewise, an employer may look at a pool of job candidates' resumes and decide that none of the applicants have the skills necessary to do the job, when in fact they do. Finally, frictional unemployment may be temporary due to certain life events, such as a woman taking maternity leave from her job, or a teacher taking a sabbatical.

Another way to understand frictional unemployment is to think of it as a period in which a person is searching for employment opportunities, or simply the period in between jobs. Unemployment is always present in the economy, resulting from temporary transitions made by workers and employers, or from workers and employers having inconsistent or incomplete information.

Cyclical Unemployment

Cyclical unemployment is job loss that occurs when the economy enters into a period of recession and there are more people seeking work than there are jobs available. In reaction to less consumer demand for goods and services, businesses lay off workers as production need decreases. These workers are then temporarily unemployed until the cycle changes and employers can rehire when the economy expands and consumer demand increases. Cyclical unemployment is a part of the business cycle. The most common method used by economists to calculate the cyclical unemployment rate is to use the unemployment rate at the peak of the business cycle and then subtract the unemployment rate at the bottom of the business cycle. The difference between these two numbers is what economists call the cyclical unemployment rate.

Structural Unemployment

Structural unemployment is unemployment that occurs when an industry goes through a transformation in the way it produces the good or service of its industry, and the skills of the former employees do not match the new skills necessary in the new industry.

Seasonal Unemployment

Seasonal unemployment occurs as a result of a job only being able to be performed during specific seasons of the year. Often the term "seasonal" conjures up visions of the summer jobs of high school and college students or the part-time jobs retail stores add during a holiday season. While those jobs are included in the Current Establishment Survey (see below), seasonal unemployment also includes jobs that are weather dependent. More specific to northern states, seasonal unemployment includes career jobs such as highway construction and housing construction.

Natural Rate of Unemployment

Remember the definition of unemployed is someone who is both willing and able to work. Frictional unemployment includes those who are between jobs and new entrants into the work force. Between frictional unemployment and structural unemployment in some industries in the economy, it is virtually inconceivable to imagine that every person willing and able to work is working. The natural rate of unemployment refers to the lowest rate of unemployment that a society can reasonably achieve, knowing there will always be some frictional and structural unemployment in the economy. What then is the unemployment rate at which the economy can be considered to be at full employment? The natural rate of unemployment can also be viewed as the point at which the economy is operating at full employment, or the point at which unemployment has reached equilibrium. The natural rate of unemployment is an arguable point between economists. Whether that unemployment rate is 3, 4, or 5 percent, economists agree that there is a percentage window at which full employment is considered achieved, even without the percentage being zero. At that point, most adults who want to be working are in fact working.

Non-Accelerating Inflation Rate of Unemployment (NAIRU)

Under the philosophy of John Maynard Keynes, an economy can reasonably continue to add jobs, i.e., lower unemployment, without creating demand-pull inflation as long as the economy is in an economic downturn or recession. However, when the economy recovers and economic growth is at the peak of the business cycle, a significantly low unemployment rate translates into a large increase of people and money demanding goods and services. This scenario poses the challenge of determining what low unemployment rate will translate in too much new demand such that prices are forced to rise—i.e., inflation. The lowest unemployment rate possible to achieve without translating into inflation is called the Non-Accelerating Inflation Rate of Unemployment, or NAIRU. This unemployment measure enters economists' discussions when an economy is operating at close to or at full potential. At this point, economists become concerned about an overheating economy and inflationary prospects are high, often instigated by excessive consumer demand for goods and services.

Measures of Unemployment

Unemployment measures are arguably the most awaited economic metrics by economists, politicians, and investors. To get as clear a picture of the labor force as possible, unemployment has three key types of measures: household survey, establishment survey, and weekly unemployment claims. Each measure reveals a distinct aspect of the labor force. Unemployment data are collected and released by the Bureau of Labor Statistics (BLS), an agency of the Department of Labor. Unemployment data are released by the BLS on the first Friday of each month at precisely 8:30 a.m. The BLS makes revisions to its data as far back as two months. Sometimes these revisions can be quite significant and impact or alter the decisions of investors and politicians. Since consumer spending is approximately two-thirds of the U.S. economy, unemployment data become a portrait of the economic spending habits and income profile of consumers.

Current Personal Survey (also known as the Household Survey)

The current personal survey data are collected by the BLS through surveying 60,000 homes across the country. All sectors of the economy are surveyed, including farm and nonfarm workers, domestic helpers, and those who are self-employed. According to the BLS, they have a response rate to the survey of approximately 95 percent. The survey includes questions on whether the respondent is employed or not, and if so, if it is part- or full-time, and if the respondent is not employed, is the respondent looking for work. With the data collected from the current personal survey, the BLS determines the size of the civilian labor force, the number of people employed, and the unemployment rate. Every survey has its shortcomings, and the household survey is no exception. The current personal survey suffers the same deficiency as all surveys, which is the honesty of the respondents.

Current Establishment Survey (also known as the Establishment Survey)

Also known as the payroll survey, the BLS surveys over 400,000 companies and government agencies in 500 different industries. The surveyed companies employ approximately 45 percent of the labor force, or 40 million workers. This survey is different from the current personal survey in a number of ways. One, it only looks at nonfarm workers and is not concerned with age. Two, the current establishment survey does not distinguish between full time or part time. The key focus of this survey is to determine the number of jobs created or eliminated. Third, since the current establishment survey gather data from only employers and workplaces, it does not count self-employed workers who work out of their homes. While both the current establishment and current personal surveys collect very different information, they tend to move in the same direction, showing similar unemployment pictures of the economy.

Weekly Unemployment Claims

The third unemployment measure is the weekly claims for unemployment insurance. This leading indicator is based on the actual numbers of unemployment claims filed, as recorded by each state's unemployment agency. Since it is measured by actual claims numbers, its accuracy makes it a good indicator of future economic conditions. From the trend of these data, it is possible to gauge the number of unemployed who are no longer receiving payments, and potentially the number of discouraged workers.

A discouraged worker is an individual of working age who is unemployed and is not currently pursuing a job. Although they are usually willing and able to work, discouraged workers have given up finding gainful employment due to a variety of factors. Due to these real or perceived limitations in the job market, these individuals have become "discouraged." Discouraged workers are not included in the unemployment rate and they are not considered to be in the labor force.

The level of employment can have a significant impact on the growth of an economy. An economy at less than full employment has underutilized resources, which translates into fewer people participating as both producers and consumers. Yet an economy at a level considered full employment is an economy with full, or close to full, utilization of the resources and capacity of consumers purchasing goods and services. There is often a fine line between the two scenarios.

David A. Dieterle
Ekaterini Chrisopoulos-Vergos

See Also Bureau of Labor Statistics; Cyclical Unemployment; Department of Labor; Gross Domestic Product (GDP); Keynes, John Maynard; Keynesian Economics

Further Reading

Baumohl, Bernard. 2008. *The Secrets of Economic Indicators*. 2nd ed. Philadelphia: Wharton School Publishing.

Johnson, Rose. N.d. "The Types of Unemployment: Cyclical, Frictional and Structural." *eHow Money*. Accessed October 25, 2013. http://www.ehow.com/info_8614302_types-unemployment-cyclical-frictional-structural.html#ixzz2jX3uRuRX.

Miller, Roger Leroy. 2010. *Economics Today*. 16th ed. Upper Saddle River, NJ: Pearson Education.

U.S. Bureau of Labor Statistics. N.d. "How the Government Measures Unemployment." http://www.bls.gov/cps/cps_htgm.htm.

WiseGeek. N.d. "What Is Frictional Unemployment?" Accessed October 25, 2013. http://www.wisegeek.com/what-is-frictional-unemployment.htm.

Resources for Teachers

Bureau of Labor Statistics. N.d. "Unemployment." http://www.bls.gov/bls/proghome.htm#unemployment.

Edvantage. N.d. "Unemployment." http://www.theedvantage.org/economics/unemployment.

Foundation for Teaching Economics. N.d. "Lesson 5: Labor Markets." http://www.fte.org/teacher-resources/lesson-plans/efllessons/lesson-5-labor-markets/.

Niederjohn, Scott. 2009. "The Unemployment Game." econedlink. http://www.econedlink.org/lessons/index.php?lid=785&type=educator.

Riley, Geoff. N.d. "Unemployment: Natural Rate by." tutor2u. Accessed August 25, 2013. http://tutor2u.net/economics/revision-notes/a2-macro-natural-rate-of-unemployment.html.

United States Census Bureau

The U.S. Census Bureau collects data on the quality of life of the United States citizens and the state of the economy. There are two types of U.S. Census Bureau programs: economic and demographic. Most widely known for its data collection on the United States population and housing every 10 years, the U.S. Census Bureau also collects data every five years on the economy and government. The economic, agriculture, and government censuses taken every five years comprise more than 98 percent of U.S. economic activity. Data on U.S. foreign trade are also collected by the Census Bureau.

The data collected are used in many different ways, including allocation and planning. One of the most important is that the population and housing data collected each decade are used to determine the number and location of congressional seats in the House of Representatives. At the federal level, census data are also used to distribute federal funds to local governments. Many state and local governments use the data to identify their legislative districts. The census data are also used by local governments to identify and plan where roads may be built, to determine school district boundaries, or to determine the distribution and location of public health care facilities. A second area of service by the U.S. Census Bureau is providing age-related data from its population census. The federal government uses Census Bureau data to plan and budget for Social Security and other age-related government benefits and federal programs.

The first census of the U.S. population (censuses had been conducted in the 13 American colonies as well) was taken in 1790, as ordered in the U.S. Constitution. The census was carried out by Secretary of State Thomas Jefferson. It was used only as a head count, and only classified the population by age (over 16 or under 16 for white males), race, and sex. The first censuses were taken by local census takers, who asked only a few basic questions, then tabulated and reported the results locally. This simple process became more complex and the questions more detailed as the country grew and the value of the data became more known by both political and business leaders. Today, the Census Bureau conducts over 200 surveys.

In the early days of the census, U.S. marshals were responsible for collecting information. They had no training on what information to gather and no recording forms, or even schedules on when to conduct the census. In 1879, part-time trained census takers were hired to replace the marshals and conduct the 1880 and subsequent door-to-door censuses. The U.S. Census Bureau began using mail questionnaires beginning with the 1960 census. Today, census takers are only used for remote areas, special circumstances such as shelters and soup kitchens, and nonresponse follow-ups. The 2010 census was the first census in which the census takers used hand-held GPS devices.

The census expanded its information gathering in 1810 to include economic data such as manufacturing and products being produced. In 1840, it expanded again to include gathering data on additional economic sectors of agriculture, fisheries, and mining. The 1850 census data expanded even further to include for the first time demographic data on taxes, church attendance, and crime. With each additional census, the amount of data collected continued to increase. The U.S. Census Bureau became a permanent agency of the federal government by an act of Congress in 1902, and was located in the U.S. Department of Commerce.

As a permanent government agency, the U.S. Census Bureau greatly expanded its data-gathering abilities through the twentieth century. During the twentieth century, the Census Bureau significantly expanded its ability to accumulate economic information. It created three new surveys that continue in use today: the American Housing Survey, the Current Population Survey, and the Survey of Income and Program Participation. These new programs go far beyond the historical decade population survey.

Not only was the Census Bureau expanding its date-gathering capabilities, it was leading the world in technology innovation. The U.S. Census Bureau was the first nonmilitary government agency to enter the computer age. In 1950, the census that year was tabulated by a UNIVAC I computer, one of the most modern, fastest computers of its time. The global positioning systems (GPS) we now enjoy in our cars and cell phones are directly attributed to the cartographic innovations of the U.S. Census Bureau through the 1970s and 1980s. Census data-gathering has grown from neighborhood walks and local surveys, from computer tape and CD-ROMs, to the Internet.

The U.S. Census Bureau headquarters are located in Suitland, Maryland. The bureau also has 12 regional offices, in Atlanta; Boston; Charlotte, North Carolina; Chicago; Dallas; Denver; Detroit; Kansas City, Kansas; Los Angeles; New York; Philadelphia; and Seattle. The president appoints the Census Bureau director with confirmation of the Senate.

David A. Dieterle

See Also Bureau of Economic Analysis; Bureau of Labor Statistics; Department of Commerce; National Bureau of Economic Research (NBER); Office of Management and Budget (OMB)

Further Reading

Trethan, Phaedra. N.d. "The U.S. Census Bureau: Counting Heads and Then Some." U.S. Government Info, About.com. Accessed June 3, 2014. http://usgovinfo.about.com/od/censusandstatistics/a/aboutcensus.htm.

United States Census Bureau. N.d. "Home Page." http://www.census.gov/.

United States Census Bureau. N.d. "State and County Quick Facts." http://quickfacts.census.gov/qfd/index.html#.

United States Census Bureau: American Fact Finder. N.d. "Community Facts." http://factfinder2.census.gov/faces/nav/jsf/pages/index.xhtml.

Resources for Teachers

Aljazeera America. N.d. "Census Bureau." http://america.aljazeera.com/topics/topic/organization/census-bureau.html.

United States Census Bureau. N.d. "Home Page." http://www.census.gov/.

United States Census Bureau. N.d. "Statistics in Schools: For Teachers, Teaching Resources." http://www.census.gov/schools/for_teachers/.

United States Mint

The United States Mint is part of the Department of the Treasury and is responsible for producing, manufacturing, and distributing coins as well as providing security for the nation's $100 billion in gold and silver assets.

Article 1, Section 8 of the United States Constitution states, "The Congress shall have power . . . [t]o coin money, regulate the value thereof, and of foreign coin, and fix the standard of weights and measures." With this statement, the Constitution placed the power of creating a monetary system to Congress. The task of developing this system fell to the first Secretary of the Treasury, Alexander Hamilton. As soon as he began his term in 1789, Hamilton was quick to organize the nation's finances and come up with ideas about how to make the United States an industrial powerhouse. His ideas included establishing a national bank, funding the national debt, taking on the war debts of individual states, and encouraging manufacturing. With Hamilton's assistance, Congress passed the Coinage Act on April 2, 1792. The Coinage Act created the U.S. Mint and authorized construction of a building to house it. At that time, the nation's capital was in Philadelphia. When construction began, the U.S. Mint was the first federal building erected under the Constitution.

The primary mission of the U.S. Mint is to serve the American people by manufacturing and distributing precious metal and collectible coins and national medals, and providing security for assets entrusted to them. One of its most important jobs is to manufacture and distribute coins. The production of these coins primarily takes place at the Philadelphia and Denver mints.

The U.S. Mint operates six facilities across the United States, with each facility performing unique functions. These facilities include the Mint headquarters in Washington, D.C., and production facilities in Philadelphia, Pennsylvania; West Point, New York;

Denver, Colorado; and San Francisco, California. In addition, there is the United States Bullion Depository at Fort Knox, Kentucky, which does not produce anything but serves as a storage facility for the nation's $100 billion in gold and silver bullion.

The facility in Washington, D.C., is responsible for policy formulation, administrative guidance, program management, research and development, marketing operations, customer services, and order processing. The Philadelphia Mint is responsible for all engraving, manufacturing of coin and medal dies, and production of circulating coins. The Denver Mint is also responsible primarily for circulating coins. Both the Philadelphia and Denver Mints are open to the public for tours. The San Francisco Mint is responsible for producing proof coins for numismatic collectibles as well as some commemorative coins. The West Point Mint is responsible for manufacturing gold, silver, and platinum bullion and proof and uncirculated coins, and also strikes some commemorative coins.

Ekaterini Chrisopoulos-Vergos

See Also Constitution of the United States (see Appendix); National Deficit vs. Debt; United States Treasury

Further Reading

Department of Treasury. N.d. "U.S. Mint Overview." http://www.treasury.gov/about/organizational-structure/offices/Treasurer-US/Pages/usMint-overview.aspx.

National Archives. N.d. "America's Founding Fathers: Delegates to the Constitutional Convention." http://www.archives.gov/exhibits/charters/constitution_founding_fathers_new_york.html.

The United States Mint. N.d. "About Us." http://www.usMint.gov/about_the_Mint/.

The United States Mint. N.d. "History of the Mint." http://www.usMint.gov/education/historianscorner/?action=history.

Resources for Teachers

teachinghistory.org. N.d. "U.S. Mint." http://teachinghistory.org/history-content/national-resources/22477.

United States Mint. N.d. "Lesson Plans by Subject." http://www.usmint.gov/kids/teachers/lessonPlans/subject/.

The United States Mint. N.d. "Roles in History." http://www.usMint.gov/education/historianscorner/?action=roles.

United States Treasury

The United States Treasury is one of the oldest executive departments. It was created through an act of Congress in 1789. In its inception, the primary function of the Department of Treasury was the management of the monetary resources of the United States and issuing reports on the public credit. However, the roles and responsibilities of the various bureaus have become increasingly complex.

The U.S. Treasury Department is an executive agency tasked with promoting the economic well-being and financial security of the United States. The mission of the U.S.

Treasury Department is to sustain a stable economy and stimulate the conditions for economic growth, as well as to protect the reliability of the U.S. monetary and financial systems, and manage the finances of the U.S. government. The Treasury Department is linked to the Federal Reserve System, which acts as the central bank for the United States Treasury.

The Treasury Department acts as the guardian of U.S. financial resources and is a key player in the world economy. It is organized into various departmental offices, which include domestic finance, economic policy, office of the general counsel, international affairs, legislative affairs, management, public affairs, tax policy, terrorism and financial intelligence, and the office of the treasurer. These departments, headed by assistant secretaries and undersecretaries, are collectively responsible for formulating policy and managing the department as a whole. The larger component of the Treasury is its several operating bureaus, which are responsible for carrying out specific tasks. These bureaus make up the overwhelming majority of the Treasury's workforce and include such divisions as the U.S. Mint, the Bureau of Engraving and Printing, and the Internal Revenue Service (IRS).

The basic functions of the Treasury, carried out by the various bureaus, include collecting taxes, duties, and monies paid to and due to the United States; paying all bills of the United States; issuing bonds, currency, and coinage; managing government accounts and the public debt; supervising national banking institutions; enforcing federal finance and tax laws; and investigating and prosecuting tax evaders, counterfeiters, and forgers. This means that the Treasury is responsible for regulating national banks, determining international economic policy, collecting income and excise taxes, issuing securities, and manufacturing coins and bills for circulation.

The U.S. Treasury is headed by the Secretary of the Treasury, appointed by the president and confirmed by the Senate. There have been 76 Treasury secretaries, from Alexander Hamilton in 1789 to Jacob (Jack) Lew (appointed by President Obama and confirmed by the Senate in 2013). The Secretary of the Treasury acts as the chief financial officer of the government. He or she reports to the president of the United States, and serves as a member of the president's cabinet; publishes annual reports on the state of the nation's finances; and has the primary responsibility for formulating and recommending tax policy and other domestic and international economic and financial policy initiatives.

Another important role within the Treasury Department is the treasurer, who has oversight over the Bureau of Engraving and Printing and the U.S. Mint, and deals with any issues pertaining to coinage and currency. There is also an inspector general who reports to the deputy secretary with an independent and objective review of the department's operations. The inspector general must keep Congress fully informed about the problems and deficiencies relating to the administration of the department's programs and operations.

The Treasury Department currently has a budget of about $13 billion, and a staff of more than 100,000 employees. The functions of the Treasury Department have become more expansive to respond to the increasing needs of a more sophisticated and developed nation. The Treasury Department works with the White House administration to pursue policy initiatives that are in line with the presidential administration, such as raising the debt limit, making housing affordable, or reforming Wall Street.

The department also works with other federal agencies, as well as with foreign governments and international financial institutions. Its goals in doing so are to encourage global economic growth, increase standards of living, and if possible, predict and prevent economic crises. The Treasury Department does what it can to improve national security by identifying security threats and supporting the financial systems by providing safeguards against those threats. A reorganization of the department in 2003 moved several law enforcement agencies out of the Treasury Department, including the Bureau of Alcohol, Tobacco and Firearms, which moved to the Department of Justice; and the Secret Service and Customs Service, which moved to the Department of Homeland Security.

Michelle D. Holowicki

See Also Bureau of Engraving and Printing; Internal Revenue Service (IRS); Taxes; United States Mint; U.S. Treasury Bills, Notes, and Bonds

Further Reading

Sunner, Michael William. 2012. *Borrowing through the U. S. Treasury's Fast Money Tree: The Need to Balance Austerity and Growth in the 21st Century*. Bloomington, IN: AuthorHouse.

U.S. Department of Treasury. N.d. "Home." http://www.treasury.gov/Pages/default.aspx.

Wann, Peter. 1989. *Inside the U.S. Treasury Market*. Westport, CT: Quorum Books.

Resources for Teachers

The Federal Reserve System. N.d. "The Federal Reserve in the U.S. Payments System." http://www.federalreserve.gov/pf/pdf/pf_7.pdf.

U.S. Department of the Treasury. N.d. "About: Kids Zone." http://www.treasury.gov/about/education/Pages/kids-zone.aspx.

U.S. Department of the Treasury. N.d. "About: Lesson Plans for Teachers." http://www.treasury.gov/about/education/pages/Lesson-Plans-for-Teachers.aspx.

United States v. South-Eastern Underwriters Association, 322 U.S. 533 (1944)

A Supreme Court Case Determining Insurance as Commerce

Economic Concepts

Competition; commerce; consumer rights; fair trade; monopoly

Economic Impact

This case defined insurance as commerce and established that it could be regulated under the commerce clause. The case explored the government's ability to maintain consumer equity, competition, and fair trade practices.

Economic Summary

The Supreme Court's responsibility in *United States v. South-Eastern Underwriters Association* was to determine whether insurance constitutes commerce, and if so, if insurance companies can be regulated by the power the commerce clause grants to Congress to regulate transactions across state lines. Until this case in 1944, insurance was not considered commerce, as defined by the commerce clause of the U.S. Constitution and interpreted by the courts. However, the business of providing financial stability through insuring property for monetary loss was comparable to the auto and coal industries in size and employment.

Monopolies were a national concern in the late nineteenth century. Congress passed the Sherman Antitrust Act in 1890 in an attempt to prevent monopolies, collusion, price-fixing, conspiracy, and intimidation tactics that would discourage competition and fair trade. Insurance was not considered commerce, and therefore did not adhere to the laws and regulations of the Sherman Act. This case established that insurance was indeed commerce. In addition, transactions of the insurance industry took place between various states and therefore were subject to the regulation of the federal government.

Case Summary

Historically, the timing for this case is set well into the United States' fight against fascism, when patriotic values and national attitudes of unity to win World War II were prevalent. By 1944, the insurance industry had grown to represent a substantial portion of the economy. The *South-Eastern Underwriters Association* case challenged the American free enterprise principles of fair trade, honest prices, and true competition. The case dealt with collusion, conspiracy, and price-fixing, and whether or not insurance was a form of commerce.

Insurance refers to a contract in which one party agrees to indemnify (compensate for loss or damage) another for a previously agreed upon category, in exchange for a premium (payment). This is significant in regard to U.S. industrial development because it provided an economic stabilizer. The Great Depression had underscored the importance of this stabilizing mechanism. It spread the loss from an individual or a few to a greater number of people, or a collection of premium payers. The insurance company is the safekeeper of these pools of money. By the 1940s, the insurance industry generated revenue comparable to an average of all-revenue receipts for the federal government. Within the previous decade, it had employed as many people as the automobile and coal mining industries combined. Insurance touched almost every home and person, as well as places of employment, constituting a significant portion of the U.S. economy.

Several decades earlier, and coincidental to the growth of the insurance industry, was the growth of trusts and monopolies. These monopolies in steel, railroads, and oil had the power to restrict production, crush small businesses, and concentrate large power in the hands of a few to the detriment of the many. In 1890, the U.S. Congress passed the Sherman Antitrust Act in response to this era of great fear and corruption. It was named after its author, Senator John Sherman, and signed by President Benjamin Harrison. The goal of this federal legislation was to protect competition, and consequently, consumers.

The Sherman Act was passed almost unanimously in both the House and the Senate, giving antitrust or competition law nonpartisan status in the Congress of 1890.

The South-Eastern Underwriters Association (SEUA) (underwriters evaluate potential risk for insurance companies and review applications for coverage giving either approval or denial) and its affiliates were indicted in a district court in northern Georgia for alleged violations of the Sherman Antitrust Act. The defendants failed to deny any activities of colluding to fix prices or intimidation tactics to limit competition. SEUA simply demurred (a demurrer does not dispute the facts, just objects on the grounds that there is not sufficient cause of action) with the intention they could get away with any of these such activities.

The insurance industry claimed that fire insurance was not included as interstate commerce according to the commerce clause of the Constitution, and therefore could not be prosecuted under the Sherman Antitrust Act of 1890. *Paul v. Virginia, 75 U.S. 168 (1869)* had established this precedent. The rationale in the *Paul* case maintained that insurance policies were not commodities that were transported, bartered, or traded from state to state. They did not represent a tangible commodity that could be taken to market. On the contrary, insurance policies were intangible, personal contracts. The parties involved may live in different states, but when any actual transaction took place, it was as a contract within a local setting subject to state laws. The defendants obtained a judgment sustaining the demurrer. Under the Criminal Appeals Act, the federal government appealed this case to the Supreme Court.

On January 11, 1944, the Supreme Court heard the case. There were two alleged conspiracies. First, the fixing and maintaining of arbitrary and noncompetitive premium rates on fire and other allied lines (allied lines include sprinkler leakage, explosion, tornado, riot, and civil commotion coverage, as well as water damage, etc., which are usually purchased together with fire protection) within several of the Southern states, (Alabama, Florida, Georgia, North Carolina, South Carolina, and Virginia). The second alleged conspiracy involved monopolizing trade and commerce in the same lines of insurance in and among the same states, since SEUA had orchestrated the actions. Tactics included boycotts and other types of intimidation and coercion. SEUA did not argue otherwise.

It was the majority opinion of the Supreme Court in *United States v. South-Eastern Underwriters Association* that insurance was commerce. Justice Black referred to Chief Justice Marshall's definition of commerce in *Gibbons v. Odgen* (1824). This definition included more than just traffic and trade of goods. Chief Justice Marshall employed a comprehensive definition that it had to be such, otherwise Congress may lack the power necessary to discharge its constitutional duty to govern interstate commerce. The Constitution did not have to name every industry in its text to include it in its intent. The transmission of an electronic impulse over a telegraph line between two states was considered commerce, and subject to vital federal regulation (*Pensacola Telegraph Co. v. Western Union Telegraph Co.*, 1877). Furthermore, it held that insurance, even though it might transpire locally, did in fact happen over state lines and therefore functioned as interstate commerce, making it subject to federal regulation and statutes. The dissenting opinion argued that this was an issue more appropriately regulated by state law. Chief Justice Stone and Justice Jackson, in their separate dissenting opinions, expressed their desire to use judicial restraint.

In March 1945, following the ruling on *U.S. v. South-Eastern Underwriters Association*, Congress passed the McCarran-Ferguson Act, addressing where and when it was appropriate and applicable to have state regulation and taxation versus federal regulation with regard to the insurance industry.

Kathleen C. Simmons

See Also Fascism; Sherman Antitrust Act of 1890

Related Cases

Gibbons v. Ogden, 22 U.S. 1 (1824)

Paul v. Virginia, 75 U.S. 168 (1869)

Pensacola Telegraph Co. v. Western Union Telegraph Co., 96 U.S. 1 (1877)

New York Life Insurance Co. v. Deer Lodge County, 231 U.S. 495 (1944)

Polish National Alliance v. National Labor Relations Board, 322 U.S. 643 (1944)

Further Reading

Bittker, Boris I., and Brannon P. Denning. 1999. *Bittker on the Regulation of Interstate and Foreign Commerce*. New York: Aspen Law & Business.

Justia.com, U.S. Supreme Court Center. N.d. "*Paul v. Virginia*, 75 U.S. 168 (1869)." http://supreme.justia.com/cases/federal/us/75/168/.

Resources for Teachers

Cornell University Law School, Legal Information Institute. N.d. "*United States v. South-Eastern Underwriters Ass'n et al.*" http://www.law.cornell.edu/supremecourt/text/322/533.

Justia.com, U.S. Supreme Court Center. N.d. "*United States v. South-Eastern Underwriters, 322 U.S. 533 (1944)*." http://supreme.justia.com/cases/federal/us/322/533/case.html.

U.S. Treasury Bills, Notes, and Bonds

Treasury bills (T-bills), notes (T-notes), and bonds (T-bonds) are marketable securities from the U.S. government. The government sells these savings and investment instruments to the general public, banks, and other financial institutions, investment and brokerage houses, wealth sovereign funds, and other nations. The funds raised are used to pay off maturing government debt and raise the cash needed to operate the federal government. One does not actually receive a certificate with the purchase of a U.S. Treasury bill, note, or bond. One's investment is followed in a system of accounts that generates continuing statements and balances. What differentiates T-bills, T-notes, and T-bonds is that each has a longer term to maturity (T-bills are the shortest and T-bonds the longest). They each have a stated interest rate, paid semiannually until the Treasuries mature.

Treasury Bills

Treasury bills are short-term obligations issued with a term of less than one year. Because they are sold at a discount from face value, they do not pay interest before maturity. The interest is the difference between the purchase price and the face value. They are often used for achieving the same saving goals or purpose as a money market fund or a savings account. Since their short maturity provides liquidity, they are often used for easy access to their money by the holder. Conversion from the Treasury bill to cash can be quickly completed by a bank or broker.

A Treasury bill is also similar to the popular zero-coupon bond. Unlike the T-bills cousins, the T-note or T-bond, a zero-coupon bond does not make periodic interest payments. A Treasury bill is purchased at a discount from its face value (par value). The receiver of the bill will then receive the full face value at the time of maturity.

Treasury Notes

Treasury notes are intermediate to long-term investments. The maturities of T-notes are typically 2, 3, 5, 7, and 10 years. Treasuries of this maturity are often purchased by individuals for their long-term savings or investment needs. Since interest is paid twice a year, these make sound, safe investment tools for one's retirement or other long-range goal.

Treasury Bonds

For the Treasury, the goal is to provide additional debt that will appeal to investors while keeping financing costs low. Bonds are sold by the U.S. Treasury Department. Treasury bonds cover terms from longer than 10 years to 30 years. Interest is paid semiannually, as with the T-note.

Treasury bonds are often called floating-rate notes. Floaters are securities with rates set periodically. Floaters can offer shorter-term safety, hedging against the potential of rising interest rates.

U.S. Savings Bonds

Probably the most popular of all the U.S. Treasuries to the noninvesting, nonfinancial career person is the U.S. Series EE or Series I savings bond. An individual can purchase up to $5,000 in any given year. The bond can then be redeemed at any time after 12 months. If the bond is redeemed prior to the 12 months, an interest penalty is imposed. A popular gift among parents and grandparents, the Series EE savings bonds are sold at one-half their face value. So to buy a $100 Series EE U.S. savings bond as a gift only costs $50. If the bond purchase is made electronically, the face value can range from $25 up to $5,000. Purchases of paper Series EE bonds are sold in the more traditional denominations ($10, $25, $50, $100, etc.).

The interest rate paid at maturity on Series EE bonds is dependent on when the bond was issued by the government. If the bond was issued later than May 2005, the interest rate is fixed based on the 10-year U.S. Treasury note. The fixed interest rate is a bit of a misnomer, since the 10-year U.S. Treasury note interest rate is adjusted semiannually. Series EE bonds issued between May of 1997 and April 2005 earn interest based on a floating rate.

Like the T-bill, the holder of the Series EE bond does not receive the interest until the bond is redeemed. If the bond is redeemed within five years, three months' interest is forfeited. The U.S. Treasury guarantee is the maturity date of Series EE bonds will not go beyond 17 years. If one really wants to earn interest on Series EE bonds, he or she can let them earn interest for up to 30 years.

Many of the characteristics of the Series EE bonds apply to the Series I saving bonds. The major difference between them is the built-in inflation adjustment mechanism of the Series I bond. The main distinction is the way in which interest is paid. A Series I bond pays interest that is partially fixed and partially adjusted for inflation. Another benefit of holding Series EE or Series I bonds is that the income tax on the interest earned does not have to be paid until the bonds are redeemed. Parents and grandparents are big fans of the Series EE and Series I bonds as a way to help pay for college.

Treasury Inflation-Protected Securities (TIPS)

Treasury Inflation-Protected Securities, or TIPS, were introduced by the U.S. Treasury in 1997 as a hedge against inflation. These securities used the consumer price index (CPI) to determine and adjust the value of the principal, taking into account the current impact of inflation on the principal's real value. TIPS pay a fixed rate of interest. This interest is then paid semiannually on the new inflation-adjusted value of the principal.

When the TIPS mature, the holder receives either the higher inflation-adjusted principal if indeed inflation has impacted the initial value or, if deflation (a general decrease in the price level) occurred, the holder of the TIPS receives the original principal amount. Due this inflation-adjusted mechanism, interest rates on TIPS are usually lower than other Treasuries with the same maturity.

There are several ways to purchase U.S. Treasuries. They can be bought, and redeemed, through commercial banks, brokers, or investment professionals. They can be purchased directly from the government, usually by broker-dealers, although some individuals can go the direct route. Another way to own U.S. Treasuries is to buy into a mutual fund specializing in Treasuries. The popular Series EE bond can be purchased at local banks or directly from the U.S. Treasury. Some employers offer a Series EE bond-buying program as a benefit to its employees.

Maura Donnelly
David A. Dieterle

See Also Deflation; Federal Reserve System; Inflation; Inflation, Measures of; United States Treasury

Further Reading

Library of Economics and Liberty. 2008. *The Concise Encyopedia of Economics*. "Bonds." http://www.econlib.org/library/Enc/Bonds.html.

Mobius, Mark. 2012. *Bonds: An Introduction to the Core Concepts*. New York: John Wiley and Sons.

Roger, Arnold A. 2014. "Chapter 26: Stocks, Bonds, Futures, and Options." In *Macroeconomics*. 11th ed. Mason, OH: South-Western Cengage Learning.

Resources for Teachers

Federal Reserve Bank of Dallas. N.d. "Lesson 6: Save and Invest; Bonds—Lending Your Money." http://www.dallasfed.org/assets/documents/educate/pubs/wealth_classroom/06_lesson.pdf.

SIFMA. N.d. "About Government/Agency Bonds." Accessed November 30, 2013. http://www.investinginbonds.com/learnmore.asp?catid=9&subcatid=50&id=104.

Treasury Direct. N.d. "Treasury Securities and Programs." http://www.treasurydirect.gov/indiv/products/products.htm.

V

Vickrey, William

Born: June 21, 1914, in Victoria, British Columbia; Died: October 11, 1996, in Harrison, New York; American; microeconomics, price theory, public finance, taxation, Nobel Prize (1996); Major Works: *Agenda for Progressive Taxation* (1947), "A Proposal for Revising New York's Subway Fare Structure" (1955).

William Vickrey was an American economist noted for his contributions in public finance, including taxation, public price theory, public utility pricing, and transportation. Vickrey was considered the first to suggest congestion pricing for public transportation, raising prices during high-traffic times and in high-use areas and lowering prices in less-used areas and during low-traffic times. In 1948, he was the first to suggest electronic payment of tolls on toll roads to reduce traffic congestion in tollbooth areas. In the area of income tax, Vickrey asserted that the optimal income tax burden for individuals should be based on long-term earnings, not yearly earnings. He was awarded the Nobel Prize in 1996. Vickrey died in 1996.

William Spencer Vickrey was born on June 21, 1914, in Victoria, British Columbia. An American economist, he was educated in both Europe and the United States, graduating from Phillips Andover Academy in 1931. He attended Yale University and received his BS in mathematics in 1935. He studied economics while at Columbia University, where he received both his MA degree (1937) and his PhD (1948).

In 1945, Vickrey became a naturalized U.S. citizen. It was during the interim between his two graduate degrees that Vickrey began his work in the area of taxation. He worked for the National Resources Planning Board in Washington, D.C., and the Division of Tax Research in the U.S. Treasury Department. As a Quaker, he objected vigorously to World War II. It was during this time that he designed a new inheritance tax for Puerto Rico. His doctoral dissertation, "Agenda for Progressive Taxation," completed in 1948, was later reprinted in 1972 as an economic classic. This 496-page work revealed that one's optimal income tax should not be based on one's year-to-year earnings, but rather on a citizen's long-term economic situation.

Vickrey's teaching career began as a lecturer in economics at Columbia University in 1946. As a New Yorker, he proposed the congestion pricing principle for its subway system. This principle, first written in 1952, was considered risky by elected officials as it recommended that subway fares be increased during peak times and in high-traffic sections and be lowered in others. This principle regarded time-of-day pricing as a way to balance the supply and demand of market forces. In 1958, he became a full professor and served as chairman of the Department of Economics from 1964 to 1967. He was named

McVickar Professor of Political Economy in 1971. He received an honorary degree from the University of Chicago in 1979. He retired as McVickar Professor Emeritus in 1982.

During his more than 60-year academic career, Vickrey researched a large range of subjects, including taxation, public utilities, transportation, and urban problems. More specifically, these included the efficient pricing of public utilities (electric power) in 1939 and 1940 for the Twentieth Century Fund. He was also considered to be a crusader for the efficiency of public services. In 1948, he created the idea that tollbooths, which significantly slowed traffic flow, should have a means to use vehicle identifiers to be read electronically without slowing down the traffic. This electronic system is still in place today. In 1950, he and his colleague Carl Shoup helped develop a comprehensive program for revising the tax system of Japan. In 1951, he studied transit fares in New York City for the Mayor's Committee on Management Survey.

A basic economic principle is that incentives affect people's behavior. Asymmetric information is the term that refers to the fact that government officials never know as much about the people their policies affect as the people affected know about themselves. Vickrey theorized that a buyer and seller have unequal information about a transaction. Vickrey devised what is now called the Vickrey auction, where bids are sealed and the highest bid wins but the second-highest bid is the price paid.

Vickrey was interested in many interdisciplinary fields and was known for showing up at seminars around the university. His interests also included ethics and philosophy; he wrote a number of papers in both areas. He lectured widely and served as a consultant in the United States and overseas and to the United Nations. Vickrey was the founding member of Taxation, Resources, and Economic Development. A popular economist, he was a member of or associated with many professional and civic organizations. He was an active supporter of organizations promoting world peace.

In 1996, three days before his death, Vickrey shared the Nobel Prize in Economics with James Mirrlees for their fundamental contributions to the economic theory of incentives under asymmetric information. Vickrey was elected to the National Academy of Sciences and served as president of the American Economic Association in 1992. He was a fellow of the Econometric Society and received the F. E. Seidman Distinguished Award in Political Economy.

William Vickrey died on October 11, 1996, in Harrison, New York.

Carol Lynn Nute

See Also Mirrlees, James; Public Goods; Taxes

Selected Works by William Vickrey

Vickrey, William. 1993. "My Innovative Failures in Economics." *Atlantic Economic Journal* 21: 1–9.

Vickrey, William. 1992. "Today's Task for Economists." *American Economic Review* 82: 1–10.

Vickrey, William. 1987. "Progressive and Regressive Taxation." In *The New Palgrave: A Dictionary of Economics*. Vol. 3. Edited by John Eatwell, Murray Milgate, and Peter Newman, 1021–25. London: Macmillan.

Vickrey, William. 1964. *Microstatics*. New York: Harcourt, Brace, and World.

Vickrey, William. 1963. "Pricing in Urban and Suburban Transport." *American Economic Review* 52, no. 2: 452–65.

Vickrey, William. 1962. "Auctions and Bidding Games." In *Recent Advances in Game Theory*. 15–27. Princeton University Conference.

Vickrey, William. 1961. "Counterspeculation, Auctions, and Competitive Sealed Tenders." *Journal of Finance* 16: 8–37.

Vickrey, William. 1960. "Utility, Strategy and Social Decision Rules." *Quarterly Journal of Economics* 74: 507–35.

Vickrey, William. 1955. "A Proposal for Revising New York's Subway Fare Structure." *Journal of the Operations Research Society of America* 3: 38–68.

Vickrey, William. 1948. "Some Objections to Marginal Cost Pricing." *Journal of Political Economy* 56: 218–38.

Vickrey, William. 1947. *Agenda for Progressive Taxation*. New York: Ronald Press.

Vickrey, William. 1939. "Averaging of Income for Income Tax Purposes." *Journal of Political Economy* 47: 379–97.

Selected Works about William Vickrey

"Biography." 1996. NobelPrize.org. http://www.nobelprize.org/nobel_prizes/economics/laureates/1996/vickrey-bio.html.

National Academies Press. 2014. "William S. Vickrey by Dreze, Jacques H." http://www.nap.edu/html/biomems/wvickrey.html.

Victoria Transport Policy Institute. 1992. "Principles of Efficient Congestion Pricing, by William Vickrey, Columbia University, June 1992." http://www.vtpi.org/vickrey.htm/.

"William S. Vickrey." 2008. In *The Concise Encyclopedia of Economics*. Edited by David R. Henderson. The Library of Economics and Liberty. http://www.econlib.org/library/Enc/bios/Vickrey.html.

Volcker, Paul

Born: September 5, 1927, in Cape May, New Jersey; American; financial economist, monetarist, chairman of the Federal Reserve Board (1979–1987); Major Work: *Good Intentions Corrupted: The Oil-for-Food Scandal and the Threat to the U.N.* (with Jeffrey A. Meyer and Mark G. Califano) (2006).

Paul Volcker became chair of the Federal Reserve Board in 1979, during a period of historically high inflation rates accompanied by low economic growth rates, known as stagflation. During such periods, economic policy makers are presented with a dilemma, since policy to control inflation will often result in depressed economic conditions, including high unemployment. Volcker, unlike previous Federal Reserve Board chairs, implemented an unpopular monetary policy to lower inflation rates. At the time, his actions were widely criticized. Though the policy was unpopular and there were negative consequences, Volcker was successful in lowering and controlling the inflation rate.

Paul Adolph Volcker was born on September 5, 1927, in Cape May, New Jersey, and grew up in Teaneck, New Jersey. He graduated from Princeton University in 1949, obtained an MA from Harvard University in 1951, and studied at the London School of Economics after graduate school. Volcker has been awarded more than 50 honorary degrees recognizing his contributions as an economist.

Volcker's first job began in 1952 as an economist at the Federal Reserve Bank of New York before leaving government employment to become a financial economist at Chase Manhattan Bank in 1957. In 1962, he returned to government service in the Department of the Treasury as the director of financial analysis and was promoted in 1963 to deputy undersecretary for monetary affairs. Volcker returned to the private sector in 1965 as vice president of Chase Manhattan Bank. Again returning to government service in 1969, he was appointed to the position of undersecretary for monetary affairs at the Treasury Department. While serving in this capacity, he was an important participant in ending the Bretton Woods Agreement, which had established exchange rates based on gold and removing the United States from the gold standard. In ending the Bretton Woods Agreement, the dollar and the other currencies were allowed to float in determining their values. Volcker became a senior fellow at the Woodrow Wilson School of Public and International Affairs at Princeton University in 1974 before becoming president of the Federal Reserve Bank of New York in 1975 until 1979.

Volcker was appointed as chairman of the Federal Reserve Board in 1979. His appointment took place in the midst of an economic period known as stagflation. During stagflation, inflation rates are abnormally high and economic growth rates are low. Inflation peaked at 13.5 percent in 1981. Immediately upon becoming chairman, Volcker implemented a monetary policy targeting money supply growth as a method to drastically lower inflation rates. In order to accomplish this, Volcker increased the federal funds rate to a high of 20 percent and the prime rate rose to 21.5 percent in 1981. This policy was widely criticized, since the effect was to radically increase unemployment (9.7% and 9.8% in 1982 and 1983, respectively) and produce high interest rates (30-year fixed mortgage rates exceeded 13%), which further slowed economic activity. However, by 1983, his policy successfully lowered the inflation rate to 3.2 percent. Volcker's policy worked and inflation was brought under control. For many Americans, he went from the villain to the conqueror. Volcker left as chair of the Federal Reserve Board of Governors in 1987, and was replaced by Alan Greenspan.

After leaving the Federal Reserve, he joined the small investment banking firm of James D. Wolfensohn, Inc. In 1996, Volcker became chair of the Independent Committee of Eminent Persons (which became commonly known as the Volcker Commission), which investigated money held in Swiss banks by Holocaust victims. The result of Volcker's commission's investigation was to draw attention to a relationship between the Swiss banks and the Nazis. Their findings led to a $1.25 billion settlement to Holocaust survivors and their families. Volcker has served on a number of committees and foundations including: chairman of the International Accounting Standards Committee Foundation (2000–2006); head of an investigation of accounting practices of Arthur Andersen, which was responsible for auditing Enron (2002); led the UN's investigation of the UN oil-for-food program for Iraq (2004–2005); and chairman of the Economy Recovery Advisory Board under President Barack Obama (2009–February 2011).

While serving on the Economy Recovery Advisory Board, in 2009 he proposed what became known as the Volcker Rule, which would have severely restricted commercial banks from capital market and trading activities—hedge funds, private equity funds, commodities trading, and derivatives—by separating commercial banks from investment banks. The rule proposed by Volcker was not enacted, but a less stringent version was passed in the Financial Reform Act of 2010.

Descriptions of Volcker include "irascibly honest," "an inflexible man of integrity," "Mr. Incorruptible," and "a fair and strong leader in troubled times." Standing at six feet seven inches tall and armed with a determined personality, Volcker was an imposing and unyielding policy maker who was successful in doing what other chairmen were unable to do. He reined in inflation during a time of double-digit inflation rates, but is also criticized for putting the American economy into recession. Politically, Volcker is considered a Democrat; however, his reputation during government service has generally been that of being nonpartisan. Volcker's economic perspective is one of caution, faith in markets, and common sense.

Jean Kujawa

See Also Burns, Arthur; Contractionary Monetary Policy; Expansionary Monetary Policy; Greenspan, Alan; Monetary Policy

Selected Works by Paul Volcker

Meyer, Jeffrey A., Mark G. Califano, and Paul Volcker. 2006. *Good Intentions Corrupted: The Oil-for-Food Scandal and the Threat to the UN*. New York: Public Affairs.

Volcker, Paul A., and Toyoo Gyohten. 1992. *Changing Fortunes*. New York: Times Books.

Selected Works about Paul Volcker

Morris, Charles. 2009. *The Sages: Warren Buffett, George Soros, Paul Volcker, and the Maelstrom of Markets*. New York: Public Affairs.

Neikirk, William R. 1987. *Volcker: Portrait of the Money Man*. New York: Congdon & Weed.

Treaster, Joseph. 2004. *Paul Volcker: The Making of a Financial Legend*. Hoboken, NJ: Wiley.

Volstead Act (See Prohibition)

Voluntary Exchange

A fundamental issue in economics is the allocation of scarce resources, goods, and services. In most free market and mixed market economic regimes, this fundamental issue of allocation is best addressed through voluntary exchange. This very basic yet fundamental concept of voluntary exchange is often ignored due to its simplicity; however, voluntary exchange should not be discounted, as it is foundational to understanding economics and the history of markets.

Voluntary exchange is best defined as a transaction in which a buyer and seller exercise their economic freedom by working out their own terms of exchange that are mutually beneficial to the parties involved. In order for voluntary exchange to function properly in a market economy, individuals who enter into these mutually beneficial exchange relationships must recognize these exchange relationships as mutually beneficial, and they have to be able to commit to fulfill their contractual obligations.

In modern economies, most institutions structure our relationships in a manner that enables us to benefit from transacting or engaging in voluntary exchange. The main way in which institutions encourage voluntary exchange is through the use of incentives. For example, financial institutions pay people interest for keeping their money in that institution. This interest encourages people to transact with the bank, and the end result is that both parties involved in the transaction, the bank and the customer, benefit from the transaction. The customer is benefiting as he or she is earning money on the deposit, and the bank is benefiting as it now has more funds to loan out, which means that it will earn interest as people pay back their loans. However, if one of the parties involved in the exchange does not fulfill the terms of the contract, that exchange will no longer be viewed as mutually beneficial, and others will have no incentive to engage in similar transactions. These transactions result in economic growth, and if they are not occurring, it will most likely result in stagnation in an economy.

Economic Performance as It Relates to Voluntary Exchange

Ever since the days of Adam Smith, it has been recognized that the ability to exchange contributes greatly to economic efficiency, which in turn promotes economic growth. By allowing people to voluntarily engage in transactions, it enables natural comparative advantage and the division of labor, which both bring out prosperity in various ways, such as the use of specialization, learning by doing, and technological innovation. All three of these result in a more efficient use of resources, which helps address the fundamental problem of scarcity in economics. From this, one can conjecture that allowing individuals the ability to exchange influences economic performance over time.

For example, central to our account of how the West grew rich are periods of expanding exchange relationships. These relationships include the late medieval commercial revolution, the rise of the Atlantic economies, the commercial ascendency of the Dutch Republic and England, and the nineteenth-century growth of the international economy through the promotion of free trade. In all of these historical periods, economic growth was seen, and it is believed that this growth was a product of institutions changing in ways that encouraged rather than prohibited exchange. Despite these time periods having different social and political environments surrounding their institutional changes, the importance of institutions governing voluntary exchange is evident in all of them. It was concluded that what must be present in facilitating voluntary exchange are things such as the establishment of a political unit that is able to govern the contracts to ensure that both parties are holding up their end of the exchange, and the enabling of not only local transactions but also long-distance trade based on the theory of comparative advantage. Whether local or long distance, it is crucial that there is a governing body to ensure that the parties involved in the exchange both follow through according to the contract of exchange. If the contract of exchange is not upheld on both ends, it is no longer mutually beneficial, and therefore it no longer results in transactions that promote prosperity.

Despite little to no quantitative research on voluntary exchange, the basic premise of voluntary exchange—that it is voluntary and therefore mutually beneficial—is evidence enough that as long as institutions are present to govern the transactions and ensure that all parties follow through, transactions will continue to occur. When transactions continually occur, there will be economic growth and prosperity.

Emily N. Manoogian

See Also Friedman, Milton; Hayek, Friedrich von; Market Capitalism; Mises, Ludwig von; North American Free Trade Agreement (NAFTA); Smith, Adam

Further Reading

Damodaran, A. 1996. *Voluntary Exchange of Information.* Delhi: Government of India, Ministry of External Affairs.

Greif, Avner. 2000. *The Fundamental Problem of Exchange: A Research Agenda in Historical Institutional Analysis.* Cambridge: Cambridge University Press.

Preston, Larry M. 1984. "Freedom, Markets, and Voluntary Exchange." *The American Political Science Review* 78, no. 4: 959–70.

Resources for Teachers

Foundation for Teaching Economics. N.d. "Lesson 10: International Markets." http://www.fte.org/teacher-resources/lesson-plans/efllessons/lesson-10-international-markets/.

Fraser Institute. N.d. "The Magic of Markets: How Trade Creates Wealth." http://www.fraserinstitute.org/uploadedFiles/fraser-ca/Content/education-programs/teachers/classroom-resources/Lesson-Plan-Trade.pdf.

National Council on Economic Education. N.d. "Why Nations Trade." EcEdWeb Economics Lesson. http://ecedweb.unomaha.edu/lessons/feog1.htm.

Niederjohn, Scott. 2010. "The Trading Game." econedlink. http://www.econedlink.org/lessons/index.php?lid=855&type=educator.

Wagner Act (See National Labor Relations Act of 1935)

Welfare State

A welfare state emphasizes programs that provide citizens with a minimum standard of living, seek to redistribute income, and bridge the gap of inequality that exists.

A welfare state contributes to short-term stability for those who meet requirements for welfare (or social welfare) programs. A welfare state may include public programs such as Temporary Aid to Needy Families (TANF); unemployment compensation; and other transfer payments, such as Social Security and Medicare, that work to aid those who meet the criteria for benefits. The effect of these programs is to redistribute equity based on taxes and transfer payments. The welfare state may also include some private benefits employees receive from their employers, nonprofit charities, or government subsidies. This can be in the form of health insurance in which the employee only pays a portion of his or her health care costs, with the rest being covered by the employer.

The welfare state is heavily tied to full-employment policies that are meant to support it. If more people are working, there are more people paying taxes, and some of this tax revenue can be used to support the welfare state. In addition, programs like unemployment compensation allow workers to be selective about accepting a job; this may cause some to hold out for a higher paying job and remain unemployed longer.

The modern welfare state is attributed to the programs of Otto von Bismarck of Germany in the 1870s. Bismarck's programs included sickness insurance and medical care, pensions, and a minimum wage. These programs helped him to win the support of Germany's working class, and by 1913, most of Germany's workers were covered by social programs. These ideas later spread to other countries, such as the United Kingdom, in the 1900s. The United States would adopt welfare state programs in the 1930s during the Great Depression.

The extent of a welfare state varies by country and region. There tends to be a more extensive welfare state in Europe than in other regions. Market economists such as the late Milton Friedman and supply-side economists such as Arthur Laffer argued that countries with an extensive welfare state have less economic growth when compared to countries with fewer government-sponsored provisions. They believed that low-skilled workers hurt the economy, pushing wages down and increasing unemployment rates.

Comparatively, the United States can be said to be a partial welfare state, with fewer provisions when compared to European countries. The effectiveness or level of a welfare state relates to other factors, such as unemployment and fiscal policy. There are more demands on a welfare state when there is high unemployment or when the economy is struggling, such as during a recession or depression. If a country has a high debt, this generally means less money for a welfare state.

The United States began to establish the infrastructure of a modern welfare state as a result of the Great Depression and the New Deal programs instituted by President Franklin D. Roosevelt. The Social Security Act of 1935 gave benefits to retirees as well as the unemployed and disabled. Initially, the intent of the program was to help alleviate the poverty of the large numbers of people who were unemployed as a result of the Depression. Prior to this act, the elderly were dependent on charity and personal savings when they could no longer physically work. The program would later be expanded through the Federal Income Tax Contributions Act of 1937 in order to collect payroll taxes from people in employment. The revenue from these taxes would be used to fund Social Security payments to those receiving benefits.

In the 1960s, the U.S. welfare state expanded under President Lyndon B. Johnson's War on Poverty programs of the Great Society. President Johnson drew much attention to poverty and the standard of living in the United States; he signed Social Security Amendments in 1965, which established the Medicare and Medicaid programs. The programs aimed to provide health insurance for the elderly and the poor, and were a result of years of research on poverty and income inequality. The implementation of these programs led to a further study of the welfare state, and it was realized that poverty must be addressed to help people achieve a higher standard of living.

In a modern welfare state, most social programs are created to benefit the unhealthy and the poor. Sometimes the welfare state is referred to as "workfare" because people need to meet certain requirements to get benefits, such as having a job. Workfare works best when unemployment is low. Political parties and interest groups also play a role, and some seek to reexamine the benefits that people receive as a result of the welfare state.

Today, there are many political and economic pressures on the welfare state. Conservatives favor retrenchment when it comes to the welfare state, while progressives and populists favor expansion. The conservatives fear that if unemployment becomes too high during periods of economic recession, the welfare expansion will place too large a burden on government spending. Progressives promote expansion of the welfare state to be sure the social safety net will cover all who are entitled.

Angela M. LoPiccolo

See Also Entitlements; Great Society; Keynesian Economics; New Deal; Social Security Act of 1935

Further Reading

Alesina, Alberto, Edward Glaeser, and Bruce Sacerdote. 2001. "Why Doesn't the United States Have a European-Style Welfare State?" *Brookings Papers on Economic Activity:* 187–277.

Atkinson, Anthony Barnes. 1996. "The Economics of the Welfare State." *The American Economist* 40: 5–15.

Khodour-Casteras, David. 2008. "Welfare State and Labor Mobility: The Impact of Bismarck's Social Legislation on German Emigration before World War I." *The Journal of Economic History* 68: 211–43.

Korpi, Walter. 2003. "Welfare-State Regress in Western Europe: Politics, Institutions, Globalization, and Europeanization." *Annual Review of Sociology* 29: 589–609.

Lindbeck, Assar. 1997. "Full Employment and the Welfare State." *The American Economist* 41: 3–14.

Palier, Bruno, ed. 2010. *A Long Goodbye to Bismarck? The Politics of Welfare Reform in Continental Europe.* Amsterdam: Amsterdam University Press.

Pierson, Paul. 1996. "The New Politics of the Welfare State." *World Politics* 48: 143–79.

Sheikh, Anwar. 2003. "Who Pays for the 'Welfare' in the Welfare State? A Multicountry Study." *Social Research* 70: 531–50.

United States Social Security Administration. N.d. "Social Security." http://www.ssa.gov/.

Vogel, Joachim. 2003. "Welfare State." *Social Indictors Research* 64: 373–91.

Waddell, Brian. 2001. "Limiting National Interventionism in the United States:" The Warfare-Welfare State as Restrictive Governance Paradigm." *Capital & Class* 74: 109–39.

Wildasin, David E. 2004. "Economic Integration and the Welfare State." *CESifo Forum* 5:19–26.

Resources for Teachers

Barr, Nicholas. 2012. *Economics of the Welfare State.* Oxford: Oxford University Press.

Folbre, Nancy, and Douglas Wolf. 2013. "The Intergenerational Welfare State." *Population and Development Review* 38: 36–51.

Hacker, Jacob S. 2002. *The Divided Welfare State: The Battle over Public and Special Benefits in the United States.* Cambridge: Cambridge University Press.

Huber, Evelyne, and John D. Stephens. 2001. *Development and Crisis of the Welfare State: Parties and Politics in Global Markets.* Chicago: University of Chicago Press.

PBS. N.d. "How Insurance Has Shaped Our World: Lesson Overview." http://www.pbs.org/wnet/ascentofmoney/lessons/how-insurance-has-shaped-our-world/lesson-overview/57/.

Wilensky, Harold L. 1975. *The Welfare State and Equality: Structural and Ideological Roots of Public Expenditures.* Berkeley: University of California Press.

West Coast Hotel Co. v. Parrish, 300 U.S. 379 (1937)

Supreme Court Case on Minimum Wage

Economic Concepts

Contracts; laissez-faire economics; minimum wage; transaction costs

Economic Impact

The constitutionality of minimum wage and negotiating contracts

Economic Summary

The Great Depression set the stage for the *West Coast Hotel Co. v. Parrish* in 1937. The specific circumstances of the case involve the constitutionality of minimum wage laws. The case served as an early example of a shift in thought regarding the role of government in the economy from the traditional laissez-faire (an economic environment where transactions are free from government intervention) to more active participation (e.g., Roosevelt's New Deal legislation).

In a broader social view, this case was about women as socioeconomically disadvantaged workers; the responsibility of businesses to adhere to wages that allow people to meet basic living demands; the extent to which the U.S. Constitution guarantees individuals freedom of contract (the liberty to contract with another without government restrictions); and the appearance of political manipulation of the Supreme Court by the president to realign review powers safeguarding New Deal policies.

Case Summary

The West Coast Hotel Company owned the Cascadian Hotel in Wenatchee, Washington, where Elsie Parrish and her husband were employed in 1933. Elsie Parrish was paid a weekly wage of $12 for 48 hours of cleaning hotel rooms. A couple of decades earlier, in 1913, the state of Washington had passed an act establishing working standards for businesses hiring women and minors. The particular vulnerability of women to be potentially exploited by employers was deemed by the Washington State Legislature as meriting legal protection.

The 1913 act established the state-based Industrial Welfare Commission to set minimum standards for working conditions, hours, and wages. A minimum wage of $14.50 for 48 hours of work was stipulated in the law. Washington was not the only state to pass such legislation. New York, Washington, D.C., and others had passed similar minimum wage standards for women as well. Elsie Parrish requested compensation in the amount of $216.96. This accrued amount was the difference in wages actually paid to her and what should have been paid to her during her employment from 1933 to 1935, according to the state minimum wage statutes.

The West Coast Hotel Company did not adhere to these state standards on the grounds that the standards infringed upon its freedom of contract as an employer and were oppressive to its business operations. Elsie Parrish sued the West Coast Hotel Company in Washington's Chelan County Superior Court. Judge Parr heard the case and ruled in favor of the respondent, West Coast Hotel. The court held that minimum wage legislation for women was an unconstitutional infringement on the freedom of contract, as protected by the due process clause of the Fifth Amendment to the U.S. Constitution, which limits the power of the federal government. The judge stated that the Supreme Court's ruling in *Adkins v. Children's Hospital* (1923) had established that minimum wage laws for women were unconstitutional. The *Adkins* case involved a Washington, D.C., statute regarding minimum wage for women and was, according to Judge Parr, appropriate to this case as well. Elsie Parrish appealed her case to the Washington State Supreme Court. The State Supreme Court upheld the legislature's statute supporting minimum wage for women and declared that *Adkins* was not applicable in the case of Washington's law. West Coast Hotel Company appealed its case to the U.S. Supreme Court, and in 1936 was granted certiorari (a writ to the lower court to send the case for review). The question for the Supreme Court was whether or not to overrule *Adkins*.

The following events happened to coincide with these legal proceedings and should be noted due to the contribution they made to the lasting significance of this case. In

November 1936, Franklin Roosevelt was reelected president. Roosevelt's New Deal policy continued, though several programs were struck down by the Supreme Court as unconstitutional. Subsequently, President Roosevelt submitted to Congress a proposal for legislation to add one federal judge for every federal judge over the age of 70. This would allow the president to add six justices of his political ideology to the Supreme Court. This would change the composition of the Supreme Court from 9 justices to 15, gaining a majority of New Deal like-mindedness on the Court. This proposal was announced on December 19, 1936. Of the nine justices on the Supreme Court who heard this case, four were over 70 years old and voted against President Roosevelt's New Deal policies (Justices Sutherland, Van Devanter, Butler, and McReynolds). In addition, Justice Owen Roberts voted with these four conservative justices, constituting a conservative majority that determined much of President Roosevelt's New Deal legislation unconstitutional.

The Supreme Court heard the arguments in *West Coast Hotel Co. v. Parrish* on December 16, 1936, and announced the opinion of the Court in March 1937. Justice Roberts, who prior to this case voted in favor of Adkins, changed his vote to the opposite opinion, leaving the four older justices in the dissenting opinion. The dissenting opinion affirmed the *Adkins* case, using the argument that freedom of contract made minimum wage laws unconstitutional. The majority opinion was written by Chief Justice Hughes, who included the current conditions of the economy as a reason to revisit *Adkins*. Thus he gave insight into the capacity of the Constitution to adapt to changing times, which was a clear indication of a change in judicial philosophy. In addition, the majority argued that minimum wage laws for women were not arbitrary, due to the fact that denial of a living wage cast a direct burden for their support on the community and harmed the general welfare. The Court also distinguished the fact that the Constitution did not speak of freedom of contract; rather, it spoke of freedom only in the context of liberty, which is not absolute and uncontrollable. Within the context of a society, liberty is safeguarded, but these limitations to individual liberty are what allow a government to enact laws to protect the general welfare. The Court also noted that due to practical realities, employers and employees did not share equal freedom in negotiating contracts.

The Supreme Court overruled the *Adkins* case and the judgment of the Supreme Court of the state of Washington was affirmed. This case had enduring significance in that it gave a green light to states to pass minimum wage laws. Furthermore, it opened the floodgates to other New Deal legislation. Two weeks later, the Supreme Court upheld the National Labor Relations Act of 1935 (Wagner Act), and six weeks later, the Social Security Act, which gave the appearance of a simultaneous change of judicial ideology coinciding with Roosevelt's plan to add six federal judges to the Supreme Court who agreed with his New Deal philosophy.

Whether or not President Roosevelt's idea to stack the court with judges who favored his New Deal politics affected the decision of Justice Roberts is unclear. After the *West Coast Hotel Co. v. Parrish* decision, President Roosevelt's plan to add federal judges lost steam. However, Roosevelt encouraged the justices who were 70 years old and older to take advantage of the Judiciary Act of 1869, where Congress voted to fund pensions for retiring judges at their full salary. Whatever conclusions may be drawn from these coincidental events, the fact remains that after this case, there was a marked change in Supreme Court majority opinions from a conservative judicial philosophy to increased government regulation and participation in the economy, and no increase in the number of judges on the Supreme Court.

Kathleen C. Simmons

See Also National Labor Relations Act of 1935 (Wagner Act); New Deal; Social Security Act of 1935

Related Cases

Lochner v. New York, 198 U.S. 45 (1905)

Adkins v. Children's Hospital, 261 U.S. 525 (1923)

Further Readings

Cornell University Law School, Legal Information Institute. N.d. "*West Coast Hotel Co. v. Parrish* (No. 293) 185 Wash. 581; 55 P.2d 1083, affirmed." http://www.law.cornell.edu/supct/html/historics/USSC_CR_0300_0379_ZS.html.

OYEZ, U.S. Supreme Court Media, ITT Chicago, Kent College of Law. N.d. "*Adkins v. Children's Hospital*." http://www.oyez.org/cases/1901-1939/1922/1922_795/.

OYEZ, U.S. Supreme Court Media, ITT Chicago, Kent College of Law. N.d. "*West Coast Hotel Co. v. Parrish*." http://www.oyez.org/cases/1901-1939/1936/1936_293.

Resources for Teachers

FDR and the Supreme Court. N.d. "Lesson Plans for FDR and the Supreme Court." http://newdeal.feri.org/court/lesson.htm.

Internet Archive, Community Video. N.d. "Through the Years [1 of 4] Important Washington Cases and Their Enduring Significance, Washington Courts Historical Society." http://archive.org/details/ThroughTheYears1Of4ImportantWashingtonCasesAndTheirEnduring?start=3839.5.

Williams, Walter

Born: March 31, 1936, in Philadelphia, Pennsylvania; American; government in economy, minimum wage, private property, libertarianism; Major Works: *The State against Blacks* (1982), *South Africa's War against Capitalism* (1990), *Do the Right Thing: The People's Economist Speaks* (1995), *Race and Economics: How Much Can Be Blamed on Discrimination?* (2011).

Walter Williams has served as the John M. Olin Distinguished Professor of Economics at George Mason University in Fairfax, Virginia, since 1980. He is the author of 10 books and over 150 publications in scholarly journals such as *Economic Inquiry* and the *American Economic Review*, as well as popular publications such as *Newsweek* and *National Review*. He frequently appears on television and radio programs such as *Nightline*, *Face the Nation*, or the *Rush Limbaugh* show. He is known for his libertarian views, including the limited role of government intervention with respect to minorities.

Walter Edward Williams was born on March 31, 1936, in Philadelphia, Pennsylvania. His mother, Catherine, raised him in a single-parent home, and the family lived at one point in the Richard Allen housing projects. He is second cousin to basketball player Julius Erving, otherwise known as "Dr. J." After graduating from Philadelphia public schools, Williams spent two years as a taxi driver before becoming a private in the U.S. Army. Williams began as a sociology major at California State College in Los Angeles before switching to economics. Although he earned a D in his first course, he persevered and ultimately earned his bachelor's degree in economics from California State College in Los Angeles in 1965. He received his MA in 1968 and his PhD in 1972, both in economics from the University of California, Los Angeles. Williams studied under Nobel laureates Armen Alchian and Milton Friedman. He also began a lasting friendship with visiting economist Thomas Sowell. Williams began to question whether government social programs like minimum wage and affirmative action were truly helping those in need. Williams then taught for eight years at Temple University in Philadelphia before joining the economics faculty at George Mason University in Fairfax, Virginia, in 1980.

Williams's work expresses doubts about the effectiveness of government social programs to promote prosperity. In his 1982 book *The State against Blacks*, Williams argues that government initiatives such as affirmative action only serve to hurt minorities and stifle their economic progress. He writes that college admission standards should be equal for all, and that minorities do not benefit from artificial measures designed to boost their enrollment numbers. Williams believes that substandard test performance by minorities is the result of substandard secondary education and family breakdown. He writes that the government has a monopoly on public education, which leads to a low quality with lack of competition. Government programs such as welfare reward childbirth out of wedlock, thus contributing to the collapse of black communities. PBS used his book *The State against Blacks* as the basis for the documentary *Good Intentions*.

In addition, Williams argues that minimum wage laws price low-skill workers out of the market and increase unemployment. In 1977, the Joint Economic Committee of Congress asked him to write about minimum wage. Williams reported that black teenage unemployment was lower than that of whites before minimum wage and higher afterward. His research also found that the Davis-Bacon Act of 1931, which required high worker wages for federally financed construction projects, was designed to discriminate against workers based on their race.

Similarly, in *South Africa's War against Capitalism* (1990), Williams argues that South African apartheid was not created for white exploitation but as a reaction to World War I, designed to encourage the hiring of higher-paid white workers. Williams again promotes his belief that capitalism without government intervention will provide the highest standard of living for all.

Williams's overall support of deregulation and laissez-faire government can be described as libertarian. Williams is one of few scholars to defend individuals' rights to sell bodily organs. He continues to write a nationally syndicated weekly column carried in approximately 140 newspapers and on multiple Web sites. He regularly participates in national debates, conferences, and lectures, as well as providing expert testimony before congressional committees on public policy issues. He serves on the boards of Grove City College, Reason Foundation, and Chase Foundation, and on the advisory boards of the Cato Institute,

Landmark Legal Foundation, Institute of Economic Affairs, and the Heritage Foundation. He has received numerous awards and fellowships, such as the Foundation for Economic Education Adam Smith Award, a Hoover Institution National Fellowship, and a Ford Foundation Fellowship, to name a few. Williams is a member of the Mont Pelerin Society and the American Economic Association.

Kathryn Lloyd Gustafson

See Also Classical Economics; Friedman, Milton; Private Property; Sowell, Thomas

Selected Works by Walter Williams

Williams, Walter. 2011. *Race and Economics: How Much Can Be Blamed on Discrimination?* Stanford, CA: Hoover Institution Press.

Williams, Walter. 1995. *Do the Right Thing: The People's Economist Speaks*. Stanford, CA: Hoover Institution Press.

Williams, Walter. 1990. *South Africa's War against Capitalism*. Rev. ed. Cape Town: Juta.

Williams, Walter. 1982. *The State against Blacks*. New York: McGraw-Hill.

Selected Works about Walter Williams

Miller, John J. 2011. "Walter Williams." *Hey Miller*, March 19. Accessed August 25, 2012. http://www.heymiller.com/2011/03/walter-williams/.

National Cable Satellite Operation. 2012. "Q&A Walter E. Williams." March 18. Accessed August 25, 2012. http://www.q-and-a.org/Program/?ProgramID=1383.

Riley, Jason L. 2011. "The State against Blacks." *Wall Street Journal*, January 22. http://online.wsj.com/article/SB10001424052748704881304576094221050061598.html.

Williams, Walter E. 2010. *Up from the Projects: An Autobiography*. Stanford, CA: Hoover Institution Press.

Wilson-German Tariff Act (See Revenue Act of 1894)

World Bank

The World Bank, formerly known as the International Bank for Reconstruction and Development (IBRD), was officially founded in July 1944 in the city of Bretton Woods, New Hampshire. The agreement to form the IBRD was largely contributed by representatives from the United Kingdom and the United States.

The World Bank is a cooperative made up of 188 member countries. These member countries can also be considered as shareholders. They are represented by a board of governors that is the ultimate policy maker at the World Bank. The governors are member countries' ministers of finance or ministers of development. They meet once a year at the annual meetings of the boards of governors of the World Bank Group and the International Monetary Fund. The World Bank is headed by a president nominated by the board of executive directors. A president is entitled to a renewable five-year term. The World Bank is an institution made up of two independent organizations, the International Bank for Reconstruction and Development (IBRD) and the International Development Association (IDA), which assist the poorest countries with their development needs.

The World Bank is recognized as an international financial institution with a goal of ending poverty in the world. The World Bank is headquartered in Washington, D.C. The organization has more than 10,000 employees and has 120 offices worldwide. The World Bank has staff members from various working backgrounds, including economists, public policy experts, sector experts, and social scientists. The World Bank's mission is to work toward ending poverty by providing loans to developing nations for capital programs.

The World Bank has established different methods of ending poverty in developing nations. The different methodologies include investments in environmental and natural resource management, education, health, public administration, infrastructure, and financial and private sector development. Most projects are jointly funded in conjunction with private investors, commercial banks, governments, and other interested institutions.

The establishment of the Innovative Knowledge Sharing initiative has brought programs and educational tools to developing nations. Through the Innovative Knowledge Sharing, the World Bank supports developing countries with policy advice, research and analysis, technical assistance, investment advice to developing countries on their investments, and supporting capacity development in countries that the bank is serving. The World Bank sponsors, hosts, and participates in a wide range of conferences and forums on issues pertaining to development, usually with the help of outside partners.

The World Bank has continuously worked to help developing nations end poverty using five of its internal institutions. The International Bank for Reconstruction and Development (IBRD) was founded in 1944. It aims to reduce poverty in middle-income countries and creditworthy poorer countries by promoting sustainable development through loans, guarantees, risk management products, and analytical and advisory services.

The International Development Association (IDA) was founded in 1944, and aims to reduce poverty by providing loans also referred to as "credits" and grants for programs that boost economic growth, reduce inequalities, and improve people's living conditions. The International Finance Corporation (IFC) was launched in 1950. It is the largest global development institution focused exclusively on the private sector. The IFC helps developing countries achieve sustainable growth by financing investment, mobilizing capital in international financial markets, and providing advisory services to businesses and governments.

The Multilateral Investment Guarantee Agency (MIGA), founded in 1988, aims to promote foreign direct investment into developing countries to support economic growth, reduce poverty, and improve people's lives. MIGA fulfills this mandate by offering political risk insurance (guarantees) to investors and lenders. The International Centre for Settlement of Investment Disputes (ICSID) was created as an impartial international forum providing facilities for the resolution of legal disputes between eligible parties through conciliation or arbitration procedures.

Bernard P. Kanjoma

See Also Bretton Woods Agreement; International Monetary Fund (IMF); World Trade Organization (WTO)

Further Reading

Gerber, James. 2011. *International Economics*. 6th ed. San Diego: Pearson Education.

International Bank for Reconstruction and Development. N.d. "Background." http://web.worldbank.org/WBSITE/EXTERNAL/EXTABOUTUS/EXTIBRD/0,,contentMDK:21130269~menuPK:3168298~pagePK:64168445~piPK:64168309~theSitePK:3046012,00.html World Bank.

International Centre for Settlement of Investment and Disputes (ICSID). N.d. "World Bank/International Centre for Settlement of Investment and Disputes." https://icsid.worldbank.org/ICSID/Index.jsp.

International Finance Corporation. N.d. "International Finance Corporation/World Bank." http://www.ifc.org/wps/wcm/connect/corp_ext_content/ifc_external_corporate_site/home.

Multilateral Investment Guarantee Agency. N.d. "Who We Are." http://www.miga.org/.

World Bank. N.d. "About." http://www.worldbank.org/en/about.

Resources for Teachers

IMF Center. N.d. "Lesson 1: Ten Basic Questions about Globalization." http://www.imf.org/external/np/exr/center/students/hs/think/lesson1.pdf.

The World Bank. N.d. "Vietnam: Personalized Lessons Keep Children from Ethnic Minorities in School." http://www.worldbank.org/en/news/feature/2013/09/04/vietnam-personalised-lessons-keep-children-from-ethnic-minorities-in-school.

World Trade Organization (WTO)

The intent of the World Trade Organization (WTO) is to supervise and liberalize international trade. The organization was officially introduced on January 1, 1995, under the Marrakech Agreement. The WTO replaced the General Agreement on Tariffs and Trade (GATT), which was established in 1948. The WTO is headquartered in Geneva, Switzerland. As of early 2013, the WTO had a membership of 159 countries. Besides the 159 members of the WTO, there are also observing members. The current number of observing members is 25. To apply for membership in the WTO, every country has to meet certain criteria set by the WTO. The economic development of a country applying for membership has a significant impact on whether the WTO approves a nation for membership. The leader of the WTO is referred to as a director-general. The WTO secretariat consists of experts in various professional fields of lawyers, economists, statisticians, and communications experts.

As the global economy developed and evolved, one main issue was the lack of an international organization to serve as arbiter when two countries had a trade conflict. One of the World Trade Organization's responsibilities is to serve in that role as a liaison to settle trade disputes between countries. Similarly, the WTO operates as a system of trade rules monitoring national trade policies. The WTO ensures that countries and governments are adhering to its rules, such as protecting consumers and preventing the spread of diseases between nations. It also provides technical assistance and training for developing countries and cooperates with other international organizations. The WTO can also aid nations as a place where governments negotiate trade agreements.

The WTO is a complex organization that is responsible for various trade topics. The WTO considers trade negotiations, including agreements that cover goods, services and intellectual property. It continually discusses the importance of the principles of liberalization with member nations, with allowable exceptions. The WTO promotes individual countries' commitments to lower their customs tariffs and various trade barriers.

All WTO members are obligated to have their trade policies and practices reviewed by the WTO to ensure that proper procedures are met. Implementing and monitoring WTO agreements require governments to make their trade policies known by notifying the WTO about laws and measures adopted. WTO councils and committees ensure that these requirements are being followed and that WTO agreements are being properly implemented.

The WTO has implemented procedures for resolving trade quarrels under the organization's dispute settlement understanding. This understanding is vital for enforcing the rules and thereby ensuring that trade among countries is flowing smoothly.

WTO agreements contain special provisions for developing countries to build trade capacity. These provisions may include longer time periods to implement agreements and commitments, measures that help increase trading opportunities, support to help developing nations build their trade capacity, and assistance to handle disputes and to implement technical standards. The WTO is responsible for organizing technical cooperation missions for developing countries annually.

The WTO ensures that aid for trade is geared toward helping developing countries develop the skills and infrastructure necessary to expand their trade. The WTO enforces regular dialogue with nongovernmental organizations, parliamentarians, and other international organizations. The WTO regularly educates the media and the general public on various aspects of the WTO and the ongoing negotiations among nations, with the aim of enhancing cooperation and increasing awareness of WTO activities. This is one of the biggest tasks the WTO has in order to keep its members informed on current trade issues necessary to be shared to the general public.

The WTO's secretariat organizational structure has subsidiary committees that help oversee various departments. There is a ministerial conference that has the following subsidiary groups. The Council for Trade in Goods is made up of 14 committees, and each committee has a specific task. Members of the WTO participate in the committees. The body has its own chair and 10 members. The body also has several groups relating to textiles. The Council for Trade-Related Aspects of Intellectual Property Rights is a second major group. This group centers on information regarding intellectual property and the WTO. It also provides news and official records of the activities on intellectual property. The WTO's work with other international organizations in this field is critical because other international organizations share information with the WTO in order to enhance trade security measures. The Council for Trade in Services and the Trade Negotiations Committee, also referred to as TNC, is the committee that deals with current trade talks. Because of the importance of this committee, the chair of this committee is the WTO's director-general.

In addition to trading policies, the WTO has initiated principles of national treatment and nondiscrimination. National treatment is the requirement that foreign goods are treated similarly to the same domestic goods once they enter a nation's markets. Nondiscrimination is also known as nondiscriminatory trading. It is embodied in the concept of most-favored nation (MFN) status. Most-favored nation status requires all WTO members to treat each other the same way the other nations treat their most-favored trading partner. This is a prohibition of trade discrimination. It is the intent of the WTO that all members consider all other members as a MFN regarding trade relations.

Bernard P. Kanjoma

See Also European (Economic) Community; International Monetary Fund (IMF); World Bank

Further Reading

Gerber, James. 2011. *International Economics*. 6th ed. San Diego: Pearson Education.

World Trade Organization. 2014. "Understanding the WTO: Who We Are." http://www.wto.org/english/thewto_e/whatis_e/who_we_are_e.htm.

World Trade Organization. 2014. "The WTO." http://www.wto.org/english/thewto_e/thewto_e.htm.

Resources for Teachers

Mace, Jon. 2009. "Teaching the WTO." tutor2u. Accessed November 24, 2013. http://www.tutor2u.net/blog/index.php/ib-diploma/comments/teaching-the-wt.

World Trade Organization. 2006. "WTO Structure." http://www.wto.org/english/thewto_e/whatis_e/tif_e/organigram_landscape_e.pdf.

World Trade Organization. 2014. "WTO Videos." http://www.wto.org/english/res_e/webcas_e/webcas_e.htm.

Yellen, Janet

Born: August 13, 1946, in Brooklyn, New York; American; macroeconomics, unemployment, fiscal policy, monetary policy; Major Work: *The Fabulous Decade: Macroeconomic Lessons from the 1990s* (2001).

Janet Yellen has served the academic sector in the classroom and the public sector as an advocate for the American people. She shared her knowledge of economics at Harvard University, the London School of Economics and Political Science, and the University of California, Berkeley, and she applied that knowledge while serving on the Board of Governors of the Federal Reserve System. Yellen currently holds the position of chair of the Board of Governors of the Federal Reserve System.

Janet Louise Yellen was born on August 13, 1946, in Brooklyn, New York. She graduated summa cum laude from Brown University in 1967 with a degree in economics and earned her PhD from Yale University in 1971. Yellen taught at Harvard as an associate professor from 1971 until 1976. She also taught at the London School of Economics and Political Science from 1978 until 1980, when she accepted a position with the University of California, Berkeley. She is professor emeritus of the Haas School of Business and has served as the Eugene E. and Catherine M. Trefethen Professor of Business and Professor of Economics. She specializes in macroeconomics, with an emphasis in the causes and effects of unemployment.

President Bill Clinton nominated Yellen as the chair of the Council of Economic Advisers in 1997, after she served as a member of the Board of Governors of the Federal Reserve, a position to which she was appointed in 1994. Her efforts were primarily focused on the stabilization of foreign exchange rates and international trade. Her work during the 1990s helped lead her into numerous leadership positions during the latter part of the decade and into the twenty-first century.

Yellen was named president and chief executive officer of the Twelfth District Federal Reserve Bank at San Francisco in 2004. Her work on the current state of the U.S. economy has prompted her testimony toward guiding appropriate macroeconomic and monetary policy for the betterment of the American people. She believes that policy should improve the lives of those it governs. Her emphasis has been on promoting policy that will both reduce the breadth, depth, and frequency of economic downturns as well as focus on long-term, sustainable growth over time. These policy changes are paramount in promoting a higher standard of living for the American people. Her work has emphasized understanding the disparity of wage increases over the past 30 years, and exploring the implications of attaining education and the impact of technology on the workforce.

Yellen's contributions to the economic community have been vast, as she has worked in the Federal Reserve System and in the classroom. She has written papers, taught classes, and helped shape monetary policy in the United States. Aside from these positions she was a member of the Council on Foreign Relations, the American Academy of Arts and Sciences, Federal Open Market Committee, the Group of 30, the executive committee of the Bay Area Council, and a research associate of the National Bureau of Economic Research. She served as president of the Western Economic Association, vice president of the American Economic Association, and fellow of the Yale Corporation, and worked with a number of other organizations.

Yellen was named vice chair of the Board of Governors of the Federal Reserve System in October 2010. In January 2014, Janet Yellen became the first female chair of the Federal Reserve System Board of Governors.

William S. Chappell

See Also Bernanke, Ben; Contractionary Monetary Policy; Expansionary Monetary Policy; Federal Reserve System; Greenspan, Alan; Monetary Policy; National Bureau of Economic Research (NBER); Volcker, Paul

Selected Works by Janet Yellen

Akerlof, George, Andrew Rose, Janet Yellen, and Helga Hessenius. 1991. "East Germany in from the Cold: The Economic Aftermath of Currency Union." *Brookings Papers on Economic Activity* 22, no. 1: 1–106.

Yellen, Janet. 1998. "The Continuing Importance of Trade Liberalization." *Business Economics* (January 1).

Yellen, Janet. 1998. *The Inequality Paradox: Growth of Income Disparity*. Washington, DC: National Policy Association.

Yellen, Janet. 1997. "Trends in Income Inequality and Policy Responses." *Looking Ahead* (October).

Yellen, Janet, George Akerlof, and Michael Katz. 1996. "An Analysis of Out-of-Wedlock Childbearing in the United States." *Journal of Economics* 111, no. 2 (May): 277–317.

Yellen, Janet, and Alan Binder. 2001. *The Fabulous Decade: Macroeconomic Lessons from the 1990s*. New York: Century Foundation Press.

Selected Works about Janet Yellen

Council of Economic Advisers. N.d. "Dr. Janet L. Yellen." http://clinton4.nara.gov/WH/EOP/CEA/html/yellen.html.

Federal Reserve. N.d. "Janet L. Yellen." http://www.federalreserve.gov/aboutthefed/bios/board/yellen.htm.

Lang, Kevin. 2007. *Poverty and Discrimination*. Princeton, NJ: Princeton University Press.

Youngstown Sheet & Tube Co. v. Sawyer, 343 U.S. 579 (1952)

Supreme Court Case That Upheld the Private Ownership of the Factors of Production and Ownership/Labor Relationship

Economic Concepts

Capitalist system; factors of production; free enterprise system; labor strike; market economy; mixed economy; stabilization; wage and price controls; wages

Economic Impact

In this case, the executive branch of government, which is constitutionally charged with enforcing the law rather than making it, in effect made policy that tipped the scales in favor of government control of the means of production in the name of national security. The case addressed whether the president of the United States could, by executive order, essentially nationalize an industry in the name of national defense. The Supreme Court upheld the means of production as private property and the relationship between ownership and labor in a market economy.

Economic Summary

In a capitalist system, private ownership of the factors of production is a foundational principle. In the case of *Youngstown Sheet & Tube Co. v. Sawyer*, the president of the United States seized operations of private steel manufacturing by executive order. For President Truman, the decision came on the heels of the Korean conflict and was essential to keep armaments necessary for national security in production. The police action in Korea was, at worst, a potential World War III, and at best a test of American resolve during the Cold War era. This case is commonly referred to as the Steel Seizure Case, and it begs the question of how much power the federal government has in a free enterprise system.

In September 1950, Congress passed the Defense Production Act in response to the military involvement in Korea. This act authorized the president to, among other things, requisition property, impose wage and price controls, and settle wage disputes in the course of national defense. Congress did not declare the conflict in Korea a war. President Truman engaged Secretary of Commerce Charles Sawyer to take authority over the steel industries to avoid a labor strike that, in the president's opinion, would delay production of steel vital to the defense effort. The Steelworkers Union, which was invited to speak at the trial as an amicus curiae (friend of the court), had submitted a wage proposal that was met by the steel industry with the demand for a commensurate increase in the price of steel. The president's Wage and Price Stabilization Commission feared the impact this would have on inflation and did not approve the price increase.

The extent to which a market economy is free and the degree to which rules defining private property are secure is a matter of politics and public policy. The term "mixed economy" has been used to describe this balance between market forces and governmental power.

Case Summary

In a surprise move by Kim II Sung in June of 1950, North Korea invaded South Korea. The United Nations voted to condemn this invasion and provide assistance to South Korea. On June 25, 1950, President Harry Truman sent U.S. troops to support the United Nations. There were no congressional measures or wartime controls in place to stabilize the economy at this time, and the nation was experiencing a post–World War II inflationary period. In September 1950, Congress passed the Defense of Production Act. This act had several parts, but in one major section, it authorized the president to requisition property, force industry to expand production, and impose wage and price controls.

The allocation of raw materials to national security was also a part of this legislation. Hence, President Truman created the Wage Stabilization Board in an effort to control prices and avoid inflation. This, however, did not work well with the steel industry. The United Steelworkers Union offered a wage increase that the steel industry rejected. The steel industry's request for higher prices to meet wage increases was rejected as well by the government's Wage Stabilization Board. In response, the union prepared to strike.

The Truman administration believed that this interruption of steel production would jeopardize the strength of the U.S. Navy and Air Force in the current police effort in South Korea, and the domestic economy in general. Therefore, on April 8, 1952, he ordered Charles Sawyer, his secretary of commerce, to take possession of and operate most of the nation's steel mills. It was announced on television and radio. The lawyers for the steel industry filed an immediate restraining order (legal barrier to an action) with a U.S. district judge and the hearing took place the following day.

The motion was denied, and the case was assigned to another district judge, who heard the steel companies' motion for a preliminary injunction (legal stop to an action) and asked the question to the assistant attorney general where the president's authority to seize private property came from; the response was Article II of the Constitution and all the powers implied therein. The plaintiffs began with a persuasive summary of what the constitutional framers had outlined executive power to include, and ended with the image of a president overreaching those intentions. An injunction was issued, and thereafter the steelworkers, union began its strike.

The government appealed immediately to a D.C. Circuit Court of Appeals. On April 30, the appellate court held in favor of the government, placing a stay on the action of the district court. Meanwhile the steel companies had already filed and were granted certiorari (request for a lower court to send the records of the case to a higher court) by the Supreme Court.

The case was heard on May 12, 1952. The government pointed to the long record of seizures of private property during wartime, from the Revolutionary War to Lincoln during the Civil War, Wilson during World War I, and Roosevelt during World War II. The steel industry argued that only Congress had the power to enact laws that allowed the seizure of private property. John W. Davis gave an extensive speech on behalf of the steel industry, saying that too much power in the hands of an executive is exactly what the framers wanted to safeguard against when they wrote Article II of the Constitution. Meanwhile, the solicitor general for the Truman administration concluded the respondent's argument by claiming that this was wartime and the president did have the power to seize the mills. Unfortunately, the justices responded with the statement that Congress had in fact not declared war. The Supreme Court heard additional statements from the steelworkers' union and railroad unions.

The Court ruled in a surprising 6–3 vote in favor of the steel industry. Justice Black delivered the opinion of the Court. He stated that Congress had been informed by the president of the danger a strike would pose on national defense, yet chose to take no action, signaling that the legislative branch thought that action was not necessary. Indeed, no action was necessary, due to legislation already in place to handle such national crisis: the Defense Production Act. However, Justice Black continued, the government admitted that it did not meet the conditions necessary in this act for the president to take possession of private property. Justice Black added that the president's power as commander in chief of the armed forces also did not justify such a broad interpretation, whereby military authorities could settle a labor dispute using possession of private property. In conclusion, Justice Black stated that if previous presidents had acted in such a capacity without authority from Congress, it did not discount the fact that only Congress has the vested power to make all laws necessary and proper to carry out the functions of the government. The Supreme Court upheld the judgment of the district court.

Although Justice Black wrote the opinion of the Court, each of the justices who voted in the majority wrote individual opinions. Justice Jackson's concurring opinion, frequently referenced by legal scholars, agrees with Justice Black, but warns that presidents and judges alike cannot confuse the issue of a power's legitimacy with the grounds it is called upon to endorse, making policies that deal with wages or price stabilization and forgetting that the Constitution established the legislative powers to do just that. Five different concurring opinions contributed to future difficulty in interpreting executive power.

In his dissent, Chief Justice Vinson wrote for all three justices that were not in the majority. He stated that the power of future presidents to act in times of national crisis and military emergency was crucial, and therefore they could not agree with the majority, who in their numbers could agree on the ruling but not on the reasoning. As the last chief justice appointed by a Democratic president (Truman), Fred M. Vinson warned that extraordinary measures were needed when the nation was experiencing extraordinary times, as it was in 1952. In addition, he stated that when Congress approved Truman's defense budget, by funding the president's policies, it had given approval of them for all intents and purposes. To limit the president's power to statutes could endanger the nation and have global effects as well. In contrast, Justice Frankfurter speculated that history does more than teach us nothing; rather, in his concurring opinion he emphasizes the appropriate use of government's use of power within the necessary system of checks and balances. The *Youngstown* case was a check on executive power and a weight on the side of property rights.

Kathleen C. Simmons

See Also Economic Systems; Inflation; Private Property

Related Cases

La Abra Silver Mng. Co. v. United States, 175 U.S. 423 (1899)

Hooe v. United States, 218 U.S. 322 (1910)

United States v. North American Co., 253 U.S. 330 (1920)

Myers v. United States, 272 U.S. 52 (1926)

Springer v. Philippine Islands, 277 U.S. 189 (1928)

Larson v. Domestic & Foreign Corp., 337 U.S. 682 (1949)

Further Reading

Justia, U.S. Supreme Court. 1952. "*Youngstown Sheet & Tube Co. v. Sawyer*, 343 U.S. 579 (1952)." http://supreme.justia.com/cases/federal/us/343/579/case.html. (Transcript, Justice Black's majority opinion and all concurring and dissenting opinions)

OYEZ, ITT Chicago, Kent College of Law. N.d. "*Youngstown Sheet & Tube Co. v. Sawyer*, 343 U.S. 579. (1952)." http://www.oyez.org/cases/1950-1959/1951/1951_744. (Facts of the case)

Teaching Materials

Adler, David Gray. 2008. *Youngstown Sheet and Tube Co. v. Sawyer* (1952): A DocNotes Analysis. Dallas: Schlager Group.

4LawSchool, the Law School Authority. N.d. "*Youngstown Sheet and Tube Co. v. Sawyer* Case Brief." Accessed April 12, 2013. http://www.4lawschool.com/conlaw/tub.shtml.

Primary Documents

Supreme Court Cases—Opinions of the Court

McCulloch v. Maryland, 17 U.S. 316 (1819)
A Supreme Court Case Regarding the Federal Government's Authority to Establish a National Bank

In 1790, Alexander Hamilton, the first U.S. Secretary of the Treasury, was adamant regarding the importance of a central bank to the stability of property within a nation. The First Bank of the United States was started to help facilitate the management of Revolutionary War debt. The Second National Bank was established with the intention of serving the nation's commercial and banking needs.

Unlike the power to create post offices, the power to create banks is not stated in the Constitution. However, the powers to lay and collect taxes, borrow money, regulate commerce, declare war, and raise and support armies and navies are among those listed in the Constitution. These powers include a considerable portion of the industry of the nation. The United States did not create a bank simply to be in the banking business, but rather as a means of carrying out its expressed duties. The architects of the Constitution intended that there to be enough powers inherent in the government in addition to those necessary and proper to carry out the government's responsibilities.

Source: http://www.oyez.org/cases/1792-1850/1819/1819_0

U.S. Supreme Court
McCulloch v. Maryland, **17 U.S. 316 (1819)**
ERROR TO THE COURT OF APPEALS OF THE STATE OF MARYLAND

MARSHALL, Chief Justice, delivered the opinion of the Court.

In the case now to be determined, the defendant, a sovereign State, denies the obligation of a law enacted by the legislature of the Union, and the plaintiff, on his part, contests the validity of an act which has been passed by the legislature of that State. The Constitution of our country, in its most interesting and vital parts, is to be considered, the conflicting powers of the Government of the Union and of its members, as marked in that Constitution, are to be discussed, and an opinion given which may essentially influence the great operations of the Government. No tribunal can approach such a question without a deep sense of its importance, and of the awful responsibility involved in its decision. But it must be decided peacefully, or remain a source of hostile legislation, perhaps, of hostility of a still more serious nature; and if it is to be so decided, by this tribunal alone can the decision be made. On the Supreme Court of the United States has the Constitution of our country devolved this important duty.

The first question made in the cause is—has Congress power to incorporate a bank?

It has been truly said that this can scarcely be considered as an open question entirely unprejudiced by the former proceedings of the Nation respecting it. The principle now contested was introduced at a very early period of our history, has been recognised by many successive legislatures, and has been acted upon by the Judicial Department, in cases of peculiar delicacy, as a law of undoubted obligation . . .

* * *

. . . JUDGMENT. This cause came on to be heard, on the transcript of the record of the Court of Appeals of the State of Maryland, and was argued by counsel; on consideration whereof, it is the opinion of this Court that the act of the Legislature of Maryland is contrary to the Constitution of the United States, and void, and therefore that the said Court of Appeals of the State of Maryland erred, in affirming the judgment of the Baltimore County Court, in which judgment was rendered against James W. McCulloch; but that the said Court of Appeals of Maryland ought to have reversed the said judgment of the said Baltimore County Court, and ought to have given judgment for the said appellant, McCulloch. It is, therefore, adjudged and ordered that the said judgment of the said Court of Appeals of the State of Maryland in this case be, and the same hereby is, reversed and annulled. And this Court, proceeding to render such judgment as the said Court of Appeals should have rendered, it is further adjudged and ordered that the judgment of the said Baltimore County Court be reversed and annulled, and that judgment be entered in the said Baltimore County Court for the said James W. McCulloch.

Gibbons v. Ogden, 22 U.S. 1 (1824)
A Supreme Court Case That Gave the Federal Government the Ability to Maintain Uniform and Equal Rule of Law within the Whole of the United States

The Supreme Court addressed the monopoly in transportation issue as well as the issue of states' responsibility versus the authority of the federal government to make laws regarding business and commerce, specifically interstate transportation. As it has on many occasions throughout history, this case was also a case of creative destruction, as technology was changing the face of an industry, in this case the transportation industry.

Source: http://supreme.justia.com/cases/federal/us/22/1/case.html

U.S. Supreme Court
***Gibbons v. Ogden*, 22 U.S. 1 (1824)**
APPEAL FROM THE COURT FOR THE TRIAL OF IMPEACHMENTS AND CORRECTION OF ERRORS OF THE STATE OF NEW YORK

Mr. Chief Justice MARSHALL delivered the opinion of the Court, and, after stating the case, proceeded as follows:

The appellant contends that this decree is erroneous because the laws which purport to give the exclusive privilege it sustains are repugnant to the Constitution and laws of the United States.

They are said to be repugnant:

1st. To that clause in the Constitution which authorizes Congress to regulate commerce.

2d. To that which authorizes Congress to promote the progress of science and useful arts.

The State of New York maintains the Constitutionality of these laws, and their Legislature, their Council of Revision, and their Judges, have repeatedly concurred in this opinion. It is supported by great names—by names which have all the titles to consideration that virtue, intelligence, and office can bestow. No tribunal can approach the decision of this question without feeling a just and real respect for that opinion which is sustained by such authority, but it is the province of this Court, while it respects, not to bow to it implicitly, and the Judges must exercise, in the examination of the subject, that understanding which Providence has bestowed upon them, with that independence which the people of the United

Page 22 U. S. 187

States expect from this department of the government. . . .

* * *

. . . I have not touched upon the right of the States to grant patents for inventions or improvements generally, because it does not necessarily arise in this cause. It is enough for all the purposes of this decision if they cannot exercise it so as to restrain a free intercourse among the States.

DECREE. This cause came on to be heard on the transcript of the record of the Court for the Trial of Impeachments and Correction of Errors of the State of New York, and was argued by counsel. On consideration whereof, this Court is of opinion that the several licenses to the steamboats the Stoudinger and the Bellona to carry on the coasting trade, which are set up by the appellant Thomas Gibbons in his answer to the bill of the respondent, Aaron Ogden, filed in the Court of Chancery for the State of New York, which were granted under an act of Congress, passed in pursuance of the Constitution of the

Page 22 U. S. 240

United States, gave full authority to those vessels to navigate the waters of the United States, by steam or otherwise, for the purpose of carrying on the coasting trade, any law of the State of New York to the contrary notwithstanding, and that so much of the several laws of the State of New York as prohibits vessels, licensed according to the laws of the United States, from navigating the waters of the State of New York by means of fire or steam is repugnant to the said Constitution, and void. This Court is therefore of opinion that the decree of the Court of New York for the Trial of Impeachments and the Correction of Errors affirming the decree of the Chancellor of that State, which perpetually enjoins the said Thomas Gibbons, the appellant, from navigating the waters of the State of New York with the steamboats the Stoudinger and the Bellona by steam or fire, is erroneous, and ought to be reversed, and the same is hereby reversed and annulled, and this Court doth further DIRECT, ORDER, and DECREE that the bill of the said Aaron Ogden be dismissed, and the same is hereby dismissed accordingly.

Juillard v. Greenman, 110 U.S. 421 (1884)
A Supreme Court Case Upholding the Legal Tender Acts in Peacetime

The Legal Tender cases were a series of cases filed during and after the Civil War, culminating in *Juilliard v. Greenman*. The Civil War brought an economic urgency to the Union. In 1862, Congress passed the Legal Tender Act, allowing United States notes to be printed to help finance the war debt. Paper money depreciates in terms of gold and silver, which was used prior to its issuance. Cheap money chases out expensive money, and old debts were soon paid with controversial paper. During Reconstruction, these cases challenged the authority of Congress to print paper money. In *Hepburn v. Griswold* in 1870, the Supreme Court said paper currency was unconstitutional, but in 1884, with the *Juilliard* case, it came to the opposite interpretation. Article I, Section 8 of the Constitution grants Congress the power to coin money, but gold and silver are the metals mentioned. Whether the framers could fathom plastic as currency is a matter of speculation; however, some would argue that if their prohibition of paper money were implemented, the American economy would be sent into disarray at best, and at worst, would cease to exist. This case settled once and for all the constitutional dispute between paper money and a currency limited to gold and silver.

Source: http://www.law.cornell.edu/supremecourt/text/110/421

THE LEGAL-TENDER CASES. *JUILLIARD V. GREENMAN*
110 U.S. 421 (4 S.Ct. 122, 28 L.Ed. 204)
Decided: March 3, 1884

Juilliard, a citizen of New York, brought an action against Greenman, a citizen of Connecticut, in the circuit court of the United States for the Southern district of New York, alleging that the plaintiff sold and delivered to the defendant, at his special instance and request, 100 bales of cotton, of the value and for the agreed price of $5,122.90; and that the defendant agreed to pay that sum in cash on the delivery of the cotton, and had not paid the same or any part thereof, except that he had paid the sum of $22.90 on account, and was now justly indebted to the plaintiff therefor in the sum of $5,100; and demanding judgment for this sum, with interest and costs. The defendant in his answer admitted the citizenship of the parties, the purchase and delivery of the cotton, and the agreement to pay therefor, as alleged; and averred that, after the delivery of the cotton, he offered and tendered to the plaintiff, in full payment, $22.50 in gold coin of the United States, 40 cents in silver coin of the United States, and two United States notes, one of the denomination of $5,000 and the other of the denomination of $100, of the description known as United States legal tender notes, purporting by recital thereon to be legal tender, at their respective face values, for all debts, public and private, except duties on imports and interest on the public debt, and which, after having been presented for payment, and redeemed and paid in gold coin, since January 1, 1879, at the United States subtreasury in New York, had been reissued and kept in circulation under and in pursuance of the act of congress of May 31, 1878, c. 146; that at the time of offering and tendering these notes, and coin to the plaintiff the sum of $5,122.90 was the entire amount due and owing in payment for the cotton, but the plaintiff declined to receive the notes in payment of $5,100 thereof; and that the defendant had ever since remained, and still was, ready and willing to pay to the plaintiff the sum of $5,100 in these notes, and brought these notes into court, ready to be paid to the plaintiff, if he would accept them. . . .

* * *

. . . No question of the scope and extent of the implied powers of congress under the constitution can be satisfactorily discussed without repeating much of the reasoning of Chief Justice MARSHALL in the great judgment in *McCulloch v. Maryland*, 4 Wheat. 316, by which the power of congress to incorporate a bank was demonstrated and affirmed, notwithstanding the constitution does not enumerate, among the powers granted, that of establishing a bank or creating a corporation. . . .

* * *

. . . Among the enumerated powers of government, we find the great powers to lay and collect taxes; to borrow money; to regulate commerce; to declare and conduct a war; and to raise and support armies and navies. The sword and the purse, all the external relations, and no inconsiderable portion of the industry of the nation, are intrusted to its government. . . .

* * *

. . . To coin money, regulate the value thereof, and of foreign coin, and fix the standard of weights and measures. The section which contains the grant of these and other principal legislative powers concludes by declaring that the congress shall have power—

* * *

. . . The other judgments delivered by Chief Justice MARSHALL contain nothing adverse to the power of congress to issue legal tender notes. . . .

* * *

. . . It follows that the act of May 31, 1878, c. 146, is constitutional and valid, and that the circuit court rightly held that the tender in treasury notes, reissued and kept in circulation under that act, was a tender of lawful money in payment of the defendant's debt to the plaintiff.

Judgment affirmed.

Pollock v. Farmers' Loan & Trust Company, 157 U.S. 429 (1895)
This Supreme Court Case Disallowed Congress's Power to Tax All Forms of Income

The power of Congress to tax is very extensive. The Constitution provides for it with one exception and two qualifications. Congress cannot tax exports, and it must impose direct taxes by the rule of apportionment, and indirect taxes by the rule of uniformity. At this time in history, most revenue the federal government acquired was through tariffs, duties, and other consumption taxes (i.e., sales taxes).

The Supreme Court's responsibility in *Pollock v. Farmers' Loan & Trust Company* was to settle the issue of whether or not a tax on income earned from property violated Article I, Section 2, Clause 3 of the U.S. Constitution. This article requires that direct taxes imposed by the national government be apportioned among the states on the basis of population.

The Economic Panic of 1893 resulted in the United States experiencing a financial contraction in the business cycle that was characterized by high unemployment rates and difficulties in accessing capital. In response, Congress passed the Wilson-Gorman Tariff Act of 1894. Believing this income tax violated the Constitution, Charles Pollock sued the Farmers' Loan & Trust Company in 1895. The Supreme Court reversed its previous ruling (in the *Springer* case) and agreed in part with Pollock. Afterwards, it became difficult for Congress to impose a national income tax that applied to all forms of income until the 1913 ratification of the Constitution's Sixteenth Amendment.

Source: http://www.law.cornell.edu/supremecourt/text/157/429#writing-USSC_CR_0157_0429_ZO

***Pollock v. Farmers' Loan and Trust Company* (No. 898)**
157 U.S. 429
Argued: March 7, 8, 11, 12, 13, 1895
Decided: April 8, 1895

FULLER, J., Opinion of the Court

MR. CHIEF JUSTICE FULLER, after stating the case as above reported, delivered the opinion of the court.

The jurisdiction of a court of equity to prevent any threatened breach of trust in the misapplication or diversion of the funds of a corporation by illegal payments out of its capital or profits has been frequently sustained. *Dodge v. Woolsey*, 18 How. 331; *Hawes v. Oakland*, 104 U.S. 450. [p554]

As in *Dodge v. Woolsey*, this bill proceeds on the ground that the defendants would be guilty of such breach of trust or duty in voluntarily making returns for the imposition of, and paying, an unconstitutional tax, and also on allegations of threatened multiplicity of suits and irreparable injury.

The objection of adequate remedy at law was not raised below, nor is it now raised by appellees, if it could be entertained at all at this stage of the proceedings; and, so far as it was within the power of the government to do so, the question of jurisdiction, for the purposes of the case, was explicitly waived on the argument. The relief sought was in respect of voluntary action by the defendant company, and not in respect of the assessment and collection themselves. Under these circumstances, we should not be justified in declining to proceed to judgment upon the merits. *Pelton. v. National Bank*, 101 U.S. 143148; *Cummings v. National Bank*, 101 U.S. 153 157; *Reynes v. Dumont*, 130 U.S. 354. . . .

* * *

. . . The opinion thus concludes:

Our conclusions are that direct taxes, within the meaning of the Constitution, are only capitation taxes, as expressed in that instrument, and taxes on real estate, and that the tax of which the plaintiff in error complains is within the category of an excise or duty.

While this language is broad enough to cover the interest as well as the professional earnings, the case would have been more significant as a precedent if the distinction had been brought out in the report and commented on in arriving at judgment, for a tax on professional receipts might be treated as an excise or duty, and therefore indirect, when a tax on the income of personalty might be held to be direct. . . .

* * *

. . . The requirement of the Constitution is that no direct tax shall be laid otherwise than by apportionment—the prohibition is not against direct taxes on land, from which the implication is sought to be drawn that indirect taxes on land would be constitutional, but it is against all direct taxes—and it is admitted that a tax on real estate is a direct tax. . . .

* * *

. . . By a joint resolution of February 21, 1895, the time for making returns of income for the year 1894 was extended, and it was provided that, in computing incomes under said act, the amounts necessarily paid for fire insurance premiums and for ordinary repairs shall be deducted;

and that

in computing incomes under said act, the amounts received as dividends upon the stock of any corporation, company, or association shall not be included in case such dividends are also liable to the tax of two percentum upon the net profits of said corporation, company, or association although such tax may not have been actually paid by said corporation, company, or association at the time of making returns by the person, corporation, or association receiving such dividends, and returns or reports of the names and salaries of employees shall not be required from employers unless called for by the collector in order to verify the returns of employees.

Lochner v. New York, 198 U.S. 45 (1905)
A Supreme Court Case on Minimum Working Hours

The Fourteenth Amendment to the U.S. Constitution, as interpreted in 1905 by the Fuller Court (1903–1905), prohibits states from interfering with most employment contracts. The right to buy and sell labor is a fundamental freedom that in a federal system of governing is protected from arbitrary statutes and acts of state legislatures. Unless there is a reasonable threat to public welfare or realistic concern for public health and safety, regulation of wages between employer and employee cannot be interfered with using the police power of the state. So whether you shoe horses or bake biscuits, your right to buy and sell your labor is exactly that: your right to be protected from arbitrary, unfair, and discriminatory treatment by state legislatures.

Source: http://supreme.justia.com/cases/federal/us/198/45/case.html

U.S. Supreme Court
Lochner v. New York, 198 U.S. 45 (1905)
No. 292
Argued February 23, 24, 1905
Decided April 17, 1906
198 U.S. 45
ERROR TO THE COUNTY COURT OF ONEIDA COUNTY, STATE OF NEW YORK

MR. JUSTICE PECKHAM, after making the foregoing statement of the facts, delivered the opinion of the court.

The indictment, it will be seen, charges that the plaintiff in error violated the one hundred and tenth section of article 8, chapter 415, of the Laws of 1897, known as the labor law of the State of New York, in that he wrongfully and unlawfully required and permitted an employee working for him to work more than sixty hours in one week. There is nothing in any of the opinions delivered in this case, either in the Supreme Court or the Court of Appeals of the State, which construes the section, in using the word "required," as referring to any physical force being used to obtain the labor of an employee. . . .

It is assumed that the word means nothing more than the requirement arising from voluntary contract for such labor in excess of the number of hours specified in the statute. There is no pretense in any of the opinions that the statute was intended to meet a case of involuntary labor in any form. All the opinions assume that there is no real distinction, so far as this question is concerned, between the words "required" and "permitted." The mandate of the statute that "no employee shall be required or permitted to work," is the substantial equivalent of an enactment that "no employee shall contract or agree to work," more than ten hours per day, and, as there is no provision for special emergencies, the statute is mandatory in all cases. It is not an act merely fixing the number of hours which shall constitute a legal day's work, but an absolute prohibition upon the employer's permitting, under any circumstances, more than ten hours' work to be done in his establishment. The employee may desire to earn the extra money which would arise from his working more than the prescribed

Page 198 U. S. 53

time, but this statute forbids the employer from permitting the employee to earn it.

The statute necessarily interferes with the right of contract between the employer and employes concerning the number of hours in which the latter may labor in the bakery of the employer. The general right to make a contract in relation to his business is part of the liberty of the individual protected by the Fourteenth Amendment of the Federal Constitution. . . .

* * *

. . . It is manifest to us that the limitation of the hours of labor as provided for in this section of the statute under which the indictment was found, and the plaintiff in error convicted, has no such direct relation to, and no such substantial effect upon, the health of the employee as to justify us in regarding the section as really a health law. It seems to us that the real object and purpose were simply to regulate the hours of labor between the master and his employees (all being men sui juris) in a private business, not dangerous in any degree to morals or in any real and substantial degree to the health of the employees. Under such circumstances, the freedom of master and employee to contract with each other in relation to their employment, and in defining the same, cannot be prohibited or interfered with without violating the Federal Constitution.

The judgment of the Court of Appeals of New York, as well as that of the Supreme Court and of the County Court of Oneida County, must be reversed, and the case remanded to

Page 198 U. S. 65

the County Court for further proceedings not inconsistent with this opinion.

Reversed.

Standard Oil Co. of New Jersey v. United States, 221 U.S. 1 (1911)
A Supreme Court Case Upholding the Sherman Antitrust Act

Standard Oil Company was the largest and richest trust in America at the beginning of the twentieth century. By 1904, it owned a Leviathan's share of all the oil production in the United States, and had interests in other markets as well. Through a process of acquisition, Standard Oil ingested all market competition. Through vertical integration, Standard Oil controlled aspects of oil production from drilling to refining and finally retail sales to customers. John D. Rockefeller, along with the other trustees, implemented product standardization that greatly enhanced sales by streamlining production, reducing costs, and undercutting competition. However, when power is unchecked or not limited by competition, that power has the potential to become corrupt. A monopoly exists when one company has all the power to control the market. Standard Oil monopolized the petroleum industry. This power dominance was contrary to the principles of free enterprise, whereby competition is fundamental. In this case, there were no viable substitutes, and prices could be set and supply could be minimized. Congress passed the Sherman Antitrust Act in 1890 to deal with monopolies that threatened consumers. The Supreme Court used the Sherman Antitrust Act to check the power of monopolies and restore the principles of the market.

Source: http://supreme.justia.com/cases/federal/us/221/1/case.html

U.S. Supreme Court
Standard Oil Co. of New Jersey v. United States, 221 U.S. 1 (1910)
Argued March 14, 15, 16, 1910
Restored to docket for reargument April 11, 1910
Reargued January 12, 13, 16, 17, 1911
Decided May 15, 1911
221 U.S. 1
APPEAL FROM THE CIRCUIT COURT OF THE UNITED STATES FOR THE EASTERN DISTRICT OF MISSOURI

MR. CHIEF JUSTICE WHITE delivered the opinion of the court.

The Standard Oil Company of New Jersey and 33 other corporations, John D. Rockefeller, William Rockefeller, and five other individual defendants prosecute this appeal to reverse a decree of the court below. Such decree was entered upon a bill filed by the United States under authority of § 4 of the act of July 2, 1890, c. 647, p. 209, known as the Anti-Trust Act, and had for its object the enforcement of the provisions of that act. The record is inordinately voluminous, consisting of twenty-three volumes of printed matter, aggregating about twelve thousand pages, containing a vast amount of confusing and conflicting testimony

Page 221 U. S. 31

relating to innumerable, complex and varied business transactions, extending over a period of nearly forty years. In an effort to pave the way to reach the subjects which we are called upon to consider, we propose at the outset, following the order of the bill, to give the merest possible outline of its contents, to summarize the answer, to indicate the course of the trial, and point out briefly the decision below rendered.

The bill and exhibits, covering one hundred and seventy pages of the printed record, was filed on November 15, 1906. Corporations known as Standard Oil Company of New Jersey, Standard Oil Company of California, Standard Oil Company of Indiana, Standard Oil Company of Iowa, Standard Oil Company of Kansas, Standard Oil Company of Kentucky, Standard Oil Company of Nebraska, Standard Oil Company of New York,

Standard Oil Company of Ohio, and sixty-two other corporations and partnerships, as also seven individuals were named as defendants. The bill was divided into thirty numbered sections, and sought relief upon the theory that the various defendants were engaged in conspiring "to restrain the trade and commerce in petroleum, commonly called 'crude oil,' in refined oil, and in the other products of petroleum, among the several States and Territories of the United States and the District of Columbia and with foreign nations, and to monopolize the said commerce."

The conspiracy was alleged to have been formed in or about the year 1870 by three of the individual defendants, viz: John D. Rockefeller, William Rockefeller, and Henry M. Flagler. The detailed averments concerning the alleged conspiracy were arranged with reference to three periods, the first from 1870 to 1882, the second from 1882 to 1899, and the third from 1899 to the time of the filing of the bill.

The general charge concerning the period from 1870 to 1882 was as follows:

Page 221 U. S. 32

"That during said first period, the said individual defendants, in connection with the Standard Oil Company of Ohio, purchased and obtained interests through stock ownership and otherwise in, and entered into agreements with, various persons, firms, corporations, and limited partnerships engaged in purchasing, shipping, refining, and selling petroleum and its products among the various States for the purpose of fixing the price of crude and refined oil and the products thereof, limiting the production thereof, and controlling the transportation therein, and thereby restraining trade and commerce among the several States, and monopolizing the said commerce.". . .

* * *

. . . We so think, since we construe the sixth paragraph of the decree not as depriving the stockholders or the corporations, after the dissolution of the combination, of the power to make normal and lawful contracts or agreements, but as restraining them from, by any device whatever, recreating directly or indirectly the illegal combination which the decree dissolved. In other words, we construe the sixth paragraph of the decree not as depriving the stockholders or corporations of the right to live under the law of the land, but as compelling obedience to that law.

. . . As therefore the sixth paragraph, as thus construed, is not amenable to the criticism directed against it, and cannot produce the harmful results which the arguments suggest it was obviously right. We think that, in view of the magnitude of the interests involved and their complexity, that the delay of thirty days allowed for executing the decree was too short, and should be extended so as to embrace a period of at least six months. So also, in view of the possible serious injury to result to the public from an absolute cessation of interstate commerce in petroleum and its products by such vast agencies as are embraced in the combination, a result which might arise from that portion of the decree which enjoined carrying on of interstate commerce not only by the New Jersey corporation, but by all the subsidiary companies until the dissolution of the combination by the transfer of the stocks in accordance with the decree, the injunction provided for in § 7 thereof should not have been awarded.

Our conclusion is that the decree below was right, and

Page 221 U. S. 82

should be affirmed except as to the minor matters concerning which we have indicated the decree should be modified. Our order will therefore be one of affirmance, with directions, however, to modify the decree in accordance with this opinion. The court below to retain jurisdiction to the extent necessary to compel compliance in every respect with its decree.

And it is so ordered.

Helvering v. Davis, 301 U.S. 619 (1937)
A Supreme Court Case Upholding Social Security

The case of *Helvering v. Davis* must be viewed through the lens of the Great Depression. The devastation of this extreme market collapse brought social as well as economic and political changes to the fabric of American life. President Roosevelt offered the nation a New Deal. Congress passed the Social Security Act of 1935, which provided income to elderly, blind, unemployed, widowed, and orphaned, as well as creating other state health initiatives. Funds were appropriated that originated from employee income taxes as well as employer excise taxes. As shareholder of a corporation subject to these taxes, Davis opposed them, claiming that they were in conflict with the Tenth Amendment to the Constitution. Whether or not Social Security is the best remedy for business cycle aliments in a free market economy remains to be seen, but the constitutionality of the issue was settled. A new approach to government involvement in the economy began. This case set the stage for cooperative federalism and a new era in government involvement in the economy.

Source: http://www.law.cornell.edu/supremecourt/text/301/619

HELVERING V. DAVIS
301 U.S. 619
Helvering v. Davis (No. 910)
Argued: May 5, 1937
Decided: May 24, 1937
89 F.2d 393, reversed.
CARDOZO, J., Opinion of the Court
MR. JUSTICE CARDOZO delivered the opinion of the Court.

The Social Security Act (Act of August 14, 1935, c. 531, 49 Stat. 620, 42 U.S.C. c. 7, (Supp.)), is challenged once again.

In Steward Machine Co. v. Davis, decided this day, ante, p. 548, we have upheld the validity of Title IX of the act, imposing an excise upon employers of eight or more. In this case, Titles VIII and II are the subject of attack. Title VIII lays another excise upon employers in addition to the one imposed by Title IX (though with different exemptions). It lays a special income tax upon employees to be deducted from their wages and paid by the employers. Title II provides for the payment of Old Age Benefits, and supplies the motive and occasion, in the view of the assailants of the statute, for [p635] the levy of the taxes imposed by Title VIII. The plan of the two titles will now be summarized more fully.

Title VIII, as we have said, lays two different types of tax, an "income tax on employees" and "an excise tax on employers." . . .

* * *

. . . We find it unnecessary to make a choice between the arguments, and so leave the question open.

Fourth. The tax upon employers is a valid excise or duty upon the relation of employment.

As to this, we need not add to our opinion in Steward Machine Co. v. Davis, supra, where we considered a like question in respect of Title IX. [p646]

Fifth. The tax is not invalid as a result of its exemptions. Here again, the opinion in *Steward Machine Co. v. Davis*, supra, says all that need be said.

Sixth. The decree of the Court of Appeals should be reversed, and that of the District Court affirmed.

Reversed.

West Coast Hotel Co. v. Parrish, 300 U.S. 379 (1937)
A Supreme Court Case on Minimum Wage

The Great Depression set the stage for the *West Coast Hotel Co. v. Parrish* in 1937. The specific circumstances of the case involve the constitutionality of minimum wage laws. The case served as an early case regarding shifts in thought regarding the role of government in the economy from the traditional laissez-faire (an economic environment where transactions are free from government intervention) to more active participation, i.e., Roosevelt's New Deal legislation.

In a broader social view, this case was about women as socioeconomically disadvantaged workers; the responsibility of businesses to adhere to wages that allow people to meet basic living demands; the extent to which the U.S. Constitution guarantees individuals freedom of contract (the liberty to contract with another without government restrictions); and the appearance of political manipulation of the Supreme Court by the president to realign review powers safeguarding New Deal policies.

Source: http://www.law.cornell.edu/supremecourt/text/300/379#writing-USSC_CR_0300_0379_ZO

300 U.S. 379
West Coast Hotel Co. v. Parrish (No. 293)
Argued: December 16, 17, 1936
Decided: March 29, 1937
185 Wash. 581; 55 P.2d 1083, affirmed.
Syllabus
Opinion, Hughes
Dissent, Sutherland

HUGHES, C. J., Opinion of the Court
MR. CHIEF JUSTICE HUGHES delivered the opinion of the Court.

This case presents the question of the constitutional validity of the minimum wage law of the State of Washington.

The Act, entitled "Minimum Wages for Women," authorizes the fixing of minimum wages for women and minors. . . . It provides:

SECTION 1. The welfare of the State of Washington demands that women and minors be protected from conditions of labor which have a pernicious effect on their health and morals. The State of Washington, therefore, exercising herein its police and sovereign power declares that inadequate wages and unsanitary conditions of labor exert such pernicious effect.

SEC. 2. It shall be unlawful to employ women or minors in any industry or occupation within the State of Washington under conditions of labor detrimental to their health or morals, and it shall be unlawful to employ [p387] women workers in any industry within the State of Washington at wages which are not adequate for their maintenance.

SEC. 3. There is hereby created a commission to be known as the "Industrial Welfare Commission" for the State of Washington, to establish such standards of wages and conditions of labor for women and minors employed within the State of Washington as shall be held hereunder to be reasonable and not detrimental to health and morals, and which shall be sufficient for the decent maintenance of women.

Further provisions required the Commission to ascertain the wages and conditions of labor of women and minors within the State. . . .

* * *

. . . Public hearings were to be held. If, after investigation, the Commission found that, in any occupation, trade or industry, the wages paid to women were "inadequate to supply them necessary cost of living and to maintain the workers in health," the Commission was empowered to call a conference of representatives of employers and employees together with disinterested persons representing the public. The conference was to recommend to the Commission, on its request, an estimate of a minimum wage adequate for the purpose above stated, and, on the approval of such a recommendation, it became the duty of the Commission to issue an obligatory order fixing minimum wages. Any such order might be reopened, and the question reconsidered with the aid of the former conference or a new one. Special licenses were authorized for the employment of women who were "physically defective or crippled by age or otherwise," and also for apprentices, at less than the prescribed minimum wage. . . .

* * *

. . . The appellant conducts a hotel. The appellee, Elsie Parrish, was employed as a chambermaid and (with her husband) brought this suit to recover the difference between the wages paid her and the minimum wage fixed pursuant to the state law. The minimum wage was $14.50 per week of 48 hours. The appellant challenged the act as repugnant to the due process clause of the Fourteenth Amendment of the Constitution of the United States. The Supreme Court of the State, reversing the trial court, sustained the statute and directed judgment for the plaintiffs. *Parrish v. West Coast Hotel Co.*, 185 Wash. 581, 55 P.2d 1083. The case is here on appeal.

The appellant relies upon the decision of this Court in *Adkins v. Children's Hospital*, 261 U.S. 525, which held invalid the District of Columbia Minimum Wage Act, which was attacked under the due process clause of the Fifth Amendment. . . .

* * *

. . . There is no "doctrinaire requirement" that the legislation should be couched in all embracing terms. . . . This familiar principle has repeatedly been applied to legislation which singles out women, and particular classes of women, in the exercise of the State's protective power. . . . Their relative need in the presence of the evil, no less than the existence of the evil itself, is a matter for the legislative judgment.

Our conclusion is that the case of *Adkins v. Children's Hospital*, supra, should be, and it is, overruled. The judgment of the Supreme Court of the State of Washington is

Affirmed.

Kellogg Co. v. National Biscuit Co., 305 U.S. 111 (1938)
A Supreme Court Case on Trademarks and Patents

Imitation may be the highest form of flattery, but in a competitive market, it can rob an innovator of his or her profit and stifle his or her motivation to create. Legal protections for property that you have invented, thought of, discovered, or created are commonly known as intellectual property rights. Trademark and patent rights are included in this category. Although these rights do not ensure the profitable success of the inventor or originator, they do offer an incentive to entrepreneurs to keep innovating. Some might argue that Americans' ability to innovate and think creatively has been one of the key factors in the nation becoming an economic world leader. In the *Kellogg* case, the courts clarified judicial precedents for intellectual property rights in the United States. The rule of law as applied to intellectual property helps safeguard against unfair trade practices as well as motivating productivity.

Source: http://supreme.justia.com/cases/federal/us/305/111/case.html

U.S. Supreme Court
Kellogg Co. v. National Biscuit Co., 305 U.S. 111 (1938)
Nos. 2 and 56
Argued October 10, 1938
Decided November 14, 1938
305 U.S. 111
CERTIORARI TO THE CIRCUIT COURT OF APPEALS FOR THE THIRD CIRCUIT

MR. JUSTICE BRANDEIS delivered the opinion of the Court.

This suit was brought in the federal court for Delaware [Footnote 1] by National Biscuit Company against Kellogg Company to enjoin alleged unfair competition by the manufacture and sale of the breakfast food commonly known as shredded wheat. The competition was alleged to be unfair mainly because Kellogg Company uses, like the plaintiff, the name shredded wheat and, like the plaintiff, produces its biscuit in pillow-shaped form. . . .

* * *

. . . Kellogg Company is undoubtedly sharing in the goodwill of the article known as "Shredded Wheat," and thus is sharing in a market which was created by the skill and judgment of plaintiff's predecessor and has been widely extended by vast expenditures in advertising persistently made. But that is not unfair. Sharing in the goodwill of an article unprotected by patent or trademark is the exercise of a right possessed by all, and in the free exercise of which the consuming public is deeply interested. There is no evidence of passing off or deception on the part of the Kellogg Company, [Footnote 5] and it has taken every reasonable precaution to prevent confusion or the practice of deception in the sale of its product.

Fourth. By its "clarifying" decree, the Circuit Court of Appeals enjoined Kellogg Company from using the picture of the two shredded wheat biscuits in the bowl only in connection with an injunction against manufacturing the pillow-shaped biscuits and the use of the term shredded wheat, on the grounds of unfair competition. [Footnote 6]

Page 305 U. S. 123

The use of this picture was not enjoined on the independent ground of trademark infringement. Since the National Biscuit Company did not petition for certiorari, the question whether use of the picture is a violation of that trademark although Kellogg Company is free to use the name and the pillow-shaped biscuit is not here for review.

Decrees reversed with direction to dismiss the bill.

United States v. South-Eastern Underwriters Association, 322 U.S. 533 (1944)
A Supreme Court Case Determining Insurance as Commerce

The Supreme Court's responsibility in the *United States v. South-Eastern Underwriters Association* was to determine whether insurance constitutes commerce, and if so, can insurance companies be regulated by the power that the commerce clause grants to Congress to regulate transactions across state lines. Until this case in 1944, insurance was not considered commerce, as defined by the commerce clause of the U.S. Constitution and interpreted by the courts. However, the business of providing financial stability through insuring property for monetary loss was comparable to the auto and coal industries in size and employment.

Monopolies were a national concern in the late nineteenth century. Congress passed the Sherman Antitrust Act in 1890 in an attempt to prevent monopolies, collusion, price fixing, conspiracy, and intimidation tactics that would discourage competition and fair trade. Insurance was not considered commerce, and therefore did not adhere to the laws and regulations of the Sherman Act. This case established that insurance was indeed commerce. In addition, transactions of the insurance industry took place between various states, and therefore were subject to the regulation of the federal government.

Source: http://www.law.cornell.edu/supremecourt/text/322/533

UNITED STATES V. SOUTH-EASTERN UNDERWRITERS ASS'N ET AL.
322 U.S. 533 (64 S.Ct. 1162, 88 L.Ed. 1440)
No. 354.
Argued: Jan. 11, 1944
Decided: June 5, 1944
opinion, BLACK
dissent, STONE
dissent, JACKSON

Mr. Justice BLACK delivered the opinion of the Court.

For seventy-five years this Court has held, whenever the question has been presented, that the Commerce Clause of the Constitution does not deprive the individual states of power to regulate and tax specific activities of foreign insurance companies which sell policies within their territories. Each state has been held to have this power even though negotiation and execution of the companies' policy contracts involved communications of information and movements of persons, moneys, and papers across state lines. Not one of all these cases, however, has involved an Act of Congress which required the Court to decide the issue of whether the Commerce Clause grants to Congress the power to regulate insurance transactions stretching across state lines. Today for the first time in the history of the Court that issue is squarely presented and must be decided.

Appellees—the South-Eastern Underwriters Association (S.E.U.A.), and its membership of nearly 200 private stock fire insurance companies, and 27 individuals—were indicted in the District Court for alleged violations of the Sherman Anti-Trust Act. The indictment alleges two conspiracies. The first, in violation of § 1 of the Act, was to restrain interstate trade and commerce by fixing and maintaining arbitrary and non-competitive premium rates on fire and specified 'allied lines' 1 of insurance in Alabama, Florida, Georgia,

North Carolina, South Carolina, and Virginia; the second, in violation of § 2, was to monopolize trade and commerce in the same lines of insurance in and among the same states. 2. . . .

* * *

. . . 'But even if the court shared the gloomy forebodings in which the defendants indulge, it could not refuse to respect the action of the legislative branch of the government if what it has done is within the limits of its constitutional power. The suggestions of disaster to business have, we apprehend, their origin in the zeal of parties who are opposed to the policy underlying the act of Congress or are interested in the result of this particular case; at any rate, the suggestions imply that the court may and ought to refuse the enforcement of the provisions of the act if, in its judgment, Congress was not wise in prescribing as a rule by which the conduct of interstate and international commerce is to be governed, that every combination, whatever its form, in restraint of such commerce and the monopolizing or attempting to monopolize such commerce, shall be illegal. These, plainly, are questions as to the policy of legislation which belong to another department, and this court has no function to supervise such legislation from the standpoint of wisdom or policy. * * *' Harlan, J., affirming decree, *Northern Securities Co. v. United States*, 193 U.S. 197, 351, 352, 24 S.Ct. 436, 462, 48 L.Ed. 679. . . .

* * *

. . . The argument that the Sherman Act necessarily invalidates many state laws regulating insurance we regard as exaggerated. Few states go so far as to permit private insurance companies, without state supervision, to agree upon and fix uniform insurance rates. Cf. *Parker v. Brown*, 317 U.S. 341, 350—352, 63 S.Ct. 307, 313, 314, 87 L.Ed. 315. No states authorize combinations of insurance companies to coerce, intimidate, and boycott competitors and consumers in the manner here alleged, and it cannot be that any companies have acquired a vested right to engage in such destructive business practices. 50

Reversed.

Youngstown Sheet & Tube Company v. Sawyer, 343 U.S. 579 (1952)
Supreme Court Case That Upheld the Private Ownership of the Factors of Production and Ownership/Labor Relationship

In this case, the executive branch of government, which is constitutionally charged with enforcing the law rather than making it, in effect made policy that tipped the scales in favor of government control of the means of production in the name of national security. The case addressed whether the president of the United States could, by executive order, essentially nationalize an industry in the name of national defense. The Supreme Court upheld the means of production as private property and the relationship between ownership and labor in a market economy.

Source: http://supreme.justia.com/cases/federal/us/343/579/case.html

U.S. Supreme Court
Youngstown Sheet & Tube Co. v. Sawyer, 343 U.S. 579 (1952)
Decided June 2, 1952*
343 U.S. 579
CERTIORARI TO THE UNITED STATES COURT OF APPEALS FOR THE DISTRICT OF COLUMBIA CIRCUIT

MR. JUSTICE BLACK delivered the opinion of the Court.

We are asked to decide whether the President was acting within his constitutional power when he issued an order directing the Secretary of Commerce to take possession of and operate most of the Nation's steel mills. The mill owners argue that the President's order amounts to lawmaking, a legislative function which the Constitution has expressly confided to the Congress, and not to the President. The Government's position is that the order was made on findings of the President that his action was necessary to avert a national catastrophe which would inevitably result from a stoppage of steel production, and that, in meeting this grave emergency, the President was acting within the aggregate of his constitutional powers as the Nation's Chief Executive and the Commander in Chief of the Armed Forces of the United States. . . .

* * *

. . . Two crucial issues have developed: First. Should final determination of the constitutional validity of the President's order be made in this case which has proceeded no further than the preliminary injunction stage? Second. If so, is the seizure order within the constitutional power of the President? . . .

* * *

. . . It is said that other Presidents, without congressional authority, have taken possession of private business enterprises in order to settle labor disputes. But even if this be true, Congress has not thereby lost its exclusive constitutional authority to make laws necessary and proper to carry out the powers vested by the Constitution

Page 343 U. S. 589

"in the Government of the United States, or any Department or Officer thereof."

The Founders of this Nation entrusted the lawmaking power to the Congress alone in both good and bad times. It would do no good to recall the historical events, the fears of power, and the hopes for freedom that lay behind their choice. Such a review would but confirm our holding that this seizure order cannot stand.

The judgment of the District Court is

Affirmed.

* Together with No. 745, *Sawyer, Secretary of Commerce v. Youngstown Sheet & Tube Co. et al.*, also on certiorari to the same court.

Menominee Tribe v. United States, 391 U.S. 404 (1968)

A Supreme Court Case on Property Rights and Rule of Law Assessing the Hunting and Fishing Rights Granted through a Previous Federal Government Treaty

In 1961, Congress enacted the Menominee Termination Act. The act terminated the Menominee Tribe of Indians' traditional hunting and fishing rights in Wisconsin. The Indians felt that this act violated their property rights to the state of Wisconsin's water and land common-pool resources as given them in the earlier Wolf River Treaty. The court case centered on the Menominee Indians' property rights as they related to water and land common-pool resources in the state of Wisconsin. Also at issue was whether the U.S. government would be subject to the rule of law, and if property rights that the government had earlier granted would be upheld. A secondary economic relevance would be the precedence set for states to collect hunting and fishing fees, i.e., generate state revenue, from the hunting and fishing activity of the states' Indian populations.

Source: http://www.law.cornell.edu/supremecourt/text/391/404#writing-type-1-DOUGLAS

Menominee Tribe of Indians, Petitioner, v. United States.
No. 187.
Reargued: April 26, 1968
Decided: May 27, 1968
opinion, DOUGLAS
dissent, STEWART, BLACK
Charles A. Hobbs, Washington, D.C., for petitioner.
Louis F. Claiborne, Washington, D.C., for respondent.
Bronson C. LaFollette, Madison, Wis., for State of Wisconsin, as amicus curiae, at the invitation of the Court.

Mr. Justice DOUGLAS delivered the opinion of the Court.

The Menominee Tribe of Indians was granted a reservation in Wisconsin by the Treaty of Wolf River in 1854. 10 Stat. 1064. By this treaty the Menominees retroceded certain lands they had acquired under an earlier treaty and the United States confirmed to them the Wolf River Reservation 'for a home, to be held as Indian lands are held.' Nothing was said in the 1854 treaty about hunting and fishing rights. Yet we agree with the Court of Claims 1 that the language 'to be held as Indian lands are held' includes the right to fish and to hunt. The record shows that the lands covered by the Wolf River Treaty of 1854 were selected precisely because they had an abundance of game. See *Menominee Tribe of Indians v. United States*, 95 Ct.Cl. 232, 240—241 (1941). The essence of the Treaty of Wolf River was that the Indians were authorized to maintain on the new lands ceded to them as a reservation their way of life which included hunting and fishing. 2

What the precise nature and extent of those hunting and fishing rights were we need not at this time determine. For the issue tendered by the present decision of the Court of Claims, 388 F.2d 998, 179 Ct.Cl. 496, is whether those rights, whatever their precise extent, have been extinguished. . . .

* * *

. . . Our conclusion is buttressed by the remarks of the legislator chiefly responsible for guiding the Termination Act to enactment, Senator Watkins, who stated upon the occasion of the signing of the bill that it 'in no way violates any treaty obligation with this tribe.' 13

We find it difficult to believe that Congress, without explicit statement, would subject the United States to a claim for compensation 14 by destroying a property rights conferred by treaty, particularly when Congress was purporting by the Termination Act to settle the Government's financial obligations toward the Indians. 15

Accordingly the judgment of the Court of Claims is affirmed.

Affirmed.

Corning Glass Works v Brennan, 417 U.S. 188 (1974)
A Supreme Court Case on Equal Pay for Women

Traditionally, women have struggled to gain equality in the workplace with men. The wage gap has been lessening since the Fair Labor Standards Act of 1938, but despite such federal legislation, pay disparities have continued between female and male workers and in various demographic groups. *Corning Glass Works v. Brennan* was the first time the Supreme Court considered an Equal Pay Act claim based on an employer paying women less than men for the same work. While some wage discrepancies are due to differences in occupations, experience, skills, and other legitimate factors, there is still a considerable gap that exists without explanation between men and women. This case is a milestone in the long journey to remedy this market phenomenon.

Source: http://supreme.justia.com/cases/federal/us/417/188/case.html

U.S. Supreme Court
***Corning Glass Works v. Brennan*, 417 U.S. 188 (1974)**
No. 73-29
Argued March 25, 1974
Decided June 3, 1974*
417 U.S. 188
CERTIORARI TO THE UNITED STATES COURT OF APPEALS FOR THE SECOND CIRCUIT

MR. JUSTICE MARSHALL delivered the opinion of the Court.

These cases arise under the Equal Pay Act of 1963, 77 Stat. 56, § 3, 29 U.S.C. § 206(d)(1), [Footnote 1] which added to § 6 of the Fair Labor Standards Act of 1938 the principle of equal pay for equal work regardless of sex. The principal question posed is whether Corning Glass Works violated the Act by paying a higher base wage to male night shift inspectors than it paid to female inspectors performing the same tasks on the day shift, where the higher wage was paid in addition to a separate night shift differential paid to all employees for night work. In No. 73-29, the Court of Appeals for the Second Circuit, in a case involving several Corning plants in Corning, New York, held that this practice violated

Page 417 U. S. 191

the Act. 474 F.2d 226 (1973). In No. 73-695, the Court of Appeals for the Third Circuit, in a case involving a Corning plant in Wellsboro, Pennsylvania, reached the opposite conclusion. 480 F.2d 1254 (1973). We granted certiorari and consolidated the cases to resolve this unusually direct conflict between two circuits. 414 U.S. 1110 (1973). Finding ourselves in substantial agreement with the analysis of the Second Circuit, we affirm in No. 73-29 and reverse in No. 73-695. . . .

* * *

. . . After considering the rather complex method in which the new wage rates for employees hired prior to January, 1969, were calculated and the company's stated purpose
Page 417 U. S. 209

behind the provisions of the new agreement, the District Court in No. 73-29 concluded that the lower base wage for day inspectors was a direct product of the company's failure to equalize the base wages for male and female inspectors as of the effective date of the Act. We agree it is clear from the record that, had the company equalized the base wage rates of male and female inspectors on the effective date of the Act, as the law required, the day inspectors, in 1969, would have been entitled to the same higher "red circle" rate the company provided for night inspectors. [Footnote 29] We therefore conclude that, on the facts of this case, the company's continued discrimination in base wages between night and day workers, though phrased in terms of a neutral factor other than sex, nevertheless operated to perpetuate the effects of the company's prior illegal practice of paying women less

Page 417 U. S. 210

than men for equal work. Cf. *Griggs v. Duke Power Co.*, 401 U. S. 424, 401 U. S. 430 (1971).

The judgment in No. 73-29 is affirmed. The judgment in No. 73-695 is reversed, and the case remanded to the Court of Appeals for further proceedings consistent with this opinion.

It is so ordered.

Lechmere, Inc. v. National Labor Relations Board, 502 U.S. 527 (1992)
A Supreme Court Case on Private Property Rights and Rights of Union Organizers to Access Employees

Private property is fundamental in a free enterprise economy. *Lechmere, Inc., v. NLRB* is about balancing the private property rights of employers with the rights of employees in the process of deciding to join a union. In a capitalist system, when private property rights are secure, competition is defined by peaceful means and guided by the rule of law. To maintain this balance, Congress passed the National Labor Relations Act in 1935. Section 7 established an employee's right to join a union and take part in collective bargaining, and an administrative board to enforce all requirements thereof. Any ambiguity within the act, Congress deferred to the board for final resolve. In the *Lechmere* case, the Supreme Court changed this default setting from the rule of deference to Court-based adjudication favoring the protection of private property rights.

Source: http://supreme.justia.com/cases/federal/us/502/527/case.html

Lechmere, Inc., v. NLRB – 502 U.S. 527 (1992)
OCTOBER TERM, 1991
LECHMERE, INC. v. NATIONAL LABOR RELATIONS BOARD
CERTIORARI TO THE UNITED STATES COURT OF APPEALS FOR THE FIRST CIRCUIT
No. 90-970. Argued November 12, 1991–Decided January 27, 1992

JUSTICE THOMAS delivered the opinion of the Court.

This case requires us to clarify the relationship between the rights of employees under § 7 of the National Labor Relations Act (NLRA or Act), 49 Stat. 452, as amended, 29 U. S. C. § 157, and the property rights of their employers. . . .

* * *

. . . The Board's conclusion in this case that the union had no reasonable means short of trespass to make Lechmere's employees aware of its organizational efforts is based on a misunderstanding of the limited scope of this exception. Because the employees do not reside on Lechmere's property, they are presumptively not "beyond the reach," *Babcock*, 351 U.S., at 113, of the union's message. Although the employees live in a large metropolitan area (Greater Hartford), that fact does not in itself render them "inaccessible" in the sense contemplated by Babcock. See *Monogram Models, Inc.*, 192 N. L. R. B. 705, 706 (1971). Their accessibility is suggested by the union's success in contacting a substantial percentage of them directly, via mailings, phone calls, and home visits. Such direct contact, of course, is not a necessary element of "reasonably effective" communication; signs or advertising also may suffice. In this case, the union tried advertising in local newspapers; the Board said that this was not reasonably effective because it was expensive and might not reach the employees. 295 N. L. R. B., at 93. Whatever the merits of that conclusion, other alternative means of communication were readily available. Thus, signs (displayed, for example, from the public grassy strip adjoining Lechmere's parking lot) would have informed the employees about the union's organizational efforts. (Indeed, union organizers picketed the shopping center's main entrance for months as employees came and went every day.) Access to employees, not success in winning them over, is the critical issue—although success, or lack thereof, may be relevant in determining

541
whether reasonable access exists. Because the union in this case failed to establish the existence of any "unique obstacles," Sears, 436 U. S., at 205-206, n. 41, that frustrated access to Lechmere's employees, the Board erred in concluding that Lechmere committed an unfair labor practice by barring the nonemployee organizers from its property.

The judgment of the First Circuit is therefore reversed, and enforcement of the Board's order is denied.

It is so ordered.

MCI Telecommunications Corp. v. American Telephone and Telegraph Co., 512 U.S. 218 (1994)

A Supreme Court Case Acknowledging Technology as a Market Structure Change Agent

In 1913, American Telephone and Telegraph (AT&T), a conglomerate of Bell Companies, had made an agreement with Congress giving the company a phone service monopoly. In 1934, Congress passed the Federal Communications Act, with the goal of securing an economical and well-functioning system of national and global communications infrastructure. In the almost 80-year history of the act, the progression of technology and business acumen paralleled the growth of government regulation. The Federal Communications Commission (FCC) had extensive oversight in technologies such as wireless, satellite, and microwave communications. The FCC employed various techniques to maintain fair trade practices, i.e., competition, reasonable rates, and lack of price discrimination.

The *MCI Telecommunications Corp. v. American Telephone and Telegraph* case, however, reflected the majority opinion that limited the discretionary ability and power of the commission powers, referring back to Congress the authority of intent. The result of this decision was the Telecommunications Act of 1996, allowing economies of scale to work within the industry, and toward decreased regulation of the communications industry.

Source: http://www.law.cornell.edu/supremecourt/text/512/218#writing-type-1-SCALIA

512 U.S. 218114 S.Ct. 2223129 L.Ed.2d 182 (512 U.S. 218114 S.Ct. 2223129 L.Ed.2d 182)
MCI TELECOMMUNICATIONS CORPORATION*, Petitioner, v. AMERICAN *TELEPHONE AND TELEGRAPH COMPANY. UNITED STATES, et al., Petitioners v. AMERICAN TELEPHONE AND TELEGRAPH COMPANY et al.
Nos. 93-356, 93-521.
Argued: March 21, 1994
Decided: June 17, 1994

Justice SCALIA delivered the opinion of the Court.

Section 203(a) of Title 47 of the United States Code requires communications common carriers to file tariffs with the Federal Communications Commission, and § 203(b) authorizes the Commission to "modify" any requirement of § 203. These cases present the question whether the Commission's decision to make tariff filing optional for all non-dominant long distance carriers is a valid exercise of its modification authority. . . .

* * *

. . . * Like most cases involving the role of the American Telephone and Telegraph Company (AT & T) in our national telecommunication system, these have a long history. An understanding of the cases requires a brief review of the Commission's efforts to regulate and then deregulate the telecommunications industry. When Congress created the Commission in 1934, AT & T, through its vertically integrated Bell system, held a virtual monopoly over the Nation's telephone service. The Communications Act of 1934, 48 Stat. 1064, as amended, authorized the Commission to regulate the rates charged for communication services to ensure that they were reasonable and non-discriminatory. The requirements of § 203 that common carriers file their rates with the Commission and charge only the filed rate were the centerpiece of the Act's regulatory scheme.

In the 1970s, technological advances reduced the entry costs for competitors of AT & T in the market for long distance telephone service. The Commission, recognizing the feasibility of greater competition, passed regulations to facilitate competitive entry. By 1979, competition in the provision of long distance service was well established, and some urged that the continuation of extensive tariff filing requirements served only to impose unnecessary costs on new entrants and to facilitate collusive pricing. The Commission held hearings on the matter, see Competitive Carrier Notice of Inquiry and Proposed Rulemaking, 77 F.C.C.2d 308 (1979), following which it issued a series of rules that have produced this litigation. . . .

* * *

. . . We do not mean to suggest that the tariff-filing requirement is so inviolate that the Commission's existing modification authority does not reach it at all. Certainly the Commission can modify the form, contents, and location of required filings, and can defer filing or perhaps even waive it altogether in limited circumstances. But what we have here goes well beyond that. It is effectively the introduction of a whole new regime of regulation (or of free-market competition), which may well be a better regime but is not the one that Congress established.

The judgment of the Court of Appeals is

Affirmed.

Seminole Tribe of Florida v. Florida, 517 U.S. 44 (1996)

This Supreme Court Case Determined the Extent of an Indian Nation's Economic Autonomy

The Seminole tribes struggled through economic challenges as their way of living changed from their traditional economy to a market-based economy. The Indian gaming industry was an evolution of ideas, starting with bingo and graduating to class III high-stakes gambling (high stakes games such as casinos, racetracks, etc.). The revenue from these businesses and other associated enterprises allowed the Seminole Indian tribes to support health facilities, schools, roads, and other such infrastructure and distribute dividends from the profits throughout the entire remaining tribe members. With this case, the Supreme Court determined the extent of an Indian nation's economic autonomy.

Source: http://caselaw.lp.findlaw.com/scripts/getcase.pl?court=US&vol=000&invol=U10198

SEMINOLE TRIBE OF FLORIDA, PETITIONER v. FLORIDA et al.
CERTIORARI TO THE UNITED STATES COURT OF APPEALS FOR THE ELEVENTH CIRCUIT No. 94-12. (1996)

CHIEF JUSTICE REHNQUIST delivered the opinion of the Court.

The Indian Gaming Regulatory Act provides that an Indian tribe may conduct certain gaming activities only in conformance with a valid compact between the tribe and the State in which the gaming activities are located. 102 Stat. 2475, 25 U.S.C. 2710(d)(1)(C). The Act, passed by Congress under the Indian Commerce Clause, U.S. Const., Art. I, 10, cl. 3, imposes upon the States a duty to negotiate in good faith with an Indian tribe toward the formation of a compact, 2710(d)(3)(A), and authorizes a tribe to bring suit in federal court against a State in order to compel performance of that duty, 2710(d)(7). We hold that notwithstanding Congress' clear intent to abrogate the States' sovereign immunity, the Indian Commerce Clause does not grant Congress that power, and therefore 2710(d)(7) cannot grant jurisdiction over a State that does not consent to be sued. We further hold that the doctrine of *Ex parte Young*, 209 U.S. 123 (1908), may not be used to enforce 2710(d)(3) against a state official. [*SEMINOLE TRIBE OF FLORIDA v. FLORIDA, ___ U.S. ___ (1996)*, 2] . . .

* * *

. . . I

Congress passed the Indian Gaming Regulatory Act in 1988 in order to provide a statutory basis for the operation and regulation of gaming by Indian tribes. See 25 U.S.C. 2702. The Act divides gaming on Indian lands into three classes—I, II, and III—and provides a different regulatory scheme for each class. Class III gaming—the type with which we are here concerned—is defined as "all forms of gaming that are not class I gaming or class II gaming," 2703(8), and includes such things as slot machines, casino games, banking card games, dog racing, and lotteries. 1 It is the most heavily regulated of the three classes. The Act provides that class III gaming is lawful only where it is: (1) authorized by an ordinance or resolution that (a) is adopted by the governing body of the Indian tribe, (b) satisfies certain statutorily prescribed requirements, and (c) is approved by the National Indian Gaming Commission; (2) located in a State that permits such gaming for any purpose by any person, organization, or entity; and (3) "conducted in conformance with a

Tribal-State [*SEMINOLE TRIBE OF FLORIDA v. FLORIDA,* ___ *U.S.* ___ (1996), 3] compact entered into by the Indian tribe and the State under paragraph (3) that is in effect." 2710(d)(1). . . .

* * *

. . . Here, of course, we have found that Congress does not have authority under the Constitution to make the State suable in federal court under 2710(d)(7). Nevertheless, the fact that Congress chose to impose upon the State a liability which is significantly more limited than would be the liability imposed upon the state officer under *Ex parte Young* strongly indicates that Congress had no wish to create the latter under 2710(d)(3). Nor are we free to rewrite the statutory scheme in order to approximate what we think Congress might have wanted had it known that 2710(d)(7) was beyond its authority. If that effort is to be made, it should be made by Congress, and not by the federal courts. We hold that *Ex parte Young* is inapplicable to petitioner's suit against the Governor of Florida, and therefore that suit is barred by the Eleventh Amendment and must be dismissed for a lack of jurisdiction.

IV

The Eleventh Amendment prohibits Congress from making the State of Florida capable of being sued in federal court. The narrow exception to the Eleventh Amendment provided by the Ex parte Young doctrine cannot be used to enforce 2710(d)(3) because Congress enacted a remedial scheme, 2710(d)(7), specifically designed for the enforcement of that right. The Eleventh Circuit's dismissal of petitioner's suit is hereby affirmed. 18

It is so ordered. [*SEMINOLE TRIBE OF FLORIDA v. FLORIDA,* ___ *U.S.* ___ (1996), 32]

Alaska Dept. of Environmental Conservation v. EPA, 540 U.S. 461 (2004)
A Supreme Court Case on the Environment, Economic Growth, and Federalism

Standards for safeguarding the environment are set at both the state and national levels. Most of the economic burden associated with protecting the environment and economic growth is incurred by local industry. Meeting clean air standards includes expenses that increase the cost of doing business. In a competitive market, these added expenditures to clean up existing factories and build new ones have long-term effects on a state's economic development. In addition, there is a political relationship between economic growth and protecting the environment. In the case of *Alaska Dept. of Environmental Conservation (ADEC) v. EPA*, the relationship between the state of Alaska and a federal bureaucratic agency snowballed into a classic battle between states' rights and federal power.

Source: http://www.law.cornell.edu/supct/html/02-658.ZO.html

***ALASKA DEPT. OF ENVIRONMENTAL CONSERVATION V. EPA* (02-658) 540 U.S. 461 (2004)**
298 F.3d 814, affirmed.
SUPREME COURT OF THE UNITED STATES
No. 02—658
ALASKA DEPARTMENT OF ENVIRONMENTAL CONSERVATION, PETITIONER v. ENVIRONMENTAL PROTECTION AGENCY et al.
ON WRIT OF CERTIORARI TO THE UNITED STATES COURT OF APPEALS FOR THE NINTH CIRCUIT
[January 21, 2004]

Justice Ginsburg delivered the opinion of the Court.

This case concerns the authority of the Environmental Protection Agency (EPA or Agency) to enforce the provisions of the Clean Air Act's (CAA or Act) Prevention of Significant Deterioration (PSD) program. Under that program, no major air pollutant emitting facility may be constructed unless the facility is equipped with "the best available control technology" (BACT). As added by §165, 91 Stat. 735, and amended, 42 U.S.C. § 7475(a)(4). BACT, as defined in the CAA, means, for any major air pollutant emitting facility, "an emission limitation based on the maximum degree of [pollutant] reduction . . . which the permitting authority, on a case-by-case basis, taking into account energy, environmental, and economic impacts and other costs, determines is achievable for [the] facility. . . ." §7479(3). . .

* * *

. . . In the case before us, "the permitting authority" under §7479(3) is the State of Alaska, acting through Alaska's Department of Environmental Conservation (ADEC). The question presented is what role EPA has with respect to ADEC's BACT determinations. Specifically, may EPA act to block construction of a new major pollutant emitting facility permitted by ADEC when EPA finds ADEC's BACT determination unreasonable in light of the guides §7479(3) prescribes? We hold that the Act confers that checking authority on EPA. . . .

* * *

. . . The Court of Appeals resolved the merits in a judgment released July 30, 2002. 298 F.3d 814 (CA9). It held that EPA had authority under §§113(a)(5) and 167 to issue the contested orders, and that the Agency had properly exercised its discretion in doing so. Id., at 820—823. . .

* * *

. . . Centrally at issue in this case is the question whether EPA's oversight role, described by Congress in CAA §§113(a)(5) and 167, see supra, at 7, extends to ensuring that a state permitting authority's BACT determination is reasonable in light of the statutory guides. . . .

* * *

. . . In sum, we conclude that EPA has supervisory authority over the reasonableness of state permitting authorities' BACT determinations and may issue a stop construction order, under §§113(a)(5) and 167, if a BACT selection is not reasonable. We further conclude that, in exercising that authority, the Agency did not act arbitrarily or capriciously in finding that ADEC's BACT decision in this instance lacked evidentiary support. EPA's orders, therefore, were neither arbitrary nor capricious. The judgment of the Court of Appeals is accordingly

Affirmed.

Kelo v. City of New London, Connecticut, 545 U.S. 469 (2005)
A Supreme Court Case on Private Property Rights and Role of Eminent Domain

In the United States, it is customary to think that home ownership is secure. Private property rights give good reason to trust in this assurance. Following the decision in *Kelo v. City of New London, Connecticut,* the question of how secure individuals are in their right to ownership of private property has been brought into question. In this case, the governmental power to take private property through eminent domain was granted to a private corporation, which in turn condemned individuals' homes and leased the property to private businesses with the intended purpose of economic revitalization for the area at large.

The Supreme Court's responsibility in this case was not to determine whether New London's master plan would be successful in carrying out the desired economic impact, but rather to interpret the U.S. Constitution. The federal judiciary's responsibility was to determine whether the reason private property was taken from individuals for public use was within the meaning of the Fifth Amendment to the U.S. Constitution. In a close vote, the Court indicated that indeed the city did not violate the takings clause of the Fifth Amendment.

Source: http://www.law.cornell.edu/supct/html/04-108.ZO.html

SUPREME COURT OF THE UNITED STATES
No. 04—108
SUSETTE KELO, et al., PETITIONERS v. CITY OF NEW LONDON, CONNECTICUT, et al.
ON WRIT OF CERTIORARI TO THE SUPREME COURT OF CONNECTICUT
[June 23, 2005]

Justice Stevens delivered the opinion of the Court.

In 2000, the city of New London approved a development plan that, in the words of the Supreme Court of Connecticut, was "projected to create in excess of 1,000 jobs, to increase tax and other revenues, and to revitalize an economically distressed city, including its downtown and waterfront areas." 268 Conn. 1, 5, 843 A. 2d 500, 507 (2004). In assembling the land needed for this project, the city's development agent has purchased property from willing sellers and proposes to use the power of eminent domain to acquire the remainder of the property from unwilling owners in exchange for just compensation. The question presented is whether the city's proposed disposition of this property qualifies as a "public use" within the meaning of the Takings Clause of the Fifth Amendment to the Constitution. . . .

. . . In affirming the City's authority to take petitioners' properties, we do not minimize the hardship that condemnations may entail, notwithstanding the payment of just compensation.21 We emphasize that nothing in our opinion precludes any State from placing further restrictions on its exercise of the takings power. Indeed, many States already impose "public use" requirements that are stricter than the federal baseline. Some of these requirements have been established as a matter of state constitutional law,22 while others are expressed in state eminent domain statutes that carefully limit the grounds upon which takings may be exercised.23 As the submissions of the parties and their amici make clear, the necessity and wisdom of using eminent domain to promote economic development are certainly matters of legitimate public debate.24 This Court's authority, however, extends only to determining whether the City's proposed condemnations are for a "public use" within the meaning of the Fifth Amendment to the Federal Constitution. Because over a century of our case law interpreting that provision dictates an affirmative answer to that question, we may not grant petitioners the relief that they seek.

The judgment of the Supreme Court of Connecticut is affirmed.

It is so ordered.

Citizens United v. Federal Election Commission, 558 U.S. ___ (2010)
A Supreme Court Case Upholding First Amendment Rights

The Bipartisan Campaign Reform Act of 2002 (BCRA) was passed by Congress in an effort to change the manner in which money is obtained and used for political campaigning in the United States, hopefully for the better. The focus in the *Citizens United v. FEC* case was on corporations, nonprofits, and labor unions and their right, without government restraint, to contribute to these political campaigns. However, when an individual votes or contributes to a politician's campaign, it is with the expectation he or she will be looked out for as a constituent.

Large corporations or unions are not like people who can cast a ballot. When they contribute to campaigns, the expectation is much different. The quid pro quo could include a corporation's receiving economic rent through special legislation that will benefit its business, less severe regulation, tax credits, or perhaps some political appointments. In an effort to adjust this imbalance and limit the contributions these organizations could make toward getting leaders elected to political office, Congress abridged their First Amendment rights to free speech. The constitutional question before the Court was whether Congress had the authority to stifle free speech by these legal organizations whose contributions had external economic effects on the nation. Following this decision, changes indeed did take place in the manner in which money was channeled toward and spent upon political campaigns in an effort to obtain economic rents. Large firms, sensitive to government policies, are able to contribute unlimited assets to the political economy with few restrictions. The economic and political results of this case still remain to be seen. Nevertheless, it can be argued that the impact of this case has altered the finances of the political landscape more so than any case in recent history.

Source: http://www.law.cornell.edu/supct/html/08-205.ZO.html

Citizens United v. Federal Election Comm'n (No. 08-205)
Reversed in part, affirmed in part, and remanded.
SUPREME COURT OF THE UNITED STATES
CITIZENS UNITED, APPELLANT v. FEDERAL ELECTION COMMISSION
On Appeal from the United States District Court for the District of Columbia
[January 21, 2010]

Justice Kennedy delivered the opinion of the Court.

Federal law prohibits corporations and unions from using their general treasury funds to make independent expenditures for speech defined as an "electioneering communication" or for speech expressly advocating the election or defeat of a candidate. 2 U. S. C. §441b. Limits on electioneering communications were upheld in *McConnell v. Federal Election Comm'n*, 540 U. S. 93, 203–209 (2003). The holding of *McConnell* rested to a large extent on an earlier case, *Austin v. Michigan Chamber of Commerce*, 494 U. S. 652 (1990). *Austin* had held that political speech may be banned based on the speaker's corporate identity.

In this case we are asked to reconsider *Austin* and, in effect, *McConnell*. It has been noted that "Austin was a significant departure from ancient First Amendment principles," *Federal Election Comm'n v. Wisconsin Right to Life, Inc.*, 551 U. S. 449, 490 (2007) (WRTL) (Scalia, J., concurring in part and concurring in judgment). We agree with that conclusion and hold that stare decisis does not compel the continued acceptance of Austin. The Government may regulate corporate political speech through disclaimer and disclosure requirements, but it may not suppress that speech altogether. We turn to the case now before us. . . .

* * *

. . . Citizens United is a nonprofit corporation. It brought this action in the United States District Court for the District of Columbia. A three-judge court later convened to hear the cause. The resulting judgment gives rise to this appeal. . . .

* * *

. . . The case was reargued in this Court after the Court asked the parties to file supplemental briefs addressing whether we should overrule either or both Austin and the part of McConnell which addresses the facial validity of 2 U. S. C. §441b. See 557 U. S. ___ (2009).

II

Before considering whether Austin should be overruled, we first address whether Citizens United's claim that §441b cannot be applied to Hillary may be resolved on other, narrower grounds. . . .

* * *

. . . Some members of the public might consider Hillary to be insightful and instructive; some might find it to be neither high art nor a fair discussion on how to set the Nation's course; still others simply might suspend judgment on these points but decide to think more about issues and candidates. Those choices and assessments, however, are not for the Government to make. "The First Amendment underwrites the freedom to experiment and to create in the realm of thought and speech. Citizens must be free to use new forms, and new forums, for the expression of ideas. The civic discourse belongs to the people, and the Government may not prescribe the means used to conduct it." *McConnell*, supra, at 341 (opinion of Kennedy, J.).

The judgment of the District Court is reversed with respect to the constitutionality of 2 U. S. C. §441b's restrictions on corporate independent expenditures. The judgment is affirmed with respect to BCRA's disclaimer and disclosure requirements. The case is remanded for further proceedings consistent with this opinion.

It is so ordered.

Affordable Health Care Act Cases, 567 U.S.___ (2012)
Supreme Court Cases Regarding Government-Provided Health Care

It is rational to assume that virtually all Americans at some time in their lives will enter the health care market. In addition, it is safe to infer that without health insurance (the financial means to pay for products and services in the health care market), many Americans will experience economic hardship during this exchange. Some will not be able to pay at all. For them, the products or services are provided without cost. The cost is shifted to those with the means to pay. Thus, the consequences of this market on the nation are to economically burden the individuals who have the ability to pay and redistribute income to pay the cost of health care for those who cannot. As in the case of Social Security, the authority of the federal government to attempt to remedy the financial shortcomings and aid the general welfare comes into question with *Health and Human Services v. Florida et al.* This case was a combination of two other cases, all three of which posed fundamental constitutional questions. The Court viewed this case not in terms of whether it was good or poor public policy, but rather from the perspective of whether Congress had adhered to constitutional principles.

Source: http://www.oyez.org/cases/2010-2019/2011/2011_11_400

SUPREME COURT OF THE UNITED STATES
Nos. 11–393, 11–398 and 11–400
NATIONAL FEDERATION OF INDEPENDENT BUSINESS, et al., PETITIONERS
11–393 v.
KATHLEEN SEBELIUS, SECRETARY OF HEALTH AND HUMAN SERVICES, et al.
DEPARTMENT OF HEALTH AND HUMAN SERVICES, et al., PETITIONERS
11–398 v.
FLORIDA et al.
FLORIDA, et al., PETITIONERS
11–400 v.
DEPARTMENT OF HEALTH AND HUMAN SERVICES et al.
On Writs of Certiorari to the United States Court of Appeals for the Eleventh Circuit
[June 28, 2012]

Chief Justice Roberts announced the judgment of the Court and delivered the opinion of the Court with respect to Parts I, II, and III–C, an opinion with respect to Part IV, in which Justice Breyer and Justice Kagan join, and an opinion with respect to Parts III–A, III–B, and III–D.

Today we resolve constitutional challenges to two provisions of the Patient Protection and Affordable Care Act of 2010: the individual mandate, which requires individuals to purchase a health insurance policy providing a minimum level of coverage; and the Medicaid expansion, which gives funds to the States on the condition that they provide specified health care to all citizens whose income falls below a certain threshold. We do not consider whether the Act embodies sound policies. That judgment is entrusted to the Nation's elected leaders. We ask only whether Congress has the power under the Constitution to enact the challenged provisions.

In our federal system, the National Government possesses only limited powers; the States and the people retain the remainder. . . .

* * *

. . . None of this is to say that the payment is not intended to affect individual conduct. Although the payment will raise considerable revenue, it is plainly designed to expand health insurance coverage. . . .

* * *

. . . The Affordable Care Act is constitutional in part and unconstitutional in part. The individual mandate cannot be upheld as an exercise of Congress's power under the Commerce Clause. That Clause authorizes Congress to regulate interstate commerce, not to order individuals to engage in it. In this case, however, it is reasonable to construe what Congress has done as increasing taxes on those who have a certain amount of income, but choose to go without health insurance. Such legislation is within Congress's power to tax.

As for the Medicaid expansion, that portion of the Affordable Care Act violates the Constitution by threatening existing Medicaid funding. Congress has no authority to order the States to regulate according to its instructions. Congress may offer the States grants and require the States to comply with accompanying conditions, but the States must have a genuine choice whether to accept the offer. The States are given no such choice in this case: They must either accept a basic change in the nature of Medicaid, or risk losing all Medicaid funding. The remedy for that constitutional violation is to preclude the Federal Government from imposing such a sanction. That remedy does not require striking down other portions of the Affordable Care Act.

The Framers created a Federal Government of limited powers, and assigned to this Court the duty of enforcing those limits. The Court does so today. But the Court does not express any opinion on the wisdom of the Affordable Care Act. Under the Constitution, that judgment is reserved to the people.

The judgment of the Court of Appeals for the Eleventh Circuit is affirmed in part and reversed in part.

It is so ordered.

The Constitution of the United States

We the People of the United States, in Order to form a more perfect Union, establish Justice, insure domestic Tranquility, provide for the common defence, promote the general Welfare, and secure the Blessings of Liberty to ourselves and our Posterity, do ordain and establish this Constitution for the United States of America.

Article I.

Section 1.

All legislative Powers herein granted shall be vested in a Congress of the United States, which shall consist of a Senate and House of Representatives.

Section 2.

The House of Representatives shall be composed of Members chosen every second Year by the People of the several States, and the Electors in each State shall have the Qualifications requisite for Electors of the most numerous Branch of the State Legislature.

No Person shall be a Representative who shall not have attained to the Age of twenty five Years, and been seven Years a Citizen of the United States, and who shall not, when elected, be an Inhabitant of that State in which he shall be chosen.

Representatives and direct Taxes shall be apportioned among the several States which may be included within this Union, according to their respective Numbers, which shall be determined by adding to the whole Number of free Persons, including those bound to Service for a Term of Years, and excluding Indians not taxed, three fifths of all other Persons. The actual Enumeration shall be made within three Years after the first Meeting of the Congress of the United States, and within every subsequent Term of ten Years, in such Manner as they shall by Law direct. The Number of Representatives shall not exceed one for every thirty Thousand, but each State shall have at Least one Representative; and until such enumeration shall be made, the State of New Hampshire shall be entitled to chuse three, Massachusetts eight, Rhode-Island and Providence Plantations one, Connecticut five, New-York six, New Jersey four, Pennsylvania eight, Delaware one, Maryland six, Virginia ten, North Carolina five, South Carolina five, and Georgia three.

When vacancies happen in the Representation from any State, the Executive Authority thereof shall issue Writs of Election to fill such Vacancies.

The House of Representatives shall chuse their Speaker and other Officers; and shall have the sole Power of Impeachment.

Section 3.

The Senate of the United States shall be composed of two Senators from each State, chosen by the Legislature thereof for six Years; and each Senator shall have one Vote.

Immediately after they shall be assembled in Consequence of the first Election, they shall be divided as equally as may be into three Classes. The Seats of the Senators of the first Class shall be vacated at the Expiration of the second Year, of the second Class at the Expiration of the fourth Year, and of the third Class at the Expiration of the sixth Year, so that one third may be chosen every second Year; and if Vacancies happen by Resignation, or otherwise, during the Recess of the Legislature of any State, the Executive thereof may make temporary Appointments until the next Meeting of the Legislature, which shall then fill such Vacancies.

No Person shall be a Senator who shall not have attained to the Age of thirty Years, and been nine Years a Citizen of the United States, and who shall not, when elected, be an Inhabitant of that State for which he shall be chosen.

The Vice President of the United States shall be President of the Senate, but shall have no Vote, unless they be equally divided.

The Senate shall chuse their other Officers, and also a President pro tempore, in the Absence of the Vice President, or when he shall exercise the Office of President of the United States.

The Senate shall have the sole Power to try all Impeachments. When sitting for that Purpose, they shall be on Oath or Affirmation. When the President of the United States is tried, the Chief Justice shall preside: And no Person shall be convicted without the Concurrence of two thirds of the Members present.

Judgment in Cases of Impeachment shall not extend further than to removal from Office, and disqualification to hold and enjoy any Office of honor, Trust or Profit under the United States: but the Party convicted shall nevertheless be liable and subject to Indictment, Trial, Judgment and Punishment, according to Law.

Section 4.

The Times, Places and Manner of holding Elections for Senators and Representatives, shall be prescribed in each State by the Legislature thereof; but the Congress may at any time by Law make or alter such Regulations, except as to the Places of chusing Senators.

The Congress shall assemble at least once in every Year, and such Meeting shall be on the first Monday in December, unless they shall by Law appoint a different Day.

Section 5.

Each House shall be the Judge of the Elections, Returns and Qualifications of its own Members, and a Majority of each shall constitute a Quorum to do Business; but a smaller Number may adjourn from day to day, and may be authorized to compel the Attendance of absent Members, in such Manner, and under such Penalties as each House may provide.

Each House may determine the Rules of its Proceedings, punish its Members for disorderly Behaviour, and, with the Concurrence of two thirds, expel a Member.

Each House shall keep a Journal of its Proceedings, and from time to time publish the same, excepting such Parts as may in their Judgment require Secrecy; and the Yeas and Nays of the Members of either House on any question shall, at the Desire of one fifth of those Present, be entered on the Journal.

Neither House, during the Session of Congress, shall, without the Consent of the other, adjourn for more than three days, nor to any other Place than that in which the two Houses shall be sitting.

Section 6.

The Senators and Representatives shall receive a Compensation for their Services, to be ascertained by Law, and paid out of the Treasury of the United States. They shall in all Cases, except Treason, Felony and Breach of the Peace, be privileged from Arrest during their Attendance at the Session of their respective Houses, and in going to and returning from the same; and for any Speech or Debate in either House, they shall not be questioned in any other Place.

No Senator or Representative shall, during the Time for which he was elected, be appointed to any civil Office under the Authority of the United States, which shall have been created, or the Emoluments whereof shall have been encreased during such time; and no Person holding any Office under the United States, shall be a Member of either House during his Continuance in Office.

Section 7.

All Bills for raising Revenue shall originate in the House of Representatives; but the Senate may propose or concur with Amendments as on other Bills.

Every Bill which shall have passed the House of Representatives and the Senate, shall, before it become a Law, be presented to the President of the United States: If he approve he shall sign it, but if not he shall return it, with his Objections to that House in which it shall have originated, who shall enter the Objections at large on their Journal, and proceed to reconsider it. If after such Reconsideration two thirds of that House shall agree to pass the Bill, it shall be sent, together with the Objections, to the other House, by which it shall likewise be reconsidered, and if approved by two thirds of that House, it shall become a Law. But in all such Cases the Votes of both Houses shall be determined by yeas and Nays, and the Names of the Persons voting for and against the Bill shall be entered on the Journal of each House respectively. If any Bill shall not be returned by the President within ten Days (Sundays excepted) after it shall have been presented to him, the Same shall be a Law, in like Manner as if he had signed it, unless the Congress by their Adjournment prevent its Return, in which Case it shall not be a Law.

Every Order, Resolution, or Vote to which the Concurrence of the Senate and House of Representatives may be necessary (except on a question of Adjournment) shall be presented to the President of the United States; and before the Same shall take Effect, shall be approved by him, or being disapproved by him, shall be repassed by two thirds of the Senate and House of Representatives, according to the Rules and Limitations prescribed in the Case of a Bill.

Section 8.

The Congress shall have Power to lay and collect Taxes, Duties, Imposts and Excises, to pay the Debts and provide for the common Defence and general Welfare of the United States; but all Duties, Imposts and Excises shall be uniform throughout the United States;

To borrow Money on the credit of the United States;

To regulate Commerce with foreign Nations, and among the several States, and with the Indian Tribes;

To establish an uniform Rule of Naturalization, and uniform Laws on the subject of Bankruptcies throughout the United States;

To coin Money, regulate the Value thereof, and of foreign Coin, and fix the Standard of Weights and Measures;

To provide for the Punishment of counterfeiting the Securities and current Coin of the United States;

To establish Post Offices and post Roads;

To promote the Progress of Science and useful Arts, by securing for limited Times to Authors and Inventors the exclusive Right to their respective Writings and Discoveries;

To constitute Tribunals inferior to the supreme Court;

To define and punish Piracies and Felonies committed on the high Seas, and Offences against the Law of Nations;

To declare War, grant Letters of Marque and Reprisal, and make Rules concerning Captures on Land and Water;

To raise and support Armies, but no Appropriation of Money to that Use shall be for a longer Term than two Years;

To provide and maintain a Navy;

To make Rules for the Government and Regulation of the land and naval Forces;

To provide for calling forth the Militia to execute the Laws of the Union, suppress Insurrections and repel Invasions;

To provide for organizing, arming, and disciplining, the Militia, and for governing such Part of them as may be employed in the Service of the United States, reserving to the States respectively, the Appointment of the Officers, and the Authority of training the Militia according to the discipline prescribed by Congress;

To exercise exclusive Legislation in all Cases whatsoever, over such District (not exceeding ten Miles square) as may, by Cession of particular States, and the Acceptance of Congress, become the Seat of the Government of the United States, and to exercise like Authority over all Places purchased by the Consent of the Legislature of the State in which the Same shall be, for the Erection of Forts, Magazines, Arsenals, dock-Yards, and other needful Buildings;—And

To make all Laws which shall be necessary and proper for carrying into Execution the foregoing Powers, and all other Powers vested by this Constitution in the Government of the United States, or in any Department or Officer thereof.

Section 9.

The Migration or Importation of such Persons as any of the States now existing shall think proper to admit, shall not be prohibited by the Congress prior to the Year one thousand eight hundred and eight, but a Tax or duty may be imposed on such Importation, not exceeding ten dollars for each Person.

The Privilege of the Writ of Habeas Corpus shall not be suspended, unless when in Cases of Rebellion or Invasion the public Safety may require it.

No Bill of Attainder or ex post facto Law shall be passed.

No Capitation, or other direct, Tax shall be laid, unless in Proportion to the Census or enumeration herein before directed to be taken.

No Tax or Duty shall be laid on Articles exported from any State.

No Preference shall be given by any Regulation of Commerce or Revenue to the Ports of one State over those of another; nor shall Vessels bound to, or from, one State, be obliged to enter, clear, or pay Duties in another.

No Money shall be drawn from the Treasury, but in Consequence of Appropriations made by Law; and a regular Statement and Account of the Receipts and Expenditures of all public Money shall be published from time to time.

No Title of Nobility shall be granted by the United States: And no Person holding any Office of Profit or Trust under them, shall, without the Consent of the Congress, accept of any present, Emolument, Office, or Title, of any kind whatever, from any King, Prince, or foreign State.

Section 10.

No State shall enter into any Treaty, Alliance, or Confederation; grant Letters of Marque and Reprisal; coin Money; emit Bills of Credit; make any Thing but gold and silver Coin a Tender in Payment of Debts; pass any Bill of Attainder, ex post facto Law, or Law impairing the Obligation of Contracts, or grant any Title of Nobility.

No State shall, without the Consent of the Congress, lay any Imposts or Duties on Imports or Exports, except what may be absolutely necessary for executing it's inspection Laws: and the net Produce of all Duties and Imposts, laid by any State on Imports or Exports, shall be for the Use of the Treasury of the United States; and all such Laws shall be subject to the Revision and Controul of the Congress.

No State shall, without the Consent of Congress, lay any Duty of Tonnage, keep Troops, or Ships of War in time of Peace, enter into any Agreement or Compact with another State, or with a foreign Power, or engage in War, unless actually invaded, or in such imminent Danger as will not admit of delay.

Article II.

Section 1.

The executive Power shall be vested in a President of the United States of America. He shall hold his Office during the Term of four Years, and, together with the Vice President, chosen for the same Term, be elected, as follows:

Each State shall appoint, in such Manner as the Legislature thereof may direct, a Number of Electors, equal to the whole Number of Senators and Representatives to which the State may be entitled in the Congress: but no Senator or Representative, or Person holding an Office of Trust or Profit under the United States, shall be appointed an Elector.

The Electors shall meet in their respective States, and vote by Ballot for two Persons, of whom one at least shall not be an Inhabitant of the same State with themselves. And they shall make a List of all the Persons voted for, and of the Number of Votes for each; which List they shall sign and certify, and transmit sealed to the Seat of the Government of the United States, directed to the President of the Senate. The President of the Senate shall, in the Presence of the Senate and House of Representatives, open all the Certificates, and the Votes shall then be counted. The Person having the greatest Number of Votes shall be the President, if such Number be a Majority of the whole Number of Electors appointed; and if there be more than one who have such Majority, and have an equal Number of Votes, then the House of Representatives shall immediately chuse by Ballot one of them for President; and if no Person have a Majority, then from the five highest on the List the said House shall in like Manner chuse the President. But in chusing the President, the Votes shall be taken by States, the Representation from each State having one Vote; A quorum for this purpose shall consist of a Member or Members from two thirds of the States, and a Majority of all the States shall be necessary to a Choice. In every Case, after the Choice of the President, the Person having the greatest Number of Votes of the Electors shall be the Vice President. But if there should remain two or more who have equal Votes, the Senate shall chuse from them by Ballot the Vice President.

The Congress may determine the Time of chusing the Electors, and the Day on which they shall give their Votes; which Day shall be the same throughout the United States.

No Person except a natural born Citizen, or a Citizen of the United States, at the time of the Adoption of this Constitution, shall be eligible to the Office of President; neither shall any Person be eligible to that Office who shall not have attained to the Age of thirty five Years, and been fourteen Years a Resident within the United States.

In Case of the Removal of the President from Office, or of his Death, Resignation, or Inability to discharge the Powers and Duties of the said Office, the Same shall devolve on the Vice President, and the Congress may by Law provide for the Case of Removal, Death, Resignation or Inability, both of the President and Vice President, declaring what Officer shall then act as President, and such Officer shall act accordingly, until the Disability be removed, or a President shall be elected.

The President shall, at stated Times, receive for his Services, a Compensation, which shall neither be increased nor diminished during the Period for which he shall have been elected, and he shall not receive within that Period any other Emolument from the United States, or any of them.

Before he enter on the Execution of his Office, he shall take the following Oath or Affirmation:—"I do solemnly swear (or affirm) that I will faithfully execute the Office of President of the United States, and will to the best of my Ability, preserve, protect and defend the Constitution of the United States."

Section 2.

The President shall be Commander in Chief of the Army and Navy of the United States, and of the Militia of the several States, when called into the actual Service of the United States; he may require the Opinion, in writing, of the principal Officer in each of the executive Departments, upon any Subject relating to the Duties of their respective Offices, and he shall have Power to grant Reprieves and Pardons for Offences against the United States, except in Cases of Impeachment.

He shall have Power, by and with the Advice and Consent of the Senate, to make Treaties, provided two thirds of the Senators present concur; and he shall nominate, and by and with the Advice and Consent of the Senate, shall appoint Ambassadors, other public Ministers and Consuls, Judges of the supreme Court, and all other Officers of the United States, whose Appointments are not herein otherwise provided for, and which shall be established by Law: but the Congress may by Law vest the Appointment of such inferior Officers, as they think proper, in the President alone, in the Courts of Law, or in the Heads of Departments.

The President shall have Power to fill up all Vacancies that may happen during the Recess of the Senate, by granting Commissions which shall expire at the End of their next Session.

Section 3.

He shall from time to time give to the Congress Information of the State of the Union, and recommend to their Consideration such Measures as he shall judge necessary and expedient; he may, on extraordinary Occasions, convene both Houses, or either of them, and in Case of Disagreement between them, with Respect to the Time of Adjournment, he may adjourn them to such Time as he shall think proper; he shall receive Ambassadors and other public Ministers; he shall take Care that the Laws be faithfully executed, and shall Commission all the Officers of the United States.

Section 4.

The President, Vice President and all civil Officers of the United States, shall be removed from Office on Impeachment for, and Conviction of, Treason, Bribery, or other high Crimes and Misdemeanors.

Article III.

Section 1.

The judicial Power of the United States shall be vested in one supreme Court, and in such inferior Courts as the Congress may from time to time ordain and establish. The Judges, both of the supreme and inferior Courts, shall hold their Offices during good Behaviour, and shall, at stated Times, receive for their Services a Compensation, which shall not be diminished during their Continuance in Office.

Section 2.

The judicial Power shall extend to all Cases, in Law and Equity, arising under this Constitution, the Laws of the United States, and Treaties made, or which shall be made, under their

Authority;—to all Cases affecting Ambassadors, other public Ministers and Consuls;—to all Cases of admiralty and maritime Jurisdiction;—to Controversies to which the United States shall be a Party;—to Controversies between two or more States;—between a State and Citizens of another State,—between Citizens of different States,—between Citizens of the same State claiming Lands under Grants of different States, and between a State, or the Citizens thereof, and foreign States, Citizens or Subjects.

In all Cases affecting Ambassadors, other public Ministers and Consuls, and those in which a State shall be Party, the supreme Court shall have original Jurisdiction. In all the other Cases before mentioned, the supreme Court shall have appellate Jurisdiction, both as to Law and Fact, with such Exceptions, and under such Regulations as the Congress shall make.

The Trial of all Crimes, except in Cases of Impeachment, shall be by Jury; and such Trial shall be held in the State where the said Crimes shall have been committed; but when not committed within any State, the Trial shall be at such Place or Places as the Congress may by Law have directed.

Section 3.

Treason against the United States, shall consist only in levying War against them, or in adhering to their Enemies, giving them Aid and Comfort. No Person shall be convicted of Treason unless on the Testimony of two Witnesses to the same overt Act, or on Confession in open Court.

The Congress shall have Power to declare the Punishment of Treason, but no Attainder of Treason shall work Corruption of Blood, or Forfeiture except during the Life of the Person attainted.

Article IV.

Section 1.

Full Faith and Credit shall be given in each State to the public Acts, Records, and judicial Proceedings of every other State. And the Congress may by general Laws prescribe the Manner in which such Acts, Records and Proceedings shall be proved, and the Effect thereof.

Section 2.

The Citizens of each State shall be entitled to all Privileges and Immunities of Citizens in the several States.

A Person charged in any State with Treason, Felony, or other Crime, who shall flee from Justice, and be found in another State, shall on Demand of the executive Authority of the State from which he fled, be delivered up, to be removed to the State having Jurisdiction of the Crime.

No Person held to Service or Labour in one State, under the Laws thereof, escaping into another, shall, in Consequence of any Law or Regulation therein, be discharged from such Service or Labour, but shall be delivered up on Claim of the Party to whom such Service or Labour may be due.

Section 3.

New States may be admitted by the Congress into this Union; but no new State shall be formed or erected within the Jurisdiction of any other State; nor any State be formed by the Junction of two or more States, or Parts of States, without the Consent of the Legislatures of the States concerned as well as of the Congress.

The Congress shall have Power to dispose of and make all needful Rules and Regulations respecting the Territory or other Property belonging to the United States; and nothing in this Constitution shall be so construed as to Prejudice any Claims of the United States, or of any particular State.

Section 4.

The United States shall guarantee to every State in this Union a Republican Form of Government, and shall protect each of them against Invasion; and on Application of the Legislature, or of the Executive (when the Legislature cannot be convened), against domestic Violence.

Article V.

The Congress, whenever two thirds of both Houses shall deem it necessary, shall propose Amendments to this Constitution, or, on the Application of the Legislatures of two thirds of the several States, shall call a Convention for proposing Amendments, which, in either Case, shall be valid to all Intents and Purposes, as Part of this Constitution, when ratified by the Legislatures of three fourths of the several States, or by Conventions in three fourths thereof, as the one or the other Mode of Ratification may be proposed by the Congress; Provided that no Amendment which may be made prior to the Year One thousand eight hundred and eight shall in any Manner affect the first and fourth Clauses in the Ninth Section of the first Article; and that no State, without its Consent, shall be deprived of its equal Suffrage in the Senate.

Article VI.

All Debts contracted and Engagements entered into, before the Adoption of this Constitution, shall be as valid against the United States under this Constitution, as under the Confederation.

This Constitution, and the Laws of the United States which shall be made in Pursuance thereof; and all Treaties made, or which shall be made, under the Authority of the United States, shall be the supreme Law of the Land; and the Judges in every State shall be bound thereby, any Thing in the Constitution or Laws of any State to the Contrary notwithstanding.

The Senators and Representatives before mentioned, and the Members of the several State Legislatures, and all executive and judicial Officers, both of the United States and of the several States, shall be bound by Oath or Affirmation, to support this Constitution; but no religious Test shall ever be required as a Qualification to any Office or public Trust under the United States.

Article VII.

The Ratification of the Conventions of nine States, shall be sufficient for the Establishment of this Constitution between the States so ratifying the Same.

The Word, "the," being interlined between the seventh and eighth Lines of the first Page, the Word "Thirty" being partly written on an Erazure in the fifteenth Line of the first Page, The Words "is tried" being interlined between the thirty second and thirty third Lines of the first Page and the Word "the" being interlined between the forty third and forty fourth Lines of the second Page.

Attest William Jackson Secretary

done in Convention by the Unanimous Consent of the States present the Seventeenth Day of September in the Year of our Lord one thousand seven hundred and Eighty seven and of the Independance of the United States of America the Twelfth In witness whereof We have hereunto subscribed our Names,

G°. Washington
Presidt and deputy from Virginia

Delaware
Geo: Read
Gunning Bedford jun
John Dickinson
Richard Bassett
Jaco: Broom

Maryland
James McHenry
Dan of St Thos. Jenifer
Danl. Carroll

Virginia
John Blair
James Madison Jr.

North Carolina
Wm. Blount
Richd. Dobbs Spaight
Hu Williamson

South Carolina
J. Rutledge
Charles Cotesworth Pinckney
Charles Pinckney
Pierce Butler

Georgia
William Few
Abr Baldwin

New Hampshire
John Langdon
Nicholas Gilman

Massachusetts
Nathaniel Gorham
Rufus King

Connecticut
Wm. Saml. Johnson
Roger Sherman

New York
Alexander Hamilton

New Jersey
Wil: Livingston
David Brearley
Wm. Paterson
Jona: Dayton

Pennsylvania
B Franklin
Thomas Mifflin
Robt. Morris
Geo. Clymer
Thos. FitzSimons
Jared Ingersoll
James Wilson
Gouv Morris

The Bill of Rights: A Transcription
The Preamble to The Bill of Rights
Congress of the United States
begun and held at the City of New-York, on
Wednesday the fourth of March, one thousand seven hundred and eighty nine.

THE Conventions of a number of the States, having at the time of their adopting the Constitution, expressed a desire, in order to prevent misconstruction or abuse of its powers, that further declaratory and restrictive clauses should be added: And as extending the ground of public confidence in the Government, will best ensure the beneficent ends of its institution.

RESOLVED by the Senate and House of Representatives of the United States of America, in Congress assembled, two thirds of both Houses concurring, that the following Articles be proposed to the Legislatures of the several States, as amendments to the Constitution of the United States, all, or any of which Articles, when ratified by three fourths of the said Legislatures, to be valid to all intents and purposes, as part of the said Constitution; viz.

ARTICLES in addition to, and Amendment of the Constitution of the United States of America, proposed by Congress, and ratified by the Legislatures of the several States, pursuant to the fifth Article of the original Constitution.

Note: The following text is a transcription of the first ten amendments to the Constitution in their original form. These amendments were ratified December 15, 1791, and form what is known as the "Bill of Rights."

Amendment I

Congress shall make no law respecting an establishment of religion, or prohibiting the free exercise thereof; or abridging the freedom of speech, or of the press; or the right of the people peaceably to assemble, and to petition the Government for a redress of grievances.

Amendment II

A well regulated Militia, being necessary to the security of a free State, the right of the people to keep and bear Arms, shall not be infringed.

Amendment III

No Soldier shall, in time of peace be quartered in any house, without the consent of the Owner, nor in time of war, but in a manner to be prescribed by law.

Amendment IV

The right of the people to be secure in their persons, houses, papers, and effects, against unreasonable searches and seizures, shall not be violated, and no Warrants shall issue, but upon probable cause, supported by Oath or affirmation, and particularly describing the place to be searched, and the persons or things to be seized.

Amendment V

No person shall be held to answer for a capital, or otherwise infamous crime, unless on a presentment or indictment of a Grand Jury, except in cases arising in the land or naval forces, or in the Militia, when in actual service in time of War or public danger; nor shall any person be subject for the same offence to be twice put in jeopardy of life or limb; nor shall be compelled in any criminal case to be a witness against himself, nor be deprived of life, liberty, or property, without due process of law; nor shall private property be taken for public use, without just compensation.

Amendment VI

In all criminal prosecutions, the accused shall enjoy the right to a speedy and public trial, by an impartial jury of the State and district wherein the crime shall have been committed, which district shall have been previously ascertained by law, and to be informed of the nature and cause of the accusation; to be confronted with the witnesses against him; to have compulsory process for obtaining witnesses in his favor, and to have the Assistance of Counsel for his defence.

Amendment VII

In Suits at common law, where the value in controversy shall exceed twenty dollars, the right of trial by jury shall be preserved, and no fact tried by a jury, shall be otherwise re-examined in any Court of the United States, than according to the rules of the common law.

Amendment VIII

Excessive bail shall not be required, nor excessive fines imposed, nor cruel and unusual punishments inflicted.

Amendment IX

The enumeration in the Constitution, of certain rights, shall not be construed to deny or disparage others retained by the people.

Amendment X

The powers not delegated to the United States by the Constitution, nor prohibited by it to the States, are reserved to the States respectively, or to the people.

Amendment XI

Passed by Congress March 4, 1794. Ratified February 7, 1795.

Note: Article III, section 2, of the Constitution was modified by amendment 11.

The Judicial power of the United States shall not be construed to extend to any suit in law or equity, commenced or prosecuted against one of the United States by Citizens of another State, or by Citizens or Subjects of any Foreign State.

Amendment XII

Passed by Congress December 9, 1803. Ratified June 15, 1804.

Note: A portion of Article II, section 1 of the Constitution was superseded by the 12th amendment.

The Electors shall meet in their respective states and vote by ballot for President and Vice-President, one of whom, at least, shall not be an inhabitant of the same state with themselves; they shall name in their ballots the person voted for as President, and in distinct ballots the person voted for as Vice-President, and they shall make distinct lists of all persons voted for as President, and of all persons voted for as Vice-President, and of the number of votes for each, which lists they shall sign and certify, and transmit sealed to the seat of the government of the United States, directed to the President of the Senate; — the President of the Senate shall, in the presence of the Senate and House of Representatives, open all the certificates and the votes shall then be counted; — The person having the greatest number of votes for President, shall be the President, if such number be a majority of the whole number of Electors appointed; and if no person have such majority, then from the persons having the highest numbers not exceeding three on the list of those voted for as President, the House of Representatives shall choose immediately, by ballot, the President. But in choosing the President, the votes shall be taken by states, the representation from each state having one vote; a quorum for this purpose shall consist of a member or members from two-thirds of the states, and a majority of all the states shall be necessary to a choice. [And if the House of Representatives shall not choose a President whenever the right of choice shall devolve upon them, before the fourth day of March next following, then the Vice-President shall act as President, as in case of the death or other constitutional disability of the President. —]* The person having the greatest number of votes as Vice-President, shall be the Vice-President, if such number be a majority of the whole number of Electors appointed, and if no person have a majority, then from the two highest numbers on the list, the Senate shall choose the Vice-President; a quorum for the purpose shall consist of two-thirds of the whole number of Senators, and a majority of the whole number shall be necessary to a choice. But no person constitutionally ineligible to the office of President shall be eligible to that of Vice-President of the United States.

*Superseded by section 3 of the 20th amendment.

Amendment XIII

Passed by Congress January 31, 1865. Ratified December 6, 1865.

Note: A portion of Article IV, section 2, of the Constitution was superseded by the 13th amendment.

Section 1.

Neither slavery nor involuntary servitude, except as a punishment for crime whereof the party shall have been duly convicted, shall exist within the United States, or any place subject to their jurisdiction.

Section 2.

Congress shall have power to enforce this article by appropriate legislation.

Amendment XIV

Passed by Congress June 13, 1866. Ratified July 9, 1868.

Note: Article I, section 2, of the Constitution was modified by section 2 of the 14th amendment.

Section 1.

All persons born or naturalized in the United States, and subject to the jurisdiction thereof, are citizens of the United States and of the State wherein they reside. No State shall make or enforce any law which shall abridge the privileges or immunities of citizens of the United States; nor shall any State deprive any person of life, liberty, or property, without due process of law; nor deny to any person within its jurisdiction the equal protection of the laws.

Section 2.

Representatives shall be apportioned among the several States according to their respective numbers, counting the whole number of persons in each State, excluding Indians not taxed. But when the right to vote at any election for the choice of electors for President and Vice-President of the United States, Representatives in Congress, the Executive and Judicial officers of a State, or the members of the Legislature thereof, is denied to any of the male inhabitants of such State, being twenty-one years of age,* and citizens of the United States, or in any way abridged, except for participation in rebellion, or other crime, the basis of representation therein shall be reduced in the proportion which the number of such male citizens shall bear to the whole number of male citizens twenty-one years of age in such State.

Section 3.

No person shall be a Senator or Representative in Congress, or elector of President and Vice-President, or hold any office, civil or military, under the United States, or under any State, who, having previously taken an oath, as a member of Congress, or as an officer of the United States, or as a member of any State legislature, or as an executive or judicial officer of any State, to support the Constitution of the United States, shall have engaged in insurrection or rebellion against the same, or given aid or comfort to the enemies thereof. But Congress may, by a vote of two-thirds of each House, remove such disability.

Section 4.

The validity of the public debt of the United States, authorized by law, including debts incurred for payment of pensions and bounties for services in suppressing insurrection or rebellion, shall not be questioned. But neither the United States nor any State shall assume or pay any debt or obligation incurred in aid of insurrection or rebellion against the United States, or any claim for the loss or emancipation of any slave; but all such debts, obligations and claims shall be held illegal and void.

Section 5.

The Congress shall have the power to enforce, by appropriate legislation, the provisions of this article.

*Changed by section 1 of the 26th amendment.

Amendment XV

Passed by Congress February 26, 1869. Ratified February 3, 1870.

Section 1.

The right of citizens of the United States to vote shall not be denied or abridged by the United States or by any State on account of race, color, or previous condition of servitude—

Section 2.

The Congress shall have the power to enforce this article by appropriate legislation.

Amendment XVI

Passed by Congress July 2, 1909. Ratified February 3, 1913.

Note: Article I, section 9, of the Constitution was modified by amendment 16.

The Congress shall have power to lay and collect taxes on incomes, from whatever source derived, without apportionment among the several States, and without regard to any census or enumeration.

Amendment XVII

Passed by Congress May 13, 1912. Ratified April 8, 1913.

Note: Article I, section 3, of the Constitution was modified by the 17th amendment.

The Senate of the United States shall be composed of two Senators from each State, elected by the people thereof, for six years; and each Senator shall have one vote. The electors in each State shall have the qualifications requisite for electors of the most numerous branch of the State legislatures.

When vacancies happen in the representation of any State in the Senate, the executive authority of such State shall issue writs of election to fill such vacancies: Provided, That the legislature of any State may empower the executive thereof to make temporary appointments until the people fill the vacancies by election as the legislature may direct.

This amendment shall not be so construed as to affect the election or term of any Senator chosen before it becomes valid as part of the Constitution.

Amendment XVIII

Passed by Congress December 18, 1917. Ratified January 16, 1919. Repealed by amendment 21.

Section 1.

After one year from the ratification of this article the manufacture, sale, or transportation of intoxicating liquors within, the importation thereof into, or the exportation thereof from the United States and all territory subject to the jurisdiction thereof for beverage purposes is hereby prohibited.

Section 2.

The Congress and the several States shall have concurrent power to enforce this article by appropriate legislation.

Section 3.

This article shall be inoperative unless it shall have been ratified as an amendment to the Constitution by the legislatures of the several States, as provided in the Constitution, within seven years from the date of the submission hereof to the States by the Congress.

Amendment XIX

Passed by Congress June 4, 1919. Ratified August 18, 1920.

The right of citizens of the United States to vote shall not be denied or abridged by the United States or by any State on account of sex.

Congress shall have power to enforce this article by appropriate legislation.

Amendment XX

Passed by Congress March 2, 1932. Ratified January 23, 1933.

Note: Article I, section 4, of the Constitution was modified by section 2 of this amendment. In addition, a portion of the 12th amendment was superseded by section 3.

Section 1.

The terms of the President and the Vice President shall end at noon on the 20th day of January, and the terms of Senators and Representatives at noon on the 3rd day of January, of the years in which such terms would have ended if this article had not been ratified; and the terms of their successors shall then begin.

Section 2.

The Congress shall assemble at least once in every year, and such meeting shall begin at noon on the 3d day of January, unless they shall by law appoint a different day.

Section 3.

If, at the time fixed for the beginning of the term of the President, the President elect shall have died, the Vice President elect shall become President. If a President shall not have been chosen before the time fixed for the beginning of his term, or if the President elect shall have failed to qualify, then the Vice President elect shall act as President until a President shall have qualified; and the Congress may by law provide for the case wherein neither a President elect nor a Vice President shall have qualified, declaring who shall then act as President, or the manner in which one who is to act shall be selected, and such person shall act accordingly until a President or Vice President shall have qualified.

Section 4.

The Congress may by law provide for the case of the death of any of the persons from whom the House of Representatives may choose a President whenever the right of choice shall have devolved upon them, and for the case of the death of any of the persons from whom the Senate may choose a Vice President whenever the right of choice shall have devolved upon them.

Section 5.

Sections 1 and 2 shall take effect on the 15th day of October following the ratification of this article.

Section 6.

This article shall be inoperative unless it shall have been ratified as an amendment to the Constitution by the legislatures of three-fourths of the several States within seven years from the date of its submission.

Amendment XXI

Passed by Congress February 20, 1933. Ratified December 5, 1933.

Section 1.

The eighteenth article of amendment to the Constitution of the United States is hereby repealed.

Section 2.

The transportation or importation into any State, Territory, or Possession of the United States for delivery or use therein of intoxicating liquors, in violation of the laws thereof, is hereby prohibited.

Section 3.

This article shall be inoperative unless it shall have been ratified as an amendment to the Constitution by conventions in the several States, as provided in the Constitution, within seven years from the date of the submission hereof to the States by the Congress.

Amendment XXII

Passed by Congress March 21, 1947. Ratified February 27, 1951.

Section 1.

No person shall be elected to the office of the President more than twice, and no person who has held the office of President, or acted as President, for more than two years of a term to which some other person was elected President shall be elected to the office of President more than once. But this Article shall not apply to any person holding the office of President when this Article was proposed by Congress, and shall not prevent any person who may be holding the office of President, or acting as President, during the term within which this Article becomes operative from holding the office of President or acting as President during the remainder of such term.

Section 2.

This article shall be inoperative unless it shall have been ratified as an amendment to the Constitution by the legislatures of three-fourths of the several States within seven years from the date of its submission to the States by the Congress.

Amendment XXIII

Passed by Congress June 16, 1960. Ratified March 29, 1961.

Section 1.

The District constituting the seat of Government of the United States shall appoint in such manner as Congress may direct:

A number of electors of President and Vice President equal to the whole number of Senators and Representatives in Congress to which the District would be entitled if it were a State, but in no event more than the least populous State; they shall be in addition to those appointed by the States, but they shall be considered, for the purposes of the election of President and Vice President, to be electors appointed by a State; and they shall meet in the District and perform such duties as provided by the twelfth article of amendment.

Section 2.

The Congress shall have power to enforce this article by appropriate legislation.

Amendment XXIV

Passed by Congress August 27, 1962. Ratified January 23, 1964.

Section 1.

The right of citizens of the United States to vote in any primary or other election for President or Vice President, for electors for President or Vice President, or for Senator or Representative in Congress, shall not be denied or abridged by the United States or any State by reason of failure to pay any poll tax or other tax.

Section 2.
The Congress shall have power to enforce this article by appropriate legislation.

Amendment XXV
Passed by Congress July 6, 1965. Ratified February 10, 1967.

Note: Article II, section 1, of the Constitution was affected by the 25th amendment.

Section 1.
In case of the removal of the President from office or of his death or resignation, the Vice President shall become President.

Section 2.
Whenever there is a vacancy in the office of the Vice President, the President shall nominate a Vice President who shall take office upon confirmation by a majority vote of both Houses of Congress.

Section 3.
Whenever the President transmits to the President pro tempore of the Senate and the Speaker of the House of Representatives his written declaration that he is unable to discharge the powers and duties of his office, and until he transmits to them a written declaration to the contrary, such powers and duties shall be discharged by the Vice President as Acting President.

Section 4.
Whenever the Vice President and a majority of either the principal officers of the executive departments or of such other body as Congress may by law provide, transmit to the President pro tempore of the Senate and the Speaker of the House of Representatives their written declaration that the President is unable to discharge the powers and duties of his office, the Vice President shall immediately assume the powers and duties of the office as Acting President.

Thereafter, when the President transmits to the President pro tempore of the Senate and the Speaker of the House of Representatives his written declaration that no inability exists, he shall resume the powers and duties of his office unless the Vice President and a majority of either the principal officers of the executive department or of such other body as Congress may by law provide, transmit within four days to the President pro tempore of the Senate and the Speaker of the House of Representatives their written declaration that the President is unable to discharge the powers and duties of his office. Thereupon Congress shall decide the issue, assembling within forty-eight hours for that purpose if not in session. If the Congress, within twenty-one days after receipt of the latter written declaration, or, if Congress is not in session, within twenty-one days after Congress is required to assemble, determines by two-thirds vote of both Houses that the President is unable to discharge the powers and duties of his office, the Vice President shall continue to discharge the same as Acting President; otherwise, the President shall resume the powers and duties of his office.

Amendment XXVI

Passed by Congress March 23, 1971. Ratified July 1, 1971.

Note: Amendment 14, section 2, of the Constitution was modified by section 1 of the 26th amendment.

Section 1.

The right of citizens of the United States, who are eighteen years of age or older, to vote shall not be denied or abridged by the United States or by any State on account of age.

Section 2.

The Congress shall have power to enforce this article by appropriate legislation.

Amendment XXVII

Originally proposed Sept. 25, 1789. Ratified May 7, 1992.

No law, varying the compensation for the services of the Senators and Representatives, shall take effect, until an election of representatives shall have intervened.

Source: The U.S. National Archives and Records Administration, www.archives.gov

Timeline of Supreme Court Cases Aligned with National Content Standards in Economics

(Chronological Order)

STANDARD 1: SCARCITY

Productive resources are limited. Therefore, people cannot have all the goods and services they want; as a result, they must choose some things and give up others.

Lochner v. New York, 198 U.S. 45 (1905)

Youngstown Sheet & Tube Co. v. Sawyer, 343 U.S. 579 (1952)

Berman v. Parker, 348 U.S. 26 (1954)

Hawaii Housing Authority v. Midkiff, 467 U.S. 229 (1984)

Kelo v. City of New London, Connecticut, 545 U.S. 469 (2005)

STANDARD 2: DECISION MAKING

Effective decision making requires comparing the additional costs of alternatives with the additional benefits. Many choices involve doing a little more or a little less of something: few choices are "all or nothing" decisions.

Berman v. Parker, 348 U.S. 26 (1954)

Menominee Tribe v. United States, 391 U.S. 404 (1968)

Hawaii Housing Authority v. Midkiff, 467 U.S. 229 (1984)

Kelo v. City of New London, Connecticut, 545 U.S. 469 (2005)

STANDARD 3: ALLOCATION

Different methods can be used to allocate goods and services. People acting individually or collectively must choose which methods to use to allocate different kinds of goods and services.

Hylton v. United States, 3 U.S. 171 (1796)

Hooe v. United States, 218 U.S. 322 (1805)

Springer v. United States, 277 U.S. 189 (1880)

Pollock v. Farmers' Loan & Trust Company, 157 U.S. 429 (1895)

La Abra Silver Mng. Co. v. United States, 175 U.S. 423 (1899)

Lochner v. New York, 198 U.S. 45 (1905)

Standard Oil Co. of New Jersey vs. United States, 221 U.S. 1 (1911)

United States v. North American Co., 253 U.S. 330 (1920)

Myers v. United States, 272 U.S. 52 (1926)

Springer v. Philippine Islands, 277 U.S. 189 (1928)

United States v. Creek Nation, 295 U.S. 103 (1935)

United States v. Butler, 297 U.S. 1 (1936)

Helvering v. Davis, 301 U.S. 619 (1937)

Shoshone Tribe v. United States, 299 U.S. 476 (1937)

Steward Machine Co. v. Davis, 301 U.S. 548 (1937)

Kellogg Co. v. National Biscuit Co., 305 U.S. 111 (1938)

United States v. Klamath Indians, 304 U.S. 119 (1938)

Larson v. Domestic & Foreign Corp., 337 U.S. 682 (1949)

Youngstown Sheet & Tube Co. v. Sawyer, 343 U.S. 579 (1952)

Berman v. Parker, 348 U.S. 26 (1954)

Hawaii Housing Authority v. Midkiff, 467 U.S. 229 (1984)

MCI Telecommunications Corp. v. American Telephone and Telegraph Co., 512 U.S. 218 (1994)

Kelo v. City of New London, Connecticut, 545 U.S. 469 (2005)

National Federation of Independent Business v. Sebelius, 567 U.S. ___ (2012)

Affordable Health Care Act Cases, 567 U.S. ___ (2012)

STANDARD 4: INCENTIVES

People usually respond predictably to positive and negative incentives.

Singer Mfg. Co. v. June Mfg. Co., 163 U.S. 169 (1896)

Holzapfel's Compositions Co. v. Rahtjen's American Composition Co., 183 U.S. 1 (1901)

Saxlehner v. Wagner, 216 U.S. 375 (1910)

Kellogg Co. v. National Biscuit Co., 305 U.S. 111 (1938)

Youngstown Sheet & Tube Co. v. Sawyer, 343 U.S. 579 (1952)

Kelo v. City of New London, Connecticut, 545 U.S. 469 (2005)

STANDARD 5: TRADE

Voluntary exchange occurs only when all participating parties expect to gain. This is true for trade among individuals or organizations within a nation, and among individuals or organizations in different nations.

Lochner v. New York, 198 U.S. 45 (1905)

STANDARD 6: SPECIALIZATION

When individuals, regions, and nations specialize in what they can produce at the lowest cost and then trade with others, both production and consumption increase.

Hooe v. United States, 218 U.S. 322 (1805)

Singer Mfg. Co. v. June Mfg. Co., 163 U.S. 169 (1896)

Holden v. Hardy, 169 U.S. 366 (1898)

La Abra Silver Mng. Co. v. United States, 175 U.S. 423 (1899)

Holzapfel's Compositions Co. v. Rahtjen's American Composition Co., 183 U.S. 1 (1901)

Lochner v. New York, 198 U.S. 45 (1905)

Muller v. Oregon, 208 U.S. 412 (1908)

Saxlehner v. Wagner, 216 U.S. 375 (1910)

United States v. North American Co., 253 U.S. 330 (1920)

Adkins v. Children's Hospital, 261 U.S. 525 (1923)

Myers v. United States, 272 U.S. 52 (1926)

Springer v. Philippine Islands, 277 U.S. 189 (1928)

West Coast Hotel Co. v. Parrish, 300 U.S. 379 (1937)

Kellogg Co. v. National Biscuit Co., 305 U.S. 111 (1938)

Larson v. Domestic & Foreign Corp., 337 U.S. 682 (1949)

Youngstown Sheet & Tube Co. v. Sawyer, 343 U.S. 579 (1952)

California v. Cabazon Band of Mission Indians, 480 U.S. 202 (1987)

Lechmere, Inc. v. National Labor Relations Board, 502 U.S. 527 (1992)

STANDARD 7: MARKETS AND PRICES

A market exists when buyers and sellers interact. This interaction determines market prices and thereby allocates scarce goods and services.

Pollock v. Farmers' Loan & Trust Company, 157 U.S. 429 (1895)

Holden v. Hardy, 169 U.S. 366 (1898)

Lochner v. New York, 198 U.S. 45 (1905)

Muller v. Oregon, 208 U.S. 412 (1908)

Standard Oil of New Jersey v. United States, 221 U.S. 1 (1911)

Adkins v. Children's Hospital, 261 U.S. 525 (1923)

Helvering v. Davis, 301 U.S. 619 (1937)

West Coast Hotel Co. v. Parrish, 300 U.S. 379 (1937)

United States v. South-Eastern Underwriters Association, 322 U.S. 533 (1944)

Maislin Industries, U.S., Inc. v. Primary Steel, Inc., 497 U.S. 116 (1990)

Lechmere, Inc. v. National Labor Relations Board, 502 U.S. 527 (1992)

MCI Telecommunications Corp. v. American Telephone and Telegraph Co., 512 U.S. 218 (1994)

Kelo v. City of New London, Connecticut, 545 U.S. 469 (2005)

National Federation of Independent Business v. Sebelius, 567 U.S. ___ (2012)

Affordable Health Care Act Cases, 567 U.S. ___ (2012)

STANDARD 9: COMPETITION AND MARKET STRUCTURE

Competition among sellers usually lowers costs and prices, and encourages producers to produce what consumers are willing and able to buy. Competition among buyers increases prices and allocates goods and services to those people who are willing and able to pay the most for them.

Bank of the United States v. Deveaux, 9 U.S. 61 (1809)

McCulloch v. Maryland, 17 U.S. 316 (1819)

Gibbons v. Ogden, 22 U.S. 1 (1824)

Briscoe v. Bank of Kentucky, 36 U.S. 259 (1837)

Paul v. Virginia, 75 U.S. 168 (1869)

Veazy Bank v. Fenno, 75 U.S. 533 (1869)

Juilliard v. Greenman, 110 U.S. 421 (1884)

Pollock v. Farmers' Loan & Trust Company, 157 U.S. 429 (1895)

United States v. E.C. Knight Co., 156 U.S. 1 (1895)

Singer Mfg. Co. v. June Mfg. Co., 163 U.S. 169 (1896)

Anderson v. United States, 171 U.S. 604 (1898)

Hopkins v. United States, 171 U.S. 578 (1898)

United States v. Joint Traffic Association, 171 U.S. 505 (1898)

Holzapfel's Compositions Co. v. Rahtjen's American Composition Co., 183 U.S. 1 (1901)

Montague & Co. v. Lowrey, 193 U.S. 38 (1904)

Pensacola Telegraph Co. v. Western Union Telegraph Co., 193 U.S. 38 (1904)

Ex Parte Young, 209 U.S. 123 (1908)

Saxlehner v. Wagner, 216 U.S. 375 (1910)

Standard Oil Co. of New Jersey v. United States, 221 U.S. 1 (1911)

New York Life Insurance Co. v. Deer Lodge County, 231 U.S. 495 (1913)

United States v. Creek Nation, 295 U.S. 103 (1935)

Helvering v. Davis, 301 U.S. 619 (1937)

Shoshone Tribe v. United States, 299 U.S. 476 (1937)

Kellogg Co. v. National Biscuit Co., 305 U.S. 111 (1938)

United States v. Klamath Indians, 304 U.S. 119 (1938)

Polish National Alliance v. National Labor Relations Board, 322 U.S. 643 (1944)

United States v. South-Eastern Underwriters Association, 322 U.S. 533 (1944)

NLRB v. Babcock & Wilcox Co., 351 U.S. 105 (1956)

Menominee Tribe v. United States, 391 U.S. 404 (1968)

Permian Basin Area Rate Cases, 390 U.S. 747 (1968)

Central Hardware Co. v. NLRB, 407 U.S. 539 (1972)

Corning Glass Works v Brennan, 417 U.S. 188 (1974)

Bryan v. Itasca County, 426 U.S. 373 (1976)

Buckley v. Valeo, 424 U.S. 1 (1976)

Hudgens v. National Labor Relations Board, 424 U.S. 507 (1976)

Seminole Tribe of Florida v. Butterworth, 658 F.2nd 310 (1981)

California v. Cabazon Band of Mission Indians, 480 U.S. 202 (1987)

Austin v. Michigan Chamber of Commerce, 494 U.S. 652 (1990)

Maislin Industries, U.S., Inc. v. Primary Steel, Inc., 497 U.S. 116 (1990)

Lechmere, Inc. v. National Labor Relations Board, 502 U.S. 527 (1992)

MCI Telecommunications Corp. v. American Telephone and Telegraph Co., 512 U.S. 218 (1994)

McConnell v. Federal Election Commission, 540 U.S. 93 (2003)

Federal Election Commission v. Wisconsin Right to Life, Inc., 551 U.S. 449 (2007)

Citizens United v. Federal Election Commission, 558 U.S. ___ (2010)

National Federation of Independent Business v. Sebelius, 567 U.S. ___ (2012)

Affordable Health Care Act Cases, 567 U.S. ___ (2012)

STANDARD 10: INSTITUTIONS

Institutions are created and evolve to help individuals and groups accomplish their goals. Banks, labor unions, markets, corporations, legal systems, and not-for-profit organizations are examples of important institutions. A different kind of institution, clearly defined and enforced property rights, is essential to a market economy.

Bank of the United States v. Deveaux, 9 U.S. 61 (1809)

Briscoe v. Bank of Kentucky, 36 U.S. 259 (1837)

Veazy Bank v. Fenno, 75 U.S. 533, 548 (1869)

Juilliard v. Greenman, 110 U.S. 421 (1884)

Buckley v. Valeo, 424 U.S. 1 (1976)

Austin v. Michigan Chamber of Commerce, 494 U.S. 652 (1990)

McConnell v. Federal Election Commission, 540 U.S. 93 (2003)

Federal Election Commission v. Wisconsin Right to Life, Inc., 551 U.S. 449 (2007)

STANDARD 11: MONEY AND INFLATION

Money makes it easier to trade, borrow, save, invest, and compare the value of goods and services. The amount of money in the economy affects the overall price level. Inflation is an increase in the overall price level that reduces the value of money.

Hepburn v. Griswold, 75 U.S. 603 (1869)

Dooley v. Smith, 80 U.S. 604 (1871)

Railroad Company v. Johnson, 82 U.S. 195 (1872)

Maryland v. Railroad Company, 89 U.S. 105 (1874)

Juilliard v. Greenman, 110 U.S. 421 (1884)

STANDARD 13: INCOME

Income for most people is determined by the market value of the productive resources they sell. What workers earn primarily depends on the market value of what they produce.

Pollock v. Farmers' Loan & Trust Company, 157 U.S. 429 (1895)

Holden v. Hardy, 169 U.S. 366 (1898)

Lochner v. New York, 198 U.S. 45 (1905)

Muller v. Oregon, 208 U.S. 412 (1908)

Adkins v. Children's Hospital, 261 U.S. 525 (1923)

West Coast Hotel Co. v. Parrish, 300 U.S. 379 (1937)

Hodgson v. Miller Brewing Co., 457 F.2d 221, 227 (CA7 1972)

Corning Glass Works v Brennan, 417 U.S. 188 (1974)

Seminole Tribe of Florida v. Butterworth, 658 F.2nd 310 (1981)

Lechmere, Inc. v. National Labor Relations Board, 502 U.S. 527 (1992)

STANDARD 14: ENTREPRENEURSHIP

Entrepreneurs take on the calculated risk of starting new businesses, either by embarking on new ventures similar to existing ones or by introducing new innovations. Entrepreneurial innovation is an important source of economic growth.

Hooe v. United States, 218 U.S. 322 (1805)

Gibbons v. Ogden, 22 U.S. 1 (1824)

Singer Mfg. Co. v. June Mfg. Co., 163 U.S. 169 (1896)

La Abra Silver Mng. Co. v. United States, 175 U.S. 423 (1899)

Holzapfel's Compositions Co. v. Rahtjen's American Composition Co., 183 U.S. 1 (1901)

Saxlehner v. Wagner, 216 U.S. 375 (1910)

United States v. North American Co., 253 U.S. 330 (1920)

Myers v. United States, 272 U.S. 52 (1926)

Springer v. Philippine Islands, 277 U.S. 189 (1928)

Kellogg Co. v. National Biscuit Co., 305 U.S. 111 (1938)

Larson v. Domestic & Foreign Corp., 337 U.S. 682 (1949)

Youngstown Sheet & Tube Co. v. Sawyer, 343 U.S. 579 (1952)

California v. Cabazon Band of Mission Indians, 480 U.S. 202 (1987)

MCI Telecommunications Corp. v. American Telephone and Telegraph Co., 512 U.S. 218 (1994)

Seminole Tribe of Florida v. Florida, 517 U.S. 44 (1996)

STANDARD 15: ECONOMIC GROWTH

Investment in factories, machinery, new technology, and in the health, education, and training of people stimulates economic growth and can raise future standards of living.

Singer Mfg. Co. v. June Mfg. Co., 163 U.S. 169 (1896)

Holzapfel's Compositions Co. v. Rahtjen's American Composition Co., 183 U.S. 1 (1901)

Saxlehner v. Wagner, 216 U.S. 375 (1910)

Kellogg Co. v. National Biscuit Co., 305 U.S. 111 (1938)

Alaska Dept. of Environmental Conservation v. EPA, 540 U.S. 461 (2004)

STANDARD 16: ROLE OF GOVERNMENT AND MARKET FAILURE

There is an economic role for government in a market economy whenever the benefits of a government policy outweigh its costs. Governments often provide for national defense, address environmental concerns, define and protect property rights, and attempt to make markets more competitive. Most government policies also have direct or indirect effects on peoples' incomes.

Ware v. Hylton, 3 U.S. 199 (1796)

Martin v. Hunter's Lessee, 14 U.S. 304 (1816)

Cohens v. Virginia, 19 U.S. 264 (1821)

Gibbons v. Ogden, 22 U.S. 1 (1824)

Holden v. Hardy, 169 U.S. 366 (1898)

Muller v. Oregon, 208 U.S. 412 (1908)

Adkins v. Children's Hospital, 261 U.S. 525 (1923)

Helvering v. Davis, 301 U.S. 619 (1937)

Steward Machine Co. v. Davis, 301 U.S. 548 (1937)

West Coast Hotel Co. v. Parrish, 300 U.S. 379 (1937)

Kellogg Co. v. National Biscuit Co., 305 U.S. 111 (1938)

United States v. South-Eastern Underwriters Association, 322 U.S. 533 (1944)

Buckley v. Valeo, 424 U.S. 1 (1976)

Austin v. Michigan Chamber of Commerce, 494 U.S. 652 (1990)

McConnell v. Federal Election Commission, 540 U.S. 93 (2003)

Alaska Dept. of Environmental Conservation v. EPA, 540 U.S. 461 (2004)

Kelo v. City of New London, Connecticut, 545 U.S. 469 (2005)

Federal Election Commission v. Wisconsin Right to Life, Inc., 551 U.S. 449 (2007)

STANDARD 17: GOVERNMENT FAILURE

Costs of government policies sometimes exceed benefits. This may occur because of incentives facing voters, government officials, and government employees; because of actions by special interest groups that can impose costs on the general public; or because social goals other than economic efficiency are being pursued.

Pollock v. Farmers' Loan & Trust Company, 157 U.S. 429 (1895)

STANDARD 19: UNEMPLOYMENT AND INFLATION

Unemployment imposes costs on individuals and the overall economy. Inflation, both expected and unexpected, also imposes costs on individuals and the overall economy. Unemployment increases during recessions and decreases during recoveries.

Holden v. Hardy, 169 U.S. 366 (1898)

Lochner v. New York, 198 U.S. 45 (1905)

Muller v. Oregon, 208 U.S. 412 (1908)

Adkins v. Children's Hospital, 261 U.S. 525 (1923)

West Coast Hotel Co. v. Parrish, 300 U.S. 379 (1937)

National Labor Relations Board v. Babcock & Wilcox Co., 351 U.S. 105 (1956)

Central Hardware Co. v. National Labor Relations Board, 407 U.S. 539 (1972)

Hudgens v. National Labor Relations Board, 424 U.S. 507 (1976)

Lechmere, Inc. v. National Labor Relations Board, 502 U.S. 527 (1992)

Legislative Acts with Economic Impact

Agricultural Adjustment Act of 1936

Alaska Native Land Claims Settlement Act (ANCSA) of 1971

Aldrich-Vreeland Act

America Invents Act (Leahy-Smith Act)

Anti-Injunction Act

Bakeshop Act of 1895

Bank Holding Company Act of 1956

Banking Act of 1933 (Glass-Steagall Act)

Banking Act of 1935

Bayh-Dole Act

Bipartisan Campaign Reform Act of 2002 (BCRA)

Budget and Accounting Act of 1921

Budget Enforcement Act of 1990

Bureau of Labor Act of 1884

Civil Rights Act of 1964

Clayton Antitrust Act of 1914

Clean Air Act (CAA)

Clean Air Act of 1963

Clean Air Act of 1970 (CAA)

Coinage Act of 1792 (Mint Act)

Communications Act of 1934

Defense Production Act

Depository Institutions Deregulation and Monetary Control Act of 1980

Dodd-Frank Nall Street Reform and Consumer Protection Act

Economic Opportunity Act of 1964

Elementary and Secondary Education Act of 1965
Emergency Home Finance Act of 1970
Employment Act of 1946
Equal Pay Act of 1963
Fair Labor Standards Act of 1938
Federal Communications Act of 1935
Federal Deposit Insurance Corporation Act of 1991
Federal Election Campaign Act of 1974 (FECA)
Federal Employees and Labor Laws Equal Pay Act of 1963 (EPA)
Federal Housing Enterprises Financial Safety and Soundness Act of 1992
Federal Reserve Act of 1913
Federal Tax Act
Federal Trade Commission Act of 1914
Financial Institutions Reform, Recovery, and Enforcement Act of 1989
Financial Reform Act of 2010
Financial Services Modernization Act of 1999 (Repealed the Banking Act of 1933)
Fordney-McCumber Tariff Act of 1922
Frazier-Lemke Farm Bankruptcy Act
Gramm-Leach-Bliley Act of 1999
Higher Education Act
Housing and Urban Development Act of 1968
Immigration Reform and Control Act of 1986
Indian Gaming Regulatory Act of 1988
International Banking Act of 1978
Interstate Commerce Act of 1887
Lanham-Trademark Act
Leahy-Smith Act (America Invents Act)
McCarran-Ferguson Act
Menominee Termination Act
National Bank Act of 1863
National Environmental Policy Act of 1970 (NEPA)
National Housing Act
National Industrial Recovery Act
National Labor Relations Act of 1935 (Wagner Act)

National Prohibition Act of 1920 (Volstead Act)

Navigation Acts

Organic Act of 1913 (Created the Department of Labor)

Pure Food and Drug Act of 1906

Reciprocal Trade Agreements Act of 1934

Revenue Act of 1894 (Wilson-Gorman Tariff Act)

Securities Exchange Act of 1933

Securities Exchange Act of 1934

Servicemen's Readjustment Act of 1947 (GI Bill)

Sherman Antitrust Act of 1890

Social Security Act

Tariff Act of 1930 (Smoot-Hawley Tariff Act)

Telecommunications Reform Act

Title VII of the Civil Rights Act of 1964

Title IX of the Education Act

Volstead Act (National Prohibition Act of 1920)

Wagner Act (National Labor Relations Act of 1935)

Wilson-Gorman Tariff Act (Revenue Act of 1894)

Online Resources for Educators and Researchers

Web Sites for Classroom Lessons

Bill of Rights Institute	billofrightsinstitute.org
BLS, "Occupational Outlook Handbook"	www.bls.gov/ooh
Bureau of Economic Analysis	www.bea.gov
Bureau of Engraving and Printing	www.moneyfactory.gov
Bureau of Labor Statistics	www.bls.gov
Citizens United	www.citizensunited.org/
Common Sense Economics	www.commonsenseeconomics.com
Council for Economic Education	www.councilforeconed.org
Council for Economic Education	msh.councilforeconed.org/lessons
Discovery Education	www.discoveryeducation.com
EcEdWeb	ecedweb.unomaha.edu
econedlink	www.econedlink.org/lessons
Economics Classroom	www.econclassroom.com
EconWorks	econworks.org
EDsitement	edsitement.neh.gov
edtechteacher: Best of History Web Sites	besthistorysites.net
Education World	www.educationworld.com
Edvantage	www.theedvantage.org
eHow Money	www.ehow.com/ehow-money
Environmental Protection Agency	www.epa.gov
e21: Economic Policies for the 21st Century	www.economics21.org
European Central Bank	www.ecb.europa.eu
FDR and the Supreme Court	newdeal.feri.org

Federal Deposit Insurance Corporation (FDIC)	www.fdic.gov
Federal Reserve Bank of Atlanta	www.frbatlanta.org
Federal Reserve Bank of Boston	www.bostonfed.org
Federal Reserve Bank of Chicago	www.chicagofed.org
Federal Reserve Bank of Cleveland	www.clevelandfed.org
Federal Reserve Bank of Dallas	www.dallasfed.org
Federal Reserve Bank of Kansas City	www.kc.frb.org
Federal Reserve Bank of Minneapolis	www.minneapolisfed.org
Federal Reserve Bank of New York	www.newyorkfed.org
Federal Reserve Bank of Philadelphia	www.philadelphiafed.org
Federal Reserve Bank of Richmond	www.richmondfed.org
Federal Reserve Bank of San Francisco	www.frbsf.org/education
Federal Reserve Bank of St. Louis	www.stlouisfed.org/education_resources
Federal Reserve Board of Governors	www.federalreserve.gov
federalreserveeducation.org	www.federalreserveeducation.org
Federal Resources for Educational Excellence	free1.ed.gov
Federal Trade Commission	www.consumer.ftc.gov
Fraser Institute	www.fraserinstitute.org
FRB of Atlanta, Center for Quantitative Research	www.frbatlanta.org/cqer
FRED (Federal Reserve Bank of St. Louis)	research.stlouisfed.org/fred2
Foundation for Teaching Economics	www.fte.org
Franklin D. Roosevelt Presidential Library and Museum	www.fdrlibrary.marist.edu
Gooru	www.goorulearning.org
History.com	www.history.com
How the Court Works	www.supremecourthistory.org
Indian Land Tenure Foundation, Lessons of Our California Land	www.landlessons.org
International Monetary Fund Center	www.imf.org
Internet Archive, Community Video	archive.org
Investor.gov	www.investor.gov
IRS: Understanding Taxes, Teachers	apps.irs.gov/app/understandingtaxes

Just Facts	www.justfacts.com
Justia.com, U.S. Supreme Court Center	supreme.justia.com
Kahn Academy	www.1.kahnacademy.org
LBJ Presidential Library	www.lbjlibrary.org
Learning to Give	learningtogive.org
Legal Information Institute, Cornell University Law School	www.law.cornell.edu
Lesson Corner	www.lessoncorner.com
LessonPlanet	www.lessonplanet.com
Library of Congress classroommaterials	www.loc.gov/teachers/
Library of Economics and Liberty	www.econlib.org
National Archives and Records Administration	www.archives.gov/education
National Archives, DOCS Teach	docsteach.org
National Bureau of Economic Research	www.nber.org
National Labor Relations Board	nlrb.gov
New York Times	www.nytimes.com
New York Times, Politico	www.politico.com
100 Years: Federal Reserve System	www.federalreservehistory.org
Online Library of Liberty	oll.libertyfund.org
Our Documents	www.ourdocuments.gov
OwlTeacher	www.owlteacher.com
OYEZ, ITT Chicago, Kent College of Law	www.oyez.org
PBS	www.pbs.org
Practical Money Skills for Life	www.practicalmoneyskills.com
Scholastic	teacher.scholastic.com
Securities and Exchange Commission Historical Society	www.sechistorical.org
Shmoop: We Speak Student	www.shmoop.com
SIFMA	www.investinginbonds.com
Stanford History Education Group	sheg.stanford.edu
Supreme Court of the United States	www.supremecourt.gov
Teacher 2 Teacher	t2t.lacoe.edu
Teaching Channel: Great Teaching, Inspiring Classrooms	www.teachingchannel.org

Teaching Economics as If People Mattered	www.teachingeconomics.org
Teaching Future Historians	dig.lib.niu.edu/teachers
teachinghistory.org	teachinghistory.org
Tenement Museum	www.tenement.org
This Day in History	www.history.com/this-day-in-history
Treasury Direct	www.treasurydirect.gov
tutor2u	tutor2u.net
United States Department of Labor	www.dol.gov
United States Department of Veteran Affairs	www.benefits.va.gov/gibill
United States Mint	www.usmint.gov/kids/teachers
United States Mint	www.usmint.gov/kids
United States Mint	www.usmint.gov
University of Toronto; G8 Information Centre	www.g8.utoronto.ca
U.S. Citizenship and Immigration Services	www.uscis.gov
U.S. Debt Clock	www.usdebtclock.org
U.S. Department of the Treasury	www.treasury.gov
Wall Street Journal	www.online.wsj.com
World Bank	www.worldbank.org
World Trade Organization	wto.org

Government Data Web Sites

Economic Growth (Gross Domestic Product)	
Bureau of Economic Analysis	www.bea.gov/gdp
Federal Reserve System	www.federal reserve.gov
St. Louis Federal Reserve Bank	www.research.stlouisfed.org
U.S. Census Bureau	www.census.gov
Price Stability (Inflation-Deflation)	
Bureau of Labor Statistics	www.bls.gov
Consumer Price Index	www.bls.gov/cpi
Labor Productivity & Costs	www.bls.gov/lpc
Producer Price Index	www.bls.gov/ppi
Unemployment	
Bureau of Labor Statistics	www.bls.gov

Mass Layoffs Report	www.bls.gov/mls
Reports from the Federal Reserve	
Federal Open Market Committee (FOMC) Statement	www.federalreserve.gov/newsevents.htm
Federal Reserve Bank of Chicago Midwest Survey	www.chicagofed.org/economic_research_and_data/cfnai.cfm
Federal Reserve Bank of Kansas City Manufacturing Conditions	www.kc.frb.org/mfgsurv/mfgmain.htm
Federal Reserve Bank of New York Empire Survey	www.ny.frb.org/research/regional_economy/
Federal Reserve Bank of Richmond Manufacturing Conditions	www.richmondfed.org/research/
Federal Reserve Board of Governors Beige-Book	www.federalreserve.gov/frbindex.htm
U.S. International Trade	
Bureau of Economic Analysis	www.bea.gov/newsreleases/international/transactions/transnewsrelease.htm
Bureau of Labor Statistics	www.bls.gov/mxp
Current Account Balance	
Export and Import Prices	
U.S. Dollar	
Federal Reserve/Foreign Exchange Rates	www.federalreserve.gov/releases/h10/summary
Consumer Measures	
Bureau of Economic Analysis	
Bureau of Labor Statistics	
Real Earnings	www.bls.gov/news.release/realer.toc.htm
Federal Reserve Board Consumer Debt	www.federalreserve.gov/releases/g19
U.S. Census	
E-Commerce Retail Sales	www.census.gov/mrts/www/ecomm.html
Money, Credit, and Interest	
Federal Funds and Treasury Securities (Historical Interest Rates)	www.federalreserve.gov/releases/h15/data.htm
Federal Reserve Bank of St. Louis	
Commercial and Industrial Loans Outstanding by Commercial Banks	research.stlouisfed.org/fred2/series/BUSLOANS/49
Consumer Loans by All Commercial Banks	research.stlouisfed.org/fred2/series/CONSUMER/49

Federal Reserve Board	
U.S. Money Supply	www.federalreserve.gov/releases/h6/current
U.S. Bank Reserves	www.federalreserve.gov/releases/h3/

Glossary

Affirmative action – Policies intended to counter discrimination in employment, education, and business by taking into account factors such as race, color, religion, gender, national origin, and sexual orientation.

Agreement – An agreed-upon arrangement between several parties.

Agricultural Adjustment Act – A legislative law passed by Congress as part of the New Deal. The act restricted agricultural production, paying subsidies to farmers for not planting or for killing off livestock. The act was struck down by the Supreme Court in 1936.

American Federation of Labor – Founded in 1886 in Columbus, Ohio, by craft unions, it was one of the first federations of labor unions.

American Temperance Society and the Woman's Christian Temperance Union (WCTU) – Led by Francis Willard, these organizations argued that alcoholic beverages were the cause of many of the social ills of the time period.

Amicus curiae – Someone who is not a party to a legal case, but on whom the court's decision may have an impact.

Antidumping duty – A tariff levied on imports, usually in retaliation for selling a product below fair value.

Anti-Injunction Act – A federal act that prohibited a federal court, in most cases, from issuing an injunction against a state court.

The Anti-Saloon League – Founded in 1893, it worked to create political support for Prohibition under the leadership of Wayne B. Wheeler. The Anti-Saloon League quickly became an incredibly successful lobbying group, drawing diverse groups of Americans from all walks of life, and including Republicans, Democrats, suffragists, and Populists, to create a constitutional amendment supporting the nationwide prohibition of alcohol.

Antitrust – Government legislation to prevent monopolies and deter companies from conducting business in collusive or anticompetitive activity.

Article II of the Constitution of the United States – It created the executive branch of the federal government and established criteria for election to the executive branch, as well as its powers.

Article V of the Constitution of the United States – Established the procedure for amending the Constitution: the requirement of a two-thirds vote of both houses of Congress to propose an amendment, and three-fourths of the states to ratify such proposals.

Automatic stabilizers – Government policies, such as taxes and spending, that take effect to reduce economic impacts.

Average tax rate – The total tax paid divided by total income.

Bakeshop Act of 1895 – An act passed by the New York State Assembly establishing minimum sanitation standards; it prohibited domestic animals from being kept in bakeries and prohibited the bake room from being used as a sleeping room by the workers.

Balance of payments – A system of accounts that measures the trade, financial, and foreign aid transactions between a nation's domestic economic components during a specific period of time.

Balance of trade – The difference between a nation's exports and imports of goods.

Bank Holding Company Act 1956 – Considered by some the most important banking legislation after World War II, the act regulated bank expansion and protected the separation of banking and nonbanking activity.

Bank of International Settlements (BIS) – An international organization that serves as a central bank for national central banks.

Bargaining table – A term used for collective bargaining.

Barriers to trade – Transparent forms of protectionism include tariffs and quotas, while nontransparent forms include specific manufacturing standards, licenses, fees, and patents.

Barter system – Market interactions between a buyer and seller conducted without a form of money, but on a duo-coincidence of wants.

Beef War of 1999 – The European Union banned the import of U.S. beef from cows raised using hormones. The United States responded by placing tariffs on European clothing and certain foods.

Belovezh Accords – The agreement signed on December 8, 1991, that declared the Soviet Union effectively dissolved and established the Commonwealth of Independent States in its place.

Black Tuesday – October 29, 1929, a day on which the stock market volume traded was a record volume and market loss of $14 billion.

Bolshevik Revolution – Also known as Red October or the October Uprising, the armed military seizure of governmental power by the socialist Bolshevik political party in October 1917.

Bootleggers – Smugglers of alcohol into the United States from Canada, the Caribbean, and Europe; their activities led to a rise in organized crime and corruption in the United States.

Boycott – The act of intentionally not participating in buying or using a good or service from a business, person, or organization as a protest and expression of dissatisfaction with a social, ethical, or political policy or business decision of the business, person, or organization.

Breach of contract – A failure to honor an agreed-upon legal contract through noncompliance or incompletion.

Bretton Woods Conference – A conference held in the small New Hampshire town of Bretton Woods in July 1944. The conference established the international financial and economic order after World War II. The foundations of both the World Bank and the International Monetary Fund were laid here.

Budget Enforcement Act of 1990 – Federal legislation creating new budget controls, including spending caps and a pay-as-we-go process for entitlements and taxes.

Budget Sequestration – Automatic spending cuts of the U.S. federal budget.

Bureau of Economic Analysis (BEA) – An agency located within the U.S. Department of Commerce that provides economic data, including the U.S. Gross Domestic Product.

Bureau of Labor Statistics (BLS) – An agency of the U.S. Department of Labor whose responsibility includes collecting, analyzing, and distributing important economic data regarding employment, inflation, and economic growth.

Business cycle – Also known as the economic cycle, the stages of an economy over time including contraction, peak, expansion, and trough.

Business Employment Dynamics (BED) – A set of statistics created by the Quarterly Census of Employment and Wages program of the Bureau of Labor Statistics.

Capitalism – The economic system also known as free enterprise, involving a market economy where the answers to the key economic questions (what to produce, how to produce, for whom to produce) are answered in the marketplace, in the interactions between buyers and sellers.

Carson, Rachel – Biologist and science writer, author of *Silent Spring* (1962); considered a pioneer of the environmental movement.

Central bank – The national bank that serves other banks and is responsible for a nation's money supply, monetary policy, and commercial bank regulations.

Centrally planned economy – Also known as a command or planned economy, it is an economy where the three main questions (what to produce, how to produce, and for whom to produce) are addressed, answered, and implemented by a central authority (government).

Certificates of deposit – A common type of interest-bearing investment instrument for a fixed duration; usually a large denomination with an interest rate higher than more conventional savings accounts.

Certiorari – A writ to a lower court from a higher court to send the case for review.

Cheap money – Money without intrinsic value, or backed by gold or silver.

Checks – Also known as demand deposits, these are a form of financial transaction for a demand-deposit account.

Chief Justice Charles Hughes – Chief justice of the Supreme Court from 1930 to 1941.

Chief Justice Warren E. Burger – Chief justice of the Supreme Court from 1969 to 1986.

Children's Health Insurance – Government health insurance for indigent children.

Circuit Court of Appeals – Twelve regional circuits of the federal U.S. court system with two charges: one, they hear appeals from lower district courts within their specific circuit; two, they hear and adjudicate decisions from federal administrative agencies.

Circular flow of economic activity – A pictorial depiction of an economy identifying the key markets (product, resource, financial, foreign) and the interaction of the key participants (households, businesses, government, financial institutions, and foreign companies) within each of the markets.

Civil Aeronautics Board (CAB) – A federal agency responsible for regulating air transportation within the United States, including airfares and interstate routes by commercial airlines; it was disbanded in 1984.

Civilian labor force – The sum of civilians who are employed and the civilians age 16 or over who are unemployed but are actively pursuing employment.

Civilian noninstitutional population – The U.S. population of those 16 years of age and older who reside in the 50 states and the District of Columbia.

Classical liberalism – A political ideology that promotes restricting government involvement in the economy to providing rule of law and economic freedom.

Clean Air Act of 1963 – The first federal legislation aimed at reducing air pollution.

Clean Air Act of 1970 (CAA) – Initiated more sophisticated and comprehensive regulations to reduce air emissions.

Coase theorem – Describes the economic efficiency that can be achieved by an economic allocation or outcome in the presence of externalities; first presented by Nobel laureate Ronald Coase.

Coinage Act of 1792 – Also known as the Mint Act, it established the United States Mint and the U.S. coinage system.

Cold War – From approximately the late 1940s to the early 1990s, an ongoing global condition of both political and military tensions primarily between the United States and the Soviet Union.

Collective bargaining – The process of negotiating between employer and employees to establish working conditions, including wages, benefits, and conditions of the workplace.

Collusion – An agreement between parties to restrict competition of a market; the agreement may be legal or illegal in the United States.

Command economy – An economy in which the three main questions (what to produce, how to produce, and for whom to produce) are addressed, answered, and implemented by a central authority (government).

Commander in chief – The leader of a nation's armed forces; in the United States, it is the president of the United States.

Commerce clause – A provision in the Constitution of the United States giving Congress power over interstate trade and trade with foreign countries; also includes trades with Indian tribes.

Commercial banking – A financial institution that participates in individual and business banking activity, including taking deposits and making personal and business loans.

Commodities – The generic term to describe the natural resources such as coal, oil, and natural gas that are used in the production of final goods.

Common carrier – A company that transports goods for the general public, such as communications.

Common-pool resource – A resource such as water or fish where exclusive or defined use is hard or impossible to enforce.

Communications Act of 1934 – Transferred the regulation of the interstate telephone service from the Interstate Commerce Commission to the Federal Communications Commission (FCC).

Communism – A political system of government in which the state holds authoritarian control and power is held by one political party, including control of the economy, and all resources of the economy are owned by the government.

Communist League – Established in 1847 in London, the Communist League is considered the first Marxist political party; it promoted the political and economic philosophies of Karl Marx, and disbanded in 1852.

Comparative advantage – A situation in which one person, company, or nation can produce a good or service with lower opportunity costs than another; useful for determining the most efficient allocation of resources; leads to trade between the two entities and increased wealth.

Comparative economic systems – The study of different economic organizations, including market, command, and mixed economies.

Competition – In economics, the act of several persons, businesses, or nations vying to be the most efficient, the most effective, or the most favorable for the allocation of resources.

Congressional Budget Office – A federal agency within the U.S. legislative branch of government, established in 1974 to provide timely, nonpartisan economic data and analysis to Congress.

Congress of Industrial Organizations (CIO) – Founded in 1935, a U.S. labor union organization based on industrial industries; it was part of the American Federation of Labor.

Consideration – In law, it is intended to persuade one party to enter into a contract.

Consumer Expenditure Survey (CES) – A program of the Bureau of Labor Statistics (BLS) consisting of surveys providing information on the buying habits of U.S. consumers.

Consumer Price Index (CPI) – An index indicating monthly changes in the prices paid by consumers of a representative market basket of goods and services.

Consumer rights – Also known as consumer protection, consumer rights promote consumer education and safety.

Consumer sovereignty – A term expressing the freedom of consumers to choose the goods and services they desire, thus determining which goods and services will be produced in a market economy.

Continentals – Bills of credit issued by the states that depreciated and ultimately lost their value during the Revolutionary War under the Articles of Confederation.

Contract – A voluntary, lawful agreement between two or more parties.

Contraction, economic – The portion of the business cycle in which a nation's economy slows down.

Coordination costs – The costs related to making, reaching, and enforcing agreements (see Transaction costs).

Copyright – The legal protection of a creative work, giving the originator of the work exclusive rights for a period of time.

Core Inflation – An inflation rate measure excluding price measures for food and energy.

Cost-push inflation – A form of inflation caused by increases in the cost of resources (land, labor, capital), causing a decrease in aggregate supply.

Council of Economic Advisers – Established in 1946 as an agency of the Executive Office of the President of the United States, it advises the president on economic policies, provides objective empirical research, and prepares the annual *Economic Report of the President.*

Currency – A term referring to the money used as a nation's medium of exchange, store of value, or standard of value.

Current Employment Statistics (CES) – A monthly program that surveys businesses and government agencies to provide industry data on employment and earnings.

Current Population Survey (CPS) – Jointly conducted by the U.S. Census Bureau and Bureau of Labor Statistics (BLS), this survey provides labor force data on the U.S. population.

Cyclical unemployment – The component of the unemployment rate determined by the economic growth or recession in the business cycle.

Damages – In legal terms, an award—usually monetary—issued in a legal suit.

Debt ceiling – Also known as the debt limit, it is a congressionally declared limit on the extent to which Department of Treasury debt can exceed revenues.

Deficit spending – A governmental unit's spending more during a fiscal year than it gains in revenue.

Deflationary spiral – The continued decreasing of the general price level of an economy over time, resulting in significant decreases in resource and investment values.

Demand-pull inflation – Inflation caused by increases in aggregate demand not matched by comparable increases in aggregate supply.

Demurred – In legal terms, an objection or delay.

Department of Commerce and Labor – Created in 1903, it was divided into two separate departments in 1913, the Department of Commerce and the Department of Labor.

Department of Labor – A federal department charged with promoting welfare and working conditions of wage earners, job seekers, and retirees.

Depression – A term used to describe an extremely severe economic recession characterized by negative economic growth, very high unemployment, and deflation over an extended period of time.

Deregulation – Freeing an industry from regulations imposed on it by government.

Detariffing – The act of a nation removing tariff regulations.

Development economics – The branch of economics that studies the conditions and variables conducive to economic growth, especially for developing nations.

Discount rate – Interest rate charged by the regional banks of the Federal Reserve System to their member banks for overnight loans.

Discouraged workers – Unemployed individuals who are not counted as part of the labor force.

Disincentive – A regulation or policy that deters a particular action by companies or individuals.

Disinflation – A lower rate of inflation from a previous inflation measure, as opposed to the negative measure, deflation.

Doctrine of secondary meaning – Legal protection of an otherwise unprotected trademark that arises when advertising and time make that mark signify a particular product.

Due process clause – It protects the legal rights of each individual under the law.

Dynamic economic view – A view of the economy's condition over time.

Economic forecasting – The process of making economic predictions regarding future unemployment, inflation, economic growth activity, and other data for a specific time period.

Economic growth – Increases in real per-capita GDP over a given period of time.

Economic index – A statistical measure of the economy that highlights changes in a specific group of individual data derived from numerous sources; the Dow Jones, GDP deflator, and consumer price index are examples of economic indices.

Economic institutions – Nonhuman entities within an economy, including businesses, governments, and unions.

Economic rent – A payment for the use of a resource above its opportunity cost.

Economic systems – An economy's method of allocating its resources, goods, and services; it is determined by who (markets, central authority, or some combination) answers the main economic questions (what to produce, how to produce, for whom to produce).

Economics of government – A subgroup of economics that studies the economic effects and impacts of government and government policies on an economy.

Economics of law – A subgroup of economics that studies the economic effects and impacts of a nation's laws on its economy.

Economics of war and peace – A subgroup of economics that studies the economic effects and impacts of a nation's conditions of war and peace on its economy.

Emergency Home Finance Act of 1970 – The federal legislation that created the Federal Home Loan Mortgage Corporation (Fannie Mae).

Eminent domain – A term used to define government's right to require the sale of privately held property for a government-defined common-good use.

Employee – A person whose wages are paid by a second source, such as another individual, business, or corporation.

Employer – An individual, business, or corporation who hires employees.

Enlightenment, Age of – A cultural movement in eighteenth-century Europe and the American colonies to create societal reforms through reason and science.

Entrepreneurship (entrepreneurs) – A component of human resources; the willingness and ability of an individual to use productive resources (land, labor, capital) to raise financial capital, organize, take risks, manage, and otherwise combine resources to create a business or organization.

Environmental economics – A study of economics concerned with creating and promoting economic solutions to environmental issues.

Environmental Protection Agency – Federal agency whose mission is to protect the environment and promote environmental quality.

Equal Employment Opportunity Commission (EEOC) – A federal agency charged with the enforcement of federal laws that prohibit discrimination against a job applicant due to race, gender, age, or national origin.

Equal Pay Act – This act amended the Fair Labor Standards Act to prohibit unequal pay based on gender.

Equation of exchange – Also known as the quantity theory of money, the equation of exchange identifies the relationship between an economy's money supply (M), price level (P), velocity of money (V), and value of its goods and services (Q) as PQ = MV. This equation states that the number of monetary units (M) times the number of times each unit is spent (V) equals the quantity of goods and services sold (Q) times the prices paid for the goods and services (P).

Euro – The monetary unit of the European Union (€), first appearing in January 2002.

European Central Bank – The central bank responsible for the monetary policies of the Eurozone Monetary Union; located in Frankfurt, Germany.

European Monetary Zone (EMZ) – Also known as the Eurozone, this is the monetary union for those members of the European Union who chose to join; the Euro is the monetary unit of the EMZ.

Exchange rates – The price of one nation's currency expressed in terms of another nation's currency.

Exports – The outflow of goods and services from one nation to another nation.

Externality – The positive or negative consequence of an economic transaction that impacts a third party.

Fair Employment Practices Agencies (FEPAs) – State or local equivalents of the federal Equal Employment Opportunities Commission.

Fair Labor Standards Act of 1938 – Federal statute that established the minimum wage.

Fair trade – The practice of a business buying at a guaranteed price directly from the producers in the developing world.

Fascism – A system of government where all authority is centralized; governed by a dictator.

Federal Communications Commission (FCC) – The federal commission that regulates interstate and international communications of television, cable, satellite, radio, and wire in the United States and territories and the District of Columbia.

Federal Deposit Insurance Corporation (FDIC) – An independent federal agency that creates stability and confidence in the U.S. financial system by insuring deposits and providing regulating and receivership oversight.

Federal Election Campaign Act of 1974 (FECA) – Designed to enhance the disclosure of political contributors.

Federal Election Commission (FEC) – A federal commission to administer and enforce federal campaign finance statutes.

Federal Housing Administration (FHA) – Federal agency that provides mortgage insurance for loans on single-family homes and multifamily homes approved by the FHA.

Federal Open Market Committee (FOMC) – A body of the Federal Reserve System responsible for the decisions regarding interest rates and quantity of the U.S. money supply through the buying and selling of U.S. securities (bills, notes, bonds).

Federal Poverty Level (FPL) – In 2013, the FPL for a family of four was $23,550; the level is changed annually. Many state minimum eligibility levels exceed the federal minimum.

Federal Reserve System – Since 1913, it has been the central banking system of the United States, responsible for the monetary policies and money supply and regulation of the U.S. banking system.

Federalism – National, state, and local governments interact collectively to solve problems; the United States is a federalist system with a national government and lower state and local governments.

The Federalist Papers – A series of articles, essays, and pamphlets written by Alexander Hamilton, John Jay, and James Madison to ratify the U.S. Constitution.

Fifth Amendment of the U.S. Constitution – A Bill of Rights amendment that sets limits on the powers of the U.S. government.

Financial Reform Act of 2010 (Dodd-Frank Wall Street Reform and Consumer Protection Act) – Signed into law in 2010 by President Obama, it called for significant changes to regulations of the financial markets resulting from the financial crisis of 2007–2009.

Financial Services Modernization Act of 1999 – An act that repealed the Banking Act of 1933.

Fordney-McCumber Tariff Act (1922) – Federal tariff implemented by the United States to protect U.S. factories and farms.

Foreign aid – Payments by developed nations to developing nations for which no repayment is required.

Foreign debt – When a nation's repayment loan obligations to another nation exceed its ability to repay the loan over time.

Formal contract – A contract in which the parties have signed formal documents.

Fourteenth Amendment to the U.S. Constitution – The amendment that grants citizenship to all those born in the United States, regardless of race.

Fractional reserve banking – A system of banking in which financial institutions are required to maintain reserves that are only a percentage of total deposits.

Frazier-Lemke Farm Bankruptcy Act – Enacted in 1934 by Congress, it was an attempt by government to limit the banking industries' ability to repossess farms.

Free-rider problem – A condition when the users of public goods assume others will pay the costs of the public good; one example is a user of a city park who lives in another city and does not pay taxes to the park's city for its maintenance and upkeep.

Free-trade agreements – Agreements by countries to provide open borders for free trade and population movements, creating a free-trade area; the North American Free Trade Agreement (NAFTA) is an example of a free-trade agreement.

Frictional costs – Transaction costs or coordination costs.

Frictional unemployment – The component of the unemployment rate determined by the continual portion of the labor force actively looking for employment.

Full employment – When the unemployment rate is equal to the frictional unemployment.

General Agreement on Tariffs and Trade (GATT) – A multilateral trade agreement created in 1947 during the United Nations Conference on Trade and Employment in Geneva to achieve substantial tariff reductions and reductions of other trade barriers. The agreement was dissolved in 1994 when it was replaced by the new World Trade Organization (WTO).

Gilded Age – This was a term coined by Mark Twain that captured the attitude of less-than-accurate expectations of immigrants toward the United States at that time. It was a period of economic growth from approximately 1870 to 1898.

Glass ceiling – A nontransparent barrier to entry to certain levels of leadership; the term is used when describing discrimination against women in their attempts to reach top levels of corporate leadership.

Global economics – The study of the world economy (also known as the global economy) and how national economies interact with each other in a global marketplace.

Globalization – The process of integrating national economies into a single global economy through improved technology in telecommunications, including the Internet and transportation.

Gold standard – A fixed exchange rate system that uses gold as its standard of value.

Government budget constraint – A relationship between monetary policy options and fiscal policy options at a specific point of time.

Government failure – Also known as nonmarket failure, it is similar to market failure, where government program costs outweigh benefits resulting in misallocation of resources.

Government Sponsored Enterprises (GSE) – Corporations created by the U.S. Congress as public service entities, but that operate as privately held corporations; Fannie Mae and Freddie Mac are examples of GSEs.

Great Depression – The worldwide depression of the twentieth century that preceded World War II; it began in the 1930s and lasted through the mid-1940s and the beginning of World War II.

Greenbacks – So called because the back is printed in green, they were the first noninterest-bearing notes printed by the government to pay for the war debt.

Gresham's law – Commonly known as "bad money driving out good," this occurs when a government overvalues one money and undervalues the second money so that the undervalued money disappears and the overvalued or bad money overwhelms the economy.

Gross Domestic Income (GDI) – A measure of a nation's economy measured by the value of wages, profits, interest, and rents income within a nation's borders over a given period of time.

Gross Domestic Product (GDP) – A measure of a nation's economy by the final market value of goods and services produced by businesses, households, government, and the effects of net trade (exports minus imports) within a nation's borders over a given period of time.

Gross National Product (GNP) – A measure of a nation's economy by the final market value of goods and services produced by the nation's businesses, households, and government, and the effects of net trade (exports - imports), regardless of geographical location.

Headline inflation – An inflation rate that includes all components of the consumer price index, including food and energy.

Health insurance mandate – Requirement that an employer or an individual have private company insurance or participate in a national plan such as Medicaid or Medicare.

Human rights – Term used to define the fundamental rights of individuals simply by being a global human citizen.

IMF conditionality – Conditions placed on nations by the International Monetary Fund that they must meet in order to receive funding assistance from the IMF.

Immigration – The movement of people to a country or region where they are not native.

Imperialism – Economic imperialism results when a nation's rates of consumption outpace production, forcing the country to export capital to foreign countries in order to exploit foreign markets and labor forces to supply its needs.

Implementation lag – Defines the time between a government's passing a law or policy and the time when the law or policy can be put into effect.

Import and Export Price Indices (IEPI) – Bureau of Labor Statistics data reporting increases or decreases of price indices on imports and exports.

Imports – The inflow of goods and services from one nation to another nation.

Incentives – Positive rewards for participating in an activity.

Income distribution – A measurement of different income levels in an economy and the percentage of income earners in each income level.

Income effect – When market changes create a change in the quantity demanded of a good or service, which alters the purchasing power of the consumer, either increasing or decreasing the consumer's ability to purchase goods and services.

Index – A statistical measure of an economy, such as a stock market index or consumer price index.

Industrial Revolution – A period in history during the eighteenth and nineteenth centuries when economies transitioned from agricultural-based economies to manufacturing-based economies, including improved transportation and communication technology.

Industrialization – The transforming of an economy from an agrarian to an industry-based economy.

Infant-industry argument – The idea that government should impose tariffs to protect an industry that is trying to get started from import competition.

Inflation – A general rise in the price level of all goods and services (demand-pull) in an economy; the general rise in the costs of resources (supply-push) in an economy; when the quantity of the money supply exceeds the current price level of the quantity of goods and services produced (monetary inflation).

Inflation-unemployment rate trade-off – First proposed by A. W. H. Phillips, the thesis that during times of economic growth, a nation will experience either inflation with low unemployment or relative price stability with high unemployment.

Informal contract – A binding legal contract that has not been formally consummated.

Infrastructure – An economy's major public services, including roads, sewers, water, schools, medical facilities, and updated telecommunications.

Injunction – Legal stop to an action.

Institutions – A formal or informal set of rules of behavior, limits, or constraints on an economic, social, and political society.

Intellectual property rights – Protecting artists' creative works, such as books, music, and movies, through copyright law.

Interest – The price/cost of money expressed in nominal (stated interest rate) or real (foundation interest rate) terms.

Interest groups – Also known as lobby, campaign, or special interest groups, they are assembled to promote and influence public policy and public opinion in their favor and create economic rents for their membership.

International Bank for Reconstruction and Development (IBRD) – Owned by member nations and founded as part of the Bretton Woods Conference, it makes loans to developing nations to improve infrastructure such as education, health, and transportation.

International economics – A branch of economics that studies the interdependence of economic activity between nations and the economic development of nations, including resource movements, trade, and investment.

International finance – A branch of economic study concerned with the money flows between nations and the international monetary systems, including balance of payments, exchange rates, international trade, and foreign direct investment.

International Monetary Fund (IMF) – Founded during the Bretton Woods Conference to administer an international foreign exchange rate system and lend to member countries having balance-of-payments problems; lender of last resort for national governments and central banks.

International policy reform – A future state or condition determined by government action and policy to stimulate future international trade or development.

International trade – Trade between companies from different nations; the study of the flow of goods and services and productive resources across international boundaries.

Isolationism – Protectionist policy of a nation in which it intentionally refuses to form alliances, treaties, or other economic partnerships.

Job Openings and Labor Turnover Survey (JOLTS) – A Bureau of Labor Statistics (BLS) survey that generates data on job openings, separations, and hires.

Judicial review – The prerogative of the courts to review the actions of the legislative and executive branches of government.

Labor force participation rate – The total number of people participating in a nation's labor market who are employed.

Labor movement – A formal action by workers to organize into a labor union to achieve better working conditions including wages and benefits.

Labor unions – A formal organization of wage earners gathered for the express purpose of improving wages, benefits, and working conditions.

Laissez-faire – An economic term used to describe an economy free from government intervention in economic activity, including trade and market transactions; a French phrase for "let you (plural) do," generally translated as "let it be" or "to leave alone."

Legal tender – A currency that is recognized by law as legal and must be accepted in payment of debts.

Lender of last resort – The role of a central bank or institution willing and able to lend to a bank with temporary liquidity problems to prevent the position spreading to a general loss of confidence in other banks or financial institutions.

Liberty of contracts – The freedom of individuals, organizations, and corporations to enter into formal legal contracts without government interference.

Living wage – Also known as a subsistence wage, an income level essential for a wage earner to meet his or her basic needs of housing, clothing, and food.

Lobbyists – Individuals involved in the act of lobbying to promote and influence policy, laws, and regulations to benefit their constituencies.

Lochner era – Named for the *Lochner v. New York* Supreme Court case, a time in American history when the Supreme Court struck down several laws interfering with personal property rights and individual economic liberties.

Love Canal – A Niagara Falls, New York, neighborhood that gained international fame when it was disclosed that the site had been a major toxic waste dump.

Macroeconomics – The study of a nation's economy as a whole, measuring changes in unemployment, money supply, national income, and general price level.

Madison, James – The fourth president of the United States; the "Father of the Constitution" and author of the Bill of Rights.

Majority rule – Process of electing an alternative by receiving one vote more than half the population voting.

Mandates – In law, a formal notice of a decision being made by an appeals court.

Marbury v. Madison **(1803)** – A landmark Supreme Court decision that laid the foundation for judicial review under Article III of the Constitution.

Market economy – An economy where the key economic questions (what to produce, how to produce, for whom to produce) are addressed, answered, and implemented in the marketplace in the transactions between buyers and sellers.

Market failures – An economic situation or transaction in which too few or too many resources are going to a specific economic activity.

Market price – Also known as economic price, this is the price offered in the marketplace.

Markets – The interaction of a buyer (consumer, household) and seller (producer, business) exchanging goods or services in a variety of different settings.

Marxism – A worldview for social, political, and economic change based on the division between social classes, and influenced by the writings of Karl Marx.

Mass Layoff Survey – A Bureau of Labor Statistics (BLS) monthly survey on layoffs of wage earners by corporations of more than 50 initial claims for unemployment insurance during any five-week period.

Medicaid – Government health insurance for the indigent.

Medicare – Government health insurance for the elderly.

Microeconomics – The study of decision making by individuals, firms, and organizations.

Minimum wage – A legislated price floor set by a government to determine the lowest possible hourly wage rate that can be legally paid to workers.

Mixed economy – An economy in which the key economic questions (what to produce, how to produce, for whom to produce) are addressed, answered, and implemented through a combination of transactions between buyers and sellers and a central authority (government).

Monetarism – An ideology of economic thought most prominently held by Milton Friedman that views the money supply as the key variable in measuring a nation's economic growth and price stability.

Monetary economics – A branch of economics that studies and analyzes the functions of money as a medium of exchange, store of value, and unit of account; it studies the roles of central banks and the money in an economic system.

Monetary policy – Macroeconomic policies related to interest rates and money supply, usually determined by the nation's central bank.

Money – The currency of a nation's economy used as a medium of exchange, a store of value, and a standard of value.

Money supply – The quantity of money circulating in an economy.

Moral hazard – The prospect of riskier behavior when borrowers know that they may not have to be responsible for a loan; behavior that generates significant social costs.

Moral philosophy – Also known as ethics, the defining and defending of conduct that is considered right or wrong.

Muckraking – A term coined by Theodore Roosevelt in 1906 comparing journalists who expose corruption or scandal in business or politicians to John Bunyan's character in *Pilgrim's Progress*; the man with the muck rake foregoes paradise to focus on the bad things of the world.

Municipal bonds – Often an income tax–free investment instrument offered by municipalities such as states, cities, schools, or other public agencies; can be offered for either general obligation or a specific purpose.

National Compensation Survey (NCS) – A Bureau of Labor Statistics (BLS) survey that comprises the Employment Cost Index (ECI) and Employer Costs for Employee Compensation (ECEC).

National Environmental Policy Act (NEPA) – Required federal agencies to include environmental values and environmental impact studies in their decision making when considering governmental actions.

National income accounting – A estimate measure of an economy's national income and its components, including wages, profits, rents, and interest income; one approach to measuring an economy's aggregate performance.

National Industrial Recovery Act – Enacted in 1933, during the Great Depression, it authorized President Franklin D. Roosevelt to regulate industry in an effort to stimulate the economy through the establishment of several governmental public works programs.

National Labor Relations Board (NLRB) – An independent agency of the U.S. government located in Washington, D.C., that oversees elections of labor union representations and investigates charges of unfair labor practice.

National Prohibition Act of 1920 – Also known as the Volstead Act, this act legislated the implementation of Prohibition, as directed by the Eighteenth Amendment of the Constitution.

Natural rate of unemployment – The idea that there is always some level of unemployment, even at levels considered full employment in an economy.

Navigation Acts – A series of English laws that restricted foreign shipping trade between the countries and the colonies.

Negative externality – A third-party effect from an economic exchange in which the external costs of the exchange are greater than the external benefits.

New Deal – Economic programs in the United States during the 1930s designed to combat the Great Depression.

Non-Accelerating Inflation Rate of Unemployment (NAIRU) – A very low unemployment rate, at which the number of employed and their corresponding purchasing power places a demand that exceeds the current production of goods and services.

Nonexclusion principle – An individual cannot be excluded from receiving the benefits of a good or service such as national defense, public education, or local police or fire protection.

Office of Management and Budget (OMB) – The largest office within the Executive Office of the President of the United States; assists the president in the preparation, oversight, and administration of the federal budget.

Okun's Law – Named for economist Arthur Okun, it describes the relationship between the unemployment rate and economic growth as measured by the Gross Domestic Product (GDP); a 1 percent decrease in the unemployment rate translates into a 3 percent increase in GDP.

Opportunity cost – The next best alternative cost (trade-off) of a decision; every decision has a cost because every decision involves forgoing an alternative good, service, or activity.

Organisation for Economic Co-operation and Development (OECD) – Established in 1961, it is an international organization of 34 developed nations committed to free trade and democracy with the goal of stimulating global trade and global economic growth; headquarters are located in Paris, France.

Ownership – The process of possessing the rights to defined property, including the ability to defend and sell as one wishes.

Panic of 1873 – An international financial crisis that lasted as long as a decade in some countries.

Paper notes – Paper money issued by the U.S. government without intrinsic value or backed by gold or silver; also known as greenbacks (see Greenbacks).

Patent – Provides private property protection to an inventor for a specified period of time.

Patent and Trademark Office – A federal office responsible for granting patents and trademarks, and protecting the holders of patents and trademarks against infringements.

Per capita income – Measure of a nation's standard of living based on a nation's total income divided by its population.

Perestroika – The economic restructuring of the Soviet economic system during the late 1980s that was initiated by Soviet leader Mikhail Gorbachev.

Personal consumption expenditures (PCE) – A report of the Bureau of Economic Analysis (BEA), which indicates changes in personal expenditures of households.

Phillips curve – Named for A. W. H. Phillips, the curve shows the trade-off or inverse relationship between unemployment and inflation.

Planned economy – Also known as a command economy, this is an economy where the three main questions (what to produce, how to produce, for whom to produce) are addressed, answered, and implemented by a central authority (government).

Political economy – Early terminology from moral philosophy used to describe the study of buying, selling, and producing, along with the governmental laws and societal customs; used to describe the relationships between government and economy in a national context.

Positive externality – A third-party effect from an economic exchange where the external benefits of the exchange are greater than the external costs.

Poverty – Defined in absolute terms as the inability to satisfy basic needs through income, or described in relative terms as a measure of income inequality, where an individual's or family's income is below a predetermined income level (this level differs from one society or nation to the next).

Price controls – Imposed by a government, establishing either minimum or maximum prices to be charged for goods or services.

Prior restraint – Stopping speech before it can be made.

Private costs – Costs of production that are borne by a private individual or business.

Private goods – Goods that are produced by privately owned businesses or produced by private individuals.

Producer Price Index (PPI) – An index produced by the Bureau of Labor Statistics (BLS) to measure the average change of prices of output being charged by domestic producers during a specified period of time.

Product standardization – Establishing consistent features for a good or service.

Productivity – Measuring the economic growth of an economy through the relationships of inputs and outputs; increased outputs using the same inputs, or the same outputs using fewer inputs.

Productivity report – A quarterly report of the Bureau of Labor Statistics (BLS) that measures the level of output based on a per unit of labor.

Prohibition Bureau – A special agency that was created inside the U.S. Treasury Department to enforce the Prohibition Act.

Property rights – The ability of an owner of private property to have defined property, to defend that property, and to receive the benefits of the property's value, including the right to transfer or exchange the property.

Protectionism – A nation's ability to limit imports (quotas) or tax imports in order to keep domestic industries competitive (tariffs).

Public choice theory – The use of economic analysis and economic tools to study the behavior of public officials and citizens as voters; public choice theory often uses tools such as game theory or decision theory.

Public finance – Revenue generated through taxes, fees, fines, and levies to be used by public institutions for the purpose of providing public goods.

Public goods – Goods and services offered by a public institution that are nonexcludable (individuals cannot be prohibited from receiving their benefit); consumption of public goods and services is shared without diminishing the benefit of the user.

Public policy – A government law or regulation imposed by a governmental unit on its constituency.

Public utility pricing – A pricing scheme in which a government subsidy is necessary to maintain production because the price is equal to marginal costs and is below the average cost.

Pure Food and Drug Act (1906) – The beginning of major consumer protection initiatives by the federal government; it led to the establishment of the Food and Drug Administration.

Quantitative easing – A monetary policy of a central bank through which the central bank purchases private market securities (primarily mortgages) to increase the money supply and lower interest rates.

Quid pro quo – A Latin phrase referring to one doing something for or giving something to someone and receiving something in return.

Recession – The declining economic growth portion of the business cycle, as measured by two consecutive quarters of negative economic growth.

Reciprocal Trade Agreements Act (1934) – Signed by President Roosevelt, it promoted the United States entering into tariff agreements with other nations.

Regional trade agreement – An agreement between groups of nations for the express purpose of granting special trade benefits and access to each domestic market; NAFTA is an example.

Rent-seeking – An action of lobbyists and special interest groups to increase the value of clients' or members' actions without increasing productivity; i.e., achieving economic rent.

Required reserve – In a fractional reserve banking system, the reserve ratio percent of daily deposits required by policy of the Federal Reserve for a financial institution to keep on its books at the conclusion of each business day.

Resolution Trust Corporation – A U.S. government–owned management company whose purpose was to liquidate assets of financial institutions, specifically savings and loan associations, that had been declared insolvent by the Office of Thrift Supervision during the 1980s savings and loan crisis.

Restraining order – In law, a court order to a person or entity to either stop an action or prevent a party from pursuing an act.

Revenue – The amount received by a business through the sale of a good or service, or a government total of taxes, fees, and fines received.

Rockefeller, John D. (1839–1937) – Founder of the Standard Oil Company, he became one of the world's wealthiest people and an influential philanthropist.

Roosevelt, President Theodore – The 26th president of the United States, he was known as the "trust-buster" for his efforts to break up the Standard Oil Trust.

Rule of law – A system of laws under which all people, whether they work in the public or private sector, are equal under a set of transparent laws administered fairly and efficiently.

Savings Bonds – The most popular U.S. Treasury note, available in denominations up to $5,000.

Seasonal unemployment – The component of the unemployment rate that is determined by those industries dependent on time of year and weather-related industries.

Sequestration – In law, the seizure of property to be distributed to creditors.

Service Mark – A trademark such as a company logo, name, or slogan for a service or nonprofit.

Shared consumption – The concept that more than one individual can enjoy the benefits of a good or service simultaneously without diminishing the benefit received by the others; a key criteria of a public good.

Sin taxes – A term used to identify taxes levied by governmental entities on goods deemed unhealthy; taxes on smoking products and alcohol are examples.

Sixteenth Amendment to the U.S. Constitution – The amendment that gave the federal government the power to levy and collect taxes, including the income tax.

Social insurance – A government program that transfers risk to an organization that provides benefits to those who represent a defined population; such programs have defined eligibility requirements and are funded through taxes or shared public-private funding.

Social liberalism – The view that the government has a social foundation, and hence the proper role of government includes addressing social issues like health and education, as well as defending the rule of law.

Social Security – Old-Age, Survivors, and Disability Insurance (OADI); a federal program of the Social Security Act of 1935 to provide income to qualifying retired individuals; the single greatest expenditure in the federal budget.

Socialism – The economic system known as the "command economy," in which a central authority answers the key economic questions (what to produce, how to produce, for whom to produce).

Solicitor General – An appointee of the federal government designated to represent the United States before the Supreme Court.

Special drawing rights (SDRs) – A reserve asset created by the International Monetary Fund (IMF) for countries, specifically developing countries, to use in settling international payments.

Square Deal – Programs of President Theodore Roosevelt to address social issues during his presidency.

Stagflation – A term coined to describe an economy experiencing stagnant economic growth (lower real Gross Domestic Product [GDP]) and inflation at the same time.

Standard of living – A term to describe a level of material well-being, including income, employment factors, poverty rate, affordable housing, gross domestic product, hours of work needed for living basics, access to health care, availability of education, infrastructure, safety, and other metrics related to a nation's quality of life.

Steel Tariff of 2002 – To protect the domestic steel industry, the United States imposed temporary tariffs on imported European steel; Europe sued, and the tariffs were ruled illegal in 2003.

Strict constitution doctrine – President James Madison's idea of limiting federal usurpation of state powers.

Structural unemployment – The component of the unemployment rate that is determined by a change in an industry where former employees do not meet qualifications to remain employed in the new restructured industry.

Subsidy – Government aid or payment to a domestic producer to encourage infant industries or protect domestic industries and make them more competitive with foreign competition.

Substitution effect – The economic concept that when the price of a good or service rises, consumers will search for a substitute good or service.

Sunday laws – Laws designed to restrict or ban some or all Sunday shopping for religious reasons.

Tariff – A tax on imports, usually levied by developed nations to protect domestic industries and by developing nations to generate revenue.

Taxes – One form of revenue generated by governments, used to produce public goods or redistribute income.

Taxing and spending clause of the U.S. Constitution – Requires most Americans to purchase health insurance.

Tenth Amendment to the U.S. Constitution – The last amendment to the Bill of Rights, which gave powers not assigned to the federal government to the states.

Theory of public choice – The study of how groups participate in decision making.

Title VII of the Civil Rights Act of 1964 – This federal law identified as illegal the practice of discrimination on the basis of race, ethnicity, religion, gender, or nationality.

Title IX of the Education Act – This federal law prohibits discrimination on the basis of sex in educational institutions.

Trade – The voluntary exchange between two entities for the express purpose of improving the standard of living for both.

Trade agreements – Trade pacts between nations to promote free trade, or preferential trade, or to identify a tariff, quota, or other trade restriction.

Trademark – A unique or innovative logo, picture, phrase, or emblem to identify a business, corporation, or manufacturer, filed with the U.S. Patent and Trademark Office.

Trade-offs – Another term for opportunity cost.

Trade war – When two or more nations create trade barriers or protectionist measures against each other as a retaliatory response to imposed protectionist measures.

Traditional economy – An economy based on culture and heritage.

Tragedy of the commons – The overuse of public goods with no regard for the costs of use.

Transaction costs – The costs related to making, reaching, and enforcing agreements.

Transfer payments – Distribution of income from governments to individuals by way of money payments with no goods or services in return.

Transitional economies – The economies of once-developing nations whose economic measures reflect significant growth, yet are still too low for them to be considered developed nations; the BRIC nations of Brazil, Russia, India, and China are examples of transitional economies.

Treasury bills – Short-term U.S. Treasury obligations issued with a term of less than one year.

Treasury bonds – Long-term U.S. Treasury obligation with a term of 10 years or more.

Treasury Inflation-Protected Securities (TIPS) – Introduced by the U.S. Treasury in 1997 as a hedge against inflation.

Treasury notes – Intermediate to long-term U.S. Treasury investments, typically with maturities of 2, 3, 5, 7, and 10 years.

TRICARE – Civilian health benefits for military personnel and retirees and their dependents.

Troubled Asset Relief Program (TARP) – A program created by the federal government and administered by the Treasury Department in an attempt to short-circuit the growing financial crisis of 2007–2008.

Truman, Harry – The 33rd president of the United States, who initiated a broad legislative agenda known as the Fair Deal.

Trust – A new business arrangement that emerged in the early 1880s in which shareholders assigned their shares in a company to trustees who held the decision-making power of the company.

Unemployment – The total number of adults 16 and over who are not working but are willing and able to work and actively looking for work.

Unemployment insurance – A transfer payment to those who are willing and able to work but currently not working.

Unemployment rate – A measure of people who are not working but are willing and able to do so.

Unfair trade practices – A trade practice that is considered to favor one party over another, giving one party an advantage within a trading partnership.

United Nations Conference on Trade and Development (UNCTAD) – Established in 1964 as a UN intergovernmental body, it assists and serves developing nations with trade, investment, and development opportunities.

Unskilled labor – The component of the workforce characterized by jobs with low skill levels and low education levels, with low wages and limited advancement.

U.S. Department of Commerce – A cabinet-level department charged with promoting economic growth and creating jobs by collecting, analyzing, and reporting economic and demographic data.

U.S. Department of Housing and Urban Development (HUD) – A federal agency responsible for the Federal Housing Administration, Fannie Mae, and Freddie Mac.

U.S. Department of Treasury – Established in 1789 by Congress, the cabinet-level executive department was created to manage government revenue, print paper currency, mint coins for circulation, collect federal taxes, and manage U.S. government debt instruments.

V-chips – Devices that enable parents to keep their children from accessing offensive content.

Vertical integration – A business model when a company increases its production capabilities and efficiencies by merging or buying companies below or above its resources, production, and/or distribution chain.

Veterans Administration (VA) – A federal government agency responsible for the operation and administration of the health care system for military veterans and disabled veterans in the United States; the nation's largest health care system.

Volcker Rule – A component of the Financial Reform Act of 2010 proposed by Paul Volcker to limit a U.S. bank's ability to make certain speculative investments that do not profit its customers.

Voluntary exchange – Elective trade between a buyer and a seller in which both anticipate being better off as a result of the exchange.

Voluntary Export Exchange (VER) – This type of quota, as the name suggests, is the exporting nation voluntarily limiting an export to an importing nation.

Wage and price controls – Government controls to restrict wage and price increases.

Welfare economics – The branch of economics that uses microeconomic tools, methods, and theory to assess the economic well-being of individuals and their economic activities as groups, societies, and communities.

Welfare state – A political unit where a government has a major role in the protection and promotion of the individual through specific government economic and social organizations; modern welfare states include Iceland, Sweden, and Norway, where significant revenue transfer from individuals to the state funds public services such as education and health care.

Wilson, Woodrow – The 28th president of the United States, who was a leader of the Progressive movement.

Woman's Christian Temperance Union (WCTU) – Led by Francis Willard, it argued that alcoholic beverages were the cause of many of the social ills, leading to the era of Prohibition.

Workfare – A system of welfare in which adults are required to perform some form of work in order to receive aid.

Working poor – Individuals who work but whose income level is below the poverty level.

Works Progress Administration (WPA) – Part of President Roosevelt's New Deal, the federal government directly hired several million unemployed Americans for tasks ranging from raking leaves to building airports.

World Bank – Established during the Bretton Woods Conference following World War II, it is a multinational agency whose purpose is to make loans to developing nations to improve the development of a nation's infrastructure such as schools, hospitals, sanitation, and roads.

World Trade Organization (WTO) – An independent organization created during GATT talks for the express purpose of serving as the main international body to promote international trade among developed and developing nations; it also serves as the refereeing body for international trade disputes.

Writ of error – A writ issued by an appellate court directing the court of record to send a trial record to the appellate court to be looked at for potential errors.

Select Bibliography

Austrian School

Boettke, Peter J., ed. 1994. *The Elgar Companion to Austrian Economics*. London: Edward Elgar.

Gloria-Palermo, Sandye. 1999. *Evolution of Austrian Economics: From Menger to Lachmann*. London: Routledge.

Grassl, Wolfgang, and Barry Smith. 2010. *Austrian Economics: Historical and Philosophical Background*. Beckenham, AU: Taylor and Francis.

Koppl, Roger. 2008. *Explorations in Austrian Economics*. Bingley, UK: Emerald Group.

Schulak, Eugen Maria, and Herbert Unterkofler. 2011. *The Austrian School of Economics: A History of Its Ideas, Ambassadors, and Institutions*. Auburn, AL: Ludwig von Mises Institute.

Bolshevik Revolution

Corney, Frederick C. 2004. *Telling October: Memory and the Making of the Bolshevik Revolution*. New York: Cornell University Press.

Edward, Carr Hallett. 1978. *The Bolshevik Revolution, 1917–1923*. Vol. 1, History of Soviet Russia. New York: W.W. Norton.

Sutton, Anthony C. 1974. *Wall Street and the Bolshevik Revolution: The Remarkable True Story of the American Capitalists Who Financed the Russian Communists*. New York: Buccaneer Books.

Bretton Woods Conference

Irwin, Neil. 2013. *The Alchemists: Three Central Bankers and a World on Fire*. New York: Penguin Press.

McKinnon, Ronald I. 2013. *The Unloved Dollar Standard: From Bretton Woods to the Rise of China*. Oxford: Oxford University Press.

Steil, Benn. 2013. *The Battle of Bretton Woods: John Maynard Keynes, Harry Dexter White, and the Making of a New World Order*. Princeton, NJ: Princeton University Press.

Capitalism

Fulcher, James. 2004. *Capitalism: A Very Short Introduction*. Oxford: Oxford University Press.

Schumpeter, Joseph A. 1950. *Capitalism, Socialism, and Democracy*. 3rd ed. Oxford: Routledge.

Zingales, Luigi A. 2010. *Capitalism for the People: Recapturing the Lost Genius of American Prosperity*. New York: Basic Books.

Central Banking

Blinder, Alan S. 1998. *Central Banking in Theory and Practice*. Lionel Robbins Lectures. Boston: MIT Press.

Davies, Howard, and David Green. 2010. *Banking on the Future: The Fall and Rise of Central Banking*. Princeton, NJ: Princeton University Press.

Singleton, John. 2011. *Central Banking in the Twentieth Century*. Cambridge: Cambridge University Press.

Civil War

Ekelund, Robert B., Jr., and Mark Thornton. 2004. *Tariffs, Blockades and Inflation: The Economics of the Civil War*. Wilmington, DE: Scholarly Resources Inc.

Kagan, Neil, ed. 2013. *Smithsonian Civil War: Inside the National Collection*. Washington, DC: Smithsonian Books.

Classical Economics

Barber, William J. 2009. *A History of Economic Thought*. Middletown, CT: Wesleyan University Press.

Gilder, George, and Steve Forbes. 2012. *Wealth and Poverty: A New Edition for the Twenty-First Century*. Washington, DC: Regnery.

Kurz, Heinz D., and Neri Salvadori. 2007. *Interpreting Classical Economics: Studies in Long-Period Analysis*. London: Routledge.

Morgan, Mary S. 2012. *The World in the Model: How Economists Work and Think*. Cambridge: Cambridge University Press.

Rickards, James. 2012. *Currency Wars: The Making of the Next Global Crisis*. New York: Portfolio Trade.

Smith, Matthew. 2011. *Thomas Tooke and the Monetary Thought of Classical Economics*. London: Routledge.

Sowell, Thomas. 2007. *On Classical Economics*. New Haven, CT: Yale University Press.

Wolff, Richard D., and Stephen A. Resnick. 2012. *Contending Economic Theories: Neoclassical, Keynesian, and Marxian*. Boston: MIT Press.

The Communist Manifesto

Blaisdell, Bob, ed. 2003. *The Communist Manifesto and Other Revolutionary Writings: Marx, Marat, Paine, Mao Tse-Tung, Gandhi and Others*. Mineola, NY: Dover.

Marx, Karl, and Frederick Engels. 2010. *The Communist Manifesto*. London: Arcturus.

Marx, Karl, and Frederick Engels. 2007. *The Communist Manifesto: Complete with Seven Rarely Published Prefaces*. Minneapolis, MN: Filiquarian.

Comparative Economic Systems

Conklin, David W. 1991. *Comparative Economic Systems: Objectives, Decision Modes and the Process of Choice*. New York: Cambridge University Press.

Gregory, Paul R., and Robert C. Stuart. 2004. *Comparative Economic Systems in the Twenty-First Century*. 7th ed. Mason, OH: South-Western, Cengage Learning.

Rosser, J. Barkley, Jr., and Marina V. Rosser. 2004. *Comparative Economics in a Transforming World Economy*. 2nd ed. Cambridge, MA: Massachusetts Institute of Technology.

Fascism

Goldberg, Jonah. 2007. *Liberal Fascism: The Secret History of the American Left from Mussolini to the Politics of Meaning*. New York: Doubleday.

Paxton, Robert O. 2004. *The Anatomy of Fascism*. New York: Vintage Books.

Rockwell, Llewellyn H., Jr. 2013. *Fascism vs. Capitalism*. Auburn, AL: Ludwig von Mises Institute.

Federal Reserve System

Beckhart, Benjamin Haggott. 1972. *Federal Reserve Systems*. New York: Columbia University Press.

Greider, William. 1987. *Secrets of the Temple: How the Federal Reserve Runs the Country*. New York: Simon and Schuster.

Harris, Ethan S. 2008. *Ben Bernanke's Fed: The Federal Reserve after Greenspan*. Cambridge, MA: Harvard Business School Press.

Meltzer, Allan H. 2010. *A History of the Federal Reserve*. Volume 2, Book 1, 1951–1969. Chicago: University of Chicago Press.

Meltzer, Allan H. 2004. *A History of the Federal Reserve*. Volume 2, Book 2, 1970–1986. Chicago: University of Chicago Press.

Fiscal Policy

Alesina, Alberto, and Francesco Giavazzi, eds. 2013. *Fiscal Policy after the Financial Crisis*. Chicago: University of Chicago Press.

Friedman, Milton. 1969. *Monetary vs. Fiscal Policy: A Dialogue*. New York: The Graduate School of Business Administration, New York University.

Friedman, Milton

Butler, Eamonn. 2011. *Milton Friedman: A Concise Guide to the Ideas and Influence of the Free-Market Economist*. Hampshire, UK: Harriman House.

Ebenstein, Lanny. 2007. *Milton Friedman: A Biography*. Basingstoke, UK: Palgrave Macmillan.

Friedman, Milton, and Rose Friedman. 1998. *Two Lucky People: Memoirs*. Chicago: University of Chicago Press.

General Theory on Equilibrium of Employment, Interest, and Money

Keynes, John Maynard. 2006. *The General Theory of Employment, Interest and Money*. Ocala, FL: Atlantic.

Great Depression

McElvaine, Robert S., ed. 2007. *Down and Out in the Great Depression: Letters from the Forgotten Man*. Chapel Hill: University of North Carolina Press.

Shlaes, Amity. 2008. *The Forgotten Man: A New History of the Great Depression*. New York: Harper Perennial.

Hayek, Friedrich von

Caldwell, Bruce. 2004. *Hayek's Challenge: An Intellectual Biography of F. A. Hayek*. Chicago: University of Chicago Press.

Ebenstein, Alan. 2001. *Friedrich Hayek: A Biography*. New York: St. Martin's Press.

Ebenstein, Alan. 2003. *Hayek's Journey*. New York: Palgrave Macmillan.

Hayek, F. A. 1994. *Hayek on Hayek: An Autobiographical Dialogue*. Edited by Stephen Kresge and Leif Wenar. Chicago: University of Chicago Press.

Wapshott, Nicholas. 2012. *Keynes Hayek: The Clash That Defined Modern Economics*. New York: Norton.

Housing Crisis (Bubble) of 2008

Blinder, Alan S. 2013. *After the Music Stopped: The Financial Crisis, The Response and the Work Ahead*. New York: Penguin Books.

Chincarini, Ludwig B. 2012. *The Crisis of Crowding: Quant Copycats, Ugly Models, and the New Crash Normal*. Hoboken, NJ: John Wiley & Sons.

Higgins, Karen L. 2013. *Financial Whirlpools: A Systems Story of the Great Global Recession*. Oxford: Elsevier.

Sowell, Thomas. 2009. *The Housing Boom and Bust*. New York: Basic Books.

Immigration

Bush, Jeb, and Clint Bolick. 2013. *Immigration Wars: Forging an American Solution*. New York: Threshold.

Daniels, Roger. 2002. *Coming to America: A History of Immigration and Ethnicity in American Life*. New York: Harper Perennial.

International Monetary Fund

Copelovitch, Mark S. 2010. *The International Monetary Fund in the Global Economy: Banks, Bonds, and Bailouts*. Cambridge: Cambridge University Press.

Danaher, Kevin, and Muhammed Yunus. 1999. *Fifty Years Is Enough: The Case against the World Bank and the International Monetary Fund*. Brooklyn, NY: South End Press.

Eichengreen, Barry J. 2008. *Globalizing Capital: A History of the International Monetary System*. Princeton, NJ: Princeton University Press.

McQuillan, Lawrence, and Peter Montgomery. 1999. *The International Monetary Fund*. Stanford, CA: Hoover Institute Press.

Vreeland, James Raymond. 2013. *The International Monetary Fund: Politics of Conditional Lending*. Global Institutions. New York: Routledge.

Keynes, John Maynard

Keynes, John Maynard. 2010. *Essays in Persuasion*. Kila, MT: Kessinger.

Minsky, Hyman. 2008. *John Maynard Keynes*. New York: McGraw-Hill.

Skidelsky, Robert. 1980. *John Maynard Keynes: 1883–1946: Economist, Philosopher, Statesman*. New York: Macmillan.

Skidelsky, Robert Jacob Alexander. 2010. *Keynes: A Very Short Introduction*. Oxford: Oxford University Press.

Skidelsky, Robert Jacob Alexander. 2009. *Keynes: The Return of the Master*. London: Public Affairs.

Skousen, Mark. 2007. *The Big Three in Economics: Adam Smith, Karl Marx, and John Maynard Keynes*. Armonk, NY: M. E. Sharpe.

Wapshott, Nicholas. 2012. *Keynes Hayek: The Clash That Defined Modern Economics*. New York: Norton.

Labor Strikes

Franklin, Stephen. 2001. *Three Strikes: Labor's Heartland Losses and What They Mean for Working Americans*. New York: The Guilford Press.

Rhomberg, Chris. 2012. *The Broken Table: The Detroit Newspaper Strike and the State of American Labor*. New York: Russell Sage Foundation.

Zinn, Howard, Dana Frank, and Robin D. G. Kelley. 2001. *Three Strikes: Miners, Musicians, Salesgirls and the Fighting Spirit of Labor's Last Century*. Boston: Beacon Press.

Laffer Curve

Denny, Jim, and Michael Reagan. 2011. *The New Reagan Revolution: How Ronald Reagan's Principles Can Restore America's Greatness*. New York: Thomas Dunne Books.

Laffer, Arthur B., and Stephen Moore. 2010. *Return to Prosperity: How America Can Regain Its Economic Superpower Status*. New York: Threshold Editions.

Lenin, Vladimir

Lenin, Vladimir. 1987. *Essential Works of Lenin: "What Is to Be Done?" and Other Writings*. Mineola, NY: Dover Publications.

Service, Robert. 2000. *Lenin: A Biography*. Cambridge, MA: Belknap Press.

Volkogonov, Dmitri. 1994. *Lenin: A New Biography*. New York: Free Press.

Marx, Karl

Marx, Karl. 1983. *The Portable Karl Marx*. Translated by Eugene Kamenka. New York: Penguin Books.

Simon, Lawrence H., and Karl Marx. 1994. *Selected Writings*. Indianapolis: Hackett.

Medicaid

Engel, Jonathan. 2006. *Poor People's Medicine: Medicaid and American Charity Care since 1965*. Durham, NC: Duke University Press Books.

Olson, Laura Katz. 2010. *The Politics of Medicaid*. New York: Columbia University Press.

Thompson, Frank J. 2012. *Medicaid Politics: Federalism, Policy Durability, and Health Reform*. American Governance and Public Policy Series. Washington, DC: Georgetown University Press.

Medicare

Marmor, Theodore R. 2000. *The Politics of Medicare*. 2nd ed. Social Institutions and Social Change. Piscataway, NJ: Aldine Transaction.

Oberlander, Jonathan. 2003. *The Political Life of Medicare* American Politics and Political Economy. Chicago: University of Chicago Press.

Starr, Paul. 2013. *Remedy and Reaction: The Peculiar American Struggle over Health Care Reform, Revised Edition*. New Haven, CT: Yale University Press.

Mercantilism

Heckscher, Eli F. 1994. *Mercantilism*. London: Routledge.

Stern, Philip, and Carl Wennerlind, eds. 2013. *Mercantilism Reimagined: Political Economy in Early Modern Britain and Its Empire*. New York: Oxford University Press.

Wallerstein, Immanuel. 2011. *The Modern World—System II: Mercantilism and the Consolidation of the European World-Economy, 1600–1750*. Berkeley: University of California Press.

Minimum Wage

Flinn, Christopher J. 2011. *The Minimum Wage and Labor Market Outcomes*. Boston: MIT Press.

Waltman, Jerold. 2000. *The Politics of Minimum Wage*. Champaign: University of Illinois Press.

New Deal

Hiltzik, Michael. 2011. *The New Deal: A Modern History*. New York: Free Press.

Katznelson, Ira. 2013. *Fear Itself: The New Deal and the Origins of Our Time*. New York: Liveright.

Prohibition

Behr, Edward. 2011. *Prohibition: The 13 Years That Changed America*. New York: Arcade Publishing.

Okrent, Daniel. 2011. *Last Call: The Rise and Fall of Prohibition*. New York: Scribner.

Rule of Law

Bingham, Tom. 2011. *The Rule of Law Paperback.* London: Penguin Global.

Tamanaha, Brian Z. 2004. *On the Rule of Law: History, Politics, Theory*. Cambridge: Cambridge University Press.

Smith, Adam

Buchan, James. 2006. *The Authentic Adam Smith: His Life and Ideas.* New York: Norton.

Colander, David, and A. W. Coats, eds. 1989. *The Spread of Economic Ideas.* Cambridge: Cambridge University Press.

Rae, John. 2010. *Life of Adam Smith.* Charleston, SC: Nabu Press.

Socialism

Harrington, Michael. 1989. *Socialism: Past and Future.* New York: Little, Brown.

Maass, Alan, and Howard Zinn. 2010. *The Case for Socialism.* Chicago: Haymarket Books.

Nichols, John. 2011. *The "S" Word: A Short History of an American Tradition . . . Socialism.* Brooklyn, NY: Verso.

Soviet Union

Lovell, Stephen. 2009. *The Soviet Union: A Very Short Introduction.* Oxford: Oxford University Press.

Suny, Ronald Grigor. 1997. *The Soviet Experiment: Russia, The USSR, and the Successor States.* New York: Oxford University Press.

The Wealth of Nations

Smith, Adam. 2010. *The Wealth of Nations: The Economics Classic.* Mankato, MN: Capstone.

Welfare State/Workfare

Mittelstadt, Jennifer. 2005. *From Welfare to Workfare: The Unintended Consequences of Liberal Reform, 1945–1965.* Gender and American Culture. Chapel Hill: University of North Carolina Press.

Peck, Jamie. 2001. *Workfare States.* New York: The Guilford Press.

World Bank

Danaher, Kevin, and Muhammed Yunus. 1999. *Fifty Years Is Enough: The Case against the World Bank and the International Monetary Fund.* Brooklyn, NY: South End Press.

Klees, Steven J., Joel Samoff, and Nelly P. Stromquist. 2012. *The World Bank and Education: Critiques and Alternatives.* Rotterdam, NL: Sense.

Marshall, Katherine. 2008. *The World Bank: From Reconstruction to Development to Equity.* New York: Routledge.

World Bank. 2011. *A Guide to the World Bank.* Washington, DC: World Bank Publications.

World Trade Organization

Cottier, Thomas, and Manfred Elsig, eds. 2011. *Governing the World Trade Organization: Past, Present and Beyond Doha.* Cambridge: Cambridge University Press.

Hoekman, Bernard M., and Michel M. Kostecki. 2010. *The Political Economy of the World Trading System.* New York: Oxford University Press.

Narlikar, Amrita, Martin Daunton, and Robert M. Stern. 2012. *The Oxford Handbook on the World Trade Organization.* Oxford Handbooks in Politics. New York: Oxford University Press.

World War I

Clark, Christopher. 2013. *The Sleepwalkers: How Europe Went to War in 1914*. New York: Harper.

Tuchman, Barbara W. 2009. *The Guns of August: The Outbreak of World War I.* New York: Random House.

World War II

Holmes, Richard. 2009. *World War II: The Definitive Visual History*. New York: DK Publishing.

New York Times and Richard Overy, ed. 2013. *The New York Times Complete World War 2: All the Coverage from the Battlefields and the Home Front*. New York: Black Dog & Leventhal Publishers.

Contributors

Martha Rowland Blenman
University of Michigan-Dearborn
Dearborn, MI

William S. Chappell
HCS Early College High School
Conway, SC

Ekaterini Chrisopoulos-Vergos
Merritt Academy
New Haven, MI

Stephen H. Day
North Carolina State University
Raleigh, NC

David A. Dieterle
Walsh College (Troy, MI)
University of Michigan-Flirt

Maura Donnelly
High School of Economics and Finance
New York, NY

Steven J. Eschrich
International Academy (Okma)
Bloomfield Hills, MI

Aimee Register Gray
Crescent High School
Anderson, SC

Kathryn Lloyd Gustafson
Farmington High School
Farmington, MI

Joseph Lee Hauser
Boiling Springs High School
Boiling Springs, SC

Michelle D. Holowicki
Brighton High School
Brighton, MI

Kerry Hritz
Wayne Memorial High School
Wayne, MI

Bernard P. Kanjoma
Walsh College
Troy, MI

Jean Kujawa
Lourdes University
Sylvania, OH

Cynthia Blitz Law
White Station Middle School
Memphis, TN

Dave Leapard
Eastern Michigan University
Ypsilanti, MI

Samantha Lohr
HCS Early College High School
Conway, SC

Angela M. LoPiccolo
Dakota High School
Macomb, MI

Elham Mahmoudi
University of Michigan
Ann Arbor, MI

Emily N. Manoogian
International Academy
Troy, MI

Carol Lynn Nute
River Bluff High School
Lexington, SC

Tracy L. Ripley
New Buffalo High School
New Buffalo, MI

Jeremy Robinson
Farmington Harrison High School
Farmington Hills, MI

Shima Sadaghiyani
Avondale High School
Auburn Hills, MI

Timothy P. Schilling
Davenport University
Grand Rapids, MI

Kathleen C. Simmons
Almamo Community College

Sara Standen
Carman-Ainsworth High School
Flint, MI

Nevena Trajkov
Eastern Michigan University
Ypsilanti, MI

John E. Trupiano
Desert Mountain High School
Scottsdale, AZ

Joseph A. Weglarz
University of Detroit Mercy
Detroit, MI

Ninee Shoua Yang
Centers for Disease Control and Prevention
Atlanta, GA

About the Editors

David A. Dieterle, PhD, is professor and lecturer of economics at Walsh College, Troy, MI, and the University of Michigan-Flint. He is a national teaching fellow for the Foundation for Teaching Economics. Formerly, he served in economic education centers and councils in Ohio, Nebraska, Illinois, Wisconsin, and Michigan. His published works include Greenwood's *Economic Thinkers: A Biographical Encyclopedia*; *Economic Experiences: Teachers Manual*; and *Energy and Economics: An Activities Book*. Dieterle holds a doctorate from Michigan State University.

Kathleen C. Simmons is adjunct instructor of political science at San Antonio College and St. Phillips College. Formerly, she taught AP economics and government, receiving multiple awards from the Comal ISD in New Braunfels, TX. Her published works include Greenwood's *Economic Thinkers: A Biographical Encyclopedia* and various writings for the National Council for Economic Education, Junior Achievement, and the Foundation for Teaching Economics. Simmons holds a master's degree from Texas State University.

Index

Page numbers in **bold** type indicate main entries in the encyclopedia.